Behavior Management

Applications for Teachers and Parents

THOMAS J. ZIRPOLI

KRISTINE J. MELLOY

**University of St. Thomas
St. Paul, Minnesota**

Merrill, an imprint of
Macmillan Publishing Company
New York

Maxwell Macmillan Canada
Toronto

Maxwell Macmillan International
New York   Oxford   Singapore   Sydney

To Susan, Steve, Christopher, and Julia

Cover art: Jeremy Frey, Southeast School, Franklin County Board of Mental Retardation and Developmental Disabilities

Editor: Ann Castel
Developmental Editor: Molly Kyle
Production Editor: Mary Irvin
Art Coordinator: Peter A. Robison
Artist: Jane Lopez
Cover Designer: Robert Vega
Production Buyer: Patricia A. Tonneman
Electronic Text Management: Ben Ko, Marilyn Wilson Phelps

This book was set in Century Schoolbook and Swiss 721 by Macmillan Publishing Company and was printed and bound by R. R. Donnelley/Virginia. The cover was printed by Phoenix Color Corp.

Macmillan Publishing Company
866 Third Avenue
New York, NY 10022

Macmillan Publishing Company is part of the Maxwell Communication Group of Companies.

Maxwell Macmillan Canada, Inc.
1200 Eglinton Avenue East, Suite 200
Don Mills, Ontario M3C 3N1

Library of Congress Cataloging-in-Publication Data
Zirpoli, Thomas J.
    Behavior management : applications for teachers and parents /
    Thomas J. Zirpoli, Kristine J. Melloy.
        p.   cm.
    Includes bibliographical references and index.
    ISBN 0–02–431725-X
    1. Behavior modification—United States. 2. Children—United States—Conduct of life. 3. Behavior assessment of children—United States. 4. classroom management—United States.   I. Melloy, Kristine J.   II. Title.
    LB1060.2.Z57 1993
    370.15—dc20
                                                                92-17780
                                                                CIP

Printing: 2   3   4   5   6   7   8   9   Year: 3   4   5   6   7

Preface

This book provides readers with the technical basics of applied behavior analysis as well as the everyday applications of behavior management. We communicate this information in language that is understandable to professionals, paraprofessionals, and parents. Readers will observe several major differences with this text as compared to other behavior management or applied behavior management texts. These differences are based upon our own values regarding the management of behavior and the recognition of current trends in our society.

Behavior management is a necessary skill for all caregivers of children, not just professional teachers. We recognize that in today's society, children are cared for by many individuals besides parents and teachers. Thus, throughout this book, the term "caregiver" is employed as a generic term for teachers, paraprofessionals, aides, nurses, parents, day-care providers, and any other individuals who care for children, and the vignettes illustrating applications of behavior management principles are adaptable for all.

Some readers might be surprised to find a chapter devoted to formal behavioral assessment (Chapter 2). However, because more than 250 million standardized tests are administered each year to American school children, many as a result of perceived "behavioral problems," we want to be sure that our readers understand the purpose of formal behavioral assessments, when and how they should be employed, and their limitations.

Cognitive behavior management and social skills training, while significant methods in the behavior management literature, have been largely ignored in current behavior management texts. In view of this, Chapters 6 and 7 include information that will help fill that void for readers who would like to gain an understanding of behavior management beyond the traditional methods of applied behavior analysis. In addition, these chapters reinforce our belief that the best behavior management strategy is the teaching and reinforcement of appropriate behaviors.

We recognize the growing preschool field and the expansion of day-care and other services provided for infants and toddlers. Although the basic principles of behavior management apply for all children, caregivers must understand that infants and young children have unique characteristics that demand special consideration. The growing number of early childhood programs require that we address this population directly; we acknowledge the special issues of young children in Chapter 10.

Adolescent issues are a primary concern to many educators and parents. The number of adolescents referred to out-of-home treatment facilities is at an all-time high. Clearly, this population requires special attention in the field of behavior management and we address these special issues in Chapter 11.

A person's behavior is influenced by his or her ethnic background, culture, and family customs. In Chapter 12 we urge caregivers to learn about and become sensitive to the cultural influences on children's behavior. While writing about these multicultural issues, there is always the danger of stereotyping. We have tried to avoid this trap, recognizing the uniqueness of all individuals, while at the same time acknowledging the influence of traditions and customs of those who share a common ethnic and cultural background.

Finally, we recognize that the best and most effective behavior management strategy is the teaching and reinforcement of appropriate behaviors and social skills. This belief is integrated throughout the text. We understand that some readers may be concerned with the inclusion of differential reinforcement in Chapter 5. Although traditionally thought of as techniques to decrease challenging behavior, we have thoughtfully and purposely focused on their ability to increase appropriate behavior.

This text includes the basic mechanics of applied behavior analysis (Chapters 1, 3, 4, 5, and 8). In many areas, the text breaks from the traditional applied behavior analysis texts and includes current topics and issues in behavior management (Chapters 2, 6, 7, 9, 10, 11, & 12). We hope our readers will find these additional chapters informative. We also hope that our readers will share their thoughts with us on how, in the next edition, this text may be improved. We welcome and look forward to your comments.

AUDIENCE

This text is designed for use in both undergraduate and graduate behavior management or applied behavior management courses. The text is appropriate for the preservice and inservice training of regular and special educators; preschool, elementary, and secondary educators; educational administrators; counselors; psychologists; and social workers.

ACKNOWLEDGMENTS

First, we thank the following individuals who made chapter contributions to this project: Mitchell Yell, University of South Carolina, who contributed Chapter 6 on cognitive behavior modification; Doug Warring and Sally Hunter,

University of St. Thomas, for their contribution of Chapter 12 on cultural influence on behavior; and Susan Bishop Zirpoli, who co-authored Chapter 10 on early childhood issues.

Second, we extend a special appreciation to Brother Leonard Courtney, University of St. Thomas, who served as our first reviewer and proofreader for each of our chapters. He contributed this service as a friend who appreciated our work and wanted to demonstrate his support for our efforts. Thank you, Brother Leonard.

Third, we thank those who made less obvious, but very important contributions: Patti Blasco, Karen Carr, Romona DeRosales, Linda Emerick, Kerry Frank, Michelle Lefebvre, Charlene Nelson, and Ann Ryan, University of St. Thomas; Bryan James, Maple Grove, Minnesota; and Mary McEvoy, University of Minnesota.

We would also like to thank the reviewers of the manuscript for their timely and helpful reviews: David Anderson, Bethel College; Paul Beare, Moorehead State University; Robert L. Carpenter, State University of New York, Binghamton; Nancy Contrucci, U. of Wisconsin-Eau Claire; E. Paula Crowley, Illinois State University; Rebecca Fewell, Tulane University; Gay Goodman, University of Houston; Diane Klein, Cal State University-Los Angeles; Louis Lanunziata, University of North Carolina, Wilmington; Douglas Lin, Central Washington University; James McCrory, Mary Baldwin College; Dean Richey, Tenn Tech University; Brenda Scheuermann, Southwest Texas State University; Craig Smith, Georgia College; Scott Sparks, Ohio University; and Philip Swicegood, Sam Houston State University.

We also appreciate the advice, assistance, and support from the professionals at Merrill/Macmillan, especially Ann Castel, Molly Kyle, and Mary Irvin.

Thomas J. Zirpoli
Kristine J. Melloy

Contents

CHAPTER 2
Formal Behavioral Assessment   39

CHAPTER 3
Informal Behavioral Assessment   79

CHAPTER 4
Single Subject Designs   123

PART THREE
Understanding and Managing Challenging Behaviors   297

CHAPTER 8
Behavior Reduction Strategies   299

CHAPTER 9
Specific Behavior Challenges   345

PART FOUR

Special Considerations for Special Populations   395

CHAPTER 10
Issues in Early Childhood Behavior   397

CHAPTER 11
Issues in Adolescent Behavior   435

PART ONE

Understanding Behavior

CHAPTER 1

Foundations of Behavior Modification

Why do people behave the way they do? It was probably first a practical question: How could a person anticipate and hence prepare for what another person would do? Later it would become practical in another sense: How would another person be induced to behave in a given way? Eventually it became a matter of understanding and explaining behavior. It could always be reduced to a question about causes.

—*Skinner, 1974, p. 10*

Behavior modification is an active intervention approach whereby caregivers (1) observe, measure, and evaluate current observable behavioral patterns; (2) identify environmental antecedents and consequences; (3) establish new behavioral objectives; and (4) advance the learning of new behavior or modify current behavior via the manipulation of identified antecedents and consequences. Behavior modification is not a single technique used to modify behavior; it is a term that has been used to describe a variety of specific techniques that have a firm foundation in the research literature. These techniques have been successfully employed to teach new behaviors and skills, expand current appropriate behaviors, and decrease inappropriate behaviors across a wide range of populations, settings, and situations (Kazdin, 1989; Rimm & Masters, 1974). As noted by Kazdin (1989), behavior modification has been successfully applied to both clinical (for example, abusive behaviors, depression, sexual deviance) and nonclinical behavior problems (for example, academic performance, noncompliance, tantrums).

The term *behavior* is defined broadly by many who study behavior and behavior modification. Behavior may refer to both *covert* responses (such as feelings and emotions) and *overt* responses (such as tantrums and aggression) (Rimm & Masters, 1974). The true behaviorist, however, is largely concerned with overt responses or behaviors that are observable and measurable. Baer, Wolf, and Risley (1968) stated that something must be observable and quantifiable to qualify as a behavior. A behavior is considered *observable* when it can be seen and *measurable* when it can be described in terms of clear criteria (Donnellan & LaVigna, 1988). These two criteria must be met in order to make the direct observation of behavior meaningful and reliable.

Morris identified *classical conditioning, operant conditioning,* and *social learning* as the "general theoretical positions . . .that form the basis of contemporary behavior modification approaches" (1985, p. 4). Each of these, in addition to *behavior therapy* and *applied behavior analysis,* makes up the primary "streams" of behavior modification and will be discussed here.

CLASSICAL CONDITIONING

Classical conditioning (also called *Pavlovian conditioning*) refers to the relationship between stimuli and reflex responses. *Stimulus* refers to any "condition, event, or change in the physical world" (Cooper, Heron, & Heward, 1987,

p. 18). Stimuli include light, noise, touch, temperature, taste of food, smells, textures, and so on, that evoke/elicit responses or respondent behavior.

Stimuli may be unconditioned or conditioned. An *unconditioned stimulus* (UCS) is naturally stimulating or unlearned. Examples include food and sex. A person does not have to learn that food and sex are reinforcing. A *conditioned stimulus* (CS) is one that has been learned or conditioned. For example, a child may learn to fear anyone wearing white clothing after spending months in a hospital that included painful treatments by medical personnel dressed in white. Meeting a certain person may serve as a conditioned stimulus for happiness or fear, depending on previous experiences with that person.

Respondent behaviors are usually not controlled by the individual and are frequently referred to as involuntary, reflex behaviors or unconditioned responses. An unconditioned stimulus usually produces an unconditioned response. For example, a bright light (unconditioned stimulus) focused on a person's eyes will probably produce many unconditioned responses such as closing the eyelids, covering the eyes, and turning away. These respondent behaviors are not learned; they occur automatically as a result of the stimulus (light).

Ivan Petrovich Pavlov
(1849–1936)

Ivan P. Pavlov (1849–1936), a Russian physiologist and 1904 Nobel Prize winner, is commonly referred to as the father of classical conditioning. During his research on animal digestion, Pavlov studied how different foods placed in the digestive system elicited unconditioned reflexes such as the production of gastric secretions and saliva. More significantly, Pavlov discovered that these responses could be stimulated when certain stimuli associated with the presentation of food were also present in the environment. For example, Pavlov observed that his dogs would begin to produce saliva when his assistant merely opened the cage door at meal time.

In 1927 Pavlov conducted his now famous study demonstrating that he could condition a dog to produce saliva (an unconditioned response) following the ringing of a bell. In his study, Pavlov paired the presentation of food (an unconditioned stimulus) with the ringing of a bell (a neutral stimulus to the dog). Over time, Pavlov found that merely ringing the bell, even in the absence of food, caused the dog to salivate. The ringing of the bell had become a learned or *conditioned stimulus* producing a learned or *conditioned response* (salivation). Pavlov went on to discover that the bell could lose its ability to elicit the production of saliva if it were repeatedly rung without the presentation of food. The dog learned that the bell was no longer associated with food and, thus, no longer acted as a conditioned stimulus for salivation. A model of Pavlov's classical conditioning of a salivation response in his dog is provided in Figure 1.1.

Pavlovian conditioning has expanded significantly since the days of Pavlov. Rescorla (1988) described the modern day understanding of classical conditioning as much more complex than the simple, but inadequate explanation provided earlier:

> Pavlovian conditioning is not a stupid process by which the organism willy-nilly forms associations between any two stimuli that happen to co-occur. Rather, the organism is better seen as an information seeker using logical and perceptual relations among events, along with its own preconceptions, to form a sophisticated representation of its world (Rescorla, 1988, p. 154)

Rescorla and others have expanded the traditional understanding of classical conditioning. Balsam and Tomie (1985) noted that learning must be under-

Figure 1.1. *Model of Pavlov's classical conditioning by the pairing of food and bell to elicit a conditioned salivation response in a dog.*

Before classical conditioning:
Food presented   Salivation
(Unconditioned Stimulus)   (Unconditioned Response)

During classical conditioning:
Food + bell presented   Salivation
(Unconditioned + Conditioned   (Unconditioned Response)
  Stimulus)

After classical conditioning:
Bell only presented   Salivation
(Conditioned Stimulus)   (Conditioned Response)

stood beyond the identification of conditioned and unconditioned stimuli. The properties of the stimuli and the context in which these stimuli are presented not only become part of the stimulus (called a *stimulus package*), but play a role in the type of response forms that follow. A conditioned stimulus presented in one environment may elicit a different response in a second environment. For example, how a child responds to another child's provocation within the classroom environment may be very different from how the child would respond to the same stimulus within the child's neighborhood. Indeed, behavior is far more complex than a simple understanding of the pairing of stimuli and associated responses; many other variables are involved. Pavlov, however, must be credited with providing the foundation for classical conditioning, which "continues to be an intellectually active area, full of new discoveries and information relevant to other areas of psychology" (Rescorla, 1988, p. 151). Classical conditioning provides the basis for many current behavior therapy techniques, described later in this chapter.

As stated by Kazdin, Pavlov was also noted for his precise scientific methods:

> Pavlov used precise methods that permitted careful observation and quantification of what he was studying. For example, in some of his studies, drops of saliva were counted to measure the conditioned reflex. His meticulous laboratory notes and his rigorous methods helped greatly to advance a scientific approach toward the study of behavior. (1989, p. 9)

Another animal psychologist who made significant contributions toward the understanding of human behavior and the advancement of the scientific method for psychological research was John B. Watson (1878–1958). Watson, influenced by the work of Pavlov, lead the way in the study of behavior on the American front. Watson pushed for major changes in traditional psychological thinking. He called himself a behaviorist (Watson, 1919) and advocated a different psychological approach to understanding behavior that he referred to as *behaviorism* (Watson, 1925). Learning, according to Watson, could explain most behaviors.

Like Pavlov, Watson conducted experiments using the principles of classical conditioning. In a famous study with an 11-month-old baby named Albert, Watson and Rayner (1920) paired a startling loud noise with the touching of a white rat. While Albert was playing with the rat, the noise was sounded each time he touched the rat. After only seven pairings, Albert, who was startled by the loud noise (unconditioned stimulus), was conditioned to also fear the white rat (a previously neutral stimuli). Even without the loud noise, Albert would cry when he was presented with the white rat. The rat had become a conditioned stimulus that elicited the conditioned response of fear.

Watson urged the psychological establishment to study overt behavior (behavior that is observable) rather than mental phenomena that could not be directly observed (for example, emotions, feelings, thoughts, and instinct). In his *Psychology from the Standpoint of a Behaviorist*, Watson criticized psychologists for their use of subjective and unproven interventions and the lack of a scientific methodology as modeled by Pavlov. Although Watson (1924), by his own admission, went "beyond my facts" (1924, p. 104) and extended his research findings on conditioning and learning to explain all behavior, he nevertheless set the stage for a new psychology.

OPERANT CONDITIONING

An *operant* is a behavior or response that is controlled or at least influenced by events within the environment (Skinner, 1974). For example, as a result of environmental influences, a child may learn to say "please" when asking for assistance. Children learning to talk quietly when visiting their school library is also an example of operant behavior. It is important to differentiate operant behavior from the previously described respondent behaviors, such as blinking in response to a bright light, which are involuntary or reflexive.

Operant conditioning refers to the relationship between overt events in the environment and changes in specific target behaviors. These events are classified as either antecedents or consequences. *Antecedents* are events in the environment that precede a target behavior or operant. For example, when John hits Mike after Mike takes a toy from John, the antecedent for hitting is the action of Mike taking a toy away from John. An observant caregiver could easily identify the antecedent to John hitting Mike. However, the relationship between an antecedent and a behavior may not be so obvious or direct. For example, when a child comes to school hungry and attends poorly to the teacher, hunger is an indirect antecedent to the poor attention. Unless a caregiver were told that the child was hungry, he or she may not be able to identify hunger as the antecedent to the child's poor behavior in the classroom.

A *consequence* refers to events in the environment that occur *after* a target behavior or response. For example, when a teacher pays attention to a child for disruptive classroom behavior (i.e., talking out, making noise), the attention serves as a consequence for the disruptive behavior. This relationship was explained by Donnellan and LaVigna:

> A consequence is defined as an environmental stimulus or event that contingently follows the occurrence of a particular response and, as a result of that contingent relationship, strengthens or weakens the future occurrence of that response. (1988, p. 20)

In operant conditioning, the consequence is identified as a *reinforcer* if the preceding behavior increases or is maintained at a current rate, duration, or intensity. The consequence is identified as a *punisher* if the preceding behavior decreases in rate, duration, or intensity. This relationship among antecedents, behaviors, and consequences serves as the foundation for operant conditioning as well as for most applications employed in applied behavior analysis. According to behaviorists, when this relationship is understood, the manipulation of antecedents and consequences may be used to teach new skills and modify current behaviors.

Operant conditioning also has its roots in animal research. Edward L. Thorndike (1874–1949) was one of the first researchers to apply basic operant conditioning principles and study the relationship between animal behavior (responses) and environmental conditions, especially the relationship between behavior and consequences. In his *law of effect,* Thorndike talked about the relationship between acts that produced "satisfaction" and the likelihood of that act (behavior) to recur (1905, p. 203). In his *law of exercise,* Thorndike (1911) also outlined how behaviors became associated with specific situations. The study of these associations between responses and consequences and between responses and situations is sometimes referred to as *associationism.* Thorndike's work provided a solid foundation for future research on positive reinforcement (*law of effect*) and stimulus control (*law of exercise*).

Thorndike (1911) demonstrated that the provision of reinforcement as a consequence increased the rate of learning. In his famous cat experiments, Thorndike used food to reinforce cats when they learned how to remove a barrier and escape from a box. He noted that, after repeated trials, the time it took the cat to escape from the box to get to the food decreased.

Thorndike's research on reinforcement influenced the work of B. F. Skinner (1904–1990) whose name has become synonymous with operant conditioning and behavior modification. Skinner (1938) also conducted many of his early studies using laboratory animals such as rats and pigeons. He expanded on Thorndike's research on the relationships between various consequences and behavior. Skinner also helped clarify the differences between operant conditioning and Pavlov's classical conditioning (Kazdin, 1989):

> The consequences which shape and maintain the behavior called an operant . . .have become part of the history of the organism. To alter a probability is not to elicit a response, as in a reflex. (Skinner, 1974, pp. 57–58)

Skinner described the concept of operant conditioning and the relationship between behavior and consequences as "simple enough":

> When a bit of behavior has the kind of consequence called reinforcing, it is more likely to occur again. A positive reinforcer strengthens any behavior that produces it: a glass of water is positively reinforcing when we are thirsty, and if we draw and drink a glass of water, we are more likely to do so again on similar occasions. (Skinner, 1974, p. 51)

Skinner is also noted for expanding his laboratory research to the promotion of operant conditioning as a method for improving societal conditions. His book *Walden Two* (1948) outlined how these principles could be used to develop a utopian society. His next book, *Science and Human Behavior* (1953), promoted the application of operant conditioning in education, government, law, and religion.

B. F. Skinner
(1904–1990)

Skinner (1953) stated that behaviorists needed to be more concerned with the *description* of behavior, and the antecedents and consequences related to behavior, rather than the explanation of behavior. Also, Skinner emphasized the importance of the current situation regarding a specific behavior rather than the long-term history of the behavior problem. For example, Skinner was more interested in teaching a child to sit in his seat within a classroom environment (by reinforcing the child for sitting) than trying to explain or understand *why* the child frequently ran around the classroom.

Skinner did not totally reject the philosophy of cognitive psychology or, as he called it, "the world within the skin" (1974, p. 24). He did, however, seem to grow wary of the minimal progress made in understanding behavior under the traditional principles of cognitive psychology: "Behaviorism, on the other hand, has moved forward" (Skinner, 1974, p. 36). Operant conditioning clearly emphasizes the study of observable, overt behaviors that can be measured and studied by methods of direct observation (see Chapter 3).

Tawney and Gast (1984, p. 14) listed Skinner's contributions as follows:

- Discovery of operant conditioning.
- Demonstration of how reinforcement contingencies can change the rate of behaviors.
- Promotion of the use of valid and reliable methods of behavioral observation and research of single organisms.
- Establishment of strategies for the experimental analysis of behavior.
- Promotion of the study of observable behavior.

The work of Pavlov, Skinner, Thorndike, and Watson represented a major shift from the work of Sigmund Freud (1856–1939) and others who promoted a more traditional psychoanalytic approach. While the behavioral approach focuses on overt behaviors and environmental events related to those behaviors, the psychoanalytic approach focuses on psychological forces such as drives, impulses, needs, motives, conflicts, and personality traits existing within the individual. Whereas the behavioral approach views inappropriate behavior as conditioned or learned, the psychoanalytic approach views inappropriate behavior primarily as the result of some maladaptive psychological process or some underlying defect in personality. In other words, the source of the child's inappropriate behavior existed within the child.

Dissatisfaction with the psychoanalytic approach has revolved around several issues. First, assessment procedures commonly used in the psychoanalytic approach remove the child from the situation in which inappropriate behaviors occur. The psychiatrist or psychologist preparing the assessment may never observe the child within the environment where the problem behaviors occur. Direct observations are usually limited to behaviors observed within the professional's office. Problem behaviors exhibited within the child's everyday life situations and environments may not even occur within the confines of the professional's office. For example, Brown (1990) found that regardless of their behavior outside the clinic, 85% of children behaved appropriately in the clinic. Frequently, the professional's understanding of the inappropriate behavior is limited to a qualitative description of the behavior provided by caregivers.

Second, the identification of underlying psychological causes of behavior yields little information that can be used in the development of an intervention plan. For example, if a psychologist identifies a specific personality trait as the cause of inappropriate behavior exhibited within the classroom, this information does not help the child's teacher establish a program to decrease the occurrence of the inappropriate behavior within the classroom. In fact, there is usually limited communication between therapists and caregivers.

Third, the generalization of therapy or treatment (for example, psychotherapy or psychoanalysis) effects to functional environments such as the home or classroom has been disappointing. Rimm and Masters (1974) stated that psychoanalysis and related schools of therapy have failed to provide hard data to support their effectiveness. Kazdin (1988, 1989) found that while there are more than 200 forms of psychotherapy identified for children and adolescents, the effectiveness of many of these treatments lacks significant empirical support and they remain virtually unknown. Table 1.1 provides an outline of differences between the psychoanalytic and behavioral approaches.

BEHAVIOR THEORY

Behavior therapy may be considered an extension or practical application of classical conditioning. While some believe that behavior modification and behavior therapy are synonymous and share the same principles and methods (for example, Kanfer & Phillips, 1970), others disagree. Rimm and Masters (1974) stated that while behavior modification and behavior therapy share many of the same principles, behavior modification stresses operant conditioning and behavior therapy stresses classical conditioning. Also, behavior therapy and classical conditioning have been used primarily with covert behaviors and mental illness such as anxiety and neuroses, while behavior modification and operant conditioning have been used primarily with overt behaviors that are observable and measurable, such as aggression and tantrums. Tawney and Gast stated that behavior therapy "refers primarily to clinical treatment of so-called behavior disorders" (1984, p. 10). Rimm and Masters (1974, pp. 6–16) listed the following general assumptions about behavior therapy:

◆ Behavior therapy tends to concentrate on maladaptive behavior rather than on some presumed underlying cause.

Table 1.1. *Psychoanalytic versus behavioral approach.*

Variable	Psychoanalytic Approach	Behavioral Approach
Behavioral focus	Covert behaviors such as drives, impulses, and motives	Overt behaviors such as walking and talking
View of inappropriate behavior	Maladaptive psychological process or underlying defect in personality	Conditioned or learned
Assessment approach	Conducted by psychiatrist or psychologist outside the environment where behavior occurs. Limited direct observations	Direct observation of child's behavior within natural environments
Concern for environmental influences	Low	High
Concern for psychological influences	High	Low
Empirical support	Low	High
Direct application for teachers and parents	Low	High

- Behavior therapy assumes that maladaptive behaviors are, to a considerable degree, acquired through learning, the same way that any behavior is learned.
- Behavior therapy assumes that psychological principles, especially learning principles, can be extremely effective in modifying maladaptive behavior.
- Behavior therapy involves setting specific, clearly defined treatment goals.
- The behavior therapist adapts his or her method of treatment to the client's problem.
- Behavior therapy concentrates on the here and now.
- Any techniques subsumed under the label "behavior therapy" are assumed to have been subjected to empirical test and have been found to be relatively effective.

In 1963 Eysenck founded the first professional journal to focus on behavior therapy. Titled *Behavior Research and Therapy,* it was followed by other journals such as *Behavior Therapy* (founded by Franks in 1970) and *Behavior Therapy and Experimental Psychiatry* (founded by Wolpe in 1970).

Several treatment strategies are frequently associated with behavior therapy, including systematic desensitization, flooding, aversion therapy, covert conditioning, modeling, and biofeedback (Kazdin, 1978). A brief description of each of these follows.

Systematic Desensitization

Joseph Wolpe, a South African medical doctor, used a form of classical conditioning to reduce anxiety in cats. Building on Pavlov's research, Wolpe (1958) demonstrated that the strength of anxiety-producing stimuli could be reduced when paired with nonanxiety-producing stimuli. First, Wolpe exposed cats to only a small amount of the anxiety-producing stimuli. He then exposed the cats to positive stimuli such as food. Eating food and engaging in other positive behaviors in the presence of small amounts of the anxiety-producing stimuli reduced the anxiety response. Over time, Wolpe slowly increased the amount of anxiety-producing stimuli paired with the competing positive stimuli (eating food) until the anxiety response was eliminated.

Wolpe later extended his work and developed an anxiety reduction treatment for humans called *systematic desensitization.* According to Wolpe (1958), systematic desensitization was an example of *counterconditioning* or the substitution of an inappropriate emotional response with an appropriate response. The majority of Wolpe's desensitization research focused on the substitution of anxiety. Rimm and Master's stated that "Wolpe assumes that individuals learn to experience anxiety in the presence of certain stimuli through a process of classical, or Pavlovian, conditioning" (1974, p. 76).

Using the same fundamental principles with humans, Wolpe paired relaxation with gradually increasing amounts of anxiety-producing stimuli. Wolpe taught his subjects how to become relaxed through relaxation exercises. The subjects were then encouraged to pair an imagined representation of the anxiety-producing stimuli with their relaxation skills. Wolpe systematically increased the anxiety-producing stimuli as his subjects became better able to relax in the presence of smaller amounts of the stimuli. Over time, the human subjects were able to overcome the anxiety response in the presence of the original anxiety-producing stimuli. Today, systematic desensitization is used to reduce a variety of behaviors from eating disorders to sexually deviant behaviors. These methods are usually employed in clinical settings by trained therapists.

Flooding

Like desensitization, flooding is used to treat anxiety. Unlike desensitization in which the anxiety-producing stimulus is presented in a hierarchical fashion, flooding involves the repeated presentation of the anxiety-producing stimulus at full strength until the stimulus no longer produces anxiety. In effect, the stimulus loses its ability to elicit anxiety. This technique has been effective in reducing or eliminating anxiety associated with specific social situations, test-taking, specific animals (spiders and snakes), and others (Kazdin, 1978).

Aversion Therapy

Aversion therapy involves the pairing of aversive stimuli (pain, being sick, losing a job) with other stimuli (alcohol, cigarettes, drugs) in order to discourage the behavior associated with the second stimuli (drinking, smoking, taking drugs). Aversion therapy employs both classical conditioning (the pairing of an aversive stimuli with another stimuli) and operant conditioning (the use of an aversive stimuli as a consequence for a target behavior). Aversion therapy has been effective in treating alcohol abuse, cigarette smoking, overeating, and "sexual attraction toward socially censured stimuli" (Kazdin, 1978, p. 220). However, the use of aversives to modify a person's behavior, especially in operant conditioning, has been seriously questioned on both ethical and efficacy grounds. The use of aversion therapy has been discouraged by many professional organizations, current texts, and individual therapists (LaVigna & Donnellan, 1986; Meyer & Evans, 1989). We agree with this contemporary assessment of aversion therapy and hope this text will promote the use of non-aversive methods of behavior change as the intervention of first choice. These issues will be discussed later in this chapter and again in Chapter 8.

Covert Conditioning

Covert conditioning, developed by Joseph R. Cautela (1972), is a covert (imagined) form of classical and operant conditioning. Those who practice covert conditioning believe that overt behavior can be changed when an individual

imagines target behaviors paired with reinforcing or punishing consequences—depending on the desired outcome. For example, an individual may
imagine drinking and getting sick or the individual may imagine avoiding a
drink and receiving reinforcement from others for demonstrating self-control.
This procedure is used primarily with older adolescents and adults. Many
questions have been raised regarding the efficacy of covert conditioning. The
primary question involves the generalization of covert behavior changes to
overt behavior changes. The efficacy of covert conditioning has not been clearly determined.

Modeling

Modeling refers to the observation and learning of new behaviors from others.
Within a therapeutic application, modeling may involve a child who is afraid of
dogs watching other children play with dogs. This type of modeling application
has been successfully used to "treat" other fears (for example, snakes, heights,
water) (Bandura, 1971). The classic example of modeling as a behavior therapy
technique was reported by Jones (1924) who helped a young boy overcome his
fear of rabbits and other furry objects. The young boy, Peter, and three other
boys were placed in a room with a rabbit. After watching the other three boys
play with the rabbit, Peter's anxiety about touching the rabbit was decreased
and he was soon touching the rabbit. An applied use of modeling as an instructional prompt for teaching new skills and behaviors, such as social skills
(Bandura, 1977), is discussed in greater detail below and in Chapter 7.

Biofeedback

Biofeedback involves providing an individual with immediate information
(visual and/or auditory) about a physiological process (e.g., heart rate, pulse
rate, blood pressure, skin temperature) and the use of operant conditioning
(reinforcement and/or punishment) to modify the physiological process. The
objective of biofeedback is to teach individuals how to control or manipulate
"otherwise involuntary or unfelt" physiological processes (Basmajian, 1983, p.
1). Biofeedback "may be understood as one component in a self-control
approach towards health and sickness" (Broder, 1980, p. 96) and has been used
to "treat" hypertension, headaches, general anxiety, stress pain, insomnia,
speech disorders, seizures, and other problems (Kazdin, 1978; Basmajian,
1983).

   A considerable body of research supports biofeedback training as effective
in teaching individuals to control various physiological processes (Orne, 1979).
On the other hand, there is evidence that relaxation training and frequent rest
breaks are equally effective in reducing anxiety and chronic pain (Cummings &
Trabin, 1980; Orne, 1979). According to Cummings and Trabin, the effectiveness of biofeedback is largely related to individuals' attitudes, which "affect
their diligence in carrying out the practice regimen" involved in biofeedback
therapy (1980, p. 145). Middaugh (1990) adds that the most important variable

regarding the efficacy of biofeedback is the selection of the right technique for the right individual.

Other questions regarding biofeedback are concerns about the generalization of clinical effects to functional environments where the stimuli for anxiety and other problems originate. In other words, are the physiological changes generalized to the individual's functional environments? Basmajian stated that there is evidence that some individuals are able to generalize biofeedback effects in functional environments and can, for example, "willfully elevate their blood pressure" (1983, p. 1).

Except for the treatment of headaches and seizures (Womack, Smith, & Chen, 1988), urinary incontinence (Killam, Jeffries, & Varni, 1985), and anal incontinence (Duckro, Purcell, Gregory, & Schultz, 1985), the use of biofeedback as a behavior management technique for children and adolescents has not received significant attention in the research literature. Some researchers have been successful in modifying children's attention, impulsiveness (Omizo & Williams, 1982), and hyperactivity (Denkowski, Denkowski, & Omizo, 1984) using biofeedback and relaxation training methods.

APPLIED BEHAVIOR ANALYSIS

The term *applied behavior analysis* refers to the direct application of the principles of behavior modification in nonlaboratory, everyday situations and settings. Horner described applied behavior analysis as "the application of behavioral principles to produce socially significant changes in behavior" (1991, p. 607). Kazdin defined applied behavior analysis as an "extension of operant conditioning principles and methods of studying human behavior to clinical and socially important human behaviors" (1989, p. 23). For example, using behavioral principles to improve classroom performance (on-task behaviors, number of math problems completed, use of manners, etc.) would be considered an applied use of behavior modification. The use of behavior modification principles and techniques in applied settings began in the late 1950s and early 1960s (Kauffman, 1989). Early research using behavior modification with people in applied settings employed persons living in institutional settings. This research included people with disability labels such as severely mentally retarded, psychotic, autistic, and emotionally disturbed. As time passed, and as the successful use of behavior modification became documented in the professional literature, the same techniques were also used with people who had mild disabilities and with populations who were nondisabled.

In the first issue of the *Journal of Applied Behavior Analysis* (founded by Wolf in 1968), Baer, Wolf, and Risley (1968) outlined several basic elements of applied behavior analysis that are still applicable today. These elements included a basic understanding or belief that:

◆ while both applied and basic research ask "what controls the behavior under study," applied research looks beyond variables that are convenient for study or important to theory (p. 91);

- behaviors should be observed and studied within their natural environments (the real world), rather than in the laboratory;

- applied research is "eminently pragmatic"; it is interested in physical behaviors, not what an individual can be made to say or feel (p. 93);

- the real world application of applied behavior analysis may not allow the same precise measurement possible in the laboratory, but that "reliable quantification of behavior can be achieved, even in thoroughly difficult settings" (p. 93);

- behaviors and techniques used to modify behavior should be "completely identified and described" so that a "trained reader could replicate that procedure well enough to produce the same results, given only a reading of the description" (p. 5);

- procedures of applied behavior analysis "strive for relevance to principle," rather than "a collection of tricks" to change behaviors (p. 96; referring to the principles of behavior modification of the time);

- a behavioral technique should be judged as having an application for society (applied) when it produces a behavior change that is "large enough" to have "practical value" (p. 96); and

- The generality or durability of behavioral change over time is an important concern that should "be programmed, rather than expected or lamented" (p. 97).

In a second review of the important elements of applied behavior analyses, Baer, Wolf, and Risley restated that applied behavior analysis ought to be *applied, behavioral, analytic, technological, conceptual, effective,* and capable of appropriate *generalized outcomes* (1987, p. 313). These are consistent with the dimensions of applied behavioral analysis outlined earlier and listed by the same authors some twenty years earlier (Baer, Wolf, & Risley, 1968). According to the authors, these dimensions "remain functional" (p. 314).

SOCIAL LEARNING THEORY

Bandura stated that "behavior, other personal factors, and environmental factors all operate as interlocking determinants of each other":

> Personal and environmental factors do not function as independent determinants, rather they determine each other. Nor can "persons" be considered causes independent of their behavior. It is largely through their actions that people produce the environmental conditions that affect their behavior in a reciprocal fashion. (Bandura, 1977, p. 9)

Bandura (1977) referred to this integrated approach as a process of *reciprocal determinism.*

Bandura also stressed the importance of modeling on the acquisition of behavior. According to Bandura (1977), an individual observes a behavior, cognitively retains the information observed, and performs the modeled behavior.

This performance is then regulated by reinforcement and motivational processes (e.g., the integration of environmental and cognitive influences on behavior). For example, Bandura (1969) found that young children imitated aggressive behavior viewed during a film. Bandura warned about the influential source of social learning provided by the developing mass media, especially television and films:

> The mass media play an influential role in shaping behavior and social attitudes. With increasing use of symbolic modeling, parents, teachers, and other traditional role models may occupy less prominent roles in social learning. (Bandura, 1977, p. 39)

Kauffman referred to social *learning* theory as an extension of the behavioral model "to include observational learning and person variables—thoughts, feelings, and other internal states—in an analysis of behavior" (1985, p. 32). Kauffman (1989) later changed his terminology to social *cognitive* theory. Wicks-Nelson and Israel (1991) noted the emphasis of cognitive processes, such as attention, memory, and problem-solving skills, in the social learning perspective. Kazdin stated that the development of social learning theory was an attempt to integrate the "aspects of different learning paradigms and to take cognitive processes into account" (1989, p. 21–22).

The student of social learning theory strives to understand how behavior is influenced by classical and operant conditioning principles, along with the influences of the child's social and cognitive development. Human behavior, according to social learning theory, is much too complex to understand without this integrated approach.

Table 1.2 provides an overview of the general theoretical streams of behavior management that have been outlined in this chapter. Table 1.3 provides an overview of historical researchers discussed in this chapter and their important contributions to the science of behavior management.

BASIC CONCEPTS OF APPLIED BEHAVIOR MODIFICATION

Behavior

We have said a lot about behavior thus far. Indeed, behavior modification cannot be understood, certainly not applied, without an understanding of what we mean when we talk about a child's behavior. As we have previously stated, behaviors may be covert (emotions) or overt (tantrums), but behavior modification tends to focus on overt behaviors. Behaviors may be in the form of unconditioned reflexes (eye blinks) or purposeful intent (giving someone a kiss). Some behaviors are conditioned or learned (avoiding a hot stove) and some are simply the result of modeling (a baby girl acting like her older sister). Behaviors may be as simple as body movements (touching) or very complex, involving the integration of many behaviors (telling a story). Our everyday lives are filled with many examples of behaviors that can be observed, mea-

Table 1.2. *General theoretical streams of behavior management and related researchers.*

Theoretical Stream	Focus of Behavioral Research	Researchers
Classical conditioning	Relationship between stimuli and reflex responses (conditioned and unconditioned).	Pavlov Watson
Operant conditioning	Relationship between overt events in the environment (antecedents and consequences) and changes in behavior.	Thorndike Skinner
Behavior therapy	Practical applications of classical conditioning used primarily with covert behaviors and mental illness.	Eysenck Wolpe Cautela
Applied behavior analysis	Practical applications of operant conditioning in nonlaboratory, everyday situations and settings.	Baer Wolf Risley Kazdin
Social learning or cognition theory	Relationship among behavior and child's social and cognitive development. Integrates classical and operant learning principles.	Bandura

Table 1.3. *Historical figures in behavioral research and important contributions.*

Researcher	Important Contributions
I. Pavlov (1849–1936)	A Russian physiologist and Nobel Prize winner. Considered to be the father of classical conditioning. Conducted research on animal digestion and unconditional reflexes. Conditioned a dog to produce saliva in response to a bell by pairing bell with presentation of food. Promoted the use of precise scientific methods.
J. B. Watson (1878–1958)	Called himself a "behaviorist." Wrote *Psychology from the Standpoint of a Behaviorist* in 1919 and *Behaviorism* in 1925. Noted for his research in classical conditioning of fear responses. Urged the psychological establishment to study overt behavior rather than mental phenomena.
E. L. Thorndike (1874–1949)	Applied operant conditioning to the study of animal behavior. His *Law of Effects* (1905) and *Law of Exercise* (1911) outlined his research on reinforcement and stimulus control.
B. F. Skinner (1904–1990)	Considered to be the father of operant conditioning. Noted for his study of rat and pigeon behavior in the "Skinner Box." Expanded on Thorndike's research on the relationship between behavior and consequences. His book *Walden Two* (1948) and *Science and Human Behavior* (1953) promoted the use of operant conditioning as a method of improving social conditions. Emphasized the study of observable, overt behaviors that could be measured.
J. Wolpe (1915–)	A South African medical doctor noted for his classical conditioning and behavior therapy research. Developed an anxiety reduction treatment called systematic desensitization.
A. Bandura (1925–)	Noted for his research on social learning theory and the use of modeling to teach behavior. Promoted an integrated approach where personal and environmental factors operate as interlocking determinants of each other. Warned of the social influence of the mass media.

sured, studied, and modified. Whether they are the unconditioned responses of internal emotions or the result of environmental conditions, behaviors provide the focal point of behavior modification.

Antecedents

Except for the provision of a basic definition of antecedents as events occurring prior to specific behaviors, little else has been said about antecedents. Indeed, within the science of behavior modification, the relationship between behavior and consequences seems to receive a disproportionate amount of attention. But antecedents are extremely important and must be recognized as equally important. While consequences focus on what happens after the occurrence of a target behavior and the modification of future behavior, the study of antecedents provides us with the opportunity to modify a behavior before it occurs. Clearly, certain environmental conditions are likely to elicit behaviors in individuals that may be avoided or prevented by means of simple environmental modifications. By making these changes, the antecedents to certain behaviors are removed and the likelihood of seeing certain behaviors is decreased or eliminated. For example, placing children within an environment containing few rules and little supervision is likely to promote the occurrence of many inappropriate behaviors.

In general, antecedents are thought of as stimuli that occur prior to behaviors. Definitions and discussion of stimuli are outlined in the following sections. While stimuli refer to specific events or prompts prior to a target behavior, antecedents refer to the broader picture of influences that exist within the environment prior to a target behavior. Therefore, when monitoring the antecedents to a target behavior, a long list of interrelated stimuli may be observed. For example, in Vignette 1.1, antecedents related to the behavior of Jill running out of the classroom may include the onset of the reading lesson, the behavior of another child in her reading group, her general seating arrangement, or a combination of all these factors. Bandura wrote about the important role antecedents play in the formation of behavior and behavioral expectations:

> Without anticipatory capacities people would be forced to act blindly in ways that might prove to be unproductive, if not hazardous. Information about the probable effects of specific actions or events is conveyed by environmental stimuli. One can be informed of what to expect by the distinctive features of places, persons, or things, or by social signals in the language, gestures, and actions of others. (1977, p. 58)

Consequences

The relationship between behaviors and consequences represents the heart of behavior modification. Consequences are events or changes in the environment following a target behavior. For example, in Vignette 1.1, what were the consequences of Jill's running away behavior? Who provided these conse-

Vignette 1.1.   Example of Classroom Antecedents and Consequences
Related to Running Away Behavior.

Jennifer, an elementary school teacher, had a young girl, Jill, in her first-grade
class who frequently ran out of the classroom and onto the playground.
Unfortunately, Jennifer's classroom, located on the first floor, had a direct-
access door to the playground. Although Jennifer tried to keep the door locked,
Jill had learned how to unlock the door and run into the playground before
anyone could stop her. Jennifer noticed that this behavior usually occurred
shortly after the children were directed into their companion reading groups.
Although Jill was progressing well with her reading, Jennifer also noticed that
Jill did not get along with one of the boys in her reading group.

Jennifer could not leave her students unsupervised. Thus, while monitoring Jill from the classroom window, she would call her principal, report that
Jill had run into the playground (again), and ask the principal to bring Jill
back to the classroom. At this point the principal would go to the playground,
bring Jill back into the school's main office, and talk to Jill about the dangers
of running away from her classroom. The principal was a very gentle man and
all the young children in the school liked him. After talking with Jill for about
five minutes, the principal would provide her with a drink of water, or sometimes juice, and return her to Jennifer's classroom. Upon returning to the
classroom, Jennifer would thank the principal and direct Jill to rejoin her
reading group.

quences? In your opinion, were these consequences primarily reinforcing or
punishing? Do you think Jill will want to run away again?

Cooper, Heron, and Heward (1987) outlined two forms of consequences.
In the first form, a consequence is represented by the *addition* of a new stimulus to the environment. For example, a child asking for a snack in an appropriate polite manner (target behavior) may be followed by attention from the
caregiver and a snack (new stimulus). In Vignette 1.1, Jill was presented with
the principal's attention and a drink of juice (stimulus) as a consequence for
running away from her classroom (target behavior).

In the second form, a consequence is represented by the *removal* of a
stimuli already present within the environment. For example, when a child is
behaving in an inappropriate manner, a caregiver may decide to ignore the
child (remove attention) until the maladaptive behavior is terminated.

A consequence may also be represented by a *change* in current environmental stimuli following a target behavior. For example, while attention to a
behavior may be added or terminated as outlined earlier, the level of attention
may be modified or changed as a consequence of a child's behavior. For example, a caregiver's changing facial expression while listening to a child tell a

story represents an ever-changing consequence for the child's ongoing behavior. In summary, a consequence may be represented by the addition, removal, or change in environmental stimuli following a target behavior.

In addition to the form a consequence may take, a second and very important element of consequences is the effect of the consequence on the preceding target behavior. The question of "effect" refers to how the consequence influences or changes the target behavior. For example, the probability of the target behavior occurring again may be increased or decreased, or the actual rate of occurrence may increase or decrease as a result of the consequence. Other possible behavioral changes may include an increase or decrease in duration and intensity. All of these behavioral changes are related to the consequence(s) that followed the behavior. Thus, a reciprocal relationship between behavior and consequence is established. Each has an influence on the other and each can be manipulated in an effort to modify the other. A more complete review of consequences (positive and negative) is provided in Chapters 5 and 8.

Stimuli

As described earlier, stimuli are events or activities within the environment that are capable of forming a relationship with behavior either as an antecedent or as a consequence. For example, turning the lights on and off in a classroom may be an antecedent stimuli for the children to look at the teacher and pay attention. A pat on the back by a caregiver is a stimulus that could be provided as a consequence following a child's outstanding performance. In this case, the stimulus (a pat on the back) is in the form of a reinforcer. A stimulus may become a *discriminative stimulus* (S^D) (also discussed in Chapter 5) for a specific behavior when it is repeatedly associated with that behavior. In the previous example, turning the lights on and off may become an S^D for looking at the teacher and paying attention (behavior). A bell in school may serve as a stimulus for children to change classes. Although the sound of a bell does not naturally elicit children to change classes, it may became a conditioned or learned stimulus after it is consistently used to signal children to change classes. The end of a specific morning TV program may become a stimulus for a child to leave home for school. When the relationship between the S^D and behavior is firmly established, then the behavior is considered to be under *stimulus control*.

We must make a distinction between an S^D and an *S-delta*. While an S^D is an antecedent that serves as an appropriate cue for a behavior and results in reinforcement, an S-delta is an antecedent that does not serve as the appropriate cue for a behavior and, thus, does not result in reinforcement. For example, if a teacher claps her hands in an effort to get the children's attention and the children continue to play (and the teacher's behavior is not reinforced), the stimulus (clapping hands) in this case would not be considered an S^D, but an S-delta.

Stimulus generalization refers to the performance of a behavior following a stimulus (prompt or cue) not presented during the initial stimulus-response training. For example, if the teacher merely reached for the light switch and the children responded as they were taught to respond (looking and paying attention) to the lights being turned on and off, we would say that stimulus generalization had occurred from one stimulus (turning the lights on and off) to another stimulus (reaching for the light switch).

Responses

A response is a behavior that is observable and measurable. Individuals are constantly responding as they move around and complete daily tasks. Many of these behaviors or responses are under stimulus control (getting up in the morning in response to the alarm clock, following a schedule throughout the day, responding to others in a manner consistent with a previous history of knowing that person, and so on). Many behaviors are in response to new stimuli that are added to the environment such as a new student walking into the classroom or a sudden change in the schedule. Many behaviors are in response to internal feelings such as being hungry and getting something to eat or feeling tired and taking a nap.

Response generalization refers to changes in behaviors other than the behavior that was targeted for change or modification. In keeping with our previous example, if the teacher turned the lights on and off and the children *also* put their hands on their desk and sat up straight, these additional behaviors exhibited by the children represent a response generalization from the target behaviors (looking at the teacher and paying attention).

Reinforcement

The relationships formed between stimuli and responses provide the foundation for behavior modification and related disciplines. Reinforcement, discussed in greater detail in Chapter 5, is a type of stimulus that serves as a consequence for a response/behavior. However, by definition, a stimulus may not be considered a reinforcer unless it affects the preceding behavior in one of the ways outlined in the following list. Used appropriately (see Chapter 5), reinforcement has several potential effects on the response it follows. For example:

- ◆ Reinforcement may *maintain* the current rate, duration, or intensity of a response.
- ◆ Reinforcement may increase the *probability* that a new response will occur again.
- ◆ Reinforcement may *increase* the future rate, duration, or intensity of a response.
- ◆ Reinforcement may strengthen a response that is weak and inconsistent.

Because of these properties, behaviorists believe that reinforcement provides the key to understanding the etiology and modification of behavior.

Reinforcement is a powerful tool used to teach new behaviors and change current behaviors; reinforcement is the foundation of Skinner's operant conditioning. It is the treatment of choice for today's contemporary application of behavior modification and, specifically, applied behavior analysis.

An important property of reinforcement that caregivers must understand is that the effects of reinforcement do not differentiate between appropriate and inappropriate behaviors. Reinforcement is under the control of the user who may, even unknowingly, apply it following any behavior, appropriate or inappropriate. Reinforcement may be, and frequently is, used to maintain or increase inappropriate, as well as appropriate, behaviors. The most common example of this is the child who has temper tantrums that are reinforced when caregivers give in to the child's demands. A primary objective of this text is to provide a greater understanding of how reinforcement may be used to increase appropriate behaviors and how the removal of reinforcement may be used to decrease inappropriate behaviors.

Punishment

Punishment (discussed in greater detail in Chapter 8), like reinforcement, is also a type of stimuli that may serve as a consequence for behavior. By definition, a stimuli may be classified as a punisher only if the preceding response/behavior changes in one of the following ways:

♦   The probability of a new behavior occurring again is decreased.
♦   The future rate, duration, and/or intensity of a current behavior is decreased or eliminated.
♦   Other dimensions of the behavior are weakened.

Like reinforcement, punishment does not differentiate between appropriate and inappropriate behaviors. Unknowingly, caregivers may punish appropriate behaviors, as well as behaviors perceived to be inappropriate. For example, when we become angry at young children for asking too many questions, we may be punishing age-appropriate behavior. Moreover, punishment procedures tend to have many undesirable side effects (discussed in Chapter 8). In this text, we hope to encourage parents and teachers to concentrate on methods of reinforcement to manage behavior.

Prompts and Cues

Although some consider "cues" to involve *verbal* guidance and "prompts" to involve *physical* guidance, in this text we use the terms synonymously and use the term "prompt" to describe both terms. Prompts are antecedent stimuli that supplement discriminative stimuli in order to produce a specific target behavior. Donnellan, LaVigna, Negri-Shoultz, and Fassbender defined a prompt as "the assistance provided to the learner after the presentation of the instructional stimulus, but *before* the response. This procedure is used to assure a correct response" (1988, p. 53). For example, a teacher may supplement ringing a bell (an S^D for starting an activity) with the verbal prompt, "Children, what are you supposed to do when you hear the bell?"

The use of prompts to supplement a discriminative stimuli is usually a temporary instructional aid and should be systematically phased out as soon as possible. In the previous example, the teacher does not want to use the additional verbal prompt for the whole school year. The goal is for the students to respond to the S^D without additional prompts. This is accomplished when the teacher slowly phases out the use of prompts and reinforces students for responding to the S^D.

Several different types of prompts are briefly described and discussed in the following sections.

Natural Prompts

A natural prompt is an environmental stimuli that naturally occurs prior to target behaviors. Natural prompts are always preferable, whereas unnatural or artificial prompts should be replaced with natural prompts whenever possible. For example, if a caregiver wants a child to make his or her bed each morning without being told (a verbal prompt), then the caregiver must teach the child to make the bed immediately after getting out of it. Initially, a verbal prompt may be necessary ("Did you make your bed?"), but when the target behavior is reinforced ("Thank you for making your bed this morning!") as the artificial prompt is phased out, the natural prompt (getting out of bed) will soon serve as the S^D for making the bed. Figure 1.2 provides a list of target behaviors and the natural prompts frequently associated with each. The less dependent children are on artificial prompts and the more they are reinforced for responding appropriately to natural prompts, the easier behavior management becomes for caregivers.

Figure 1.2. *Target behaviors and natural prompts.*

Target Behaviors	Natural Environmental Prompts
Getting up in the A.M.	Alarm clock
Going to school on time	Clock or watch
Being quiet and listening	Teacher or someone else begins to talk
Changing classes	School bell Classroom clock
Being loud and playful	Entering the gym or playground
Raising your hand	When you need help When you have a question When you know the answer to a teacher's question.

Verbal Prompts

Verbal prompts are the most common type of prompt used with children and include the following (Cuvo & Davis, 1980):

- ◆ Giving directions or instructions regarding a whole target behavior. This may serve as the S^D for the expected appropriate behaviors ("Class, it's time for lunch" or "John, it's time for bed").
- ◆ Specific prompts concerning expected behaviors within a task ("Line up by the door" or "Go to your bedroom"). These provide additional verbal prompts (instructional prompts) for the specific behaviors included within the whole target behavior—going to lunch or going to bed.
- ◆ Asking questions ("What should you do now?").

In the following example, a verbal direction serves as the S^D for a child to go to bed:

- ◆ *Behavior:* Going to bed.
- ◆ *Discriminative Stimulus (S^D):* A specific time, such as 8:00 P.M., or a verbal S^D such as "John, it is time for bed."
- ◆ *Additional Instructional Verbal Prompts:*
  1. "Go to your bedroom."
  2. "Put on your pajamas."
  3. "Get into bed."
  4. "Stay in bed."

Initially, a caregiver may have to use the S^D and additional instructional verbal prompts when teaching the child what is expected when the S^D is given. Over time, the caregiver should phase out the use of the additional verbal prompts and allow each step in the sequence of going to bed to act as the natural prompt for the next behavior. Thus, *going to the bedroom* serves as a natural prompt for *putting on pajamas,* and so on.

When gestural, modeling, and physical prompts are necessary, caregivers are encouraged to pair these prompts with verbal prompts. As the more intrusive prompts are relinquished, the verbal prompt serves as the S^D for the appropriate behavior. Over time, even the verbal prompt may be phased out as still more natural prompts (environmental conditions, time of day, and so on) serve as the S^D for the appropriate behavior.

Gestural Prompts

A gestural prompt refers to a simple gesture, usually a pointing prompt, that visually directs an individual in a particular direction. For example, in addition to the verbal prompt "Go to your bedroom," a caregiver may also point in the direction of the bedroom. In this case, the gestural prompt (pointing) is paired with the verbal prompt ("Go to your bedroom"). Over time, the gestural and verbal prompts should be phased out and the child should receive reinforcement for completing the target behavior following the S^D, "John, it's time for bed."

Modeling Prompts

Modeling prompts "consist of demonstrating part or all of the desired behavior to the student who imitates or repeats the action immediately" (Snell & Zirpoli, 1987, p. 126). As with gestural prompts, modeling should be paired with an appropriate verbal prompt or verbal S^D that the child will be expected to respond to after the modeling prompt is phased out. For example, when instructing a group of children on expected behavior during story time, the teacher may model where the children should sit, how they should sit quietly with their hands to themselves without disturbing others, how they should look at the teacher or the pictures in the storybook, and so on. Then, following the verbal S^D, "Children, it is time to read a story," the teacher may ask the children to imitate or practice this behavior while a story is being read to them. Appropriate behaviors are then reinforced ("John, I like the way you are listening!").

Sometimes the practitioner may ask another student to model a particular behavior for the other children. Regardless of who is providing the model, Bandura (1971) recommended that:

◆ the children's attention should be gained prior to the presentation of the model,
◆ the children readily imitate the model, and
◆ the modeled behavior be kept short and simple, especially for young children.

Kazdin (1989, p. 21) stated that the imitation of a model by an observer is more likely when:

◆ the model (child) is similar to the observer,
◆ the model is more prestigious than the observer,
◆ the model is higher in status and expertise than the observer, and
◆ several models perform the same behavior.

Physical Prompts

A physical prompt consists of physically guiding a child in the performance of a target behavior. Obviously, physical prompts are the most intrusive prompt form and are recommended only as a last resort. Physical prompts should be phased out as soon as possible since they are very unnatural and, when used to modify a child's behavior, may promote hostility and defensiveness.

ASSUMPTIONS OF BEHAVIOR MODIFICATION

Most practitioners employing the principles of behavior modification do not deny the possible relationship between a child's challenging behaviors and real psychological, physiological, or other emotional disturbances. Most behaviorists do not disregard the influences of heredity, nor are they insensitive to a child's developmental stage when evaluating a behavior problem. Many challenging behaviors observed in infants and toddlers are "normal" behaviors that facilitate the child's development of more mature behaviors and skills. To disregard these considerations completely is incongruent with years of research in developmental and general psychology. Trying to change a behavior that is consistent with a child's developmental age (e.g., stranger anxiety) or genetic condition (e.g., Rett syndrome) would be insensitive to the current psychological and biological needs of the child.

With that stated, however, note that behavior modification does place a *primary* emphasis on overt behaviors and current influences (antecedents and consequences) within the environment that are observed to be related to those behaviors. The following is a list of general assumptions of behavior modification:

- ◆ Most behaviors are learned.
- ◆ Behaviors are stimulus specific.
- ◆ Behaviors can be taught and modified.
- ◆ Behavior change programs must be individualized.
- ◆ Emphasis on intervention is on the here and now.
- ◆ Focus of etiology is on child's environment.
- ◆ Behavior change goals are specific and clearly defined.

Most behaviorists believe that at least some of these assumptions have exceptions. These assumptions, however, do represent the general philosophy of behaviorism. A brief discussion of each of these basic assumptions is provided below.

Most Behaviors Are Learned

Behaviorists believe that the majority of behaviors observed in children are learned. That is, children tend to exhibit behaviors that are reinforced and avoid behaviors that have not been previously reinforced or have been punished. Behavior modifiers believe that there is no difference between appropriate and inappropriate behaviors—both are learned in the same manner. The goal of behavior modification is to provide learning experiences for individuals that promote appropriate, prosocial behaviors.

Behaviors Are Stimulus Specific

Behaviorists believe that individuals behave differently within different environments. That is, the behavior a child shows within a particular situation indicates only how the child typically behaves in that specific situation. This is because each environment contains its own set of antecedents (e.g., people, tasks, and expectations) and consequences (reinforcers and punishers) for behavior. In addition, individuals have different histories of reinforcement and punishment within different environments. For example, a child may have learned that within one environment (the home) tantrums are reinforced. In another environment (the school), however, tantrums are not reinforced. As a result, the child's rate of tantrums is likely to be different in the home (frequent tantrum behaviors) compared to the school (little or no tantrum behaviors).

Behaviors Can Be Taught and Modified

Because behavior is learned, behavior modifiers can teach new behaviors and modify current behaviors that are inappropriate or considered antisocial. Behaviorists are quick to point to the many research studies that document the efficacy of behavior modification and the lack of evidence supporting the traditional psychoanalytic approach. Since behavior modification is effective in teaching new behaviors and modifying current behaviors, it serves as a functional approach for caregivers in everyday situations.

Behavior Change Programs Must Be Individualized

Behaviorists believe that individuals function in different environments with different antecedents and consequences. Each of us has developed many different associations among many different behaviors, antecedents, and consequences. Also, individuals respond differently to different types of environmental stimuli and responses. What one child finds reinforcing, another may find punishing. Thus, behavior change programs must be individualized for each child and the child's environment. The idea of using a single behavior modification technique as the management strategy for all children within a given environment is not congruent with the basic assumptions of behavior modification.

Emphasis on Intervention Is on the Here and Now

Unlike the psychoanalytic approach in which a considerable amount of time and effort is invested by delving into an individual's past experiences, the behaviorist is not very concerned with past events. Instead, the behavior modifier concentrates on current events within an individual's environment in order to identify the influences on the person's current behavior. The behaviorist sees no benefit from identifying and discussing underlying causes of childhood fears, anxieties, relationships with others, and so on; these have no role in changing current behaviors. Again, the behaviorist points to the lack of evidence supporting the usefulness of identifying and discussing historical events when attempting to modify current behaviors within the home and classroom.

Focus of Etiology Is on Child's Environment

While the psychoanalytic approach concentrates primarily on the individual and looks for an explanation of problem behaviors within the individual, the behaviorist concentrates on the individual's environment and looks for an explanation of problem behaviors within that environment. The behavior modifier is interested in environmental, situational, and social determinants of behavior. While the psychoanalytic approach views inappropriate behavior mainly as the result of a flawed personality and other internal attributes, the behavioral approach considers antecedents and consequences as the most significant factors related to appropriate and inappropriate behavior. It is not necessary for the child to have "insight" as to why he or she is behaving in a certain way for that behavior to be modified.

Behavior Change Goals Are Specific and Clearly Defined

The behavioral approach is based on a planned and systematic approach to teaching new behaviors or modifying current behaviors. Objectives are clearly observable and measurable and are stated in specific terms. Behaviorists talk about reducing specific behaviors such as "talking when the teacher is talking," "hitting others," and "getting out of seat"; these are specific behaviors. The strategies used in the behavioral approach are also very specific and must be applied systematically. Objectives, methods, reinforcement strategies, intervention strategies, and so on, are outlined in writing so that the program may be implemented in a consistent manner by all caregivers who have contact with the child.

MYTHS AND MISCONCEPTIONS OF BEHAVIOR MODIFICATION

Many myths and misconceptions are associated with behavior modification that have lead to public and professional hostility toward behavioral principles and techniques (Gelfand & Hartmann, 1984; Kazdin, 1975, 1978). These misconceptions have developed over the long history of behavior modification as the term *behavior modification* and the techniques associated with the term have been abused and misused. The association of behavior modification with nonbehavioral methods such as drug therapy, electroconvulsive therapy, psychosurgery, and sterilization provides an example of common errors made among the uninformed. As stated by Kazdin (1978):

It cannot be overemphasized that these techniques are not a part of behavior modification. They are not derived from psychological research nor do they depend upon reversible alterations of social and environmental conditions to change behavior. (1978, p. 341)

Although many of these *medical* interventions do change or modify behavior and, thus, may be confused with behavior modification techniques, "clear differences exist between medical and behavioral interventions" (Kazdin, 1978, p. 341). Unfortunately, these differences are not understood by many individuals who are misinformed about both the medical and behavioral techniques.

The perception of punishment as the primary strategy of behavior modification has also lead to negative reactions, even among professionals, when the term is suggested as a method to manage behavior. Alberto and Troutman went so far as to discourage teachers from using the term *behavior modification* when communicating with others about behavioral techniques:

We simply suggest that teachers avoid using the term with uninformed or misinformed people. In many cases, other professionals, including administrative staff and fellow teachers, may be as confused as parents and school board members. It may be as necessary to educate these fellow professionals as it is to teach children. (1990, p. 41)

Some suggested replacing the terminology used in behavior modification with more humanizing language (Saunders & Reppucci, 1978; Wilson & Evans, 1978). Kazdin and Cole (1981) found that individuals labeled identical intervention procedures as less acceptable when they were described in behavioral terms (reinforcement, punishment, contingencies) compared to humanistic terms (personal growth and development).

Why has behavior modification developed such a poor image in the minds of so many? First, as previously stated, there has been a gross misuse of the term *behavior modification*. The term is frequently associated with unpopular techniques that have nothing to do with the behavioral approach. Yet, these techniques continue to be discussed under the heading of behavior modification in the mass media, books, and other sources.

Second, a long history exists of documented abuses of behavior modification techniques, especially with individuals who were unable to protect themselves from these abuses. As previously stated, behavior modification was first applied to people living within institutional settings. Most of these individuals were children and individuals with various mental, emotional, and physical disabilities. In addition, behavioral techniques have been employed by inadequately trained professionals and paraprofessionals who, at best, had a surface understanding of the variety of techniques applicable within the behavioral approach.

In an interview with Coleman (1987), B. F. Skinner talked about the decline of behaviorism and blamed the decline on the association between behaviorism and punishment. Skinner was an opponent of punishing methods such as spanking and other aversive techniques used to control behavior. On numerous occasions before his death in 1990, Skinner encouraged caregivers to use positive behavior management approaches and to avoid the use of aversive interventions. Changing the negative image of behavior modification will require a significant amount of education for professionals and the general public. An attempt to outline additional concerns regarding the use of behavior modification and a brief discussion of each is provided next.

Myth: Changing Another Person's Behavior Is Coercive

The idea that behavior modification is coercive because it is used to change another person's behavior is an interesting position. For some, trying to change another person's behavior is a violation of that person's freedom and other rights. To address this issue, we must first consider what our responsibilities are regarding the children placed in our care. Do caregivers have a responsibility to prepare children for their place within society, to teach them the social skills necessary to survive in the world, and to teach behaviors that will allow them to interact effectively and communicate with others within the home, school, work place, and general community? Most caregivers, especially teachers and parents, would respond yes. In our opinion, then, the question is not whether it is coercive to change another person's behavior; we do this daily in our homes and schools. Rather, the significant questions are as follows: *Who* decides if a child's behavior should be modified? *What* behaviors should be modified? *Which* techniques should be used? (Gelfand & Hartmann, 1984). These three questions raise several ethical issues that deserve considerably more discussion than the scope of this introductory chapter can supply. However, each question will be addressed in Chapter 8.

Myth: Behavior Modification Is a Form of Bribery

Some caregivers believe that reinforcing children for appropriate behavior is simply a form of "bribery" used to get children to behave appropriately. In a worst case situation, the children may even turn the tables and try to bribe the caregiver (for example, "I'll behave if you give me a cookie."). Kazdin (1975) stated that people who confuse reinforcement with bribery do not understand the definition and intent of each.

Kazdin described the difference between bribery and reinforcement this way:

> Bribery refers to the illicit use of rewards, gifts, or favors to pervert judgment or corrupt the conduct of someone. With bribery, reward is used for the purpose of changing behavior, but the behavior is corrupt, illegal, or immoral in some way. With reinforcement, as typically employed, events are delivered for behaviors which are generally agreed upon to benefit the client, society, or both. (1975, p. 50)

Clearly, there are significant differences between bribery and giving children attention for appropriate behaviors. Moreover, if children don't get our attention following appropriate behavior, they will try to get our attention by acting inappropriately.

Myth: Children Will Learn to Behave Appropriately Only for Reinforcement

The fear that using reinforcement will lead to manipulation by children is generally unsupported (Kazdin, 1975). Manipulative behavior, however, can be promoted in children. For example, if a caregiver provides a reinforcer to a child for terminating a tantrum, the child is likely (1) to have future tantrums and (2) to demand a reinforcer before terminating future tantrums. However, if the caregiver provides reinforcement to the same child following a specific period of time when no tantrums occurred, the child is less likely to have future tantrums. In the first case, the child learned that *having a tantrum* was reinforced. In the second case, the child learned that the *absence of a tantrum* was reinforced.

Myth: Children Should "Work" for Intrinsic Reinforcers

Although "doing the right thing" for its intrinsic value is certainly an admirable situation, extrinsic reinforcers are a part of everyday life. People who say that extrinsic reinforcement is inappropriate appear to have higher expectations for children than adults. How many adults would continue going to work without an occasional paycheck? How many adults appreciate a pat on the back for a job well done? How many adults work harder at activities they find reinforcing? Behavior modification applies these simple principles to the management of behavior. As previously stated, extrinsic reinforcers are a part of everyday life. Behavior management teaches caregivers how to use these natural reinforcers to teach new skills and promote appropriate behaviors. As children grow older and become more mature, we hope that they will learn the value of intrinsic reinforcement.

Myth: All Children Should Be Treated in the Same Way

The issue here is whether or not one child should be singled out for a behavior program in which the child will receive a special reinforcer for learning a new behavior. For example, if John, one of twenty-five children in a classroom, frequently gets out of his seat, is it "fair" to reinforce him for staying in his seat? What about the other children who already stay in their seats and do not need a special program? These questions focus on the issue of fairness; teachers and parents do not want their children to think that one child is receiving special attention. In fact, research shows that caregivers *do* interact differently with individual children (Bell & Harper, 1977; Zirpoli, 1990). All children have individual needs that call for individual attention. Some children need more individual attention than others. The idea of treating everyone the same is incongruent with good educational practice.

Regarding our previous example, John's teacher has a professional responsibility to identify John's needs and to use the best method for him and his behavior. If reinforcement of in-seat behavior will increase John's in-seat behavior, then John has the right to receive the most effective intervention. Although the other children who already have appropriate in-seat behavior do not need a systematic reinforcement program, good educational practice tells us that they should also receive attention for their appropriate behavior in order to maintain that behavior. The level of attention for in-seat behavior may vary because John's needs are different from his classmates. However, the other children are unlikely to have a problem with this difference; children are very sensitive to other children who have special needs. Research has shown that children recognize and accept these differences, frequently better than adults (Casey-Black & Knoblock, 1989; Melloy, 1990).

SUMMARY

Behavior modification describes a variety of techniques used to increase appropriate behaviors, decrease inappropriate behaviors, and teach new behaviors. This active intervention approach involves the observation, measurement, and evaluation of target behaviors; and the identification of environmental antecedents and consequences that maintain these behaviors.

Classical conditioning refers to the relationship between various environmental stimuli and reflex responses. Classical conditioning was initially promoted by Pavlov who demonstrated that he could condition a response (salivation) in a dog at the sound of a bell (conditioned stimulus). Today, our understanding of learning has expanded beyond the simple relationship of conditioned and unconditioned stimuli. However, the work of Pavlov, Watson (1919), and others has provided a firm foundation for many current intervention strategies.

Operant conditioning refers to the relationship between environmental events and behavior. Antecedent events occur prior to the target behavior. Consequent events occur after a target behavior. A consequent event is defined as a reinforcer if the preceding behavior increases or is maintained. A consequent event is defined as a punisher if the preceding behavior decreases in rate, duration, or intensity. Operant conditioning has its roots in the animal research conducted by Thorndike (1905, 1911) and Skinner (1938, 1953). Thorndike demonstrated the relationship between reinforcement and rates of learning. Skinner, whose name is synonymous with operant conditioning and behavior modification, helped clarify the differences between operant conditioning and classical conditioning. Skinner encouraged researchers to study observable behavior and promoted the use of valid and reliable scientific methods of behavioral research.

The primary differences between the behavioral and psychoanalytic approach include the focus on overt rather than covert behaviors, a different understanding of inappropriate behavior, a different approach to assessment, and a different understanding of the importance of environmental and psychological influences on behavior. The behavioral approach provides teachers and parents with direct applications for classroom and home settings.

Behavior therapy is considered a modern day, practical application of classical conditioning involving several treatment strategies. These strategies include systematic desensitization, flooding, aversion therapy, covert conditioning, modeling, and biofeedback. Wolpe (1958) used systematic desensitization as an anxiety-reducing procedure.

Applied behavior analysis expanded laboratory principles of operant conditioning to everyday situations and settings.

Baer, Wolf, and Risley (1968, 1987) stated that applied behavior analysis ought to be applied, behavioral, analytic, technological, conceptual, effective, and capable of generalized outcomes.

Social learning theory expanded the behavioral model and stressed the interdependence and integration of person variables (thoughts and feelings) with environmental factors. The role of modeling, for example, was researched by Bandura (1977) as a significant learning tool.

The basic concepts of applied behavior modification include behavior, antecedents, consequences, stimuli, responses, reinforcement, punishment, and prompts and cues. Prompts may be natural, verbal, gestural, modeling, or physical. Behaviorists believe that most behaviors are learned, behaviors are stimulus specific, and that behaviors can be taught and modified. Behavioral interventions focus on individualized programming, interventions for the here and now, and goals that are specific and clearly defined.

Many myths and misconceptions exist concerning behavior modification. These have developed over a long history of abusive interventions with a focus on punishment. The perception of punishment as the primary strategy of behavior modification has lead to negative reactions, even among professionals. Others believe that changing another person's behavior is coercive, that behavior modification is a form of bribery, and that children should work for intrinsic reinforcers. Current behavioral interventions, however, focus on the reinforcement of appropriate behavior and focus less on the modification of inappropriate behavior directly.

For Discussion

1. What is behavior modification? List and discuss the assumptions of behavior modification.
2. What are the differences between classical and operant conditioning? List examples of each.
3. Discuss the relationship among antecedents, behavior, and consequences in operant conditioning.
4. Discuss the primary differences between the psychoanalytic and behavioral approaches to understanding behavior.
5. What is behavior therapy? List and discuss the assumptions of behavior therapy.

6. List and discuss the treatment strategies frequently associated with behavior therapy.
7. List and give examples of the different types of prompts and cues that may be used as antecedent stimuli to teach new behaviors.

REFERENCES

Alberto, P. A., & Troutman, A. C. (1990). *Applied behavior analyses for teachers.* Columbus: Merrill/Macmillan.

Baer, D. M., Wolf, M. M., & Risley, T. R. (1968). Some current dimensions of applied behavior analysis. *Journal of Applied Behavior Analysis, 1,* 91–97.

Baer, D. M., Wolf, M. M., & Risley, T. R. (1987). Some still-current dimensions of applied behavior analysis. *Journal of Applied Behavior Analysis, 20,* 313–327.

Balsam, P. D., & Tomie, A. (1985). *Context and learning.* Hillsdale, NJ: Erlbaum.

Bandura, A. (1969). *Principles of behavior modification.* New York: Holt, Rinehart, & Winston.

Bandura, A. (1971). Psychotherapy based upon modeling principles. In A. E. Bergin & S. L. Garfield (Eds.), *Handbook of psychotherapy and behavior change: An empirical analysis.* New York: Wiley.

Bandura, A. (1977). *Social learning theory.* Englewood Cliffs, NJ: Prentice-Hall.

Basmajian, J. V. (1983). *Biofeedback: Principles and practice for clinicians.* Baltimore: Williams and Wilkins.

Bell, R. Q., & Harper, L. V. (1977). *Child effects on adults.* Hillsdale, NJ: Erlbaum.

Broder, S. N. (1980). Biofeedback: Plain as the nose on your face. *Orthomolecular Psychiatry, 9,* 90–92.

Brown, I. D. (1990, April). *Attention deficit-hyperactivity disorder and self-control training.* Paper presented at the 68th annual convention of the Council for Exceptional Children, Toronto, Ontario, Canada.

Casey-Black, J., & Knoblock, P. (1989). Integrating students with challenging behaviors. In R. Gaylord-Ross (Ed.), *Integration strategies for students with handicaps* (pp. 129–148). Baltimore: Paul H. Brookes.

Cautela, J. R. (1972). Rationale and procedures for covert conditioning. In R. D. Rubin, H. Fensterheim, J. D. Henderson, & L. P. Ullmann (Eds.), *Advances in behavior therapy,* (Vol 4). New York: Academic Press.

Coleman, D. (1987, August 16). B. F. Skinner. *The New York Times.*

Cooper, J. O., Heron, T. E., & Heward, W. L. (1987). *Applied behavior analysis.* Columbus: Merrill/Macmillan.

Council for Children with Behavioral Disorders (1990). Position paper on use of behavior reduction strategies with children with behavioral disorders. *Behavior Disorders, 15,* 243–260.

Cummings, C., & Trabin, T. E. (1980). Locus of control and patients' attitudes towards biofeedback, relaxation training and group therapy. *American Journal of Clinical Biofeedback, 3,* 144–147.

Cuvo, A. J., & Davis, P. K. (1980). Teaching community living skills to mentally retarded persons: An examination of discriminative stimuli. *Gedrag, 8,* 14–33.

Denkowski, K. M., Denkowski, G. C., & Omizo, M. M. (1984). Predictors of success in the EMG biofeedback training of hyperactive male children. *Biofeedback and Self-Regulation, 9,* 253–264.

Donnellan, A. M., & LaVigna, G. W. (1988). *Progress without punishment: Effective approaches for learners with behavior problems.* New York: Teachers College Press.

Donnellan, A. M., LaVigna, G. W., Negri-Shoultz, N. N., & Fassbender, L. L. (1988). *Progress without punishment: Effective approaches for learners with behavior problems.* New York: Teachers College Press.

Duckro, P. N., Purcell, M., Gregory, J., & Schultz, K. (1985). Biofeedback for the treatment of anal incontinence in a child with ureterosigmoidostomy. *Biofeedback and Self-Regulation, 10,* 325–334.

Gaylord-Ross, R. (1980). A decision model for the treatment of aberrant behavior in applied settings. In W. Sailor, B. Wilcox, & L. Brown (Eds.), *Methods of instruction for severely handicapped students* (pp. 135–158). Baltimore: Paul H. Brookes.

Gelfand, D. M., & Hartmann, D. P. (1984). *Child behavior analysis and therapy.* New York: Pergamon Press.

Horner, R. H. (1991). The future of applied behavior analysis for people with severe disabilities. In L. H. Meyer, C. A. Peck, & L. Brown (Eds.), *Critical issues in the lives of people with severe disabilities.* Baltimore: Paul H. Brookes.

Jones, M. C. (1924). A laboratory study of fear: The case of Peter. *The Pedagogical Seminary and Journal of Genetic Psychology, 3,* 308–315.

Kanfer, F. H., & Phillips, J. S. (1970). *Learning foundations of behavior therapy.* New York: Wiley.

Kauffman, J. M. (1985). *Characteristics of children's behavior disorders.* Columbus: Merrill/Macmillan.

Kauffman, J. M. (1989). *Characteristics of behavior disorders of children and youth.* Columbus: Merrill/Macmillan.

Kazdin, A. E. (1975). *Behavior modification in applied settings.* Homewood, IL: The Dorsey Press.

Kazdin, A. E. (1978). *History of behavior modification.* Baltimore: University Park Press.

Kazdin, A. E. (1988). *Child psychotherapy: Developing and identifying effective treatments.* Elmsford, NY: Pergamon Press.

Kazdin, A. E. (1989). *Behavior modification in applied settings.* Pacific Grove, CA: Brooks/Cole.

Kazdin, A. E., & Cole, P. M. (1981). Attitudes and labeling biases toward behavior modification: The effects of labels, content, and jargon. *Behavior Therapy, 12,* 56–68.

Kerr, M. M., & Nelson, C. M. (1989). *Strategies for managing behavior problems in the classroom.* Columbus, OH: Merrill/Macmillan.

Killam, P. E., Jeffries, J. S., & Varni, J. W. (1985). Urodynamic biofeedback treatment of urinary incontinence in children with myelomeningocele. *Biofeedback and Self-Regulation, 10,* 161–172.

Koegel, R., Rincover, A., & Russo, D. (1982). Classroom management; Progression from special to normal classrooms. In R. Koegel, A. Rincover, & A. Egel (Eds.), *Educating and understanding autistic children* (pp. 203–241). San Diego: College-Hill.

LaVigna, G. W., & Donnellan, A. M. (1986). Alternatives to punishment: Solving behavior problems with non-aversive strategies. New York: Irvington Publishers, Inc.

Melloy, K. J. (1990). *Attitudes and behavior of non-disabled elementary-aged children toward their peers with disabilities in integrated settings: An examination of the effects of treatment on quality of attitude, social status and critical social skills.* Unpublished doctoral dissertation, University of Iowa.

Meyer, L. H., & Evans, I. M. (1989). *Nonaversive intervention for behavior problems: A manual for home and community.* Baltimore: Paul H. Brookes.

Middaugh, S. (1990). On clinical efficacy: Why biofeedback does—and does not—work. *Biofeedback and Self-Regulation, 15,* 191–208.

Morris, R. J. (1985). *Behavior modification with exceptional children.* Glenview, IL: Scott, Foresman and Company.

Mowrer, O. H. (1960). *Learning theory and behavior.* New York: Wiley.

Omizo, M. M., & Williams, R. E. (1982). Biofeedback—induced relaxation training as an alternative for the elementary school learning disabled child. *Biofeedback and Self-Regulation, 7,* 139–148.

Orne, M. T. (1979). The efficacy of biofeedback therapy. *Biofeedback Therapy, 30,* 489–503.

Rescorla, R. A. (1988). Pavlovian conditioning: It's not what you think it is. *American Psychologist, 43,* 151–160.

Rimm, D. C., & Masters, J. C. (1974). *Behavior therapy: Techniques and empirical findings.* New York: Academic Press.

Saunders, J. T., & Reppucci, N. D. (1978). The social identify of behavior modification. In M. Hersen, R. Eisler, & P. Miller (Eds.), *Progress in behavior modification* (Vol. 6). New York: Academic Press.

Skinner, B. F. (1938). *The behavior of organisms: An experimental analysis.* New York: Appleton-Century.

Skinner, B. F. (1948). *Walden two.* New York: Macmillan.

Skinner, B. F. (1953). *Science and human behavior.* New York: Macmillan.

Skinner, B. F. (1974). *About behaviorism.* New York: Knopf.

Snell, M. E., & Zirpoli, T. J. (1987). Intervention strategies. In M. E. Snell (Ed.), *Systematic instruction of persons with handicaps.* Columbus: Merrill/Macmillan.

Tawney, J. W., & Gast, D. L. (1984). *Single subject research in special education*. Columbus: Merrill/Macmillan.

Thorndike, E. L. (1905). *The elements of psychology*. New York: Seiler.

Thorndike, E. L. (1911). *Animal intelligence: Experimental studies*. New York: Macmillan.

Watson, J. B. (1919). *Psychology from the standpoint of a behaviorist*. Philadelphia: J. B. Lippincott.

Watson, J. B. (1924). *Psychology from the standpoint of a behaviorist*. Philadelphia: J. B. Lippincott.

Watson, J. B. (1925). *Behaviorism*. New York: Norton.

Watson, J. B., & Rayner, R. (1920). Conditioned emotional reactions. *Journal of Experimental Psychology, 3*, 1–4.

Wicks-Nelson, R., & Israel, A. C. (1991). *Behavior disorders of childhood*. Englewood Cliffs, NJ: Prentice Hall.

Wilson, G. T., & Evans, I. M. (1978). The therapist-client relationship in behavior therapy. In A. S. Gurman & A. M. Razin (Eds.), *The therapist's contribution to effective psychotherapy: An empirical approach*. New York: Pergamon Press.

Wolpe, J. (1958). *Psychotherapy by reciprocal inhibition*. Stanford, CA: Stanford University Press.

Womack, W. M., Smith, M. S., & Chen, A. C. N. (1988). Behavioral management of childhood headache: A pilot study and case history report. *Pain, 2*, 279–283.

Zirpoli, T. J. (1990). Physical abuse: Are children with disabilities at greater risk? *Intervention in School and Clinic, 26*, 6–11.

CHAPTER 2

Formal Behavioral Assessment

From the time of their conception, children in our society are assessed, evaluated, and labeled. These processes, which are guided by the implicit assumptions about development held by significant others and society, are applied to the children's physical growth, cognitive status, social and emotional development, educational achievement, and psychological functioning. Parents, teachers, physicians, siblings, peers, and the social community all participate in this ongoing evaluative process, as do the children themselves. For most children, these evaluations occur primarily in the course of everyday social transactions and, to a lesser extent, during periodic formal evaluations best characterized as "routine." As a result of these assessments, some children are identified as deviating from a normal course of development with regard to their behavior, their physical condition, or their violation of social norms and expectations. When a negative valence is assigned to this deviation, a child is especially likely to be labeled as belonging to a category of children who show similar characteristics. It is these children and their families who may then come to the attention of society's professional assessors, who will utilize special strategies to build upon the assessments that have already taken place.

—Mash and Terdal, 1988, p. 3

The purpose of *behavioral assessment* is to identify problem areas and develop interventions that will ameliorate those problem areas (Bellack & Hersen, 1988; Mash & Terdal, 1988). Professionals spend a great deal of time evaluating children's behavior using a myriad of instruments and techniques. This practice results in a plethora of information that often goes no further than a child's chart in some clinic or permanent file in a school office. Instead of using the information gained through assessment (for example, behavior rating scales, naturalistic observation, behavioral interviews) to develop effective interventions, the information may be stashed away. The time spent administering tests to children may then result in wasted time and money on the part of the professional, parents, children, and others. Although this practice is in direct defiance of the guidelines for assessment and use of information set forward by law (for example, P.L. 94-142), it is a practice familiar to many professionals and parents.

Currently, the trend is toward *functional assessment*, which is also useful in the development of intervention strategies. In other words, the results of assessment should go beyond the need for proper identification and should result in recommendations for effective intervention. This chapter focuses on reasons for assessing children and formal behavioral assessment strategies frequently used by professionals. The purpose of this chapter is to provide teachers and parents with an overview of the types of measures they would expect to be part of an evaluation of children's behavior. The scope of this text does not allow for an in-depth description of how to administer most of these measures. Throughout the chapter, we will consider the cases of Melissa, presented in Vignette 2.1, and Mark, presented in Vignette 2.2.

Vignette 2.1.   Case Study of Melissa.

Melissa, a 9-year-old girl, was referred to a behavior management clinic for behavioral assessment of moody behavior and suicidal verbalizations. Melissa was referred to the clinic by her pediatrician, Dr. Ted Franklin, after seeing Melissa and her mother in his office. Dr. Franklin reported that Melissa was in good physical health and no developmental problems were noted. He shared that Melissa's mother and father were distressed about her behavior and needed help in determining what to do when Melissa demonstrated undesirable behavior. Melissa is the oldest of three children. She has two brothers, Tim, age 4, and Patrick, age 9 months. Melissa and her brothers live with their natural mother and father, Elizabeth and Charles Young. Melissa is in the fourth grade and has received remedial help for math and reading in previous school years. Melissa and her parents came to the behavior management clinic with hopes that the assessment would provide clues to effective behavioral interventions for Melissa.

Vignette 2.2.   Case Study of Mark.

Mark, a 12-year-old sixth-grader, was referred to Dr. Novak, the school psychologist, for assessment of behavior problems due to aggressive and disruptive behaviors demonstrated in school. Mark was referred for assessment after his teacher, Mrs. Rose, had implemented several interventions to assist Mark in developing more appropriate school behavior. Among the interventions tried were sending Mark to see the principal whenever he hit a peer or became verbally aggressive toward peers or adults. When Mark was disruptive in the classroom (e.g., calling out, walking around the room aimlessly, shoving peer's books on the floor), his teacher and peers ignored his behavior. Neither of these interventions was effective in helping Mark to change his behavior. Mark is an only child and lives with his mother, Mrs. Nelson. His mother and father are divorced, but Mark's father sees Mark two weekends per month. Mrs. Rose, Mark, and his parents hope that a formal behavioral assessment will be helpful to gather information that will assist them in developing an effective behavior change plan for Mark and others in his environment.

COMMON FEATURES OF BEHAVIORAL ASSESSMENT

Mash and Terdal (1988) suggested a "prototype" view of behavioral assessment. According to their *behavioral assessment prototype,* several common features exist with regard to strategies and procedures used, regardless of the child's age and behavioral characteristics. For example, although data from Melissa's behavioral assessment may look very different from Mark's assessment data, several features would be common to both *assessment protocols* (Mash & Terdal, 1988):

- Assessment should be based on "conceptualizations of personality and abnormal behavior that focus on the child's thoughts, feelings, and behaviors as they occur in specific situations rather than as manifestations of underlying traits or dispositions" (Mash & Terdal, 1988, p. 9). Interest is on behaviors viewed as direct samples of the child's behavioral characteristics rather than as signs of underlying causes.
- Assessment should focus on the individual child and family rather than comparisons to a norm group. This is also true when describing and understanding the characteristics of the child and family, the context in which these characteristics are expressed, and the functional relationships between situations, behaviors, thoughts and emotions.
- Assessment is primarily interested in discovering situational influences on behavior rather than historical experiences, except in cases where an earlier event (e.g., physical or sexual abuse) may help understand current behavior.
- The primary purpose of assessment is to obtain information that will assist in developing effective intervention strategies.
- During assessment a multimethod approach is employed whereby no one assessment instrument is thought to be better than another. A variety of instruments, strategies, and informants is utilized to provide information.
- Objective information collected during assessment is more useful than inferences or subjective interpretations.
- Assessment is continuous and the effectiveness of intervention strategies is constantly evaluated.

♦   Decisions about specific assessment strategies are based on empirical data available on child and family characteristics, as well as the literature on specific behavior disorders.

PURPOSES OF BEHAVIORAL ASSESSMENT

With these common features in mind, the purposes of behavioral assessment should be clarified. Bellack and Hersen (1988) defined these purposes in terms of assessment phases to include: (1) screening, (2) problem identification and analysis, (3) selection of intervention, and (4) intervention evaluation.

Screening

During screening, a child is assessed to determine if further services, such as school-based or home-based services, are necessary to address behavioral problems. The screening phase is also important when it is determined that behavioral interventions are not warranted. Obviously, a teacher or parent has determined that a problem exists if the child has been referred for assessment. If, however, behavioral interventions have been deemed not appropriate, information may be obtained to assist in determining other appropriate services.

Problem Identification and Analysis

In the second phase, problem identification and analysis, the objective is to pinpoint behavior problems and to provide information about whether or not behavioral intervention is warranted. Underlying variables that maintain the behavior problems will also be identified during this phase.

Selection of Intervention

In the third assessment phase, selection of the type of intervention, the assessor considers possible answers to questions regarding the most effective intervention for the child and his or her family. During this phase, the assessor should look at *maintaining variables* information from phase two to provide clues to treatment. Also, the assessor needs to obtain information about the environment where intervention will take place. A number of important *environmental variables,* including persons and situations, exist that can affect treatment. These variables need to be considered before making treatment selection. Reimers and Wacker (1988) found that parental acceptance of a treatment recommendation was based on whether or not the intervention was actually effective as opposed to other variables that affected treatment such as disruption to the family. The goal of assessment is to identify the most effective intervention after a complete evaluation of the child, the child's environment, and the variables associated with significant persons in the child's life.

However, even with all this information on each of these variables, we can only *predict* behavioral outcome.

Intervention Evaluation

Phase four of behavioral assessment requires an ongoing intervention evaluation designed to measure the effectiveness of the selected intervention. Unfortunately, many educators do not make adjustments in their intervention program based on their own assessment information. They continue with the same treatment, even when it is obvious that the child's problem behavior has not been replaced with more desirable behavior. Teachers and parents should be involved in treatment evaluation and should help determine whether or not treatment has resulted in the expected outcomes. First, they need to determine if the treatment has been administered as planned. Second, changes in the problem behavior need to be monitored and documented (see Chapters 3 and 4). Third, if change has occurred, it must be determined if the change can be traced to the treatment. Fourth, teachers and parents need to assess treatment costs and decide if the benefits are cost effective. Finally, a decision needs to be made about modifying the treatment or terminating treatment if desired outcomes have been achieved.

For each of these assessment phases of intervention, specific assessment instruments and strategies have been designed to address one or more of the purposes of assessment described above. The assessor needs to take responsibility for being familiar with the variety of measures available and, in adhering to a basic tenet of behavioral assessment, must be able to use a number of strategies to collect assessment data. Examples of the strategies used to evaluate Melissa and Mark are provided in their individual assessment protocols (see Table 2.1). The remainder of this chapter will provide a review of reliable and valid assessment procedures designed to collect formal behavioral data. Chapters 3 and 4 provide information on informal behavioral assessment procedures. Chapter 7 presents information on assessment of social competence, in which a combination of formal and informal assessment procedures is used.

SCREENING AND IDENTIFICATION

The purpose of screening is to isolate children who are in need of further assessment from a larger group (Bellack & Hersen, 1988; Kerr & Nelson, 1989; Martin, 1988; Mash & Terdal, 1988; Salvia & Ysseldyke, 1985). Teachers and parents are often the most knowledgeable when it comes to considering children's behavior. Melissa, from our example in Vignette 2.1, was referred for further assessment after her mother expressed concern to Dr. Franklin regarding Melissa's moody behavior. Mark was referred by his teacher who observed that his behaviors were different enough from his peers to warrant further assessment. Perhaps, however, with early intervention, Melissa and Mark

Table 2.1.   *Example of assessment protocols.*

	Melissa	Mark
Ratings by others	CBCL TRF Children's Depression Rating Scale	CBCL TRF Conner's Parent Rating Scale Conner's Teacher Rating Scale
Interviews	K-SADS (parents) Child interview format Teacher interview format	Parent interview format Child interview format Teacher interview format
Self ratings	CDI	Nowicki-Strickland Locus of Control Scale for Children
Behavioral observation	Kazdin's Behavioral Code (clinic, school)	Academic Situation Code (school)
Physical exam	Yes	Yes

would have been spared the process of formal behavioral assessment. Use of screening procedures early in their lives could have identified them as children at risk for future behavioral problems. Several screening procedures are available for early detection of behavior problems.

Due to the nature of screening, procedures are brief and usually administered to large groups of children or individuals in the quickest manner possible. For example, some measures are administered in a few minutes to individual children who have been brought into a school during *child find* as part of a screening process. The term *child find* refers to the mandate in P.L. 94-142 to locate and identify all children with disabilities (Heward & Orlansky, 1992). Those children who perform poorly on screening measures designed to assess behavioral disorders may be considered "at risk" for future problems in behavior or demonstrate characteristics of specific behavior disorders. The most common screening techniques for assessment of behavioral problems are *sociometric techniques, ratings by others,* and *self-ratings* (Kerr & Nelson, 1989).

Early identification of children who experience *externalizing* (e.g., aggressive, acting out, oppositional) and/or *internalizing* (e.g., social withdrawal, anxiousness, fears) *behavior problems* is important. The literature states that these children are at risk for developing ongoing problems into adulthood (Hops, Finch & McConnell, 1985; Kazdin & Frame, 1983; Goleman, 1990). Children who demonstrated externalizing behavior problems were more likely to drop out of school, become delinquent, and/or need mental health services. Academic underachievement and peer rejection have been some problems reported in children who demonstrated internalizing behavior problems. Screening of all children in elementary school is necessary for identifying special needs in terms of *behavioral deficits* or *excesses.* Early identification and intervention is likely to result in positive educational and social outcomes for most children.

Sociometric Techniques

Sociometric measures are popular techniques used to assess individuals in social settings such as classrooms to determine which children appear to be popular, rejected, neglected, isolated, or accepted by the other children (Kauffman, 1989; McConnell & Odom, 1987). These techniques provide general information on acceptance, desirability, and social status of children. Sociometric techniques have been most widely used to screen children who may benefit from social skills training in order to improve acceptance among peers (see Chapter 7). Once children receive intervention, sociometric techniques have been used to assess the effects of treatment on social status (Melloy, 1990). A number of researchers have used sociometric techniques to evaluate children's social status and acceptance among their peers (Conoley & Conoley, 1983; Iano, Ayers, Heller, McGettigan, & Walker, 1974; Melloy, 1990; Peery, 1979).

The most popular sociometric techniques are *peer nomination, peer rating,* and *paired comparisons* (McConnell & Odom, 1987). Peer nomination and peer rating are described in Chapter 7.

Paired comparisons are used to assess the social status of young children. In this procedure, photographs of each of the children in a class are presented in pairs to a single child for rating. The photographs are presented in all possible pairs and the child is asked to rate the pictures on some positive criterion

Students complete a peer rating as part of a behavioral assessment to identify students/peers at risk for behavior problems.

such as "I like to play with/work with (teacher inserts name of child)." Once the photograph pairs have been shown in all possible combinations to all children in the class, the number of choices each child receives is computed into a social status score. The paired comparison technique has a number of advantages including excellent test-retest reliability among preschool-aged and older children, making the use of a negative criterion unnecessary (McConnell & Odom, 1986). According to McConnell and Odom (1986) the major disadvantage of the paired comparison technique is the time involved. For example, to assess the social status of 10 children in a class, each child would need to make 36 comparisons—that's 360 comparisons!

Ratings by Others

An example of a rating scale completed by, for example, parents or teachers and used in the screening phase of assessment is the *Systematic Screening for Behavior Disorders* (SSBD) (Walker, Severson, Stiller, Williams, Haring, Shinn, & Todis, 1988). To date, this is the only comprehensive screening system that has been developed and researched adequately to be used in screening behavioral disorders. The SSBD utilizes multiple assessment methods to identify elementary-aged children who demonstrate behavioral problems. The SSBD has the potential to assist teachers to identify systematically and objectively children who demonstrate externalized and/or internalized behavior disorders (Walker, Severson, Todis, Block-Pedego, Williams, Haring, & Barckley, 1990). In the past, children with behavior problems were typically referred by their teachers based mainly on subjective decisions. Also, there has been a tendency to refer children who demonstrated externalized behavior problems (e.g., disruptive, aggressive, noncompliant, out of seat) and less often children who showed internalized behavior disorders (e.g., excessive shyness, severely withdrawn, poor peer interactions) (Walker et al., 1988).

"The SSBD is a three-stage, multiple gating screening system designed for the standardized screening and identification of students in Grades 1 to 5 who may be at risk for their externalizing or internalizing behavior disorders" (Walker et al., 1990, p. 33). During the first stage of screening, teachers are asked to rank order every child in their class based on behavioral criteria for externalized and internalized behavior disorders. Children who are ranked at the top of the list are further assessed by a teacher rating of behavior in stage 2 of the assessment process. Finally, in stage 3, children who meet criteria for behavior disorders in stage 2 are observed in classroom and playground settings to determine if their academic and social behavior deviates significantly from the behavior of their peers. Children identified in each stage may warrant further assessment, pre-referral interventions, and/or referral to a *child study team.*

Research continues on the reliability and validity of the SSBD. Preliminary results, however, indicated that this screening process showed promise for screening all elementary-aged children for purposes of identifying those at risk of developing or maintaining behavior disorders (Walker et al.,

1988; Walker et al., 1990). A complete description of the SSBD is available in Walker et al. (1988).

Self-Ratings

A number of *self-rating instruments,* or *self-reports,* are available to assist in the screening process. Children complete self-ratings, which typically include questions about behaviors and how the child feels he or she matches the description. The following are examples of questions from a self-rating on social skills: "Is it easy for me to listen to someone who is talking to me?" and "Do I tell others without getting mad or yelling when they have caused a problem for me?" (McGinnis & Goldstein, 1984, pp. 9, 11). Self-ratings have been designed to measure a variety of constructs including social skills, locus of control, level of self-control, aggression, anxiety, and depression (Bellack & Hersen, 1988; Martin, 1988; Mash & Terdal, 1988). Instruments such as the *Skillstreaming Student Skill Checklist* (McGinnis & Goldstein, 1984), the *Coopersmith Self-Esteem Inventory* (Coopersmith, 1967), the *Piers-Harris Children's Self-Concept Scale* (Piers & Harris, 1969), and the *Nowicki-Strickland Locus of Control Scale for Children* (Nowicki & Strickland, 1973) are reliable and valid instruments for measuring these various constructs (for example, Kazdin, 1988; Wolfe & Wolfe, 1988). Caution needs to be exercised, however, with regard to information from self-report instruments because children tend to answer the way they perceive others would want them to answer. Self-report instruments such as the *Nowicki-Strickland Locus of Control Scale for Children* (Nowicki & Strickland, 1973) include items built in to decrease the impact of this confounding variable. Many of these instruments were designed for administration to a group of children in 10 to 15 minutes. Mark's assessment protocol (see Vignette 2.2 and Table 2.1) included administration of the Nowicki-Strickland test instrument to his entire class of sixth graders during the first month of school. Mark and his peers answered questions such as "Do you feel that it's nearly impossible to change your parent's mind about anything?" and "Do you believe that most kids are just born good at sports?" (Nowicki & Strickland, 1973, p. 46). The information from this measure helped Mrs. Rose to identify some of the children in her class who seemed to be more significantly controlled by external and internal influences than others. Mark's score on this measure indicated that he felt more controlled by others than by his own internal motivation.

Kazdin (1988) described 16 different self-report instruments designed to assess childhood depression. Self-report instruments are especially important in assessing depression since the core symptoms of sadness, feelings of worthlessness, and loss of interest in activities are dependent on subjective feelings or perceptions. The most widely used self-report instrument for measuring childhood depression is the *Children's Depression Inventory* (CDI) (Kovacs, 1981). This 27-item instrument asks children to choose from three alternative statements that characterize them over the previous two weeks. Statements on the CDI assess cognitive, affective, and behavioral signs of depression. Melissa, from our example in Vignette 2.1 and Table 2.1, completed the CDI when she visited the clinic. Her responses on the CDI indicated significant differences from other children her age in demonstrating signs of depression.

Fears and anxieties have also been assessed using self-reports (Barrios & Hartmann, 1988; Martin, 1988; Nietzel, Bernstein, & Russell, 1988). According to Nietzel et al., "self-reports are the only means assessors have to learn about the subjective components of fear experienced by their clients" (1988, p. 297). Self-report instruments that are often used to assess children's fears and anxieties include the *Fear Survey Schedule for Children* (Ollendick, 1983), the *Revised Children's Manifest Anxiety Scale* (Castaneda, McCandless, & Palermo, 1956), and the *State-Trait Anxiety Scale for Children* (Spielberger, 1973). Complete descriptions of these instruments can be found in other sources (for example, Nietzel et al., 1988; Martin, 1988).

ASSESSMENT FOR SPECIFIC BEHAVIOR DISORDERS

Once professionals have completed the screening process of assessment, they have a "rough sketch" of children and the manner in which their behavior is perceived by themselves and significant others. Through screening, some children may be identified as needing further assessment of their behavior problems. This section will cover procedures that have been suggested for evaluating problem behaviors that may be characteristic of specific behavior disorders. Suggestions for behavioral assessment of behavior disorders that will assist in problem identification and analysis of problem behavior are provided. The identification and analysis phase of assessment allows teachers and parents to make finer discriminations of problem behavior and to obtain clues to effective intervention. Following descriptions of each type of assessment instrument, a brief description is given to familiarize parents and educators with how these instruments are used to assess specific behavior disorders such as attention deficit hyperactive disorder (ADHD), conduct disorders, depression, and withdrawal behavior.

Behavioral assessment beyond screening incorporates multiple assessment methods that rely on several informants concerning the nature of the children's difficulties across multiple situations. Informants include parents, teachers, other caregivers, and children. Informants for Melissa included herself, her parents, pediatrician, teacher, and the clinician administering the assessment measures. Mark's informants included himself, his mother, teacher, school psychologist, and pediatrician. According to a number of authors (e.g., Bellack & Hersen, 1988; Martin, 1988; Mash & Terdal, 1988) the following methods should be included in an assessment of a child who demonstrates behavioral problems:

- ◆ Behavior rating scales completed by parents and teachers;
- ◆ Parent, teacher, child interviews;

- ◆   Naturalistic behavioral observations;
- ◆   Detailed family history;
- ◆   Physical examination by a physician;
- ◆   Review of previous records of treatment;
- ◆   Laboratory measures; and
- ◆   Psychometric measures where indicated.

Ratings by Others

Teachers and parents are often asked to provide an overall perception of a child's behavior via behavioral checklists or ratings. Behavioral *ratings by others* are administered as part of the total assessment process that takes place during the problem identification and analysis phase of evaluation. The reader should note that other rating scales are more appropriate for screening purposes (e.g., the SSBD previously described in this chapter). Parents and teachers are typically asked to complete these ratings in a clinic or school setting by general psychologists, school psychologists, behavioral consultants, and others who are qualified to assess children's behavior. Melissa visited a behavior management clinic for evaluation. Prior to this visit, Dr. Anderson, the behavioral consultant, had sent the rating scales to Melissa's parents asking them to complete the measures and return them before their scheduled visit to the clinic. Mark's assessment was conducted in the school setting. Dr. Novak, the school psychologist, solicited information from Mark's teacher and mother by sending them the rating scales and asking them to return the completed measures to her.

Behavioral checklists require the teacher or parent to read a behavioral descriptor and then make a judgment about the presence or absence of the behavior in the child. Behavior rating scales typically use a *Likert-type* rating scale to judge the degree to which the behavior is perceived to be a problem (Mash & Terdal, 1988). A Likert scale (Likert, 1932) is an evaluative scale. Persons are asked to respond to each item in terms of a varied-point scale defined by labels such as "agree strongly," "agree," "undecided," "disagree," and "disagree strongly" (Melloy, 1990). These measures provide information on how a child's behavior compares to peers. Behavior ratings by others are available for preschool-aged through adolescent-aged children. A number of behavior rating scales are available. Included in this chapter, however, are examples of widely used, reliable, and valid instruments for assessing a variety of behavior problems.

Child Behavior Checklist

The *Child Behavior Checklist* (CBCL) (Achenbach & Edelbrock, 1983) is a behavior rating instrument designed to be completed by parents and parent surrogates of children aged 2 to 16. The 113-item rating scale requires parents to rate their child's behavior on a Likert-type scale using descriptors "not true," or "sometimes true," or "very true" or "often true" about their child.

The results of the rating scale assist in determining the presence of externalizing or internalizing behavior problems. *Scaled scores* are provided for the following: (a) depression, (b) obsessive-compulsive, (c) hyperactivity, (d) aggression, (e) delinquency, (f) schizoid behavior, (g) cruel behavior, (h) social withdrawal, (i) sex problems, (j) immaturity, (k) somatic complaints, and (l) communication disorders. The instrument also yields a social competence rating based on parents' answers to several questions about their child's involvement in social activities. Comparisons of parents' perceptions can be made when both parents are available to complete the rating on a child. Children who score in the top 3 to 5% for age and sex on standardized behavior rating scales of major behavior symptoms may be candidates for further assessment of behavior disorders. Sample items from the CBCL are provided in Figure 2.1.

Melissa's mother and father, and Mark's mother each completed the CBCL. Scaled scores from the depression and social withdrawal scales were of particular interest to the behavioral consultant conducting assessment for Melissa. Figure 2.2 provides a sample of the items on the CBCL that Melissa's mother completed. The hyperactivity and aggression scales, along with the social competence rating, were of particular interest to the school psychologist who assessed Mark.

For assessment of ADHD, the test administrator would be most interested in the scale scores for externalizing disorders such as conduct, aggressiveness, and hyperactivity (Achenbach & Edelbrock, 1986; Barkley, 1988). The CBCL includes conduct disorder behavior on three scales: aggression, delinquency, and cruelty (McMahon & Forehand, 1988).

Teacher's Report Form

The *Teacher's Report Form* (TRF) (Achenbach & Edelbrock, 1986), a rating scale that is completed by teachers, has scales available for boys and girls aged 6 to 16. This 113-item rating scale asks teachers to judge each behavioral

Figure 2.1. Sample items from a rating scale for parents.

Source: Achenbach, T. M. (1988). Child Behavior Checklist for Ages 4-16. Burlington, VT: University of Vermont. Reproduced with permission.

Below is a list of items that describe children. For each item that describes your child now or within the past 6 months, please circle the 2 if the item is *very true* or *often true,* 1 if the item is *somewhat* or *sometimes true,* and 0 if the item is *not true* of your child.

1. Acts too young for his/her age	0	1	2
2. Disobedient at school	0	1	2
3. Shy or timid	0	1	2
4. Threatens people	0	1	2
5. Steals at home	0	1	2
6. Withdrawn, doesn't get involved with others	0	1	2
7. Not liked by other children	0	1	2
8. Sudden changes in mood or feelings	0	1	2
9. Secretive, keeps things to self	0	1	2
10. Sleeps more than most children	0	1	2

Below is a list of items that describe children. For each item that describes your child now or within the past 6 months, please circle the 2 if the item is *very true* or *often true,* 1 if the item is *somewhat* or *sometimes true,* and 0 if the item is *not true* of your child.

1. Acts too young for his/her age	0	①	2
2. Argues a lot	0	1	②
3. Shy or timid	0	1	②
4. Cries a lot	0	1	②
5. Demands a lot of attention	0	①	2
6. Withdrawn, doesn't get involved with others	0	1	②
7. Not liked by other children	0	①	2
8. Sudden changes in mood or feelings	0	1	②
9. Secretive, keeps things to self	0	1	②
10. Sleeps more than most children	0	①	2

Figure 2.2. *Completed items on the CBCL for Melissa.*

Source: Achenbach, T. M. (1988). *Child Behavior Checklist for Ages 4-16.* Burlington, VT: University of Vermont. Copyright by T. M. Achenbach. Reproduced by permission.

descriptor as "not true," "somewhat or sometimes true," or "very true or often true" about a child in their class. Results of the behavior ratings indicate externalizing or internalizing behavior problems by providing scaled scores for (a) anxious, (b) social withdrawal, (c) unpopular, (d) self-destructive, (e) obsessive-compulsive, (f) inattentive, (g) nervous-overactive, and (h) aggressive. A score is also obtained for school performance and adaptive functioning based on the teacher's responses to items related to academic subjects. Figure 2.3 provides sample items from the TRF. Melissa's teacher, Mr. Singleton, and Mark's teacher, Mrs. Rose, completed the TRF on each of their respective stu-

Figure 2.3. *Sample items from a rating by others scale for teachers.*

Source: Achenbach, T. M. (1988). *Teacher's Report Form.* Burlington, VT: University of Vermont, Center for Children, Youth and Families. Copyright T. M. Achenbach. Reproduced by permission.

Below is a list of items that describe pupils. For each item that describes the pupil now or within the past 2 months, please circle the 2 if the item is *very true* or *often true,* circle 1 if the item is *somewhat true* or *sometimes true,* or, circle 0 if the item is *not true.*

1. Argues a lot.	0	1	2
2. Destroys property belonging to others	0	1	2
3. Doesn't get along with other pupils.	0	1	2
4. Easily jealous.	0	1	2
5. Fears going to school.	0	1	2
6. Has difficulty learning.	0	1	2
7. Talks out of turn.	0	1	2
8. Threatens people.	0	1	2
9. Overly anxious to please.	0	1	2
10. Withdrawn, doesn't get involved with others.	0	1	2

dents. The TRF scaled scores with the most interest for Melissa included the anxious and social withdrawal scales. Melissa's score on the TRF for school performance was also of interest. Scaled scores on the TRF for Mark that were of particular interest included unpopular, inattentive, and aggressive.

Behavior ratings of externalizing behaviors (e.g., inattentiveness, aggressiveness) on the TRF that deviate by at least two standard deviations above the norm may be indicative of ADHD characteristics (Barkley, 1988). The TRF scaled score for aggressiveness has been correlated with other measures of conduct disorder (McMahon & Forehand, 1988).

Conners' Rating Scales and Variations of the Conners' Scales

The *Conners' Rating Scales* (Conners, 1990) are other popular screening instruments designed to assess children's behavior. The Conners' scales are comprised of the *Conners' Parent Rating Scales* (CPRS) and the *Conners' Teacher Rating Scales* (CTRS). Long and short forms are available for both rating scales. The CPRS and the CTRS are the most commonly used rating scales for assessing ADHD (Barkley, 1988).

Parents or *parent surrogates* rate their child's behavior using a Likert-type scale to evaluate how closely the child fits a particular behavioral description on the CPRS. On the CPRS-93, parents are required to read 93 behavioral descriptors and determine if their child is (a) not at all like that, (b) just a little like that, (c) pretty much like that, or (d) very much like the behavioral descriptors. The results of the ratings may indicate presence of behavior problems in the following areas: (a) conduct disorder, (b) anxiousness-shyness, (c) restless-disorganized, (d) learning problems, (e) psychosomatic, (f) obsessive-

Figure 2.4. *Example of rating by others scale for parents.*

Source: Conners, C. K. (1989). *Conners' Parent Rating Scales,* North Tonawanda, NY: Multi-Health Systems. Reprinted with permission.

Instructions: Read each item below carefully, and decide how much you think your child has been bothered by this problem during the past month. (1 = *not at all,* 2 = *just a little,* 3 = *pretty much,* 4 = *very much*)

Problems of eating
  1. Picky and finicky   1   2   3   4
  2. Will not eat enough   1   2   3   4

Temper
  3. Temper outbursts, explosive   1   2   3   4
       and unpredictable behavior
  4. Throws and breaks things   1   2   3   4

Childish or immature
  5. Cries easily   1   2   3   4
  6. Clings to parents or other adults   1   2   3   4

Fire-setting
  7. Sets fires   1   2   3   4

compulsive, (g) antisocial, and (h) hyperactive-immature. Norms are available for the CPRS-93 for ages 6 to 14. A sample of items from the CPRS-93 is provided in Figure 2.4.

From Table 2.1 we see that the CPRS-93 was part of Mark's assessment protocol. The school psychologist asked Mark's mother to complete the CPRS-93. Parents use similar ratings of 48 behavioral descriptors on the short form, the CPRS-48. This rating scale yields factor scores for conduct disorders, learning problems, psychosomatic behavior, impulsivity-hyperactivity, and anxiety. Norms are available for the CPRS-48 for children aged 3 to 17.

On the CTRS-39, teachers rate a child's behavior using a Likert-type scale of 39 items. Teachers are asked to judge the behavioral items as "not at all," "just a little," "pretty much," or "very much like" the child. The CTRS-39 includes scaled scores for (a) hyperactivity, (b) conduct disorders, (c) emotional overindulgent, (d) anxious-passive, (e) asocial, and (f) daydream-attention problem. The short form, CTRS-28, requires the same type response by the rater and yields scores for (a) hyperactivity, (b) conduct problems, and (c) inattentive-passive. Norms are available for children aged 3 to 17. A sampling of items from the CTRS-39 is provided in Figure 2.5. Mrs. Rose completed the CTRS-39 on Mark's behavior and returned the completed measure to the school psychologist for scoring and interpretation.

Persons assessing ADHD would be most interested in the conduct and hyperactivity indexes provided by the Conners' rating scales (Achenbach & Edelbrock, 1986). According to McMahon and Forehand (1988), the Conners' scales were designed primarily as instruments to discriminate children with hyperactivity from those without hyperactivity. Several modified versions of the CTRS were designed to identify conduct disorders in children. These teacher rating scales are briefly described below.

The *Abbreviated Symptom Questionnaire* (ASQ) (Conners, 1973) consists of 10 items from the CTRS. The ASQ was designed to assess children who

Figure 2.5. *Example of rating by others scale for teachers.*

Source: Conners, C. K. (1989). *Conners' Teacher Rating Scales-39.* North Tonawanda, NY: Multi-Health Systems. Reprinted with permission.

Instructions: Read each item below carefully, and decide how much you think the child has been bothered by this problem during the past month. (1 = *not at all*, 2 = *just a little*, 3 = *pretty much*, or 4 = *very much*)

Classroom behavior:
1. Constantly fidgeting	1	2	3	4
2. Overly sensitive	1	2	3	4

Group participation:
3. Appears to be unaccepted by group	1	2	3	4
4. Appears to lack leadership	1	2	3	4

Attitude toward authority:
5. Submissive	1	2	3	4
6. Fearful	1	2	3	4

demonstrate features of both hyperactivity and conduct disorders. Loney and Milich (1982) developed the Iowa CTRS from items taken from the CTRS. The Iowa CTRS was designed to discriminate children with conduct disorders from children with hyperactivity (McMahon & Forehand, 1988). The ASQ and the Iowa CTRS have demonstrated reliability and validity in discriminating conduct disorders from hyperactivity (Milich & Fitzgerald, 1985).

Home Situations Questionnaire

The *Home Situations Questionnaire* (HSQ) (Barkley, 1981) is a rating scale that was developed to assist in differentiating children with ADHD (Barkley, 1981). McMahon and Forehand (1988) suggested that the HSQ could also be used to provide information for interviews with parents of children who demonstrated behaviors characteristic of conduct disorders.

On the HSQ, parents respond "yes" or "no" depending on the absence or presence of specific behavior problems exhibited by their child in home and

---

Name of child: _____

Name of person completing this form: _____

Does this child present any behavior problems in any of these situations? If so, indicate how severe they are.

Situation	Yes/No (Circle one)	If yes, how severe? (Circle one) Mild Severe
When playing alone	yes no	1 2 3 4 5 6 7 8 9
When playing with other children	yes no	1 2 3 4 5 6 7 8 9
When at meals	yes no	1 2 3 4 5 6 7 8 9
When getting dressed	yes no	1 2 3 4 5 6 7 8 9
When washing/bathing	yes no	1 2 3 4 5 6 7 8 9
When you are on the telephone	yes no	1 2 3 4 5 6 7 8 9
When watching TV	yes no	1 2 3 4 5 6 7 8 9
When visitors are in the home	yes no	1 2 3 4 5 6 7 8 9
When you are visiting someone else	yes no	1 2 3 4 5 6 7 8 9
When in supermarkets, stores, church, restaurants, or other public places	yes no	1 2 3 4 5 6 7 8 9
When asked to do chores at home	yes no	1 2 3 4 5 6 7 8 9
When going to bed	yes no	1 2 3 4 5 6 7 8 9
When in the car	yes no	1 2 3 4 5 6 7 8 9
When with a babysitter	yes no	1 2 3 4 5 6 7 8 9
When at school	yes no	1 2 3 4 5 6 7 8 9
When asked to do school homework	yes no	1 2 3 4 5 6 7 8 9

Figure 2.6.   *Example of rating by others scale for home situations.*

Source: Barkley, R. A. (1981). *Hyperactive children: A handbook for diagnosis and treatment.* New York: The Guilford Press. Reprinted with permission.

public situations. They are also asked to rate the severity of the problem behavior on a Likert-type scale. Two scores are derived from parent responses to the questionnaire: the number of situations in which behavior problems exist and a mean severity rating of these problems. Children with ADHD consistently demonstrate problem behaviors of a severe nature in five or more situations described on the HSQ. The HSQ has been shown to "significantly differentiate children with ADHD from children without ADHD and is sensitive to parent training and stimulant drug interventions" (Mash & Terdal, 1988, p. 84). Barkley's (1981) HSQ is provided in Figure 2.6.

School Situations Questionnaire

The *School Situations Questionnaire* (SSQ) (Barkley, 1981) is similar to the HSQ in that it is designed to assess a child's behavior in school settings and situations. The SSQ, however, is completed by the child's teacher. The teacher is asked to respond "yes" or "no" to questions regarding the presence or absence of behavior problems in twelve school settings such as in the hallway, during group work, or in the bathroom. Behavior problems are also rated with regard to severity of the problem in a particular situation. The number of problem settings and mean severity rating are the two measures available from the SSQ. This instrument discriminated children who were ADHD from those who were not and is sensitive to the effects of stimulant drug intervention (Mash & Terdal, 1988). A complete review of the SSQ is presented by Barkley (1981).

Eyberg Child Behavior Inventory

The *Eyberg Child Behavior Inventory* (ECBI) (Eyberg, 1980) is a behavior rating scale designed to assess conduct disorders in children. The 36-item ECBI is completed by parents who rate their child's behavior based on descriptions of conduct-disordered types of behavior. Norms are available for children aged 2 to 16.

Children's Depression Rating Scale

The *Children's Depression Rating Scale* (CDRS) (Poznanski, Cook, & Carroll, 1979), a 17-item rating scale concerning symptoms of depression, is completed by the person conducting the assessment of the child. The clinician's rating is based on information obtained through interviews with the child, parents, and others. The CDRS has been used for assessing childhood depression (Kazdin, 1988). When Melissa visited the clinic, Dr. Anderson completed the CDRS based on his impressions of Melissa.

Peer Nomination Inventory for Depression

The *Peer Nomination Inventory for Depression* (PNID) (Lefkowitz & Tesiny, 1980) is a peer-based instrument used to assess depression in children. Children are given twenty behavioral descriptions that fall into subscales of "depression," "happiness," and "popularity." The children are asked to supply the name of a peer who fits the description. Individual scores are obtained by summing the nominations the child receives on each of the three subscales. Figure 2.7 provides examples of the questions asked of peers on the PNID. Obviously, children who get high scores on "depression" may need further assessment to determine if depressive behaviors are perceived by the child and others. Correlations among assessment findings would indicate a need for treatment of depression.

Behavioral Interviews

Parent, teacher, and child interviews are recommended to collect varying perceptions about behavioral concerns. The person who conducts the interviews needs to be able to build a positive rapport with others and at the same time obtain valuable interview information during the assessment process. Interviewers must also be sensitive to the need for privacy within families. According to McMahon and Forehand (1988) "the primary function of the interview is to identify verbally the behaviors to be targeted for treatment and the stimulus conditions, both antecedent and consequent, currently maintaining the problem behaviors" (p. 116). The interviewer should keep this as the primary idea during the interview. In Table 2.1 we see that parent, teacher, and child interviews were used as part of the assessment for Melissa and Mark.

Parent Interviews

Interviews with parents should include:

◆ Questions regarding behavior concerns;
◆ Current complaints of the child and the history of those complaints;
◆ Interventions that have been attempted to modify the child's behavior and the success/failure of those interventions; and
◆ A review of social circumstances and developmental history.

As an example, Dr. Novak interviewed Mark's mother using questions based on the above format and similar to the questions in Figure 2.8. Through questioning, Dr. Novak attempted to find out what Mrs. Nelson's perceptions were in regard to Mark's behavior.

The *Home Situations Questionnaire* (Barkley, 1981) described earlier can provide an excellent starting point for questioning parents of children who

Figure 2.7. Example of rating by others scale for peers.

Source: Lefkowitz, M. M., & Tesiny, E. P. (1980). Assessment of childhood depression. *Journal of Consulting and Clinical Psychology, 48,* 44. Copyright 1980 by the American Psychological Association. Adapted by permission.

1. Often plays alone? (D)
2. Thinks he/she is bad? (D)
3. Often says he/she doesn't feel well? (D)
4. Is often cheerful? (H)
5. Who would he/she like to sit next to in class? (P)

demonstrate behavioral problems. By addressing problem behaviors that the parent has identified as "severe" on the HSQ, the interviewer is provided with a beginning point for the interview and, therefore, can assist the parent in opening up to provide maximum information about their child's behaviors. A formal parent interview used to assess ADHD is provided in Figure 2.8. An interview format that could be used to interview parents of children who have demonstrated conduct disorders can be found in McMahon and Forehand (1988).

Schedule for Affective Disorders and Schizophrenia

The *Schedule for Affective Disorders and Schizophrenia for School-Age Children* (K-SADS) (Chambers, Puig-Antich, & Tabrizi, 1978). This is an assessment tool used to assess childhood depression. The K-SADS consists of an unstructured interview and a structured portion that is administered to the child and his or her parents to determine the presence or absence of depressive symptoms in the child (Kazdin, 1988). Kazdin (1988) provided the structured

---

Parent_____Date_____Child's name_____

Examiner's name_____

Situations to be discussed with parents:

General overall interactions
When playing alone
When playing with other children
When at meals
When getting dressed in the morning
When washing and bathing
When parent is on the telephone
When watching TV
When visitors are at home
When in public places (supermarkets, stores, etc.)
When mother is occupied with chores or activities
When father is at home
When child is asked to do a chore
When going to bed
When doing homework
When in other situations (in car, in church, etc.)

Follow-up questions for each problematic situation:

1. Is this a problem area? If so, then proceed with questions 2 to 9.
2. What does the child do in this situation that bothers you?
3. What is your response?
4. What will the child do next?
5. If the problem continues, what will you do next?
6. What is usually the outcome of this interaction?
7. How often do these problems occur in this situation?
8. How do you feel about these problems?
9. On a scale of 0 to 9 (0 = no problems; 9 = severe problem), how severe is this problem to you?

Figure 2.8. *Example of parent interview format.*

Source: Barkley, R. A. (1988). Attention deficit disorder with hyperactivity. In E. J. Mash & L. G. Terdal (Eds.), *Behavioral assessment of childhood disorders.* (2nd ed.) New York: The Guilford Press. Reprinted with permission.

and unstructured format of the K-SADS in its entirety. For example, Dr. Anderson used the K-SADS to structure the interview with Melissa's parents when they visited him in the clinic.

Other Concerns

In addition to questions about problem behaviors, questions about the families' social circumstances are important to assess factors such as financial and marital accord. According to Mash and Terdal (1988), children's behavior problems and response to intervention may be a function of family variables (e.g., financial and marital accord; child-rearing practices; maternal anxiety). To obtain this information it would be worthwhile for professionals to administer a parent self-report instrument such as the *Beck Depression Inventory* (Beck, Rush, Shaw & Emery, 1980), the *Locke-Thomas Marital Adjustment Scale* (Locke & Thomas, 1980), *Parent Self-Report* (Peterson & Shigetomi, 1981); *Child Rearing Practice Questionnaire* (Venham, Murray, & Gaulin-Kremer, 1979), or the *Parenting Stress Index* (PSI) (Burke & Abidin, 1980).

Teacher Interviews

During teacher interviews, the interviewer attempts to obtain information about the child's behavior (Barkley, 1988; McMahon & Forehand, 1988). This information can be obtained by asking questions about problem situations in the school setting and what interventions have been tried to change problem behaviors. Such questions might include the following: "Do you notice the problem behavior occurring more frequently by (target child) than others in your class?" The interviewer should also acquire information about the child's history of behavior problems within the school. The *School Situations Questionnaire* can offer an initial questioning route for the interviewer and teacher to discuss problem behaviors demonstrated by the child. The interviewer also needs to determine the teacher/child interaction patterns and teacher motivation/willingness to carry out intervention plans.

Questions should focus on: (a) specific situations and environments where behaviors occur; (b) typical consequences for those behaviors; (c) dimensions of the behavior, which include frequency, duration, topography, and magnitude of the behavior; and (d) observed learning problems. If the child demonstrates characteristics of learning disabilities, it may be necessary to evaluate academic achievement and intellectual functioning as part of the assessment protocol. Many children with behavior disorders (e.g., ADHD, conduct disorder) demonstrated problems in academic achievement (Forness, 1990).

With regard to our case study in Vignette 2.1, Dr. Anderson interviewed Mr. Singleton in a phone conversation and asked questions about Melissa based on the above format. As part of Mark's case presented in Vignette 2.2, Mrs. Rose was interviewed in her classroom after school by Dr. Novak, the school psychologist. Dr. Novak asked questions about Mark based on the suggested format for teacher interviews described previously.

Child Interviews

Although interviews with children below age 10 tend to be unreliable, some useful information about their perceptions may be obtained (Brown, 1990; McMahon & Forehand, 1988). Also, interviewing children provides the examiner with an opportunity to become acquainted with the child from a perspective other than that provided by parent and teacher interviews. The child can also be made more comfortable in the assessment setting after a rapport with the examiner is established. The examiner should keep in mind, however, that regardless of their behavior in functional settings, 85% of children will behave *appropriately in clinical settings* (Brown, 1990). Dr. Anderson interviewed Melissa, our case example from Vignette 2.1, using the interview format suggested in Figure 2.9. His purpose for interviewing Melissa was mainly to build rapport with her since they had not met previously and to obtain some idea about Melissa's perceptions of her behavior. During these interviews questions should be asked about any concerns children may have concerning their behavior and that of their parents and teachers. Also, questions should focus on reviewing problem situations and what helps the child in school and at home.

Child's name_____   Examiner's name_____
Date_____

Situations to be discussed with the child:

Do you get along with your mom/dad?
How do you know?
Do you get along with your brothers/sisters?
How do you know?
Do you get along with your teacher?
How do you know?
Do you have friends?
How do you know when someone is your friend?
What do you do when you don't get your own way?
What do you do when you get to do something you want to?
What do you like best about school?
What is the worst thing about school?
What makes you angry? What do you do when you get angry?
What makes you happy? What do you do when you are happy?
What is your favorite thing to do with your mom? dad? sibling? teacher? friends?
What do you really hate to do at home? in school?
What are some activities you like?
What are some things that you can't eat that you like?
What are some things to eat that you like?
What are some things you like people to say or do for you when you have done something well?

Figure 2.9. *Example of child interview format.*

Source: Melloy, K. J. (1990). *Assessment protocol for ADHD.* Unpublished manuscript. University of St. Thomas, St. Paul, MN. Reprinted with permission.

Another structured interview format for children in grades 4 through 10 is offered by Patterson and Bank (1986). This format is especially useful for children who have demonstrated conduct disorders since the questions are geared toward such constructs as parental monitoring, family relations, alcohol use, substance consumption, use of positive reinforcement in the child's home, peer behavior, chores, frequency of engaging in conduct-disordered behavior, parental discipline, and problem solving (McMahon & Forehand, 1988). Mark, from Vignette 2.2, was interviewed by Dr. Novak using questions she had developed based on the Patterson and Bank (1986) format. The purpose of the interview was to gather information from Mark about his behavior.

Naturalistic Behavioral Observations

Chapter 3 provides an in-depth description of behavioral assessment using naturalistic observations. Note that accurate decisions about children's behavior should not be made without collecting data through naturalistic observations. In fact, naturalistic behavioral observations are the most widely accepted procedures for obtaining reliable and valid information about child/parent, child/teacher, or child/peer interaction patterns (McMahon & Forehand, 1988). It is important to note here that although most of the evaluation for *specific behavior disorders,* such as ADHD, conduct disorders, and depression, will take place in a clinical setting, it is imperative that the person conducting the assessment visit the child's school or home to observe behavior in those settings. Brief descriptions of several behavioral observation systems used to assess specific behavior disorders are provided in the following.

Academic Playroom Situation Code

Several observational procedures for assessing ADHD are available (Barkley, 1988; Milich, 1984). Barkley (1988) described the *Academic Playroom Situation Code* (APSC), which was designed to differentiate children with ADHD. The APSC behavioral codes include "off task," "fidgeting," "vocalizing," "talks to mother/teacher," "plays with objects," "out of seat," "negative," and "mother/teacher commands" behaviors. According to Barkley, this behavioral observation system can be used in both clinical and school settings for the purpose of ADHD assessment.

Considering Mark from Vignette 2.2, Dr. Novak used the APSC to observe Mark's behavior in math and reading classes—the classes where he seemed to be having the most trouble with his behavior. Each of the observations was at least 15 minutes in length, and three observations were made during math class and three were made during reading class. The observations were made prior to Mark's initial meeting with Dr. Novak after she obtained permission from Mark's mother for assessment. Figure 2.10 provides a graph of the baseline data from Dr. Novak's observations of Mark's on-task/off-task behavior.

Figure 2.10. Baseline data from Mark's behavioral observations.

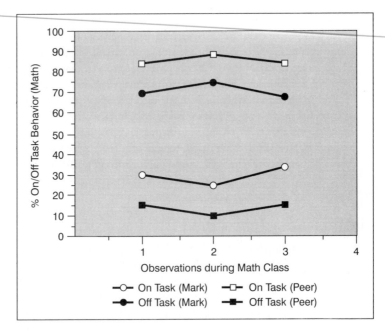

Observations during Math Class

—○— On Task (Mark)   —□— On Task (Peer)
—●— Off Task (Mark)   —■— Off Task (Peer)

Forehand Observation System and Dyadic Parent-Child Interaction Coding System

Two widely used observation systems that assist in differentiating children with conduct disorders are the Forehand observation system (Forehand & McMahon, 1981) and the *Dyadic Parent-Child Interaction Coding System* (DPICS) (Eyberg & Robinson, 1983). These systems are described in-depth in McMahon and Forehand (1988). Briefly, each of the systems is designed to assess children's conduct disorders through observations of their interaction behavior with their parent(s) in a free play situation and in a command (parent) situation. Both of these observation systems have provided reliable and valid data in clinic and home settings. The Forehand system and the DPICS have also been adapted to assess conduct disorder types of behavior in the schools. To date, however, these systems have not been used extensively in school settings and little data exist with regard to their psychometric properties (McMahon & Forehand, 1988).

Kazdin's Behavioral Codes

Kazdin (1988) described behavioral codes to use in direct observation of children to determine if they demonstrated overt behaviors affiliated with depression. Kazdin broke the codes into three categories: (a) social activity (e.g., talking, playing a game); (b) solitary behavior (e.g., playing a game alone, grooming); and (c) affect-related expressions (e.g., smiling, arguing). These and other behavioral codes were used to observe children in clinical, home, and school settings. Typically, children high in depression, "engaged in significantly less social behavior and evinced less affect-related expression than did children low in depression" (Kazdin, 1988, p. 178).

Melissa from Vignette 2.1 was observed using the Kazdin Behavioral Code in the clinic setting. Dr. Anderson requested Melissa to interact as she normally would with her mother and father during three 15-minute observation sessions. These behavioral observations were conducted in the clinic setting in a room with a one-way window. Melissa and her parents were seated in the room while Dr. Anderson positioned himself in the room on the other side of the window so that he could observe Melissa's behavior in an unobtrusive manner.

Dr. Anderson used the same coding system to observe Melissa's behavior in the school setting when he visited Melissa's school on two separate occasions prior to Melissa's visit to the clinic. Dr. Anderson conducted six 15-minute observations at the school. Three observations were made of Melissa's interaction behavior on the playground, and three observations of her behavior were made while Melissa ate lunch with her peers. For each of the observations, Dr. Anderson positioned himself close enough to Melissa so that he could see and hear Melissa interacting with her peers. Since Melissa did not know Dr. Anderson at this point, Dr. Anderson explained to the play/lunch groups that he was there simply to watch children play and eat. Figure 2.11 provides a graph of Melissa's interaction behavior with her peers on the playground.

Behavioral Avoidance Tests

These observational systems have been used to assess children's motor reactions to fear- and anxiety-producing stimuli, which include blood, darkness, medical procedures, school events, strangers, and water (Barrios & Hartmann, 1988). Typically, the child is placed in a setting that includes the feared stimulus. The child is asked to perform a series of graduated tasks that call for

Figure 2.11.   *Baseline data from behavioral observations of Melissa's interaction behavior.*

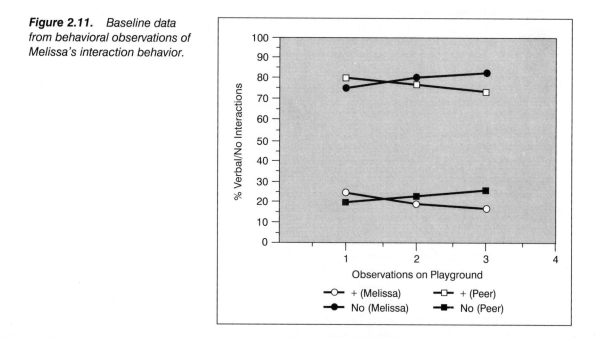

approaching the feared stimulus. An observer records the motor responses (e.g., grimacing, stiffness, crying) the child demonstrates during the observation period. The number of graduated tasks the child is able to accomplish toward the stimulus helps to determine the level of fear and anxiety the child experiences when expected to perform in the presence of the feared stimulus.

Observational Rating Systems

Many of these systems have been designed for use in medical settings to assess children's fears and anxieties (e.g., Jay & Elliott, 1984; Katz, Kellerman, & Siegel, 1980; LeBaron & Zeltzer, 1984). Other systems have been designed to assess children's motor responses to such things as public speaking, separation, social contact, and test taking (Barrios & Hartmann, 1988; Nietzel et al., 1988). One example of these observation systems is that developed by Wine (1979). This system was designed to measure the level of anxiety children felt in anticipation of an academic test. Children's behavior is observed in 15-minute sessions in the classroom. Twenty-two discrete behaviors in five categories (i.e., attending behaviors, task-related behaviors, communication behaviors, activity level behaviors, and interactional behaviors) are observed and recorded. Observation data are assessed to determine motor responses affiliated with anxiety demonstrated by the child when a test is anticipated.

Family History

A brief developmental and medical history of the child should be obtained to determine any medical factors that may be associated with current behavior problems. This information can be obtained through questioning during the parent interview and from written answers to questions about biological family member's health, developmental history of the child, medical records, and psychiatric difficulties in parents or siblings. Examples of questions that may be on a family history questionnaire include the following: "When did your child learn to walk?" "Has anyone in your family been treated for alcoholism?" "What education did the child's mother/father have?" Before treatment ideas are explored, the child must be assessed by a physician to rule out any medical problems that may be causing the behavior problem. Even in cases where medical problems seem to be the cause of behavior disorders, often the child has learned inappropriate behaviors that will need treatment in addition to any medical interventions that are warranted.

Physical Examination

To rule out treatable diseases and allergies, it is necessary to include a physical examination by a physician as part of the assessment of behavioral problems. Often, parents will first report behavior problems to a physician during routine physical examinations. It is important for physicians to collaborate with behavioral experts before making recommendations about behavior interven-

Once behavioral assessment data have been gathered, a professional scores and completes an interpretation of each measure prior to a team meeting on a child and his or her behavior.

tion. Physicians can then refer parents to appropriate professionals for adequate assessment and subsequent recommendations for intervention. A number of pediatric clinics have moved toward offering on-site comprehensive services, including behavioral assessment, as a service to families (R. J. Deeb & J. VanRoeckel, personal communication, 1990; D. P. Wacker, personal communication, 1989).

In Melissa's case, Dr. Franklin did not find any medical reasons for her behavior problems. He then referred her to a behavior management clinic where a more thorough examination of her behavior would be possible. Mark was given a physical when Dr. Novak suggested to his mother that it was important that Mark be examined by a physician in order to rule out any medical problems that might be causing his behavior problems.

Psychometric Assessment

During parent and teacher interviews, the interviewer needs to obtain information about the child's academic achievement and effects of behavior problems on that achievement. When learning disabilities are suspected, additional information is necessary regarding intellectual functioning through psychometric assessment of *global intelligence* and *academic achievement*. A number of authors provide descriptions of assessment instruments and procedures that can be used to assess these constructs (e.g., Salvia & Ysseldyke, 1985; Sattler,

1988; Taylor, 1988). These instruments will not be described in this text. This information, however, will assist in making accurate intervention decisions about the child's learning problems that may be associated with behavior problems.

Laboratory Measures

A number of laboratory measures are available to use in the assessment of children who demonstrate behavior problems. Parents and professionals should be cautioned, however, in the use of these measures as indicators of the presence of specific behavior disorders. Just as information from the other assessment procedures previously described would never be used in isolation, a laboratory measure provides only part of the information needed to determine a child's specific behavior problems and ideas for treatment. Basing treatment decisions on the information gained solely from any one measure would indeed be a mistake on the part of professionals and others. With these cautions in mind, we have provided brief descriptions of laboratory measures that are often used in clinical settings to assess children's behavior problems.

A number of laboratory measures or vigilance tasks are available that were designed to differentiate the performance of children with ADHD (Barkley, 1988). These measures typically require a child to view a computer screen while numbers or letters are projected onto the screen at a fast pace. Children are asked to respond by pressing keys that correspond to criteria they are to follow in making correct responses. The number of omissions and commissions the child makes are counted and compared to normative samples' responses. The results of these *continuous performance tests* were used to discriminate children with and without ADHD, and the tests were sensitive to the effects of stimulant drugs (Klee & Garfinkel, 1983). According to Klee and Garfinkel (1983), children without ADHD committed fewer errors on the CPT than children with ADHD. Also, when children with ADHD were treated with stimulant drugs, some of them tended to commit fewer errors on the CPT. Barkley (1988) described a number of CPTs that are available for personal computers.

For example, the *Gordon Diagnostic System* (GDS) (Gordon, 1983) is a small, childproof, computerized continuous performance test that is used in discriminating children with ADHD from those without ADHD. The instrument has been normed on children aged 3 to 16. The GDS has proven to be sensitive to intervention effects, which included stimulant drug intervention (Barkley, Fischer, Newby & Breen, 1988). The system requires the child to watch a screen while numbers are flashed onto it and to press a button when a 1 and a 9 are presented in sequence. Results are indicated for the number correct, omissions, and commissions.

A number of laboratory measures are also used to assess depression (Kazdin, 1988), fears, and anxieties in children (Barrios & Hartmann, 1988). Extensive study, however, has not been completed on the reliability and validity of these measures used with children.

A number of assessment instruments and strategies have been described in this chapter. These measures are designed to assess children's behavior. To assist the reader in understanding how assessment data are pulled together in order to plan for effective intervention, we offer a continuation of Vignette 2.1 This continued vignette provides hypothetical reports on the findings from behavioral assessment of Melissa.

Vignette 2.1.   Case Study of Melissa, continued.

Behavioral Assessment Summary Report

Name: Melissa Young

Birthdate: March 12, 1982

Education: Fourth grade

Date: Sept. 11, 1991

Age: 9-5

Examiner: Anderson

Reason for referral: Evaluation of behavior problems due to moodiness, sadness, and suicidal verbalizations.

History: Melissa lives with her mother, father, and her two brothers aged 4 years and 9 months. According to Melissa's medical file, she is in good physical health and there were no developmental problems noted. Melissa was referred to see me by her pediatrician, Dr. Ted E. Franklin. The purpose of the referral was for an evaluation of behavior problems Melissa had demonstrated at home and at school over the past year.

Examinations: Parent interview

Child behavior checklist

Child interview

Child Depression Inventory

Teacher interview

Teacher Report Form

Children's Depression Rating Scale

Direct behavior observation: school setting and clinic setting.

Findings: Melissa visited the clinic with her mother and father. Currently, Mr. and Mrs. Young are primarily concerned about Melissa's moody behavior. They described Melissa's mood changes as occurring frequently and said that one minute she is happy and enthusiastic and the next she seems very unhappy and in a bad mood. These moods seem to be precipitated by incidents in which Melissa doesn't get her own way. For example, on a shopping trip Melissa becomes very upset when told she can't buy something she desires. At home, when Melissa doesn't get her own way, she stomps from the room and goes to her bedroom. Mr. and Mrs. Young reported that sometimes these bad moods pass quickly but at other times they last longer (e.g., for a day). Melissa's parents felt that she is moodier than other children her age and that she exhibits this behavior four to five mornings a week. They also reported that when Melissa is very upset, she talks about killing herself. Mr. and Mrs. Young said that they ignore this behavior or tell her not to talk that way. Mrs. Young stated that two significant others in Melissa's life, her grandfather and an aunt, had died in the past year. Melissa was very sad about this and sometimes wishes she could die to be with her grandfather and aunt. Mr. and Mrs. Young stated that her behavior at home has gotten worse over the last year and that in addition to 4-year-old Tim, another brother was born nine months ago. Mr. and Mrs. Young have tried to divide their attention among their three children but agreed that the younger children demand more time and attention than Melissa. Recently, Mrs. Young talked with Melissa about needing her to help with the two younger children and that Melissa seemed accepting of this. Mrs. Young reported that Melissa does try to help more and that the youngest child is now sharing a room with Melissa. Melissa's parents stated that Melissa does have remorse for things she does such as fighting with her brother and hurting persons' feelings.

The consequences for Melissa's bad mood behavior have been to go to her room or to be grounded. Mr. and Mrs. Young reported that punishment did not seem to phase Melissa and that when she receives negative consequences for her behavior, she doesn't cry or seem upset. These consequences have not been effective in decreasing her bad mood behavior.

Mr. and Mrs. Young are also concerned about Melissa's behavior during homework time. They reported that Melissa has at least one hour of homework per night and that she has a very difficult time staying on task while she does her homework. Melissa has a desk in her bedroom but fiddles around and procrastinates a lot. They stated that she is easily distracted and goes in and out of her room many times to where her parents are in the house to ask for assistance. Mr. and Mrs. Young felt that the work Melissa brought home seems to be within her ability range and yet she seemed to lack confidence in being able to complete her work correctly and that she would like them to do it for her. According to Mr. and Mrs. Young, Melissa received remedial help in reading and math through Chapter 1 in third grade but so far this year she hasn't received these services. They reported that Melissa has told them she doesn't like school and that sometimes she is very difficult to deal with in the morning when they try to get her off to school.

Mr. and Mrs. Young each completed the Child Behavior Checklist (CBCL), a behavior rating instrument that provides information on a child's behavior compared to other children of the same age and sex. Both parents' responses to the CBCL were very similar. For example, on items such as "demands a lot of attention," "impulsive or acts without thinking," and "argues a lot," Mr. and Mrs. Young were in complete agreement that Melissa demonstrates this behavior very often. According to their ratings of Melissa's behavior problems on the CBCL, Mr. and Mrs. Young rated the following behaviors that Melissa demonstrates at a significantly different rate, intensity, and duration than other girls her age: arguing, demanding attention, disobeying at home, jealousy, feeling unloved, impulsive, moody, loud, whining, preference for older/younger kids, poor school work, feeling persecuted, feeling worthless, sulking, and having temper tantrums. These behavior problems resulted in significantly different ratings in the overall behavior area, "depressed behavior." According to her parent's responses to questions on social competence, Melissa appears to be as socially competent in these areas as other girls her age.

During the interview with Melissa, she stated that she got along well with her parents and siblings most of the time. She reported that she got upset most often when she didn't get her own way. Melissa also said that her younger brother, Tim, sometimes "bugs" her and that she has felt like hitting him. One time she slammed the door on him and hurt him. This made her feel bad and she became angry with herself for this. Melissa reported that now she is better able to control her anger in situations because she doesn't want to hurt Tim. Melissa stated that she gets angry the most when she is expected to do things she doesn't like to do such as reading, taking a shower, and going to bed. Melissa stated that she argues with her parents about these things.

Melissa said that her 9-month-old brother had just moved into her room and that she thought this would be okay. Melissa stated that she spends more time with Tim so that she can be helpful to her mom in taking care of the younger children. Although she doesn't babysit yet, Melissa stated that she looks forward to the time when she is allowed to do this.

Melissa reported that she likes school and her teacher. She felt that things were going better this year since she didn't need remedial help for math and reading. Melissa reported that her teacher used a behavior reward system whereby the class was able to earn tokens for a class party. She felt this was a good system and that when the class didn't receive tokens, it was due mostly to the boys' behavior but never her behavior. Melissa reported that she had friends in school and the neighborhood.

Melissa stated that there have been times when she has wanted to die, such as when her grandfather and her aunt died. She said that she has these feelings sometimes but she knew that if she died too, then people in her family would be hurt. When asked how a child who was young and healthy could die, Melissa stated that she would just hold her breath until she died.

Melissa and her parents were observed during three 15-minute behavioral observations in the clinic. During the observation, Melissa was given a reading and writing assignment to complete while her father read a magazine and her mother worked on a crossword puzzle. Behaviors that were observed included positive and negative verbal interactions, and positive and negative nonverbal interactions. While Melissa and her parents were observed, she did not engage in inappropriate behaviors. In addition to this observation, Melissa was observed in the school setting in order to obtain a more realistic assessment of her behavior. The same behaviors were observed in the school setting as had been observed in the clinic. Three 15-minute observations of Melissa's behavior were conducted during recess on the playground and three 15-minute observations were conducted during lunch in the lunchroom. During each 15-minute session, a peer was randomly chosen for observation also. During observations in these naturalistic settings, Melissa was observed to engage in only one behavior that was significantly different from her peers. Melissa was not observed to interact with anyone on the playground or in the lunchroom during 80% of the observations. In comparison, Melissa's peer engaged in positive verbal and nonverbal interactions with peers during an average of 75% of the observation time.

Melissa's teacher, Mr. Singleton completed the *Teacher Report Form,* a behavior rating scale. According to the responses that Mr. Singleton made in reference to Melissa's behavior, significant differences were noted in the behavior domains "anxiousness," "social withdrawal," "depression," and "unpopularity" when compared to other girls her age. Mr. Singleton reported on the TRF that Melissa had been tested in May 1991 using the *Wechsler Intelligence Scale for Children—Revised* and appears to have high average intellectual ability. Academic achievement scores were recorded on the TRF. Scores from the *Kaufman Test of Educational Achievement* (KTEA), which was administered in May 1991, for math, reading, and spelling were all within the average range.

SUMMARY

The purpose of behavioral assessment is to identify behavior problems in children and to gain information about effective intervention. Functional assessment of behavior is the current trend being used by professionals to evaluate children's behavior. Common features of behavioral assessment include the following:

1. Assessment should be based on children's observable behavior.
2. Assessment should focus on the child and family.
3. Assessment is primarily interested in situational influences on behavior.
4. Behaviors are viewed as direct samples of children's behavioral characteristics.
5. The primary purpose of assessment is to gain information for developing effective interventions.

6. A multimethod approach is used to assess children's behavior.
7. Objective information is more useful than inferences or subjective interpretations.
8. Assessment is continuous.
9. Decisions about assessment strategies are based on empirical information on the child and family.

The elements of behavioral assessment are screening, problem identification and analysis, treatment selection, and treatment evaluation. Specific assessment instruments are available for each assessment purpose.

Instruments and techniques used in the screening and identification phase of assessment include sociometric techniques, ratings by others, and self-ratings. During the problem identification and analysis, treatment selection, and treatment evaluation phases, professionals use a number of assessment instruments to evaluate specific behavior disorders. A number of these instruments and strategies were described including ratings by others, interviewing, behavioral observation, and laboratory measures. A matrix is provided in Table 2.2 that depicts the types of measures recommended for the assessment of specific behavior disorders. Table 2.3 outlines the names and purposes of each formal assessment described in this chapter.

Licensed psychologists and experts in behavior disorders are typically the most qualified professionals for formally assessing children's behavior problems and helping parents and teachers to make decisions about effective intervention strategies. Many children exhibit behaviors that are characteristic of specific behavior disorders but they do not fit the general criteria for a specific diagnosis (see Chapter 9). Regardless of the diagnosis or lack of diagnosis, the most important information gained from a behavioral assessment is the information considered helpful for the development of an effective intervention.

For Discussion

1. What is behavioral assessment? List and explain the common features of behavioral assessment.

Table 2.2. *General measures recommended for assessment of specific behavior disorders.*

Behavior Disorder	Behavioral Assessment Measure							
	SR	Int.	RBO	NO	FH	PE	Psy.	Lab.
ADHD		x	x	x	x	x	x	x
Conduct disorders		x	x	x	x	x		
Depression	x	x		x	x	x		
Fears and anxiety	x	x		x	x	x		

SR = self-rating; Int. = interview; RBO = rating by others; NO = naturalistic observation; FH = family history; PE = physical exam; Psy. = psychometric measure; Lab. = laboratory measure

Table 2.3. *Formal measures, acronyms, and usage.*

Test Name	Acronym	Test Usage
Standardized Screening for Behavior Disorders (Walker et al., 1988)	SSBD	Used to identify children who demonstrate behavior problems.
Skillstreaming Student Skill Checklist (McGinnis & Goldstein, 1984)	——	Self-rating instrument used to assess social skills.
Coopersmith Self-Esteem Inventory (Coopersmith, 1967)	——	Self-rating instrument used to assess children's feelings about themselves.
Piers-Harris Children's Self Concept Scale (Piers & Harris, 1969)	——	Self-rating instrument used to assess children's feelings about themselves.
Nowicki-Strickland Locus of Control Scale for Children (Nowicki & Strickland, 1973)	——	Self-rating instrument used to assess children's feelings of control.
Children's Depression Inventory (Kovacs, 1981)	CDI	Self-report instrument used to assess childhood depression
Fear Survey Schedule for Children (Ollendick, 1983)	——	Self-report instrument used to assess children's anxieties and fears.
Revised Children's Manifest Anxiety Scale (Casteneda et al., 1956)	——	Self-report measure of children's anxiety.
State-Trait Scale for Children (Spielberger, 1973)	——	Self-report measure of children's anxiety.
Child Anxiety Scale (Gillis, 1980)	——	Self-report measure of children's anxiety.
Child Behavior Checklist (Achenbach & Edelbrock, 1983)	CBCL	Parent's rating of their child's behavior.
Teacher's Report Form (Achenbach & Edelbrock, 1986)	TRF	Teacher rating of children's behavior.
Conner's Parent Rating Scales (Conners, 1990)	CPRS	Parent's rating of their child's behavior
Conner's Teacher Rating Scales (Conners, 1990)	CTRS	Teacher's rating of children's behavior.
Abbreviated Symptom Questionnaires (Connors, 1973)	ASQ	Abbreviated form of the CTRS.

2. Discuss the elements of behavioral assessment (i.e., screening, problem identification and analysis, treatment selection, and treatment evaluation).

3. Describe the various types of instruments and techniques used in a behavioral assessment.

4. Discuss reasons why behavioral assessment is important when developing interventions for children who demonstrate behavior problems.

5. Who will be involved in the behavioral assessment of a child?

REFERENCES

Achenbach, T. M. (1988). *Child Behavior Checklist for Ages 4-16*. Burlington, VT: Department of Psychiatry, University of Vermont.

Achenbach, T. M., & Edelbrock, C. (1983). *Manual for the Child Behavior Checklist and Revised Child Behavior Profile*. Burlington, VT: Department of Psychiatry, University of Vermont.

Achenbach, T. M., & Edelbrock, C. (1986). *Manual for the Teacher's Report Form and teacher version of the Child Behavior Profile*. Burlington, VT: Department of Psychiatry, University of Vermont.

Barkley, R. A. (1981). *Hyperactive children: A handbook for diagnosis and treatment*. New York: Guilford Press.

Barkley, R. A. (1988). Attention deficit disorder with hyperactivity. In E. J. Mash & L. G. Terdal (Eds.), *Behavioral assessment of childhood disorders,* (2nd ed., pp. 69–104). New York: Guilford Press.

Barkley, R. A., Fischer, M., Newby, R., & Breen, M. (1988). Development of a multimethod clinical protocol for assessing stimulant drug responding in ADD children. *Journal of Clinical Child Psychology, 17,* 14–24.

Barrios, B. A., & Hartmann, D. P. (1988). Fears and anxieties. In E. J. Mash & L. G. Terdal (Eds.), *Behavioral assessment of hildhood disorders,* (2nd ed., pp. 196–262). New York: Guilford Press.

Beck, A. T., Rush, A. J., Shaw, B. F., & Emery, G. (1980). *Cognitive therapy of depression*. New York: Guilford Press.

Bellack, A. S., & Hersen, M. (1988). *Behavioral assessment: A practical handbook* (3rd ed.). New York: Pergamon Press.

Brown, I. D. (1990, April). *Attention deficit-hyperactivity disorder and self-control training.* Paper presented at the 68th annual convention of the Council for Exceptional Children, Toronto, Ontario, Canada.

Brown, L., & Hammill, D. D. (1990). *Behavior Rating Profile—2*. Austin, TX: Pro-Ed.

Burke, A., & Abidin, R. R. (1980). *Parenting Stress Index (PSI)*. Charlottesville, VA: Pediatric Psychology Press.

Castaneda, A., McCandless, B. R., & Palermo, D. S. (1956). The children's form of the Manifest Anxiety Scale. *Child Development, 27,* 317–326.

Chambers, W. J., Puig-Antich, J., & Tabrizi, M. A. (1978). *The ongoing development of the Kiddie-SADS (Schedule for Affective Disorders and Schizophrenia for School-Age Children).* Paper presented at the meeting of the American Academy of Child Psychiatry, San Diego.

Cone, J. D., & Hoier, T. S. (1986). Assessing children: The radical behavioral perspective. In R. J. Prinz (Ed.), *Advances in behavioral assessment of children and families,* (Vol. 2, pp. 1–27). Greenwich, CT: JAI Press.

Conners, C. K. (1973). Rating scales for use in drug studies with children. *Psychopharmacology Bulletin, 9,* 24–84.

Conners, C. K. (1990). *Conners' Rating Scales manual*. North Tonawanda, NY: Multi-Health Systems, Inc.

Conoley, J. C., & Conoley, C. W. (1983). A comparison of techniques to affect sociometric status: A small step toward primary prevention in the classroom? *Journal of School Psychology, 21*, 41–47.

Coopersmith, S. (1967). *Coopersmith Self-Esteem Inventory*. San Francisco, CA: W. H. Freeman and Company.

Deno, S. L., & Fuchs, L. S. (1987). Developing curriculum-based measurement systems for data-based special education problem solving. *Focus on Exceptional Children, 19*(8), 1–16.

Eyberg, S. M. (1980). Eyberg Child Behavior Inventory. *Journal of Clinical Child Psychology, 9*, 29.

Eyberg, S. M., & Robinson, E. A. (1983). Dyadic parent-child interaction coding system: A manual. *Psychological Documents, 13* (Ms. No. 2582).

Forehand, R., & McMahon, R. (1981). Helping the noncompliant child: A clinician's guide to parent training. New York: Guilford Press

Forness, S. (1990, November). *Stimulants, psychopharmacology, and reading improvement*. Paper presented at the 14th Annual Teacher Educators of Children with Behavior Disorders Conference, Tempe, Arizona.

Goleman, D. (1990, October). Child's skills at play crucial to success, new studies find. *New York Times*, p. B1; B6.

Gordon, M. (1983). *The Gordon Diagnostic System*. DeWitt, NY: Gordon Diagnostic Systems.

Heward, W. L., & Orlansky, M. D. (1992). *Exceptional children, an introductory survey of special education* (4th ed.). New York: Merrill/Macmillan.

Hops, H., Finch, M., & McConnell, S. R. (1985). Social skills deficits. In P. H. Bornstein & A. E. Kazdin (Eds.), *Handbook of clinical behavior therapy with children* (pp. 543–598). Homewood, IL: Dorsey Press.

Iano, R. P., Ayers, D., Heller, H. B., McGettigan, J. F., & Walker, V. S. (1974). Sociometric status of retarded children in an integrative program. *Exceptional Children, 40*, 336–342.

Jay, S. M., & Elliott, C. (1984). Behavioral observation scales for measuring children's distress: The effects of increased methodological rigor. *Journal of Consulting and Clinical Psychology, 52*, 1106–1107.

Katz, E. R., Kellerman, J., & Siegel, S. E. (1980). Behavioral distress in children with cancer undergoing medical procedures: Developmental considerations. *Journal of Consulting and Clinical Psychology, 48*, 356–365.

Kauffman, J. M. (1989). *Characteristics of behavior disorders of children and youth* (4th ed.). Columbus, OH: Merrill/Macmillan.

Kazdin, A. E. (1988). Childhood depression. In E. J. Mash & L. G. Terdal (Eds.), *Behavioral assessment of childhood disorders* (2nd ed., pp. 157–195). New York: Guilford Press.

Kazdin, A., & Frame, C. (1983). Aggressive behavior and conduct disorder. In M. Richards & T. Kratochwill (Eds.), *The practice of child therapy* (pp. 167–192). Elmsford, NY: Pergamon Press.

Kerr, M. M., & Nelson, C. M. (1989). *Strategies for managing behavior problems in the classroom* (2nd ed.). Columbus, OH: Merrill/Macmillan.

Klee, S. H., & Garfinkel, B. D. (1983). The computerized continuous perfor-
     mance task: A new measure of inattention. *Journal of Abnormal Child
     Psychology, 11*, 487–496.
Kovacs, M. (1981). Rating scales to assess depression in school-aged children.
     Acta Paedopsychiatrica, 46, 305–315.
LeBaron, S., & Zeltzer, L. (1984). Assessment of acute pain and anxiety in
     children and adolescents by self-reports, observer reports, and a behavior
     checklist. *Journal of Consulting and Clinical Psychology, 52*, 729–738.
Lefkowitz, M. M., & Tesiny, E. P. (1980). Assessment of childhood depression.
     Journal of Consulting and Clincial Psychology, 48, 43–50.
Likert, R. (1932). A technique for the measurement of attitudes. *Archives of
     Psychology*, No. 140.
Locke, H. J., & Thomas, M. M. (1980). *The Locke Marital Adjustment Test: Its
     validity, reliability, weighting procedure, and modification*. Unpublished
     manuscript, University of Southern California.
Loney, J., & Milich, R. S. (1982). Hyperactivity, inattention, and aggression in
     clinical practice. In M. Wolraich & D. K. Routh (Eds.), *Advances in
     developmental and behavioral pediatrics* (Vol. 2, pp. 113–147).
     Greenwich, CT: JAI Press.
Mash, E. J., & Terdal, L. G. (1988). *Behavioral assessment of childhood
     disorders* (2nd ed.). New York: Guilford Press.
Martin, R. P. (1988). *Assessment of personality and behavior problems*. New
     York: Guilford Press.
McConnell, S. R., & Odom, S. L. (1986). Sociometrics: Peer referenced mea-
     sures and the assessment of social competence. In P. S. Strain, M. J.
     Guralnick, & H. M. Walker (Eds.), *Children's social behavior, develop-
     ment, assessment, and modification* (pp. 215–284). New York: Academic
     Press.
McConnell, S. R., & Odom, S. L. (1987). Sociometric measures. In *Dictionary of
     behavioral assessment techniques* (pp. 432–434). Elmsburg, NY:
     Pergamon Press.
McGinnis, E., & Goldstein, A. P. (1984). *Skillstreaming the elementary school
     child: A guide for teaching prosocial skills*. Champaign, IL: Research
     Press.
McMahon, R. J., & Forehand, R. (1988). Conduct Disorders. In E. J. Mash & L.
     G. Terdal (Eds.), *Behavioral assessment of childhood disorders* (2nd ed.,
     pp. 105–153). New York: Guilford Press.
Melloy, K. J. (1990). *Assessment protocol for ADHD*. Unpublished manuscript,
     St. Paul, MN: University of St. Thomas.
Melloy, K. J. (1990). *Attitudes and behavior of non-disabled elementary-aged
     children toward their peers with disabilities in integrated settings: An
     examination of the effects of treatment on quality of attitude, social status
     and critical social skills*. Unpublished doctoral dissertation, University of
     Iowa.
Milich, R. (1984). Cross-sectional and longitudinal observations of activity level
     and sustained attention in a normative sample. *Journal of Abnormal
     Child Psychology, 12*, 261–276.

Milich, R., & Fitzgerald, G. (1985). Validation of inattention/overactivity and aggression ratings with classroom observations. *Journal of Consulting and Clinical Psychology, 53,* 139–140.

Nietzel, M. T., Bernstein, D. A., & Russell, R. L. (1988). Assessment of anxiety and fear. In A. S. Bellack and M. Hersen (Eds.), *Behavioral assessment, a practical handbook* (3rd ed., pp. 280–312). New York: Pergamon Press.

Nowicki, S., & Strickland, B. (1973). Nowicki-Strickland Locus of Control Scale for Children. *Journal of Consulting and Clinical Psychology, 40*(1), 148–154.

Ollendick, T. H. (1983). Reliability and validity of the Revised Fear Survey Schedule for Children. *Behaviour Research and Therapy, 21,* 685–692.

Patterson, G. R., & Bank, L. (1986). Bootstrapping your way in the nomological thicket. *Behavioral Assessment, 8,* 49–73.

Peery, J. C. (1979). Popular, amiable, isolated, rejected: A reconceptualization of sociometric status in preschool children. *Child Development, 50,* 1231–1234.

Peterson, L., & Shigetomi, C. (1981). The use of coping techniques in minimizing anxiety in hospitalized children. *Behavior Therapy, 12,* 1–14.

Piers, E. V., & Harris, D. B. (1969). *Piers-Harris Children's Self-Concept Scale "The Way I Feel About Myself."* Los Angeles, CA: Western Psychological Services.

Poznanski, E. O., Cook, S. C., & Carroll, B. J. (1979). A depression rating scale for children. *Pediatrics, 64,* 442–450.

Reimers, T. M., & Wacker, D. P. (1988). Parents' ratings of the acceptability of behavioral treatment recommendations made in an outpatient clinic: A preliminary analysis of the influence of treatment effectiveness. *Behavioral Disorders, 14,* 7–15.

Salvia, J., & Ysseldyke, J. E. (1985). *Assessment in special and remedial education* (3rd ed.). Boston, MA: Houghton Mifflin Company.

Sattler, J. M. (1988). *Assessment of children* (3rd ed.). San Diego, CA: Jerome M. Sattler, Publisher.

Spielberger, C. D. (1973). *Manual for the State-Trait Anxiety Inventory for Children.* Palo Alto, CA: Consulting Psychologists Press.

Taylor, H. G. (1988). Learning disabilities. In E. J. Mash & L. G. Terdal (Eds.), *Behavioral assessment of childhood disorders* (2nd ed., pp. 402–450). New York: Guilford Press.

Venham, L. L., Murray, P., & Gaulin-Kremer, E. (1979). Child-rearing variables affecting the preschool child's response to dental stress. *Journal of Dental Research, 58,* 2042–2045.

Walker, H. M., Severson, H. H., Stiller, B., Williams, G., Haring, N., Shinn, M., & Todis, B. (1988). Systematic screening of pupils in the elementary age range at risk for behavior disorders: Development and trial testing of a multiple gating model. *Remedial and Special Education, 9*(3), 8–14.

Walker, H. M., Severson, H. H., Todis, B. J., Block-Pedego, A. E., Williams, G. J., Haring, N. G., & Barckley, M. (1990). Systematic screening for behavior disorders (SSBD): Further validation, replication, and normative data. *Remedial and Special Education, 11* (2), 32–46.

Wechsler, D. (1974). *Manual for the Wechsler Intelligence Scale for Children—Revised*. San Antonio, TX: The Psychological Corporation.

Wine, J. D. (1979). Test anxiety and evaluation threat: Children's behavior in the classroom. *Journal of Abnormal Child Psychology, 7*, 45–59.

Wolfe, V. V., & Wolfe, D. A. (1988). The sexually abused child. In E. J. Mash & L. G. Terdal (Eds.), *Behavioral assessment of childhood disorders* (2nd ed., pp. 670–714). New York: Guilford Press.

CHAPTER 3

Informal Behavioral Assessment

There is a need for intervention and measurement methods that are practical and which allow for the documentation of empirically and socially valid outcomes. The teacher's interest is . . .in gathering information that can be used in ongoing decision making and problem solving. Teachers require measurement systems that are useful in formative program evaluation; competent instructional decision making is ongoing and does not occur only upon completing of a program. Teachers also need evidence that the outcomes associated with their efforts are meaningful for the students themselves.

—*Meyer and Janney, 1989, p. 269*

The purpose of this chapter is first to provide caregivers with an understanding of the importance of direct behavioral observation, the measurement of behavior, and the documentation of these observations and measurements. Second, caregivers are provided with several simple, but effective, methods of behavioral observation, measurement, documentation, and analysis. Third, we want to demonstrate that behavioral observation, measurement, and documentation may be completed without significant sacrifices of caregiver time from the typical classroom or home routine. Unfortunately, many teachers consider data collection as too demanding (Bancroft & Bellamy, 1976; Fisher & Lindsey-Walters, 1987), and many teachers use intuition rather than classroom data when making instructional decisions (Grigg, Snell, & Loyd, 1989). In addition, teachers tend to discount their classroom data as invalid (Grigg et al., 1989) and unreliable (Fisher & Lindsey-Walters, 1987).

Last, caregivers are challenged to try at least one method described in this chapter to assess the dimensions of a challenging behavior. We believe that, once tried, parents and teachers will find these less formal methods of behavioral assessment valid and reliable for evaluating the majority of behaviors observed in everyday settings. Together, the formal and informal methods of behavioral assessment outlined here and in Chapter 2 will provide caregivers with functional information about children, their environment, and their behaviors.

DIRECT OBSERVATION

The purpose of direct observation is to record behavioral patterns across natural settings and situations, to measure the dimensions of specific target behaviors, and to identify the variables associated with specific target behaviors. In addition, observational data provide information on the effectiveness of behavior interventions and necessary modifications to ongoing programming (Cooper, 1981; Cartwright & Cartwright, 1984). Direct observation may include watching a single child or a group of children for a specific time period, or observing a child's performance on a specific task. It may involve a narrative recording of general behavior observed or a measurement of specific target behaviors. The desired outcome of direct observation and measurement is an objective record of behavior or performance. But before a behavior can be observed and measured, it must first be identified and defined.

Identifying Target Behaviors

A *target behavior* is the behavior that is targeted for observation, measurement, and/or modification. The target behavior is identified by caregivers as the behavior needing to be learned, increased, or decreased. Frequently, caregivers are faced with several children who may have many challenging behaviors and training needs. In such situations, caregivers are encouraged to prioritize behaviors according to their severity and need for remediation. Several questions have been recommended to assist in identifying and prioritizing target behaviors that need to be modified or eliminated (Barlow & Hersen, 1984; Kazdin, 1982):

- ◆ Is the behavior dangerous to the child or to others in the child's environment?
- ◆ Is the behavior interfering with the child's academic performance or placement?
- ◆ Is the behavior interfering with the child's social integration or causing the child to be socially isolated from peers?
- ◆ Is the behavior interfering with effective parental interactions (e.g., bonding or communication)?
- ◆ Is the reduction of the behavior likely to produce positive outcomes for the child in the areas of academic performance and social acceptance?

Cooper, Heron, & Heward (1987, p. 50) offered several questions for caregivers to consider before teaching new behaviors. The following questions are adapted from their recommendations:

- ◆ How functional is the new behavior? How many opportunities will the child have to use the new behavior in everyday settings and situations?
- ◆ Will this new behavior provide opportunities for the child to be reinforced or receive positive attention from significant caregivers?
- ◆ Will the new behavior make the child more acceptable to significant caregivers and peers?
- ◆ Will this new behavior assist the child in becoming more independent in both daily living and social functioning?

Once the target behaviors are identified, they must be clearly defined so that they can be objectively observed and measured. This, perhaps, is the most critical step in assuring accurate and reliable observations and measurements of target behaviors.

Defining Target Behaviors

Target behaviors must be defined precisely so that there will be a minimum amount of variation from one observer to the next in the interpretation of the behavior. Behaviors that are precisely defined are stated in terms that are observable and measurable. *Observable* means that you can see the behavior occur. *Measurable* means that you can quantify the frequency, duration, or other dimensions of the behavior (dimensions of behavior are discussed later in this chapter). For example, increasing John's "appropriate" behavior and/or decreasing John's "inappropriate" behavior are not target behaviors that are stated in observable and measurable terms; the behaviors are not directly observable since the observer does not have a precise behavior to observe. A target behavior defined as "increasing John's attendance in English class" is precise and may be easily observed and measured. Few individuals would have trouble understanding what to count when measuring the frequency of John's English class attendance. The following list provides additional examples of observable and nonobservable target behaviors.

Observable Target Behaviors:

Chris will *complete his assignments* during math class.

Adam will *use his fork* to pick up food during mealtime.

Julia will *talk to other children* on the playground.

John will *ask for a break* when he is angry.

Tommy will *complete all school assignments* before going home.

Jeremy will *share his toys* with other children during free play.

Jill will *practice her piano* one hour per day.

Jason will *say "Thank you"* when given gifts for his birthday.

Mike will *say "excuse me"* before interrupting others at home.

Justen will *look both ways* before crossing the street.

Melissa will *wait for her turn* during group work at school.

Nonobservable Target Behaviors:

Chris will *be a good boy* during math class.

Adam will *be polite* during mealtime.

Julia will *be cooperative* on the playground.

John will *think* before he acts when he is angry.

Tommy will *remember* to do his school work.

Jeremy will *be nice* to the other children during free play.

Jill will *apply herself* during piano practice.

Jason will *understand* the importance of saying "Thank you."

Mike will *demonstrate appropriate manners* with others.

Justen will *be careful* when crossing the street.

Melissa will *get along* with others during group work.

Notice that in most cases, the target behavior is presented in positive terms. Caregivers should try to state target behaviors in terms of how children should behave instead of stating how children should not behave.

Hawkins and Dobes (1977) stated that definitions of target behaviors should be *objective, clear, and complete*. A target behavior is *objective* when the observer can see the behavior or when the behavior is overt. Covert feelings or states are not objective. For example, "hitting other children" is overt and can be observed and measured. "Feeling angry" at other children is a state that is difficult to define, observe, and accurately measure. A target behavior is *clearly* defined when the definition is "unambiguous, easily understood, and readily paraphrased" (Barlow & Hersen, 1984, p. 111). For example, stating that a child "will behave" during group activities is not a clearly defined target behavior. Stating that the child "will stay seated" or "keep her hands on the desk" are clear and unambiguous. A *complete* definition "includes the boundaries of the behavior, so that an observer can discriminate it from other, related behaviors" (Barlow & Hersen, 1984, p. 111). For example, in the previous example, the target behavior "will behave" does not discriminate one behavior (e.g., "staying in seat") from other behaviors that could also be the intended behavior to be observed under the definition of "will behave" (e.g., "keeping hands on desk"). After a target behavior is identified and defined, caregivers must establish a behavioral objective.

Establishing Behavioral Objectives

A *behavioral objective* describes an anticipated behavior, new or modified from current behavior, subsequent to the completion of a behavior change program. As demonstrated in the first of the following examples, a behavioral objective includes several basic elements: the desired *terminal behavior* (in seat behavior), the *conditions* under which the behavior is to occur (during each 45-minute math class), a level of performance or *behavioral criteria* (45 consecutive minutes), and a specified number of *consecutive observations* (three math classes) during which the behavioral criteria must be exhibited. The terminal behavior is what the child's behavior will look like after the behavior change program is completed. If the target behavior is the behavior you wish to teach or modify, the terminal behavior defines the child's behavior when the behavioral objective has been achieved. For example, a child may have a problem staying in his seat during math class. "Staying in seat" or "getting out of seat" is the target behavior. "Staying in seat for the entire 45-minute math class" may be the terminal behavior you wish to observe at the end of your behavior change program. An appropriate behavioral objective may be stated as follows:

> John will stay in his seat during each 45-minute math class, unless he has permission from the teacher to leave his seat, for three consecutive math classes.

Behavioral criteria may be stated in many ways depending on the behavior and environmental expectations. In the preceding example, the behavioral objective for John's in-seat behavior was stated in terms of *what* behavior will be exhibited (staying in his seat), *when* the behavior will be exhibited (during each 45-minute math class), and for *how many* (three consecutive) math classes the behavior must be exhibited. Criteria may also be stated in the form of a percentage when a certain percentage of correct or appropriate responses is desired. For example:

> John will comply with teacher requests with a 90 percent compliance rate over four consecutive days

or

> John will complete 80 percent of his class assignments for five consecutive school days.

During the behavior change program, a child's behavior may be evaluated on the basis of the behavioral criteria outlined in the behavioral objective. The criteria outlined in behavioral objectives should reflect realistic expectations based on current performance (determined by a review of baseline data), academic necessity, and social norms.

Before caregivers can develop behavioral objectives, baseline observations and data collection must be completed (as described later in this chapter). Baseline observations not only provide information about current performance levels from which behavioral objectives are developed, but help determine if the target behavior is as problematic as perceived. With this information, caregivers can establish objectives that are challenging, yet realistic. Table 3.1 provides a review of the above terms and their definitions.

DIMENSIONS OF BEHAVIOR

After a target behavior has been identified and defined, and a behavioral criteria established, two additional questions remain: What are the dimensions or "characteristics" of the child's behavior that should be observed and measured, and how will the dimensions of the target behavior be measured (Tawney & Gast, 1984, p. 112). This section addresses the first question regarding the dimensions of behavior. The five primary dimensions of behavior are *frequen-*

Table 3.1.   *Definitions for writing behavioral objectives and examples.*

Term	Definition	Example
Target behavior	The behavior you want to teach or modify. When teaching a new behavior, the target and terminal behavior may be the same.	Temper tantrums at the grocery store or asking "please" when making a request.
Terminal behavior	The desired behavior.	The absence of temper tantrums.
Behavioral criteria	A desired performance level of the terminal behavior. When the child reaches this performance level, the program is complete.	Zero tantrums for five consecutive shopping trips to the grocery store.
Behavioral objective	A statement including the terminal behavior and the behavioral criteria.	John will have zero tantrums for five consecutive shopping trips to the grocery store.

cy, duration, rate, latency, and *intensity.* Each of these is defined and discussed below.

Frequency

Frequency or *number* refers to a simple count of the number of times a behavior occurs during a specific time period. If one frequency count is to be compared with a second, the observation period must be constant across both. For example, if you observe Chris having 5 tantrums on day one and 10 tantrums on day two, the duration of the observation periods across the two days must be the same for the two frequency counts to be directly comparable. In other words, you can't assume that Chris had more tantrums on the second day since the increase may be due to a longer observation period. Since caregivers do not always have a constant observation period from day to day, frequency counts alone are not recommended.

When a constant observation period can be established, frequency counts are best used when the target behavior has a clear starting and stopping point (Foster, Bell-Dolan, & Burge, 1988). For example, counting the number of times one child *hits* another child is easily counted. However, counting the number of times a child *talks* to another child may be more complicated since clear starting and stopping points between *talks* may be blurred.

Kazdin recommended that frequency only be used when each occurrence of the target behavior "takes a relatively constant amount of time each time it is performed" (1989, p. 58). Using our previous example, each *hit* probably takes the same time to perform while each *talk* may not. A child could talk for one second to one child ("Hi!") or have a five-minute conversation with a second child. A simple frequency count ("2") would not discriminate the two *talking* behaviors as different. For behaviors that may vary in duration, caregivers are encouraged to measure frequency and duration.

Another caution regarding the use of frequency counts alone is knowing the number of response opportunities. For example, if a teacher reports that a student completed five assignments during math class, this information is incomplete without knowing the total number of assignments requested. Knowing that the student completed 5 out of 5 or 5 out of 10 assignments communicates a more complete picture of the student's performance than the frequency count alone. A second example involves the measurement of compliance. If a teacher reports a frequency count of eight compliances during a school day, without reporting the total number of opportunities to be compliant, the information is incomplete and not very useful. A frequency count of 8 compliances out of 10 opportunities represents a different level of performance than 8 compliances out of 20 requests.

Duration

Duration data are recommended when caregivers are concerned about how long a behavior continues once started or the amount of time consumed when a behavior is performed. Duration is a necessary dimension to measure when caregivers want to increase or decrease the amount of time a child performs a behavior or participates in an activity. In addition to how often some behaviors occur, the duration of behaviors, such as crying, temper tantrums, listening, or working on a task, is a significant dimension that should be measured. For example, if a child has a 60-minute temper tantrum one day and a 5-minute tantrum the next, information that the child had one tantrum each day (frequency) does not provide a complete picture of the child's behavior. In this example, the duration of tantrum behavior has significantly decreased from the first to the second day. This change in behavior would not have been noted if the duration of the behavior was not measured.

There are two types of duration: *total duration* (Tawney & Gast 1984) and *response duration* (Kazdin, 1989). Total duration refers to the total amount of time a child performs a target behavior during an observation period. For example, if a child had two tantrums during a one-hour observation period and each tantrum lasted 5 minutes each, the total duration was 10 minutes. Caregivers would be interested in measuring total duration if they were trying to increase or decrease the total amount of time a child was engaged in an activity or behavior within a specific time period or activity. For example, a caregiver may wish to increase a child's total time on task in a reading class. Total duration may be used to estimate the percent of total observation time in which a child is engaged in a behavior (Kazdin, 1989). For example, if a child worked on task for a total duration of 30 minutes during a 45-minute class period, it may be stated that the child was on task for 66.6% of the class period ($30/45 = 0.666 \times 100 = 66.6\%$).

A response duration refers to the amount of time a child performs each individual target behavior. In the above example, the response duration for the first and second tantrum was five minutes. Caregivers would be interested in measuring response duration if they were trying to increase or decrease the amount of time a child exhibits a specific behavior. Referring back to our temper tantrum example, it is helpful to know the duration of each individual tantrum, not total duration, when trying to decrease tantrum behavior. In addition, the use of response duration allows caregivers to estimate a median response duration per behavior occurrence.

Rate

Rate refers to the frequency of a target behavior divided by the number of minutes or hours of observation time. This will yield a rate-per-minute or rate-per-hour measurement:

frequency of behavior/observation time = rate

For example, if John is noncompliant 10 times during a five-hour observation period, John's hourly rate of noncompliance is 2. This was calculated by dividing the frequency (10) of noncompliance into the number (5) of observation hours (10/5 = 2).

Frequency of noncompliance/total observation hours = rate per hour of noncompliance

Rate is often stated in terms of minutes. For example, if a teacher observes Julia kick her desk six times during a 30-minute social studies class, then Julia's kicking rate per minute is 0.20. This was calculated by dividing the frequency (6) of kicking by the number (30) of observation minutes (6/30 = 0.20).

frequency of kicking/total observation minutes = rate per minute

Rates are useful when the observation periods are not constant and vary in duration. The measurement of the rate allows caregivers to compare the frequency of behavior across observation periods even if the duration of the observation period varies from day to day. For example, if Julia kicks her desk 12 times during another one-hour observation period, her minute rate of kicking is 0.20 (12/60 = 0.20). The minute rate (0.20) from the first observation period may be compared with the rate (0.20) from the second observation period since the difference in the duration of the observation period was accounted for during the rate calculation. In this case, a summary of Julia's performance for the two days may conclude that the rate of her kicking was constant (0.20 per minute). On the other hand, if the teacher reported frequency alone (6 kicks on day one and 12 kicks on day two), an observer might incorrectly conclude that Julia's kicking behavior doubled on the second day.

Caregivers are recommended to use rate when reporting the number of times a behavior occurred unless the observation periods are constant. However, given the busy schedules of classrooms and homes, observation periods are very unlikely to be constant and caregivers should plan on using rates when reporting behavioral data.

Latency

Latency refers to the amount of time it takes for a child to begin a behavior once he or she has been provided a direction or instruction to complete a task or modify a behavior. Latency is most useful when caregivers are concerned about children's compliance or behaviors related to following directions. For example, when a caregiver asks a child to help pick up toys after a free-time activity, latency is recorded by keeping track of the number of minutes or seconds between the initial request to pick up the toys and when the child actually starts to pick up the toys. When caregivers are working with children who tend to be noncompliant, the objective is to reduce the latency period to an acceptable level (5 to 10 seconds). This is accomplished by reinforcing children when they show improvement in decreasing their latency period and when they respond appropriately within an acceptable period of time. Refer to Chapter 7 for additional discussion on compliance and noncompliance.

There may be times when caregivers want to increase latency periods. A common example is the child who responds incorrectly to a teacher's directions because he or she begins an activity before the teacher provides all the instructions. Children who are too quick to answer a teacher's question, without allowing some time to think about the question, may commit many errors because of short latencies. When this is a problem, teachers may want to require a certain latency period (thinking time) before children are allowed to volunteer an answer.

Intensity or Magnitude

Intensity refers to the force or strength of a behavior. Intensity of behavior is a useful measurement with behaviors such as acts of aggression, temper tantrums, verbal responses, or other noises and body movements. For example, since the variability in crying behavior is considerable, caregivers working with a child who cries when he or she is brought to daycare each morning may be interested in measuring intensity, in addition to the frequency and duration of crying. A child who cries for five minutes once each morning may, with just frequency and duration measures, seem to be making poor progress adjusting to daycare. However, the intensity measurement may record a significant change in the child's crying behavior from "loud screaming" to "mild whining."

Intensity measures are either estimates based on a predetermined qualitative scale or, for a more objective measure, an automated apparatus used to measure a behavior's intensity. For example, Greene, Bailey, & Barber (1981) used an automated apparatus to measure noise levels during a program to decrease disruptive behavior on school buses. In most cases, however, caregivers do not have access to such automatic equipment and, moreover, qualitative estimates of intensity will probably serve the needs of most teachers and parents. When an objective method of measuring the intensity of a target behavior is not possible, the following are some example scales that may be used, depending on the behavior:

◆   "very strong," "strong," "weak," and "very weak"
◆   "mild," "moderate," "severe," "very severe"
◆   "very loud," "loud," "quiet," "very quiet"
◆   "very fast," "fast," "slow," "very slow."

We must stress, however, that the above "ratings" provide very subjective measurements of behavior. When these are used, precise criteria should be established per rating and reliability checks by independent observers should be completed.

MEASUREMENT OF BEHAVIOR

Wacker provided two primary reasons why caregivers should measure behavior: to document what occurred and to identify the variables responsible for the occurrence. "Measurement, in short, provides us with guidance regarding what we should do next" (1989, p. 254). In addition, a systematic process of behavioral measurement can:

◆   Help caregivers identify learning and behavior problems.
◆   Provide information concerning program effectiveness.
◆   Identify the need for program modifications.
◆   Facilitate communication with parents, administrators, other teachers, and support personnel.

Tawney and Gast (1984, p. 84) provided several guidelines for the measurement and evaluation of behavior. These guidelines are expanded on in the following list:

◆   Define the target behavior in measurable and observable terms.
◆   Collect sufficient data to provide the information necessary to make programming decisions. It is not necessary to collect data constantly on all behaviors.
◆   Become familiar with data collection alternatives so intelligent decisions can be made regarding the most effective measurement method per child and behavior.
◆   Select a data collection method that is practical. In other words, choose a method that can be consistently and reliably used within the constraints of the environment. A simple data collection system is more likely to be used than a demanding one.

♦ Integrate data collection into the daily routine. Again, data collection should not take an extraordinary effort on the part of caregivers.

♦ Review and evaluate the data regularly and use the data to make programming decisions.

The primary purpose of data collection is to provide caregivers with objective information with which to make informed programming decisions. It is disturbing to observe caregivers collect data only to fulfill an organizational requirement, place the data in a file, and never use the data for program evaluation.

Several types of data collection methods or observational recording systems are used to monitor behavior. An understanding of these different methods will allow caregivers to select the simplest and most informative data collection procedure. A description of the primary types of behavioral observation and measurement methods is outlined in the next sections.

Anecdotal Observation: The ABC Analysis

Anecdotal observation, sometimes referred to as an ABC analysis, was first described by Bijou, Peterson, and Ault (1968). During an anecdotal observation, the observer records everything observed about an individual's behavior. For example, if an anecdotal observation was completed for Jason during a 15-minute free-time period, the observer would record Jason's behavior, whom he played with, what he played with, what he said, and so on. The product of this anecdotal observation would probably include a narrative describing Jason's behavior during the 15-minute observation period. From this information, specific target behaviors may be identified for modification. It is important to note that ABC recording presents an objective description of actual behavior, not interpretations of that behavior. For example, "Jason hit Mike," not "Jason was angry."

In addition to behavioral observation and measurement, an anecdotal observation may also include an analysis of antecedent and consequent events occurring within the observed environment. This assessment of antecedent and consequent events, along with behavioral observations, is also called ABC analysis. As stated by Lennox and Miltenberger, understanding behavior is incomplete without an understanding of the "events surrounding the target behavior and, subsequently, to determine the extent to which specific events may be related to the occurrence of the behavior" (1989, p. 306). The focus of an ABC analysis is on "external events that appear to influence the behavior" (Snell & Grigg, 1987, p. 78).

To complete an ABC analysis or anecdotal record of the antecedents, behaviors, and consequences within a child's environment, practitioners should prepare an observation form that will facilitate record keeping during the observation period. The observation form may be a simple sheet of paper divided into three sections: antecedent events, observed behaviors, and consequent events. An example of an anecdotal observation form, suitable for an ABC analysis, is provided in Figure 3.1.

Child's Name: <u>Michael</u>   Observer: <u>Ms. Garris</u>
Environment: <u>Playground</u>   Date: <u>11/5/92</u>
Observation Time Start: <u>12:30 pm</u>   Stop: <u>12:45 pm</u>

Antecedent Events	Observed Behavior	Consequent Events
12:36: Children running around in a circle.	Michael pushed Tim from behind.	Tim turned around and yelled at Michael to "Stop!"
12:42: Children standing in a circle and talking.	Michael told Tim "You're a nerd," and hit him on the head.	Tim said nothing and did nothing. Michael laughed.
12:45: Bell rings for kids to return to classroom. Kids begin to run toward building.	Michael hit Tim on the back as the two were running toward the building.	Tim continued to run toward the building. Did not give Tim a response. Michael laughed.

Figure 3.1.   *Example record form for an ABC analysis.*

An ABC analysis provides caregivers with:

◆ A descriptive record of a child's behavior during a specific observational period. The observational period could coincide with activities or settings in which the child's behavior has been especially problematic.

◆ A descriptive record of the child's environment, the significant people in the child's environment, and their interactions with the child, and the activities occurring within the child's environment.

◆ Information about antecedent events occurring prior to the child's immediate behavior. This information will help caregivers identify events that may elicit specific behaviors. For example, what are the adult or peer behaviors (requests, demands, proximity) that occur prior to the child's behavior?

◆ Information about consequent events occurring after the child's behavior. This information will help caregivers identify events that may maintain, reinforce, or punish specific behavior. For example, what comments do others make following the child's behavior?

This information will help caregivers identify target behaviors, events that are maintaining inappropriate behavior, appropriate behaviors that are not reinforced, social skills that need to be learned, and environmental conditions that need modification in order to promote appropriate behaviors and decrease the probability of inappropriate behaviors. The anecdotal record is recommended as the first step during the informal assessment of children's behavior. Observation and measurement of specific target behaviors is the next step.

Frequency Recording/Event Recording

When observing for an individual target behavior, an easy method of measuring the target behavior is to simply count the behavior every time it occurs during a specific time period. This method of data collection is called *frequency recording* or *event recording*. The result of a frequency recording is a frequency count or rate of occurrence per observation period. For example, a teacher may use event recording to count how many times a student hits other students during a 30-minute recess period. Koorland, Monda, and Vail (1988) made the following recommendations concerning event recording:

- ◆ Event recording should be used only when the target behavior is "discrete, uniform in duration, brief, and repeatable" (p. 59).
- ◆ The observation periods per day may be fixed or variable. Thus, caregivers may decide to count a target behavior once per day, twice per day, or whatever schedule is convenient with the caregiver's schedule.
- ◆ The duration of each observation period may vary. When the observation period is constant, a frequency count may be reported per observation. When the observation periods vary, however, the rate of the behavior must be determined by dividing each number of occurrences per observation period with the number of minutes per observation period.

Figure 3.2 provides an example of an event recording data form used to count hitting behavior. Data collected include the number of times hitting was observed, the length of the observation periods in minutes, and the rate of hitting per minute. Note that the observation periods vary in length and the rate per minute is calculated for each observation so that the data are comparable. The rate of the target behavior, per minute, may also be charted on a graph as demonstrated in Figure 3.2.

Duration Recording

It is important to record the duration of a behavior when caregivers are concerned with the amount of time a child engages in a target behavior. Caregivers may record duration along with frequency by making a note of the time the target behavior begins and ends. A duration can then be calculated. For example, if a child begins to tantrum at 10:15 and ends at 10:25, the duration of the tantrum is 10 minutes.

Duration may be recorded in two ways. First, caregivers may be interested in the *average duration* of a behavior over a specific period of time. For example, if a child had three tantrums during one class period lasting 10, 5, and 3 minutes each, the average duration is 6 minutes (10 + 5 + 3 = 18/3 = 6). Second, caregivers may also be interested in the *total duration* of the target behavior. Using our same example, the total duration of tantrum behavior is 18 minutes.

Figure 3.2. *Example of event recording data form and graph of recorded raw data.*

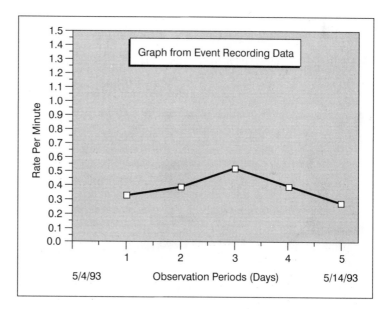

Child's Name: <u>Mike</u>   Observer: <u>Ms Garris</u>
Environment: <u>Playground</u>   Date: <u>1/1/93 – 1/5/93</u>
Target Behavior: <u>Hitting others</u>

Day/Time	Observation Period	Frequency of Behavior	Rate per Minute
1/1/93	30 minutes	10	.33 per min.
1/2/93	20 minutes	08	.40 per min.
1/3/93	15 minutes	08	.53 per min.
1/4/93	30 minutes	12	.40 per min.
1/5/93	20 minutes	06	.30 per min.

Interval Recording

Interval recording refers to the division of a specific observation period into equal intervals of smaller time periods or intervals. The observer then indicates if the target behavior occurred (+) or did not occur (-) during each interval. Note that the frequency of the target behavior during each interval is *not* recorded. This is a limitation of interval recording. A second limitation is that the size of the intervals will partly determine the recorded rate (percentage of intervals) of the target behavior. If the intervals are too long, a summary of the intervals may always indicate a target behavior rate of 100%, regardless of real decreases in the target behavior. For example, although a child's frequency of hitting may have decreased from 10 to 5 per interval, the observer would indicate only a "+" to indicate that the target behavior (hitting) occurred during that particular interval. As a result, the observer may then report that hitting was still occurring during 100% of the intervals. Although this statement would be correct, the decrease in the actual frequency of hitting may not be documented. On the other hand, intervals that are too short may result in the recording of artificially low rates of behavior. (Note in Figure 3.4 how the resulting percentages may be manipulated by changing the duration of the intervals.)

The size of each interval within the total observation period may range from 5 to 30 seconds. Kazdin (1989) recommended 10- to 15-second intervals; Cooper, Heron, and Heward (1987) recommended 6- to 15-second intervals; and Alberto and Troutman (1990) stated that the intervals should not be longer than 30 seconds. Repp, Nieminen, Olinger, and Brusca (1988) found that shorter intervals produced more accurate data than longer intervals. The total observation period for interval recording may range from 10 to 60 minutes, depending on the caregiver's schedule.

An example of an interval-recording form is provided in Figure 3.3. A 10-minute observation period is divided into 30-second intervals. Since there are twenty 30-second intervals during a 10-minute observation period, the 10-minute observation period is divided into 20 intervals. Thus, the total number of intervals depends on the total observation time and the length of the intervals.

Once the length of the total observation period and the size of the intervals have been decided, the next step is to observe the child and indicate if the target behavior occurred or did not occur during each interval. It does not make a difference how many times the target behavior occurred during each interval. During the observation period, mark a "+" if the behavior occurred

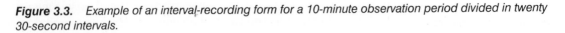

> Child's Name: _____   Observer: _____
> Environment: _____   Date: _____
> Target Behavior: _____
> Start Time: 9:00 am   Stop time: 9:10 am
>
> 10-minute observation period: 30-second intervals
>
> 9:00   9:01   9:02   9:03   9:04   9:05   9:06   9:07   9:08   9:09
>
> | 1 | 2 | 3 | 4 | 5 | 6 | 7 | 8 | 9 | 10 | 11 | 12 | 13 | 14 | 15 | 16 | 17 | 18 | 19 | 20 |
> |---|---|---|---|---|---|---|---|---|----|----|----|----|----|----|----|----|----|----|----|
> | | | | | | | | | | | | | | | | | | | | |
>
> *Key:* Mark a "+" in the interval if the target behavior occurred; mark a "–" in the interval if it did not occur.

Figure 3.3. *Example of an interval-recording form for a 10-minute observation period divided in twenty 30-second intervals.*

at any time during each interval and a "-" if the behavior did not occur during the interval. An example is provided in Figure 3.4. At the end of the interval, caregivers may calculate the percent of intervals the target behavior occurred and did not occur. This is calculated by dividing the number of intervals with a "+" by the total number of intervals. In our hypothetical data provided in Figure 3.4, the target behavior was observed in 14 of the 20 intervals. By dividing 14 by 20, it is determined that the target behavior occurred during 70 of the total intervals.

The two primary methods of interval recording are *partial-interval recording* and *whole-interval recording*. Partial-interval recording requires the observer to record whether the behavior occurred or did not occur at any time during the interval. The frequency or duration of the behavior within the interval is not monitored. Whole-interval recording, however, requires that the observer record the occurrence of the behavior only if the behavior was present throughout the entire interval. Thus, the duration of the behavior is monitored. The decision to use partial- or whole-interval recording depends primarily on the observed behavior. The partial-interval approach is preferred for behaviors that are short in duration (hitting and touching), while the whole-interval approach is appropriate for behaviors that occur for an extended dura-

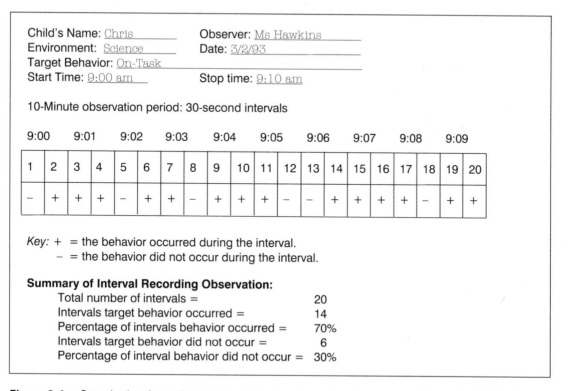

Key: + = the behavior occurred during the interval.
    − = the behavior did not occur during the interval.

Summary of Interval Recording Observation:

Total number of intervals =	20
Intervals target behavior occurred =	14
Percentage of intervals behavior occurred =	70%
Intervals target behavior did not occur =	6
Percentage of interval behavior did not occur =	30%

Figure 3.4.   *Sample data for an interval recording form for a 10-minute observation period divided into twenty 30-second intervals.*

tion (off-task and talking). Repp et al. (1988) noted that in comparison with continuous measurement, partial-interval recording tends to overestimate the continuous measures while whole-interval recording underestimates.

Caregivers may use interval recording to monitor the behavior of several children or behaviors at the same time. However, caregivers should not try to monitor more than three children or behaviors during a single observation period. Figure 3.5 shows a sample recording form used to monitor talking behavior across three children during a five-minute observation period divided into ten 30-second intervals. A similar form could also be used to observe three different behaviors for one child.

Time Sampling

Time sampling, sometimes referred to as *momentary time sampling,* refers to another common method of behavior measurement. Like interval recording, time sampling requires the observer to divide the total observation period into smaller time intervals. However, unlike interval recording in which the observer records if the behavior occurred at *any* time during the interval, time sampling requires the observer to record if the behavior was observed at the *end* of the interval. For example, if an observer was monitoring Julia's on-task behavior, the observer would look at Julia at the end of each interval and record a "+" if she was on-task at that *moment* or a "-" if she was not on-task. Time sampling is most appropriately used when monitoring behaviors that have

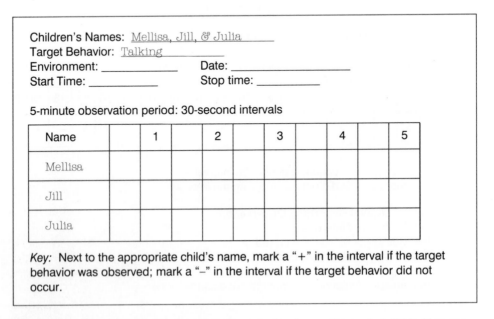

Children's Names: Mellisa, Jill, & Julia _____
Target Behavior: Talking _____
Environment: _____   Date: _____
Start Time: _____   Stop time: _____

5-minute observation period: 30-second intervals

Name		1		2		3		4		5
Mellisa										
Jill										
Julia										

Key: Next to the appropriate child's name, mark a "+" in the interval if the target behavior was observed; mark a "–" in the interval if the target behavior did not occur.

Figure 3.5. *Interval recording form for a five-minute observation period divided into ten 30-second intervals for three children.*

some duration. For example on-task/off-task, in-seat/out-of-seat, and talking are examples of behaviors that may be monitored with time sampling.

The total length of observation for time sampling may be significantly longer than interval recording since the observer is actually required to look at the child only at the end of each interval. In addition, while the intervals in interval recording are usually seconds long, the intervals in time sampling are usually minutes long. For example, a 60-minute observation period may be divided into twelve 5-minute intervals. Like interval recording, the observer records the percentage of intervals for which the target behavior was recorded (number of "+" divided by the total number of intervals). A recording form for such an observation is provided in Figure 3.6.

Two concerns arise with regard to time sampling. First, it is important to note that, as the length of the intervals increases, the amount of observed or sampled behavior decreases. As the amount of observed behavior decreases, the collected data are less likely to be consistent with the actual occurrence of the target behavior. Thus, we recommend that interval periods for time sampling not exceed five minutes. Second, if the child knows that a caregiver is monitoring his or her behavior and that the caregiver is looking at the child only at the end of a specific time interval, the child may modify his or her behavior so that the target behavior is not observed at the end of the interval. If this is a problem or a potential concern, caregivers have three options: keep the interval length a secret, use interval recording instead of time sampling, or vary the length of the interval. While varying the length of the intervals, caregivers maintain an average interval period (e.g., five minutes) while the actual intervals may range, for example, from two to eight minutes.

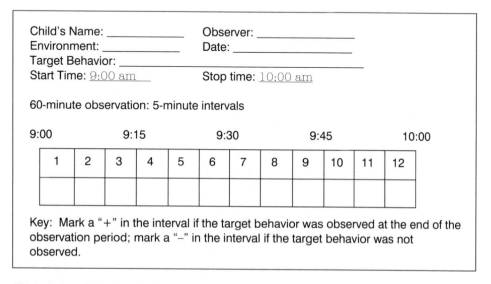

Child's Name: _____   Observer: _____
Environment: _____   Date: _____
Target Behavior: _____
Start Time: 9:00 am   Stop time: 10:00 am

60-minute observation: 5-minute intervals

9:00   9:15   9:30   9:45   10:00

1	2	3	4	5	6	7	8	9	10	11	12

Key: Mark a "+" in the interval if the target behavior was observed at the end of the observation period; mark a "−" in the interval if the target behavior was not observed.

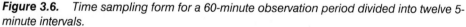

Figure 3.6.   *Time sampling form for a 60-minute observation period divided into twelve 5-minute intervals.*

As with interval recording, time sampling allows observers to calculate the percentage of total intervals the behavior was observed and not observed. For example, if the behavior was observed at the end of 6 out of a total of 12 intervals, we would report that the behavior was observed during 50% of the total intervals.

ACCURACY OF BEHAVIORAL OBSERVATION AND MEASURES

Repp et al. (1988, p. 29) outlined several factors that may "potentially affect the accuracy of data collected during direct observations: reactivity; observer drift; the recording procedure; location of the observation; reliability; expectancy; and characteristics of subjects, observers, and settings. Personal values and biases are additional sources of observer error. A description of each of these is provided in the following sections.

Reactivity

Reactivity refers to changes in a child's behavior as a result of being observed. For example, when children know that a teacher is counting how often they get out of their seats, the children may increase or decrease the target behavior in response to this knowledge. The exact effect on a child's behavior depends on the child, the behavior, the observer, and many other situational variables. Since the observer cannot be sure if his or her presence will have an impact on the child's behavior, there are times when unobtrusive observations (i.e., when the child is unaware that his or her behavior is being observed) are recommended. For example, unobtrusive observations are recommended when baseline data, discussed later in this chapter, are collected.

Observer Drift

Observer drift refers to a gradual shift by the observer of his or her understanding of the target behavior being observed and measured. For example, a caregiver counting the frequency of a child getting out of his or her seat may have a different definition of the target behavior at the end of the observational period than the original definition used at the beginning of the observational period. In this case, differences observed and recorded in the child's behavior from one day to the next may have more to do with observer drift than actual changes in the child's behavior.

To control for observer drift, the target behavior should be defined in very specific terms that will remain clear throughout the duration of a program. Moreover, caregivers should define the topography of the target behavior prior to any observation. Thus, when "out of seat" behavior is being observed, caregivers should define what "out of seat" means—what is counted and what is not counted as an "out of seat" behavior. For example, a good description of out-of-seat behavior may state "Paul will be considered to be 'out of seat' when his buttocks are at least 12 inches from his chair." This clearly defines "out of seat" behavior such that caregivers know when to count the target behavior as occurring. Observer drift is more common when target behaviors are vaguely defined.

The Recording Procedure

The *recording procedure* refers to the procedure selected to measure the dimensions of a behavior (e.g., frequency and duration). The primary methods of measuring behavior include event recording, interval recording, and time sampling. As we have discussed, some procedures produce a more accurate picture of the behavior than others depending on the dimensions of the behavior to be measured.

Location of the Observation

At the beginning of this chapter, we discussed the importance of direct observation within natural settings. That is, if a child is exhibiting an inappropriate behavior within a classroom setting, it is important that the child's behavior be observed and measured within the classroom. Direct observations in natural settings provide a more accurate picture of the child's typical behavior within functional environments. Observations within natural environments also allow the observer to monitor caregiver behavior, peer behavior, and other environmental influences related to the inappropriate behavior. These same considerations hold true for inappropriate behavior exhibited in other environments.

Direct observation is a necessary and significant element to behavioral assessment.

Observer Expectations

Observer expectations refer to the expectations caregivers have about the children they observe. For example, when a teacher hears "things" from other teachers about a child's behavior, the teacher develops certain expectations about the child's behavior. These expectations may bias a teacher's observation of the child.

Caregiver's expectations may also affect how children behave. Observer expectations are less likely to influence observational data when target behaviors are clearly defined. Also, the periodic use of independent observers for reliability checks will help monitor these influences on teacher observations.

Characteristics of Subjects, Observers, and Settings

Characteristics of subjects, observers, and settings refer to variables such as gender differences, the complexity of the behavior being observed, and familiarity with the setting and children being observed (Repp et al., 1988). Results of studies suggested that gender differences may affect the way observers score children's behaviors. In fact, the gender of both the child and the observer may influence the data collected during direct observation (Repp et al., 1988; Yarrow & Waxler, 1979). Using both male and female observers to observe and measure children's behaviors is an excellent solution to gender influences. However, given the overwhelming proportion of female teachers in our schools, this may not be practical within school environments.

Regarding the setting, research has shown that "familiarity with the setting may make observation easier and thereby increase observer accuracy" (Repp et al., 1988, p. 32). This is certainly a positive finding for classroom teachers and parents who are interested in observing and measuring behaviors within their own school or home setting.

Personal Values and Bias

Personal values refer to social, cultural, or religious values that affect a caregiver's perception of children's behavior. For example, different personal values regarding behavior will affect a caregiver's definition of "appropriate" and "inappropriate" behavior. Observer bias refers to beliefs or emotional feelings about individual children. For example, among caregivers, teachers may report different observations than parents who were asked to observe for the same behavior. Whether or not a caregiver likes a child, how the child looks, and the gender of the child are other variables that may bias the caregiver's perceptions and observations (Bell & Harper, 1977; Zirpoli & Bell, 1987).

Many variables may provide a threat to the accuracy of data collected during direct observation. However, these threats are easily overcome. First, caregivers should become aware of the potential threats given their specific situation and available resources. Second, as previously stated, the target behavior must be stated in observable and measurable terms. This is the most important variable regarding the accurate measurement of behavior. A clear and concise definition of the target behavior will help eliminate misunderstandings of exactly what behaviors are and are not included in the target behavior. Third, caregivers may want to practice using their data collection method and correct any "bugs" before a full-scale implementation. Fourth, reliability data should be completed periodically in order to check for the reliability of data across caregivers. Checking reliability is discussed below. Repp et al. (1988, p. 33) outlined five additional recommendations to improve the accuracy of data collected during direct observations:

◆ *Train observers well regarding the definition and measurement of the target behavior.* This is especially important for caregivers within educational environments where many caregivers may be involved in collecting data.

◆ *Use an adaptation period for both caregivers and children.* This is necessary only when the caregiver is a stranger to the child and reactivity becomes a potential problem. This is not an issue for parents or teachers who are collecting data within their own classrooms.

◆ *Observe unobtrusively.* Try to integrate data collection into the teaching or caregiving routine.

◆ *Use permanent products* (e.g., videotapes, audiocassettes, etc.). This is not always possible or practical when teaching or caring for children in the home. However, there may be times when a teacher may need to document a child's behavior on film in order to show others and receive suggestions and other assistance.

◆ *Observe frequently and systematically.* Obviously, a longer period of observation is likely to document a more accurate "picture" of a child's typical behavior than a shorter period. However, a systematic approach to data collection need not take a significant amount of caregiver's time.

Data Collection Aids

Caregivers do not have to purchase sophisticated and expensive recording devices when collecting data. For example, caregivers may use a simple wrist counter or golf counter to record frequency during event recording. Also, caregivers may use a wristwatch with a second-hand or a stopwatch to monitor duration. Other less technical, homemade aids or techniques follow.

Pocket Counting

Pocket counting refers to the transfer of pennies or other small objects from one pocket to another each time a target behavior is observed. At the end of the observation period, the caregiver simply counts the number of pennies in the receiving pocket to measure the frequency of the target behavior. The frequency count can then be recorded on the appropriate data collection form.

The Empty Jar

Caregivers may drop pennies or other small objects into a jar each time a target behavior occurs. At the end of the observation period, the caregiver simply counts the number of objects in the jar to measure the frequency of the target behavior. We observed one teacher drop paper strips into jars placed on the students' desks each time appropriate behavior was observed. At the end of the day the student with the most paper strips was provided with a special reinforcer. The paper strips also provided the teacher with a frequency count of appropriate behaviors exhibited per student or small groups of students.

Masking Tape on the Wrist

Another teacher told us about placing masking tape on her wrist. A few select names and target behaviors were written on the tape and the teacher recorded slash-marks next to the appropriate behavior. At the end of class the teacher counted the slash-marks, which served as a frequency count per target behavior. Of course, a clipboard with a data collection form would serve the same purpose. Caregivers could tape a watch or stopwatch to the clipboard in order to measure both frequency and duration. However, some caregivers may consider a clipboard obtrusive and difficult to carry while teaching or completing other caregiver responsibilities.

These recording tools ease the task of data collection in addition to facilitating accuracy and reliability. Caregivers should use their imagination and creativity when planning data collection methods and procedures. The most effective methods achieve the following:

- ◆ Make data collection easier than if no tools were used.
- ◆ Do not interfere with teaching or other caregiver duties.
- ◆ Are simple to operate.
- ◆ Ensure accurate monitoring of the target behavior.

RELIABILITY OF OBSERVATIONS

When measuring a target behavior, reliability refers primarily to the accuracy of data collected across observers. This kind of reliability is most commonly called *interrater reliability*. Other terms include *interobserver reliability* or *interobserver agreement*. For example, when observing a child's out-of-seat behavior, two observers are said to have perfect (100%) interrater reliability when both observers observe and record the child getting out of his or her seat the same number of times. However, if one caregiver observes 5 occurrences of the behavior while a second caregiver observes 10, the interrater reliability between the two observers is only 50 (5/10 = 0.5 x 100 = 50%).

Reliability measures provide independent confirmation that the data collected by one observer are accurate. Kazdin (1989) cited three primary reasons why reliability is important. First, the assessment of an individual's behavior

should be a function of the individual's true behavior, not a function of inconsistent data collection. If caregivers are going to use direct observation to evaluate the effectiveness of an intervention program, the data collected must be
reliable. Second, monitoring reliability identifies and minimizes the possible
biases of individual observers. Having a second observer periodically monitor
the same target behavior provides a check and balance on the first observer's
observation and recorded data. Last, reliability provides evidence regarding
how well the target behavior is defined. High reliability scores reflect a well-
defined target behavior. Low reliability scores may reflect a target behavior
that is not clearly identified and defined. This may result in an inconsistent
application of the intervention plan and must be corrected. Inconsistency is
the primary deficiency of many behavior management programs.

Caregivers will obtain satisfactory reliability measures when target
behaviors are clearly defined and when all observers are adequately trained.
Observer training should include an overview of the program, the topography
of the target behavior(s) to be observed, and the measurement techniques to
be employed during observation.

Reliability measures greater than 70 to 80% are usually considered adequate. Of course, the closer the reliability is to 100 the better. When reliability
is lower than 70%, serious questions should be raised regarding the accuracy of
the data collected. Behavior change programming decisions are difficult to
make with inconsistent or deficient data. The method used to calculate reliability depends to a large extent on the dimension of behavior measured or the
type of data collection procedure used.

Reliability of Frequency Counts

If a frequency count or event recording procedure is employed, interrater reliability may be calculated by dividing the lower frequency by the higher frequency. Referring back to the previous example, one observer recorded 5 out-of-seat
behaviors and the second observer recorded 10 out-of-seat behaviors. The
lower frequency (5) is then divided by the higher frequency (10) and a quotient
of 0.5 is the result. The quotient (0.5) is then multiplied by 100 and an interrater reliability of 50 is calculated as demonstrated below:

$$05 = \text{frequency recorded by first observer}$$
$$10 = \text{frequency recorded by second observer}$$
$$\text{reliability} = 05/10 = 0.5 \times 100 = 50\%$$

Reliability of Duration and Latency Measures

A similar procedure is used to calculate interrater reliability when two
observers are measuring the duration or latency of a target behavior. Instead
of frequency, these measures involve a measurement of time. To find the reliability between the two time periods, the shorter duration/latency observed is

divided by the longer duration/latency observed. For example, if one observer records that a child was on task for 10 minutes and a second observer records that the same child was on task for 15 minutes, their interrater reliability would equal 66.6 or 67% as demonstrated below:

$$10 \text{ minutes} = \text{duration observed by first observer}$$
$$15 \text{ minutes} = \text{duration observed by second observer}$$
$$\text{reliability} = 10/15 = 0.67 \times 100 = 67\%$$

Reliability for Interval Recording and Time Sampling

To calculate interrater reliability for interval and time sampling procedures, a slightly more complex method is required. As previously outlined, both interval recording and time sampling involve the division of an observation period into smaller intervals of time. Two concerns arise regarding the reliability of data collected using these two procedures. First, observers want to know if the *number* of intervals that the target behavior was recorded across the two observers is reliable. We will call this *frequency reliability*. This is calculated in the same manner as event recording reliability. Thus, if one caregiver observes the behavior in 7 intervals and the second caregiver observes the behavior in 12 intervals, their frequency reliability is calculated as follows:

$$7/12 = 0.58 \times 100 = 58\%$$

The second reliability concern during interval recording or time sampling may be referred to as *agreement reliability*. This second reliability is more important than frequency reliability because it communicates a more accurate picture of the interrater reliability between two observers. In looking at Figure 3.7, note that both caregivers recorded that the child was on task 5 out of the 10 intervals. Thus, their frequency reliability is 100% ($5/5 = 1 \times 100 = 100\%$). Also note, however, that both observers *agree* on when the child was on task (interval 7) and when the child was not on task (interval 3) only in 2 out of the 10 intervals. That is, during interval 7 both observers marked a "+," indicating that they observed the child to be on task, and during interval 3 both observers marked a "-," indicating that they did not observe on-task behavior. Interestingly, although they both recorded that the child was on task 5 out of the 10 intervals and received a 100% frequency reliability, the observers hardly agree at all! To calculate the agreement reliability for interval recording and time sampling, the following formula is recommended:

$$\text{agreements/total intervals} \times 100 = \% \text{ of agreement}$$

It is not necessary to measure interrater reliability during every observation period. In fact, most teachers and parents will not be interested in collecting reliability data unless requested. If reliability data are required, a weekly reliability check (1/5 or 20% of observation periods) is usually adequate. That is, for every five days of data collection, there should be one day when an indepen-

Observer 1:

Interval

1	2	3	4	5	6	7	8	9	10
+	+	−	+	−	−	+	−	+	−

Observer 2:

1	2	3	4	5	6	7	8	9	10
−	−	−	−	+	+	+	+	−	+

Agreement between observers one and two:

1	2	3	4	5	6	7	8	9	10
No	No	Yes	No	No	No	Yes	No	No	No

Key: += On task behavior observed during interval
       − = On task behavior not observed during interval

Summary:
   Agreements = 2
   Total intervals = 10
   2/10 = .20 X 100 = 20% agreement

   Frequency Reliability = 100%
   Agreement Reliability = 20%

Figure 3.7.   *Interrater reliability (frequency and agreement) of two interval recording observations of on-task behavior.*

dent observation is recorded and compared with the caregiver's data. For long-term interventions, every other week should be satisfactory.

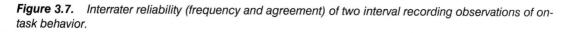

RECORDING OBSERVATIONS

Having discussed how to observe and measure behaviors, it is time to review some recording methods that will simplify the observation process and facilitate the collection of reliable measurements. Methods used to record behavioral observations include permanent product recording, various data collection forms, and coding systems. In addition, several data collection aids are available for caregivers to use that may increase the accuracy of data collected.

Permanent Recording

Permanent products are materials that are produced as a result of behavior. Caregivers may then measure and evaluate the product of the behavior. For example, when a teacher gives students a paper and pencil math test, the test becomes a permanent product of the student's math performance. The teacher may then use the test to measure and evaluate the students' math performance. Researchers have used permanent product recording to measure a variety of academic skills (Stern, Fowler, & Kohler, 1988), independent living skills (Williams & Cuvo, 1986), and safety skills (Sowers-Hoag, Thyer, & Bailey, 1987). Other examples of permanent products include completed puzzles, artwork, writing projects, building projects, and so on. Usually, the child's performance or behavior is not measured during the completion of the product (e.g., taking the test or writing the paper). Rather, the product is measured and evaluated after it is completed.

As discussed in Chapter 6, children can be taught how to observe and record data regarding their own behavior. The results of this self-monitoring may also produce permanent products, generated by the children, which caregivers may use to evaluate behavior. As discussed in Chapter 6, children usually generate permanent products that accurately reflect their behavior.

When an audio- or video-recorder is used during direct observation of children's behavior, the completed tape provides caregivers with the ultimate permanent product of behavior. The recorded behavior can then be observed immediately or stored for future observation of specific target behaviors, which can be measured and remeasured at the caregiver's convenience.

Data Collection Forms

A data collection form is a prepared sheet of paper used to record raw data collected during behavioral observations. Sometimes referred to as *raw data sheets,* these forms are prepared to assist the observer in recording data effectively and accurately. Many examples of data collection forms are provided throughout this chapter. Note that the forms are very simple in design. Caregivers are encouraged to design their own data collection forms according to their individual needs.

Figure 3.8 provides an additional sample form that caregivers may use for event recording and/or duration measurement. Data collection forms should include, at a minimum, the child's name, the target behavior, the environment or situation in which the child is being observed, the name of the observer, and dates of observation. Data collection forms may also include space for observer comments.

Coding Systems

Coding systems refer to a list of codes added to a data collection form that assists caregivers in recording observed behaviors in an efficient manner. Coding systems are especially useful when many target behaviors are being

Child's Name: _____   Observer: _____

Environment: _____   Dates: From _____ to _____

Target Behavior: _____

Recording Code: _____

Date/Time	Frequency of Behavior	Start Time	Stop Time	Total Frequency	Total Duration

Observation Comments:

Figure 3.8.   *Sample data collection form for event and/or duration recording.*

observed at the same time. When using a coding system, each target behavior is given a code. Readers are encouraged to keep the coding system as simple as possible. During the observation period the observer simply records the code corresponding to the target behavior(s) observed. Coding systems can be used when caregivers are making anecdotal observations or during interval recordings. When used during interval recordings, the observer records within each interval the code of any target behavior observed during the interval. Figure 3.9 provides an example of an interval recording form using a coding system. Caregivers can calculate the percentage of intervals each target behavior was observed by counting the number of intervals each code was recorded and dividing by the total number of intervals.

Another option includes having the codes prerecorded within each interval. The observer can then simply circle the appropriate code corresponding to the behavior(s) observed within each interval.

DISPLAYING OBSERVATIONAL DATA

Once observational data have been recorded on data collection forms, displaying the raw data on a graph provides caregivers with a picture of the data. Ideally, graphs should be updated on a regular basis as new raw data are collected. Graphs provide caregivers with important information on behavioral

Child's Name: Jeremy, Jason, Justin

Target Behavior: See coding system

Coding System: T = Talking appropriately to other children,
C = Working on the computer,
D = On-task at desk,
G = playing a game with others,
A = playing alone.

Environment: Classroom free time

Date: _____

Start Time: _____

Stop time: _____

5-minute observation period: 30-second intervals

Name		1		2		3		4		5
Jeremy										
Jason										
Justin										

Note: Next to the appropriate child's name, record the appropriate code or codes within each interval indicating which target behaviors were observed during each 30-second interval. Record a "-" if none of the target behaviors were observed.

Figure 3.9.   *Sample interval recording form using a coding system (5-minute observation period divided into ten 30-second intervals).*

trends and intervention comparisons over time that are usually difficult to decipher by looking at a list of numbers recorded on raw data sheets. Moreover, graphs provide caregivers with an effective mode of communication when reporting a child's progress to other caregivers. For example, during parent-teacher meetings, a simple graph reflecting a child's behavior from the beginning of the school year provides an effective way for teachers to display student progress. With the use of a simple graph, caregivers can determine if a child's performance is increasing, decreasing, or remaining stable. Kerr and Nelson (1989, p. 91) outlined three primary reasons for using graphs:

1. To summarize data in a convenient manner for daily decision-making.
2. To communicate program effects.
3. To provide feedback to caregivers involved with the program.

Graphs also provide feedback to children about their performance or progress toward a goal. Children can look at a graph and visually inspect their own progress. Moreover, many children find a graphic display of their progress very reinforcing. The graph may become part of the treatment program as the child is visually reinforced by the accelerating trends noted on the graph. Also, children can be taught to chart their own performance data on their own graphs. The graphs can be displayed on a bulletin board at school or on the refrigerator at home so the child can monitor his or her progress. Make it fun!

Line Graphs

A line graph is the most common graph used to chart a child's performance over time. The line graph, as previously demonstrated in Figure 3.2, consists of a *horizontal axis* and a *vertical axis*. The horizontal axis is frequently referred to as the *abscissa* or *x-axis*. The *x*-axis is used to indicate the passage of time and intervention changes or phases over the duration of the intervention program. Note in Figure 3.10 that the *x*-axis is marked in equal intervals of time. These intervals may represent program sessions, days, weeks, and so on. The *x*-axis should be clearly labeled as is the one in Figure 3.10. In this example, the *x*-axis indicates the days that aggression was observed and counted. Recording the dates of these observations under the *x*-axis is a good idea.

The vertical axis is frequently referred to as the *ordinate* or *y-axis*. The *y*-axis is always drawn on the left side of the *x*-axis and is used to indicate the values of a behavioral dimension (e.g., frequency, rate, duration, etc.) Thus, the *y*-axis may represent the frequency, rate, duration, latency, or percentage measurements of behavior. In our example, the *y*-axis represents the frequency of aggressive behavior. Like the *x*-axis, the *y*-axis is clearly labeled to indicate what dimension of behavior is being charted and marked at equal intervals starting at zero at the point where the *x*- and *y*-axes intersect. As you move up the *y*-axis, the values of frequency, rate, and so on, increase. As you move from left to right on the *x*-axis, time progresses.

Figure 3.10. *Example of a line graph of frequency aggression over 10 days of observation.*

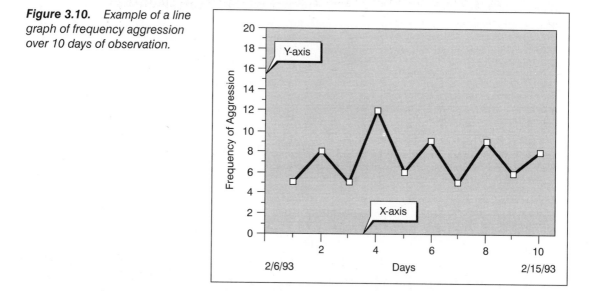

Each data point on the graph indicates an intersection point between a value from the *y*-axis and a point in time from the *x*-axis. For example, in Figure 3.10, the first data point indicates that the child was aggressive five (5) times on the first day, eight (8) times on the second day, five (5) times on the third day, and so on. When data points are charted on a graph, they may show one of four patterns or trends: accelerating, decelerating, stable, or variable. All of these data trends will be reviewed, along with examples, in our discussion on baseline and intervention measures below.

Cumulative Graphs

As illustrated in Figure 3.11, caregivers may display the same data charted in Figure 3.10 on a cumulative graph. In a cumulative graph, the frequency of aggression for each day is added to the previous day's data. In our example, the child was aggressive 5 times on the first day and 8 times on the second day. In a typical line graph, each data point would be charted independently. But in a cumulative graph, the first data point reflects the 5 aggressive acts observed on the first day, and the second data point reflects an additional 8 aggressive acts observed on the second day. Thus, the second data point represents 13 aggressive acts observed over the first two days of observation. Each additional data point indicates the number of behaviors observed that day *plus* the number of behaviors observed in all previous days of the program.

Cumulative graphs are used when the total number of behaviors observed is required from day to day. For example, a teacher's supervision may require a daily report on the total number of target behaviors observed from a specific start date or during a specific time period. Cumulative graphs are also useful when recording skill acquisition over a specific time period. For example, a

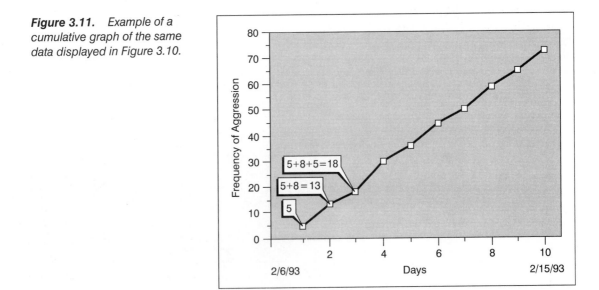

Figure 3.11. *Example of a cumulative graph of the same data displayed in Figure 3.10.*

reading teacher may need to keep a cumulative record of the number of new words learned by an individual student.

As demonstrated in Figure 3.11, the cumulative graph may give the impression that the frequency of the target behavior (aggression) is increasing very rapidly. A graph like this might give the wrong impression to caregivers who do not understand the nature of a cumulative graph. Thus, in most cases, caregivers are encouraged to use a noncumulative line graph to chart behaviors.

Bar Graphs

Another way to display raw data is with a bar graph or histogram. Like the line graph, the bar graph also has an x-axis and a y-axis. However, instead of data points to indicate the frequency, rate, and duration of the target behavior, the bar graph uses vertical bars. Each vertical bar represents one observation period. The height of the bar corresponds with a value on the y-axis. Figure 3.12 is a display of the same raw data used in the line graph shown in Figure 3.10. Since five aggressive acts were observed on the first day of observation, the first bar in Figure 3.12 is drawn to the value of 5 on the y-axis. Since eight aggressive acts were observed on the second day, the second bar is drawn to the value of 8 on the y-axis. The corresponding frequency count of the first four bars of our example are recorded on top of each bar.

Bar graphs present an excellent opportunity for caregivers to get children involved in monitoring their own behavior. While caregivers can place a mark where the top of a bar should stop, children can draw in the space from zero to the line. Also, caregivers can draw "empty" bars and have young children "fill" or color the bars. Again, this feedback will provide children with information

Figure 3.12. *Example of a bar graph using the same raw data given in the line graph of Figure 3.10.*

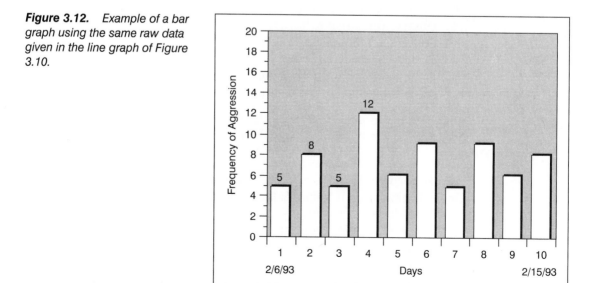

about their own behavior and reinforcement for increasing or decreasing behaviors.

Baseline and Intervention Measures

Baseline data refer to the measurement of a target behavior prior to the implementation of any intervention plan intended to modify the behavior. For example, if Mike frequently reports to school without his homework completed, a baseline measurement may include a count of the number of days during an observation period (four to five days) that Mike's homework was completed. During this baseline observation period, the teacher simply observes and measures the rate of homework completion. The teacher may also choose to measure the amount of homework completed. For example, if Mike had four homework assignments due on Monday and completed two, his teacher would record that Mike completed 50% of his Monday homework.

Baseline data are essential for developing realistic behavioral objectives. In the example above, it would be difficult for Mike's teacher to establish realistic objectives and goals for Mike without baseline data indicating his current performance levels. Baseline data provide a benchmark from which Mike's teacher can outline future performance objectives. Without baseline data, the teacher may establish objectives that are not challenging or objectives that are unrealistic, given Mike's current performance.

Caregivers should follow several steps when they want to obtain a baseline measure on a target behavior. These steps outline the important relationship between collecting baseline data and the establishment of behavioral objectives. Each of these steps is discussed in this chapter

- ◆ Identify the target behavior.
- ◆ Define the target behavior in measurable and observable terms.
- ◆ Observe the target behavior.
- ◆ Collect data on the target behavior.
- ◆ Review the data.
- ◆ Establish behavioral objectives based on current performance measures as outlined in the baseline data.

Baseline data serve many purposes. Referring back to our example, Mike's teacher may use the baseline data on Mike's homework for the following purposes:

- ◆ To document Mike's current homework completion performance.
- ◆ To help decide if Mike's homework completion performance needs to be modified.
- ◆ To provide objective data to Mike's parents and other significant caregivers about his homework completion performance.
- ◆ To justify the initiation of a homework completion program.
- ◆ To serve as comparative data for future intervention program data.

An important question about baseline data involves the number of observation periods necessary for a reliable baseline measurement. That is, how many observations of the target behavior are appropriate before the intervention plan can be introduced? The general rule is that caregivers should collect data points until the baseline data are stable (typically four to five). As previously stated, a data point refers to a point on a graph representing a single observation period. Thus, if Mike's teacher observed and measured his homework completion for five days, the teacher would have five baseline data points. When these data points are transferred to a graph, a "picture" of Mike's homework completion performance can be reviewed. Figure 3.13 provides a hypothetical example of Mike's homework completion baseline data and a graph of

Figure 3.13. *Mike's hypothetical baseline raw data and graph for homework completion performance.*

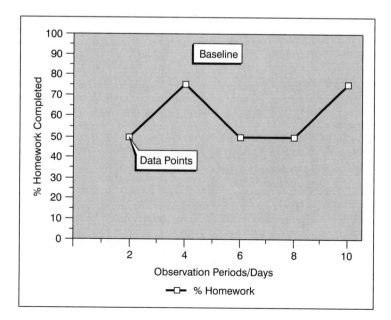

| Student's Name: | Mike |
| Target Behavior: | Homework Completion |

Observation Period	**Percentage of homework completed**
Monday	50 percent of homework completed
Tuesday	75 percent of homework completed
Wednesday	50 percent of homework completed
Thursday	75 percent of homework completed
Friday	50 percent of homework completed

the same data collected during the five days of baseline observation. Note that in this example the *y*-axis indicates the *percentage* of homework completed each day.

As previously stated, baseline data should be collected for four to five days or until the data are stable. Data are *stable* when they do not appear to have either an upward or downward trend and the data points do not vary significantly from each other. An *accelerating* trend refers to a pattern of data points that is increasing in value across time, from left to right along the *x*-axis. A *decelerating* trend refers to a pattern of data points that is decreasing across time. If the baseline data points show an accelerating or decelerating trend, caregivers may want to extend the baseline collection period beyond the normal four to five observations until a more stable measurement is obtained. For example, if the baseline data show an accelerating trend, Mike's teacher may want to take a wait-and-see attitude since an accelerating trend indicates that Mike's homework completion performance is improving without intervention. Mike may have discovered that his teacher is keeping track of his homework and, as a result, an improvement in his homework completion is observed. If the trend continues, Mike's teacher may consider the act of monitoring Mike's homework performance an effective intervention. If the baseline data trend is decelerating, Mike's teacher may not want to wait for additional evidence that an intervention program is necessary since, in this case, a decelerating trend indicates that Mike's homework completion performance is decreasing. For inappropriate behavior (e.g., aggression), however, a decelerating trend would be welcomed and caregivers may want to take a wait-and-see attitude before starting an intervention plan.

A *variable* trend refers to a pattern of data points that varies from day to day and does not show a definite accelerating or decelerating trend. According to Tawney and Gast, a "minimum of three separate, and preferably consecutive, observation periods are required to determine the level of stability and trend of data" (1984, p. 160). Figure 3.14 shows some hypothetical data with accelerating, decelerating, stable, and variable trends.

Once baseline data have been collected and caregivers have decided that an intervention program is necessary, data collection should continue through the intervention phase of the program. While baseline refers to the data collected *prior* to the introduction of an intervention, *intervention data* refer to the measurement of a target behavior *during* the intervention phase or phases of a behavior change program. Using the previous example, suppose that Mike's teacher decides to initiate a homework completion program that includes giving Mike a verbal prompt before he leaves school each day (such as "Mike, don't forget to do your homework!"), plus extra attention when he completes more than 75% of his homework assignments. Intervention data would include a measurement of Mike's homework completion performance starting on the first day of the homework completion program and every day after until the program's behavioral criteria has been reached.

Intervention data are separated from baseline data by simply drawing a line down the graph between the two data types. Note in Figure 3.15 that the

Figure 3.14 (pp. 115–116).
Examples of data showing accel-
erating, decelerating, stable, and
variable trends.

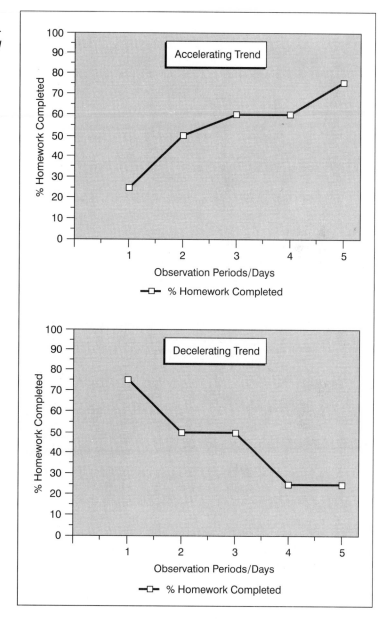

word "Baseline" is inserted on the left side of the graph. In this same manner, the word "Intervention" or "Treatment" should be inserted on the right side of the graph where the data points representing intervention data are graphed. For example, let's say that Mike's teacher decides to introduce the homework completion program (outlined above) for five consecutive school days. If the results look encouraging, Mike's teacher may decide to continue the intervention program. During the five days of intervention, Mike's teacher continued

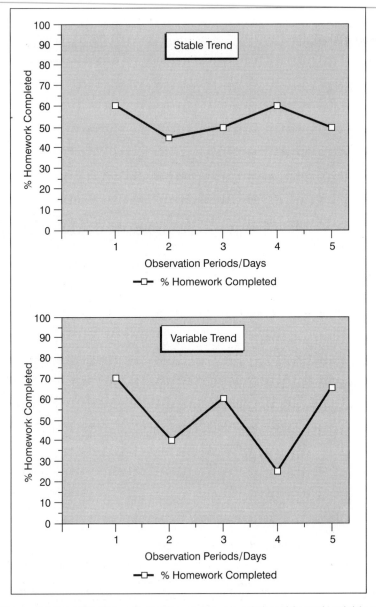

Figure 3.14 continued.   *Examples of data showing stable and variable trends.*

Figure 3.15. *Mike's hypothetical intervention data and graph for homework completion performance.*

| Student's Name: | Mike |
| Target Behavior: | Homework Completion |

Observation Period	Percentage of homework completed
Monday	50 percent of homework completed
Tuesday	75 percent of homework completed
Wednesday	100 percent of homework completed
Thursday	100 percent of homework completed
Friday	100 percent of homework completed

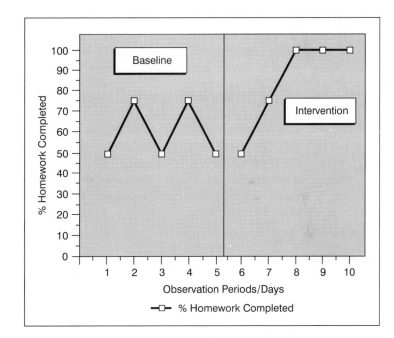

to observe and measure Mike's homework completion performance in the same manner that the baseline data were collected. Figure 3.15 outlines Mike's hypothetical intervention data and a graph of the five data points collected by Mike's teacher during the five days of intervention. These intervention data are added to the baseline data previously recorded on the graph. Note the line between the baseline data and the intervention data. Mike's teacher may now compare the intervention data with the baseline data and decide if Mike's homework completion performance has improved since the implementation of the homework completion program.

Like baseline data, intervention data charted on a graph may also indicate an accelerating, decelerating, stable, or variable trend. For example, after showing a variable trend during baseline, Mike's intervention data showed an accelerating trend as his homework completion increased from 50% on the first day of intervention to 75% on the second day and 100% on the third, fourth, and fifth days. In this case, since we want Mike's homework completion to increase, an accelerating trend on the intervention side of the graph means that Mike's homework completion is increasing and caregivers should continue the current program. If, however, the intervention data showed a decelerating, stable, or variable trend, caregivers should review and modify Mike's behavior change program.

If modifications are made to the intervention plan, a second line should be drawn down the graph, similar to the line separating baseline from the first intervention plan, separating the first and second intervention plan. The second plan may be a simple program modification or a totally new intervention. Regardless, each "new" intervention or phase of the program should be separated from each other and labeled accordingly. Caregivers may then review the data collected and charted across interventions and compare the effectiveness of each. Examples of multi-intervention programs charted on a single graph are provided below in our discussion of single subject designs.

Again, the purpose of data collection and graphing is to provide feedback about current programming so that caregivers may distinguish effective from ineffective interventions. By comparing the intervention data with the baseline data, and by looking at the data trends within each intervention plan, caregivers should be able to make decisions regarding the effectiveness of their interventions and make modifications accordingly. Also, the graph provides caregivers with an effective manner of communicating intervention results to others.

SUMMARY

The purpose of direct observation is to record behavioral patterns across natural settings and situations, to measure the dimensions of specific target behaviors, and to identify the variables associated with these target behaviors. Data from direct observations allow caregivers to monitor and evaluate the effectiveness of behavior change programs. Before a target behavior can be observed, however, it must be identified and defined in observable and measurable terms.

After an initial baseline observation to determine current performance levels of the target behavior, caregivers can establish behavioral objectives, which include the desired terminal behavior and performance criteria. Once these are established, caregivers must identify the dimensions of the behavior to be measured and determine how the dimensions will be measured. The five primary dimensions of behavior are frequency, duration, rate, latency, and intensity. Frequency refers to a simple count of the number of times a behavior occurs. Duration refers to the time period for which a behavior continues once started. Rate refers to the frequency of a target behavior divided by the amount of observation time. Latency refers to the amount of time it takes for a child to begin a behavior once directions are provided. Last, intensity refers to the force or strength of a behavior.

Measurement of behavior may include anecdotal observations or an ABC analysis. Anecdotal observations provide caregivers with a descriptive record of a behavior and related antecedents and consequences. Other measurement methods include event recording, interval recording, and time sampling.

The accuracy of behavioral observations are influenced by reactivity; observer drift; the recording procedure; the location of the observation; observer expectations; characteristics of subjects, observers, and settings; and personal values and biases. Recommendations to reduce error in direct observations include having precise definitions of target behaviors, training observers, using adaptation periods for both observer and children, using unobtrusive observations, using permanent product recording, and observing frequently and systematically.

Interrater reliability refers to the accuracy of data collected across observers. Caregivers will obtain satisfactory reliability measures when target behaviors are clearly defined and when all observers are adequately trained. Reliability measures may be calculated for frequency, duration, and latency measures, as well as for event, interval, and time sampling recording.

Caregivers may record their observations using permanent product recording, a variety of data collection forms, and coding systems. Data collection aids include wrist counters, watches, and other homemade devices and techniques. These tools ease the task of data collection and facilitate accuracy and reliability.

Caregivers are encouraged to display collected data on graphs in order to summarize data in a convenient manner, communicate program effects, and provide feedback to caregivers and the child. The line graph is the most common graph, however, cumulative and bar graphs are also used to display data. Graphs are used to chart both baseline and intervention data. While baseline data refer to the data collected prior to the introduction of an intervention, intervention data refer to the measurement of a target behavior during the behavior change program. A visual analysis of differences between baseline and intervention data and of the trends of the data provide caregivers with information regarding the effect of the intervention.

For Discussion

1. Discuss the importance of stating target behaviors in observable and measurable terms. Give examples of behaviors stated in observable and nonobservable ways.
2. Discuss the four elements of well-stated behavioral objectives. Provide examples.
3. Discuss the various dimensions of behavior. Provide examples of each.
4. Discuss the various methods of data collection and the types of behavior and situations in which each would be used.
5. Discuss the variables that may influence the accuracy of behavioral observations and what may be done to control for these influences.

REFERENCES

Alberto, P. A., & Troutman, A. C. (1990). *Applied behavior analysis for teachers.* Columbus, OH: Merrill/Macmillan.

Bancroft, J., & Bellamy, G. T. (1976). An apology for systematic observation. *Mental Retardation, 14,* 27–29.

Barlow, D. H., & Hersen, M. (1984). *Single case experimental designs: Strategies for studying behavior change.* New York: Pergamon Press.

Bell, R. Q., & Harper, L. V. (1977). *Child effects on adults.* Hillsdale, NJ: Lawrence Erlbaum.

Bijou, S. W., Peterson, R. F., & Ault, M. H. (1968). A method to integrate descriptive and experimental field studies at the level of data and empirical concepts. *Journal of Applied Behavior Analysis, 1,* 175–191.

Cartwright, C. A., & Cartwright, G. P. (1984). *Developing observation skills.* New York: McGraw Hill.

Cooper, J. O. (1981). *Measuring behavior.* Columbus, OH: Merrill/Macmillan.

Cooper, J. O., Heron, T. E., & Heward, W. L. (1987). *Applied behavior analysis.* Columbus, OH: Merrill/Macmillan.

Fisher, M., & Lindsey-Walters, S. (1987, October). *A survey report of various types of data collection procedures used by teachers and their strengths and weaknesses.* Paper presented at the annual conference of the Association for Persons with Severe Handicaps, Chicago.

Foster, S. L., Bell-Dolan, D. J., & Burge, D. A. (1988). Behavioral observation. In A. S. Bellack & M. Hersen (Eds.), *Behavioral assessment: A practical handbook.* New York: Pergamon Press.

Gast, D. L., & Tawney, J. W. (1984). The visual analysis of graphic data. In J. W. Tawney & D. L. Gast (Eds.), *Single subject research in special education* (pp. 142–186). Columbus, OH: Merrill/Macmillan.

Greene, B. F., Bailey, J. S., & Barber, F. (1981). An analysis and reduction of disruptive behavior on school buses. *Journal of Applied Behavior Analysis, 14*, 177–192.

Grigg, N. C., Snell, M. E., & Loyd, B. (1989). Visual analysis of student evaluation data: A qualitative analysis of teacher decision-making. *Journal of The Association for Persons with Severe Handicaps, 14*, 23–32.

Hawkins, R. P., & Dobes, R. W. (1977). Behavioral definitions in applied behavior analysis: Explicit or implicit. In B. C. Etzel, J. M. LeBlanc, & D. M. Baer (Eds.), *New directions in behavioral research: Theory, methods, and applications* (pp. 167-188). Hillsdale, NJ: Lawrence Erlbaum.

Kazdin, A. E. (1982). *Single-case research designs: Methods for clinical and applied settings*. New York: Oxford University Press.

Kazdin, A. E. (1989). *Behavior modification in applied settings*. Pacific Grove, CA: Brooks/Cole Publishing.

Kerr, M. M., & Nelson, M. C. (1989). *Strategies for managing behavior in the classroom*. Columbus, OH: Merrill/Macmillan.

Koorland, M. A., Monda, L. E., & Vail, C. O. (1988). Recording behavior with ease. *Teaching Exceptional Children, 21*, 59–61.

Lennox, D. B., & Miltenberger, R. G. (1989). Conducting a functional assessment of problem behavior in applied settings. *The Journal of The Association for Persons with Severe Handicaps, 14*, 304–311.

Meyer, L., & Janney, R. (1989). User-friendly measures of meaningful outcomes: Evaluating behavioral interventions. *Journal of The Association for Persons with Severe Handicaps, 4*, 263–270.

Repp, A. C., Nieminen, G. S., Olinger, E., & Brusca, R. (1988). Direct observation: Factors affecting the accuracy of observers. *Exceptional Children, 55*, 29–36.

Snell, M. E., & Grigg, N. C. (1987). Instructional assessment and curriculum development. In M. E. Snell (Ed.), *Systematic instruction of persons with severe handicaps*. Columbus, OH: Merrill/Macmillan.

Sowers-Hoag, K., Thyer, B., & Bailey, J. (1987). Promoting automobile safety belt use by young children. *Journal of Applied Behavior Analysis, 21*, 103–109.

Stern, G., Fowler, S., & Kohler, F. (1988). A comparison of two intervention roles: Peer monitor and point earner. *Journal of Applied Behavior Analysis, 21*, 103–109.

Tawney, J. W., & Gast, D. L. (1984). *Single subject research in special education*. Columbus, OH: Merrill/Macmillan.

Wacker, D. P. (1989). Introduction to special feature on measurement issues in supported education: Why measure anything? *Journal of The Association for Persons with Severe Handicaps, 14*, 254.

Williams, G., & Cuvo, A. (1986). Training apartment upkeep skills to rehabilitation clients. *Journal of Applied Behavior Analysis, 19*, 39–41.

Yarrow, M. R., & Waxler, C. Z. (1979). Observing interactions: A confrontation with methodology. In R. B. Cairns (Ed.), *The analysis of social interactions: Methods, issues, and illustrations*. Hillsdale, NJ: Lawrence Erlbaum.

Zirpoli, T. J., & Bell, R. Q. (1987). Unresponsiveness in children with severe disabilities: Potential effects on parent-child interactions. *The Exceptional Child*, *34*, 31–40.

CHAPTER 4

Single Subject Designs

Measurement alone does not permit the identification of functional relationships between independent and dependent variables. This is accomplished only when a behavior is measured within the framework of an appropriately chosen single subject research design. Through such pairing it is possible to formatively evaluate a particular intervention's effect on behavior and subsequently use that information to affect positive behavior change with students.

—*Gast and Tawney, 1984, p. 142.*

Most teachers and parents do not use elaborate single subject designs to demonstrate the effectiveness of their behavior change programs. However, as with our discussion on behavioral observation, measurement, and recording procedures in the previous chapter, we hope to demonstrate that caregivers may employ these simple research designs in the classroom or in the home with little difficulty and some exciting results. Since this text was written for teachers, parents, and other caregivers, we will not go into great detail about these designs. Instead, we will provide caregivers with an overview of some basic single subject designs, discuss their importance and application, and refer our readers to other sources where these and other more complicated research designs are discussed in far greater detail (for example, Barlow & Hersen, 1984; Tawney & Gast, 1984).

THE PURPOSE OF SINGLE SUBJECT DESIGNS

When people think about research they usually think about large samples of "subjects" participating in one of two groups: an *experimental group* where a "treatment" or intervention is presented, and a *control group* where the intervention is not presented. These *group designs* involve many subjects and each group's average performance is usually compared in order to evaluate *experimental control.*

Under ideal circumstances, caregivers may attribute the differences found between the performance of the experimental and control groups to the intervention applied in the experimental group and the absence of the intervention in the control group. These attributions refer to *intervention* or *treatment effects.* By using these research designs, researchers can demonstrate the effectiveness of their interventions (e.g., teaching style, behavior change program, new curriculum) and communicate these findings to others.

The purpose of single subject designs is also to demonstrate experimental control and intervention effects. However, instead of having to work with large groups of individuals, single subject designs allow researchers and caregivers to demonstrate experimental control and intervention effects while working with a single individual or a few individuals. As stated by Odom:

> The term 'single subject' is somewhat of a misnomer because usually more than one subject is involved, although the number of subjects is almost always small. (1988, p. 16)

Sidman (1960), an early proponent of single subject designs, stated that group research designs, in which an average group performance is measured, do not communicate important individual performances. He stated that, in many cases, the performance of individual children does not resemble the group average. For example, when a teacher initiates a specific behavior reduction program (such as trying to decrease hitting) for an individual student, an average classroom performance score is unlikely to let the teacher know how effective the program is for that individual student.

Single subject designs are ideal for caregivers who wish to demonstrate a relationship between a behavior change program and behavioral changes exhibited by a single child or a small group of children (Martin, 1985). For example, a classroom teacher may want to demonstrate that a behavior program developed for a small group of children is likely to be effective with other children in the school. In this case each data point in the single subject design graph represents the performance of a single class or other intact group of children; the data point represents the total group score or average score. For example, in a program to increase appropriate classroom behavior, a teacher could develop a single subject design for one student or for the whole class. When charting the frequency of appropriate behavior for one student, the data points on the graph represent the performance of the one student. When charting the frequency of appropriate behavior for the whole class, however, the data points on the graph represent the performance of the whole group. This latter example is demonstrated in Vignette 4.1.

Martin (1985, pp. 90–91) outlined the following four advantages of single subject designs over large group research designs:

- They provide a powerful method of studying the effectiveness of an intervention or several interventions on a single subject or small group of subjects.
- The results of single subject experimental designs are easy to interpret, usually by a visual inspection of the charted data points.
- They allow caregivers to decide when to initiate or modify interventions.
- The use of statistics, necessary in group research designs, is not usually necessary with single subject designs.

When using single subject designs, comparisons are made between *conditions* employed during the behavior change program. A condition refers to the baseline phase and various intervention phases used to modify an individual's behavior and are called *baseline* and *intervention conditions*.

1. *Baseline Condition:* In a single subject design the baseline condition is usually referred to as condition A. During this condition, baseline data are collected on a specific target behavior before an intervention strategy is employed.
2. *Intervention Condition:* Usually referred to as condition B. Data collection continues throughout the intervention condition.

Vignette 4.1.   Example of a Classroom Teacher Initiating Baseline and Intervention Conditions to Study the Effect of a New Seating Arrangement on Student Interactions.

Marty, a first grade teacher, wanted to try a new seating arrangement for her 28 students. Her students' desks were arranged in seven rows of four. After she implemented her new seating plan, however, her students were arranged in seven groups of four, with their desks facing each other in a circle. Marty believed that her new seating plan would increase appropriate student interactions and decrease inappropriate interactions (e.g., touching the backs of other students, having to turn away from the teacher to ask a student behind you a question, and so on).

Before Marty rearranged the classroom she decided to collect baseline data on the type and number of appropriate student interactions in her classroom. To do this she picked three target behaviors that, in her opinion, indicate appropriate student interactions:

◆ Asking another child for help,
◆ Praising another child's work, and
◆ Working cooperatively on a class assignment with another child.

Marty collected frequency data for each target behavior from 10 A.M. to 11 A.M. for five consecutive days. She then recorded her data on a simple line graph.

On the following Monday, Marty initiated her new seating plan. When the students arrived at school the desks were arranged according to Marty's new plan. To measure the effect of her new seating plan, Marty continued to collect data on the same target behaviors, from 10 A.M. to 11 A.M. for five consecutive days. She recorded this intervention data on the same graph as her baseline data. She drew a line between the baseline and intervention data points and recorded "Baseline" and "Intervention" on the left and right side of the graph.

By looking at her graph Marty noticed that the frequency of the target behaviors had increased significantly since the implementation of her new seating plan. Although it is possible that other factors may have made the difference in the students' behavior, Marty is sure that her new seating plan was the significant factor for her students.

In Vignette 4.1, Marty's students were in the "baseline condition" when they were in their old seating arrangement. When Marty initiated her new seating plan, the "intervention condition" began. Each data point on Marty's graph represents the total number of appropriate student interactions, defined by her three target behaviors, from 10 A.M. to 11 A.M. each day.

If variations to the intervention condition were employed or if new interventions were initiated, each of these would be considered a new condition (i.e., conditions C, D, E, and so on). For example, Marty's first intervention can be referred to as condition B. It was her first intervention plan initiated after baseline (condition A). If, after a few weeks, Marty decided to modify her new seating plan, the modified intervention would be called condition C. These variations to the basic baseline/intervention designs will be discussed later in this chapter.

A comparison of data across "conditions" allows caregivers to determine the most effective intervention. For example, if Marty looked at her data and found that higher rates of appropriate student interactions occurred during condition B than condition C, she might decide to go back to the seating arrangement used in condition B and delete the modifications made during condition C. When conditions are employed in a predetermined order, as in single subject designs, caregivers can demonstrate cause and effect relationships between specific interventions and children's behavior.

TYPES OF SINGLE SUBJECT DESIGNS

The type of single subject design employed depends on the order in which baseline and intervention conditions are presented. In some designs, baseline is followed by several intervention phases. In other designs, the baseline period is repeated while the intervention condition is withdrawn. Caregivers may also develop designs to represent intervention effects across subjects, settings, and other conditions. The designs reviewed in this chapter include the A-B, A-B-A, A-B-A-B, alternative treatment, changing criterion, and multiple baseline designs. Each of these designs, along with examples, is discussed below.

The A-B Design

In the most simple of single subject designs, the *A-B design,* only two conditions, baseline (A) and intervention (B), are used. We have already seen examples of A-B designs in Figure 3.14, discussed in the previous chapter, and in Vignette 4.1. In addition to the data trends that may be identified *within* each condition of the A-B design, the most important variable within this design is the change in data recorded from the first condition (baseline) to the second condition (intervention). Small changes in the data recorded across conditions indicate a weak intervention effect. That is, regardless of the implementation of the intervention, the recorded data indicate little change in the child's behavior. A large intervention effect would be reflected by large differences observed in the data recorded during the baseline and intervention conditions. In Vignette 4.1, Marty could determine if there was an intervention effect by looking at the changes in data trends across the different seating plans (the original seating plan of condition A and the new seating plan of condition B).

Caregivers may determine if there is a "small" or "large" change in the data by conducting a simple visual analysis or "eyeballing" the graph for obvious differences. "A visual interpretation of graphed data is the most common form of analysis" (Odom, 1988, p. 14). For example, in Figure 4.1, two A-B designs are presented for two hypothetical programs developed to increase school attendance for two high school students. For the first student (Example 1) school attendance was reinforced with special activity passes (e.g., field trips, computer time, and other preferred activities). For the second student (Example 2), a one-day in-school suspension followed the student's return to school each time he skipped school. Baseline data were collected for four consecutive weeks followed by four weeks of intervention. The students' attendance percentage per week (1 day = 20%, 2 days = 40%, 3 days = 60%, 4 days = 80%, and 5 days = 100%) was graphed during baseline and intervention conditions. When looking at the differences between conditions A and B for each example, what do you conclude about the intervention effects for each attendance program? Which program would you judge as having the greatest impact on school attendance?

In Example 1, a visual inspection of the graph seems to reveal an intervention effect. Data collected during the intervention phase indicate that school attendance was higher during the reinforcement program compared to data collected during the baseline condition. In Example 2, an intervention effect is not apparent because significant differences between baseline and intervention data are not apparent. As a result, caregivers using the two attendance programs may conclude that the reinforcement program is more effective than the in-school suspension program.

Although the visual analysis of single subject design data serves the needs of most educators and parents, "some authors have argued that the poor interrater reliability associated with visual analysis is a major limitation of single subject methods" (Ottenbacher & Cusick, 1991, p. 48). More formal estimates than the visual analysis of single subject design data involve mathematical calculations to determine the stability and changes in the direction of trend lines. These methods are beyond the scope of this text. For more information on visual analysis of single subject designs and methods that supplement visual analysis, readers are referred to Bailey (1984); Gibson and Ottenbacher (1988); Mueser, Yarnold, and Foy (1991); Parsonson and Baer (1986); and Tawney and Gast (1984).

Figure 4.1. *A-B designs demonstrating a possible intervention effect (Example I) and no intervention effect (Example 2) on school attendance.*

Example 1:

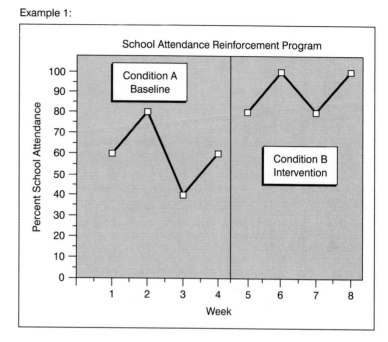

Example 2:

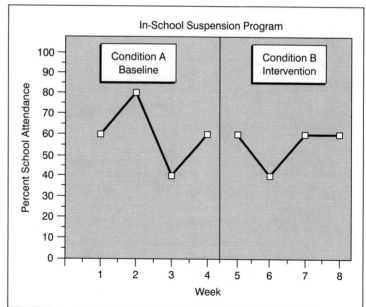

A considerable limitation with the A-B design is that we can only *presume* that behavioral changes noted during the intervention condition are a function of the intervention. Thus, we cannot be *assured* that the intervention program is responsible for the observed behavioral changes (Parsonson & Baer, 1986).

Other variables concerning caregiver behavior, influences in the home, and other environmental conditions may be more responsible for behavioral changes during the four days of intervention than the reinforcement program. For example, suppose the parents of the student in Example 1 heard about their son's attendance problems and decided to drive their child to school each day. The change in school attendance may be more closely related to a change in parental behavior than the effects of the reinforcement program implemented by the school. Thus, the A-B design has many internal and external validity problems (Campbell & Stanley, 1966) and is considered a *quasi-experimental design* since an association between the intervention condition and behavioral changes may not be made without "major reservations" (Barlow & Hersen, 1984, p. 142). For many caregivers, the increase in school attendance would be accepted as a direct outcome from the reinforcement program and the possibility that other variables are responsible for these changes would not be a primary concern. As stated by Gay:

> Single subject designs are most frequently applied in clinical settings where the primary emphasis is on therapeutic impact, not contribution to a research base. However, if the development of a school-wide attendance program depended upon the results from this research, a stronger research design would be recommended. These are described below. (1987, p. 296)

The A-B-A Design

An important feature of the A-B-A design is the employment of a second baseline condition after the withdrawal or termination of the intervention condition. Whereas the A-B design has a baseline and intervention condition, the A-B-A design has a baseline, intervention, and second baseline condition as outlined below:

Condition A	**Condition B**	**Condition A**
Initial	Initial	Intervention Withdrawn
Baseline	Intervention	Baseline Reintroduced

If Marty from Vignette 4.1 decided that she did not like her new seating arrangement (condition B) and returned her classroom to the original seating plan (condition A), this would be an example of an A-B-A design. She would continue to collect data and chart the frequency of appropriate student interactions after the return to condition A. Marty could then evaluate her new seating by comparing her intervention data (condition B) with the data charted during the first and second baseline conditions.

The withdrawal of the intervention and the reintroduction of the baseline condition is referred to as a *withdrawal design* (Gay, 1987) and, sometimes, a *reversal design* (Alberto & Troutman, 1990). However, Gay argued that the A-B-A design is not a true reversal design:

The A-B-A withdrawal designs are frequently referred to as reversal designs, which they are not, since treatment is generally withdrawn following baseline assessment, not reversed. A reversal design is but one kind of withdrawal design, representing a special kind of withdrawal. (1987, p. 302)

In a reversal design, one intervention is withdrawn and a second intervention, opposite from the first, is implemented. This is called an *A-B-C design*. Both B and C conditions are interventions, but are opposite to each other. For example, condition B may require a classroom teacher to reinforce *in-seat* behavior, while condition C, the reversal condition, requires the teacher to reinforce *out-of-seat* behavior. In this example, the reversal design may demonstrate the relationship between reinforcement and students' in- and out-of-seat behaviors.

The purpose of the A-B-A design is to more clearly demonstrate the relationship between student performance and an intervention. As previously stated, the change in student performance from condition A to condition B, as in the A-B design, may be coincidental. However, if student performance returns to baseline levels during the *second* baseline condition, caregivers may attribute changes in student performance to the implementation and removal of the intervention. Note, however, that a return to baseline may not result in data points that mirror the first baseline condition. Some student learning during the intervention condition may be maintained into second baseline condition.

While the A-B design tries to establish a relationship between student performance and the implementation of an intervention, the A-B-A design tries to establish a relationship between student performance and the implementation *and* withdrawal of an intervention. Thus, the A-B-A design has the potential to demonstrate a more powerful intervention effect than the simpler A-B design:

Whereas the A-B design permits only tentative conclusions as to a treatment's influence, the A-B-A design allows for an analysis of the controlling effects of its introduction and subsequent removal." (Barlow & Hersen, 1984, 152)

In continuing with our example first presented in Figure 4.1, suppose that after four weeks of the school attendance reinforcement program the teacher decides to terminate the reinforcement program, but continue to measure the student's attendance for another four weeks. In effect, the teacher is deciding to return to the baseline condition in which data on attendance is collected without an intervention program. The A-B-A design has three conditions including:

1. *Condition A*: Initial baseline data collected for four consecutive weeks.
2. *Condition B*: Intervention plan is employed for four consecutive weeks. Student is reinforced for attendance. Attendance data continues to be collected and recorded.

3. *Condition A:* Intervention plan is withdrawn and baseline data collection condition reintroduced for four consecutive weeks.

Figure 4.2 provides an example of an A-B-A design using our hypothetical data collected during all three conditions of our school attendance reinforcement program.

   The increase in school attendance during the intervention condition and the decrease in school attendance after the intervention was withdrawn demonstrate a strong intervention effect on school attendance. Would you recommend a return to the reinforcement program? If your answer is yes, we agree. Also, a return to the intervention condition leads us to another type of single subject design—the A-B-A-B design.

The A-B-A-B Design

In the A-B-A-B design, the intervention condition is reintroduced after the second baseline condition. The A-B-A-B design has four conditions to include:

1. *Condition A*: Initial baseline data are collected and recorded.
2. *Condition B*: Intervention plan is initiated. In our example, the student is reinforced for attendance according to the attendance program. Attendance data continue to be monitored and recorded throughout the intervention condition.

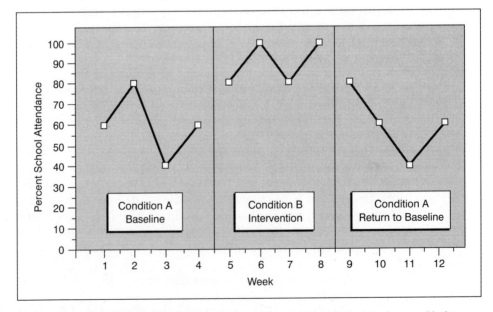

Figure 4.2.   *An A-B-A design demonstrating a change in student attendance with the implementation of the intervention (school attendance reinforcement program) and a withdrawal of the intervention.*

3. *Condition A*: Intervention plan is withdrawn and the baseline condition reintroduced.
4. *Condition B:* Baseline condition is withdrawn and intervention plan is introduced for a second time. Student is again reinforced for attendance. Attendance data continues to be monitored and recorded.

The A-B-A-B design has several advantages over the A-B-A design. First, the A-B-A-B design ends during an intervention condition:

> While the A-B-A design "represents the simplest single subject research paradigm for demonstrating cause-effect relationships . . .an applied researcher would seldom select this design at the outset to evaluate intervention effectiveness due to the practical and ethical considerations of ending an investigation in a baseline condition. (Tawney & Gast, 1984, 195-200)

For example, if a caregiver was trying to decrease self-injurious behavior exhibited by a child, it would be unethical to withdraw an effective intervention plan in order to demonstrate an intervention effect.

Second, the A-B-A-B design provides three comparisons or opportunities for the intervention, or the lack of intervention, to demonstrate an effect on student behavior (condition A to B, B to A, and A to B). Third, the A-B-A-B design provides a replication of the first A-B sequence or a replication of the introduction of the intervention. Since both A and B conditions are withdrawn and introduced a second time, the efficacy of the intervention, introduced after a baseline condition, may be demonstrated on two occasions (Barlow & Hersen, 1984). This replication is not perfect, however, because some effects from the first A-B experience may remain going into the second A-B experience. While the A-B-A design is an extension of the A-B design, the A-B-A-B design is an extension of the A-B-A design. This is demonstrated in Figure 4.3. Note that when the reinforcement program (intervention condition) is reintroduced, the student's attendance increases as it did during the first intervention condition.

The Alternating Treatments Design

The *alternating treatments design,* also referred to as an *alternating* or *changing conditions design, multiple schedule design* (Hersen & Barlow, 1976), and a *multi-element baseline design* (Ulman & Sulzer-Azaroff, 1975), involves the "relatively rapid alternating" of interventions for a single subject. "Its purpose is to assess the relative effectiveness of two (or more) treatment conditions" (Gay, 1987, p. 299). This design is also an expansion of the basic A-B design. However, instead of a withdrawal of the intervention and a reintroduction of the baseline condition, a second and *different* intervention strategy is introduced while student performance continues to be monitored. This second intervention, following conditions A and B, is called condition C. The number of different intervention conditions (D, E, and so on) added to the alternating treatment design depends on the number of interventions the caregiver or

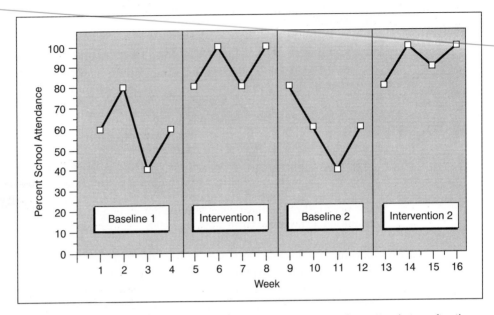

Figure 4.3.   *An A-B-A-B design demonstrating a change in student attendance after the reintroduction of the school attendance reinforcement intervention.*

researcher is interested in testing. Figure 4.4 provides an example of this design using two different intervention conditions (B and C) as follows:

1. *Condition A:* Baseline data collected on target behavior.
2. *Condition B:* First intervention strategy employed for a specific period of time.
3. *Condition C:* First intervention strategy terminated and a second intervention introduced for a specific period of time.

Frequently, each new intervention added in an alternating treatment design is a modification of the previous intervention. For example, let's say that a teacher wants to increase appropriate behavior during a homeroom period. The intervention in condition B may include verbal reinforcement at the end of the class period contingent upon appropriate behavior. Condition C may include the use of the same reinforcement program *plus* a positive note sent home. Condition D may include the use of the reinforcement, a note home, *and* a public announcement regarding the student's outstanding behavior by the school principal.

By reviewing the data collected on student behavior during each intervention condition, caregivers can compare the results of each intervention and decide which program *appears* to be the most effective. However, as in the basic A-B design, the alternating treatment design with a single baseline *does not* establish a cause and effect relationship between intervention and behav-

Figure 4.4. *The three conditions of an A-B-C design.*

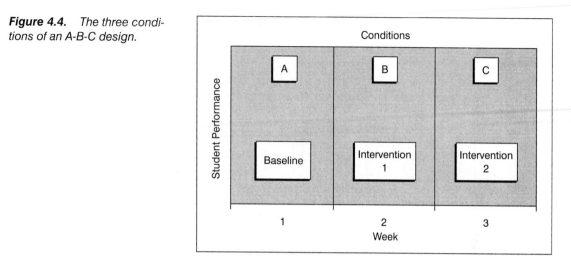

ior. Data collected during each intervention may reflect cumulative intervention effects rather than the effects of any one intervention.

Another variation of the alternating research design is the repeated baseline alternating research design. In this design, the caregiver decides to return to the baseline condition before the introduction of each new intervention condition. Thus, one may have an A-B-A-C or an A-B-A-C-A-D design as provided in Figure 4.5 and as described below:

1. *Condition A:* Baseline data collected on target behavior.
2. *Condition B:* First intervention strategy employed for a specific period of time.
3. *Condition A:* Withdrawal of intervention and return to baseline condition.
4. *Condition C:* Baseline condition is withdrawn and a second and different intervention is introduced for a specific period.
5. *Condition A:* Second intervention is withdrawn and a third baseline condition is introduced.
6. *Condition D:* Baseline condition is withdrawn and a third intervention is introduced for a specific period.

The repeated baseline variation of the alternating treatment design provides caregivers with an opportunity to compare baseline to intervention changes in the child's performance for each intervention tested. This somewhat reduces the cumulative treatment effects found in other designs in which treatments are employed consecutively without a baseline period between each intervention.

Another variation of the alternating treatment design is a repeated or rotating design. For example, in an A-B-C-B-C-B-C design the interventions B

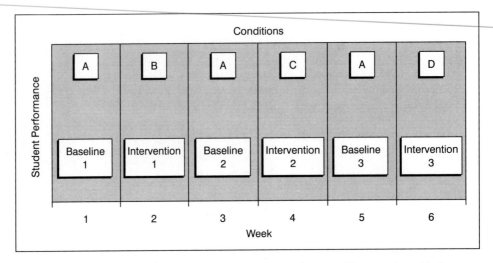

Figure 4.5. *An alternating treatment design with baseline condition employed between each intervention condition.*

and C are each presented three times in a rotating fashion as demonstrated in Figure 4.6.

In many of the examples provided above, the duration of each condition is one week. However, as in all the designs discussed in this chapter, the actual duration of each condition may vary. For example, caregivers may employ each individual intervention for one day or for several days. Also, the duration of each intervention does not have to be equal. For example, while the duration of condition B may equal one day, the duration of condition C may equal one month.

The interpretation of these varied and more complicated designs depends on the same variables described in the basic designs. Caregivers need to ask the following questions regarding the data collected across conditions:

- What are the data trends within each condition?
- Regarding the direction of the data trends, how do the data trends differ from baseline to intervention conditions? A change in direction from baseline to intervention conditions may indicate an intervention effect.
- What is the difference between the mean baseline performance and the mean intervention performance? Large differences may be associated with a strong relationship between the intervention and the child's behavior.
- How rapid is the change between baseline and intervention conditions? The rapidity of behavior change may be related to the strength of the intervention effect.

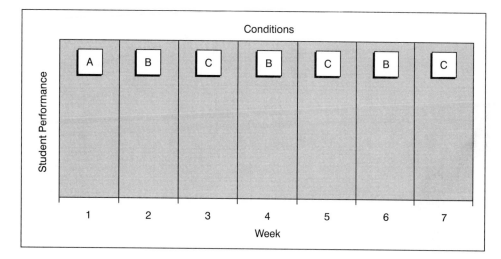

Figure 4.6.   *An A-B-C-B-C-B-C alternative treatment design.*

◆   How do the data trends differ across different intervention conditions? Large differences may indicate different intervention effects across conditions.

The Changing Criterion Design

First described by Sidman (1960) and named by Hall (1971), the *changing criterion design* is used to increase or decrease the performance of a single behavior by gradually increasing the criterion for reinforcement across several intervals of time. Gay described the changing criterion design as follows:

> In this design, a baseline phase is followed by successive treatment phases, each of which has a more stringent criterion for acceptable behavior level. Thus, each treatment phase becomes the baseline phase for the next treatment phase. The process continues until the final desired level of behavior is being achieved consistently. (1987, p. 303)

Like the A-B design, the changing criterion design has two major phases. After the baseline condition, an intervention is initiated. However, the intervention condition is "divided into subphases." Within each subphase of the intervention condition, the child must obtain a predetermined level of performance to earn reinforcement. Once that criterion level has been consistently achieved, a new criterion is established. Each increase in the performance criterion brings the student closer to the program objective. As stated by Hartmann and Hall:

> When the rate of the target behavior changes with each stepwise change in the criterion, therapeutic change is replicated and experimental control is demonstrated. (1976, p. 527)

For example, suppose a teacher wanted to increase Justin's participation in class discussion to a rate of 10 responses per class period. The first step in a changing criterion design is to assess the child's current performance (baseline) of the target behavior (class discussion). Justin's teacher collected baseline data for four consecutive days and recorded a rate of 0 for all four days. Since the teacher's goal is 10 responses per class session, the teacher must now determine:

◆ The number of steps to be implemented between the current performance level (0) and the ultimate criterion or program objective level (10),

◆ The reinforcement to be provided to the child contingent on behavior that meets or exceeds the established criterion, and

◆ The specific reinforcement criterion for each of the steps.

Justin's teacher decided to divide her program into five steps, use 15 minutes on the class computer as the reinforcement, and to increase the criterion by two responses per step, as follows:

Criterion for step one: 2 responses per class
Criterion for step two: 4 responses per class
Criterion for step three: 6 responses per class
Criterion for step four: 8 responses per class
Criterion for step five: 10 responses per class

After the baseline period, the intervention condition begins. The teacher begins the intervention condition by telling Justin that he may earn 15 minutes on the computer during class free-time by participating in class discussion at a rate of two times per class period. After this criterion is achieved and a stable performance is observed, Justin's teacher changes the criterion to four responses per class period. After this criterion is achieved and a stable performance is observed, the next criterion level is implemented, and so on. Justin must be told that the criterion has been changed before the implementation of the next intervention subphase. Figure 4.7 provides an overview of Justin's performance (see data points) per criterion level (indicated by the vertical line per subphase). Note the rapid rate at which Justin's performance increased and the relationship between the increases in his performance and each change in the criterion for reinforcement. Justin's teacher has established a clear relationship between the reinforcement program and the rate of Justin's class participation.

Multiple-Baseline Designs

In many cases it may be impossible, for practical or ethical reasons, to withdraw an intervention and return to a baseline condition. For example, if an intervention involves some type of academic instruction, returning to a true

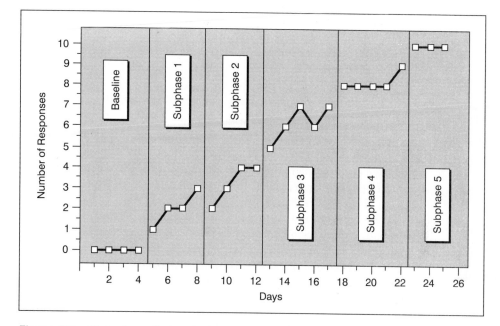

Figure 4.7.   *Changing criterion design over 26 days.*

baseline condition is impossible since the teacher cannot remove information learned during the intervention condition from the student's memory. In this situation, teachers may incorrectly identify the A-B design as the only alternative.

When a cause-and-effect relationship is desired and it is not possible to extend beyond the simple A-B design with a single subject, caregivers should consider a multiple-baseline design. The multiple-baseline design is, in fact, an extension of the A-B design, but in a different way than discussed up to this point. The multiple-baseline design retains the basic concept of the A-B design while extending these principles beyond a single subject. Instead of providing replication of intervention effects with a single subject, replication is achieved across a small sample of subjects, behaviors, or settings. This allows caregivers to establish a cause-and-effect relationship between the intervention and behavioral changes.

The three basic types of multiple-baseline designs are *across subjects,* *across behaviors,* and *across settings.* In each case, an A-B design is employed across three subjects, behaviors, or settings, and the intervention condition is applied to each subject, behavior, or setting at different intervals.

The Multiple-Baseline-Across-Subjects Design

In this design, the same intervention is employed across three children. The initiation of the intervention, however, is staggered across the three *subjects* as demonstrated in Vignette 4.2.

Vignette 4.2. Classroom Application of a Multiple-Baseline-Across-Subjects Design.

Margaret, a licensed elementary teacher who operates an after-school program, has three children (John, Mike, and Julia, ages 8, 8, and 9, respectively) in her program who exhibit hitting behavior. To decrease the hitting behavior, Margaret developed a behavior change program that involved the reinforcement of specific periods of no hitting.

Margaret's first step was to collect four days of baseline data on each of the three children's hitting frequency. With the baseline data collected, she was now ready to initiate her intervention plan. Not sure that her program would work, Margaret decided to first try her plan only with John while she continued to collect baseline data for the other two students. Margaret observed and charted John's hitting behavior every day. After four days, Margaret noticed that John's hitting behavior had decreased significantly. She then decided to start the same program with Mike while continuing to collect baseline data on Julia's hitting. Then, after four more days, Margaret initiated the same program with Julia. All three students were now involved in Margaret's program.

Margaret noticed a significant decrease in the frequency of hitting behavior for all three children, but only after the initiation of her reinforcement program. She decided that her program was effective in decreasing hitting behavior and felt confident that the program could work with other students with similar behaviors.

The data that Margaret collected from observing the hitting behavior of her three students is presented in Figure 4.8. In this case, a multiple-baseline-across-subjects design was used to test an intervention program aimed at decreasing hitting behavior across three subjects. After a baseline condition, the same intervention condition was applied for each of the three children, but at different intervals. Four days of baseline data were collected for each of the three children. For John, the intervention was employed on the fifth day. Meanwhile, Margaret continued to collect baseline data for Mike and Julia. For Mike, the intervention was initiated on the ninth day after eight days of baseline. Meanwhile, the intervention condition continued for John while the baseline condition continued for Julia. Finally, the intervention was applied for Julia on the thirteenth day. All three children were now receiving the intervention condition.

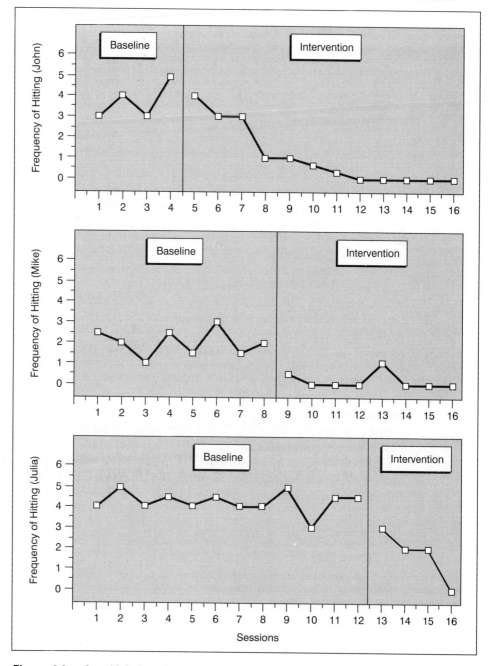

Figure 4.8.   *A multiple-baseline-across-subjects design.*

The Multiple-Baseline-Across-Behaviors Design

In this design the same intervention is applied to a single child across three different behaviors. As with other multiple-baseline designs, the initiation of the intervention is staggered. In this case, the initiation of the intervention is staggered across the three *behaviors* as demonstrated in Vignette 4.3.

Vignette 4.3. Classroom Application of a Multiple-Baseline-Across-Behaviors Design.

Gregg is a third-grade teacher. One of his students, Christopher, exhibited several aggressive behaviors (hitting, yelling, and kicking) until Gregg initiated a new classroom reinforcement program. In this program, Gregg provided his children with exaggerated verbal reinforcement for appropriate interactions with other children that did not include hitting, yelling, and kicking. Gregg hoped that Christopher would observe the other children receive attention for appropriate behavior and that Christopher would model his peers. When Christopher was aggressive, Gregg decided to ask Christopher to stand away from the other children for five minutes of time-out (usually in a classroom corner).

Gregg did not want to tackle all of Christopher's inappropriate behaviors at the same time. Instead, he decided to complete four days of baseline observation on all three behaviors, decide which one was the biggest problem, and initiate his time-out program with only one behavior at a time. He decided to start with Christopher's hitting behavior.

After four days of baseline observation and data collection, Gregg initiated his program. Verbal praise was provided following appropriate interactions between students, including Christopher, and Christopher was sent to the time-out corner immediately after he hit another child. Meanwhile, Gregg continued to collect baseline data for Christopher's other two behavior problems (yelling and kicking). By charting the frequency of Christopher's hitting, Gregg noticed a significant decrease in Christopher's hitting frequency.

After four more days, Gregg incorporated Christopher's yelling behavior in his program. Thus, hitting and yelling behavior were followed by five-minute periods of time-out. Meanwhile, Gregg continued to collect baseline data for Christopher's kicking behavior.

On the twelfth day of programming, Gregg included Christopher's kicking behavior into his program. Now, all three of Christopher's inappropriate behaviors were followed by the five-minute time-out while appropriate interactions continued to be verbally reinforced.

Gregg continued his program for the rest of the school year because he liked the idea of verbally reinforcing appropriate classroom behaviors. Since Christopher's aggressive behaviors only occurred occasionally, the occasional use of a five-minute time-out period provided Gregg with an effective consequence for aggression. In fact, Gregg decided to use this approach as a consequence for aggression exhibited by the other students in his classroom.

The data charted by Gregg during his multiple-baseline-across-behaviors design is provided in Figure 4.9. In this example, the teacher (Gregg) had a problem with one student who exhibited three different behaviors (hitting, yelling, and kicking) that needed to be decelerated. By initiating the same program for the three behaviors at different intervals, Gregg established a relationship between the initiation of his intervention and a deceleration of each of the three behaviors. In this case, as in Vignette 4.2, the duration of baseline and intervention conditions was four days. The actual number of days for any of the conditions, however, will vary according to the child, behavior, and setting.

The Multiple-Baseline-Across-Settings Design

In the multiple-baseline-across-settings design, the same intervention is applied to a single child across three different settings or environments. As with other multiple-baseline designs, the initiation of the intervention is staggered. In this case, the initiation of intervention is staggered across three *settings* as demonstrated in Vignette 4.4.

Vignette 4.4.   Classroom Application of a Multiple-Baseline-Across-Settings Design.

Brenda, a special education consultant for a large school system, was talking to several sixth-grade teachers about a boy named Tommy. Tommy had some attention deficits that resulted in a significant amount of off-task behaviors in his math, science, and English classes.

Baseline measures indicated that Tommy was off-task an average of 30 minutes for each of the 45-minute classes. Brenda recommended a cognitive behavior modification (see Chapter 6) program that included:

- ◆ Teaching Tommy how to monitor his own on-task behavior;
- ◆ Teaching Tommy how to record his own on-task behavior performance;
- ◆ Teaching Tommy how to evaluate his on-task performance according to specific criteria established by his teachers; and
- ◆ The development of a reinforcement menu (see Chapter 5) and program for appropriate on-task behaviors.

Brenda recommended that the teachers use a multiple-baseline-across-settings design to evaluate the effectiveness of their program. This design was recommended since they were interested in increasing Tommy's on-task behavior in three different classes.

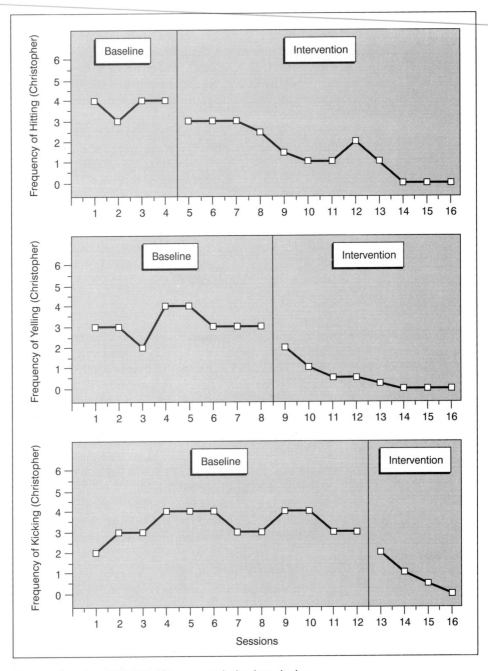

Figure 4.9.   *A multiple-baseline-across-behaviors design.*

At the start, the program was initiated in Tommy's math class. Tommy's math teacher explained the program to him and initiated the program the same day. Meanwhile, Tommy's science and English teachers continued to collect baseline data on his on-task duration data in science and English classes.

On the fifth day, Tommy's science teacher initiated the same program while his English teacher continued collecting and charting baseline data on Tommy's on-task duration in English class. Finally, on the ninth day, Tommy's English teacher told Tommy that she too would use the same program used in his other two classes. The on-task program was now being employed across Tommy's three classes. All three teachers communicated daily to ensure that they consistently followed the program.

In Vignette 4.4, the same behavior change program was initiated by three different teachers across three different settings. By implementing the same on-task program across settings and at different intervals, the teachers demonstrated a relationship between Tommy's on-task behavior and their intervention plan. Data collected and charted by the three teachers are presented in Figure 4.10. Notice that Tommy's on-task behavior remains low across all three settings until the intervention plan is initiated. As the intervention is initiated per setting, Tommy's on-task behavior increases for that setting. A cause-and-effect relationship between Tommy's on-task behavior and the intervention plan is established.

In the vignettes and examples provided here, the intervention condition was applied across three levels of subjects, behaviors, or settings. This reflects the most common application of the multiple-baseline designs. Other variations of the multiple-baseline design, however, may employ more than three levels. A minimum of two levels is required. Also, although four days (or sessions) per condition were used in all our examples, other variations of this design may include more or less than four sessions. Four, however, is usually the minimum number required if a stable data trend is to be established.

Several questions about the recorded data on a multiple-baseline design must be evaluated before a cause-and-effect relationship can be established:

◆ Are there significant changes from baseline to intervention conditions within each individual A-B design per subject, behavior, or setting? Note these differences in Figures 4.8, 4.9, and 4.10.

◆ What are the data trends or direction of data during the intervention conditions compared to the baseline conditions per subject, behavior, or setting?

◆ Does the data improve per subject, behavior, and setting *only* after the intervention condition is applied? In Figures 4.8, 4.9, and 4.10, note how the baseline data remain stable until the intervention condition is initiated across subjects, behaviors, and settings.

◆ How rapid did the data change once the intervention condition was initiated?

◆ Did baseline data remain stable before the intervention condition was introduced per child, behavior, or setting? For example, in Figure 4.8, note how the frequency of hitting remains high during the baseline

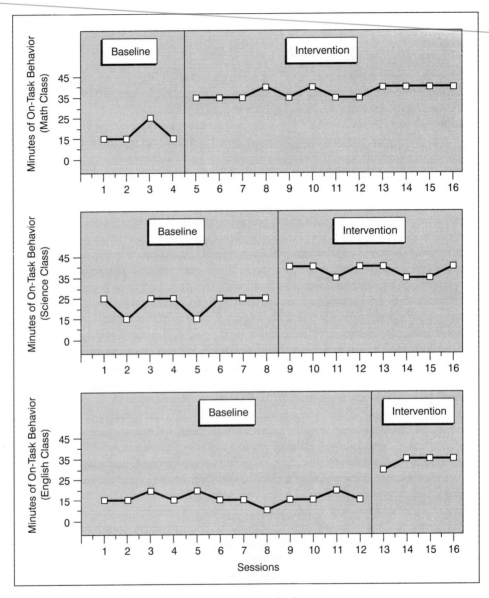

Figure 4.10. *A multiple-baseline-across-settings design.*

condition across Mike and Julia even after the intervention program is implemented for John.

◆ Does the data collected during intervention conditions remain stable across subjects, behaviors, and settings? Note in Figure 4.8 how John's hitting rate remains low during the intervention condition independent of Mike and Julia's data.

The multiple-baseline designs offer caregivers a simple experimental design with the unique feature of testing interventions across several children, behaviors, and settings (Kazdin, 1982). Like the A-B-A-B design, the multiple-baseline design replicates the intervention effect, but beyond a single child, behavior, or setting. The design may demonstrate a clear cause-and-effect relationship "by showing that behavior changes when and only when the intervention is applied" (Kazdin, 1982, p. 128).

SUMMARY

The purpose of single subject designs is to allow caregivers to demonstrate experimental control and intervention effects with a single child or with a small group of children. Thus, these designs are ideal for classroom teachers, parents, and other caregivers who want to demonstrate the effectiveness of their behavior reduction strategies.

When using single subject designs, comparisons are made between or among conditions employed during different phases of a behavior change program. Baseline and intervention conditions represent the two primary conditions employed in single subject designs. These are labeled conditions A and B. Intervention conditions may vary and, thus, may be labeled C, D, E, and so on, to indicate a new or modified intervention plan.

Types of single subject designs include the A-B, A-B-C, A-B-A-B, alternating treatment, changing criterion, and multiple-baseline designs. All of these designs are variations of each other and serve specific functions related to the demonstration of experimental control and intervention effects.

The A-B design is the most simple of the single subject designs and employs a baseline and one intervention condition. When using the A-B design we can only presume that behavioral changes noted during the intervention condition are a function of the intervention. The A-B-A design employs a withdrawal of the intervention condition and a return to baseline condition. The purpose of the A-B-A design is to more clearly demonstrate the relationship between student performance and the intervention. The A-B-A-B design employs a return to condition B after a short return to baseline as in the A-B-A design. The A-B-A-B design has many advantages over the previously described designs.

The alternating treatment or changing conditions design involves the alternating of intervention conditions for a single subject or group of subjects. The changing criterion design is used to increase or decrease student performance by gradually increasing the criterion for reinforcement across several intervals of time. Finally, the multiple-baseline designs provide for the replication of intervention conditions across subjects, behaviors, or settings.

For Discussion

1. Discuss the purpose of single subject designs.
2. Discuss how the effectiveness of an intervention is demonstrated or not demonstrated in the A-B, A-B-A, and A-B-A-B designs.
3. Discuss how the effectiveness of an intervention is demonstrated when using multiple baseline designs.

REFERENCES

Alberto, P. A., & Troutman, A. C. (1990). *Applied behavior analysis for teachers.* Columbus, OH: Merrill/Macmillan.

Bailey, D. B. (1984). Effects of lines of progress and semilog-arithmetic charts on ratings of charted data. *Journal of Applied Behavior Analysis, 17,* 359–365.

Barlow, D. H., & Hersen, M. (1984). *Single case experimental designs: Strategies for studying behavior change.* New York: Pergamon Press.

Campbell, D. T., & Stanley, J. C. (1966). *Experimental and quasi-experimental designs for research.* Boston, MA: Houghton Mifflin Company.

Gast, D. L., & Tawney, J. W. (1984). The visual analysis of graphic data. In J. W. Tawney & D. L. Gast (Eds.), *Single subject research in special education* (pp. 142–186). Columbus, OH: Merrill/Macmillan.

Gay, L. R. (1987). *Competencies for analysis and application.* Columbus, OH: Merrill/Macmillan.

Gibson, G., & Ottenbacher, K. (1988). Characteristics influencing the visual analysis of single-subject data: An empirical analysis. *Journal of Applied Behavioral Science, 24,* 298–313.

Hall, R. V. (1971). *Managing behavior—Behavior modification: The measure of behavior.* Lawrence, KS: H & H Enterprises.

Hartmann, D. P., & Hall, R. V. (1976). The changing criterion design. *Journal of Applied Behavior Analysis, 9,* 527–532.

Hersen, M., & Barlow, D. H. (1976). *Single-case experimental designs: Strategies for studying behavior changes.* New York: Pergamon Press.

Kazdin, A. E. (1982). *Single-case research designs: Methods for clinical and applied settings.* New York: Oxford University Press.

Martin, D. W. (1985). *Doing psychology experiments* (2nd ed.). Pacific Grove, CA: Brooks/Cole Publishing Company.

Mueser, K. T., Yarnold, P. R., & Foy, D. W. (1991). Statistical analysis for single-case designs. *Behavior Modification, 15,* 134–155.

Odom, S. L. (1988). Research in early childhood special education. In S. L. Odom & M. B. Karnes (Eds.), *Early intervention for infants and children with handicaps* (pp. 1–22). Baltimore, MD: Paul H. Brookes.

Ottenbacher, K. J., & Cusick, A. (1991). An empirical investigation of inter-rater agreement for single-subject data using graphs with and without trend lines. *Journal of The Association for Persons with Severe Handicaps, 16,* 48–55.

Parsonson, B. S., & Baer, D. M. (1986). The graphic analysis of data. In A. Poling and R. W. Fuqua (Eds.), *Research methods in applied behavior analysis: Issues and advances* (pp. 157–186). New York: Plenum Press.

Sidman, M. (1960). *Tactics of scientific research: Evaluating experimental data in psychology.* New York: Basic Books.

Tawney, J. W., & Gast, D. L. (1984). *Single subject research in special education.* Columbus, OH: Merrill/Macmillan Publishing.

Ulman, J. D., & Sulzer-Azaroff, B. (1975). Multi-element baseline design in educational research. In E. Ramp & G. Semb (Eds.), *Behavior analysis: Areas of research and application* (pp. 377–391). Englewood Cliffs, NJ: Prentice-Hall.

PART TWO

Increasing Appropriate Behavior

CHAPTER 5

Establishing a Reinforcement Program

There are a number of advantages to using (positive) programming as a strategy for the reduction of behavior problems in applied settings. Together, these advantages make programming the most preferable alternative to the use of punishment. They include its positive and constructive nature; its long term and lasting effects; its potential for the prevention of future problems; its efficiency; its social validity and the contribution it makes to the learner's dignity.

—LaVigna and Donnellan, 1986, p. 32

All children exhibit at least some appropriate behaviors throughout each day. Too often, however, caregivers ignore children when they behave appropriately and are doing what they were asked to do. To increase or maintain appropriate behaviors, children should be reinforced when they engage in desired behavior, rather than waiting for the occurrence of misbehavior to provide attention. Research has demonstrated that when children are reinforced for appropriate behaviors they will exhibit appropriate behavior more frequently (Donnellan, LaVigna, Negri-Shoultz, & Fassbender, 1988; Mason, McGee, Farmer-Dougan, & Risley, 1989; Skinner, 1938, 1969). On the other hand, children who get most of their attention after they have behaved inappropriately will soon learn to behave inappropriately in order to gain attention (Bandura, 1973; Wolery, Kirk, & Gast, 1985). Children quickly learn what behaviors—appropriate and inappropriate—will get the most attention from others (Carr & Durand, 1985; Kauffman, 1989; Kerr & Nelson, 1989; Sasso, Melloy, & Kavale, 1990).

REINFORCEMENT

Definition

A stimulus takes on the value of a reinforcer only if it has been demonstrated that the *response/behavior* it followed was maintained (at the current rate, duration, or intensity) or increased (from the current rate, duration, or intensity). A stimulus is defined as a reinforcer or not a reinforcer contingent on the effect of that stimulus on the future response rate of the *target behavior*. If the rate, duration, or intensity of a target behavior is not maintained, or increased, following the provision of X stimulus, then X cannot be considered a reinforcer. For example, when a classroom teacher provides her students with social praise following appropriate behavior in the cafeteria, the social praise may be defined as an effective reinforcer if the praise maintains or increases the students' appropriate cafeteria behavior in the future. However, if the teacher notes that student behaviors in the cafeteria have not been maintained, then the teacher's social praise cannot be considered an effective reinforcer for maintaining appropriate student behavior in the cafeteria. The teacher needs to consider another, more powerful reinforcer, or a variation to her social praise. For example, a token economy program may be initiated.

It should also be noted that a stimulus may act as a reinforcer for one behavior, but not for a second behavior, even if both behaviors are exhibited by the same child. For example, while a student may maintain appropriate classroom behavior in response to social praise, other reinforcers, such as positive notes home or a token economy program, may be necessary to maintain acceptable academic performance in a different class. Caregivers cannot assume that an object or activity will be reinforcing to a child; this can only be determined by testing the effect of the potential reinforcer on the child's behavior, as discussed later in this chapter.

Reinforcement may be positive or negative. Both *positive reinforcement* and *negative reinforcement* increase behavior. The word "positive" refers to the *presentation* of a stimulus following a behavior; it does not refer to the nature of the stimulus presented. In turn, the word "negative" refers to the *removal* of a stimulus; it does not refer to the nature of the stimulus removed. Also, as discussed later, reinforcers may be *primary* or *secondary*. Both primary and secondary reinforcement increase or maintain target behaviors.

Reinforcement is most effective in maintaining or increasing a target behavior when it is individualized for a particular child and when it is presented contingent on the target behavior (Donnellan et al., 1988). Other factors associated with the effective use of reinforcement include:

- ◆ *Immediacy of the reinforcement.* As the interval between the behavior and reinforcement increases, the relative effectiveness of the reinforcer decreases. At least initially, an effective reinforcement program provides reinforcement immediately after the target behavior. Later, the latency between the behavior and reinforcement may be increased.

- ◆ *Combine verbal praise with the reinforcement.* When presenting the reinforcer, remind the child of the behavior that entitled him or her to the reinforcer. This builds an association between the appropriate behavior and reinforcer. Also, the learned association between the reinforcer and verbal praise will increase the reinforcement properties of verbal praise.

- ◆ *Schedule of reinforcement.* During the initial phase of the reinforcement schedule, reinforce the child after each and every occurrence of the target behavior. This also builds an association between the appropriate behavior you want to increase and reinforcement. Later in the program, continuous schedules of reinforcement should be faded to intermittent schedules. These schedules are discussed later in this chapter.

- ◆ *Type of reinforcement.* Some reinforcers will be more effective than others depending on the child's individual preferences. By asking the child and by testing different potential reinforcers, caregivers can generate a reinforcement menu.

◆ *Quality and quantity of reinforcement.* The quality of a reinforcer refers to its freshness and the immediacy of its effect on behavior. Caregivers need to determine the right quantity of reinforcers to deliver—just enough to make the program interesting yet not too much so that the child becomes satiated.

◆ *Who provides the reinforcement.* Reinforcers are more effective when they are provided by significant others or from people loved, liked, or admired. When provided by people the child does not like or trust, they may lose some or all of their reinforcing properties.

◆ *Consistency.* The reinforcement program should be followed consistently. Moreover, all other caregivers who come in contact with the child should understand and implement the program consistently.

Positive Reinforcement

Positive reinforcement (R+) is defined as the contingent *provision* of a stimulus (such as a treat, object, or activity) following a target behavior, which results in an increase or maintenance of the frequency, duration, and/or intensity of the target behavior (Skinner, 1938, 1969). For example, letting a child spend extra time playing with the classroom computer (stimulus) after the child completed specific classroom tasks (response) may be considered positive reinforcement *if* the future rate of the target behavior (completing specific classroom tasks) is increased or maintained. Positive reinforcement is recommended as the intervention of first choice when trying to teach new behaviors, increase appropriate behaviors, or decrease inappropriate behavior.

Negative Reinforcement

Negative reinforcement (R-) is defined as the contingent *removal* of a stimulus following a target behavior, which results in an increase or maintenance of the frequency, duration, and/or intensity of the target behavior (Pfiffner & O'Leary, 1987). Usually, the stimulus removed is an aversive stimulus. Negative reinforcement is *not* punishment; again, the effect of negative reinforcement is an *increase* in the target behavior, not a *decrease,* which would be the effect of a punishing stimulus.

Two variations of negative reinforcement can be used. In the first variation, the child performs the target behavior to escape an *ongoing* aversive stimulus (Iwata, 1987). For example, when a caregiver tells a child he must remain in the time-out corner until tantrum behavior is no longer exhibited, that caregiver is using negative reinforcement. The purpose here is to teach the child to perform a target behavior (nontantrum behavior) in order to have the aversive stimulus (remaining in the time-out corner) removed. In a second variation, the child performs the target behavior in order to avoid a *potential* or *likely* aversive stimulus. For example, when a child performs a target behavior (studying a history lesson) in order to avoid a threatened, aversive stimulus (receiving a failing grade), then the target behavior is maintained by negative reinforcement.

Using negative reinforcement is quite different from positive reinforcement, and the disadvantages of negative reinforcement are numerous. Negative reinforcement involves the presentation of an aversive event that may be removed contingent on the target behavior. Another significant disadvantage of negative reinforcement in applied settings is the escape and avoidance behavior produced when children are trying to behave appropriately in order to avoid an aversive stimulus. For example, consider the differences between two classrooms. In classroom A, the children behave appropriately because their teacher recognizes their appropriate behavior and the students enjoy her attention (positive reinforcement). The children in classroom A are likely to enjoy school and have a healthy attitude about learning. In contrast, the students in classroom B behave appropriately only to avoid their teacher's aversive behavior (negative reinforcement). The children in classroom B probably do not like going to school and are not motivated, except by fear and anxiety, to do well. Some of the students may try to avoid or escape this situation by skipping school or dropping out of school altogether. These side effects represent the primary reasons why negative reinforcement is not recommended as a preferred intervention. The relationships among the type of reinforcement, stimulus, and outcome for target behavior are as follows:

Reinforcement	Stimulus	Target Behavior
Positive	Presented	Increases
Negative	Removed	Increases

Types of Reinforcers

The list of potential reinforcers for children is limited only by a caregiver's imagination. Reinforcers may be verbal statements, foods and drinks, objects, time to participate in preferred activities, and so on. Caregivers should not limit their understanding of reinforcers to giving candy to children. In fact, young children will quickly become satiated when food, especially candy, is used as a reinforcer. *Satiation* refers to a condition in which a current reinforcer loses its reinforcement value. That is, the target behavior is no longer maintained by the reinforcer. For example, when food is used as a reinforcer, children may become too full to want additional reinforcers. Thus, caregivers are encouraged to consider other types of reinforcers before edibles; more attention should be given to the use of reinforcing activities and other social opportunities children enjoy. These types of reinforcers may serve both as reinforcers and learning opportunities for children of all ages.

Primary Reinforcers

Primary reinforcers are stimuli that are naturally reinforcing to individuals. Food, liquids, warmth, and sex are examples of primary reinforcers. In other words, they are unlearned or unconditioned. Individuals do not have to be taught that eating tasty food or drinking refreshing drinks will make them feel good (naturally reinforcing).

Secondary Reinforcers

Secondary reinforcers are stimuli that are *not* naturally reinforcing. Their value to the individual has been learned or conditioned through an association, or *pairing,* with primary reinforcers. For example, when a caregiver pairs verbal praise (a potential secondary reinforcer) with the delivery of a glass of juice (a primary reinforcer) to a child, the verbal praise takes on some of the reinforcement value associated with the glass of juice. The purpose here is to *fade-out,* or decrease, the use of juice as a reinforcer and *fade-in,* or increase, the value of verbal praise. If successful, verbal praise will become a secondary reinforcer capable of maintaining or increasing the target behavior.

High-preferenced activities (for example, playing a computer game, free-time, recess) frequently serve as excellent secondary reinforcers. Premack (1959) promoted the idea of using high-preferenced activities as reinforcement for the completion of low-preferenced activities. A classroom example of using the *Premack principle* is telling a child that he must complete all his math problems before he can join the other children in playing a game. The objective

Allowing extra time on the computer or other desired classroom activities may serve as effective and functional reinforcers.

here is to increase the completion rate of a low-preferred activity (completing math problems) by scheduling a high-preferred activity (playing a game) immediately after.

Socially Valid Reinforcers

A reinforcer is considered socially valid when its provision is congruent with the norms of the child's social setting. The variables that determine what is socially valid include culture, setting, age of the child, the specific situation, and the relationship between the caregiver and the child. For example, patting a child on the buttocks may be a socially acceptable form of reinforcement among football players on the football field (setting); in a different setting (a classroom), this same form of reinforcement may not be socially acceptable. In a second example involving the child's age, using stickers may be socially acceptable for young children but socially unacceptable for older children. Social praise, rather than stickers, would be more valid for older children. Thus, it is important to consider all these variables when selecting reinforcers and developing a reinforcement menu. The following list provides some suggestions for reinforcers.

Tangible	Social	Activities
Stars	Verbal recognition	Free-time
Rubber stamps	Verbal praise	Time with teacher
Check marks	Student of the day	Read a story
Points	First in line	Pass out materials
Toys	Leader of the day	Feed class pet
Edibles	Phone call home	Use of computer
Magazines	Note home	Bring toy to school
Puzzles	Activity leader	Listen to tape

As stated, a reinforcer is considered socially valid when it is consistent with the norms of the child's social setting. Sometimes, however, effective reinforcement means using reinforcers, at least temporarily, that may not be consistent with the "typical" social behavior of a setting. For example, giving children points for completing classroom or home tasks may not be a natural consequence or socially congruent with the "real" world. In fact, many caregivers refuse to reinforce children for expected behaviors. Used temporarily, however, as an initial step to manage behavior and with the objective of eventually fading the point system to a more natural or typical social reinforcement (verbal praise), the use of extrinsic reinforcement is clearly a worthy investment.

Identifying Reinforcers

One way to identify reinforcers is to ask children to help develop a list or menu of potential reinforcers. Of course, caregivers maintain veto power over children's suggestions for the *reinforcement menu*. However, research has determined that child-preferred activities serve as effective reinforcers in behavior management programs (e.g., Koegel, Dyer, & Bell, 1987). In addition to asking the child directly, another method of developing a list of effective reinforcers is through trial-and-error or *reinforcement assessment*. A systematic assessment, conducted by direct observation, of different reinforcers and their influence on behavior is likely to produce the most accurate list of children's preferences—more accurate than when caregivers make reinforcement decisions alone. For example, Green, Reid, White, Halford, Brittain, and Gardner (1988) found that the results of a systematic trial-and-error assessment of potential reinforcers did not correlate with a list of reinforcers generated by caregivers alone. Others, using different assessment methods, have also found that client selection of effective reinforcers was more accurate than caregiver predictions (Datillo, 1986).

Also, having a reinforcement menu is important because a single reinforcer may quickly lose its appeal. Children become satiated when the same reinforcement is used too frequently. Moreover, caregivers should note that what may be reinforcing one day may not be reinforcing another day, even with the same child. Having a variety of reinforcers to select from allows caregivers to keep the reinforcement program fresh and exciting for caregivers and children (Egel, 1981).

Too often, caregivers blame a reinforcement program for "not working" instead of evaluating the effectiveness of the selected reinforcers. Children's reinforcement preferences change across time and activities. Within a classroom setting, Mason et al. found "that maladaptive behaviors decreased significantly as a function of on-going reinforcer assessment" (1989, p. 177). When caregivers suspect that a child is satiated on a single reinforcer, changing to an alternative reinforcer or varying the reinforcers may stimulate the child's interest. Egel (1981) compared the effects of using the same reinforcer against a variety of reinforcers to increase the responsiveness of children in a classroom setting. He found that when the same reinforcer was presented, correct responding and on-task behavior declined over time. Varying the reinforcers, however, produced significantly improved and consistent responding. Egel's study "provides further documentation of the importance of providing variation within the teaching situation" (p. 31).

Caregivers may prevent satiation by:

◆ Varying the reinforcer or using a different reinforcer for each target behavior
◆ Monitoring the amount of reinforcement delivered and using only enough to maintain the target behavior
◆ Avoiding edible reinforcers (if you must use edibles, vary and apply minimally)
◆ Moving from a constant to an intermittent schedule of reinforcement as soon as possible
◆ Moving from primary to secondary reinforcers as soon as possible.

Caregivers should also review the schedule of typical activities in which children participate within the educational setting and ask the following questions:

♦   How may some of these activities, which are known reinforcers to the children, be used to reinforce appropriate behaviors?
♦   How may some children, as a result of appropriate behaviors, have greater access to preferred activities within the educational setting?
♦   How may the Premack principle be employed in my setting?

Manipulating a child's schedule according to the Premack principle increases the chance that less desirable tasks and activities will be completed if more desirable activities follow. The following is an example of scheduling so that preferred activities follow less desirable activities:

Time	Activity
8:00 am	Arrival and greeting; play time*
8:30 am	Opening activities with group
8:45 am	Story in small group*
9:00 am	Math instruction
9:20 am	Structured free play*
9:35 am	Reading instruction
10:00 am	Snack*
10:15 am	Clean-up
10:30 am	Puzzles and games*
10:45 am	Physical fitness activity
11:00 am	Creative drama*
11:45 am	Lunch*
12:15 pm	Clean-up
12:30 pm	Free play outside*
1:00 pm	Social Studies instruction
2:00 pm	Snack*
2:15 pm	Science instruction
3:00 pm	Structured free play*
3:30 pm	Token exchange
3:45 pm	Preparation for home*

* = Indicates preferred activity.

Establishing a reinforcement system in the educational setting does not have to be a significant modification to an already established program. Often, effective modifications take the form of simple changes in activity schedules and a commitment on the part of caregivers to increase their attention to appropriate behaviors. As we mentioned at the beginning of the chapter, it is easy for caregivers to fall into the habit of ignoring appropriate behaviors and, instead, focus their attention on inappropriate behaviors. Development of a reinforcement program may help caregivers ensure that they will pay attention to appropriate behaviors.

ESTABLISHING A REINFORCEMENT PROGRAM

When developing a reinforcement program, caregivers need to balance spontaneity and structure. That is, although the program needs to be planned and systematically applied, caregivers also need to be spontaneous in delivering reinforcers. We will outline some important elements in developing a reinforcement program.

Establishing Clear Rules and Guidelines

Caregivers need to be clear and direct in outlining what behaviors are expected and what behaviors are not acceptable within the children's different environments. Clear instructions outline behavioral expectations in *specific* and *observable* terms. For example, the rule "Respect others" does have an appealing sound and is certainly a worthy goal for all children. However, the rule fails to outline the specific behaviors that demonstrate respect for others and the specific behaviors that violate this rule. Caregivers need to be more specific, such as "Never hit other children," "Say 'Excuse me' before interrupting others," "Ask permission before taking things that don't belong to you," "Say 'Please' and 'Thank you,'" and so on. These examples are specific and observable.

Rules and guidelines for behavior should be stated in positive terms whenever possible. Instead of saying "Don't take things without permission," say "Ask permission before taking things." Small differences such as this make significant differences in the children's environment by creating a positive and affirming atmosphere. When most rules state what children *cannot* do, then the focus of caregivers' attention will likely be on punishment of inappropriate behaviors. When the rules state what children *can* do, then caregivers will tend to focus on the reinforcement of appropriate behaviors. Rules concerning some inappropriate behaviors, however, such as hitting, need to be stated very directly. As a guideline, plan to state at least three "appropriate" behavior rules for every "inappropriate" behavior rule.

Rules and behavioral guidelines are taught through direct instruction. In addition, rules are likely to be followed more consistently if they are posted somewhere in the educational setting, and if the children are reinforced for following them. Also, periodic (such as daily or weekly) review ensures that children understand the rules and, therefore, know what is expected of them (Rosenberg, 1986).

Setting the Example

Once rules are established, caregivers need to be consistent in following the rules and must be themselves models of appropriate behavior for the children.

If caregivers ask children to say "please" and "thank you," then caregivers should say "please" and "thank you" when talking to the children. If the rule says "No hitting," then caregivers should set the example. If caregivers spank children, they should not be surprised if their children are aggressive and attempt also to solve their problems by hitting. Remember, children learn from watching others, especially significant others such as parents and teachers.

The Delivery of Reinforcers

After you have established some behavior guidelines and discussed them with the children, and after you have outlined a reinforcement menu, the next step is to develop a reinforcement delivery program. Reinforcers are most effective in increasing behaviors when they are delivered:

◆   Immediately after the behavior you intend to increase,
◆   When they are fresh (the child is not satiated with the reinforcer),
◆   By caregivers whom the child admires.

The methods of delivering reinforcers to children are as endless as the selection of reinforcers. Again, caregivers are encouraged to use their imaginations. The important guidelines here are for caregivers to be *consistent* and to *make it fun*. If the reinforcement program is developed for an entire classroom, teachers may want to establish a token economy reinforcement program as described later in this chapter. When this program is targeted to change a specific behavior for one child, then the following steps will be helpful.

First, as previously stated, try to describe the behavior you want to change in positive terms. For example, Robert, a child in your program, will not sit in his chair for longer than a few seconds at a time. Instead of stating the program goal in terms of *decreasing* Robert's out-of-seat behavior, state the goal in terms of *increasing* Robert's in-seat behavior. This will force caregivers to focus on reinforcing the appropriate behavior (Robert's in-seat behavior), instead of the inappropriate behavior (Robert's out-of-seat behavior).

Second, collect baseline data on how often Robert currently stays in his seat. Baseline data, as outlined in Chapter 3, are a measurement of a child's behavior before the introduction of a behavior change program. This involves measuring, for 30 to 60 minutes per day, for about four days, the number of seconds or minutes (duration) Robert is currently staying in his seat. Calculate the average duration (total duration of sitting divided by number of observation periods), and this average will serve as the baseline for Robert's sitting behavior. An example of baseline data would be to determine, through direct observation, that Robert currently averages 90 seconds of in-seat behavior per 30 minutes of classroom observation.

Third, the caregiver should establish an appropriate *program goal*. That is, given the child's age and program needs, how many minutes is it reasonable to expect Robert to sit? Consistent with the earlier example, let's say the program goal is to teach Robert to stay in his seat for 15 consecutive minutes.

Baseline data, the program goal, and the overall behavior change program should be shared with Robert. The caregiver should explain to him why his in-seat behavior needs to increase and how he will be reinforced for longer periods of in-seat behavior.

Fourth, given the gap between the baseline data or current level of performance (90 seconds of in-seat behavior) and the program goal (15 minutes of in-seat behavior), the caregiver should determine a *reinforcement schedule*. The caregiver needs to reinforce behaviors (i.e., longer periods of sitting) that will bring the child closer to the program goal. Given our example, phase one of the reinforcement schedule may include reinforcing the child each time he stays in his seat for 2 consecutive minutes. Phase two may include reinforcing the child each time he stays in his seat for 3 consecutive minutes. Phase three may include reinforcing the child for 5 consecutive minutes of in-seat behavior, and so on. The last phase of the reinforcement schedule would include reinforcing the child for 15 consecutive minutes, the program goal.

The speed of progression from one phase to the next will depend on the child's progress for each phase. A *performance criterion* for moving from one phase of the reinforcement schedule to the next should be established. For example, the criterion for moving from phase one to phase two may state that "Robert must meet the objective of phase one, staying in his seat for two consecutive minutes, for two consecutive observation periods." When this criterion is reached, the reinforcement schedule changes as outlined in phase two.

Several other reinforcement schedule variations are available. Understanding these different reinforcement delivery schedules will help caregivers develop effective and individualized reinforcement delivery plans.

SCHEDULES OF REINFORCEMENT

A reinforcement schedule refers to the frequency or timing of the delivery of reinforcement following a specific target behavior or general appropriate behavior. A reinforcer may be delivered on a *continuous* or *intermittent* schedule. When a child is reinforced each and every time the target behavior is exhibited, a continuous schedule of reinforcement is being employed. Although not always the case, initiation of a continuous reinforcement program is usually best until an association between the target behavior and reinforcement is established. Initiating a program with a continuous schedule is recommended for young children or when teaching a new behavior. As discussed above, this schedule should then be faded to an intermittent, or more natural, socially acceptable schedule.

When a child is reinforced after some occurrences, but not each and every one of the specific target behaviors, an intermittent schedule of reinforcement is being employed. An intermittent schedule is used after the child has learned that there is an association between the target behavior and the reinforcer, and the caregiver wants to fade (sometimes referred to as "thinning") to a more natural reinforcement schedule. We will outline variations of the continuous and intermittent schedules of reinforcement.

Ratio Reinforcement Schedules

A ratio reinforcement schedule consists of reinforcing a person contingent on an established *number of occurrences* of the target behavior. Although the specific number of occurrences may be fixed or variable, a ratio schedule is always based on the number of behavior occurrences exhibited. For example, reinforcing a child after a specific number of tasks is completed means that a ratio schedule of reinforcement is being employed.

Fixed Ratio Schedules

Reinforcing a child each and every time the target behavior occurs is called a *fixed ratio of one* (FR1) schedule of reinforcement (also called a continuous schedule of reinforcement). If, however, a caregiver reinforces a child every second time the target behavior is exhibited, then this would be considered a *fixed ratio of two* or FR2 schedule of reinforcement. Reinforcing a child every third time the target behavior is exhibited would be an example of a *fixed ratio of three* or FR3, and so on. An advantage of fixed ratio schedules is that they provide a systematic schedule of reinforcement; caregivers know exactly when to reinforce the target behavior based on a fixed number of behaviors.

Variable Ratio Schedules

When a child is reinforced following a variable ratio schedule, reinforcement is delivered following an *average* number of behavior occurrences. For example, when a child is reinforced on an average of every third time he says "Please," the schedule would be considered a *variable ratio of three* or VR3. Variable ratio schedules of reinforcement are not recommended because the delivery of reinforcers for appropriate behavior may become less systematic and consistent. It may be difficult for some caregivers to monitor the delivery of reinforcement based on an average number of behaviors. Because a fixed ratio schedule is easier to monitor, it will probably result in a more consistent application of the reinforcement program.

Interval Reinforcement Schedules

An interval schedule of reinforcement provides reinforcement after an established *interval of time* has elapsed, contingent on the occurrence of a target behavior during the interval. Although the specific interval or length of time between reinforcers may be fixed or variable, an interval schedule is always based on the passage of time. Delivery of reinforcement following a specific period of time is best employed for behaviors that can be measured in terms of duration. In-seat and on-task behaviors, for example, can be measured by duration as well as frequency. Thus, when trying to decrease children's out-of-seat behavior, reinforcing periods of in-seat behavior through an interval reinforcement schedule, as demonstrated in Vignette 5.1, will be more functional and effective than with a ratio schedule.

Vignette 5.1.   Example of Using an Interval Schedule of Reinforcement.

Ann, a seventh-grade teacher, had a student named Paul who frequently got out of his seat and walked around the classroom during a 30-minute study hall period. The study hall period was from 2:30 to 3:00 each school day. This behavior was disruptive to the other students trying to study or complete assignments. After collecting some baseline data, Ann discovered that Paul remained in his seat an average of five consecutive minutes before getting out of his seat. Ann decided that since Paul was already on a token economy program (discussed later in this chapter) she would reinforce Paul's in-seat behavior on an interval schedule of reinforcement. Her goal was to teach Paul to remain seated (except when he received permission to get out of his seat) for 15 consecutive minutes.

Ann had a meeting with Paul and told him that he could earn an extra token whenever he stayed in his seat for five consecutive minutes. Time would start at 2:30 (the beginning of study hall) and Paul would have opportunities to earn an extra token at 2:35, 2:40, 2:45, 2:50, 2:55, and 3:00. During this first phase of the program Paul could earn a total of six extra tokens per day. Ann used the classroom clock to keep track of the time. She reinforced Paul with a token at the end of each five-minute interval *if* he remained seated during the previous five-minute interval.

After the first week of programming, Ann told Paul that he was doing very well and that he now needed to remain seated for 10 consecutive minutes to earn extra tokens. However, Ann raised the number of tokens Paul could earn from one to three. During this second phase, Paul could earn a total of nine extra tokens (three at 2:40, 2:50, and 3:00).

After another week on phase two, Ann had another meeting with Paul and told him that he now had to remain seated for 15 consecutive minutes to receive extra tokens. She now raised the number of extra tokens Paul could earn to six. Paul now had two opportunities to receive reinforcement (2:45 and 3:00). Paul did very well with this program and frequently earned the full 12 extra tokens during the 30-minute study hall period. Ann always paired the provision of tokens with social praise.

Two primary applications exist for interval reinforcement schedules. In the first application, the child is reinforced after a specific interval of time contingent on the appropriate behavior performance. For example, when trying to increase in-seat behavior, Ann reinforced Paul after a set interval of time. During the first week of Ann's reinforcement program, Paul was reinforced after five consecutive minutes of in-seat behavior. At the end of each time interval, Ann had to decide if Paul earned the promised reinforcement (extra tokens). If Paul did not remain seated during the previous interval, reinforcement was not provided.

In a second application, caregivers could decide to begin a new time interval every time the targeted inappropriate behavior (e.g., getting out of seat) is exhibited. If, in Vignette 5.1, Ann wanted to use this second application, she would reset the interval each time Paul got out of his seat. For example, if Paul got out of his seat at 2:31 and returned to his seat at 2:32, his next reinforcement opportunity would be five minutes later at 2:37. A new five-minute interval would begin once Paul returned to his seat.

Fixed Interval Schedules

When a child is reinforced following a specific interval of time (for example, for every 10 consecutive minutes of appropriate behavior), a *fixed interval of 10 schedule* or FI10 of reinforcement has been applied. Reinforcement for every five consecutive minutes of appropriate behavior is a *fixed interval of 5* or FI5, and so on. As with fixed ratio schedules, fixed interval schedules provide teachers and parents with a systematic reinforcement schedule; they know exactly when to reinforce the target behavior based on a fixed interval of time. In Vignette 5.1, Paul was reinforced on a fixed interval of 5 minutes of in-seat behavior during phase one, a fixed interval of 10 minutes during phase two, and a fixed interval of 15 minutes during the last phase of his in-seat behavior program.

Variable Interval Schedules

When a child is reinforced following a variable interval schedule, reinforcement is delivered following an *average* interval of time. For example, reinforcing a child for staying on-task for an average of every 10 minutes would be considered a *variable interval of 10* or VI10. As with variable ratio schedules, variable interval schedules of reinforcement are not recommended at the beginning of a behavior change program when consistency is very important. Again, it may be difficult for some caregivers to monitor the delivery based on an average interval of time and to maintain a consistent program of reinforcement delivery. Once a new behavior has been established, however, more intermittent reinforcement schedules, interval and ratio, are very effective (Baer, Blount, Detrich, & Stokes, 1984). A summary of reinforcement schedules is provided in Table 5.1.

DIFFERENTIAL REINFORCEMENT OF BEHAVIOR

Differential reinforcement refers to two primary applications of reinforcement to maintain or increase the occurrence of appropriate behavior. First, a behavior may be reinforced only when it is exhibited following an appropriate *discriminative stimulus* (S^D). For example, the behavior of talking in class may be appropriate under some situations, but not appropriate in others. By reinforc-

Table 5.1.   *Summary of reinforcement schedules.*

	Fixed	**Variable**
Ratio	Reinforcement is delivered contingent upon a *fixed* number of occurrences of the target behavior.	Reinforcement is delivered contingent upon an *average* number of occurrences of the target behavior.
Interval	Reinforcement is delivered after a *fixed* interval of time has elapsed, contingent upon the occurrence of a target behavior during the interval.	Reinforcement is delivered after an *average* interval of time has elapsed, contingent upon the occurrence of a target behavior during the interval.

ing talking only when it follows certain antecedents (e.g., when the teacher asks a question) and not reinforcing talking at other times, teachers can apply differential reinforcement to talking behavior.

A second application of differential reinforcement refers to the reinforcement of one target behavior while other behaviors are ignored. Thus, as the reinforced behavior increases, it becomes differentiated from other behaviors, related or unrelated, that are likely to decrease in the absence of reinforcement. When reinforcing behaviors that are incompatible with, or provide an alternative to, inappropriate behaviors, caregivers are using differential reinforcement to increase appropriate behaviors. Generally, differential reinforcement increases the rate, duration, or intensity of behaviors that children already have in their repertoire, but do not perform at acceptable levels. For example, a child may know how to raise his hand to get a teacher's attention, but frequently calls out the teacher's name in the middle of an assignment, interrupting the other students. When the teacher responds to the hand-raising instead of calling-out behavior, the child learns which behavior is effective in getting the teacher's attention.

Most differential reinforcement procedures are traditionally cited as behavior reduction procedures in other texts. Indeed, these procedures indirectly reduce targeted inappropriate behavior by reinforcing other or incompatible behaviors. Since reinforcement is the key element of these procedures, however, we decided to discuss them within this chapter.

Differential Reinforcement of Other Behaviors

Differential reinforcement of other behaviors (DRO), first described and used by Reynolds (1961), refers to the delivery of reinforcement after the child *has not exhibited* a target behavior during a predetermined interval of time, regardless of other behaviors occurring during the interval. For example, a caregiver may wish to reinforce a child for not hitting other children during recess, even though the child exhibited other inappropriate behaviors. A DRO schedule may also be used for providing reinforcement contingent on the absence of several inappropriate behaviors during a specific interval. For example, if a child screams and occasionally kicks others, reinforcement may be provided contingent on the absence of both screaming and kicking, or contingent on the absence of only screaming or only kicking. Because the DRO procedure entails the reinforcement of the *omission* of specified inappropriate behaviors, the term *differential reinforcement of the omission* of behavior is sometimes used (Deitz & Repp, 1983).

The primary purpose of this procedure is to target the reduction of a *specific* inappropriate behavior in a child who has perhaps several, less severe, inappropriate behaviors, which are put on hold. Prioritizing inappropriate behaviors and targeting the reduction of one behavior at a time may be an acceptable solution for caregivers who are working with children who have multiple behavior problems.

A DRO schedule has several different applications. In the first application, the DRO schedule is fixed (such as every 10 minutes; every 30 minutes). If the inappropriate behavior does not occur during the predetermined fixed interval, the child is reinforced. If the inappropriate behavior does occur at any time during the interval, the child is not reinforced at the end of the interval; a new interval begins only at the end of the preceding interval. For example, a child who frequently fights with other children may be placed on a DRO with a fixed interval of 30 minutes beginning at 9:00 am and ending at 3:00 pm. At 9:30 am, and at each 30-minute interval thereafter, caregivers would determine if the child exhibited fighting behavior. If fighting behavior did not occur, the child would qualify for a reinforcer. If fighting behavior occurred at any time during the 30-minute period, the child would not qualify for a reinforcer. With this DRO 30-minute fixed schedule, the child could earn up to 12 reinforcers (one each at 9:30, 10:00, 10:30, 11:00, 11:30, 12:00, 12:30, 1:00, 1:30, 2:00, 2:30, 3:00). Providing reinforcement when a targeted behavior has not been exhibited for an entire predetermined interval has also been referred to as *whole-interval DRO* (Repp, Barton, & Brulle, 1983).

A second variation, labeled *momentary DRO* (Repp et al., 1983), also uses a fixed, predetermined interval of time during which the occurrence of a target behavior is monitored. However, the child is reinforced only if the target behavior is not being emitted at the specific moment of observation—the end of each interval. For example, if a caregiver were using a momentary DRO-5 (minutes), the child would be observed every five minutes. If, at that moment, the target behavior was not occurring—even if it had occurred at another moment during the interval—the child would be reinforced. If, at that moment, the target behavior was occurring, the child would not earn reinforcement, regardless of the child's behavior during the rest of the interval. The child's next opportunity for earning a reinforcer would be at the end of the next interval (five minutes). In a comparison of whole-interval DRO and momentary DRO, Repp et al. found the whole-interval DRO to be more effective, especially in the initial stages of programming. They suggested that momentary DRO may be used as part of a maintenance program.

In a third variation of DRO, described by Donnellan et al. (1988) as a *DRO-reset* schedule, the interval of time is reset, or starts over, each time the targeted inappropriate behavior occurs. Using the previous example, if the child fought with another child at 9:15, the 30-minute interval would immediately be reset at 9:15 and end at 9:45 instead of 9:30. On the DRO-reset schedule, the child is reinforced for every 30 minutes during which no fighting occurs. The clock is always reset after each fight. With the DRO-fixed schedule, the child who has a fight at 9:15 would not have another opportunity for reinforcement until 10:00 (45 minutes after his last fight), the end of the next interval.

In a fourth variation of the DRO schedule, the expected interval of appropriate behavior increases over time in relation to the child's progress. Research has demonstrated that DRO schedules are more effective when the interval is short at the start of the program and gradually increases than when the interval is initially long (Repp & Slack, 1977). This variation may be referred to as a *DRO-increasing-interval* schedule or a *DRO-fading* schedule. The purpose of this variation is to fade or decrease the provision of reinforcement gradually from a frequent-opportunity schedule to a less-frequent-opportunity schedule. Using this procedure, the child is reinforced for the absence of a targeted inappropriate behavior for a specific interval (e.g., 30 minutes). However, after a predetermined number of successful intervals (e.g., three 30-minute intervals), the duration of the interval increases (e.g., from 30 to 45 minutes). Now the child must not exhibit the inappropriate behavior for a longer interval to qualify for reinforcement. If the inappropriate behavior does occur, the length of the interval stays the same. In effect, fading the reinforcement delivery schedule is determined by the child's progress. As the child progresses to longer intervals of appropriate behavior, caregivers may wish to increase the quantity or quality of reinforcement. Otherwise, the child may feel penalized for making progress (i.e., getting reinforced less often for behaving appropriately for longer periods of time). These four variations of DRO are outlined as follows:

Variation	Reinforcement (R+) Delivery
Whole-Interval	R+ delivered if target behavior not emitted at any time during interval.
Momentary	R+ delivered if target behavior not occurring at the moment of observation at the end of interval.

Variation	Reinforcement (R+) Delivery
Reset-interval	R+ delivered if target behavior not emitted for a full interval period of time. Clock reset after each target behavior.
Increasing-interval	R+ delivered if target behavior not emitted at any time during interval. Duration of interval gradually increases as student makes progress.

Fading reinforcement schedules are an important element to any reinforcement program. Busy caregivers are not likely to reinforce target behaviors consistently every 10, 15, or 30 minutes for extended periods. Also, the child needs to learn to behave appropriately in response to a more natural, intermittent schedule of reinforcement. On the other hand, it is important for caregivers to understand that all children have different needs and that some children will continue to need a greater level of support than others.

LaVigna and Donnellan (1986) listed three cautions concerning the use of DRO. First, because reinforcement is provided as a result of the *nonoccurrence* of a targeted inappropriate behavior, a specific appropriate behavior is not reinforced. Other types of differential reinforcement programs may be more effective for caregivers increasing specific appropriate behaviors. Second, provision of reinforcement contingent on nonoccurrence of a targeted inappropriate behavior may lead to inadvertent reinforcement of other inappropriate behaviors as well as appropriate behaviors. Last, under a DRO-reset schedule, the child may learn to exhibit the inappropriate behavior *immediately* after the timer is set and, after the timer is reset, still receive reinforcement at the end of the new interval. In effect, the child still receives a reinforcer at the end of each interval, even if the inappropriate behavior occurred. This problem could be eliminated by changing to a DRO-fixed schedule and not resetting the interval after each inappropriate behavior. Then, the child would not receive a reinforcer at the end of the interval because the inappropriate behavior had been exhibited at the beginning of the interval. A new interval would begin only at the end of the previously scheduled interval.

Differential Reinforcement of Alternative Behaviors

Differential reinforcement of alternative behaviors (DRA) refers to reinforcement of a more appropriate *form* of a targeted inappropriate behavior. Unlike DRO, DRA is more specific about the targeted behaviors to be reinforced. For example, when a caregiver reinforces a child for politely *asking* for a treat instead of *demanding* a treat, the caregiver is reinforcing an alternative, socially appropriate form of a behavior that has the same intent—to get a treat.

The DRA procedure has several advantages. First, it emphasizes reinforcement of specific, appropriate behaviors. Unlike the DRO procedure, where the caregiver must monitor the occurrence or absence of inappropriate behaviors, the DRA procedure forces caregivers to focus on occurrence of appropriate behaviors. Second, the DRA procedure encourages caregivers to review alternative behaviors that may be taught (if not already in the child's repertoire) or increased (if already in the child's repertoire). Too frequently, caregivers are eager to punish inappropriate behaviors without considering alternative behaviors they could reinforce. Again, focusing on reinforcement instead of punishment will have a significant, positive influence on the child's home and classroom environment. Third, the DRA procedure has a double effect on the child's behavior. Not only does appropriate behavior increase when reinforced, but the targeted inappropriate behavior is likely to decrease. In contrast, when punishment of inappropriate behavior is used alone, decreases in inappropriate behaviors are unlikely to occur in conjunction with increases in appropriate behaviors. Last, the DRA procedure is simple, easy to teach, and easy to implement.

Implementation of a DRA procedure can vary in several ways. Appropriate alternative behaviors may be reinforced based on a ratio schedule (number of appropriate behaviors) or an interval schedule (duration of appropriate behaviors). In addition, these ratio and interval schedules of reinforcement may be fixed or variable.

Differential Reinforcement of Incompatible Behaviors

Differential reinforcement of *incompatible* behaviors (DRI) refers to the reinforcement of behaviors that are topographically incompatible with targeted inappropriate behaviors. *Topographically incompatible* means that it is physically impossible for the incompatible and the target behaviors to occur at the same time. This procedure is also referred to as the reinforcement of *competing* behaviors (DRC) (Donnellan et al., 1988). Reinforcement of incompatible or competing behaviors is even more specific than DRO or DRA as to what types of behaviors are targeted. For example, keeping your hands in your lap is incompatible with hitting others and on-task behavior is incompatible with off-task behavior. Thus, when a caregiver reinforces hands-in-lap behavior, hitting-others behavior is likely to decrease, and the reinforcement of on-task behavior is likely to reduce off-task behavior.

Of course, not all inappropriate behaviors have topographically incompatible behaviors that would be appropriate or functional to reinforce. For example, although sitting still (the absence of movement or behavior) is incompatible with overactivity, self-stimulation, and a variety of behaviors identified as inappropriate in certain settings, reinforcing children for not moving is not recommended. Instead, caregivers should identify alternative, functional

Table 5.2. *DRO, DRA, and DRI examples.*

| Target behavior | Behavior Reinforced Per Program | | |
	DRO	DRA	DRI
Out of seat	Absence of	Asking permission	In seat
Off-task	Absence of	—	On task
Hitting	Absence of	Cooperation/talking	Hands in lap
Self-Stimulation	Absence of	Playing with toys	Keeping still
Non-Compliance	Absence of	—	Compliance
Temper Tantrum	Absence of	Taking/asking	—
Talking-Out	Absence of	Raising hand	Being quiet
Throwing Objects	Absence of	Playing basketball	Writing
Hands in Mouth	Absence of	Brushing teeth	Hands in lap
Running	Absence of	Walking	Standing still
Foul Language	Absence of	Appropriate language	Being quiet

behaviors to increase using a DRA or DRO procedure. Table 5.2 lists examples of differential reinforcement programs.

Differential Reinforcement of Lower Rates of Behavior

Differential reinforcement of lower rates (DRL) of behavior, first described by Skinner (1938), refers to the reinforcement of small *decreases* in the rate of a target behavior compared to the baseline rate of that behavior. Unlike the DRA, DRI, and DRO procedures, the DRL procedure is especially useful when trying to decrease the frequency of a behavior that has a high rate of occurrence. With a DRA or DRI procedure, few appropriate behaviors may occur during the high rate of inappropriate behavior, thus leaving few opportunities to reinforce alternative (DRA) or incompatible (DRI) behaviors. In addition, when there is a high rate of inappropriate behavior, reinforcement delivered under a DRA or DRI schedule may inadvertently become associated with the inappropriate behavior. A DRO procedure may also be problematic when an inappropriate behavior occurs at a high rate. Since this procedure calls for providing reinforcement contingent on the absence of the targeted inappropriate behavior for a specific interval, the child may never qualify for a reinforcer.

A DRL procedure may also be recommended for a behavior considered appropriate and functional except for a high rate of occurrence. Asking to use the bathroom is an appropriate behavior; however, when it occurs frequently throughout the school day, it may disrupt the classroom and have an adverse effect on the student's academic performance. In this case, the classroom teacher would be interested in decreasing the rate of the behavior to an acceptable level, rather than trying to eliminate the behavior.

The use of DRL may take on one of two forms. In the first form, reinforcement is provided contingent on a target behavior as long as a predetermined interval of time has passed since the target behavior last occurred (Skinner, 1938). The teacher would determine that a child could leave the classroom for the bathroom if a certain length of time had passed since the child's previous request. The objective with this form of DRL is to increase the intervals between target behaviors from the current baseline interval to a more socially acceptable level.

In a second form of DRL, reinforcement is provided contingent on a lower rate of the target behavior within a specific interval of time (Dietz & Repp, 1973). In keeping with our example, caregivers may decide to monitor the average hourly rate of the target behavior (asking to use the bathroom) and then reinforce the child each hour, contingent on a lower hourly rate of the target behavior. For example, the child may be reinforced for making two or fewer requests to use the bathroom per hour. As the child progresses in reducing the rate of the target behavior, reinforcement becomes contingent on a new criterion (an even lower hourly rate of the target behavior), until an acceptable level is achieved.

An important element in both DRL and differential reinforcement of higher rates of behavior, is the completion of a baseline measurement of the target behavior. Before setting new criteria or objectives for reduced rates of behavior, an accurate baseline measurement is a must. Baseline data will reveal a benchmark for expected behavior or behavior change. For example, if caregivers did not know the hourly baseline rate (how often the child asked to use the bathroom), they would not know whether the behavior had decreased during intervention or if the decrease was significant enough for the child to earn a reinforcer. If caregivers know that the baseline rate of the target behavior was ten requests per hour, however, then they know that the first step in their DRL program should be to reinforce the child contingent on an hourly rate of fewer than ten requests (for example, eight or fewer per hour). After the child has consistently (three or four consecutive hours) stayed below the baseline rate, a new and lower rate (such as six per hour) is established. Now, to earn a reinforcement, the child must exhibit the target behavior fewer than six times per hour. Additional reductions in the criteria for reinforcement should be made as the child progresses. Figure 5.1 outlines a sample DRL program to decrease cursing behavior.

Differential Reinforcement of Higher Rates of Behavior

Differential reinforcement of higher rates (DRH) of behavior (also called a changing criterion design) refers to the reinforcement of *increases* in the rate of a target behavior compared to the baseline rate of that behavior. DRH is typically used to increase behaviors that are already in the child's repertoire, but do not occur frequently or consistently enough. A child may know how to say "please" and "thank you," but may say the two terms infrequently. Reinforcing the child for saying "please" and "thank you" at a higher rate is likely to increase the use of the behaviors that already exist in the child's repertoire.

Child's Name: John (15 years)

Target Behavior: Cursing during gym class.

Baseline Data: John was observed for five consecutive days during gym class (45 minutes each). John cursed an average of 5 times during each 45-minute gym class (range = 4–6).

Program Goal: John will reduce his cursing rate to one or fewer per 45-minute gym class.

Reinforcement Menu: John may pick one reinforcement from the list below per reinforcement opportunity.

- Ten minutes of playing with a video game of his choice during study hall.
- Ten minutes of listening to an audio tape of his choice (with earphones only) during study hall.
- Fifteen minutes of computer time.

Reinforcement Schedule:

   Phase one: John may select <u>one</u> reinforcer when his cursing rate is less than 5 per 45-minute gym class.

   Phase two: John may select <u>one</u> reinforcer when his cursing rate is less than 4 per 45-minute gym class.

   Phase three: John may select <u>two</u> reinforcers when his cursing rate is less than 3 per 45-minute gym class.

   Phase four: John may select <u>two</u> reinforcers when his cursing rate is less than 2 per 45-minute gym class.

Performance Criteria for Phase Change: John will move to each new phase of this program after achieving the current phase objective for three consecutive gym periods. For example, after John has achieved the objective for phase one, reducing the rate of cursing to less than 5 for three consecutive gym classes, he is moved to phase two.

Figure 5.1. *Example of teacher's DRL program to decrease cursing behavior.*

Application of DRH is similar to the application of DRL, except that the purpose of DRH is to *increase* the rate of a target behavior within a specific interval of time. As with DRL, caregivers must first complete a baseline observation of the target behavior to establish a current rate. Then, they should reinforce increases in the rate, above baseline, until the rate of the target behavior occurs at an acceptable level. Figure 5.2 outlines a sample DRH program to increase a child's use of "please."

SHAPING AND CHAINING NEW BEHAVIORS

Shaping

In the previous section we discussed how differential reinforcement is used to increase and decrease the rate, duration, or intensity of behaviors that, for the most part, children already have in their repertoires. *Shaping* refers to the differential reinforcement of *successive approximations* of a terminal behavior.

Child's Name: Julia (5 years old)

Target Behavior: Saying "please" when making a request.

Baseline Data: A four-day baseline measure was taken by caregivers, from 8:30 until 12 noon, on the rate of saying "please" when making a request. Julia averaged 12.5% correct responses by saying "please" two out of 16 requests (Range = 0-4).

Program Goal: Julia will say "please" when making a request 95 percent of the time as measured during daycare from 8:30 until 12 noon, for three consecutive days.

Reinforcement Menu: Julia may select from the following reinforcement menu:
- One additional story read by a caregiver.
- An extra cup of juice during snack time.
- A choice of stickers.
- Five minutes playing with a computer game.

Reinforcement Schedule (Criteria for reinforcement, per phase):

Phase one: Julia will say "please" at a rate greater than 13 percent of total requests made during morning daycare.

Phase two: Julia will say "please" at a rate greater than 25 percent of total requests made during morning daycare.

Phase three: Julia will say "please" at a rate greater than 50 percent of total requests made during morning daycare.

Phase four: Julia will say "please" at a rate greater than 75 percent of total requests made during morning daycare.

Phase five: Julia will say "please" at a rate greater than 90 percent of total requests made during morning daycare.

Performance Criteria for Phase Change: Julia will move to the next phase of this program after achieving the phase objective for three consecutive sessions. For example, after Julia has achieved the objective for phase one, saying "please" at a rate greater than 13 percent of total requests made during morning daycare, for three consecutive sessions, she is moved to phase two.

Figure 5.2. *Example of a teacher's use of a reinforcement of higher rates of appropriate behavior program to increase a child's use of "please."*

Generally, shaping is used to teach *new* behaviors and skills—behaviors that are not already part of the child's repertoire. A successive approximation to a terminal behavior may be any intermediate behavior that, when combined with other intermediate behaviors, forms the topography of the terminal behavior. Within each step, or successive approximation, responses that meet the criteria for that step are reinforced, while other responses are not (differential reinforcement). As the child moves from one step to the next, the criterion for reinforcement changes as expectations increase. Each step in the shaping process brings the child's behavior closer to the terminal behavior. Vignette 5.2 demonstrates how shaping was used to teach a child how to walk independently from her classroom to a resource room.

Vignette 5.2.   The Use of Shaping to Teach Independent Travel from Classroom to Resource Room.

Aldy, a first grader, was a new student at Luke Elementary. Born and raised in Indonesia, Aldy was attending school in America for the first time. Because of her poor English language skills, Aldy was scheduled to attend an ESL (English as a second language) class every day in the school's resource room. Unfortunately, Luke Elementary is a large school and the resource room is a significant distance from Aldy's classroom. Aldy, not used to large school buildings, was very anxious about getting lost. Aldy's teacher, Marie, decided to use shaping to teach Aldy how to walk independently from the classroom (point A) to the resource room (point D).

Marie noted that on the way to the resource room Aldy would have to pass the rest rooms (point B) and the school cafeteria (point C). To teach Aldy how to walk independently from point A to point D, Marie first showed Aldy how to walk from point A to B with supervision, then without supervision. Correct performance of this behavior was practiced and reinforced for five days (the time it took for Aldy to learn how to walk independently from the classroom to the rest rooms).

In a second step, Marie showed Aldy how to walk from point A to point C with supervision, then without supervision. In this second step, the criterion for reinforcement was changed. Aldy was now required to walk all the way to point C without supervision, not just point B. This was also practiced until Aldy could independently walk from the classroom to the cafeteria. Correct responses were reinforced.

In the last step, Marie showed Aldy how to walk from point A to point D with supervision, then without supervision. Within three weeks Aldy learned to independently walk from her classroom to the resource room.

In Vignette 5.2, each of the three steps has two substeps, walking *with* then *without* supervision. Each of the steps and substeps is a successive approximation to the new terminal behavior of walking independently from point A to point D without supervision. Appropriate performance of successive approximations of the terminal behavior were reinforced to shape Aldy's behavior according to the topography of the terminal behavior.

The process of shaping includes several steps:

◆ Determine the terminal behavior or behavioral goal.
◆ Determine the successive approximations or steps necessary to complete the terminal behavior.

◆ Identify a "starting point" or behavior that the child currently performs that approximates either the terminal behavior or the first step to the terminal behavior (Aldy already walks to the rest room, point B, with the rest of her class).

◆ Reinforce closer approximations of the terminal behavior until the behavioral criterion for each successive approximation, or step, has been achieved [reinforce improvement, not perfection (Panyon, 1980)].

◆ Move from one step to the next until the terminal behavior has been learned/shaped [withhold reinforcement for behaviors that are not clear steps toward the terminal behavior (Panyon, 1980)].

Shaping is generally thought of as a method of teaching *new* behaviors or skills. It may be used to *modify* the rate, duration, or intensity of current behaviors. Thus, while the basic topography of the behavior remains the same, the dimensions of the topography are gradually modified. Examples of this second application of shaping include increasing motor activities, in-seat behavior, the number of correct responses per specific time interval, and so on.

Shaping may also be used to *decrease* the rate, duration, or intensity of current behaviors. Again, the child is not learning a new response (the purest application of shaping); the child is learning a new topography of a current response. For example, by reinforcing small decreases in the volume of a child's talking within a classroom setting, shaping may be used to modify a current behavior (talking too loud) to a more socially acceptable level of performance.

One of the primary advantages of shaping is the emphasis on reinforcing appropriate behaviors (successive approximations) as a strategy for teaching new or modified behaviors. Also, the process involved in shaping new behaviors forces caregivers to evaluate the child's current performance (baseline), to review the topography of the terminal behavior, and to establish a systematic program for the delivery of reinforcement.

Chaining

Chaining refers to the performance of a series or sequence of behaviors rather than just one independent behavior. For example, if a classroom teacher wants students to walk into the classroom, hang up their coats, put their lunch boxes into their lockers, and sit at their desks, these four behaviors may be taught separately or together as one *behavior chain*. Each of the four behaviors serves as a link in the behavior chain. Each link serves as the S^D for the performance of the next link (response) and as a conditioned reinforcer for the previous link:

Step 1:   Walking into the classroom.
Step 2:   Hanging up their coats.

Step 3:   Putting their lunch boxes into their lockers.
Step 4:   Sitting at their desks.

Alberto and Troutman stated "many complex human behaviors consist of such chains—often with dozens or even hundreds of component steps" (1990, p. 318). In our example, walking into the classroom serves as the S^D for the students to hang up their coats. Hanging up their coats serves as the S^D for putting their lunch boxes in their lockers, and putting their lunch boxes away serves as the S^D for sitting at their desks.

The development of a behavior chain, or any chain of skills, is called a *task analysis.* In the previous example, the four behavior links make up a task analysis of the teacher's expectations for her students when they walk into the classroom. Below we provide a task analysis for washing hands. Notice how much more detail is provided in the washing hands task analysis compared with the first example (teacher's expectations). The amount of detail contained in the behavior chain must depend on the complexity of the behavior and the characteristics of the child. More difficult tasks and behaviors may require a more detailed task analysis.

In the initial stages of teaching a behavior chain, caregivers should reinforce the child for correctly completing each behavior *and* for completing each behavior in the correct sequence. After the child has learned the appropriate sequence of behaviors, reinforcement may be faded from after the performance of each link to after the performance of the whole chain of behaviors. In addition, this behavior chain can be linked to other behavior chains and serve as the S^D for a second chain. For example, the completion of the behavior chain for coming into the classroom may serve as the S^D for the beginning of another behavior chain (e.g., stop talking, establish eye contact with the teacher, and wait for directions). There are two primary variations to teaching behavior chains—forward chaining and backward chaining.

Forward Chaining

Forward chaining refers to the teaching of each behavior link, starting with the *first* link, and moving "down" to the next link in the chain, until all the behaviors in the chain have been learned and can be performed in the appropriate sequence. A basic decision to be made in using forward chaining is whether to use serial training, concurrent task training, or total task training. In *serial training,* behaviors are taught in order, one at a time, to a set of criteria before the next behavior is added and taught. For example, when teaching a student the sequence of behaviors for coming into the classroom, step 1 (walking into the classroom) would be taught to a specific performance criterion before step 2 (hanging up their coats) is taught. In *concurrent task training,* two or more behaviors in the behavior chain are taught at the same time (Snell & Zirpoli, 1987). Thus, step 1 and step 2 of the behavior chain would be taught concurrently. Research has found that concurrent training may be more effective than serial training (Waldo, Guess, & Flanagan, 1982). Concurrent training may be more interesting and motivating to both student and teacher. Also, concurrent training may be more readily integrated into the daily routine because training is conducted within the context of other tasks (Dunlap & Koegel, 1980). *Total task training* refers to teaching of all steps in the behavior chain simultaneously. Total task training is actually an extension of concurrent training, has the same advantages of concurrent training, and is considered the most effective method for less difficult behavior chains (Johnson & Cuvo, 1981; Spooner & Spooner, 1984).

Backward Chaining

Backward chaining refers to the teaching of each behavior link in a behavior chain, starting with the *last* link and moving "up" the behavior chain, until all the behaviors in the chain have been learned and can be performed in the appropriate sequence. For example, if a caregiver were teaching a child a simple behavior chain for washing hands, as outlined in the following list, the caregiver would physically assist the child through all the steps in the chain until the last step (step 10—Hang up the towel). At that point, the caregiver begins instruction on step 10. This sequence continues until the child can complete step 10 independently. After the criterion for step 10 is achieved, the caregiver begins instruction on the second-to-the-last step (step 9—Dry your hands with the towel) in the sequence. At this point, the caregiver would assist the child through all of the preceding steps (1–8), provide instruction for step 9, and let the child complete the last step (10) independently. Each preceding step becomes the S^D for the next step in the behavior chain and serves as the conditioned reinforcer for the previous step. For example, step 9 becomes the S^D for step 10 and the conditioned reinforcer for step 8.

Stimulus: **Caregiver states that it is time to eat lunch.**

Step 1	Turn on the water.
Step 2	Wet your hands.
Step 3	Pick up the soap.
Step 4	Rub soap on your other hand.
Step 5	Put the soap down.
Step 6	Rub your hands together.
Step 7	Rinse your hands.
Step 8	Turn off the water.
Step 9	Dry your hands with the towel.
Step 10	Hang up the towel.

Research on which method is better, forward or backward chaining, is mixed. Spooner and Spooner remind us that "different learners do better with different procedures" (1984, p. 123). In general, forward chaining is recommended because it presents a more natural teaching sequence than backward chaining and allows more effective use of concurrent and total task training. When making these programming decisions (i.e., forward or backward chaining and serial, concurrent, or total task training), caregivers should consider the difficulty level of the behavior chain and the child's intellectual ability.

TOKEN ECONOMY REINFORCEMENT PROGRAMS

A *token economy* program is a symbolic reinforcement system (Kazdin & Bootzin, 1972; Kazdin, 1977). It is called an economy system because it is based on a monetary system. The most common form of tokens is money. Just as one who has a job receives money for the completion of specific tasks, which can then be exchanged for food, housing, and other material objects, the same principle applies in a token economy reinforcement program. Children receive tokens for specific appropriate behaviors, which they may exchange for objects or activities that have been identified as reinforcing. After the children have learned to associate the tokens with the purchase of reinforcers, the tokens become valuable and desirable.

Several advantages of token economy programs exist, especially for classroom teachers or other caregivers who work with large groups of children:

◆   Tokens can be distributed to large groups of children with minimum effort. Throughout the day, caregivers can give tokens to individual

Token economy programs are effective for managing large groups of children.

children or small groups of children as a simple but effective method of displaying positive attention to appropriate behaviors (Speltz, Shimamura, & McReynolds, 1982).

◆ Tokens allow caregivers to delay the provision of reinforcers during busy periods of the day.

◆ Tokens allow caregivers to provide a single reinforcer (the token) to many children who may have different reinforcer preferences. The children learn, however, that accumulating tokens throughout the day will allow them to purchase the reinforcer of their preference at a later time.

◆ Since the provision of tokens is followed by children's choosing from a variety of reinforcers, tokens are seldom subject to satiation.

◆ Tokens can be provided to children without interrupting teaching and other activities (Stainback, Payne, Stainback, & Payne, 1973).

Characteristics of Tokens

Tokens may be tally marks or points recorded on the board or check marks recorded on a piece of paper at the child's seat. Tokens may also be plastic chips, points, happy faces, stickers, stars, pennies, pieces of colored paper, pieces of cloth, ribbons, marbles, or any small, attractive object. Tokens should be something children can see, touch, and count. With the exception of tally and check marks, tokens should not be so large or small that children are unable to handle, store, and save them for later purchases. Also, caregivers want to be sure that tokens cannot be obtained from other sources via counterfeiting or stealing.

Most important, children must understand that they can exchange the tokens for various reinforcers and how many tokens they will need to purchase each reinforcer. Initially, caregivers may need to guide children through the exchange system to demonstrate how the program works.

Establishing a Token Economy Program

Several important steps are necessary to establish a token economy reinforcement program. Each of these steps is described in Vignette 5.3.

Vignette 5.3.   Example Token Economy Program.

Marge, a fifth-grade teacher, had a class of 30 students. Several of her students demonstrated challenging behaviors such as noncompliance, running around the classroom, hitting, interrupting others, yelling, and so on. Marge thought about starting individual behavior reduction programs for each of her "problem students," but decided instead to initiate a classroom-wide token economy program. In this way, she thought she could focus her attention and energy on reinforcing children for appropriate behaviors and, thus, indirectly decrease most of the inappropriate classroom behaviors at the same time.

Marge's first step was to *identify the target behaviors she wanted to increase.* She tried to think of appropriate behaviors that were incompatible with many of the challenging behaviors her students were exhibiting. She developed a list of five target behaviors that would be reinforced within her token economy program. These included:

◆   following the teacher's directions
◆   walking in the classroom
◆   keeping hands to self
◆   raising hand to be recognized before speaking out
◆   talking in a quiet voice.

Marge's second step was to *identify the medium of exchange,* or what would serve as tokens for her program. She decided to use colored strips of construction paper (one inch wide and five inches long).

Her third step was to *identify reinforcers the children would be able to purchase with the tokens they earned.* To develop this list, Marge wisely decided to tell her students about her plan and asked them for reinforcement suggestions. Her students were very helpful and had many ideas for reinforcers. Several of their ideas, however, were not acceptable and Marge communicated this to the students. She also included many activities as reinforcers. With her students' help, Marge developed a list of 15 reinforcers for the reinforcement menu. These included: five minutes extra time on the computer; five minutes extra free-time; being first in line for one day; being the class leader for one day; a pad of stationery paper (several were donated); one baseball card (donated); a new ballpoint pen (donated); picking a game during gym class; a positive note home; serving on a panel of judges for the next class competition; an extra show-and-tell session; pick your own seat assignment for one day; extra trip to the water fountain; pick and read a story to the class; and an extra trip to the library.

Marge wrote the five target behaviors and the reinforcement menu on two big sheets of cardboard. Each list was hung on the front classroom wall for all the student to see.

Having decided that the students would earn one token each time she observed one of her students exhibiting any of the target behaviors, Marge's next step was to *identify the price or number of tokens necessary to purchase each reinforcer on the reinforcement menu.* To do this, she followed these simple guidelines:

◆   The greater the supply of an item listed on the reinforcement menu, the lower the price, or the fewer number of tokens necessary to purchase that reinforcer. For example, Marge had hundreds of baseball cards. Thus, these could be purchased by the students for only one token.

- ◆ The lower the supply of the item, the higher the price. For example, Marge had only ten stationery pads. These, she decided, could be purchased for ten tokens.
- ◆ The greater the demand for an item, the higher the price. For example, many of the students wanted to buy extra time on the class computer. The cost, she decided, would be 10 tokens.
- ◆ The lower the demand for an item, the lower the price. For example, the students were not very interested in picking and reading a story to the class. Because this was an activity Marge wanted to promote, she only charged one token for this activity.
- ◆ The greater time required (for an activity), the higher the price. For example, extra free time removed the students from five minutes of academic time. Thus, Marge required 15 tokens for this item on the reinforcement menu.
- ◆ The less time required, the lower the price. For example, it took little time to write a positive note home and, besides, Marge viewed this as an effective strategy for promoting positive teacher-parent relationships. Thus, the positive note home cost only one token.

Marge's next decision was to *pick a time when the students would have the opportunity to exchange their tokens for reinforcers.* She decided that the classroom exchange period would be every Friday, after lunch. Marge explained to the students that they did not have to exchange their tokens; they could save them if they wanted. She also told her students that she would modify the price of each reinforcer after each exchange period, based on supply and demand, but that price changes would not be made between exchange periods.

For a token economy to be most effective in increasing appropriate behavior, a child should never experience a zero token balance by the exchange period. Caregivers should make an effort to identify at least one appropriate behavior, in even the most challenging child, to enable that child to participate in the token economy program. Finally, children should have the opportunity to purchase something small, even if they have earned only one token. In Marge's program, several items could be purchased for one token. Several characteristics of an effective token economy program include:

- ◆ Tokens should be something children can see, touch, and count.
- ◆ Tokens should not be so small or large that children can't store them, handle them, and count them. Tally marks or checks may be effective with some, especially older, children.
- ◆ Children must be able to exchange the tokens for actual reinforcers.

- ◆ Children should not be able to obtain tokens from sources other than the caregiver. If stealing is a potential problem, the caregiver may choose to store the tokens.
- ◆ Children must understand that the tokens they earn can be exchanged for various reinforcers. To learn how the system works, some children may have to be "walked" through the exchange process immediately after earning tokens.
- ◆ Caregivers must respect the differences in children's spending habits; some children like to save their tokens and some like to spend all their tokens at each exchange.
- ◆ Each child should have the opportunity to earn at least one token per exchange period. Also, no maximum should be placed on the number of tokens a child may earn.
- ◆ Children who earn only a few tokens, or even just one, should have the opportunity to exchange their tokens for small reinforcers.

CONTINGENCY CONTRACTING

Contingency contracting involves the establishment of a written behavioral contract between a child and caregivers regarding the performance of specific target behaviors and the exchange of specific consequences. Written contracts may be used with individual children or with groups of children and provide caregivers with a positive approach to reducing inappropriate behaviors (DeRisi & Butz, 1975). Contracts are useful behavior management tools that may be employed in the home and in a variety of educational settings:

> Contracting is a technique used to structure behavioral counseling by making each of the necessary elements of the process so clear and explicit that they may be written into an agreement for behavior change that is understandable and acceptable to everyone involved. (DeRisi & Butz, 1975, p. 1)

Saxon stated that the establishment of behavioral contracts was "an effective way to achieve mutual benefits" for both child and caregiver (1979, p. 523). While the child's role is to carry out the contracted behaviors, the caregiver's role is to create a supportive environment and to reinforce the performance of contracted target behaviors.

Contingency contracting has been successfully used to teach self-control (Raubolt, 1983), to modify assaultive and disruptive behaviors (Bagarozzi, 1984), to decrease alcohol abuse (Vannicelli, Canning, & Griefen, 1984), to treat bulimia (Brisman & Siegel, 1985), and to modify parent-child and teacher-student interactions (Stuart, Jayaratne, & Tripodi, 1976). The use of behavioral contracts to modify academic performance has had mixed results (Arwood, Williams, & Long, 1974). Contracts have been employed with children as young as six years old and with older children and adults (Bagarozzi, 1984).

Raubolt (1983) recommended the use of individual behavioral contracts over group psychotherapy. He outlined significant flaws in group psychotherapy that included the length of treatment, the difficulty of meeting the needs of a diverse group of children, the complex and delicate problem of choosing and grouping children, and the constraints that must be placed on the behavior of aggressive individuals in group settings. Brisman and Siegel (1985) found that contracts facilitated self-monitoring for individuals and peer-review for group contracts.

DeRisi and Butz (1975, p. 7) outlined several steps in establishing a behavioral contract. These steps have been modified and expanded on here:

◆ Select the target behavior(s) you want to increase. Limit the number of target behaviors to two or three.

◆ Describe the target behavior(s) in observable and measurable terms so that the child's progress may be observed and measured.

◆ Identify reinforcers that the child will find motivating.

◆ Establish general guidelines and timelines of the contract—who will do what and what will be the consequences.

◆ Write the contract so that all individuals involved can understand it; use age-appropriate wording.

◆ Require individuals involved to sign the contract indicating their understanding and agreement to the terms of the contract.

◆ Consistently reinforce the performance of the target behavior in accordance with the terms of the contract.

◆ Monitor and collect data on performance of target behavior(s).

◆ Discuss and rewrite the contract when data do not show improvement in the performance of the target behavior. Contract modifications should be signed by all individuals involved.

Advantages of Contracts

Contracts have many advantages when used to modify behavior. Behavioral contracts encourage caregivers to communicate their expectations clearly and provide children with a clear understanding of the rewards and consequences available for their behavior. Caregivers are encouraged to use their imagination in the development of behavioral contracts and to make them positive tools for changing behavior. Other advantages of contingency contracts are as follows:

◆ They are easy to use in natural environments and do not restrict child's participation in normal educational activities (Bagarozzi, 1984; Kerr & Nelson, 1989).

◆ Caregiver focus is placed on positive reinforcement of appropriate behaviors agreed on in the contract.

◆ Behavioral expectations of child and caregivers are outlined in writing.

◆ Reinforcement is presented in a systematic manner.
◆ Consequences for the performance or nonperformance of the target behavior are specific and clearly understood by child and caregivers.
◆ Contracts may be modified and rewritten as necessary to meet the needs of the current situation.
◆ Contracts may be employed with an individual child or a group of children.

Examples of simple behavioral contracts that may be used in home and educational settings are provided in Figures 5.3, 5.4, 5.5, and 5.6.

Figure 5.3. *Sample contract between child and parent.*

CONTRACT

I _____
Child's name here

Will _____
_____
_____
_____

I _____
Parent's name here

Will _____
_____
_____
_____

_____   _____
Child's signature   Parent's signature

_____
Date

Figure 5.4. *Sample contract between child and parent.*

CONTRACT

Contract between _____ and _____
If I do _____
_____
_____

Then I can: _____
_____
_____

_____   _____
Child's signature   Parent's signature

_____
Date

Figure 5.5 *Sample contract between student and teacher.*

```
┌─────────────────────────────────────────────────────┐
│                    CONTRACT                           │
│                                                       │
│  This is an agreement between _____    │
│                                    Student's name      │
│  and _____.                     │
│              Teacher's name                            │
│                                                       │
│  This contract begins on _____ and ends on_____. │
│                                                       │
│  The terms of this contract are as follows:           │
│  Student will: _____  │
│  _____ │
│  _____ │
│  _____ │
│                                                       │
│  Teacher will:_____  │
│  _____ │
│  _____ │
│  _____ │
│                                                       │
│  If student completes his/her part of the agreement,   │
│  teacher will provide student with reinforcement as    │
│  outlined in the teacher part of the agreement above.  │
│  If student does not complete his/her part of the      │
│  agreement, teacher will withhold reinforcement.       │
│                                                       │
│  _____    _____  │
│  Student's signature         Teacher's signature       │
│                                                       │
│            _____             │
│                        Date                            │
└─────────────────────────────────────────────────────┘
```

GENERALIZATION

Generalization refers to the degree that a behavior change transfers to other settings, situations, or behaviors in addition to the setting, situation, or target behavior involved in the behavior change program. Haring referred to generalization as "appropriate responding in untrained situations" (1988, p. 5). The two primary types of generalization are *stimulus generalization* and *response generalization.*

Stimulus Generalization

Stimulus generalization refers to the degree of behavior change in settings or situations other than the training setting, even when no training occurred in the new setting (Carr, Robinson, Taylor, & Carlson, 1990). If, during science class, for example, the teacher reinforces a child for reading directions on written assignments before asking questions, and then, in math class, the child

Figure 5.6.   *Sample contract between student and teacher.*

CONTRACT

_____ will demonstrate the following
(Student's name)
appropriate behaviors in the classroom:

1. Come to school on time.
2. Come to school with homework completed.
3. Complete all assigned work in school without prompting.
4. Ask for help when necessary by raising hand and getting teacher's attention.

_____ will provide the following reinforcement:
(Teacher's name)

1. Ten tokens for the completion of each of the above four objectives. Tokens for the first two objectives will be provided at the beginning of class after all homework assignments have been checked. Tokens for objectives three and four will be provided at the end of the school day.
2. Tokens may be exchanged for activities on the Classroom Reinforcement Menu at noon on Fridays.

_____   _____
Student's signature   Teacher's signature

_____
Date

begins to read directions before asking questions, the new behavior (reading directions before asking questions) has generalized from the science to the math class.

Response Generalization

Response generalization refers to the degree that a behavior change program influences other behaviors in addition to the target behavior (Carr et al., 1990). For example, if a caregiver develops a reinforcement program to increase a child's use of "please," and the child also exhibits an increase in the use of "thank you," then the behavior change program shows a response generalization. In a second example, if a caregiver develops a behavior change program to decrease aggression (the target behavior) and the child also demonstrates a decrease in tantrums (not the target behavior), then the behavior change program shows a response generalization.

In these cases, response generalization is credited with changing behaviors other than the target behavior in the same direction (increasing or decreasing a response) as the target behavior. Response generalization may, however, change behaviors in the opposite direction of the target behavior. For example, a program resulting in a *decrease* in self-injurious behavior may also result in an *increase* in other pro-social behaviors. Also, an *increase* in on-task behaviors may result in the *decrease* of disruptive behaviors. Although the evidence tends to suggest that these behavior changes are the result of response generalization (Kazdin, 1989), few would disagree that they may also represent some spread of treatment effects.

Promoting Generalization of Behavior Change

Haring stated that "generalization is, perhaps, the most important phase of learning" (1988, p. 5). In most cases, however, generalization does not occur spontaneously. To ensure that new behaviors are used in natural settings, generalization must be integrated into the acquisition phase of teaching (Snell & Zirpoli, 1987). Several methods are used to accomplish this objective.

Teaching in Natural Settings

The term *natural setting* refers to the setting in which a behavior is most likely to occur or should occur (Gaylord-Ross & Holvoet, 1985). For example, if a teacher wants to establish a reinforcement program to increase "sharing" behavior, the best place to teach this behavior is within the environments where children are expected to share. Pulling children out of the classroom for individualized training by a behavior therapist is usually not recommended. Behaviors that are learned in this type of environment are unlikely to generalize automatically to the places where children live and go to school. The behavior therapist, teacher, and parents must collaborate to integrate skill acquisition and generalization successfully into the child's natural environments (e.g., classroom, playground, home).

Selecting Natural Antecedents for Stimulus Control

Natural antecedents refer to the events or situations that should act as natural prompts or cues for a specific target behavior (Ford & Mirenda, 1984; Snell & Zirpoli, 1987). For example, several situations occur within a classroom setting in which children are expected to stop talking and listen (e.g., when the teacher is talking, reading to the class, or giving instructions). Teaching children to stop talking and listen, following these naturally occurring situations, is another example of integrating skill acquisition and generalization. The most effective way for caregivers to identify the natural antecedents or stimuli for behaviors is through direct observation of children within natural environments.

There are times when artificial stimuli (prompts and cues) are necessary to teach appropriate behaviors or increase the opportunity for reinforcement of a target behavior. For many children, the use of artificial prompts is a necessary and important element during the initial stages of behavior acquisition. Using a tone sound from a tape recorder during the initial stages of a self-instruction program to teach in-seat behavior (see Chapter 6) is an example of an artificial prompt. These artificial prompts clearly have a useful place in behavior management. It is also important, however, to pair artificial prompts with natural stimuli and to fade them as soon as possible (Wolery & Gast, 1984). Children who learn to stop talking only when they hear an artificial prompt may not learn to stop talking in response to natural stimuli when they occur.

Selecting Natural Consequences as Reinforcers

In addition to teaching within natural settings and associating appropriate behaviors with natural antecedents and stimuli, caregivers should employ natural consequences for behaviors (Snell & Zirpoli, 1987). Thus, although a token economy program—or any other program using artificial reinforcers—may be appropriate and necessary for many children, one of the goals of reinforcement programs should be to fade artificial reinforcers (e.g., from tokens to praise) and schedules (e.g., continuous to intermittent) and to teach children to respond to natural reinforcers. Natural classroom reinforcers include positive statements made by the teacher or other children, having completed artwork or other assignments hung on the classroom bulletin board, and getting a good grade on an assignment. This may not be possible in all cases, however, and the long-term use of artificial reinforcers (e.g., tokens, extra attention) may be necessary to maintain appropriate behavior with some children.

Reinforcing Generalization

As with other behaviors discussed in this chapter, the generalization of learned behaviors for one stimulus, setting, or situation is likely to increase when generalization is systematically reinforced. Generalization may be increased by reinforcing the child for exhibiting target behaviors outside the training setting or situation or, more directly, by training *for* generalization. In a procedure referred to as *sequential modification* (Stokes and Baer, 1977), a skill or behavior is taught in one setting or situation, then additional settings or situations are systematically added to the training program until generalization is achieved in all targeted settings or situations. For example, a behavior change program may begin and continue within a specific classroom setting until the target behavior is achieved. Then caregivers gradually expand the program to other settings within the school until complete generalization (within the school) is achieved.

MAINTENANCE

Maintenance refers to the degree to which a behavior change is maintained over time after completion of a behavior change program. For example, in-seat behavior is said to be maintained when a caregiver terminates the behavior change program used to increase in-seat behavior in the first place and the duration of in-seat behavior remains at an acceptable level. If, after termination of the behavior change program, the duration of in-seat behavior decreases to an unacceptable level, then the behavior change was not maintained and the program may have to be reinstated.

Promoting the Maintenance of Behavior Change

The methods for promoting maintenance are similar to those used to promote generalization. When training is conducted within natural settings, using natural antecedents and consequences, behavior changes are likely to be maintained after artificial stimuli and consequences (and other training conditions) are faded.

The following methods are likely to promote generalization and maintenance of learned behaviors:

- ◆ Teach within settings where the behavior is likely to occur and within multiple settings; avoid artificial training areas or pull-out training. Teaching a child appropriate classroom behaviors within a resource room (artificial environment) is unlikely to generalize to the regular classroom or be maintained after the child leaves the resource room unless the same behaviors are taught and reinforced in the regular classroom.

- ◆ Implement the behavior change program with a variety of caregivers across multiple settings. All caregivers who have contact with a child should consistently follow the behavior change program.

- ◆ Identify common elements between the teaching environment and other environments within which behavior is to be generalized. This is especially important when students change classes throughout the school day. Collaboration, cooperation, and consistency are important elements for effective behavioral generalization and maintenance across school personnel and environments.

- ◆ Gradually shift from artificial stimulus controls to natural stimulus controls that occur in the child's natural environment. Be flexible, however, to the individual needs of the child.

- ◆ Shift from continuous to intermittent schedules of reinforcement as soon as possible. These decisions, as outlined in Chapter 3, should be based on the student's progress as outlined in your program data.

- ◆ Pair artificial reinforcers (e.g., tokens) with natural reinforcers and consequences (social praise) provided within the natural environment.

- ◆ Phase out artificial reinforcers that are unlikely to be provided in the natural environment.

- ◆ Introduce delays in the provision of reinforcement that would be likely to occur in the natural environment. For example, while initially students may exchange tokens at the end of each day, weekly

exchange intervals will teach children to plan and save for future consequences. Again, caregivers must, however, be sensitive to what
works for their children and be flexible enough to modify the behavior change plan as necessary.

◆   Reinforce generalization and maintenance. Tell children when you
    notice the generalization of skills across different environments, and
    verbally reinforce them when appropriate behaviors are maintained
    after the "official" program is completed.

SUMMARY

Reinforcement increases the probability that a behavior will reoccur, or at
least be maintained, at the current rate, duration, or intensity. Reinforcement
of appropriate behavior is the most effective method of increasing appropriate
and decreasing inappropriate behaviors. Reinforcers may be tangible, social, or
physical (activities). Primary reinforcers are naturally reinforcing, while secondary reinforcers are learned or conditioned through their association with
primary reinforcers. Caregivers must be sure that reinforcers are socially valid
and age-appropriate.

A reinforcement menu is a list of potential reinforcers that may be used
for an individual student or group of students to reinforce appropriate behavior. By having a variety of reinforcers to select from, children will not become
satiated with a single reinforcer.

Factors associated with effective reinforcement programs include immediacy of presentation, consistency, pairing with verbal praise, schedule of presentation, and the type, quality, quantity, and presenter of the reinforcement
to the child. Caregivers are encouraged to establish clear rules and guidelines,
model the target behavior, and consistently reinforce behaviors targeted for
increase.

Reinforcement may be delivered on a continuous or an intermittent
schedule. A continuous schedule involves the delivery of reinforcement each
and every time the target behavior is observed. When an intermittent schedule
is employed, a child is reinforced after some, but not each and every, occurrences of the target behavior. Reinforcement may also be delivered on a fixed
ratio, variable ratio, fixed interval, and variable interval schedule.

Differential reinforcement of behavior refers to the reinforcement of
behavior following an appropriate discriminative stimulus, or the reinforcement of a target behavior while other behaviors are ignored. Differential reinforcement schedules include the differential reinforcement of other behaviors,
differential reinforcement of alternative behaviors, differential reinforcement
of incompatible behaviors, and the differential reinforcement of lower and
higher rates of behaviors.

Shaping refers to the differential reinforcement of successive approximations of a terminal behavior. Shaping is generally used to teach new behaviors
and skills. Chaining refers to the performance of a series or sequence of behav-

iors rather than of one behavior independently. Chaining may be presented in a forward or backward sequence.

A token economy reinforcement program is a symbolic reinforcement system. Children are presented with tokens for objects or activities that are reinforcing. Tokens, which may take many forms, allow caregivers to delay provision of reinforcers during busy periods of the day and are effective with individual or large groups of children. Establishing a token economy program includes identification of the target behavior, the medium of exchange, the price of each item on the reinforcement menu, and when the children will exchange their tokens for reinforcers.

Contingency contracting involves the development of a written agreement between a child and caregivers regarding the performance of target behaviors and the exchange of specific consequences. Contracts are highly recommended because they are easy to use in natural environments, do not restrict the child's participation in educational activities, focus on the reinforcement of appropriate behaviors, outline behavioral expectations in writing, may be used with individuals or groups of children, and may be modified to meet the needs of different children and situations.

Generalization refers to the degree to which a behavior change transfers to other settings, situations, or behaviors beyond the training environment. There are two types of generalization—stimulus and response. Stimulus generalization refers to the degree of behavior change from training to other settings. Response generalization refers to the degree to which a behavior change program generalizes to other behaviors.

Maintenance refers to the degree to which a behavior change is maintained over time after the completion of a behavior change program. Caregivers may promote generalization and maintenance by teaching in natural environments, selecting natural antecedents for stimulus control, selecting natural consequences as reinforcers, shifting from continuous to intermittent schedules of reinforcement, introducing delays in reinforcement similar to the natural environment, and by reinforcing generalization.

For Discussion

1. Discuss the different types of reinforcement caregivers may use in different environments (school, home, etc.) to increase appropriate behavior.
2. List and discuss the factors associated with effective reinforcement programs.
3. Discuss the different types of reinforcement schedules and give examples of each.
4. Discuss the process of shaping new behaviors.
5. Discuss the important elements of an effective reinforcement program.
6. Discuss the important elements of an effective contingency contracting program.

7. What do we mean when we talk about program generalization and maintenance and how can they be facilitated?

REFERENCES

Alberto, P.A., & Troutman, A.C. (1990). *Applied behavior analysis for teachers.* Columbus, OH: Merrill/Macmillan.

Arwood, B., Williams, R. L., & Long, J. D. (1974). The effects of behavior contracts and behavior proclamations on social conduct and academic achievement in a ninth grade English class. *Adolescence, 9,* 425–436.

Baer, R. A., Blount, R. L., Detrich, R., & Stokes, T. F. (1984). Using intermittent reinforcement to program maintenance of verbal/nonverbal correspondence. *Journal of Applied Behavior Analysis, 20,* 179–184.

Bagarozzi, D. A. (1984). Applied behavioral intervention in rural school settings: Problems in research design, implementation, and evaluation. *Clinical Social Work Journal, 12,* 43–56.

Bandura, A. (1973). *Aggression: A social learning analysis.* Englewood Cliffs, NJ: Prentice-Hall.

Brisman, J., & Siegel, M. (1985). The bulimia workshops: A unique integration of group treatment approaches. *International Journal of Group Psychotherapy, 35,* 585–601.

Carr, E. G., & Durand, V.M. (1985). Reducing behavior through functional communication training. *Journal of Applied Behavior Analysis, 18,* 111–126.

Carr, E.G., Robinson, S., Taylor, J.C., & Carlson, J.I. (1990). *Positive approaches to the treatment of severe behavior problems in persons with developmental disabilities: A review and analysis of reinforcement and stimulus-based procedures.* Monograph No. 4, The Association for Persons with Severe Handicaps.

Datillo, J. (1986). Computerized assessment of preference for severely handicapped individuals. *Journal of Applied Behavior Analysis, 19,* 445–448.

Deitz, S. M., & Repp, A. C. (1973). Decreasing classroom misbehavior through the use of DRL schedules of reinforcement. *Journal of Applied Behavior Analysis, 6,* 457–463.

Deitz, S. M., & Repp, A. C. (1983). Reducing behavior through reinforcement. *Exceptional Education Quarterly, 3,* 34–46.

DeRisi, W. J., & Butz, G. (1975). *Writing behavioral contracts.* Champaign, IL: Research Press.

Donnellan, A. M., LaVigna, G. W., Negri-Shoultz, N., & Fassbender, L. L. (1988). *Progress without punishment: Effective approaches for learners with behavior problems.* New York: Teachers College Press.

Dunlap, G., & Koegel, R. K. (1980). Motivating autistic children through stimulus variation. *Journal of Applied Behavior Analysis, 13*, 619–627.

Egel, A. L. (1981). Reinforcer variation: Implications for motivating developmentally disabled children. *Journal of Applied Behavior Analysis, 14*, 345–350.

Ford, A., & Mirenda, P. (1984). Community instruction: A natural cues and correction decision model. *Journal of the Association for Persons with Severe Handicaps, 9*, 79–87.

Gaylord-Ross, R. J., & Holvoet, J. F. (1985). *Strategies for educating students with severe handicaps.* Boston, MA: Little, Brown.

Green, C. W., Reid, D. H., White, L. K., Halford, R. C., Brittain, D. P., & Gardner, S. M. (1988). Identifying reinforcers for persons with profound handicaps: Staff opinion versus systematic assessment of preferences. *Journal of Applied Behavior Analysis, 21*, 31–43.

Haring, N. G. (1988). *Generalization for students with severe handicaps: Strategies and solutions.* Seattle, WA: University of Washington Press.

Iwata, B. A. (1987). Negative reinforcement in applied behavior analysis: An emerging technology. *Journal of Applied Behavior Analysis, 20,* 361–378.

Johnson, B. F., & Cuvo, A. J. (1981). Teaching mentally retarded adults to cook. *Behavior Modification, 5*, 187–202.

Kauffman, J. M. (1989). *Characteristics of behavior disorders of children and youth,* Columbus, OH: Merrill/Macmillan.

Kazdin, A. E. (1977). *The token economy: A review and evaluation.* New York: Plenum Press.

Kazdin, A. E. (1989). *Behavior modification in applied settings.* Pacific Grove, CA: Brooks/Cole.

Kazdin, A. E., & Bootzin, R. R. (1972). The token economy: An evaluative review. *Journal of Applied Behavior Analysis, 5*, 343–372.

Kerr, M.M., & Nelson, C.M. (1989). *Strategies for managing behavior problems in the classroom.* Columbus, OH: Merrill/Macmillan.

Koegel, R. L., Dyer, K., & Bell, L. K. (1987). The influence of child-preferred activities on autistic children's social behavior. *Journal of Applied Behavior Analysis, 20*, 243–252.

LaVigna, G. W., & Donnellan, A. M. (1986). *Alternatives to punishment: Solving behavior problems with non-aversive strategies.* New York: Irvington Publishers.

Mason, S. A., McGee, G. G., Farmer-Dougan, V., & Risley, T.R. (1989). A practical strategy for ongoing reinforcer assessment. *Journal of Applied Behavior Analysis, 22*, 171–179.

Panyon, M. V. (1980). *How to use shaping.* Austin, TX: Pro-Ed.

Pfiffner, L. J., & O'Leary, S. G. (1987). The efficacy of all positive management as a function of the prior use of negative consequences. *Journal of Applied Behavior Analysis, 20*, 265–271.

Premack, D. (1959). Toward empirical behavior laws: I. Positive reinforcement. *Psychological Review, 66*, 219–233.

Raubolt, R. R. (1983). Treating children in residential group psychotherapy. *Child Welfare, 62*, 147–155.

Repp, A. C., Barton, L. E., & Brulle, A. R. (1983). A comparison of two procedures for programming the differential reinforcement of other behaviors. *Journal of Applied Behavior Analysis, 16*, 435–445.

Repp, A. C., & Slack, D. J. (1977). Reducing responding of retarded persons by DRO schedules following a history of low-rate responding: A comparison of ascending interval sizes. *The Psychological Record, 27*, 581–588.

Reynolds, G. S. (1961). Behavioral contrast. *Journal of the Experimental Analysis of Behavior, 4*, 57–71.

Rosenberg, M. S. (1986). Maximizing the effectiveness of structured classroom management programs: Implementing rule-review procedures with disruptive and distractible students. *Behavioral Disorders, 11*, 239–248.

Sasso, G. M., Melloy, K. J., & Kavale, K. A. (1990). The effects of social skills training through structured learning: Behavioral covariation, generalization, and maintenance. *Behavioral Disorders.*

Saxon, W. (1979). Behavioral contracting: Theory and design. *Child Welfare, 58*, 523–529.

Skinner, B.F. (1938). *The behavior of organisms.* New York: Appleton-Century-Crofts.

Skinner, B.F. (1969). *Contingencies of reinforcement: A theoretical analysis.* New York: Appleton-Century-Crofts.

Snell, M. E., & Zirpoli, T. J. (1987). Intervention strategies. In M.E. Snell (Ed.), *Systematic instruction of persons with severe handicaps.* Columbus, OH: Merrill/Macmillan.

Speltz, M. L., Shimamura, J. W., & McReynolds, W. T. (1982). Procedural variations in group contingencies: Effects on children's academic and social behaviors. *Journal of Applied Behavior Analysis, 15*, 533–544.

Spooner, S.B., & Spooner, D. (1984). A review of chaining techniques: Implications for future research and practice. *Education and Training of the Mentally Retarded, 10*, 114–124.

Stainback, W., Payne, J., Stainback, S., & Payne, R. (1973). *Establishing a token economy in the classroom.* Columbus, OH: Merrill/Macmillan.

Stokes, T. F., & Baer, D. B. (1977). An implicit technology of generalization. *Journal of Applied Behavior Analysis, 10*, 349–367.

Stuart, R. B., Jayaratne, S., & Tripodi, T. (1976). Changing adolescent deviant behaviour through reprogramming the behaviour of parents and teachers: An experimental evaluation. *Canadian Journal of Behavioural Sciences, 8*, 132–144.

Vannicelli, M., Canning, D., & Griefen, M. (1984). Group therapy with alcoholics: A group case study. *International Journal of Group Psychotherapy, 34*, 127–147.

Waldo, L., Guess, D., & Flanagan, B. (1982). Effects of concurrent and serial training on receptive labeling by severely retarded individuals. *Journal of the Association for the Severely Handicapped, 6*, 56–65.

Wolery, M., & Gast, D. L. (1984). Effective and efficient procedures for the transfer of stimulus control. *Topics in Early Childhood Special Education*, *4*, 52–77.

Wolery, M., Kirk, K., & Gast, D. L. (1985). Stereotypic behavior as a reinforcer: Effects and side effects. *Journal of Autism and Developmental Disorders*, *15*, 149–161.

CHAPTER 6

Cognitive Behavior Modification

Mitchell L. Yell, University of South Carolina

. . . the major aim of teaching self control is to teach the student to be the agent of change of his or her own behavior, then the controlling response itself must maintain and generalize beyond the training setting and after training ceases.

—Liberty and Michael, 1985, p. 102

*C*ognitive behavior modification (CBM) is not a specific type of intervention, rather it is a term that has been used to refer to a number of theories and interventions. Problem-solving, anger control, self-instruction, alternate response, self-control, self-management, self-monitoring, self-evaluation, and self-reinforcement training are interventions included under the rubric of cognitive behavior modification. These interventions share three basic assumptions (Hughes, 1988). First, behavior is mediated by cognitive events (thoughts, beliefs, etc.). Second, a change in cognitive mediating events results in a change of behavior. Third, all persons are active participants in their learning. Cognitive behavioral theories posit a reciprocal relationship between one's thoughts and behaviors. Cognitive behavioral interventions attempt to modify thoughts and beliefs in order to change behavior.

Cognitive behavioral interventions have been used to modify a wide variety of social and affective behaviors such as attentional deficits, impulsivity, anger, depression, noncompliance, attributions, motivation, social skills, and metacognition as well as academic deficits in reading, written expression, handwriting, math, and spelling (Alberto & Troutman, 1990; Kaplan, 1991; Wolery, Bailey, & Sugai, 1988).

A major goal of CBM is to teach persons to manage their behavior. Proponents of CBM believe that sole reliance on behavior management interventions makes the child overly dependent on the caregiver's environmental manipulations. However, when a caregiver uses the techniques and procedures of CBM to teach self-management, the person taught these skills becomes less dependent on the caregiver and on external sources of control. Several researchers have discussed the advantages of teaching individuals to manage their behavior (Alberto & Troutman, 1990; Cooper, Heron, & Heward, 1987; Wolery, Bailey, & Sugai, 1988). Some of these advantages are:

- ◆ Teaching self-management skills is a proactive rather than reactive approach to behavior management. The caregiver teaches these skills to prevent behavior problems from occurring by teaching self-control.
- ◆ Persons with self-management skills can learn and behave more appropriately even without the supervision of the caregiver. This frees the caregiver to concentrate on other matters of importance.
- ◆ Self-management might be an effective method for promoting the generalization of behavior change. When behaviors are under external control by the caregiver, the behaviors might not be controlled in

situations and settings where the caregiver is not able to apply the external control procedures. However, when individuals are able to self-manage their behaviors, these behaviors will be more likely to last and to carry over to different situations and settings without external control by caregivers.

◆ Behavioral improvements established through self-management procedures might be more resistant to extinction than behavioral improvements established through external control procedures. When behavioral improvements are established through external control procedures, these improvements may disappear when the external reinforcers are removed. However, some researchers have suggested that this is less of a problem when behaviors are improved through self-management.

A major difference between traditional behavior modification and CBM is that with the former the caregiver is taught the various procedures to modify the child's behavior, while in cognitive behavior modification the child is taught the procedures in order to modify his or her behavior. The caregiver teaches self-management procedures as they do with other behaviors, in accordance with the principles of learning (Alberto & Troutman, 1990).

The purpose of this chapter is to review separately those interventions that fall under the category of CBM. Note, however, that in practice these interventions are usually employed in packages.

ORIGINS OF COGNITIVE BEHAVIOR MODIFICATION

Cognitive behavior modification represents a synthesis among the forces of cognitive psychology and behavior modification. According to Kendall and Hollon, cognitive-behavioral approach represented a number of forces coming together. It was "a joining of forces rather than a break for independence" (1979, p. 6). Although many forces have been identified as contributing to the development of cognitive-behavioral approaches, the primary forces were trends in behavioral psychology, specifically Bandura's social-learning theory and trends in cognitive psychology, including cognitive psychology and private speech.

Trends in Behavioral Psychology

The traditional behavioral approach has emphasized the modification of behavior through control of environmental antecedents and consequences. Behavioral procedures include reinforcement, punishment, stimulus control, etc. These procedures are used to establish behaviors, increase or maintain behaviors, or reduce or eliminate behaviors (see Chapter 1). To the radical behaviorist, cognitions and feelings were denied or not considered. To moderate behaviorists, cognitions—although not denied—were considered irrelevant to the task of modifying behavior.

The 1970s were a time of growing dissatisfaction with behaviorism. Kazdin (1982) argued that conceptual stagnation was occurring within behaviorism. Little in the way of new theory was developed and the applied research seemed merely to catalog the same behavioral interventions with new populations, problems, or settings. Another source of dissatisfaction was that behavior management procedures were not fostering changes that were durable or that generalized to other settings, across behaviors, or across subjects (Meichenbaum, 1980).

The conceptual stagnation and the growing dissatisfaction with the behavioral model may have helped to foster the shift toward more cognitively oriented interventions (Kazdin, 1982). The shifting view acknowledged that behavior modification involved cognitive processes, and that cognitions were involved in the learning process (Craighead, 1982).

In 1978 Bandura advanced his concepts of reciprocal determinism. Bandura (1978) stated that environmental, cognitive, and behavioral variables interact with each other. He demonstrated the importance of self-efficacy and the importance of modeling in learning (Bandura, 1977). His theories provided the basis for social-learning theory. Bandura's work laid the cornerstone of what was to become the cognitive-behavioral model (Meyers, Cohen, & Schlester, 1989).

Behavioral research on the development of self-control and the processes of self-regulation were also important contributors to the movement toward cognitive behavior modification (Harris, 1982). Homme (1965) stated that "coverants" or operants of the mind were subject to the same laws as behavior, and that these cognitions could modify behavior. Kanfer and Karoly (1972) developed a model of self-regulation that included self-monitoring, self-evaluation, and self-reinforcement. According to Kanfer and Karoly, self-regulation occurred when a child observed his or her performance, compared it to some criterion, and reinforced himself or herself. These and other events within the behavioral field began to acknowledge the interaction of interpersonal cognitions and environmental events in human behavior.

Trends in Cognitive Psychology

Cognitive psychology posits that behavior is influenced by cognitions. Cognitive psychologists, unlike behavioral psychologists, believe the determinants of human behavior lie within the individual. Interventions are aimed at altering thoughts, perceptions, beliefs, and attributions. An important influence on cognitive behavior modification was the development of cognitive therapy. According to Craighead (1982) the writings of Ellis and Beck were the beginning points for the development of cognitive interventions. Beck (1976) believed that many problems were due to an individual's misinterpretation of events. He contended that individuals could be helped by assisting them to identify their faulty perceptions and teaching them more accurate ones. Individuals progressed through four stages in Beck's cognitive therapy: First,

the individual had to become aware of his or her thoughts; second, the individual had to recognize the thoughts that were inaccurate; third, the individual had to substitute accurate judgments for inaccurate ones; and, finally, he or she needed feedback as to the correctness of the changes. Similarly, Ellis believed that it is an individual's inaccurate perceptions of events that cause disturbances. To modify these inaccurate perceptions, Ellis (1973) developed *rational-emotive therapy* (RET). In RET individuals are taught that it is not what happens to them that makes them upset and causes them to behave counterproductively, but rather it is what they think about what happens to them. (For a more detailed explanation of RET, see the section later in this chapter.) The theories of Beck and Ellis shared two primary assumptions: (1) dysfunctional behavior was the result of inappropriate cognitive processes (what individuals thought about events) and (2) the interventions must modify these inappropriate cognitions (Craighead, 1982).

Theories concerning the relationship between private speech and behavior have also influenced the development of cognitive behavior modification. Private speech refers to overt or covert speech that is directed at oneself. Theories about the role of private speech have their roots in the work of two Soviet psychologists, Vygotsky and Luria, in the early 1960s. Vygotsky (1962) proposed that the internalization of verbal commands was the crucial step in a child's control over his or her behavior. Vygotsky's student Luria (1961), in a series of investigations, proposed a normal developmental sequence by which the child came to regulate his or her behavior. In this developmental sequence, the child's behavior was first controlled by verbalizations of adults. The next stage involved the child controlling his or her own behavior through overt verbalizations. Finally, by the age of five or six, the child's behavior was controlled by his or her own covert verbalizations. Jenson referred to verbal control of behavior as "verbal mediation." He defined verbal mediation as "talking to oneself in relevant ways when confronted with something to be learned, a problem to be solved, or a concept to be attained" (1966, p. 101). This developmental sequence generally results in the verbal mediation ability becoming automatic. These theories led to the development of interventions that attempted to modify behaviors through self-statements.

Summary of the Origin of CBM

The origins of cognitive behavior modification represent an integration of a number of schools of thought. This integration was evident in Kendall and Hollon's definition of cognitive behavior modification:

> The cognitive-behavioral approach . . .is a purposeful combination of the performance-oriented and methodologically rigorous behavioral techniques with the treatment and evaluation of cognitive-mediational phenomena. Thus internal as well as environmental variables are targets for treatment and are scientifically evaluated as contributors to behavior change. (1979, p. 3)

PROCEDURES OF COGNITIVE BEHAVIOR MODIFICATION

Self-Instructional Training

Luria's (1961) developmental theory is the basis for self-instructional training. As is the case with all normal developmental sequences, there are children for whom the normal sequence for self-regulation goes awry. It either does not occur or it occurs only partially. These children are deficient in the ability to use internal speech to control behavior. Children that have not developed mediational skills will have difficulties in solving problems. Meichenbaum and Goodman (1971) investigated this deficiency in hyperactive and impulsive children. They found that these youngsters had deficiencies in verbal mediation abilities. In a series of investigations, Meichenbaum and his colleagues attempted to duplicate Luria's developmental sequence as an intervention for children deficient in behavioral control. In these investigations, Meichenbaum asked:

> Could we systematically train hyperactive, impulsive youngsters to alter their problem-solving styles, to think before they act, in short to talk to themselves differently? Could we, in light of the specific mediational deficits observed, teach the children how to: (a) comprehend the task, (b) spontaneously produce mediators and strategies, and (c) use such mediators to guide, monitor, and control their performances? (1977, p. 31)

The remedial sequence in Meichenbaum and Goodman's self-instructional training had five basic steps:

Step 1:   *Cognitive modeling.* The caregiver models task performance while self-instructing aloud. The child observes in this stage.

Step 2:   *External guidance.* The child performs the same task under the caregiver's direction.

Step 3:   *Overt self-instructions.* The child performs the same task, self-instructing aloud.

Step 4:   *Faded self-instructions.* The child performs the task while whispering the instructions.

Step 5:   *Covert self-instructions.* The child performs the task using covert self-instructions.

Meichenbaum and Goodman (1971) taught this process to the impulsive children in the study using several performance-relevant tasks. The process involved the following content:

1. *Problem definition:* For example, "What do I have to do?"
2. *Attention focusing* and *response guidance:* For example, "What is it I have to do?"
3. *Self-reinforcement:* For example, "I did a good job."

4. *Self-evaluative, coping skills,* and *error correction:* For example, "Okay, I can start over again."

The researchers used a variety of tasks (games, complex problems, etc.) to teach the children to use self-instructions to control nonverbal behaviors. The tasks were chosen because they required children to think and plan prior to taking action. The results of these studies indicated that hyperactive, impulsive children could be taught to think before acting. They could learn to "stop, look, and listen."

Self-instructional training has also been used with aggressive children. Aggressive children tend to react to problem situations in a very impulsive manner, not taking time to "stop and think" or consider alternatives in responding to provocative situations.

Camp, Blom, Hebert, and Van Doornick (1977) examined the use of self-instructional training with these youngsters. The primary purpose of these studies was to teach aggressive children to engage in coping self-instructions when responding to provocations. *Coping* refers to the child's ability to deal with perceived aversive events in a constructive rather than negative manner (e.g., walking away from a perceived insult rather than starting a fight). Camp et al. (1977) developed the *Think Aloud* program to teach aggressive boys to use coping self-instructions. The self-instructional training methods were very similar to those developed by Meichenbaum and Goodman. The *Think Aloud* program attempted to train the aggressive boys in using self-instructions in a problem-solving sequence. The children were taught to identify the problem, generate a solution, monitor their use of the solution, and evaluate their performance by asking and answering the following questions: What is my problem? What is my plan? Am I using my plan? How did I do?

Essentially, self-instruction is the use of personal verbal prompts. Caregivers training children in self-instruction teach them to identify and guide themselves using these prompts.

A point that has been stressed throughout this book is that caregivers should approach behavior management from a proactive or preventive rather than a totally reactive manner. That is, there are many modifications we can make in the environment, the child, and/or ourselves that will serve to prevent behavioral problems. When task demands outweigh a child's performance capabilities, behavior problems may occur. For example, when an assignment is too difficult for a child, he or she may act out or become noncompliant to escape the task. It has been theorized that many behavior problems actually stem from learning problems. Torgeson (1982) has stated that learning problems in children might be due to a failure to apply basic abilities efficiently by using effective task strategies. Children who manifest these failures have been referred to as inactive learners (Torgeson, 1982). To remediate these inefficient learning strategies, caregivers should assess the cognitive task strategies needed for competence in a particular area. If these task strategies are taught to children, enabling them to become more active, self-regulating learners, the subsequent academic improvements may lead to improvements in appropriate behavior (Ryan, Weed, & Short, 1986). In this way we can act in a proactive rather than a reactive manner to prevent behavior problems.

Interventions using self-instructional procedures were originally devised for the purpose of altering behavior problems in children. However, these procedures have also been extended to academic interventions, particularly in the area of academic strategy training (Lloyd, 1980).

Self-instructional procedures, when applied to academic performance, are designed to help learners improve their academic problem-solving behaviors. The basic assumptions of CBM listed by Hughes (1988) apply when these strategies are used to improve academics. These assumptions are: (1) behavior is mediated by cognitive events; (2) a change in cognitive mediating events results in a change in behavior; and (3) all persons are active participants in their own learning.

In designing CBM strategies, researchers conduct a cognitive task analysis of the processes involved and determine what processes are used by students who are academically successful. Researchers then develop a training procedure that will enhance the use of these processes (Wong, 1989). The purpose of these training procedures is to help learners improve their academic performance by using cognitive mediation strategies.

The basic procedures in many of these interventions are similar. The teacher models the processes while using self-instructions, students then follow the examples, first overtly, and then covertly (Meichenbaum, 1977). According to Meichenbaum, the teacher modeling provides a window on the thinking processes. Eventually by learning the strategies through modeling and self-instructions the students take over their own learning.

Rinehart, Stahl, and Erickson (1986) taught summarization to grade school students using modeling and self-instructional training. The students were taught to produce summaries of reading material that included main and supporting ideas. The teachers in this study first explained to the students the purpose of summarization. Following explanations the teachers modeled writing summaries of sample paragraphs. The teachers overtly self-instructed while producing the summaries. The children did similar self-instructing. Next the teachers would model monitoring of the summaries using the following instructions: "Have I found the overall idea that the paragraph or group of paragraphs is about? Have I found the most important information that tells more about the overall idea? Have I used information that is not directly about the overall idea? Have I used any information more than once?" Students then completed summaries while the teacher provided feedback. By means of this strategy, the teacher eventually extended the summarization procedure to longer paragraphs. The researchers found that the students trained in the procedure, when compared to students not trained, improved their recall of main ideas.

In an example of a self-instructional program to teach writing skills to students with learning disabilities, Graham and Harris (1985) developed an instructional program based in part on Meichenbaum's (1977) self-instructional training. In teaching the program, the researchers assessed the student's level of performance, described the learning strategy, and modeled the strategy using self-instructions. The student practiced the steps of the strategy using self-instructions, was trained in data collection, and was trained to generalize the strategy. In modeling the strategy the teacher used the following self-instructions:

- *Problem definition:* What is it I have to do? I have to write a good story. Good stories make sense and use many action words.
- *Planning:* Look at the picture and write down good action words. Think of a good story. Write my story—make good sense and use good action words.
- *Self-evaluation:* Read my story and ask "Did I write a good story? Did I use action words?" Fix my story—can I use more good action words?
- *Self-reinforcement:* That was a great story.

After modeling the story, the teacher and student discussed the importance of using self-instructions. The student was asked to identify the self-instructions and to write examples of self-instructions in his or her own words. The self-control strategy training resulted in increases in student performance above baseline levels. The authors concluded that self-control strategy training improved and maintained composition skills among children with learning disabilities.

When using self-instructional training to teach academics, caregivers do not need to adhere precisely to any formula, but instead can follow a general procedural outline. Whether teaching a child to do long division or to do a household chore, the teacher or parent can use cognitive behavior modification by modeling the task and self-instructing while modeling. Through self-instructions the child is taught to do a kind of thinking they could not, or would not, otherwise do (Meichenbaum & Asarnow, 1979). The child's internal dialogue is used to facilitate performance.

The caregiver should use the following guidelines when using cognitive behavior modification to teach children skills or strategies. First, the caregiver should determine what it is the child needs to know and what is the current level of performance. Second, the caregiver must describe the strategy to be taught and model it to the child while using self-instructions. Third, the child should practice the strategy using self-instructions under the guidance of the caregiver. The self-instructions are spoken aloud. It is important at this stage that the child have as many opportunities to practice as possible. Fourth, when the child can successfully perform the strategy under controlled practice conditions using overt self-instructions, the child is allowed to independently practice using covert self-instructions. Students should be encouraged to monitor their use of strategies and to continue to use them. Student motivation can be increased by explaining that the skills that are being taught will help to increase performance in academic subjects.

For example, if the caregiver had determined that the child could not do long division, he or she would decide on a strategy for teaching the skill to the child. If the caregiver decided to use the divide, multiply, subtract, bring down, check model (Burkell, Schneider, & Pressley, 1990) to teach the child, he or she would explain the model and how it is used. The caregiver would then model the strategy using self-instructions (first I divide, the next step is to multiply, etc.) while doing a long division problem to successful completion. The next step would involve having the child practice long division problems while the caretaker gives the self-instructions. The child would then practice long division using self-instructions (still under the caretaker's guidance) until he or she had mastered the strategy. When the caretaker is satisfied that the child has mastered the self-instructional procedure, the child should independently practice the skill using the self-instructional strategy covertly. Evaluation of the success of the cognitive-behavioral procedures must take place during training and on completion of training.

Whatever the purpose and content of training, the methods of training will be similar. Kendall (1977) suggested that the following five basic types of instructions be taught to children:

1. *Problem definition instructions:* The child first learns to define the problem.
2. *Problem approach instructions:* The child verbalizes potential strategies to solve the problem.
3. *Attention focusing instructions:* The child focuses his or her attention on the problem by asking if he or she is using the strategy.
4. *Coping statement instructions:* If a mistake is made, the child uses statements to cope with the error and to encourage another try.
5. *Self-reinforcement instructions:* The child reinforces him or herself for doing a good job.

In using self-instructional training to teach children to be more reflective and deliberate in their responses to problems, the following guidelines will be helpful.

First, it is important that caregivers model the self-instruction process. Caregivers should perform the task and verbally self-instruct while the child is observing. It is important in modeling that caregivers use the same self-instructional process as the child will be using.

Second, caregivers must consider the ability of the child. It has been shown that if children need practice prior to performing a task or if they are unable to perform a task, self-instructions can actually interfere with their performance. Self-instructions will not enable children to perform tasks that are not in their repertoires. Similarly children must be capable of understanding the statements to be used.

Third, caretakers should systematically fade their presence in the process. If self-instructional training is to be effective, the child must be able to self-instruct independently of the caretaker.

Last, caretakers must systematically reinforce the child's accurate use of self-instructions and demonstrations of target behaviors.

Problem-Solving Training

Children are faced with conflicts, choices, and problems daily. Successful problem-solving is necessary for effective coping and independence. The ability to confront and solve these problems successfully is an important factor in social and emotional adjustment. The inability to solve problems in an effective manner can lead to future social and emotional difficulties. Researchers have attempted to remediate difficulties in problem-solving through formal training. The training represents a form of self-instruction to teach procedures for systematically approaching, evaluating, and solving interpersonal problems (Braswell & Kendall, 1988). Training in problem-solving has been effective in reducing behavior problems and aggression, controlling impulsivity, and increasing appropriate social interaction (Harris, 1982).

Goldstein (1988) stated that problem-solving typically involves a stepwise sequence of problem definition, identification of alternative solutions, choice of an optimal solution, implementation of the solution, and evaluation of the solution's effectiveness. D'Zurilla and Goldfried (1971) presented five steps that could be used to teach problem solving ability:

Step 1:   *Orientation to the problem.* Help the child learn to recognize problems and to realize that one can deal with problems in appropriate ways.

Step 2:   *Definition of the problem.* Clearly define the problem and any factors related to it.

Step 3:   *Generation of alternatives.* The caregiver and child should think of as many solutions to the problem as possible.

Step 4:   *Decision-making.* The caregiver and the child should consider all alternatives generated in the previous step and devise a plan for implementing the chosen alternative.

Step 5:   *Verification.* Implement the plan and monitor the results. If the problem is not solved, the caregiver and child should start over at step 1.

The seminal work in problem-solving was done by Spivak, Shure, and colleagues in the mid- to late 1970s. The training program developed by Spivak and Shure (1974) was called *interpersonal cognitive problem solving* (ICPS). The program was designed to teach children *how* to think, not *what* to think (Goldstein, 1988). Spivak and Shure believed that many caregivers did not effectively teach problem-solving. For example, in dealing with a young child who hits another child, caretakers might typically respond with one of the following actions: (1) They might demand that the behavior stop ("Stop because I said so"). (2) They might explain why an action is inappropriate ("You might hurt your brother"). (3) They might try to help the child understand the effect of the situation ("That hurts your brother's feelings"). (4) They might isolate the child ("Stay in your room until you're ready to play appropriately"). These responses have serious limitations if the caregiver's goal is to help the child develop effective ways of handling personal and interpersonal problems because the caretaker does the thinking for the child.

In ICPS children are taught a problem-solving process rather than solutions to problems. The core of the program is six specific problem-solving skills that are taught to children. The ICPS attempts to train children to be competent in these six skill areas:

1. *Alternative solution thinking:* Spivak and Shure felt that the ability to generate different options or potential solutions to a problem was central to effective problem-solving.
2. *Consequential thinking:* The ability to consider consequences that a behavior might lead to; this goes beyond the consideration of alternatives to the consideration of the consequences of potential solutions.
3. *Causal thinking:* The ability to relate one event to another over time with regard to why a particular event happened or will happen.
4. *Interpersonal sensitivity:* The ability to perceive that an interpersonal problem exists.
5. *Means-ends thinking:* The step-by-step planning done in order to reach a given goal. Means-ends thinking involves insight, forethought, and the ability to consider alternative goals.
6. *Perspective taking:* The ability of the individual to recognize and take into account the fact that different people have different motives and may take different actions.

Siegel and Spivak (1973) also developed an ICPS training program for older adolescents and adults. It is designed to teach basic problem-solving skills. The program teaches four problem-solving steps: (1) recognition of the problem, (2) definition of the problem, (3) alternative ways of solving the problem, and (4) deciding which solution is the best way to solve the problem.

Goldstein (1988), drawing on the work done by Spivak and Shure, developed a problem-solving training program as part of the *Prepare Curriculum*. The *Prepare Curriculum* is a series of courses designed to teach adolescents and younger children prosocial competencies. It is specifically designed for youngsters demonstrating prosocial deficiencies that fall toward either end of a continuum defined at one extreme by chronic aggressiveness, antisocial behavior, and juvenile delinquency and at the other extreme by chronic withdrawal, asocial behavior, and social isolation. The problem-solving course is taught to groups of students over an eight-week period. Group structure is provided by a set of rules and procedures explained at the beginning of a session. During each session, a poster that shows the problem-solving process being covered during that session is displayed. The program also uses a "problem log." An example of a program log is provided in Figure 6.1. The problem log is to be filled out by the students. The logs are to be an accurate record of any prob-

Figure 6.1. *Program log example.*

Source: From *The prepare curriculum: Teaching prosocial competencies,* by Arnold P. Goldstein, 1988, Champaign, IL: Research Press. Copyright 1988 by the author. Reprinted by permission.

Problem Log

Name: _____   Date _____

What is the problem? Describe it (who is involved, where did it happen, and what happened?).

What do you want to happen?

What did you do or say to solve the problem?

Did your choice solve the problem?

How well did it work (circle one)?

1	2	3	4	5
Poorly	Not so well	Okay	Good	Great

Homework:

---

lems that students encounter. The purpose of the problem log is to help students figure out what their problem situations are and to assist them to begin thinking about ways of handling the problems.

Problem logs are also used in role plays. Skills taught in the program include:

◆ *Stop and think.* Students in the program are taught that when a problem is encountered they must stop and think or they might decide too quickly. They are to use this time to think of alternate ways to handle the problem.

◆ *Problem identification.* Once the students realize a problem exists and have stopped to think, they have to state the problem clearly and specifically.

◆ *Gathering information from their own perspective.* Students have to decide how they see a problem and gather information about the problem before acting. If all the information is not available, trainees are taught to ask for it.

◆ *Gathering information from other's perspectives.* Students learn the necessity of looking at situations from other people's points of view.

◆ *Alternatives.* Students are taught that to make a good choice in any situation requires more than one way of acting.

◆ *Evaluating consequences and outcomes.* Once trainees are taught to consider a number of alternatives, they are told they must consider the consequences of each. Once a decision is made it must be evaluated.

A session-by-session outline of Goldstein's *Problem Solving Training* program is presented in the following list. The program is designed as an eight-week program. According to Goldstein, however, it may take several sessions longer depending on individual needs. Sessions may be extended over two or three weeks because all participants are given opportunities to practice skills by role playing and to receive feedback on his or her performance.

Session 1: Introduction

Rationale

Rules and procedures

Overview of problem-solving steps

Problem log

Review Session 1

Session 2: Stop and Think

Rationale

Review Session 1

Stop and think

Be a detective

Role play: stop and think

Review Session 2

Session 3: Problem Identification

Rationale

Review Session 2

Learn to define (What is the problem?)

Ways to define a problem

Role play: stop and think + problem identification

Review Session 3

Session 4: Gathering Information/Own Perspective

Rationale

Review Session 3

Fact or opinion (What do I see? What are the facts?)

Information (What do I see? What do I need to know?)

Role play: stop and think + problem identification + gathering information from own perspective

Review Session 4

Session 5: Gathering Information/Other's Perspectives

Rationale

Review Session 4

Other's views (What do others see? What do others think?)

Other's emotions (What do others feel?)

Role play: stop and think + problem identification + gathering information/own and other's perspectives

Review Session 5

Session 6: Alternatives

Rationale

Review Session 5

Options (What can I do or say?)

Brainstorming (What are my choices?)

Role play: stop and think + problem identification + gathering information/own and other's perspectives + alternatives

Review Session 6

Session 7: Evaluating Consequences and Outcomes

Rationale

Review Session 6

Consequences (What will happen if I do or say that?)

Choices (How do I decide what to do?)

Role play: stop and think + problem identification + gathering information/own and other's perspectives + evaluating consequences and outcomes

Review Session 7

Session 8: Practice

Rationale

Review Session 7

Role play: stop and think + problem identification + gathering informa-
tion/own and other's perspectives + evaluating consequences and
outcomes

Reinforcement[1]

Anger-Control Training

In anger-control training, children are taught to inhibit or control anger and
aggressive behavior through self-instructions. Three well-known anger training procedures are those developed by Novaco (1975), Feindler and her colleagues (Feindler & Fremouw, 1983; Feindler, Marriott, & Iwata, 1984), and
Goldstein and Glick (1987). These programs train children to respond to internal or external provocations with anger-control procedures rather than anger
and aggression.

Novaco defined anger arousal as an affective stress reaction. He stated:

> . . .anger arousal is a response to perceived environmental demands—most com-
> monly, aversive psychosocial events. Anger arousal results from particular
> appraisal of aversive events. External circumstances provoke anger only as medi-
> ated by their meaning to the individual. (1979, pp. 252-253)

Novaco noted the importance of the individual's appraisal of events. Because
Novaco believed that anger was created, influenced, and maintained by self-
statements, he designed a program based on Meichenbaum's self-instructional
training. The purpose of the training was to develop an individual's ability to
respond appropriately to stressful events. The goals of the program were to: (1)
prevent maladaptive anger from occurring, (2) enable the individual to regulate arousal when provocation occurred, and (3) provide the person with the
skills to manage the provocation.

Anger-control intervention consisted of three stages: cognitive preparation, skill acquisition, and application training. In the cognitive preparation
phase, trainees were educated about anger arousal and its determinants, the
identification of circumstances that trigger anger, the positive and negative
functions of anger, and anger-control techniques as coping strategies. In the
skill acquisition phase, trainees learned cognitive and behavioral coping skills.
Trainees were taught to recognize anger and to use alternative coping strategies. The self-instructional element of training was emphasized in this phase.
In the final phase, application training, the trainee practiced the skills taught
through role playing and homework assignments.

The self-instructional component of this intervention consisted of self-
statements in the four stages of the provocation sequence: (1) preparation for

---

[1]   *Source:*   From *The prepare curriculum: Teaching prosocial competencies,* by Arnold
P. Goldstein, 1988, Champaign, IL: Research Press. Copyright 1988 by the author.
Reprinted by permission.

provocation, (2) impact and confrontation, (3) coping with arousal, and (4) reflecting on the provocation. Some of these self-instructions are as follows:

Preparing for provocation

This could be a rough situation, but I know how to deal with it. I can work out a plan to handle this. Easy does it. Remember, stick to the issues and don't take it personally.

There won't be any need for an argument. I know what to do.

Impact and confrontation

As long as I keep my cool, I'm in control of the situation.

You don't need to prove yourself. Don't make more out of this than you have to.

There is no point in getting mad. Think of what you have to do.

Look for positives and don't jump to conclusions.

Coping with arousal

My muscles are getting tight. Relax and slow things down.

Time to take a deep breath. Let's take the issue point by point.

My anger is a signal of what I need to do. Time for problem solving.

He probably wants me to get angry, but I'm going to deal with it constructively.

Subsequent reflection—Conflict unresolved

Forget about the aggravation. Thinking about it only makes you upset. Try to shake it off. Don't let it interfere with your job.

Remember relaxation. It's a lot better than anger.

Don't take it personally. It's probably not as serious as you think.

Subsequent reflection—Conflict resolved

I handled that one pretty well. That's doing a good job.

I could have gotten more upset than it was worth.

My pride can get me into trouble, but I'm doing better at this all the time.

I actually got through that without getting angry.[2]

---

[2] *Source:*   Novaco, Raymond W. (1979). The cognitive regulation of anger and stress. In P. C. Kendall and S. D. Hollon (Eds.), *Cognitive-behavioral interventions: Theory, research, and procedures* (p. 269). New York: Academic Press. Copyright 1979 by Academic Press Inc. Reprinted by permission.

In the late 1970s and early 1980s, Feindler and her colleagues researched and refined the techniques of anger-control training. In a series of investigations, support was provided for the cognitive preparation and skill acquisition phases and self-instructional training developed by Novaco. The investigations refined the three processes of Novaco's training (i.e., cognitive preparation, skill acquisition, and application training) to include five sequences to be taught to students:

1. *Cues:* The physical signals of anger arousal.
2. *Triggers:* The events and internal appraisals of those events that serve as provocations.
3. *Reminders:* Novaco's self-instructional statements that were used to reduce anger arousal.
4. *Reducers:* Techniques such as deep breathing and pleasant imagery that could be used along with reminders to reduce anger arousal.
5. *Self-evaluation:* The opportunity to self-reinforce or self-correct.

Goldstein and Glick (1987) added to the work of Meichenbaum, Novaco, and Feindler in developing *Anger Control Training.* The goals of anger-control training were to teach children and adolescents to understand what caused them to become angry and aggressive and to master anger reduction techniques. According to Goldstein:

> Many youngsters believe that in many situations they have no choice: The only way for them to respond is with aggression. Although they may perceive situations in this way, it is the goal of Anger Control Training to give them the skills necessary to make a choice. By learning what causes them to be angry and by learning to use a series of anger reduction techniques, participating trainees will become more able to stop their almost "automatic" aggressive responses long enough to consider constructive alternatives. (1988, p. 256)

Anger-control training consists of modeling, role playing, and performance feedback. Group leaders describe and model the anger-control techniques and conflict situations in which they may be used. In role playing, the students take part in role plays in which they practice the just modeled techniques. Role plays are of actual provocative encounters provided by the students. Each role playing session is followed by a brief performance feedback period. In this phase the group leaders point out to the child involved in the role playing how well they used the technique. Group leaders also provide reinforcement following role plays.

A unique aspect of the program used in the role play situations is the "hassle log" shown in Figure 6.2. The hassle log is a structured questionnaire that students fill out on actual provocative encounters. The trainee has to answer questions concerning where they were when the hassle occurred, what happened, who else was involved, what the trainee did, how they handled themselves, and how angry they were. The log is constructed so that even young children can fill it out; written responses are not required and children

Figure 6.2.   Hassle log example.

Source: From *The prepare curriculum: Teaching prosocial competencies* by Arnold P. Goldstein, 1988, Champaign, IL: Research Press. Copyright 1988 by the author. Reprinted by permission.

Hassle Log

Name _____ Date _____

Morning _____   Afternoon _____   Evening _____

Where were you?
Classroom _____   Bathroom _____   Off grounds
Dorm _____   Team Office _____   Halls _____
Gym _____   Dining room _____   On a job_____
Recreation room _____   Outside/on grounds _____
Other_____

What happened?
Somebody teased me _____
Somebody took something of mine _____
Somebody told me something _____
Somebody was doing something I didn't like _____
I did something wrong _____
Somebody started fighting with me _____
Other _____

Who was that somebody:
Another student _____   Another adult _____   Other _____
Teacher _____   Staff member _____

What did you do?
Hit back _____   Told adult _____
Ran away _____   Walked away calmly _____
Yelled _____   Talked it out _____
Cried _____   Told peer _____
Broke something _____   Ignored it _____
Was restrained _____   Used anger control _____

How did you handle yourself?

      1   2   3   4   5

Poorly Not so well Okay   Good   Great

How angry were you?
Very angry _____   Moderately angry _____
Moderately angry but still OK _____   Not angry _____

---

simply check off options on the form. The trainees complete a form for each provocative encounter, whether they handle it in an appropriate manner or not. The advantage of the "hassle log" is that it provides accurate pictures of actual provocative encounters that occur, it helps trainees to learn about what makes them angry and how they handle themselves, and it provides role playing material.

During the 10-week training period, the group leaders also teach (1) the A-B-Cs of aggressive behavior (A—What led up to the behavior? B—What did you do? C—What were the consequences?); (2) how to identify cues and triggers; (3) the use of reminders and anger reducers; (4) the importance of thinking ahead (the consequences of anger); and (5) the nature of the angry behavior cycle (identifying anger-provoking behavior and changing it). A session-by-session outline of Goldstein's Anger Control Training program is presented here:

Week 1: Introduction

1. Explain the goals of Anger Control Training and "sell it to the youngsters."
2. Explain the rules for participating and the training procedures.
3. Give initial assessments of the A-B-Cs of aggressive behavior:
   a. What led up to it?
   b. What did you do?
   c. What were the consequences?
4. Review goals, procedures, and A-B-Cs; give out binders.

Week 2: Cues and Anger Reducers 1, 2, and 3.

1. Review first session.
2. Introduce the hassle log.
3. Discuss how to know when you are angry (cues).
4. Discuss what to do when you know you are angry.
   Anger reducer 1: Deep breathing
   Anger reducer 2: Backward counting
   Anger reducer 3: Pleasant imagery
5. Role play: Cues + anger reducers.
6. Review hassle log, cues, and anger reducers 1, 2, and 3.

Week 3: Triggers

1. Review second session.
2. Discuss understanding what makes you angry (triggers).
   a. External triggers
   b. Internal triggers
3. Role play: Triggers + cues + anger reducer(s).
4. Review triggers, cues, and anger reducers 1, 2, and 3.

Week 4: Reminders (Anger Reducer 4)

1. Review third session.
2. Introduce reminders.
3. Model using reminders.
4. Role play: Triggers + cues + reminders + anger reducer(s).
5. Review reminders.

Week 5: Self-Evaluation

1. Review fourth session.
2. Introduce self-evaluation.
   a. Self-rewarding
   b. Self-coaching
3. Role play: Triggers + cues + reminders + anger reducer(s) + self-evaluation.

4.   Review self-evaluation.

Week 6: Thinking Ahead (Anger Reducer 5)

1.   Review fifth session.
2.   Introduce thinking ahead.
     a.   Short- and long-term consequences
     b.   Most and least serious consequences
     c.   Internal, external, and social consequences
3.   Role play: "If-then" thinking ahead.
4.   Role play: Triggers + cues + reminders + anger reducer(s).
5.   Review thinking ahead.

Week 7: The Angry Behavior Cycle

1.   Review sixth session.
2.   Introduce the Angry Behavior Cycle
     a.   Identifying your own anger-provoking behavior
     b.   Changing your own anger-provoking behavior.
3.   Role play: Triggers + cues + reminders + anger reducer(s) + self-evaluation.
4.   Review the angry behavior cycle.

Week 8: Rehearsal of Full Sequence

1.   Review seventh session.
2.   Role play: Introduce using new behaviors (skills) in place of aggression.
3.   Role play: Triggers + cues + reminders + anger reducer(s) + interpersonal skill + self-evaluation.

Week 9: Rehearsal of Full Sequence

1.   Review hassle logs.
2.   Role play: Triggers + cues + reminders + anger reducer(s) + interpersonal skill + self-evaluation.

Week 10: Overall Review

1.   Review hassle logs.
2.   Recap anger control techniques.
3.   Role play: Triggers + cues + reminders + anger reducer(s) + interpersonal skill + self-evaluation.
4.   Reinforce and encourage to continue.[3]

Self-Management Training

In self-management training, children are taught procedures that are used to change or modify their behavior. Self-management training allows caregivers to teach children techniques that will make them less dependent on the caregiver's environmental manipulations. Procedures used in self-management

---

[3]   *Source:*   From *The prepare curriculum: Teaching prosocial competencies* by Arnold P. Goldstein, 1988, Champaign, IL: Research Press. Copyright 1988 by the author. Reprinted by permission.

training include self-monitoring, self-evaluation, and self-reinforcement. Although each of these procedures is often discussed separately, in reality they are often combined and taught as self-management packages.

Self-Monitoring

Self-monitoring or self-recording requires the child to record the frequency of a particular behavior or behaviors. It has been demonstrated that having a child collect self-monitoring data may often result in increases in desired behavior. This may be because self-monitoring procedures force the child to monitor his or her behavior. Baer (1984) stated that a further reason for behavioral improvement is that self-monitoring provides cues that increase the child's awareness of potential consequences for a particular behavior. Researchers have noted that behavior often improves simply because the student is collecting the behavioral data. Broden, Hall, and Mitts (1971) investigated the effects of self-monitoring on two disruptive students. They found that the act of recording their disruptive behaviors dramatically decreased these behaviors. This has been termed a *reactive effect*. That is, the behavior may change in the desired direction simply as a function of self-monitoring (Alberto & Troutman, 1990).

To teach self-monitoring, the caregiver must train the child to collect data on his or her behavior. Usually the data collection system requires the child to record the occurrence or nonoccurrence of the behavior. The collected data provide the child and the caregiver with feedback regarding the frequency of the behavior.

Self-monitoring systems have been used with event recording procedures (Broden, Hall, and Mitts, 1971; Kerr & Nelson, 1989) and time sampling procedures (Barkley, Copeland, & Sivage, 1980; Glynn, Thomas, & Shee, 1973). A case study of a self-monitoring procedure using event recording was provided by Kerr & Nelson (1989). The case study was of a third-grade student named Keith. Keith was constantly leaving his seat. If reprimanded by the teacher, Keith would return to his seat but would soon be out of his seat again. The student was aware that the behavior was disruptive and inappropriate but was seemingly incapable of exercising the necessary self-control to remain seated. A self-monitoring program was instituted in which Keith was taught to self-record his out-of-seat behavior. Self-recording was done on a form in which Keith was to put a tally mark down each time he left his seat without permission. The self-recording procedure was combined with a contingency contract to increase effectiveness. Figure 6.3 is an example of a self-monitoring form using an event sampling procedure. A self-monitoring intervention using a time sampling procedure was used by Barkley, Copeland, and Sivage (1980) to increase on-task behavior in three hyperactive students. The students were given self-monitoring forms. An audio tape was prerecorded with an audible tone that sounded randomly. At the signal the boys were to ask themselves if they were on-task as described prior to the study. If the students were on-task they were to record a tally mark; if they were not no mark was recorded. Bonus points were also given if the student's self-recording matched that of an

Figure 6.3 *Example of a self-monitoring form using event sampling.*

Name: _____

Date: _____

Environment: _____

////   //

Total "/" marks: 6

Record a "/" each time you talk without permission during this class period.

independent observer. Figure 6.4 is an example of a self-monitoring form using time sampling.

Caregivers may be concerned with children's accuracy in self-monitoring. In a number of investigations children have accurately recorded their behaviors, while in others, children have not been accurate. An important question is whether accuracy is a significant variable during self-monitoring. O'Leary and Dubay (1979) demonstrated that the accuracy of a child's self-collected data did not necessarily correlate with the child's behavior or academic performance. That is, when trying to increase appropriate behaviors, the act of self-monitoring alone may be more important than the accuracy of the child's data.

However, if a child is scheduled to be reinforced on the basis of self-monitoring data, some researchers believe that contingencies regarding the accura-

Figure 6.4. *Example of a self-monitoring form using time sampling.*

Name: _____

Date: _____

Environment: _____

Start time: _____ Stop time: _____

Intervals (40 1-minute intervals)

Every time you hear the beep, record a "+" if you were paying attention or a "−" if you were not paying attention.

cy of the data should apply. Otherwise, children may rate their behavior as appropriate to receive reinforcement even when inappropriate (Gross and Wojnilower, 1984). Thus children may be reinforced for inaccurate self-monitoring. When accuracy is a concern, matching procedures may be employed to check the child's data. When using matching procedures a child's data are matched with the recorded data of independent observers. The child is reinforced when his or her self-monitoring data closely match the data collected by the independent observer. In an example of a matching strategy, Drabman, Spitalnik, and O'Leary (1973) rewarded children for self-recorded data that matched the data recorded by teachers. The children were told that they would be able to keep all their points if their self-recorded data were within one point of the teachers recording. If student and teacher data matched exactly, the student would receive a bonus point. However, if the children were off by more than one point, they would lose all their points. The study demonstrated that the children could record their own behavior reliably. Following a period of student-teacher matching the researchers began to fade the matching procedures. This was accomplished by matching initially with only 50% of the randomly selected students. The percentage of students for matching was decreased gradually to zero. Throughout the reduction period children continued to self-record accurately.

In addition to reinforcing the child for matching, the child should also be reinforced for appropriate behavior exhibited during the self-monitoring program. The matching procedure should be faded as the child becomes more independent and accurate in his or her monitoring skills as in the Drabman, Spitalnik, and O'Leary (1973) study.

Children will usually have to be taught self-monitoring by caregivers. Programs to teach children to use these strategies should include the following components (Wolery, Bailey, & Sugai, 1988; Alberto & Troutman, 1990):

- ◆ *Select a target behavior.* Research has suggested that self-monitoring tends to be more effective with behaviors that have been previously managed by external management procedures. Therefore, when selecting a target behavior, the caregiver should select a behavior already managed by an external procedure. It is preferable, when possible, to select a positive behavior to monitor (e.g., raising your hand to speak rather than talking without permission).
- ◆ *Define the target behavior.* The caregiver and child together should define the behavior to be monitored. The child must be absolutely clear as to what is expected. The caregiver and child must agree on what constitutes an occurrence of the behavior to be monitored.
- ◆ *Monitor the target behavior.* Select an appropriate system of data collection and train the child in its use. The child should be trained to a high level of accuracy before concluding training. The child can also be trained to summarize and chart the data in addition to recording it. When the self-monitoring is initiated, random reliability checks may be conducted to ensure accurate recording.

♦ *Evaluate progress.* The child and caregiver should have frequent evaluation meetings so that the caregivers can provide feedback and reinforcement.

♦ *Fade self-monitoring.* When the child's behavior approaches desired levels, the self-monitoring procedures should be faded. This can be done by increasing the intervals between self-monitoring periods, by using self-monitoring less frequently, and by other fading techniques.

A classroom example of self-monitoring is presented in Vignette 6.1.

Vignette 6.1.   *A Classroom Example of Self-Monitoring.*

Nick, a second-grade student, blurted out answers in class without first raising his hand. He realized that his behavior was disruptive to the class but did not seem to be able to control it. Nick's teacher, Miss Quam, had put Nick on a behavior management system in which he was rewarded with a point every time he raised his hand for permission to speak. The system seemed to work, but Miss Quam wanted Nick to be able to control the behavior himself rather than having it controlled by an external management system. She decided to implement a self-monitoring system with reinforcement.

Miss Quam had a conference with Nick to explain the disruption caused by his blurting out answers in class. She explained that they would be working together to help Nick control this behavior. They talked about the fact that the class would not be disrupted if Nick raised his hand when he knew an answer. Together they practiced the desired behavior. Miss Quam also told Nick that he would be monitoring his own behavior. She explained to Nick that when he became aware of the correct behavior it would be easier for him to do it.

Nick was given a chart to record his hand-raising behavior. Every time Nick would raise his hand to get permission to answer a question, he was to put a slash mark on the chart. Miss Quam also marked each occasion of Nick raising his hand on a chart at her desk. At the end of each period, Nick and Miss Quam would compare charts. They would count the number of matching slashes and Nick would be given that number of points. Verbal praise would also be given. Together they practiced marking the chart. When Miss Quam was satisfied that Nick understood the procedure, she told him that they would start doing it in class the next day. Miss Quam told Nick that on Fridays they would review the charts for every day of the week to see if the procedure was helping.

The procedure was in place for two weeks and was very successful. Nick was raising his hand for permission to speak and very seldom blurted out an answer. During the evaluation meetings, Nick expressed a great deal of satisfaction with his newfound control. At this point Miss Quam decided to start fading the procedure. First she withdrew the point reinforcers. The next Monday Nick was told he only had to do the procedure twice a day rather than for each academic period. By Thursday he was told he had only to count once a day. A week later Nick was only recording his behavior on Mondays and Fridays. The hand-raising behavior continued at a high rate so Miss Quam told Nick they would only do the procedure once in a while. Following the cessation of the program, Miss Quam noted that Nick still raised his hand for permission to talk and very seldom blurted out in class.

Self-Evaluation

In self-evaluation or self-assessment the child compares his or her behavior against a preset standard to determine whether the performance meets a particular criterion (Cole, 1987). Maag (1989) referred to self-evaluation as self-monitoring followed by a covert evaluation of the behavior. Clark and McKenzie (1989) found that self-evaluation led to lower levels of disruptive behavior, increases in on-task behavior, and generalization across settings and teachers of the improved behaviors.

Smith, Young, West, Morgan, and Rhode (1988) trained four boys with behavior disorders in a self-evaluation procedure. The target behaviors were off-task and disruptive behaviors. The training was conducted in three phases. In the first phase the children were taught classroom rules. Behavior was rated on a five-point scale in accordance with how closely they followed the rules. The children rated their behavior on an evaluation card every 10 minutes. Each child was asked to record a "5" or "excellent" if he or she followed classroom rules and worked on assigned tasks for the entire interval; "4" or "very good" if he or she followed classroom rules and worked for the entire interval with the exception of one minor infraction; "3" or "average" if he or she followed the rules and worked without any serious offenses except for receiving two reminders to get to work; "2" or "below average" if he or she followed rules and worked for approximately half of the interval; "1" if he or she followed the rules and worked for half the interval but had to be separated from the group; and "0" or "unacceptable" if he or she did not follow classroom rules nor do any work during the interval. The self-evaluation card used by Smith et al. (1988) can be found in Figure 6.5. The children were told to rank their behavior on the scale and that their teachers would do the same. The teacher would mark each child's card to indicate her rating at the end of a certain period of time. The two scales would be compared and the children would receive points for matching or nearly matching the teacher. Points could be exchanged for tangible reinforcers.

In the second phase the children continued to evaluate their behavior, but they only matched evaluations with the teacher every 15 minutes. During the third phase children continued to evaluate themselves on the scale; however, they only matched evaluations with the teacher once every 30 minutes. Phase 3 was not as effective in reducing inappropriate behaviors as phases 1

Figure 6.5. *Self-evaluation card example.*

Source: Smith, D. J., Young, K. R., West, R. P., & Rhode, G. (1988). Reducing the disruptive behavior of junior high school students: A classroom self-management procedure. *Behavioral Disorders, 13,* 231–239. Copyright 1988 by Council for Children with Behavior Disorders. Reprinted by permission.

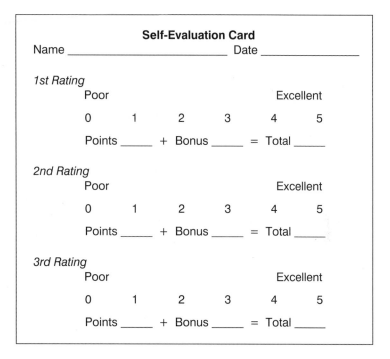

and 2. Results indicated that the self-evaluation procedures paired with teacher matching were effective in reducing off-task and disruptive behavior in the special education classroom. The authors concluded that self-evaluation paired with teacher matching was an effective intervention and that the procedures were effective even though the behaviors were not first brought under control by an external behavior management procedure. Data collected in regular classrooms did not show *treatment generalization* (see Chapter 4). According to the authors, this was anticipated because regular classroom teachers were unwilling or unable to implement the procedure. They suggested that peers in the regular classroom might be used in the program to match evaluations, thereby freeing the teachers from this responsibility.

Self-Reinforcement

In traditional behavior modification programs, the practitioner specifies the target behavior and delivers the reinforcers for performance of the behaviors. In many self-management packages the child chooses a reinforcer and delivers the reinforcer following appropriate behavior. This is referred to as *self-reinforcement.* Research has demonstrated that self-determined reinforcers can be as effective as or even more effective than caregiver-controlled reinforcers (Hayes, Rosenfarb, Wulfert, Munt, Korn, & Zettle, 1985).

Baer, Fowler, and Carden-Smith (1984) investigated a self-reinforcement strategy with a six-year-old boy who had behavioral disorders. The self-reinforcement consisted of teaching the boy to grade his daily assignments and to determine whether or not he had earned a reinforcer (a recess period). The researchers found that this procedure was an effective strategy for increasing on-task behavior and task accuracy.

Self-reinforcement, like reinforcement delivered by caregivers, must be delivered in a systematic and consistent manner. Research has indicated that initially reinforcement should be caregiver managed and delivered. As the child progresses, caregiver involvement should be decreased and the child's involvement increased. Wolery, Bailey, and Sugai (1988) offered the following guidelines for self-reinforcement:

- The child should be fluent at accurate self-monitoring.
- The child should be involved in setting the criteria for receiving reinforcement and selecting reinforcers.
- Caretakers should provide reinforcement for target behaviors displayed by the child, accurate matches between caregiver and child data, and accurate determination by the child of whether the criteria for reinforcement were met.
- Matching requirements and caregiver evaluation should be faded over time.
- Opportunities for the children to evaluate their performance, determine criteria for reinforcement, select reinforcers, and administer reinforcement should be systematically increased.
- Naturally occurring reinforcers should be used throughout the process.

Other factors that contribute to the maintenance of desired behavior are (1) continuous caregiver praise, (2) peer reinforcement for appropriate behavior, and (3) accurate self-evaluation (Drabman, Spitalnik, & O'Leary, 1973).

While most self-management packages include self-reinforcement, some have investigated the effectiveness of self-punishment. In self-punishment, the student is taught to punish rather than reinforce his or her own behaviors. In several investigations (Humphrey, Karoly, & Kirschenbaum, 1978; Kaufman & O'Leary, 1972) the self-punishment procedure used was response cost (see Chapter 8) in conjunction with a token economy (see Chapter 5). Self-punishment was compared with self-reinforcement in an investigation by Humphrey, Karoly, and Kirschenbaum (1978). The study took place in a chaotic elementary classroom. A self-reinforcement system and a self-punishment system were compared. The students in the self-reinforcement condition reinforced themselves with tokens for accurate performance on reading assignments. The students in the self-punishment condition began each morning with tokens and removed them for inaccurate work or failure to complete work on time. The researchers found that under both conditions the rate of attempted reading assignments was accelerated and accuracy was maintained. However, the self-reinforcement condition produced slightly better results.

Summary of Self-Management Training

According to Sugai and Lewis (1990), when teaching self-management skills to children, certain conditions must be maintained. During the pre-intervention phase of training, it is important that the child be involved. Together, the caregiver and child develop the goals of the self-management program as well as the criteria and contingencies necessary to meet the goals. The recording instrument must be developed at this time and should be simple and easy to use. The child must be trained in the use of the recording procedure. The caregiver needs to teach the procedure to the child and provide practice opportunities. Prior to implementing the procedure, the child must be as fluent as possible in self-monitoring. If a self-reinforcement component will be used, the caregiver should involve the child in selecting reinforcers. The child must then be trained in the use of the self-reinforcement procedure.

During the intervention phase of the procedure, a matching strategy is suggested. During this phase, the child is reinforced for appropriate behavior and accurate self-monitoring. Prompts should be provided to cue the child when to self-monitor and record (e.g., beeps on a recorder). The matching procedure, as well as the actual self-monitoring procedure, should be faded when the behavioral criteria are reached. Following the fading of the intervention, caregivers should continue to collect data to ensure that behaviors continue at appropriate levels in all settings. If the target behaviors fall below criteria the procedure may have to be reimplemented.

Sugai and Lewis (1990) suggested the following guidelines for increasing the effectiveness of self-monitoring strategies:

◆ The behavior to be self-managed should first be brought under external control so the child associates the appropriate behavior with reinforcement.

◆ Behavioral contracts for self-management can be used initially to provide structure.

◆ The child must have numerous opportunities to practice self-management with immediate feedback given.

◆ The child must be motivated to participate; this can be encouraged by involving the child in the procedure from the initial stages.

◆ To involve the child in the process and to increase motivation, caregivers should record and post the child's behavioral performance.

◆ The caregiver should periodically monitor the procedure and provide "booster" sessions if necessary.

Alternate Response Training

In alternate response training a child is taught an alternative or competing response that interferes with opportunities for an undesirable response to be emitted (Wolery, Bailey, & Sugai, 1988). If an alternative response already exists in the child's repertoire, it can be strengthened as the child is taught to use the alternative behavior. In using alternate response training a child must first be taught to self-monitor.

Relaxation training procedures designed to relieve stress and calm children have been investigated by researchers as an alternative response procedure. A widely used relaxation training procedure is progressive muscle relaxation (Maag, 1989). The training involves having children tense and relax muscles while focusing on the relaxation of particular parts of the body. Eventually the child focuses on relaxing the entire body. Muscle relaxation is a form of alternate response training that has been used to decrease disruptions and aggression and increase social skills and academic performance.

Robin, Schneider, and Dolnick (1976) developed an alternate response intervention called the *turtle technique*. The turtle technique is a procedure that was developed to teach aggressive students to manage their aggressive impulses. The procedure consists of teaching the students to pull their arms and legs close to their bodies, put their heads on their desks, and imagine that they are turtles withdrawing into their shells. The children were taught to do this when they perceived that a provocative situation was about to occur, they felt frustrated or angry, or a teacher or classmate called out "turtle." The children were also taught a muscle relaxation procedure. Once children mastered this technique they were taught to relax while doing the turtle. Eventually, the child learns to relax and imagine withdrawing from the situation rather than actually going into the turtle position. Robin, Schneider, and Dolnick (1976) found that children who had been taught the procedure behaved less aggressively. Morgan and Jenson (1988) stated that the turtle technique and other similar approaches are worthy of consideration in selecting interventions.

Aggressive behaviors in regular and special class settings were reduced by alternative social response training in an investigation by Knapczyk (1988). Participants in the study were two male junior high school students in special education programs. Both had been referred because of aggressive behavior. The treatment involved training the students in social skills that could be used as alternatives to the aggressive behavior (see Chapter 7). The students learned alternate responses through modeling and rehearsal. Videotapes were prepared and shown to the students that provided examples of events that often led to aggressive behavior. The tapes had two male students (of high social status in the school) demonstrating alternative responses to the aggression. One of the actors played the part of the participant. In response to a particular event the student actor would first simulate aggressive behaviors. The student would then demonstrate an acceptable alternative response rather than the aggressive response. The other student actor represented the reactions of peers. The teacher and participant viewed the videotapes together. Following a discussion the participant was asked to demonstrate the appropriate behavior and provide additional alternatives. Results indicated that the treatments reduced the level of aggressive behaviors and led to an increase in peer-initiated interactions. A classroom example of alternative response training is presented in Vignette 6.2.

Vignette 6.2.   Alternate Response Training.

Jerry is a fourth-grade student in a self-contained classroom for children with learning disabilities. Jerry also has problems controlling his temper. His temper tantrums frequently follow requests to do academic work. The special education teacher had implemented a point system with a response cost component in an attempt to reduce the tantrums. The program had succeeded in reducing the tantrums but did not eliminate them. Because the tantrums were so disruptive to the class and Jerry became so upset following them, the teacher referred the problem to Mr. Cleveland, the school behavior specialist.

Mr. Cleveland observed Jerry at various times during the next week. He was present during two of Jerry's tantrums. He observed that prior to a tantrum Jerry grew tense, grimaced, and frequently chewed on his fingernails. This behavior would escalate into tantrums in which Jerry would swear, throw books, damage objects, etc.

In a conversation with the special education teacher and Mr. Cleveland, Jerry expressed frustration with his tantrums. He said he didn't like to "blow up" but he couldn't help it. He also said that the tantrums made it hard for him to learn, that kids were afraid of him, and his parents were upset about them. He also said he wanted to learn to control his behavior.

Because Jerry was motivated to change his behavior and the tantrum behavior had been controlled with external management procedures, Mr. Cleveland felt that a cognitive behavioral intervention may be effective. He chose to try a form of alternate response training with Jerry.

Jerry was first taught to recognize when a tantrum was about to occur by becoming aware of the tension in his body and his angry feelings. The next step was to teach him an alternate response to the tension and anger. Together Jerry and Mr. Cleveland decided on a technique using deep breathing, self-instruction, and visualization. When Jerry felt angry and tense he was to fold his arms on his desk, put his head on his arms, breathe deeply 10 times, and say to himself "stop and think." While saying this to himself he was to think of a red stop sign with the words "stop and think" on it. Jerry was also told to go through this procedure when the teacher told him to stop and think. If Jerry performed the procedure correctly and didn't have a tantrum, he received social praise from the teacher. Following the procedure the teacher was to reissue the original request if it was an academic or behavioral direction.

Within a few weeks of using the procedure, Jerry's temper tantrums were significantly reduced. The instances of the teacher having to remind Jerry to stop and think also were almost entirely eliminated. Jerry felt more in control of his behavior.

Attribution Retraining

The cognitive-behavioral procedure of attribution retraining is based on attribution theory. Attribution theory posits that individuals seek causes for events in their environment and that these perceived causes influence subsequent behavior (Palmer & Stowe, 1989). Performance attributions can be influenced by a child's current performance, his or her history of performance, and the performance of others. The consequences of repeated failure on a child's attributions and the subsequent effects on the child's motivation and achievement have been examined by researchers (Palmer & Stowe, 1989). Attribution theorists believe that children with positive attributions impute successes to their effort and ability and failure to a lack of effort. However, when children experience repeated failure they may impute failure to their lack of ability and success to good luck. As a result of these attributions, the child becomes less likely to attempt or persist at accomplishing tasks. This lower level of persistence and effort can lead to additional failures.

Attribution retraining attempts to replace negative attributions with positive attributions and thereby increase task persistence. The positive attributions are effort-oriented statements concerning their successes and failures (Maag, 1989). Dweck (1975) investigated attributional retraining with children who had difficulty solving math problems. The children were taught to make an effort-oriented statement, such as "failure makes you try harder," when working on math problems. Results indicated that the children persisted longer on the problems. Borkowski, Weyhing, and Turner (1986) stated that attributions may also influence a child's use of learning strategies. Schunk (1983) indicated that attribution retraining may not work when a child has a specific skill deficit. However, attribution retraining is more likely to be successful when the child is not using the skills that he or she possesses.

Attribution retraining usually consists of two phases (Licht & Kistner, 1986). In the first phase, the child is set up to experience some degree of failure. The failure is not severe and might consist of a few problems among a set that are too difficult for the child. In the second phase, the child is taught to make statements that attribute the failures to insufficient effort. According to Licht and Kistner (1986) the following is of crucial importance when teaching attributional statements: The caregiver must convey to the children that increased effort leads to success rather than simply that they are not trying hard enough. It is also important that the child in attribution retraining does experience some success. Self-statements that "increased effort will lead to increased success" will be more readily accepted when the child does experience some success. If the child does experience success, this will validate the self-statements. Attribution retraining is likely to be successful if the child believes that the use of the strategy will contribute to future success.

Concerns have been raised about having children attribute their failures to lack of effort because this might convey to the children that they are lazy. Anderson and Jennings (1980) suggested that children be taught to attribute their difficulties to ineffective task strategies. This would lead to less blame on the child's part. Licht and Kistner (1986) have suggested that attribution retraining be coupled with problem-solving and strategy training. It might be advisable for the caregiver to teach attributional statements and strategies as an integrated approach.

RATIONAL-EMOTIVE THERAPY

Cognitive behavior modification has become popular only in the past decade, however, many of the ideas integral to it were developed by Albert Ellis in the 1950s (Zionts, 1985). Ellis, originally trained as a psychotherapist, doubted the effectiveness of the client-centered model of psychotherapy. He developed an "active-directive" approach to psychotherapy. In this approach Ellis would directly confront the client with what he perceived to be the answers and insights that the client would eventually reach. He also noted that, although his methods were more effective than his previous methods, the insights gained were alone not enough to overcome disturbances. He felt the clients also needed strategies to improve their disturbances. He referred to his therapeutic approach as *rational-emotive therapy* (RET).

RET is a procedure that has been referred to as cognitive, behavioral, and cognitive-behavioral (Zionts, 1985). However, RET meets Hughes's three criteria for cognitive-behavioral interventions: (1) behavior is mediated by cognitive beliefs (i.e., the rational or irrational beliefs concerning an event); (2) a change in cognitive mediating events results in a change in behavior (i.e., substituting rational for irrational beliefs, thereby changing behavior); (3) all persons are active participants in their own learning (i.e., RET requires "active-directive" work with an individual).

In RET people who are disturbed are seen as disturbed not by occurrences but rather by their irrational beliefs about occurrences. Irrational beliefs, as opposed to rational beliefs, are beliefs that interfere with an individual's goals and result in maladaptive behavior. Rational and irrational beliefs are internal statements that one makes concerning events happening in one's life. Irrational beliefs lead to disturbed behavior. RET works with a person's cognitions and behaviors in an attempt to alter these irrational beliefs and thus correct disturbed behavior. RET allows people to assume internal responsibility for feelings, cognitions, and behavior by altering belief systems (Zionts, 1985).

A central tenant of RET is A-B-C theory. This theory holds that people do not get upset by events but rather their misinterpretation of events. The particular event is labeled "A" for activating events. The behaviors, cognitions, or feelings are labeled "C" for consequences. According to RET "A does not cause C," rather the person's beliefs ("B") about the activating events ("A") cause the behavioral consequences ("C"). RET uses a procedure called *disputation* to counteract these beliefs (the "D" of the ABC theory). The fifth component of ABC theory is "E" or effect. This concerns the effect of the new belief system on the person's behavior.

Kaplan (1991) adapted RET to be used with children and youths. He explained that the disputation process (DIBs) consisted of five steps. In the first step the caregiver assists the child in describing the activating event (A) associated with a maladaptive behavior. It is very important that the child verbally describe the event accurately. The second step involves the identification of the thinking (B) triggered by the event (e.g., what does the individual think or say to him or herself when a particular event occurs?). Kaplan (1991) contends that because children typically don't speak to themselves concerning particular events this is the most difficult step of DIBs. He further states that they often require prompting to complete the steps. He suggests that caregivers might provide a list of irrational beliefs and have the child choose one that might be associated with the activating event. Another procedure is to give the child a beliefs assessment and identify any irrational beliefs that the child might have and determine if they go with a particular event. Figure 6.6 is a partial list of a sample beliefs assessment provided by Kaplan (1991). Following this procedure if the child is unable to identify the irrational belief associated with the activating event, the caregiver will have to help. The care-

---

Name: _____   Date: _____

Directions: Read each statement below and decide whether it is true or false. If you believe the statement is true, write the letter "T" next to the number of the statement. If you think that it is false, write the letter "F" next to the number. It is not necessary to think about each one for very long. Be honest. You won't get into any trouble because of your answers so answer the way you really believe.

_____ 1. Everyone should treat me fairly and it's awful if they don't.
_____ 2. Everyone must like me and it's awful if they don't.
_____ 3. I always have to win and it's terrible if I don't.
_____ 4. I never make mistakes.
_____ 5. People should not have to do anything they don't want to.
_____ 6. If people say things to me that I don't like, they must be rotten.
_____ 7. When people find fault with you, it usually means they don't like you.
_____ 8. I must be stupid if I make mistakes.
_____ 9. I can't help the way I act around others. That's just the way I am and there's nothing I can do about it.
_____ 10. It's awful when things don't go my way.
_____ 11. I feel good about myself.
_____ 12. With a little effort one can change one's behavior.
_____ 13. I must be good at everything and it's terrible if I'm not.
_____ 14. When bad things happen to you, you should think about them all the time.
_____ 15. You should never admit when you're wrong.

Figure 6.6.   *Sample beliefs assessment.*

giver must then show the child how the irrational belief and activating event go together.

In the third step, the feelings associated with the individual's thoughts and behaviors are described. If the child has difficulty, the caregiver might have to prompt him or her. If the child cannot remember the feelings associated with an event, the caregiver and child may have to recreate the event through role playing.

Following the child describing his or her feelings, in the fourth step, the child describes the behavior. Prompting may again be necessary.

The first four steps comprise a reporting of thoughts, feelings, and behavior. The fifth and sixth steps of the process are evaluations of the thoughts and behavior. In step five, the child is asked to provide evidence that support the beliefs described in the second step. The child should be prodded to cite specific past experiences. In the sixth step, the individual is asked if there is any evidence that these thoughts might be true. In going through this step, the caregiver must be prepared to directly challenge the beliefs of the individual and convince him or her of the irrationality of those beliefs. If the individual accepts the irrationality of his or her thinking in step seven he or she must think of a rational thought to substitute for the irrational one. A method that can be used to help the child actually substitute the rational for the irrational belief is to have them practice it. The following is a list of some irrational beliefs and corresponding rational beliefs.

1. I must be good at everything I do./Nobody's perfect.
2. Everyone must like me. You can please some people some of the time but you can't please all the people all the time.
3. If people do things that I don't like, they must be bad people and must be punished./I've done things that other people don't like but I'm not a bad person.
4. Everything must go my way all the time./You can't always get what you want.
5. Everyone must treat me fairly all the time./Who said life is fair?
6. I never have control over what happens to me in my life./Nobody has control over what happens but you can control some things (e.g., grades or relationships).
7. When something bad happens to me, I must never forget it and think about it all the time./Don't worry be happy!
8. I must be stupid if I make mistakes./Nobody's perfect.
9. I should never have to wait for anything I want./Waiting for something sometimes makes the getting more special.
10. I should never have to do anything I don't want to./Nobody is free to do whatever he or she wants.[4]

---

[4] *Source:*   From *Beyond behavior modification: A cognitive-behavioral approach to behavior management in the schools* by J. S. Kaplan, 1991 (p. 171). Austin, TX: Pro-Ed. Copyright 1991 by Pro-Ed. Reprinted by permission.

RET for children and youth can be done individually or in groups. It also can be done verbally or by writing an essay (Kaplan, 1991). Until the rational beliefs become ingrained, it is important that the caretaker provide the child with opportunities to practice. Rehearsing RET plans through role-playing can be helpful. Once a child reaches a stage when he or she can substitute rational for irrational beliefs, the caregiver will begin to see a reduction in maladaptive behaviors.

Zionts (1985) cautions that when using RET it is important to remember that behavioral change will occur only if the individual desires it. Throughout the intervention, motivation must be constantly checked and reinforced.

RET is often used in groups using a problem-solving format (Zionts, 1985). Zionts suggests that group meetings be held in accordance with Glasser's (1969) suggestions. The meeting should be held in a small, tight circle of chairs; the duration of the meetings should be shorter for children and longer for adolescents and adults; rules should be established for conduct; and the caregiver should sit in a different chair at each meeting.

When using RET with groups, caregivers should introduce the concepts to the groups in the first meetings (i.e., A-B-C theory, rational and irrational beliefs, etc.). When the group becomes comfortable with RET, the meetings turn to more of a discussion and problem-solving format. Actual problems encountered by group members become the grist of the group discussions. The problems are discussed in accordance with RET procedures. When a particular problem is being discussed the group should attempt to identify the behaviors ("C") that a member needs to change or identify the activating event ("A") that the member believes causes the problem. The next step is for the group to identify the irrational belief system ("B") that leads to the inappropriate behavior. Following the identification of the irrational belief the caregiver and group attempt the disputation process. The group members should also have to prove that the belief system is rational if they believe it is so.

Although the group RET procedures use a discussion rather than a lecture format, the role of the caregiver is extremely important. Caregivers should communicate empathy, that is, acceptance of the individual even when communicating nonacceptance of the individual's behaviors. RET group sessions are "active-directive" with the practitioner and group members actively confronting irrational beliefs. The caregiver often has to confront group members who are dishonest, waste time, or are unfocused. It is the role of the caregiver to facilitate discussion and to assure that irrational beliefs, not individual group members, are confronted and attacked.

Whether working in groups or with individuals, the primary purpose of RET is to allow individuals—by modifying cognitions—to begin to think rationally and to take responsibility for their feelings, thoughts, and behaviors.

DEVELOPMENT AND GENERALIZATION OF CBM PROGRAMS

Developing cognitive-behavioral programs requires more than choosing a strategy and following a program of implementation. Harris (1982) outlined a three-stage process for constructing and implementing cognitive-behavioral interventions. The first stage is *task analysis*. In this stage the caregiver must determine the cognitions and strategies necessary for successful performance in whatever is being taught. In determining the necessary strategies, the caregiver might perform the task him or herself and note the strategies used or observe those who do well on a task to determine necessary strategies. According to Meichenbaum (1976) determination of strategies involved in a task, the production of appropriate strategies, and the application and monitoring of these strategies are important considerations. The second stage is *learner analysis*. In analyzing the learner, a variety of characteristics (e.g., age, cognitive capabilities, language development, learning ability, initial knowledge state, etc.) must be considered. These characteristics will influence the development of the training procedure. It is very important that the cognitive-behavioral training procedures and requirements be matched to the learner's characteristics if the training is to be successful. The third stage is *development and implementation*. The caregiver must establish the goals of training. The next step is to select the cognitive-behavioral procedures that are appropriate given the results of the task and learner analysis. In designing the intervention, the caregiver must tailor the learning activities to the desired goals (Brown, Campione, & Day, 1981). Following the development of the cognitive-behavioral procedure the caregiver initiates training.

Previous chapters have documented powerful behavioral strategies that have been used successfully by caregivers to modify behaviors in children and adolescents. However, the effects of behavioral change programs often are not generalized to other settings or maintained in treatment settings when the intervention procedures are withdrawn (Kerr & Nelson, 1989). Morgan and Jenson (1988) referred to self-management strategies as being among the more promising strategies to facilitate generalization. When behaviors are under external control by the caregiver the behaviors might not be controlled in situations and settings in which the caregiver is not able to apply the external control procedures. When persons are able to manage their behaviors, these behaviors will be more likely to last and to carry over to different situations and settings, even without external control by caregivers. However, in a review of self-management strategies Nelson, Smith, Young, and Dodd (1991) found that treatment effects of self-management procedures do not automatically generalize. They suggest that treatment effects will generalize if generalization is systematically programmed.

Kaplan (1991) offered several suggestions that could be used by caregivers to encourage children to use CBM strategies outside of the training environment. The following is a list of some of the suggestions:

◆ *Model the strategies.* The caregiver should model the strategies taught when appropriate. Students should be able to observe the strategies in action. Caregivers should share how they are using the strategies to help modify their behavior.

◆ *Teach the strategies to mastery.* The caregiver should teach the skills and subskills in the CBM strategy taught to mastery. Periodic assessments may be necessary to determine if a child has achieved mastery. When mastery is achieved a child is much more likely to use the strategy. According to Kaplan (1991) a child has achieved mastery of a strategy when he or she is both fast and accurate in its use.

◆ *Reinforce appropriate use of strategies.* Whenever the practitioner observes a child using a CBM strategy outside of the training context, it is important that the caregiver reinforce him or her. Caregivers should also encourage the child's peers to reinforce appropriate behavior.

◆ *Program for generalization by giving homework assignments.* Give homework assignments that will require the CBM strategies to be used in environments outside of the training context.

◆ *Discuss the relevance of each strategy when it is taught.* Children must be taught how the particular strategy is relevant to them and their situations. An effective way to do this is for the caregiver to discuss the relevance of the strategy prior to training.

SUMMARY

In this chapter we have examined a number of interventions that fall under the general category of cognitive behavior modification. The review was not exhaustive but only meant to give the reader a flavor of the number of different strategies available for effecting the caregiver's desired outcomes. Cognitive-behavioral strategies have been used to modify behavior, facilitate academic performance, train problem-solving ability, and foster self-control. The major aim of cognitive-behavioral training is to teach children to be their own agents of change, in control of their behavior and learning.

For Discussion

1. What is cognitive behavior modification? List and explain the three basic assumptions and goals of CBM.
2. Discuss some advantages of teaching individuals to manage their own behavior using CBM.
3. Discuss problem-solving and anger-control training.
4. Discuss the three components of self-management training, self-monitoring, self-evaluation, and self-reinforcement.
5. List and explain Sugai and Lewis's guidelines for increasing effectiveness of self-monitoring strategies.
6. Discuss Kaplan's procedure for encouraging the generalization of CBM strategies.

REFERENCES

Alberto, P. A., & Troutman, C. A. (1990). *Applied behavior analysis for teachers* (3rd ed.). Columbus, OH: Merrill/Macmillan.

Anderson, C. A., & Jennings, D. L. (1980). When experiences of failure promote expectations of success: The impact of attributing failure to ineffective strategies. *Journal of Personality, 48,* 393–407.

Baer, D. M. (1984). Does research on self-control need more control? *Analysis and Intervention in Developmental Disabilities, 4,* 211–284.

Baer, M., Fowler, S. A., & Carden-Smith, L. (1984). Using reinforcement and independent-grading to promote and maintain task accuracy in a mainstreamed class. *Analysis and Intervention in Developmental Disabilities, 4,* 157–170.

Bandura, A. (1977). *Social learning theory.* Englewood Cliffs, NJ: Prentice-Hall.

Bandura, A. (1978). The self system in reciprocal determinism. *American Psychologist, 33,* 344–358.

Barkley, R., Copeland, A., & Sivage, C. (1980). A self-control classroom for hyperactive children. *Journal of Autism and Developmental Disorders, 10,* 75–89.

Beck, A. T. (1976). *Cognitive therapy and emotional disorders.* New York: International Universities Press.

Borkowski, J. G., Weyhing, R. S., & Turner, L. A. (1986). Attributional retraining and the teaching of strategies. *Exceptional Children, 53,* 130–137.

Broden, M., Hall, R. V., & Mitts, B. (1971). The effect of self-recording of the classroom behavior of two eighth grade students. *Journal of Applied Behavior Analysis, 4,* 191–199.

Braswell, L., & Kendall, P. C. (1988). Cognitive-behavioral methods with children. In K.S. Dobson (Ed.), *Handbook of cognitive-behavioral therapies* (pp. 167–213). New York: Guilford.

Brown, A. L., Campione, J. C., & Day, J. D. (1981). Learning to learn: On training students to learn from text. *Educational Researcher, 10,* 14–21.

Burkell, J., Schneider, B., and Pressley, M. (1990). Mathematics. In M. P. Pressley and Associates (Eds.), *Cognitive strategy instruction that really improves children's academic performance* (pp. 147–177). Cambridge, MA: Brookline Books.

Camp, B., Blom, G., Herbert, F., & Van Doornick, W. (1977). "Think aloud": A program for developing self-control in young aggressive boys. *Journal of Abnormal Child Psychology, 5,* 157–169.

Clark, L. A., & McKenzie, H. S. (1989). Effects of self-evaluation training on seriously emotionally disturbed children on the generalization of their classroom rule following and work behaviors across settings and teachers. *Behavioral Disorders, 14,* 89–98.

Cole, C. L. (1987). Self-management. In C. R. Reynolds & L. Mann (Eds.), *Encyclopedia of special education* (pp. 1404–1405). New York: John Wiley & Sons.

Cooper, J. O., Heron, T. E., & Heward, W. L. (1987). *Applied behavior analysis.* Columbus, OH: Merrill/Macmillan.

Craighead, W. F. (1982). A brief clinical history of cognitive-behavior therapy with children. *School Psychology Review, 11,* 5–13.

Drabman, R. S., Spitalnik, R., & O'Leary, K. D. (1973). Teaching self-control to disruptive children. *Journal of Abnormal Psychology, 82,* 10–16.

Dweck, C. S. (1975). The role of expectations and attributions in the alleviation of learned helplessness. *Journal of Personality and Social Psychology, 31,* 674–685.

D'Zurilla, T. J., & Goldfried, M. R. (1971). Problem solving and behavior modification. *Journal of Abnormal Psychology, 78,* 107–126.

Ellis, A. (1973). Rational-emotive therapy. In R. Corsini (Ed.), *Current psychotherapies.* Itasca, IL: F. E. Peacock Publishers.

Feindler, E. L., & Fremouw, W. J. (1983). Stress inoculation training for adolescent anger problems. In D. Meichenbaum & M. E. Jaremko (Eds.), *Stress reduction and prevention.* New York: Plenum.

Feindler, E. L., Marriott, S. A., & Iwata, M. (1984). Group anger control training for junior high school delinquents. *Cognitive Therapy and Research, 8,* 299–311.

Glasser, W. (1969). *Schools without failure.* New York: Harper & Row.

Glynn, E. L., Thomas, J. D., & Shee, S. M. (1973). Behavioral self-control of on-task behavior in an elementary classroom. *Journal of Applied Behavior Analysis, 6,* 105–113.

Goldstein, A. P. (1988). *The prepare curriculum: Teaching prosocial competencies.* Champaign, IL: Research Press.

Goldstein, A. P., & Glick, B. (1987). *Aggression replacement training: A comprehensive intervention for aggressive youth.* Champaign, IL: Research Press.

Graham, S., & Harris, K. H. (1985). Improving learning disabled students' composition skills: Self-control strategy training. *Learning Disability Quarterly, 8,* 27–36.

Gross, A. M., & Wojnilower, D. A. (1984). Self-directed behavior change in children: Is it self-directed? *Behavior Therapy, 15,* 501–514.

Harris, K. R. (1982). Cognitive-behavior modification: Application with exceptional students. *Focus on Exceptional Children, 15,* 1–16.

Hayes, S. C., Rosenfarb, I., Wulfert, E., Munt, E. D., Korn, Z., & Zettle, R. D. (1985).Self-reinforcement effects: An artifact of social standard setting? *Journal of Applied Behavior Analysis, 18,* 201–214.

Homme, L. E. (1965). Perspectives in Psychology: XXIV. Control of coverants, the operants of the mind. *Psychological Record, 15,* 501–511.

Hughes, J. N. (1988). Cognitive behavior therapy. In L. Mann and C. Reynolds (Ed.). *The encyclopedia of special education* (pp. 354–355). New York: John Wiley & Sons.

Humphrey, L. L., Karoly, P., & Kirschenbaum, D. S. (1978). Self-management in the classroom: Self-imposed response cost versus self-reward.
Behavior Therapy, 9, 592–601.

Jenson, A. (1966). The role of verbal mediation in mental development.
Journal of Genetic Psychology, 118, 39–70.

Kanfer, F. H., & Karoly, P. (1972). Self-control: A behavioristic excursion into
the lion's den. *Behavior Therapy, 3,* 398–416.

Kaplan, J. S. (1991). *Beyond behavior modification: A cognitive-behavioral
approach to behavior management in the schools* (2nd ed.). Austin, TX:
Pro-Ed.

Kaufman, S. K., & O'Leary, K. D. (1972). Reward, cost, and self-evaluation
procedures for disruptive adolescents in a psychiatric hospital school.
Journal of Applied Behavior Analysis, 5, 293–309.

Kazdin, A. E. (1982). Current developments and research issues in cognitive-
behavioral interventions: A commentary. *School Psychology Review, 11,*
75–82.

Kendall, P. C. (1977). On the efficacious use of verbal self-instructional
procedures with children. *Cognitive Therapy and Research, 4,* 331–341.

Kendall, P. C., & Hollon, S.D. (1979). *Cognitive-behavioral interventions:
Therapy, research and procedures.* New York: Academic Press.

Kerr, M. M., & Nelson, C. M. (1989). *Strategies for managing behavior
problems in the classroom* (3rd ed.). Columbus, OH: Merrill/Macmillan.

Knapczyk, D. R. (1988). Reducing aggressive behaviors in special and regular
class settings by training alternative social responses. *Behavioral
Disorders, 14,* 27–39.

Liberty, K. A., & Michael, L. J. (1985). Teaching retarded students to reinforce their own behavior: A review of process and operation in the
current literature. In N. Haring (Ed.), *Investigating the problem of skill
generalization* (3rd ed., pp. 88–106). Seattle, WA: University of
Washington.

Licht, B. G., & Kistner, J. A. (1986). Motivational problems of learning
disabled children: Individual differences and their implications for
treatment. In J. K. Torgeson and B. Y. L. Wong (Eds.), *Psychological
and educational perspectives on learning disabilities* (pp. 225–249). New
York: Academic Press.

Lloyd, J. (1980). Academic instruction and cognitive behavior modification:
The need for attack strategy training. *Exceptional Education Quarterly,
8,* 53–63.

Luria, A. (1961). *The role of speech in the regulation of normal and abnormal
behaviors.* New York: Basic Books.

Maag, J. W. (1989). Use of cognitive mediation strategies for social skills
training: Theoretical and conceptual issues. In R. B. Rutherford, Jr., &
S. A. DiGangi (Eds.), *Severe behavior disorders of children and youth*

(Vol. 12, pp. 87–100). Reston, VA: Council for Children with Behavioral Disorders.

Meichenbaum, D. (1976). Cognitive factors as determinants of learning disabilities: A cognitive functional approach. In R. M. Knights & D. J. Baker (Eds.). *The neuropsychology of learning disorders: Theoretical approaches.* Baltimore, MD: University Park Press.

Meichenbaum, D. (1977). *Cognitive behavior modification: An integrative approach.* New York: Plenum Press.

Meichenbaum, D. (1980). Cognitive behavior modification with exceptional students: A promise yet unfulfilled. *Exceptional Education Quarterly, 8,* 83–88.

Meichenbaum, D., & Asarnow, J. (1979). Cognitive-behavioral modification and metacognitive development: Implications for the classroom. In P.C. Kendall and S.D. Hollon (Eds.), *Cognitive-behavioral interventions: Theory, research, and procedures* (pp. 11–35). New York: Academic Press.

Meichenbaum, D., & Goodman, T. J. (1971). Training impulsive children to talk to themselves: A means of developing self control. *Journal of Abnormal Psychology, 77,* 115–126.

Meyers, A. W., Cohen, R., & Schlester, R. (1989). A cognitive-behavioral approach to education: Adopting a broad-based perspective. In J. N. Hughes and R. J. Hall (Eds.), *Cognitive behavioral psychology in the schools: A comprehensive handbook* (pp. 62–84). New York: Guilford.

Morgan, D. P., & Jenson, W. R. (1988). *Teaching behaviorally disordered students: Preferred practices.* Columbus, OH: Merrill/Macmillan.

Nelson, J. R., Smith, D. J., Young, R. K., & Dodd, J. (1991). A review of self-management outcome research conducted with students who exhibit behavioral disorders. *Behavior Disorders, 13,* 169–180.

Novaco, R. W. (1975). *Anger control: The development and evaluation of an experimental treatment.* Lexington, MA: Lexington.

Novaco, R. W. (1979). The cognitive regulation of anger and stress. In P. C. Kendall & S. D. Hollon (Eds.), *Cognitive-behavioral interventions: Therapy, research and procedures* (pp. 241–285). New York: Academic Press.

O'Leary, S. D., & Dubay , D. R. (1979). Application of self-control procedures by children: A review. *Journal of Applied Behavior Analysis, 2,* 449–465.

Palmer, D. J., & Stowe, M. L. (1989). Attributions. In C. R. Reynolds & L. Mann (Eds.), *Encyclopedia of special education* (pp. 151–152). New York: John Wiley & Sons.

Rinehart, S. D., Stahl, S. A., & Erickson, L. G. (1986). Some effects of summarization training on reading and studying. *Reading Research Quarterly, 21,* 422–438.

Robin, A., Schneider, M., & Dolnick, M. (1976). The turtle technique: An extended case study of self-control in the classroom. *Psychology in the Schools, 12,* 120–128.

Ryan, E. B., Weed, K. A., & Short, E. J. (1986). Cognitive behavior modification: Promoting active, self-regulatory learning styles. In J. K. Torgeson and B. Y. L. Wong (Eds.), *Psychological and educational perspectives on learning disabilities* (pp. 367–397). New York: Academic press.

Schunk, P. H. (1983). Ability versus effort attributional feedback: Differential effects on self-efficacy and achievement. *Journal of Educational Psychology, 75,* 848–856.

Siegel, J. M., & Spivak, G. (1973). *Problem-solving therapy* (Research report 23). Philadelphia: Hahnemann Medical College.

Smith, D. J., Young, K. R., West, R.P., Morgan R. P., & Rhode, G. (1988). Reducing the disruptive behavior of junior high school students: A classroom self-management procedure. *Behavioral Disorders, 13,* 231–239.

Spivak, G., & Shure, M. B. (1974). *Social adjustment of young children.* San Francisco, CA: Jossey Bass.

Sugai, G. M., & Lewis, T. (1990, November). *Teaching self-management skills as a strategy to achieve generalized responding.* Paper presented at the 14th annual conference of the Teacher Educators for Children with Behavior Disorders, Tempe, Arizona.

Torgeson, J. K. (1982). The learning disabled child as an inactive learner: Educational implications. *Topics in Learning and Learning Disabilities, 2,* 45–52.

Vygotsky, L. (1962). *Thought and language.* New York: Wiley.

Wolery, M., Bailey, D. B., & Sugai G. M. (1988). *Effective teaching: Principles and procedures of applied behavior analysis with exceptional students.* Boston, MA: Allyn and Bacon.

Wong, B. Y. L. (1989). On cognitive training: A thought or two. In J. N. Hughes & R. J. Hall (Eds.), *Cognitive behavioral psychology in the schools: A comprehensive handbook* (pp. 209–219). New York: Guilford.

Zionts, P. (1985). *Teaching disturbed and disturbing students:An integrative approach,* Austin, TX: Pro-Ed.

CHAPTER 7

Development of Social Competence

. . .young children have come under intense analysis as scientists studying the roots of social skills find that ability in interpersonal dealings can be crucial for academic achievement and success throughout life. Understandably, children who cannot read the feelings and intentions of playmates and who lack a natural sense of timing and smoothness in social interactions are among the least popular in any children's group. But new data reveal more dramatic costs of such early awkwardness: these children are more likely to fail academically, drop out of school or get into trouble with the law.

—*Goleman, 1990, p. B1*

Teachers and parents often note that some children are often socially isolated and/or rejected by their peers (Hollinger, 1987; Lefevre, Malcolm, West, & Ledingham, 1983; Melloy, 1990). This isolation and rejection leads to few opportunities to develop friendships, which results in devastating effects on children during their childhood and into adulthood (Goleman, 1990; Strain, Guralnick & Walker, 1986). Many children are not accepted by their peers, and others seem to lack in *critical social skills*, that is, the social skills necessary to interact with others) that would allow for acceptance among their peers (Hollinger, 1987). Others have stated that even when children were capable of performing critical social skills, they were not *socially competent* (i.e., able to perform the social skill at the appropriate time, with other persons, and in varied settings as well as maintain relationships with others) and this resulted in rejection by others (Asher & Renshaw, 1981; Hollinger, 1987; Putallaz & Gottman, 1981, 1982). Several authors (Cartledge & Milburn, 1983; Hollinger, 1987; Williams, Walker, Holmes, Todis, & Fabre, 1989) have suggested that the development of peer relation skills are among the most important aspects of a child's life. Children who were found to be deficit in skills critical to peer relations (such as joining in, starting and maintaining conversations, supportive actions, refraining from aggressive behavior) were consistently rated lower on sociometric measures, which indicated peer rejection and isolation.

Few topics in recent literature on children's interaction behavior have received more interest than the topics of social competence and social skills training. The literature is replete with studies that focused on how children interacted with each other and the effect these interactions had on their ability to get along with their peers. The literature in this area was consistent in one finding: Children who are rejected or neglected by their peers and who fail to make friends while they are young are at risk for future problems including academic deficits, delinquency, problems with mental health, unemployment, and alcohol (e.g., Asher & Renshaw, 1981; Bierman & Furman, 1984; Gottman, Gonso, & Schuler, 1976; Guralnick, 1986; Ladd & Asher, 1985).

Unfortunately, a number of children and youth fail to acquire any friends or have only a few friends (Gronlund, 1959; Putallaz & Gottman, 1981; Sabornie, Kauffman, & Cullinan, 1990). Because this fact is of considerable concern to a number of persons who work with children, numerous attempts have been made to identify factors important to social competence.

DEFINITION AND RATIONALE FOR SOCIAL COMPETENCE

Various definitions of social skills exist that include concepts of social behavior, assertiveness, and social competency. For example, Michelson, Sugai, Wood, and Kazdin (1983) provided a list of components that were part of most social skills definitions. They suggested that social skills "are primarily acquired through learning, comprise specific and discrete verbal and nonverbal behaviors, entail both effective and appropriate initiations and responses, maximize social reinforcement, are interactive by nature, are influenced by the characteristics of the participant and environment in which it occurs, and can be specified and targeted for intervention" (Michelson & Mannarino, 1986, p. 376). Generally, the directionality of social skills deficits and excesses is considered under the broad general categories of social withdrawal and social aggression (e.g., Gottman, Gonso, & Schuler, 1976; Hops, 1982; Michelson & Mannarino, 1986; Walker, Shinn, O'Neill, & Ramsey, 1987).

A number of authors have attempted to define *social competence,* but as yet there does not appear to be consensus among them. Putallaz and Gottman (1981, 1982) explored the concept of social competence in an attempt to determine if knowledge of social skills or performance of certain behaviors was more important relative to peer acceptance. They stated that the concept of social competence suggests that poor interpersonal functioning may be modified through social skills training. Putallaz and Gottman further pointed out that peer acceptance and having a close friend, as measured by sociometric tests, appear to be the only factors that can currently be linked empirically to the concept of social competence. They described a number of behavioral and cognitive correlates of peer acceptance and sociometric status, concluding that socially competent or popular children are usually positive and agreeable in their interactions with peers. Unpopular, less competent children, however, were disagreeable, bossy, and negative in their interactions with other children. According to these authors, popular children provided general reasons for their disagreements and described constructive alternatives when criticizing a peer compared to unpopular children who were also more likely to give aggressive solutions to conflict situations.

In a review of studies about children and how they developed friendships, Asher and Renshaw (1981) examined the hypothesis that social skillfulness is a crucial determinant of children's peer relationships. They pointed out that children are without friends for a variety of reasons including physical appearance, gender or race, opportunities for participation, and a child's social skill repertoire. They further stated that difficulty in peer relations may indeed be due to the hypothesis "that children without friends are prevented from establishing effective peer relationships by their own lack of social skills" (p. 273). Correlations between behavior and sociometric status suggested that popular children participated in peer activities, were cooperative and helpful, communicated effectively, and were friendly and supportive toward their peers. Unpopular children were rejected or neglected due to a lack of certain social skills. Their review of observational and hypothetical situation data, however, yielded differences between children of high and low sociometric status, which offered support to the assumption that children's limited social skills contributed to their low social status.

McMahon defined social competence as "responses that increase or maximize the probability of producing, maintaining, and enhancing positive effects for the child who has interacted with another" (1989, p. 12). She further stated that learning often leads to social competence (for example, getting along with others).

Finally, Kerr and Nelson defined social competence as "an individual's ability to use these skills [social skills] at the right time and place, showing social judgment or perception about how to act" (1989, p. 312). This definition seems to be generally accepted among professionals and parents to explain social competence. Therefore, we will use it in the context of this text to define social competence. Critical social skills will be defined as the behaviors (e.g., use of self-control, being on-task, expressing feelings) that are necessary to interact effectively with others in home, school, and community settings. Throughout this chapter, we will demonstrate application of the methods prescribed for assessment and intervention presented in vignettes and research examples.

TARGETING SKILLS FOR INTERVENTION

Numerous attempts have been made by educators to assist children in becoming skillful in social skills through direct instruction. The assumption was that children demonstrated *social skills deficits* (i.e., did not know how to perform a particular social behavior) and needed training in social skills to improve their behavior. These attempts seemed to have been effective in teaching children the steps of specific social skills. However, children did not necessarily become socially competent as a result of this training. Children continued to be rejected and isolated even when they had received training in social skills (Asher & Renshaw, 1981; Gresham, 1986; Melloy, 1990; Sasso, Melloy, & Kavale, 1990). Hollinger (1987) pointed out that children were not accepted even when they knew social skills because they were not socially competent, and therefore demonstrated *performance deficits* (i.e., were not able to perform the skill in a situation in which it was needed). Consider Kevin who is presented in Vignette 7.1.

Vignette 7.1.   Example of a Child with a Social Skill Performance Deficit.

Kevin was able to learn friendship-making social skills during social skills class. However, he was not able to use these skills outside of social skills class. For example, while Kevin and his peers played a kickball game during recess, Kevin sat listlessly on the sidelines when his teammates were up to bat. Since Kevin did not encourage his peers (a skill he had been taught), he was described as someone who didn't support his peers on a peer rating that his classmates completed. Observations of Kevin indicated that he had performance deficits in many social skills that were important for getting along with his peers. As a consequence, he was often isolated from his peers and did not appear to have any friends.

Children who demonstrate deficits similar to Kevin's need to receive direct instruction in social skills as a step toward becoming socially competent. Equally important, however, is the need to validate the social skills taught and to incorporate generalization training into social skills lessons. Kevin did in fact improve his social skills and performance of these skills as a result of direct instruction in social skills. Training for generalization of the social skills became an integral part of Kevin's training. This resulted in Kevin's performance of learned social skills across persons, settings, and situations. Direct instruction in critical social skills and training for generalization will be explored later in this chapter.

Social Validation of Skills to be Taught

Social validation has been defined as social skills that were deemed *socially significant* and *socially important* by society (i.e., persons in the child's environment) (Gresham, 1986). According to Gresham (1986), socially valid social skills predict important social outcomes such as peer acceptance and popularity.

Social significance refers to the behavior change goals that society wants. An example of this would be a behavior change goal that a parent may have for a child that tantrums whenever the child doesn't get his or her own way. Consider the case of Hillary and her mother in Vignette 7.2.

Vignette 7.2. Example of Socially Significant Behavior Change Goals.

Four-year-old Hillary throws a tantrum whenever she doesn't get her way. Her mother wishes that Hillary would learn the social skill of accepting "no" for an answer. By learning this important skill, Hillary's mother feels that her daughter will be able to choose something else to do or ask for a reason if she doesn't understand why she is being told "no." These behavior options would be more acceptable than tantrum behavior.

The fact that Hillary's mother has determined that accepting "no" is an important social skill to demonstrate in their home implies that it is a significant social skill and therefore one that is worthwhile to teach. On the other hand, if accepting "no" is not a skill that the parent feels is important, training in this skill would be useless, at least for the home environment.

Social importance has been defined as the importance of the effects of social skills training on significant social outcomes for the child. Gresham reviewed a number of studies and reported the following as socially important outcomes for children and youth: "peer acceptance, acceptance by significant adults, school adjustment, mental health functioning, and lack of contact with the juvenile court system" (1986, p. 167). When teachers and parents are making decisions about social skills training, they must consider whether or not the skills to be taught have been socially validated for the environments in which the child will be expected to demonstrate the skills. Hillary's mother realizes that it is important for her daughter to learn to accept "no" because this is a social skill important to many environments and social situations.

ASSESSMENT OF SOCIAL SKILLS

Assessment information is essential in making decisions about which skills need to be taught to children who demonstrate problems in social competence. In Chapter 2, formal assessment of behavior was discussed. This section will focus on assessment instruments and techniques that are designed to measure levels of social competence in children.

In the past, teachers, parents, and other professionals have relied on subjective information to assist them in determining which social skills they would teach. The results have often lead to children wasting time learning things they already knew or didn't need to learn. Consequently, even though children received social skills training, they did not improve in sociometric status or in the quantity or quality of interpersonal relations. A number of investigators have identified assessment instruments and techniques that were designed to identify social behaviors that were critical to peer-adult relations in a variety of situations. Several of these instruments and techniques are reviewed.

Frequently used social skill assessment methods used include sociometrics, ranking methods, ratings by others, behavioral role play tasks, self-reporting, naturalistic observation, and self-monitoring (Foster & Ritchey, 1985; Gresham, 1986; Gresham, Elliott, & Black, 1987; Kerr & Nelson, 1989; Maag, 1989; McMahon, 1989; McConnell & Odom, 1986; Melloy, 1990; Strain, Guralnick, & Walker, 1986). Assessment in the area of social competence is typically employed either to diagnose deficit skills or to target skills for intervention. In general, approaches such as sociometric measures, ratings by others, self-reporting, and behavioral role playing appear to be more useful for selection and diagnosis purposes. Other approaches (e.g., behavioral interview, naturalistic observations, peer assessment, and self-monitoring) are reported to assist in targeting skills for intervention (Bem & Fender, 1978; Gresham, 1986; Hoier & Cone, 1980; Strain, Odom & McConnell, 1984). Specific assessment procedures are described in the following.

Sociometric Measures

Various sociometric techniques have been used to examine the social status, social competence, and/or acceptance level of children and youth among their peers. The most commonly used sociometric assessment methods are peer nomination and peer ratings (Hops & Lewin, 1984; Martin, 1988; McConnell & Odom, 1986). Peer assessments are also described in sociometric literature because they are often used in cross-method comparison studies (McConnell & Odom, 1986).

Peer Nomination

The peer nomination method has become the most commonly applied sociometric assessment (McConnell & Odom, 1986). It was developed by Moreno (1934) and requires children to select one or more classmates with whom they would or would not like to engage in an activity (e.g., play with, hang out with, work with). Generally, social status scores are derived by adding the numbers of choices a child receives. Scores derived from such measures indicate levels of popularity or acceptance and are designed to identify "stars" in a class (those frequently nominated on positive criteria), the "isolates" (those not nominated frequently on positive criteria), and the "rejectees" (those frequently nominated on negative criteria) (Ollendick & Hersen, 1984, p. 127).

Peery (1979) used the two dimensions of social impact and social preference to describe social status. His classification categories included:

Popular	High social impact, positive social preference
Rejected	High social impact, negative social preference

| Isolate | Low social impact, negative social preference |
| Amiable | Low social impact, positive social preference |

Coie, Dodge, and Coppotelli (1982) described a "controversial" category in addition to Peery's (1979) classifications. According to Coie and his colleagues, "controversial" students were identified by their peers as children who "exhibited a high measure of social impact and high frequencies of both positive and negative nominations (1985, p. 239). McConnell and Odom (1986) pointed out that inclusion of negative criteria in sociometric assessment is a controversial aspect. They remarked, however, that the efficiency of peer nomination assessments decreased markedly when negative nominations were not used (McConnell & Odom, 1986). Also, inclusion of negative nominations allows for identification of rejected children in a class—often prime candidates for social skills training. Mrs. Kelly, described in Vignette 7.3, wanted to identify children who needed social skills training. A sociogram from one of the third-grade classes in Mrs. Kelly's school is depicted in Figure 7.1.

Vignette 7.3.   Use of Peer Nomination.

Mrs. Kelly, the principal of an elementary school, met with the curriculum committee to discuss the need for social skills training for some of the children in grades one through three. The committee decided that they would screen candidates for training using a peer nomination sociometric technique. Teachers in the first, second, and third grades were given a list of three questions to ask of the children in their classes. The questions were:

1. Who is someone in this class that you like to work with on a math problem?
2. Who is someone in this class that you like to play with at recess?
3. If you could pick anyone in this class to be in a class play, who would that person be?

Once the peer nomination had been administered in each classroom, the teachers completed a sociogram and were able to obtain preliminary information about children in the class who were popular, neglected, isolated, and amiable [using Peery (1979) definitions]. Children who were identified as being neglected or isolated in each classroom were considered at risk for needing training in social skills. According to Hops and Greenwood (1988), children who received few or no positive nominations would be considered as "neglect-

Figure 7.1. Sociogram resulting from a peer nomination process administered in a third-grade class.

Child's Name	% of classmates who indicated a positive choice for question:		
	1	2	3
Marcy	45	30	60
Joe	0	5	2*
Billy	90	95	85
Trevor	79	87	79
Carol	50	45	30
Nancy	39	56	54
Heather	76	67	65
David	67	85	75
Ronald	98	96	87
George	10	11	11**
Jennifer	0	0	0*
Timothy	1	3	5*
Sheryl	2	45	30

* Indicates children who were "rejected"
** Indicates children who were "neglected"

ed," and those receiving no positive nominations would be "rejected." Further assessment was completed on these children before decisions were made about intervention.

Peer Rating

The peer rating method of sociometric assessment involves the use of a Likert-type rating scale. Children are asked to rate each class member along a continuum of attraction-rejection (Hops & Lewin, 1984; McConnell & Odom, 1986). Typically, raters are given a class roster, read each classmate's name, and asked to rate the classmate according to how much they like or dislike to play with or work with the child. Individual scores for peer ratings are generally calculated as the sum of numerical ratings provided by all other members of the group (McConnell & Odom, 1988). For example, a peer rating scale was administered to measure social status in a study conducted with 350 elementary-aged children (Melloy, 1990). The format of the peer rating instrument included a roster of each classroom and a four-point Likert-type scale following each child's name. Points on the continuum indicated "like to play with a lot," "just kind of like to play with," "do not like to play with," and "I don't know this person." Ratings were assigned a weighted value (i.e., likes to . . .a lot = 3; just kind of . . .play with = 2; does not . . .play with = 1; and don't know . . .person = 0). The sum of the ratings was calculated and yielded an overall social status score. Scores were ranked to reveal the relative social standing of each child in the class as suggested by McConnell and Odom (1986). An example of the peer rating instrument is presented in Figure 7.2.

Peer ratings tend to result in higher reliability and stability coefficients when compared to peer nominations (McConnell & Odom, 1986). The major advantages for using the peer rating technique compared to peer nomination include: (1) every child in the class is rated, (2) higher test-retest reliability results over time, and (3) this technique is more sensitive to subtle changes in social status depending on criteria used (Hops & Lewin, 1984; McConnell & Odom, 1986). A disadvantage of the peer rating method is that children, especially younger ones, may tend to rate most classmates in the middle of the scale or to give everyone in the class the same rating (McConnell & Odom, 1986). Sociometric techniques were effective in screening individuals in need of social skills training to improve social competence.

Peer Rating

Name _____ Grade _____ Date _____

Listen as each name on the list is read. Circle the number next to each child's name that matches the description of how much you would like to play with him or her.

	Rating			
Student names	I like to play with this person a lot.	I just kind of like to play with this person.	I don't like to play with this person.	I don't know this person.
Ashley	1	2	3	4
Carissa	1	2	3	4
Kelli	1	2	3	4
Matthew	1	2	3	4
Jaclyn	1	2	3	4
Allison	1	2	3	4
Tyler	1	2	3	4
Zachary	1	2	3	4
Alex	1	2	3	4
Kacie	1	2	3	4
Cliff	1	2	3	4
Clint	1	2	3	4
Colen	1	2	3	4
Mackenzie	1	2	3	4
Theresa	1	2	3	4

Figure 7.2.   *Peer rating questionnaire.*

Source: Melloy, K. J. (1990). Attitudes and behavior of non-disabled elementary-aged children toward their peers with disabilities in integrated settings: An examination of the effects of treatment on quality of attitude, social status and critical social skills. Doctoral dissertation, The University of Iowa, Iowa City, Iowa.

Peer Assessment

The peer assessment method is often referred to as a measure of social status, although it differs from sociometric measures. Peer assessment techniques require children to judge their peer's behavior, whereas sociometric methods require children to make judgments about their feelings toward peers. Peer assessment procedures are often combined with sociometric measures to provide information about a child's relationships with peers (McConnell & Odom, 1986). They have been used to examine variables that contribute to or affect sociometric status (McConnell & Odom, 1986). In a peer assessment, children are asked to nominate or rate classmates according to a variety of behavioral criteria. Generally, children are given descriptions of children and the child "guesses" who in the class best fits the description. The number of nominations for positive and negative measures are computed to yield a qualitative score (i.e., positive or negative). The most popular peer assessments include *The Guess Who? Test* (Agard, Veldman, Kaufman, Semmel & Walters, undated), *The Shapiro Sociometric Role Assignment Test* (Shapiro & Sobel, 1981), and *The Class Play* (Bower, 1961). The following list provides a sample of the 20 descriptions/questions from *The Guess Who? Test* (Agard et al., undated).

1. Here is someone who is generally cheerful, jolly and good-natured, laughs and smiles a good deal. Guess Who_____.
2. Here is someone who generally seems rather sad, worried, or unhappy, who hardly ever laughs or smiles. Guess Who_____.
11. Here is someone who seems to trust most people. Guess Who_____.
12. Here is someone who never seems to trust anyone. Guess Who-_____.
19. Here is someone who cooperates in class and isn't noisy when the group is trying to work. Guess Who_____.
20. Here is someone who is often noisy in class. Guess Who_____.[1]

Coie, Dodge, and Coppotelli (1982) used peer assessment to measure types of behavior that contributed to the social status of children in regular classrooms. They found that behaviors that seemed to correlate with social preference were cooperativeness, supportiveness, and physical attractiveness. Social preference was negatively related to disruptiveness and aggression.

Another peer assessment technique that has been used to measure social competence is the *behavioral template approach* (Bem & Fender, 1978; Hoier & Cone, 1987; Melloy, 1990; Strain, Odom & McConnell, 1984). This procedure requires children identified as rejected through sociometric techniques to identify *hopeful playmates* (i.e., the rejected child nominates a peer with whom he or she would like to play but doesn't play with). These hopeful playmates are asked through formal peer assessment to identify the types of behavior that they like about children with whom they did play. Hoier and Cone (1987)

---

[1] *Source:*   From J. A. Agard, D. J. Veldman, M. J. Kaufman, M. I. Semmel and P.B. Walters (undated). Guess Who: An instrument of the PRIME Instrument Battery. Project PRIME, Technical Report. Reprinted by permission.

developed a behavioral template using formal peer assessments consisting of 50 behavioral descriptions that the hopeful playmate sorted into "like my friend" and "not like my friend" categories. The behaviors identified in the behavioral template were compared to the behaviors observed in rejected children. Hoier and Cone suggested that discrepancies between the behavioral template and the target child's actual behavior could be used for social skills interventions. Through several studies, they concluded that this procedure could assess the social validity of the template behaviors. A Q-sort was used across 50 behavioral descriptors. Each child sorted the 50 items into two piles labeled "like my friend" and "not like my friend." This sorting process was repeated until descriptors evolved that described 10 behaviors that were very much like the friend the child had in mind. A behavioral template was generated through these interviews. These descriptors were identified as *critical social skills* needed for positive peer interactions. Discrepancies between this behavioral template and the target child's observed behavior were suggested as goals for social skills intervention (Melloy, 1990; Strain et al., 1984). The following list provides examples of the behavioral descriptors identified by Hoier and Cone (1987).

1. Tells me I did well
2. Smiles at me, laughs
3. Gives me things without being asked
4. Shares
5. Gives me hugs, kisses, pats on the back
6. Says nice things about me
7. Says things about the way I feel
8. Tells me how he/she feels
9. Agrees with me
10. Goes along with my ideas, complies
11. Gives me reason when he/she doesn't do what I say
12. Looks at me when I am talking
13. Starts games for me
14. Talks first before I do
15. Talks a lot when we are together
16. Explains games or stories to me
17. Asks for help
18. Encourages me, tells me to keep trying
19. Looks at me when she/he is talking
20. Stays close to me when we play/hang out
21. Tells jokes
22. When I decide to do something she/he goes along
23. Includes me in what he/she is doing
24. Invites me over
25. Ask questions
26. Teases
27. Tells on others, tattles

28. Blames others
29. Takes things without asking
30. Hurts or threatens to hurts others
31. Daydreams or wanders around
32. Doesn't talk, doesn't have much to say
33. Doesn't agree with me
34. Shows off
35. Doesn't let people join in
36. Doesn't look at me when I talk to her/him
37. Doesn't let me go first
38. Spends a lot of time alone
39. Calls people names
40. Gets angry often
41. Says things about kids to hurt their feelings
42. Yells, screams
43. Makes fun of others
44. Talks about others behind their backs
45. Bothers people, interrupts games
46. Keeps others from joining what he/she is doing
47. Makes you do what he/she says, bossy
48. Doesn't do what you ask or tell her/him
49. Breaks rules, cheats
50. Fights, argues with others[2]

The behavioral template approach was used in a study conducted by Melloy (1990) to determine critical social skills in four elementary schools with children who were identified as being rejected by their peers. Following identification of deficits in these critical skills among the children, intervention in the form of social skills training took place. Treatment resulted in the rejected children becoming more competent in demonstrating critical social skills and a slight increase in interactions with their more popular peers. The procedure used to generate behavioral templates follows:

1. Interview children who are rejected by peers to identify hopeful playmates (child they would like to be friends with but are not friends with).
2. Interview the hopeful playmate to determine behaviors he or she likes in friends.
3. Interview/template generation:
   a. Ask hopeful playmate to think about their best friends.
   b. Have them sort the 50 behavior descriptors (Hoier & Cone, 1987) into two piles: "Like my friend" and "Not like my friend."

---

[2] *Source:*   From T. S. Hoier and J. D. Cone, 1987. Target selection of social skills for children. *Behavior Modification, 11,* 137–163; Appendix B. Copyright 1987 by the authors. Reprinted by permission of Sage Publications, Inc.

(Record numbers of these behaviors on the template worksheet from Figure 7.3.)

    c. Have child sort the items in the "like my friend" category into two piles: "very much like my friend" and "somewhat like my friend." (Record numbers of responses on worksheet.)

    d. Repeat previous step until only 10 descriptors remain in the "very much like my friend" category. (Record.)

    e. Have the child rank order the final 10 items from the "most important for your friend to do" to "least important for your friend to do."

4. The rank-ordered behaviors provide possible targets for social skills intervention.

5. Observe target children to determine deficits in behavior compared to those behaviors identified in the behavior template.

6. Deficit behaviors become targets for social skills intervention.[3]

Figure 7.3. *Example of a behavior template worksheet.*

Source: Melloy, K. J. (1990). Attitudes and behavior of non-disabled elementary-aged children toward their peers with disabilities in integrated settings: An examination of the effects of treatment on quality of attitudes, social status and critical social skills. Doctoral dissertation, The University of Iowa, Iowa City, Iowa.

Child's name _____ Date _____

Grade _____ Teacher _____ School _____

Name of child who identified this child as a hopeful playmate _____ (complete only after interview with hopeful playmate).

Record the number of the behavior descriptor under the categories listed below as the child sorts the descriptor cards:

       Like my friend   Not like my friend

     Very much like my friend   Somewhat like my friend

Trial 1

Trial 2

Trial 3

Final 10 behavioral descriptions:

Rank order of final 10:

1.   2.   3.   4.   5.   6.   7.   8.   9.   10.

---

[3] *Source:* From T. S. Hoier and J. D. Cone, 1987. Target selection of social skills for children. *Behavior Modification, 11,* 137–163; Appendix B. Copyright 1987 by the authors. Reprinted by permission of Sage Publications, Inc.

Figure 7.3 shows a worksheet that can be used while interviewing hopeful playmates to record responses to the interviewer. An example of a completed worksheet is provided in Figure 7.4.

Ranking Methods

Ranking methods have been used to select children for social skills training programs (Gresham, 1986; Walker, Severson, Stiller, Williams, Haring, Shinn, & Todis, 1988). Ranking methods require teachers to rank order children in their classes based on behavioral (e.g., disruptive, aggressive, talks the least) or nonbehavioral (e.g., best liked, fewest friends) criteria. Teacher rankings have been found to correspond relatively well to observed behaviors such as fre-

Figure 7.4. *Example of a completed behavior template worksheet.*

Source: Melloy, K. J. (1990). Attitudes and behavior of non-disabled elementary-aged children toward their peers with disabilities in integrated settings: An examination of the effects of treatment on quality of attitudes, social status and critical social skills. Doctoral dissertation, The University of Iowa, Iowa City, Iowa.

Behavior Template Worksheet

Child's name Joshua   Date 9/25/93

Grade 5 Teacher Mr. Rogers School Goodhue Elementary

Name of child who identified this child as a hopeful playmate
William   (complete only after interview with hopeful playmate).

Record the number of the behavior descriptor under the categories listed below as the child sorts the descriptor cards:

Like my friend	Not like my friend
33,5,38,48,2,16,13,10,22,	26,50,39,46,49,42,40,
17,17,25,19,32,21,37,24,8,	30,47,44,35,29,7,27,28,
11,20,9,23,12,15,4,18,1,6	31,3,43,45,41,36,34

Very much like my friend	Somewhat like my friend

Trial 1

6,1,18,4,15,23,8,24,21,	5,33,12,9,20,11,32,37,
13,2,25,22,17,10	38,48,16,19

Trial 2

10,18,1,8,21,24,2,17,25,	13,6,23,15,4
22	

Trial 3
(ten descriptors in Trial 2)

Final 10 behavioral descriptions:
10,8,1,21,24,2,17,25,22

Rank order of final 10:

1. 24 2. 25 3. 17 4. 2 5. 8 6. 18 7. 1 8. 21 9. 10 10. 22

quency of interactions and on-task behavior (Greenwood, Walker, & Hops, 1977). However, this method has failed to identify socially withdrawn children since withdrawn behaviors are usually not perceived as being problematic (Hops & Greenwood, 1988). Therefore, rankings are primarily useful for identifying children at the extremes of a criterion and for social validation purposes (Gresham, 1986).

Ratings by Others

Ratings by others are scales that are completed by teachers and peers that yield useful information for identifying target behaviors that may be correlates of important social outcomes such as peer acceptance and rejection (Gresham, 1986).

Teacher Rating Scales

Teacher rating scales that have been developed specifically to assess social skills include the *Social Behavior Assessment* (SBA) (Stephens, 1978). The SBA requires teachers to rate elementary-aged children on 136 social skills and the degree to which they exhibit the skill. The SBA is most useful in the selection and classification for social skills training.

Walker and McConnell (1988) developed a teacher rating scale of social competence and school adjustment. Designed for use in screening and identification of social skills deficits among children in kindergarten through sixth grade, the *Walker-McConnell Scale of Social Competence and School Adjustment* (1988) consists of 43 positively worded descriptions of social skills that were designed to sample the two primary adjustment domains within school settings: adaptive behavior and social competence. These descriptions are distributed across three subscales—two measure interpersonal social skills with adults or peers, one measures adaptive behavior required for success in the classroom. The descriptions are rated by the teacher on a five-point Likert scale ranging from "never occurs" to "frequently occurs." The instrument yields three factor scores (subscale 1: 16 items, teacher-preferred social behavior; subscale 2: 17 items, peer-preferred social behavior; subscale 3: 10 items, school adjustment behavior) and a composite score of social competence. Representative samples from the three scales are presented here:

Scale 1: Teacher-preferred Behavior:

1. Shows sympathy for others.
2. Accepts constructive criticism from peers without becoming angry.
3. Cooperates with peers in group activities or situations.

Scale 2: Peer-preferred Behavior

1. Spends recess and free time interacting with peers.
2. Interacts with a number of different peers.
3. Invites peers to play or share activities.

Scale 3: School Adjustment Behavior

1. Uses free-time appropriately.
2. Does seatwork assignments as directed.
3. Answers or attempts to answer a question when called on by the teacher.[4]

Teachers completed the Walker-McConnell scale on children who were identified as at risk for having social skill deficits through the peer nomination method described in Vignette 7.3. Children who were significantly different from the norm on the Walker-McConnell subscales were further identified as children in need of social skills training. Parental permission for further assessment was obtained prior to completion of rating scales and other assessment techniques.

Parents, Teachers, and Others

Other rating instruments are available that produce factor scores designed to assess social competence in children and youth. One of the most popular and well normed of these instruments is the *Child Behavior Checklist* (CBCL) (Achenbach & Edelbrock, 1983). The CBCL generates a factor score of social competence for children aged 2 through 16. Forms are available for parents, teachers, and the child to complete by rating questions about behavior, involvement with others, and school type skills. The following list provides a sample of items from the parent form of the CBCL.

1. Please list the sports your child most likes to take part in.
2. Compared to other children of the same age, about how much time does he/she spend in each?
3. Please list any organizations, clubs, teams, or groups your child belongs to.
4. Compared to other children of the same age, how active is he/she in each?
5. Compared to other children of his/her age, how well does your child get along with his/her brothers and sisters?[5]

Ratings by others were effective as screening devices that supply a piece of information in the assessment process of children who demonstrate deficits in social competence. Instruments such as the Walker-McConnell scale (Walker & McConnell, 1988) provide information on specific skill deficits a

---

[4] *Source:* Walker, H. M., and McConnell, S. R. (1988). *Walker-McConnell Scale of Social Competence and School Adjustment.* Austin, TX: Pro-Ed. Reprinted with permission.

[5] *Source:* Achenbach, T. M. (1981). *The Child Behavior Checklist for Ages 4–16 (CBCL/4–16).* Department of Psychiatry, University of Vermont, 1 S. Prospect Street, Burlington, VT 05401-3456. Reprinted with permission.

child may demonstrate, but that information is useful only when it is considered as part of an assessment package for the evaluation of social competence.

Once a child has been identified as having deficits in social competence, the next step is to pinpoint target behaviors for intervention. The following instruments and techniques will provide additional information that will assist teachers and parents in planning for intervention once screening data have been collected.

Behavioral Role Plays

This type of assessment is a test of performance in analog situations. Children are asked to role play social behaviors they would use in situations where social skills are needed. The person completing the assessment evaluates the child's performance in terms of appropriateness and acceptability. The behaviors demonstrated during the role play offer the evaluator insight into the child's level of social competence in a given situation and help to identify deficit behaviors. Behavioral role plays are useful in the assessment of social competence for several reasons:

- ◆ They can be used to evaluate behaviors that occur at low frequencies in natural environments.
- ◆ They represent actual behavioral enactment of a skill.
- ◆ Better control is possible in simulated settings; environments can be simulated where naturalistic observation is difficult.
- ◆ They are less expensive than collecting data via naturalistic observation (Gresham, 1986).

Although use of this method was practical in clinical settings, performances in behavioral role plays show little or no correspondence with the same behaviors assessed in naturalistic settings, and they do not predict sociometric status (Bellack, Hersen & Turner, 1976; LaGreca & Santogrossi, 1980; Van Hasselt, Hersen & Bellack, 1981). This strategy, however, is still considered to be valuable in providing information about social skill deficits, especially when alternative strategies are not practical (Becker & Heimberg, 1988).

Self-Reporting Measures

These evaluations of children's social skills are not used as frequently as other assessment techniques because of their subjectivity and lack of criterion-related validity (Gresham, 1986). Most self-reporting measures were originally developed to assess adult social functioning. Therefore, Becker and Heimberg (1988) cautioned against their use with children unless readability levels were found to be within the child's scope of ability. Gresham (1986) stated that self-reporting measures have not demonstrated predictive validity with peer acceptance, peer popularity, teacher ratings of social skills, role play performance, or social behavior in naturalistic settings. At best, self-reporting measures could provide a piece of information in a total assessment package (Becker & Heimberg, 1988; Gresham, 1986).

Several self-ratings of social skills are available including the *Student Self-Rating* provided in the program forms of *Skillstreaming the Elementary School Child* (McGinnis & Goldstein, 1984). This 60-item checklist requires the child to rate him or herself on a Likert-type scale on specific social skills and how much or how little the behavioral description is like him or her. Sasso, Melloy, and Kavale (1990) used this instrument along with a teacher rating and naturalistic observation to identify social skills deficits in a group of children with behavior disorders. The information gained from the *Student Self-Rating* in conjunction with other assessment information was effective in identifying skill deficits that led to treatment via social skills training. Children demonstrated an increased use of appropriate social skills and some generalization of the skills following treatment. Children from Vignette 7.3 who were identified as neglected and rejected completed the *Student Self-Rating* as part of their assessment.

Behavioral Interviewing

Behavioral interviewing has been successfully used in functional assessment of social behavior. According to Becker and Heimberg (1988), an interview to assess social skills should be designed to evaluate:

- ◆ settings where the behavior is problematic,
- ◆ the specific behavioral competencies necessary for effective performance in each target situation,
- ◆ whether or not the child possesses the necessary competencies,
- ◆ the antecedents and consequences for performance of the behavior in each setting, and
- ◆ additional assessment procedures needed to complete the assessment of social skills.

Behavioral interviews are used infrequently to assess social skills (Gresham, 1986) but are effectively used as a starting point for assessment leading to intervention (Becker & Heimberg, 1988). Although no empirical investigation has been conducted using the behavioral interview method as an assessment of children's social competency, 21 studies investigating the psychometric characteristics of behavioral interviews were reviewed by Gresham (1983). These studies revealed strong reliability and validity.

Naturalistic Observations

Naturalistic observations or behavioral observations of children in naturalistic settings is "the most face-valid method of assessing children's social skills"

(Asher & Hymel, 1981, p. 136). Behavior observation procedures were described in Chapter 3. The naturalistic observation methods described in this section focus on the observation of social behaviors.

Naturalistic observations have been used in numerous studies to identify children in need of social skills interventions, to target social behaviors in need of intervention, and to measure treatment outcomes (e.g., Asher, Markell & Hymel, 1981; Bierman & Furman, 1984; Dodge, Coie & Brakke, 1982; Gresham, 1981; Hartup, Glazier & Charlesworth, 1967; LaGreca & Santogrossi, 1980; McMahon, 1989; Melloy, 1990). In addition a number of studies found a significant positive relationship between sociometric acceptance and positive interactions with peers, while negative interactions with peers were found to correlate with rejection (e.g., Gottman, Gonso & Rasmussen, 1975; Gresham, 1981; Putallaz & Gottman, 1981).

Identified children from Vignette 7.3 were observed by the school psychologist using a naturalistic observation method and recording device similar to the one described in Figure 7.5.

Maheady and Sainato (1985) confirmed these findings when they examined the social interaction patterns of high and low status elementary-aged students who were behaviorally disordered. A peer rating was used to measure

Children who are socially competent are able to interact with their peers with prosocial behavior.

the social status of students in a self-contained behavior disorders class. Students who received the highest and lowest ratings were targeted for study. Social interactions between the six target subjects and their special class peers were measured via direct behavioral observations during recess. The behavioral observations revealed that students with behavioral disorders engaged in positive social interactions of a reciprocal nature during play time. No discernible differences were noted between the target-initiated interaction behavior of high and low status subjects. Specific differences were noted, however, in the interaction behavior directed at target students. High status students received higher rates of peer interactions, greater percentages of positive social initiations, and fewer negative social contacts. Low status students, on the other hand, experienced fewer peer-initiated contacts and these were often negative in nature.

Melloy (1990) used direct observation of the peer interactions among children with and without disabilities to provide data that assisted in the development of social skills interventions for children with disabilities. She identified critical social skills using the behavioral template approach and then, by means of a formal observation method, assessed discrepancies between the behavioral template and the target child's actual behavior. This data, along with information from a teacher rating, peer rating, and peer assessment, resulted in information on social skills deficits targeted for intervention. Behavioral observations were made using paper and pencil recording methods that utilized the behavioral code shown in Figure 7.5. Target behavior codes, which included peer interaction and template behaviors, were defined using information from the teacher's ratings of social competence and peer assessments. Target students' and peers' rates and quality of interaction behavior were coded. Observations were made during the school day when students were expected to interact with peers (e.g., lunch, recess). A minimum of three 10-minute observations were conducted on each of 22 target students using a six-second observe, four-second record, partial interval recording system. Generalization probes of each child's social competence level were obtained across settings (e.g., library, lunchroom) and with peers other than those targeted for intervention. The results indicated that the target students demonstrated very low levels of critical social skill behavior during baseline. Following treatment, however, all but one of the target students demonstrated higher levels of social competence as measured by direct observation and teacher ratings. The social status of the target children did not improve as a result of social skill training.

Hoge (1985) presented an extensive study regarding the validity of direct observation measures of children's classroom behavior. He was able to find consistent support for the validity of direct observation measures. In addition to being the most face-valid assessment method available, behavioral observations provide information on actual peer-adult exchanges (which minimizes subjective bias), have demonstrated sensitivity to intervention effects, and are more conducive to frequent repeated measures. These factors are considered to be advantages of the process of naturalistic observation of social behaviors.

Figure 7.5. *Peer interaction behavior recording sheet.*

Source: Melloy, K. J. (1990). Attitudes and behavior of non-disabled elementary-aged children toward their peers with disabilities in integrated settings: An examination of the effects of treatment on quality of attitudes, social status and critical social skills. Doctoral dissertation, The University of Iowa, Iowa City, Iowa.

Target Child _____ Date _____ Observation #___
Hopeful Playmate _____ Observer _____
Setting _____ Time _____
Template Behaviors: 1_____ 2 _____ 3 _____

D = child with disability	ND = Child without disability
HP = hopeful playmate	V = verbal interaction
+ = positive interaction	NV = nonverbal interaction
– = negative interaction	Tem. = template behavior
	Non-tem. = nontemplate behavior

Int.   Interaction   Behavior

---

 6 D ND HP V NV + – Tem. _____ Non-tem _____
16 D ND HP V NV + – Tem. _____ Non-tem _____
26 D ND HP V NV + – Tem. _____ Non-tem _____
36 D ND HP V NV + – Tem. _____ Non-tem _____
46 D ND HP V NV + – Tem. _____ Non-tem _____
56 D ND HP V NV + – Tem. _____ Non-tem _____
1 minute
 6 D ND HP V NV + – Tem. _____ Non-tem _____
16 D ND HP V NV + – Tem. _____ Non-tem _____
26 D ND HP V NV + – Tem. _____ Non-tem _____
36 D ND HP V NV + – Tem. _____ Non-tem _____
46 D ND HP V NV + – Tem. _____ Non-tem _____
56 D ND HP V NV + – Tem. _____ Non-tem _____
2 minutes
 6 D ND HP V NV + – Tem. _____ Non-tem _____
16 D ND HP V NV + – Tem. _____ Non-tem _____
26 D ND HP V NV + – Tem. _____ Non-tem _____
36 D ND HP V NV + – Tem. _____ Non-tem _____
46 D ND HP V NV + – Tem. _____ Non-tem _____
56 D ND HP V NV + – Tem. _____ Non-tem _____
3 minutes
 6 D ND HP V NV + – Tem. _____ Non-tem _____
16 D ND HP V NV + – Tem. _____ Non-tem _____
26 D ND HP V NV + – Tem. _____ Non-tem _____
36 D ND HP V NV + – Tem. _____ Non-tem _____
46 D ND HP V NV + – Tem. _____ Non-tem _____
56 D ND HP V NV + – Tem. _____ Non-tem _____
4 minutes
 6 D ND HP V NV + – Tem. _____ Non-tem _____
16 D ND HP V NV + – Tem. _____ Non-tem _____
26 D ND HP V NV + – Tem. _____ Non-tem _____
36 D ND HP V NV + – Tem. _____ Non-tem _____
46 D ND HP V NV + – Tem. _____ Non-tem _____
56 D ND HP V NV + – Tem. _____ Non-tem _____
5 minutes

The limitations of naturalistic observations include costliness in time and money, and insufficient information regarding the nature of difficulties in social skills, normative levels of behavior, or the importance of various social behaviors in interpersonal relationships. Some of these limitations are based on the fact that very little data exist that examined the predictive and social validity of observation codes.

Asher, Markell, and Hymel (1981) examined rate of peer interaction to determine if naturalistic observations of rate of interactions provided sufficient information on the social skills of withdrawn children. They concluded that rate of interaction observations lack information with regard to peer acceptance and quality of interactions. Because of this, children may be selected for intervention who do not differ in social skills from those with higher interaction rates. They further stated that this limitation of naturalistic observation could be eliminated if observers focused observations on the rate of interactions, the quality of children's interactions, and examined acceptance levels.

Despite these shortcomings, however, naturalistic observations will continue to be an important method to use in targeting skills for intervention and assessing treatment outcomes of social skills training programs. The reasons for this are that naturalistic observations can provide a functional analysis of behaviors in a natural setting at the time the behavior occurs. In addition, these observations play a critical role in the understanding of children's social behavior and offer a way to access correlates of acceptance reliably.

A number of social skill assessment strategies have been described. To assist the reader in making decisions about appropriate assessment instruments, Table 7.1 offers descriptions of the techniques that have been discussed thus far in Chapter 7.

The children from Vignette 7.3 were evaluated using a peer nomination method to screen individuals who appeared to be at risk for being neglected and rejected by their peers. Findings from the peer nomination resulted in children who were further assessed using a teacher rating scale, a student self-rating, and naturalistic observation. The results of this assessment are reported in Vignette 7.4.

Vignette 7.4.   Results of Assessment for Social Skill Deficits.

Mrs. Kelly and the curriculum committee used the peer nomination procedure to screen 250 first through third graders for social status (see Vignette 7.3). Following administration of the peer nomination, 25 children were identified as being either rejected, neglected, or isolated by their peers. These children were identified as being at risk for needing social skill training to improve their relations with peers. The teachers of these 25 children were asked to complete a Walker-McConnell teacher rating (Walker & McConnell, 1988) on each of the children.

Table 7.1. Social skill assessment instruments and techniques.

Assessment Method	Age	Grade	Commercial Tests Available	Teacher-made Test
Sociometric measures:				
Peer Nomination	6–12	1st–6th		Three questions developed by the teacher, other professional
Peer Rating	6–12	1st–6th		Class roster (see example in Vignette 7.2)
Peer Assessment	3–12	Preschool–6th	The Guess Who Test	Behavior Template Procedure (see Figure 7.2)
Ranking Methods	3–17	Preschool–6th	Systematic Screening of Behavior Disorders	
Ratings by Others:				
Teacher Rating Scales	5–16	K–12th	Social Behavior Assessment; Walker-McConnell Scale of Social Competence Teacher Report Form	
Parent Rating Scales	4–16	Preschool–12th	Child Behavior Checklist	
Behavioral Role Plays	3–17	Preschool–12th		Analog conditions set up by clinician in clinical settings
Self Report	7–17	1st–12th	Student Self Rating from Skillstreaming	
Behavioral Interviews	8–18	2nd–12th		Question format described in Chapter 7
Naturalistic Observations	All ages	All grades		Coding and recording systems (see Figure 7.4)

The school psychologist was responsible for giving each teacher a protocol for the Walker-McConnell and then collecting, scoring, and writing interpretations for each of the completed rating scales. The school psychologist also administered, scored, and interpreted the *Student Self-Rating* (McGinnis & Goldstein, 1984) for each of the 25 children. The school psychologist met with groups of children from each grade who had been identified as in need of further assessment. The purpose of these meetings was to administer the self-rating.

Following completion of the teacher rating and self-rating, the school psychologist identified children who deviated significantly from the norm group on both of the assessment instruments. Ten children emerged as needing further assessment. These children were observed in peer interaction behavior in school situations. Each child was observed for a minimum of six 15-minute sessions in different school settings. The school psychologist presented his findings to the child study team in the school. This group was responsible for identifying effective interventions for individual children and their individual needs. It was decided by the team that all 10 of the children who were observed would receive specific social skills training using the structured learning approach and the social skills described in *Skillstreaming the Elementary School Child* (McGinnis & Goldstein, 1984). The school psychologist was identified as the person who would teach the group social skills using the procedures described later in this chapter. The decision was made that the 15 children who were also identified as at risk, but who did not deviate significantly on the norm-referenced instruments, would be monitored by their teachers for further signs of rejection and isolation. The team left open the possibility that these children would also warrant instruction in social skills.

SOCIAL COMPETENCE TRAINING

Social competence training programs have been effective for children who are deficit in social skills (Coie, 1985; Gresham & Nagle, 1980; Gottman, Gonso, & Schuler, 1976; LaGreca & Santogrossi, 1980; McConnell, Strain, Kerr, Stagg, Lenkner & Lambert, 1984; Melloy, 1990; Oden & Asher, 1977; Sasso, Melloy & Kavale, 1990). The significance of these procedures was strengthened by findings from longitudinal research which suggested that childhood social abilities have significant implications for subsequent adult adjustment (e.g., Hartup, 1979; Kohlberg, LaCrosse & Ricks, 1972; Michelson & Mannarino, 1986; Roff, Sells & Golden, 1972). A variety of social skills training methods have been used to affect the interpersonal relations of children. These methods include coaching and practice, modeling, positive reinforcement, problem-solving techniques, and social skills training packages.

Specific Interventions

Coaching

Coaching and practice are strategies that have been used in a number of studies to improve social competence in children. Coaching involves instruction from either a peer or an adult in a particular social skill (e.g., starting a conversation). To achieve maximum effectiveness of the training, children are given opportunities to practice the skill with others through role play and naturally occurring situations. Kerr and Nelson (1989) suggested that this strategy was effective in teaching social skills to children who were withdrawn to enhance acceptance opportunities.

In one of the most widely cited social skills training studies, Ladd (1981) used a social learning model (i.e., coaching) to teach social skills to 36 children who received low scores on both a sociometric measure and on observations of targeted social skills. The investigation examined changes in low status children's behavior and peer acceptance as the result of social skills training. The target children were randomly assigned to one of three conditions: social skills training (i.e., dyads were coached and given a chance to rehearse three social skills—asking questions, leading, and offering support to others), attention control (i.e., dyads were provided with a similar type [game instruction] and amount of experimenter attention and peer interaction), and nontreatment control (i.e., children were not separated from their classrooms and did not receive any type of training). Results of the investigation showed that:

- Social skill training had a beneficial and lasting effect on children's peer acceptance in the classroom.
- Increases in the levels of "asking questions" and "leading" were significant with no measurable change in the "supportive statements" skill.
- Social skills training of skills correlated with peer acceptance resulted in improved sociometric standing for the treated children.
- The change in peers' attitudes toward the trained children was significant.
- Children in the attention control group did not evidence gains in untrained positive or neutral behaviors and peer acceptance.
- No changes in sociometric status or peer interaction behavior occurred in the control group.

Similarly, Oden and Asher (1977) were able to demonstrate improvement in children on a play sociometric rating measure compared to no change in a control group. Using a peer rating, children were identified as socially isolated. These children were assigned to one of three treatment conditions in which their play behavior was observed. Children who were paired with a peer and received coaching in social skills critical to peer acceptance demonstrated increased acceptance among their peers. Some of the trained children went from having no friends to having at least one friend.

Oden and Asher (1977) suggested that children receive instruction in social skills via coaching for five to seven minutes on each concept (skill) in the following list. Coaching was to take place following these steps, which are derived from Oden's (1980) coaching procedure:

1. Suggest concept (e.g., cooperation).
2. Probe child's knowledge of concept and request examples.
3. Repeat and rephrase child's examples that are appropriate to the concept, and disconfirm and redirect the examples that are not appropriate.
4. Probe child's understanding of counter or opposite concepts and examples.
5. Repeat and rephrase child's examples and clarify that these are or are not counter examples of the concept.
6. Probe child's understanding and reasoning of different social consequences of the social behavioral examples and the counter examples for each concept, from the perspective of both the child and the other child or person with whom the child interacts during a game.
7. Check to see if the child remembers one or two examples for each concept. Review each concept and suggest examples that were not mentioned or remembered.
8. Suggest or instruct the child to try some of the instructed "ideas" in the play session to follow immediately.
9. Inform the child of the postplay review session that will take place later and explain that the ideas will be discussed to determine how useful they are for playing with another child.[6]

Modeling

Modeling is a method that has been used in several studies to teach children social skills (e.g., Gresham & Nagle, 1980; O'Connor, 1969; Oden & Asher, 1977). Modeling is a type of vicarious learning that exposes the child to live or filmed examples of children who perform the desired social skill in an appropriate manner. The technique is seldom used in isolation because of its short-term effects (McGinnis & Goldstein, 1984; Michelson & Mannarino, 1986; Rinn & Markle, 1979). Modeling is an effective social skills intervention when used in conjunction with techniques such as coaching, role play, and feedback (Gresham & Nagle, 1980; LaGreca & Santogrossi, 1980; Lefevre, Malcolm, West, & Ledingham, 1983).

For example, Gresham and Nagle (1980) investigated the effects of coaching and modeling on the social skills of isolated children. Sociometric peer ratings and peer nominations were administered to members of 14 third- and fourth-grade classrooms to identify socially isolated children. Outcomes of

---

[6] *Source:*   Cartledge G., and Milburn, J. F. (Eds.). (1983). Teaching social skills to children: Innovative approaches. New York: Pergamon Press. Reprinted with permission.

social skills training were measured using sociometric measures and naturalistic observations of the quality and rate of peer interactions. Coaching consisted of verbal instructions, behavioral rehearsal, and feedback. Modeling was in the form of videotapes of unfamiliar grade peers modeling the social skills. Results indicated that coaching and modeling were effective in improving the social skills of the target children and increasing social status.

Positive Reinforcement

Positive reinforcement (defined and discussed in Chapter 5) is another effective, empirically based social skills technique (Cole, Meyer, Vandercook & McQuarter, 1986; Lefevre et al., 1983; Strain & Timm, 1974; Strain, Shores, & Timm, 1977). These social skills training programs were based on the positive reinforcement process (i.e., behaviors increase in frequency because they are followed by reinforcement—see Chapter 5). Positive reinforcement is given by the teacher in the form of social approval or attention or tokens that were exchanged for other rewards, privileges, or activities. Peers as well as adults have been used to facilitate appropriate social behavior (Cole et al., 1986; Lefevre et al., 1983; Michelson & Mannarino, 1986).

A number of common characteristics of positive reinforcement programs are used to facilitate social skills in children. When developing new social behaviors (e.g., use of self-control), reinforcement needs to be applied using a continuous reinforcement schedule following a desired response. Once responding occurs at a high level, reinforcement can be given on an intermittent schedule. Prompting, shading, and fading procedures (see Chapter 5) are important components of effective reinforcement programs used in teaching children to become socially competent. Walker, Greenwood, Hops, and Todd (1979) cautioned teachers and parents that providing reinforcement and praise to children who were withdrawn for behaviors such as "starting a conversation" actually suppressed interaction behavior. Reinforcement of maintaining and continuing social interactions, however, was effective in increasing levels of interaction. It is important to note here that individuals who are withdrawn may respond better to the coaching and modeling interventions that were discussed previously. Use of reinforcement for children in this population will be effective once they have acquired the social skills.

In research on the social skills of students who were severely disabled, Cole et al. (1986) examined the effects of positive reinforcement on peer interactions. The *Special Friends Program* (Voeltz, 1982) was used with 40 dyads made up of one child who was severely disabled and one regular education peer. During the baseline phase of the study, teachers in the classrooms allowed a free play session in which peer interactions and teacher behavior were observed. Following baseline, dyads were randomly assigned to one of two treatment conditions: a social instruction group and a friendly comments control group. Teachers were required to intervene with members of both groups at a rate of twice per 20-minute session using different scripts for instructional prompting or verbal reinforcement with each group. Each script consisted of two to three sentences and prompting for or rewarding demonstration of various types of cooperative play behavior. Friendly comment scripts that did not prompt cooperative play were applied to the control group. Behavioral observations were made of teacher and peer interaction behavior. Results indicated that the intervention positively affected various social play behavior initially but that these effects diminished or reversed themselves as the intervention continued. These results implied that early teacher intervention may improve interactions between peers with and without severe disabilities but needed to be withdrawn over time so that students could resolve interpersonal difficulties independently.

Use of Peers to Develop Social Competence

Use of peers to effect change in social competence has proven effective with a number of children who demonstrated deficits in social skills. When peer-mediated strategies are used to assist children in learning social skills, it is important that the peers be sensitive to the child's needs and able to appreciate the child's abilities and any deficits the child may have. Sasso and Rude (1987) suggested that use of high status peers (i.e., popular children) in training of social skills resulted in the child with deficits learning social skills and becoming more accepted in the educational environment.

Kerr and Nelson (1989) described a number of interventions that involved peers as behavior change agents. *Peer Imitation Training* requires a classmate of the child who demonstrates deficits (e.g., rejected or isolated) to model appropriate social skills. A teacher is also involved to provide prompts and reinforcement to the child who is deficit in social skills. This strategy has been most successful with young withdrawn children in teaching them to interact with peers in play situations. Peer imitation training should take place in the most natural setting possible so that the social skill is more likely to generalize. Kerr and Nelson (1989) suggested that peers chosen as models be students who attend school regularly, exhibit frequent appropriate social skills with others, can follow teacher verbal instructions and imitate a teacher model, and are able to attend to the training task for at least ten minutes per target child. The following list provides guidelines for using peer imitation to teach social skills.

1. Seat the children about two feet apart and facing one another.
2. Station a trainer behind each child in a "shadowing" style.
3. The trainer behind the peer model whispers in the child's ear to cue the target behavior.
4. The model child performs the target behavior.
5. The trainer behind the target child instructs him or her to watch the model child and asks the target child to do the behavior.
6. If the target child imitates the modeled behavior, the trainer offers verbal praises and affectionate pats.

7. If the target child does not imitate the modeled behavior, the trainer behind the target child physically guides the desired behavior.

8. The trainer gradually fades physical guidance and continues to reinforce successive approximations.

9. When the target child can successfully imitate the peer model while seated across from each other, move the training to a less structured setting, e.g., a free-play setting.

10. When the peer model exhibits an appropriate behavior, approach the target child and instruct him or her to watch the model and tell the target child to do the same.

11. Provide physical guidance if the target child fails to imitate.

12. Fade physical guidance and reinforce successive approximations.[7]

Peer social initiation is a strategy that enlists a peer trainer to make social bids to a withdrawn child or children (Kerr & Nelson, 1989). Sasso and Rude (1987) used this strategy with eight children who were severely disabled to effect social status change. In another study with middle-school children who were nondisabled and disabled, Sasso, Mundschenk, Melloy, Wacker, and Kelly (1990) found this procedure to be effective in teaching children to interact with each other during card-playing sessions. Peer trainers should be chosen using the criteria described above. Also keep in mind that even children with disabilities and very young children have been used as effective peer trainers. Trainers should not be expected to work with more than one child at a time. Kerr and Nelson (1989) noted that initially the child who is withdrawn may not respond to this strategy since typically they may demonstrate oppositional behavior. For this reason, it is important for the peer trainer and teacher to stick with the target child and not give up immediately. Prompting and reinforcement in the initial sessions will help to eliminate the oppositional behavior on the part of the target child. The following is a list of suggestions for preparing the peer trainer:

1. Explain to the peer trainer what is expected during the training sessions. Examples of the explanation are "Try your best to get other children to play with you."

2. Train the peer trainer to expect rejection. This may be accomplished by the adult and the peer trainer conducting role play situations in which the target child ignores the peer trainer. It is important for the adult to encourage the peer trainer to keep trying to initiate social interactions even when the target child ignores him or her.

3. Repeat the role play, first training the peer to make a motor-gestural initiation (e.g., handing a toy). Then train the peer trainer to make vocal-verbal initiations.

_____

[7] *Source:*   Cooke, T. P., in Kerr, M. M., and Nelson, C. M. (1989). *Strategies for managing behavior problems in the classroom* (2nd ed.), p. 327. Columbus, OH: Merrill/Macmillan. Reprinted with permission.

4. Carry out the role play using each of the toys or play materials in the natural setting. Cue the peer trainer about any toys that have particular appeal to the target child.
5. Continue practicing the role plays during daily 20-minute practice sessions until the peer trainer can reliably make repeated social initiations toward you (usually four).
6. Be sure to reinforce the peer trainer's participation during each training session.[8]

Suggestions for conducting peer social initiation intervention procedures are as follows:

1. Set aside at least six minutes for each target individual during the play session.
2. Try to use the same free-play area with the play materials suggested each day.
3. Before each intervention session, review with the peer trainer those activities that are most likely to be successful.
4. Remind the peer trainer before each session that the child may not be responsive at first, but to keep trying.
5. Remind the peer trainer when to change toys and when to begin play with another target child.
6. Reinforce the peer trainer for attempting to play with target children. If the session is going slowly, you may wish to reinforce the peer trainer during the session. Otherwise, provide the peer trainer with some form of reinforcement at the end of the session.[9]

Structured Learning Approach

A number of authors have described the effectiveness of using the *structured learning approach,* or combinations of social skills interventions, to assist children in developing social competence (Hops, Walker, & Greenwood, 1979; LaGreca & Santogrossi, 1980; Lefevre et al., 1983; McMahon, 1989; McGinnis & Goldstein, 1984; Melloy, 1990; Sasso, Melloy, & Kavale, 1990). Typically, the structured learning approach includes instructions, modeling, rehearsal and practice (role play), feedback, social reinforcement, homework assignments, and procedures to enhance generalization (McGinnis & Goldstein, 1984; Michelson & Mannarino, 1986; Midgett, Miller, & Wicks, 1989). Significant results in improved social competence have been reported in studies employing

---

8 *Source:* Kerr, M. M., and Nelson, C. M. (1989). *Strategies for managing behavior problems in the classroom* (2nd ed.), p. 329. Columbus, OH: Merrill/Macmillan. Reprinted with permission.
9 *Source:* Kerr, M. M., and Nelson, C. M. (1989). *Strategies for managing behavior problems in the classroom* (2nd ed.), p. 330. Columbus, OH: Merrill/Macmillan. Reprinted with permission.

social skills training packages as interventions for children (Melloy, 1990; Michelson, Mannarino, Marchione & Martin, 1982; Michelson & Wood, 1980; Midgett, Miller, & Wicks, 1989).

Sasso, Melloy, and Kavale (1990) initiated social skills training using the structured learning approach with three students who were behaviorally disordered (ages 8, 10, and 13). The skills taught were chosen based on the results from teacher ratings and self-ratings, which identified skills deficits and strengths. Following assessment, the students were trained in social skills through modeling, role play, performance feedback, and homework assignments that promoted generalization. The study revealed that the social skills behavior of the children increased in frequency of use of the skills as a result of the structured learning approach. In addition, negative behaviors decreased as a result of training. These effects were measured across an entire school year and were found to be maintained over time. Two of the children were observed to generalize the skills they had acquired to nontreatment settings. One of the children did not generalize the skills he had learned to nontreatment settings. This suggested that modifications may be needed in the structured learning approach when teaching social skills to children with autism. Finally, functional clusters of behavior related to peer interactions were identified. This implied that teaching these skills together may result in more effective training of social skills to children.

Melloy (1990) provided instruction in critical social skills to 13 first through sixth graders with mild mental disabilities or behavior disorders. The children in the study were all integrated into regular classrooms, but received some instruction in special education classrooms during part of their school day. Social skills training was conducted using the structured learning approach. Training occurred during twice-weekly 30-minute sessions (i.e., 60 minutes per week) over a six-week period. For each skill identified for intervention (e.g., giving a compliment, praising, sharing, how to join in), modeling, role play, performance feedback, and homework assignments were used to assist in the acquisitions of new social skills or to provide practice for newly acquired skills. The format that was used to train all skills included four distinct session components: (1) a discussion of the specific skill, the steps necessary for successful performance of the skill, and the modeling of the skill by the instructor; (2) a review of the skill steps, followed by instructor modeling, student role play activities, and instructor and peer feedback; (3) a presentation of homework practice assignments, followed by reports of success in using the skill; and (4) a session in which students reported results of homework practice and discussed possible situations in which the skill might be necessary. The training criterion was reached when the children successfully (i.e., able to perform at least 95% of the skill steps without prompts from the teacher) role-played the steps involved in each skill within the context of the training sessions.

Appropriate behavior (listening to others in the group and participating in group activities) during each session was reinforced with praise and tokens. Inappropriate behavior (disrupting the group with noise or not participating in group activities) resulted in loss of tokens and practice of appropriate behavior.

Homework assignments were provided to give practice opportunities at times other than during the social skills class. Children chose a setting, situation, and person to practice the skill. These settings included the regular classroom, playground, bus, lunchroom, home, and others. Children received guidance as necessary in choosing a homework opportunity.

Children were also asked to keep a journal describing when social skills were used and also missed opportunities to use the skills. This provided an opportunity for students to self-record and monitor their success. In addition, this information allowed for feedback from the teacher concerning the child's performance. Children were given a few minutes each week to write in their journals during the training session.

A *sufficient exemplars approach* (Stokes & Baer, 1977) was used to facilitate generalization of social skills across untrained persons, settings, and situations (Kerr & Nelson, 1989; Stokes & Osnes, 1986). Thus, training took place in a minimum of two settings (i.e., school settings other than the special education classroom) and with at least two other persons (randomly chosen peers and adults encountered in the school environment). For example, target children received social skills training on the playground when the skill being taught would naturally be used in that setting (e.g., encouraging others during recess).

Results of the study revealed that all but one of the children who received social skills training did become more socially competent in that they increased their use of critical social behaviors crucial to acceptance and friendship. The children were also observed to generalize these behaviors to other settings and persons. The following list offers a description of the first social skills training session used in the Melloy (1990) study:

1. Tell the students that the purpose of the class is to help them learn to be a better friend and to get along better with friends.
2. Develop group rules (helpful reminders) as a class.
3. Explain the token economy system (reinforcement for appropriate behavior).
4. Explain journal for self-monitoring of social skill behavior.

In subsequent sessions, each skill is taught using the structured learning approach which includes modeling of the skill, student role plays, performance feedback, and homework. Skills instruction in each social skill takes place for a minimum of three 30- to 45-minute sessions. A format for each session is described below.

Lesson #1:
1. Discuss the skill to be learned.
2. Formulate the skill steps to be learned. Write these on the board or on an easel sheet.
3. The teacher models the skill using another adult or a skilled child as a co-actor.

4. Feedback is given to the teacher by the students.

Lesson #2:

1. Discuss homework assignments from previous skills taught.
2. Review skill steps for skill currently being learned.
3. The teacher models the skill again.
4. Role plays are done by each child in the group. The main actor chooses a co-actor from other members of the group. They then role play the skill using a situation that the main actor chooses. Role plays take place for as many sessions as needed to allow each child in the group a chance to be the main actor. Try not to make this more than three sessions.
5. Students and teacher provide feedback to the main actor.
6. Homework is assigned.

Lesson #3:

1. Discuss homework assignments from previous sessions.
2. Review skill steps.
3. Continue role plays.
4. Provide feedback.
5. Assign homework.[10]

Social Skills Curricula

Young Children

A number of social skills curricula designed to improve social competence in young children (ages 5 through 12) are available for use by teachers and other practitioners in school settings. Current popular curricula are described below.

Skillstreaming the Elementary School Child (McGinnis & Goldstein, 1984) describes the teaching of 60 social skills to elementary-aged children using the structured learning approach. Lesson plans are given for teaching each social skill. Social skills are broken down into five components: classroom survival, friendship-making, dealing with feelings, alternatives to aggression, and dealing with stress. A separate program-forms book provides reproducible sheets for three types of homework assignments, progress forms, teacher and student checklists, contracts, and awards for demonstration of social skills. The curriculum is available from Research Press in Champaign, Illinois.

The second edition of *Systematic Instruction of Social Skills* (Sargent, 1988) provides lesson plans for teaching social skills to children in primary and intermediate grades. Skills lessons are included for classroom-related skills,

---

10 *Source:*   Melloy, K. J. (1990). Attitudes and behavior of non-disabled elementary-aged children toward their peers with disabilities in integrated settings: An examination of the effects of treatment on quality of attitude, social status and critical social skills. Doctoral dissertation, The University of Iowa, Iowa City, Iowa.

school building-related skills, personal skills, interaction initiative skills, and interaction response skills. The format for teaching social skills follows the structured learning approach. The appendix includes a social skills rating checklist and homework forms. The curriculum was written to be used with children who are mentally disabled but could be adapted for use with other populations as well. It is available from the Iowa Department of Education, Bureau of Special Education, Grimes State Office Building, Des Moines, Iowa 50319-0146.

Learning the Skills of Peacemaking, an Activity Guide for Elementary-Age Children on Communicating/Cooperating/Resolving Conflict (Drew, 1987) was designed to teach children skills for problem-solving. The 56 lessons offer teachers and others well-planned ideas and activities for teaching social skills regarding getting along with others and resolving conflicts. The curriculum is available from Jalmar Press, 45 Hitching Post Drive, Building 2, Rolling Hills Estates, California 90274.

Adolescents

A number of curricula are also available to teach social skills to adolescents. These curricula tend to focus on skills needed in the workplace following school but also deal with interpersonal relationships adolescents encounter in other environments. A sample of several popular curricula are described below.

Skillstreaming the Adolescent (Goldstein, Sprafkin, Gershaw, & Klein, 1980) suggests use of the structured learning approach to teach social skills to adolescents that will assist them in becoming socially competent. Lesson plans for 50 different social skills are provided in the manual, which includes suggestions for homework report forms, a student skills checklist, a grouping chart, and progress charts. The social skills are broken down into six components, including beginning social skills, advanced social skills, dealing with feelings, alternatives to aggression, dealing with stress, and planning skills. Each skill is broken into behavioral steps that can be role-played by a main actor and co-actors. The curriculum is available from Research Press in Champaign, Illinois.

The second edition of *Systematic Instruction of Social Skills* (Sargent, 1988) provides lessons in social skills for junior and senior high students who are mentally disabled. The format for instruction uses the structured learning approach to teach social skills in classroom-related skills, school building-related skills, interactive initiative skills, community-related skills, and work-related skills. It is available from the Iowa Department of Education, Bureau of Special Education, Grimes State Office Building, Des Moines, Iowa 50319-0146.

The Walker Social Skills Curriculum: The ACCESS Program (Walker, Todis, Holmes, & Horton, 1988) was designed to promote social competence among adolescents. Thirty-one social skills lessons are presented in which students are to role play common situations. A student study guide is provided to give students the opportunity to contract with caregivers for a given social skill and to complete homework assignments for each skill. Social skills lessons are given for peer-related skills, adult-related skills, and self-related skills. The curriculum is available from Pro-Ed in Austin, Texas.

Considerations for Selecting a Social Skills Curriculum

Teachers and others who are responsible for selecting social skill curricula will be happy to know that many excellent commercially available materials are on the market. Many of these materials have been well researched and are relatively inexpensive. Several of these curricula have been described in this chapter. The following points are offered for consideration when choosing social skill curricula to guide teaching of social skills to children and adolescents:

◆ The cost of the curriculum (many are available for less than $50).
◆ The age of the students who will receive instruction based on the chosen curriculum (curricula are available for preschoolers through high school aged children).
◆ The level of training needed to teach social skills using a selected curriculum. Several curricula (for example, Accepts or Skillstreaming) are formatted in a fashion that is easy to understand simply by reading the material and observing someone using the materials. Other curricula require specific training (e.g., Boy's Town).
◆ The evaluation system that is built into the social skills curriculum. Those curricula that have assessment techniques and recording devices provided in the materials will require less teacher preparation time than those curricula that do not supply these materials.
◆ The skills taught based on those offered in the curriculum need to be social skills that are critical to the needs of the children who will be taught lessons based on the curriculum.

Guidelines for Social Skills Groups

Group Size

Teaching social skills to children and youth is best accomplished in groups of 5 to 10 students. Groups of this size will allow for everyone in the group to participate in role playing and other activities designed to promote social competence. A small group also lends itself to easier behavior management and allows the teacher to give necessary attention to all members of the group. If it is necessary to teach in larger groups, it is suggested that initial discussion of the social skill to be taught and modeling of the skill could be accomplished in the large group. If more than one adult is available, it is suggested that the group be broken into smaller groups for role playing sessions.

Instructors

Most of the curricula for teaching of social skills is designed to be taught by a variety of educators. Teachers, psychologists, social workers, and guidance counselors have all proven to be effective instructors of social skills. Other adults such as paraprofessionals, teacher assistants, and parents could provide useful assistance in social skills instruction within small groups. The most important characteristic of an effective instructor of social skills is that the person teaching the skill must practice appropriate social skills and be socially competent in a variety of environments. Children are often referred to social skills training because they have demonstrated deficits in social competence—they deserve to be taught by an individual who is socially competent and equipped to model behaviors that are accepted by society.

Physical Arrangement of the Room

Social skills instruction needs to be viewed with the same importance as instruction in reading, math, and other school subjects. Children who need this type of instruction are at risk for failure in social relations during their school years and, just as importantly, as adults. Just as a teacher arranges the room to meet the needs of instruction in other subjects, he or she needs to give attention to the arrangement for instruction in social skills. Social skills instruction seems to be most effective when the group's chairs are arranged in a semicircle facing a blackboard or an easel. The space created by the semicircle provides a "stage" on which the main actor and his or her co-actors can role play. This arrangement also gives the impression that interaction among the group members is expected and necessary to the success of the lesson. The blackboard provides a space to list the behavioral steps of the social skill so that members of the group have easy access to the skill steps during the lesson.

Materials

Initially, a group should develop a *list of rules* such as "listen to others," "keep hands and feet to self," etc. Figure 7.6 provides an example of rules generated by a social skills group in an elementary class. A list of the rules should be readily accessible to members of the group so that they can keep them in mind during the group session.

Once the first lesson of the social skill has been completed, the behavioral steps of the skill should be listed on a *poster* that can be used in the group during the sessions. Later, the poster can be displayed in the room for the children to refer to as they continue to practice social skills they have learned. Skills posters are available from the publishers of *Skillstreaming the Elementary School Child* (McGinnis & Goldstein, 1984) and *Skillstreaming the Adolescent* (Goldstein et al., 1980). Posters can easily be developed also by using markers and poster board or computer software designed to make posters. An example of a poster is presented in Figure 7.7.

The teacher needs to record the children who have been the main actor in a role play, completed homework assignments, and other information about the skills lesson. Blank index cards make handy *recording devices* that can be brought to social skills class and then stored in a card file box on the teacher's desk. Some curricula include progress recording forms that can be used to document each child's progress in learning social skills. Some teachers will want

Figure 7.6. *Examples of social skills group rules.*

GOODHUE ELEMENTARY SOCIAL SKILLS GROUP

Helpful Reminders:

1. Look at the person who is talking to show you are listening.

2. Keep hands and feet to yourself.

3. Leave stuff at other table.

4. Participate.

to use a token economy (see Chapter 5) for behavior management during the social skills group. *Tokens* will need to be available for use during the session. McGinnis and Goldstein (1984) suggest use of "SCAMO" (showing caring about myself and others) tokens in a social skills group.

Group Composition

Social skills groups are typically composed of children of similar ages who demonstrate common deficits in social skills. Effective instruction has taken place in groups of children who were mentally disabled, behaviorally disordered, learning disabled, nondisabled, and combinations of these populations (Hollinger, 1987; Melloy, 1990; Renshaw & Asher, 1982; Strain et al., 1984). Children targeted for intervention are identified using the assessment techniques described previously in this chapter. Once identification takes place, teachers can group children based on common deficits, schedules, ages, grade levels, and/or classroom. There is no empirical evidence to date that clearly defines what type of children group together best. Rather, it is important that teachers and children learn the social skills necessary to work together in any combination of types of persons since in the real world, people are not always allowed to pick and choose with whom they will work and play.

*Figure 7.7.   Example of a
poster listing social skill steps.*

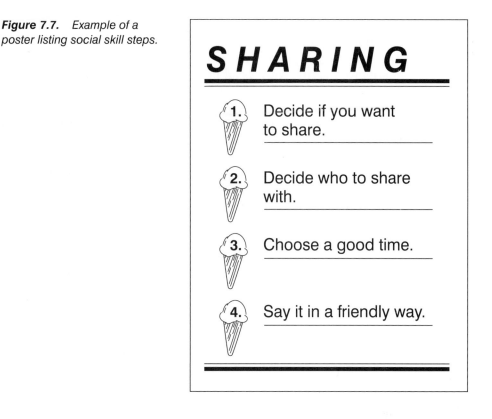

SHARING

1. Decide if you want to share.

2. Decide who to share with.

3. Choose a good time.

4. Say it in a friendly way.

Conducting the Lesson

Conducting the lesson should follow a structured learning approach. Once the room has been arranged for the social skills group to meet and the group is seated, the group rules should be reviewed. This will help to eliminate the need for the teacher to remind children about the rules for participation later in the session, saving valuable time for instruction.

After the rules have been reviewed, discussion of the social skill being learned needs to be discussed. This discussion is needed during the first session only. In subsequent sessions, the behavioral steps of the social skill will need to be reviewed. Depending on the session—first, second, or third—the teacher models the skill (session 1 and 2). The group members give the teacher feedback on his or her performance of the skill.

Then the teacher asks for volunteers to be main actors (every student in the group needs to take a turn being the main actor). The main actor then thinks about a role play situation for the skill being taught. To save class time, this could be done before social skills class as part of the child's daily assignments. When the main actor has a role play in mind, he or she picks a co-actor to act out the role play. After the role play, the teacher gives general feedback to the main actor and co-actor about how they did in the role play. Then peers are given a chance to give constructive feedback to the actors about their performance of the social skill. It is important that feedback be limited to constructive comments and that peers are not allowed to put down the actors. "Giving constructive feedback" could be one of the group rules.

If a token economy is being used to help manage group behavior, tokens are given paired with social praise throughout the session for adhering to the group rules and for participating in the role plays. Time must be set aside at the end of the class to tally tokens and record them in a "bank book" and to make time to trade in tokens for secondary reinforcers (see Chapter 5 for a description of token economies).

At the end of each session, homework assignments are given to children who have been actors. Children are given the option at the beginning of each session to discuss their assignment with the class or to hand it in without discussion.

Monitoring of Progress

Children will want to see their progress in learning of social skills. Although they should realize enhanced social relations as a result of social skills training, they will be further motivated by a written record of their progress. Several suggestions for monitoring progress are provided.

The teacher can help the child to keep track of use of a social skill on a point sheet by tallying points earned whenever the child receives reinforcement. Children can record this number on a graph that can be displayed in the classroom. Forms for charting progress are available in several social skills curricula. Caregivers can use these to document skills learned and level of social competence demonstrated by the child.

Homework assignments can be saved and bound into a book using a plastic comb, rings, or a three-ring notebook. Children could decorate their "books" and keep them for future reference.

BEHAVIOR MANAGEMENT TECHNIQUES TO IMPROVE SOCIAL SKILLS

In Chapter 5 behavior management techniques designed to increase behavior were described. Here we call your attention to the use of these procedures to increase social skills competence in children.

Increasing Social Skills Behavior

Positive Reinforcement

Positive reinforcement has been used as a strategy to improve social competence in children. This procedure was described previously in this chapter. Specifically, *token economies* are one type of positive reinforcement program that are effective in increasing social skill use by children. Children who engage in appropriate social skill behaviors are reinforced by earning tokens for their demonstration of social competence. The following list describes how to set up a token economy applied to the use of social skills:

1. Target social skill behaviors that will be reinforced when demonstrated by target children.
2. Conceptualize and present the desired social skill behavior to the child or group by emphasizing what they can do.
3. Instruct the children in desired social skill behavior. Post social skill steps and review frequently.
4. Select an appropriate token (see Chapter 4).
5. Establish rewards for which tokens can be exchanged.
6. Develop a reward menu and post it in the classroom.
7. Implement the token economy.
8. Provide immediate reinforcement for acceptable social behavior.
9. Gradually change from a continuous to a variable schedule of reinforcement.
10. Provide time for the children to exchange tokens for rewards.
11. Revise the reward menu frequently.[11]

Contingency contracts have been effective in increasing appropriate social skill behavior, especially in older children and adolescents. When contingency contracts are used to increase the likelihood that a child will increase his or her use of social skills, the child and teacher define the contract in terms of demonstration of appropriate social skills and a mutually agreed on form of reinforcement. Examples of contract forms specifically for increasing social skills can be found in McGinnis and Goldstein (1984). When formulating a contract for behavioral management of social skill behavior, the following steps are essential:

1. Select one or two social skills that you want to work on first.
2. Describe those social skills so that they may be observed and counted.
3. Identify rewards that will help provide motivation to increase social skill performance.
4. The teacher and child work out a plan for keeping track of behavior and handing out rewards.
5. Write the contract so that everyone can understand it.
6. Collect data.
7. Troubleshoot the system if the data do not show improved social skill performance.
8. Rewrite the contract if needed.
9. Continue to monitor, troubleshoot, and rewrite until the social skills that were troublesome improve.

---

[11] *Source:*   Cooper, J. O. (1987). *Token economy,* pp. 486–498, Applied behavior analysis. Columbus, OH: Merrill/Macmillan.

10.   Select another social skill on which to work.[12]

Level Systems

Level systems have been used with token economies to account for improvement in behavior targeted for intervention (Kerr & Nelson, 1989). Social skills training and acquisition lends itself to the use of a level system with a token economy to reinforce children when they engage in appropriate social behavior. Guidelines for setting up a level system to incorporate into the teaching of social skills are provided here:

1.   *Select the entry behavior that the children may have.* These may include deficits in social skills such as joining in a game, carrying on a conversation, and using self-control.
2.   *Choose the terminal behaviors that the children are expected to demonstrate before moving out of the level system.* In keeping with the examples in item 1, these behaviors may be competence in joining in, carrying on a conversation, and acting out alternatives to aggression.
3.   *Name two to four behaviors that are between the entry level and terminal behaviors.* For example, a child enters the system without the ability to join in a game with others. The first step or behavior that would need to be acquired is for the child to learn to decide if he wants to join in the game. Next, he would need to learn and decide what to say to members of the group he wishes to join. The child would then need to learn how to decide on a good time to join in. Finally, the child would need to learn how to ask to join in using a friendly voice and body language.
4.   *The teacher needs to assign privileges and reinforcers to each step toward the terminal behavior—this constitutes the levels.* For example, a child would earn 100 points each time he demonstrated the social skill (Level 1). Those points could be traded for items on a menu such as two minutes of free-time. When the child was able to demonstrate the social skill on a regular basis, he would move to an intermittent schedule of reinforcement and earn 300 points for demonstration of the skill (Level 2). Level 2 points could be traded for such things as five minutes of free-time and so on.[13]

Boy's Town Motivation System

One educational model that combines social skills training with a levels system and token economy is the *Boy's Town Motivation System* (Wells, personal com-

---

[12]   *Source:* From *Writing Behavioral Contracts: A Case Simulation Practice Manual,* (p. 7) by W. J. DeRisi and G. Butz, 1975, Champaign, IL: Research Press. Copyright 1975 by Research Press. Reprinted by permission.

[13]   *Source:* Bauer, A. M., Shea., T. M., and Keppler, R. (1986). Levels systems: A framework for the individualization of behavior management. *Behavioral Disorders,* *12*(1), 28–35. Reprinted with permission.

munication, 1990). Children involved in the Boy's Town Model are taught social skills using the structured learning approach. The motivation system of the model is designed to reinforce use of the social skills by the children. This model allows teachers to use a common approach to teaching social skills and consequating positive/negative behavior. Children on the system accumulate points to allow access to a menu of reinforcers. "Three graduated levels of support are employed by the system in order to promote learning of the skills, and systematically fade dependence upon artificial reinforcers" (Wells, 1990, p. 2). This also helps to promote generalization and maintenance of acceptable social behavior.

The levels system is comprised of three levels: a daily points system, progress level, and merit level. On the daily points system, the focus is on acquisition of social skills through frequent, direct instruction and immediate point gains and losses. Students earn their way to the progress level by accumulating points toward advancement in the system. On the progress level, students still receive direct instruction in social skills but the verbal feedback and consequences reflect qualitative differences in skill use. Instead of earning points, the child earns a positive or negative. At the end of the day, the child and teacher review his or her progress card and negotiate a rating of the child's overall performance. This rating is translated into a number of points that allows access to the reinforcer menu. Privileges and activities on the progress level reflect a higher level reward for competence in social skills. In the third level, merit, the focus is on maintaining social skill use across various settings, situations, and persons. Direct teaching of social skills continues but students receive a noncontingent allowance of points for each day that merit level criteria for behavior are met. Children at the merit level receive special privileges and recognition. Once children attain the merit level, they are able to demonstrate social skills that imply social competence. This also implies that the child is ready to be reintegrated into the regular classroom if he or she has attended special education classes. At the merit level, gradual reintegration takes place and the child is expected to meet typical school expectations and consequence systems.

The Boy's Town Model has been applied in a number of schools throughout the country with success in assisting children to become socially competent (Hendrickson, personal communication; Ebling & Schultz, personal communication; Tetterton, 1990). This model, along with others like it, represents a comprehensive teaching approach to developing social competence in children.

GENERALIZATION OF SOCIAL SKILLS TRAINING

Generalization Training Procedures

Very often children and teachers spend a lot of time learning social skills in a restrictive setting such as a special education classroom where children are able to demonstrate use of the skills. Unfortunately, children do not always naturally generalize these skills to settings other than the training setting or to people different than those they learned from. Treatment effects often do not extend to situations outside the treatment setting and therefore the changes in behavior have not been socially validated. A number of training procedures exist that are effective in teaching children to generalize social behaviors from one setting to another. Kerr and Nelson (1989) explained generalization in terms of three effects on behavior and these explanations are extended to effects of social skills training on social competence in children.

Response maintenance refers to whether or not the behavior exists once intervention has been withdrawn. For example, a child receives social skills training in "staying out of fights" and is able to demonstrate this behavior during the time he or she is being trained and reinforced for not fighting with his or her peers. However, two days after training ceases, the child gets into a fight on the playground. This implies that the child was not able to maintain the response (staying out of fights) when he or she was not receiving direct instruction in the social skill. On the other hand, if behavioral observations revealed that the child no longer got into fights 2 weeks, 6 weeks, and 12 weeks after intervention was stopped, we could assume that the social behavior of "staying out of fights" could be maintained.

Another effect is referred to as *stimulus generalization* or transfer of training. This effect is described as learning a social skill in the presence of specific discriminative stimuli such as a teacher prompt to initiate a conversation. The child would demonstrate stimulus generalization if he or she initiated a conversation following training without the teacher prompt. Stimulus generalization also occurs if the child is able to transfer training to other settings, persons, cues, or physical objects (Kerr & Nelson, 1989).

A third behavior effect is referred to as *response generalization*. This effect on behavior involves the demonstration of other behaviors that are related to the social skill behavior taught. These behaviors may be related by function (e.g., attention getting) or topography (e.g., what the behavior looks like). For example, a child steals money from his sister so that he can buy gas for his car to drive peers around that he would like to be friends with. Through social skills training, he learns strategies for making friends that are alternatives to giving material things. As a result, he makes friends and stops stealing money from his sister.

Stokes and Baer (1977) described training strategies that promote generalization of behaviors. A number of authors have shown that several of these strategies are effective in teaching children to generalize social skills, therefore developing social competence (Gresham, 1986; McConnell, 1987; McMahon, 1989; Melloy, 1990; Sasso, Melloy, & Kavale, 1990).

One of the most effective procedures to promote generalization of social skills is *training sufficient exemplars*. This procedure is designed to offer many opportunities for the child learning social skills to practice with others in settings different than the training setting. For example, if a child is learning the social skill "using self-control," she will be taught the skill steps during social skills class and then be reinforced whenever she uses the skill in the classroom. However, the child has demonstrated the most difficulty with using self-control on the playground when all of the swings have been taken. When she doesn't get a swing, she taunts the children who are swinging and yells loudly to let others know she isn't happy. Using the sufficient exemplars approach, her teacher needs to conduct social skills lessons in the use of self-control on the playground during recess with children other than those in the target child's social skills class. This training can take place in 5- to 10-minute sessions on a daily basis until the target behavior is demonstrated in the generalization setting. To train sufficient exemplars, the teacher would inform the child that they were going to work on the social skill on the playground, since that is where she had trouble using self-control. The teacher and the child would go to the playground where the skill would be modeled by the adult and then role played by the child. During training, the teacher would model alternative behavior that the target child could engage in when she felt herself losing control. Following this training session, the target child would be given opportunities to role play with other children on the playground. The teacher could enlist the help of untrained peers by briefly explaining to the peer that the target child was learning a new social skill and needed his or her help in practicing the skill. This strategy has been used effectively to increase interaction rate and quality among a group of children with behavior disorders and their nondisabled peers (Melloy, 1990).

Homework assignments in social skills promote generalization of skills by having the child report opportunities where he or she demonstrated the social behavior. Children who successfully complete homework assignments demonstrate that they have been trained with sufficient exemplars to be able to transfer the social skill.

Entrapment or the *trapping effect* has been described as a strategy that could promote generalization of social skills (McConnell, 1987; McMahon, 1989). The trapping effect is "used to describe the tactic of increasing naturally contingent reinforcement" (Kerr & Nelson, 1989, p. 361). In other words, children are taught social skills that would be naturally reinforced by peers and others in naturally occurring environments and situations. When children demonstrate these skills and are reinforced for them, the behavior becomes "trapped" in the child's social skills repertoire, and since the behavior is reinforced, the chances that it will be repeated increase. If this is to be an effective strategy, Kerr and Nelson (1989) suggest that teachers assess generalization settings to determine social behaviors that are required and/or necessary in those settings. They also suggest that the child become proficient in the skill before attempting to trap the behavior. If the child is not skillful in the social skill, the chances for reinforcement decrease, and the effect on behavior may be the opposite.

These strategies seem to be the most promising in effecting the generalization of social skills. Rutherford and Nelson (1988) reviewed 5300 behavioral studies and found that less than 1% of them included information on programming for maintenance and generalization of treatment effects. It is imperative that teachers train for the generalization of skills taught in educational settings. Otherwise, children will spend valuable time learning skills that they will not use in natural environments.

SUMMARY

Social competence has been defined by a number of authors, but there does not appear to be consensus among them. A generally accepted definition by Kerr and Nelson defined social competence as "an individual's ability to use these skills (social skills) at the right time and place, showing social judgement or perception about how to act" (1989, p. 312). Social skills are socially valid when they are judged acceptable by persons within the child's environment. In addition to learning about socially valid social skills, children must also be able to perform the skills when and where necessary. Some children demonstrate social skills deficits and need training and practice to improve these skills.

It is important that children who are deficit in social competence receive social skills training so that they are able to make friends and get along with others in their environment. Children who are not socially competent are likely to experience negative social outcomes as children, adolescents, and adults.

Many methods may be used to assess a child's social competence. Social skills assessment methods include sociometrics, ranking methods, ratings by others, behavioral role play tasks, self-reporting, naturalistic observation, and self-monitoring. Sociometric measures and ratings by others appear to be best used for screening purposes. Behavioral interviews, role plays, self-ratings, and naturalistic observations provide the best clues for intervention once children have been identified as needing social skill intervention.

Coaching, modeling, positive reinforcement, peer-mediated strategies, and structured learning approaches are effective in improving children's social skills, therefore promoting social competence. These interventions have resulted in positive outcomes, measured in social acceptance and interpersonal relationships, among children. Other variables that must be considered during social skills training include curriculum, group size, choice of instructor, the physical arrangement of the room, materials, group composition, and variables related to the presentation and monitoring of the lesson. Behavior management techniques used to teach social competence include the use of positive reinforcement, contingency contracts, level systems, and the Boy's Town Motivation System.

Children must be taught to transfer new social skills across settings, situations, and persons. Response maintenance refers to whether or not a new social skill is exhibited once training has been withdrawn. Stimulus generalization refers to the generalization of a learned response to other settings, persons, and cues. Response generalization refers to the demonstration of other social skills related to the learned skills. Strategies to promote social skills training generalization include training sufficient exemplars, entrapment, and reinforcing generalization.

For Discussion

1. Discuss the definitions of social skills and social competence. Why is it important for children to become socially competent?
2. Describe the techniques used to assess children's deficits in critical social skills.
3. Describe effective interventions for teaching children social skills.
4. What are the variables that teachers and others need to consider before they teach social skills?
5. Discuss methods for teaching children to generalize social skills.

REFERENCES

Achenbach, T. M. (1981). *The child behavior checklist for ages 4–16 (CBCL/4–16)* Burlington: University of Vermont.

Achenbach, T. M., & Edelbrock, C. S. (1983). *Manual for the child behavior checklist and revised child behavior profile.* Burlington, VT: University of Vermont, Department of Psychiatry.

Agard, J. A., Veldman, D. J., Kaufman, M. J., Semmel, M. I., & Walters, P. B. (Undated). *Guess who: An instrument of the PRIME instrument battery.* Project PRIME Technical Report.

Asher, S. R., & Hymel, S. (1981). Children's social competence in peer relations: Sociometric and behavioral assessment. In J. D. Wine & M. D. Smye (Eds.), *Social competence* (pp. 125–157). New York: Guilford Press.

Asher, S. R., Markell, R. A., & Hymel, S. (1981). Identifying children at risk in peer relations: A critique of the rate-of-interaction approach to assessment. *Child Development, 52,* 1239–1245.

Asher, S. R., & Renshaw, P. D. (1981). Children without friends: Social knowledge and social skill training. In S. R. Asher & J. M. Gottman (Eds.), *The development of children's friendships* (pp. 273–296). New York: Cambridge University Press.

Bauer, A. M., Shea, T. M., & Keppler, R. (1986). Level systems: A framework for the individualization of behavior management. *Behavioral Disorders, 12* (1) 28–35.

Becker, R. E., & Heimberg, R. G. (1988). Assessment of social skills. In A. S. Belleck & M. Hersen (Eds.), *Behavioral assessment, a practical handbook* (3rd ed., pp. 365–395). New York: Pergamon Press.

Bellack, A. S., Hersen, M., & Turner, S.M. (1976). Generalization of social skills training in chronic schizophrenics: An experimental analysis. *Behaviour Research and Therapy, 14,* 381–398.

Bem, D. J., & Fender, D. C. (1978). Predicting more of the people more of the time: Assessing the personality of situations. *Psychological Review, 85,* 485–501.

Bierman, K. L., & Furman, W. (1984). The effects of social skills training and peer involvement on the social adjustment of preadolescents. *Child Development, 55,* 151–162.

Bower, E. M. (1961). *Early identification of emotionally handicapped children in school*. Springfield, IL: Charles C. Thomas.

Cartledge, G., & Milburn, J. F. (1983). *Teaching social skills to children, innovative approaches*. New York: Pergamon Press.

Coie, J. D. (1985). Fitting social skills intervention to the target group. In B. H. Schneider, K. H. Rubin, & J. E. Ledingham (Eds.), *Children's peer relations: Issues in assessment and interventions* (pp. 141–156). New York: Springer-Verlag.

Coie, J. D., Dodge, K. A., & Coppotelli, H. (1982). Dimensions and types of social status: A cross-age perspective. *Developmental Psychology, 18,* 557–570.

Cole, D. A., Meyer, L. H., Vandercook, T., & McQuarter, R. J. (1986). Interactions between peers with and without severe handicaps: Dynamics of teacher intervention. *American Journal of Mental Deficiency, 91,* 160–169.

Cooper, J. O. (1987). Token economy. *Applied Behavior Analysis* (pp. 486–498). Columbus, OH: Merrill/MacMillan.

DeRisi, W. J., and Butz, G. (1975). *Writing Behavioral Contracts: A Case Simulation Manual* (p. 7). Champaign, IL: Research Press.

Dodge, K. A., Coie, J. D., & Brakke, N. P. (1982). Behavior patterns of socially rejected and neglected preadolescents: The roles of social approach and aggression. *Journal of Abnormal Child Psychology, 10,* 389–410.

Drew, N. (1987). *Learning the skills of peacemaking, an activity guide for elementary-age children on communicating/cooperating/resolving conflict.* Rolling Hills Estates, CA: Jalmar Press.

Foster, S. L., & Ritchey, W. L. (1985). Behavioral correlates of sociometric status of fourth-, fifth-, and sixth-grade children in two classroom situations. *Behavioral Assessment, 7,* 79–83.

Goldstein, A. P., Sprafkin, R. P., Gershaw, N. J., & Klein, P. (1980). *Skillstreaming the adolescent*. Champaign, IL: Research Press.

Goleman, D. (1990, October). Child's skills at play crucial to success, new studies find. *New York Times,* B1, B6.

Gottman, J., Gonso, J., & Rasmussen, B. (1975). Social interaction, social competence and friendship in children. *Child Development, 46,* 709–718.

Gottman, J. M., Gonso, J., & Schuler, P. (1976). Teaching social skills to isolated children. *Journal of Abnormal Child Psychology, 4,* 179–197.

Greenwood, C. R., Walker, H. M., & Hops, H. (1977). Issues in social interaction/withdrawal assessment. *Exceptional Children, 43,* 490–498.

Gresham, F. M. (1981). Assessment of children's social skills. *The Journal of School Psychology, 19,* 120–133.

Gresham, F. M. (1983). Social validity in the assessment of students' social skills: Establishing standards for social competency. *Journal of Psychological Assessment, 1,* 297–307.

Gresham, F. M. (1986). Conceptual issues in the assessment of social competence in children. In P. Strain, M. Guralnick, & H. Walker (Eds.), *Children's social behavior: Development, assessment, and modification* (pp. 143–179). New York: Academic Press.

Gresham, F. M., Elliott, S. M., & Black, F. L. (1987). Factor structure replication and bias investigation of the teacher rating of social skills. *Journal of School Psychology, 25,* 81–92.

Gresham, F. M., & Nagle, R. J. (1980). Social skills training with children: Responsiveness to modeling and coaching as a function of peer orientation. *Journal of Consulting and Clinical Psychology, 48,* 718–729.

Gronlund, N. E. (1959). *Sociometry in the classroom.* New York: Harper & Brothers.

Guralnick, M. J. (1986). The peer relations of young handicapped and non-handicapped children. In P. S. Strain, M. J. Guralnick, & H. M. Walker (Eds.), *Children's social behavior development, assessment and modification* (pp. 93–140). Orlando, FL: Academic Press.

Hartup, W. W. (1979). Peer relations and the growth of social competence. In M. W. Kent & J. E. Rolf (Eds.), *Primary prevention of psychopathology: Vol. 3 Social competence in children* (pp. 150–170). Hanover, NH: University Press of New England.

Hartup, W. W., Glazier, J., & Charlesworth, R. (1967). Peer reinforcement and sociometric status. *Child Development, 38,* 1017–1024.

Hoge, R. D. (1985). The validity of direct observation measures of pupil classroom behavior. *Review of Educational Research, 55,* 469–483.

Hoier, T. S., & Cone, J. D. (1980). *Idiographic assessment of social skills in children.* Paper presented at the Association for the Advancement of Behavior Therapy Convention, New York, NY.

Hoier, T. S., & Cone, J. D. (1987). Target selection of social skills for children: The template-matching procedure. *Behavior Modification, 11,* 137–163.

Hollinger, J. D. (1987). Social skills for behaviorally disordered children as preparation for mainstreaming: Theory, practice and new directions. *Remedial and Special Education, 8,* 17–27.

Hops, H. (1982). Social skills training for socially withdrawn/isolate children. In P. Karoly & J. J. Steffen (Eds.), *Improving children's competence, advances in behavioral analysis and therapy* (Vol. 1, pp. 39–97). Cambridge, MA: Lexington Books.

Hops, H., & Greenwood, C. R. (1988). Social skills deficits. In E. J. Mash & L. G. Terdal (Eds.), *Behavioral assessment of childhood disorders* (pp. 347–394). New York: Guilford Press.

Hops, H., & Lewin, L. (1984). Peer sociometric forms. In T. H. Ollendick & M. Hersen (Eds.), *Child behavioral assessment: Principles and procedures* (pp. 124–147). New York: Pergamon Press.

Hops, H., Walker, H. M., & Greenwood, C. R. (1979). PEERS: A program for remediating social withdrawal in school. In L. A. Hamerlynck (Ed.), *Behavioral systems for the developmentally disabled: Vol. 1, School and family environments* (pp. 48–86). New York: Bruner/Mazel.

Kerr, M. M., & Nelson, C. M. (1989). *Strategies for managing behavior problems in the classroom.* Columbus, OH: Merrill/Macmillan.

Kohlberg, L., LaCrosse, J., & Ricks, D. (1972). The predictability of adult mental health from childhood behavior. In B. Wolman (Ed.), *Manual of child psychopathology.* New York: McGraw-Hill.

Ladd, G. W. (1981). Effectiveness of a social learning method for enhancing children's social interaction and peer acceptance. *Child Development, 52,* 171–178.

Ladd, G. W., & Asher, S. R. (1985). Social skill training and children's peer relations. In L. L'Abate & M. Milan (Eds.), *Handbook of social skills training and research* (pp. 219–244). New York: Wiley.

LaGreca, A. M., & Santogrossi, D. A. (1980). Social skills training with elementary school students: A behavioral group approach. *Journal of Consulting and Clinical Psychology, 48,* 220–227.

Lefevre, M. A., Malcolm, L. W., West, L., & Ledingham, J. E. (1983). The sensitivity of a peer-nomination technique in assessing changes in children's social behavior: A case study. *Journal of the American Academy of Child Psychiatry, 22,* 191–195.

Maag, J. W. (1989). Assessment in social skills training: Methodological and conceptual issues for research and practice. *Remedial and Special Education, 10*(4), 6–17.

Maheady, L., & Sainato, D. M. (1985). Social interaction patterns of high and low status behaviorally disordered students within self-contained classroom settings: A pilot investigation. *Behavioral Disorders, 10,* 20–26.

Martin, R. P. (1988). *Assessment of personality and behavior problems.* New York: Guilford Press.

McConnell, S. R. (1987). Entrapment effects and the generalization and maintenance of social skills training for elementary school students with behavioral disorders. *Behavioral Disorders, 12,* 252–263.

McConnell, S. R., & Odom, S. L. (1986). Sociometrics: Peer referenced measures and the assessment of social competence. In P. S. Strain, M. J. Guralnick, & H. M. Walker (Eds.), *Children's social behavior, development, assessment, and modification* (pp. 215–284). New York: Academic Press.

McConnell, S. R., Strain, P. S., Kerr, M. M., Stagg, V., Lenkner, D. A., & Lambert, D. (1984). An empirical identification of social adjustment: Selection of target behaviors for a comprehensive treatment program. *Behavior Modification, 8,* 451–473.

McGinnis, E., & Goldstein, A. P. (1984). *Skillstreaming the elementary school child: A guide for teaching prosocial skills.* Champaign, IL: Research Press.

McMahon, C. (1989). *An evaluation of the multiple effects of a social skills intervention: An interactionist perspective.* Unpublished doctoral dissertation, The University of Iowa.

Melloy, K. J. (1990). *Attitudes and behavior of non-disabled elementary-aged children toward their peers with disabilities in integrated settings: An examination of the effects of treatment on quality of attitudes, social status and critical social skills.* Unpublished doctoral dissertation, University of Iowa.

Michelson, L., & Mannarino, A. (1986). Social skills training with children: Research and clinical application. In P. S. Strain, M. J. Guralnick, & H. M. Walker (Eds.), *Children's social behavior, development, assessment and modification* (pp. 373–406). Orlando, FL: Academic Press.

Michelson, L., Mannarino, A. P., Marchione, K., & Martin, P. (1982). *Relative and combined efficacy of behavioral and cognitive problem solving social skills programs with elementary school children.* Unpublished manuscript, University of Pittsburgh.

Michelson, L., Sugai, D. P., Wood, R. P., & Kazdin, A. E. (1983). *Social skills assessment and training with children.* New York: Plenum.

Michelson, L., & Wood, R. (1980). Behavioral assessment and training of children's social skills. In M. Hersen, P. Miller, & R. Eisler (Eds.), *Progress in behavior modification* (Vol. 9). New York: Academic Press.

Midgett, J., Miller, M., & Wicks, L. (1989, November). *Skillstreaming research.* Paper presented at the Teacher Educators of Children with Behavior Disorders Annual Conference, Tempe, Arizona.

Moreno, J. L. (1934). *Who shall survive? A new approach to the problem of human interrelations.* Washington, D.C.: Nervous and Mental Disease Publishing Co.

O'Connor, R. D. (1969). Modification of social withdrawal through symbolic modeling. *Journal of Applied Behavior Analysis, 2,* 15–22.

Oden, S. (1980). A child's social isolation: Origins, prevention, intervention. In G. Cartledge & J. F. Milburn (Eds.). Teaching social skills to children: Innovative approaches (pp.179–202). New York: Pergamon Press.

Oden, S., & Asher, S. R. (1977). Coaching children in social skills for friendship making. *Child Development, 48,* 495–506.

Ollendick, T. H., & Hersen, M. (Eds.), (1984). *Child behavioral assessment: Principles and procedures.* New York: Pergamon Press.

Peery, J. C. (1979). Popular, amiable, isolated, rejected: A reconceptualization of sociometric status in preschool children. *Child Development, 50,* 1231–1234.

Putallaz, M., & Gottman, J. (1981). Social skills and group acceptance. In S. Asher & J. Gottman (Eds.), *Development of children's friendships* (pp.116–146). New York: Cambridge University Press.

Putallaz, M., & Gottman, J. (1982). Conceptualizing social competence in children. In P. Karoly & J. J. Steffen (Eds.), *Improving children's competence* (pp. 1–33). Cambridge, MA: Lexington Books.

Renshaw, P., & Asher, S. (1982). Social competence and peer status: The distinction between goals and strategies. In K. Rubin & H. Ross (Eds.),

Peer relationships and social skills in childhood (pp. 375–396). New York: Springer-Verlag.

Rinn, F. C., & Markle, A. (1979). Modification of social skill deficits in children. In A. S. Bellack & M. Hersen (Eds.), *Research and practice in social skills training*. New York: Plenum Press.

Roff, M., Sells, S. B., & Golden, M. M. (1972). *Social adjustment and personality development in children*. Minneapolis, MN: University of Minnesota Press.

Rutherford, R. B. Jr., & Nelson, C. M. (1988). Generalization and maintenance of treatment effects. In J. C. Witt, S. N. Elliott, & F. M. Greshaw (Eds.). *Handbook of behavior therapy in education* (pp. 277–324). New York: Plenum.

Sabornie, E. J., Kauffman, J. M., & Cullinan, D. A. (1990). Extended sociometric status of adolescents with mild handicaps: A cross-categorical perspective. *Exceptionality, 1*(3), 197–209.

Sargent, L. R. (1988). *Systematic instruction of social skills*, 2nd ed. Iowa Department of Education, Bureau of Special Education, Grimes State Office Building, Des Moines, Iowa.

Sasso, G. M., Melloy, K. J., & Kavale, K. A. (1990). Generalization, maintenance, and behavioral covariation associated with training through structured learning. *Behavioral Disorders, 16*(1), 9–22.

Sasso, G., Mundschenk, N., Melloy, K., Wacker, D., & Kelly, L. (1990, May). *Multiple effects of peer initiation dyads and triads on the social behavior of handicapped and nonhandicapped children*. Poster presented at the Association for Behavior Analysis Conference, Nashville, TN.

Sasso, G. M., & Rude, H. A. (1987). Unprogrammed effects of training handicapped children. *Journal of Applied Behavior Analysis, 20*, 35–44.

Shapiro, S. B., & Sobel, M. (1981). Two multinomial random sociometric voting models. *Journal of Educational Statistics, 6*, 287–310.

Stephens, T. M. (1978). *Social skills in the classroom*. Columbus, OH: Cedars Press.

Stokes, T. F., & Baer, D. M. (1977). An implicit technology of generalization. *Journal of Applied Behavior Analysis, 10*, 349–367.

Stokes, T. F., & Osnes, P. G. (1986). Programming the generalization of children's social behavior. In P. S. Strain, M. J. Guralnick, & H. M. Walker (Eds.), *Children's social behavior, development, assessment, and modification* (pp. 407–443). Orlando, FL: Academic Press.

Strain, P. S., Guralnick, M. J., & Walker, H. M. (1986). *Children's social behavior, development, assessment and modification*. New York: Academic Press.

Strain, P. S., Odom, S. L., & McConnell, S. (1984). Promoting social reciprocity of exceptional children: Identification, target behavior selection, and intervention. *Remedial and Special Education, 5*, 21–28.

Strain, P. S., Shores, R. E., & Timm, M. A. (1977). Effects of peer social initiations on the behavior of withdrawn preschool children. *Journal of Applied Behavior Analysis, 10*, 289–298.

Strain, P. S., & Timm, M. A. (1974). An experimental analysis of social interaction between a behaviorally disordered preschool child and her classroom peers. *Journal of Applied Analysis, 7,* 583–590.

Tetterton, J. (1990). *Dubuque management system.* Dubuque Community School District and Keystone Education Agency, Dubuque, Iowa 52001.

Van Hasselt, V. B., Hersen, M., & Bellack, A. S. (1981). The validity of role play tests for assessing social skills in children. *Behavior Therapy, 12,* 202–216.

Voeltz, L. M. (1982). Effects of structured interaction with severely handicapped peers on children's attitudes. *American Journal of Mental Deficiency, 86,* 380–390.

Walker, H. M., Greenwood, C. R., Hops, H., & Todd, N. M. (1979). Differential effects of reinforcing topographic components of social interaction: Analysis and systematic replication. *Behavior Modification, 3,* 291–321.

Walker, H. M., & McConnell, S. R. (1988). *Walker-McConnell scale of social competence and school adjustment.* Austin, TX: Pro-Ed.

Walker, H. M., Severson, H., Stiller, B., Williams, G., Haring, N., Shinn, M., & Todis, B. (1988). Systematic screening of pupils in the elementary age range at risk for behavior disorders: Development and trial testing of a multiple gating model. *Remedial and Special Education, 9*(3), 8–14.

Walker, H. M., Shinn, M. R., O'Neill, R. E., & Ramsey, E. (1987). A longitudinal assessment of the development of antisocial behavior in boys: Rationale, methodology, and first year results. *Remedial and Special Education, 8,* 7–16.

Walker, H. M., Todis, B., Holmes, D., & Horton, G. (1988). *The Walker social skills curriculum: The ACCESS program adolescent curriculum for communication and effective social skills.* Austin, TX: Pro-Ed.

Williams, S. L., Walker, H. M., Holmes, D., Todis, B., & Fabre, T. (1989). Social validation of adolescent social skills by teachers and students. *RASE: Remedial and Special Education, 10,* 18–27, 37.

PART THREE

Understanding and Managing Challenging Behaviors

PART THREE

Understanding and Managing Challenging Behaviors

CHAPTER 8
Behavior Reduction Strategies

> *The effectiveness of a procedure in reducing a behavior problem of a learner is one of the criteria for its use, but not necessarily the most important. Treatment decisions must also include many complex value issues which cannot be empirically supported by a summary graph.*
>
> —LaVigna and Donnellan, 1986, p. 1

It is no coincidence that chapters regarding reinforcement, cognitive behavior modification, and the development of social competence were placed in this text before our discussion of specific behavior challenges and behavior reduction strategies. The use of positive reinforcement is promoted as the intervention of first choice when caregivers want to implement a behavior reduction strategy. The most effective intervention strategy for most challenging or inappropriate behaviors is the reinforcement of appropriate behaviors and behaviors that are inconsistent or incompatible with inappropriate behaviors (Donnellan & LaVigna, 1990). Even for severe behavior problems, such as self-injury, there is growing empirical support that positive or nonaversive methods can be effective without the employment of "aversive" punishers (Berkman & Meyer, 1988; Donnellan, LaVigna, Negri-Shoultz, & Fassbender, 1988; Friman, 1990; O'Brien & Repp, 1990; Underwood & Thyer, 1990). Decisions to use behavior reduction procedures, however, must extend beyond the question of effectiveness. Evans and Meyer stated that "clinical interventions must be judged in a variety of ways, and simply because something meets someone's definition of 'effectiveness' does not mean that it is right" (1990, p. 134).

The focus on appropriate behavior and positive reinforcement dramatically changes the atmosphere of any environment where individuals live and work (Meyer & Evans, 1989; Turnbull & Turnbull, 1990). This fundamental difference in philosophy makes a tremendous difference in the atmosphere of the home and educational setting and in the quality of interactions among caregivers and children (Pfiffner & O'Leary, 1987; Pfiffner, Rosen, & O'Leary, 1985). Additionally, by reinforcing appropriate behaviors, children may learn effective social skills that will "enhance successful functioning in school and other environments" (Sasso, Melloy, & Kavale, 1990, p. 9).

TERMINOLOGY

The term *behavior reduction strategies* is used here to identify procedures that, when implemented immediately after a target behavior, reduce the future probability of the target behavior recurring. The use of the term "punishment" is limited in this chapter because it has many meanings for different people and is frequently, although incorrectly, associated only with "aversive" procedures not promoted in this text. By definition, the term *punishment* "simply refers to any contingent consequence that decreases the behavior that it follows; thus, the term ought to be a neutral one as such consequences would usually be idiosyncratic to the individual" (Evans & Meyer, 1985, p. 135). The problem of finding the "correct" terminology to describe procedures that reduce the likelihood of challenging or inappropriate behaviors was articulated by Skiba and Deno:

> By introducing methodologies called punishment, psychologists and educators are placed in the awkward position of using a term that serves as a discriminative stimulus for the very practices they are trying to avoid or reform. It is not surprising that trainers of practitioners are often unsuccessful in shaping nonpunitive practice, when the word they use to describe behavior reduction is derived from the same Latin root (poena: fine, penalty) as punitive (*Oxford English Dictionary*, 1982, p. 1604).(1991, p. 301)

Appropriate Terminology for Challenging Behavior

Another challenge in the area of terminology is what to call the behavior targeted for reduction. The terms "antisocial," "challenging," "inappropriate," "excessive," and "undesirable" are frequently used. In this chapter, both "challenging" and "inappropriate" will be used to describe behaviors that are targeted for reduction either because of their excessive or antisocial nature. Although the current trend in the field is to use "challenging," situations exist in which behaviors are less challenging than they are inappropriate. An inappropriate behavior may or may not be challenging. A challenging behavior may or may not be inappropriate.

Children may exhibit inappropriate behaviors for very functional purposes such as the communication of pain and discomfort. (Doss & Reichle, 1989; Schuler, 1980) or as a way to escape demanding or threatening situations (Durand & Crimmins, 1988). Some might argue that all behaviors have a purpose and we should strive to understand the function of specific behaviors, through a functional analysis, before we strive to change them (O'Neill, Horner, Albin, Storey, & Sprague, 1990; Iwata, Vollmer, & Zarcone, 1990). Others, such as LaVigna and Donnellan, stated that behavior cannot be judged as either appropriate or inappropriate:

> Rather than being a dichotomy, desirability can be measured on a continuum and behavior has degrees of desirability. The same holds for many other adjectives, such as "appropriate" or "acceptable." Therefore, in defining a behavior in such terms, it is important to understand that one is judging the degree of appropriateness of a given behavior. (1986, p. 2)

Is There Really a Problem?

Behavior must be judged by its function (Donnellan, Mirenda, Mesaros, & Fassbender, 1984), the social context in which it is exhibited, and the impact on the individual's growth and development across settings. Indeed, perhaps the most important consideration before the implementation of a behavior change program is to ask the question "Is there really a problem?" (Snell & Zirpoli, 1987). Vignette 8.1 provides an example of how important it is for caregivers to look beyond the child and consider other variables that may be related, directly or indirectly, to a child's challenging behaviors.

Vignette 8.1.   Another Perspective of a "Problem Behavior."

By Linda J. Emerick

Sara was a lively four year old in a local preschool program. While she was always curious and appeared interested in classroom activities, her attention would quickly wander. This behavior was particularly noticeable during story time. Sara would begin the session sitting attentively, facing the teacher. Within minutes, however, she would be stretched out on the floor, playing with objects around her or trying to attract the attention of children nearby. These behaviors were disruptive and distracting to the teacher and the other students.

One way to look at the situation is to conclude that Sara is controlling, seeking attention, and immature. After all, story time is a valuable learning experience and beneficial to all. If Sara is not attentive during the readings or explanations of activities, she obviously has a problem—or does she?

Sara's teacher chose to look at her behaviors from another perspective: An environmental influence might be causing Sara to "tune out" during story time and in other situations. By questioning her, the teacher learned Sara was a precocious reader and had already heard many of the stories shared in class. In fact, she had read some of them herself at home. What was new for the other students was "old stuff" for Sara. A similar situation was occurring when instructions were given by the teacher; Sara could quickly grasp what was being asked for in most instances and did not always need the details or repetitions given.

Sara's teacher modified the learning experiences to better match Sara's abilities and characteristics by reading less familiar stories at story time and allowing Sara and other children to begin a task as soon as they could demonstrate they understood the directions. Sara's disruptive behaviors diminished as the teacher's expectations changed.

Sara's teacher responded differently from many of us in that she did not assume Sara's behavior was caused by internal factors. The behaviors were not problems in and of themselves; they reflected Sara's response to an environment that was inappropriate for her. To state it simply, sometimes the child is the last thing that needs "fixing" when "problem behaviors" occur.

As educators, we have to guard against a natural impulse to take a superficial view of children's behaviors. It would have been quicker and maybe easier for Sara's teacher to have identified a "problem behavior"; but the *real* problem underlying the behavior would have been missed. Her teacher had the right idea—let's check what *we* may be doing that is causing the behavior first.

Source: Linda Emerick, Ph.D., is an assistant professor in the Gifted and Special Education Program at the University of St. Thomas, St. Paul, Minnesota.

Gaylord-Ross (1980) outlined five questions that should be considered before a decision is made to modify a behavior:

1. Is the behavior causing physical harm to the child or others?
2. Is the behavior disruptive to the student's learning or the learning of others?
3. Does the behavior appear to be triggering additional problem behaviors or emotional reactions in the child or others?
4. Is the behavior causing the child to be socially excluded?
5. Is the behavior related to a medical condition (for example, ear infections in young children, side-effects of medication, behavior associated with a genetic condition)?

After the above considerations have been examined and the target behavior is still judged to be a problem in need of modification, caregivers should consider two alternatives to the direct modification of a target behavior. First, what positive or alternative behaviors can be increased as a method of decreasing or eliminating the inappropriate behavior? These strategies are outlined in Chapter 5. Second, are environmental variables facilitating or maintaining the inappropriate behavior, and can these environmental variables be modified? Environmental modifications are frequently very effective in decreasing inappropriate behaviors and offer caregivers an effective strategy for preventing inappropriate behaviors in the first place.

PREVENTIVE STRATEGIES

Perhaps the best behavior reduction strategy, along with the reinforcement of appropriate behavior, is the strategy of prevention. As previously stated, caregivers should monitor the environment in order to identify environmental conditions (antecedents and consequences) related to inappropriate behavior. Antecedents are the activities or conditions occurring immediately before a behavior. For example, if a child is aggressive, caregivers need to identify the activities occurring immediately before the aggressive acts. The caregiver may be able to modify the antecedents (change schedule, seating arrangement, etc.) of a behavior and, as a result, decrease the occurrence of the inappropriate behavior. By reinforcing appropriate behaviors and modifying antecedent conditions, caregivers are more likely to be effective in reducing inappropriate behaviors rather than just trying to decrease inappropriate behavior.

An excellent example of modifying environmental antecedents was documented by Rosenberg (1986) who added a brief (two minutes) review of the classroom rules before the start of a lesson to an ongoing classroom behavior management program. The teacher asked the students individually or in unison to state the classroom rules orally. Rosenberg found that "daily lessons preceded by a review of rules tend to possess a greater academic focus and are generally conducted with greater efficiency" (p. 246).

It is also important to review the *consequences* of current inappropriate behaviors. The consequences of a behavior are the responses, positive or negative, that occur immediately after a behavior. Consequences may be reinforcing, which tend to increase the occurrence of the behavior, or punishing, which tend to decrease the occurrence of the behavior. Caregivers may provide consequences to inappropriate behaviors that actually serve to reinforce and, thus, increase the likelihood of the behavior occurring again.

There are times that while caregivers think they are providing punishing consequences for inappropriate behaviors, they are actually reinforcing the behaviors they want to decrease. This is usually the case when a positive reinforcement program is *not* in place and the child receives attention only as a consequence of inappropriate behaviors. If children don't get attention for appropriate behaviors, they will probably misbehave for attention—even if the attention is in the form of punishment.

LaVigna and Willis (1991) discussed several strategies related to *interrupting the behavior chain* of inappropriate behavior. These methods are helpful in preventing and deescalating inappropriate behaviors. Suggestions for interrupting the behavior chain included proximity control, injecting humor, instructional control, problem-solving facilitation, and stimulus change.

Proximity control refers to a method of anticipating a child's potential response to an event or situation and interrupting the usual sequence of behaviors by body positioning, remaining calm, and facilitating communication. For example, a classroom teacher may notice that the students are beginning to talk too loud during a community library visit and, anticipating that the students will become louder, the teacher breaks the behavioral chain by reminding the students to talk quietly. By anticipating a potential problem, the teacher was able to position herself among the students, calmly communicate her expectations, and prevent a potential situation in which she might have to yell above the student's noise for them to hear her instructions. Vignette 8.2 provides an example of a father who anticipates his son's response to a request and interrupts the behavior chain.

Vignette 8.2.   Example of Interrupting the Behavior Chain to Prevent Challenging Behavior.

Brian, who is seven years old, wanted to go to a friend's house after school. His father, however, expected Brian to help clean the yard. Brian has a history of losing his temper and becoming aggressive when demands are made of him, especially if these demands interfere with his play time. Instead of telling Brian that he could not play with his friends because he had to help clean the yard, Brian's dad told Brian that they needed to talk. Brian's father told Brian that he understood that Brian wanted to play with his friend. His father also stated that Brian could play with his friends after he helped clean the yard. Brian's dad was able to interrupt his son's usual response by sitting next to his son and speaking in a calm, warm, and empathetic tone of voice. Together, they agreed on a mutually discussed plan of how Brian could help clean the yard and still have time to play with his friend.

Injecting humor into a situation may also interrupt a behavior chain. Humor will often reduce the tension of an explosive situation. A teacher might respond to a child who is ready to lose control by telling the student a story about a similar situation occurring in the past ("Did I ever tell you that that happened to me once?")

Instructional control or providing instructions on expected behaviors is also useful in interrupting a behavior chain. For example, after a classroom schedule is abruptly changed and the students begin to respond in frustration, the teacher provides clear instructions about what they will do next and what the expectations are for student behavior.

Problem-solving facilitation involves the provision of positive alternatives to inappropriate behavior. For example, a parent may suggest to a child "Let's sit and talk about what you can do about this" after observing that the child is ready to behave inappropriately in response to a frustrating experience. Problem-solving skills are also facilitated when caregivers talk to children about alternatives to the inappropriate behaviors children observe in their everyday environment (e.g., children fighting on the playground, world events children hear on the news). These kinds of problem-solving discussions are easily integrated into both academic and social activities.

Stimulus change refers to a range of caregiver behaviors that prevents challenging behaviors by modifying environmental stimuli that might precipitate challenging behavior. Stimulus change may include removing objects, relocating people, removing unnecessary demands and requests, changing the location or timing of events, and other rearrangements of environmental stimuli. For example, teachers frequently modify student seating arrangements in response to disruptive interactions between students. A greater effort to anticipate and prevent inappropriate behaviors through environmental modifications, rather than direct behavior modification, is encouraged. Environmental changes may be temporary while caregivers gradually reintroduce the stimulus that elicited the behavior. For example, a toy that children have fought over may be temporarily removed and gradually reintroduced in a more controlled manner.

Prevention Strategies for the Classroom

Several authors suggested the use of preventive strategies in order to promote the use of socially acceptable classroom behavior (DeLuke & Knoblock, 1987; Sabatino, 1987; Stainback, Stainback, & Froyen, 1987). Many of these strategies are based on the earlier work of Long and Newman (1976). Long and Newman discussed three categories of ecological manipulation that can be incorporated into classroom management strategies to prevent challenging behaviors. These categories included classroom environment, classroom activities, and teacher behavior. By monitoring and modifying the classroom environment (Sabatino, 1987), classroom activities, and teacher behavior (DeLuke & Knoblock, 1987), acceptable student behavior may be facilitated and unacceptable behavior prevented. Long and Newman listed several strategies for classroom teachers:

- ◆ *Inform students of what is expected of them.* Teachers are encouraged to develop classroom rules and to review the rules frequently with students. Rules may even be posted to serve as a reminder for teachers and students.
- ◆ *Establish a positive learning climate.* Teachers can establish a positive learning climate by reinforcing students for appropriate behavior, by interacting with the children in a consistent manner, and by being flexible enough to accommodate the individual needs of all the classroom students. In addition, teachers need to make learning a fun experience so that children will want to come to school and will come to school motivated to learn.
- ◆ *Provide meaningful learning experiences.* Relating academic lessons and tasks to the daily lives of children will increase student interest and provide for effective generalization of skills.
- ◆ *Avoid threats.* When rules are clearly stated and understood, threats are unnecessary. Instead of threats, teachers should remind students of the classroom rules and other behavioral expectations and consistently provide consequences for both appropriate and inappropriate behaviors.
- ◆ *Demonstrate fairness.* Teachers are more likely to interact with all students equally and consistently when classroom rules are clearly stated and understood.

◆ *Build and exhibit self-confidence.* Children who feel good about them-selves and their school work are likely to interact with others appro-priately. (See Chapter 10 for a section on building self-esteem and self-confidence.) Teachers have many opportunities to model self-con-fidence (for example, "I know I can do this") and encourage student self-confidence throughout the day.

◆ *Recognize positive student attributes.* All children have positive attributes that may be recognized to build self-esteem and self-confi-dence. Also, teachers should recognize, be sensitive to, and celebrate individual student differences.

◆ *Use positive modeling.* Children are likely to model the behavior of teachers and other significant caregivers. This provides teachers with many opportunities to teach children how to deal appropriately with anger, mistakes, and everyday frustrations.

◆ *Pay attention to the physical arrangement of the classroom.* The class-room should allow for a smooth flow of student traffic and visual monitoring of student behavior. An organized teacher and classroom environment may encourage students to be better organized.

◆ *Limit downtime.* The more time students spend in downtime, the more opportunities are available for inappropriate behaviors. Both teacher and students should be prepared for the day. The time a teacher spends preparing for class will be time saved when children are busy and challenged (and not engaged in inappropriate behavior).

Teachers and parents should always evaluate environmental variables, espe-cially antecedents and consequences and their own behavior, as the first step in reducing inappropriate behavior. When behavior reduction strategies are still necessary, caregivers are encouraged to familiarize themselves with some generally acceptable guidelines and procedural safeguards.

GENERAL BEHAVIOR REDUCTION GUIDELINES

When behavior reduction strategies are employed, several general guidelines are available that will assist caregivers to implement an effective behavior change program.

The Fair Pair Rule

A term coined by White and Haring (1976), the "fair pair" rule states that when a caregiver targets a behavior for reduction, "an alternative behavior is selected to replace the challenging behavior" (Wacker, Berg, & Northrup, 1991, p. 11). Snell and Zirpoli (1987) stated that when one behavior is targeted for reduction, an appropriate behavior should be targeted for positive rein-forcement. Preferably, the behavior targeted for increase is an appropriate substitute, or at least incompatible, with the challenging behavior targeted for decrease. "This procedure results in a repertoire of appropriate behaviors, providing the student with alternative responses rather than merely eliminating behavior. More opportunities to reinforce the student positively are also created" (Snell & Zirpoli, 1987, p.136).

Be Consistent

When children are provided with rules and behavioral guidelines it is important for caregivers to be consistent about enforcement and reinforcement. For example, if the rule states that Robert must sit in the corner for two minutes when he hits other children, caregivers must be consistent and implement the consequence each and every time the rule is broken. Mild inappropriate behaviors, such as an occasional rude comment or noncompliance, may be followed by a verbal warning—as long as this is stated in the rules. Severe inappropriate behaviors, such as hitting or other acts of aggression, should not be followed only by a warning. Consistency teaches children that there is a relationship between following the rules and reinforcement. Also, it teaches the children that there are consequences when the rules are not followed. When caregivers are not consistent, children tend to become confused about the rules and caregiver expectations. This confusion will be demonstrated by their behavior. For example, if a teacher is inconsistent with the enforcement of a classroom rule (such as "Students must receive permission from the teacher before leaving the class") some students may think that the rule is not very important or that it is not important to *always* obey the rule. Some students may generalize this attitude to other classroom rules. Thus, caregivers should not establish rules they are unable or unwilling to enforce consistently.

Avoid Reinforcing Inappropriate Behavior

Caregivers must be careful that children do not get more attention following inappropriate behaviors than they would following appropriate behaviors. Inappropriate behavior should be calmly followed with the provision of a specific consequence as outlined in your behavior change program. It is important that "the challenging behavior never results in the desired consequence" (Wacker, Berg, & Northrup, 1991, p. 11).

Caregivers should avoid long lectures and excessive one-to-one interaction with children after inappropriate behavior. This type of attention may be reinforcing to some children, especially when done in the presence of other children. For example, a male high school student may enjoy a teacher reprimand conducted in full view of classmates if he perceives the incident as a way of increasing his status among his peers. The teacher can deliver the same comments, quietly at the student's desk, without drawing a significant amount of attention to the student's inappropriate behavior. This approach may be called a "soft" reprimand.

The greatest danger in implementing a behavior reduction procedure without a reinforcement component is that children may learn to associate adult attention only with the behavior reduction procedure. A child who is "hungry" for adult attention will soon learn to act inappropriately for the attention he or she cannot gain through appropriate behavior.

Consequences for Inappropriate Behavior

The consequences a child experiences for acting inappropriately should be short and to the point. Whether we are talking about time-out or the removal of a toy or other preferred object, a short period of time is usually as effective as longer periods of time. Taking a toy away from a child for an hour or, at most, for the day following an inappropriate behavior is long enough. Consequences for inappropriate behavior should seldom be carried over into the next day. Indeed, the next day will provide caregivers with new opportunities to identify and reinforce appropriate behavior. In behavior management, longer (such as longer time-out periods, longer periods of restriction or "grounding," etc.) does not necessarily mean better. For example, if a child breaks a rule in school and the consequence is the removal of recess, the removal of one to a few recess periods should be sufficient if the child considers recess reinforcing. The removal of recess for weeks or months is counterproductive and will likely lead to further inappropriate behavior (Harris, 1985).

Deal with Inappropriate Behavior Immediately

When teachers send children to the principal's office for inappropriate behavior or when a mother says "Wait till your dad comes home," the stated consequence for the inappropriate behavior will probably not be immediately or consistently applied. In addition, children of these caregivers will learn that it is not necessary to behave appropriately in the absence of the threatened adult (e.g., the principal or dad). By teaching the child that the first caregiver either will not or cannot deal with the inappropriate behavior, the caregiver is, in effect, teaching the child that it is safe to behave inappropriately with that caregiver.

Avoid Ineffective Procedures

Yelling or shouting at children is not an effective manner in which to communicate or control inappropriate behavior. The same is true with spanking or other forms of corporal punishment, which will be discussed at greater length later in this chapter. Instead of controlling inappropriate behavior, these behaviors simply provide children with inappropriate models of behavior. When a caregiver shouts at children or resorts to the use of corporal punishment, chances are that the caregiver is out of control. In this case, the caregiver should take a break and, if possible, let someone else take over for awhile. These kinds of caregiver behaviors are not only ineffective in changing the behavior of children, they are also damaging to children's self-esteem. In the end, nothing worthwhile has been accomplished and the potential for negative outcomes is great.

Restrictiveness and Social Acceptability

Another important factor that caregivers must consider when selecting a behavior change procedure is the perceived restrictiveness and social acceptability of the procedure by others. Least restrictive procedures are always preferred over more restrictive procedures. Researchers have found general agreement among professionals regarding the restrictiveness of various behavior change procedures. For example, Morgan and Striefel (1988) studied how educators viewed the restrictiveness of various behavior change procedures, including those discussed in this chapter. They surveyed the perceptions of school psychologists, administrators, teachers, and specialists. The perceived restrictiveness of the procedures evaluated in their study, and discussed in this chapter, are outlined in Figure 8.1. Morgan and Striefel speculated that the restrictiveness of a procedure depended on several variables, including the amount of physical contact or restraint from the caregiver and the child's level of discomfort when the procedure is applied. They also found that the "social acceptability" of each procedure was influenced by the "suitability of the procedure for classroom use, risk to the student, teacher time and skill required for intervention, and effects on other students" (p. 119).

ESTABLISHING SAFEGUARDS AND PROGRAM REVIEW PROCEDURES

Once the decision is made to implement a behavior reduction program, several procedural safeguards should be put in place. Wolery and Gast outlined several "conditions under which all behavior reduction procedures, aversive or nonaversive, should be implemented" (1990, p. 137):

◆ "A decision model should be employed to ensure that individuals' rights are protected, appropriate planning is completed, best-practice implementation occurs, and appropriate review is obtained" (p. 137).

Figure 8.1. *Restrictiveness of procedures to decrease behaviors as viewed by school teachers and specialists.*

Source: Adapted from Morgan, R. L., and Striefel, S. (1988). Restrictiveness of procedures to decrease behavior: Views of school psychologist, administrators, teachers, and specialists. *Journal of Special Education, 21,* p. 108–119.

Level of Restrictiveness	Behavioral Procedure
Least Restrictive	Changing antecedent events
	Planned ignoring
	Response cost
	Nonexclusionary time-out
	Positive practice overcorrection (without physical guidance)
	Positive practice overcorrection (with physical guidance)
	Exclusionary time-out
Most Restrictive	Application of discomforting stimuli

◆ There should be an assessment of motivational factors related to the target behavior.

◆ Assessment of the target behavior should be data-based.

◆ Behavior reduction strategies should be used in conjunction with strategies to teach and reinforce appropriate and adaptive behaviors.

◆ There should be reliable measurement of the target behavior and treatment implementation.

◆ There should be periodic monitoring of side-effects of the intervention.

◆ Attention should be given to the maintenance and generalization of program outcomes.

◆ Informed consent from parents and administrative authorities must be obtained.

◆ There should be peer review of the intervention plan to ensure "that the proposed procedure reflects best-practice and has a base in the empirical literature" (p. 139).

◆ The program must be implemented in an "open" environment where interested parties may "observe, evaluate and comment" on the implementation of the program (p. 139).

◆ The program must be implemented by a competent team of caregivers.

Decisions about the management of children's behaviors should be made in collaboration with many caregivers involved. Any decision to implement a behavior reduction procedure should be a team decision, rather than an individual one. Parents are very important members of this team, and educators should make every effort to include parents in all discussions about their children. None of the behavior reduction strategies discussed in this chapter should be implemented before a discussion of the child and his or her behaviors with all significant caregivers is completed.

Program Review and Human Rights Committees

Within educational settings, the establishment of a Program Review Committee (PRC) or Human Rights Committee (HRC) is recommended. These committees may serve to review general behavior management policies and specific behavior reduction program plans for individual students. Members of the committee may include administrators, teachers, parents, and community experts in behavior management. The PRC/HRC may serve:

◆ as a "sounding board" for educators regarding individual children, challenging behaviors, or programming ideas;

◆ as a source of fresh programming ideas for specific behavior problems;

The focus of any behavior program should be the reinforcement of appropriate behaviors.

- ◆ to monitor and review ongoing behavior management programming for individual students; and
- ◆ to monitor and review general policy guidelines regarding the use of behavior management strategies within the educational setting.

While some may view the PRC/HRC as intrusive (Axelrod, 1990), these groups should be viewed both as a resource and as groups concerned with providing children with appropriate and positive learning experiences. When behavior reduction procedures are used, the PRC/HRC should ensure that caregivers are monitoring student progress and that decisions about program effectiveness are made based on reliable data.

SPECIFIC BEHAVIOR REDUCTION STRATEGIES

A number of behavior reduction strategies are available to caregivers to decrease inappropriate behavior. While some strategies are recommended, others are recommended only with modifications, and some not at all. These recommendations will be communicated within the discussion of each procedure. Some common strategies used to reduce inappropriate behavior include *extinc-*

tion, time-out, response cost, restitution, positive practice, and *overcorrection.* In addition, other more intrusive interventions (including some we do not recommend) such as *medications, restraints,* and *corporal punishment* also need to be discussed because they are frequently used and abused as behavior reduction procedures. A brief description and discussion of each of these interventions will be presented. Again, it must be stressed that none of these techniques should be used in isolation. They should always be used in conjunction with interventions that are designed to increase appropriate behavior. Caregivers should incorporate techniques to decrease behavior only when reinforcement strategies alone are not effective.

Extinction

Frequently, children engage in behaviors to elicit caregiver or peer attention. Extinction is a procedure that gradually reduces the frequency and/or intensity of a target behavior by withholding reinforcement from the previously reinforced behavior. Extinction requires caregivers to ignore behavior that, under normal circumstances, would typically lead to attention, a form of reinforcement. By withholding this reinforcement, "extinction can be used to eliminate the connection between the behavior and the positive consequences that follow it" (Kazdin, 1989, p. 174). Gilliam stated that "to discontinue the effect the behavior has on the environment (extinction)" is one of "the most fundamental" ways to eliminate behavior (1989, p. 5).

Extinction is only effective in reducing behaviors that are motivated by attention or some other form of reinforcement. For example, in what may be the first published article regarding the withholding of reinforcement to reduce an inappropriate behavior, Williams (1959) outlined an extinction program to eliminate temper tantrums in a 21-month-old boy. The boy had been sick for the first 18 months of life and had learned to associate crying behavior with parental attention. Although he had recovered, he still used the crying behavior as a way of gaining significant amounts of parental attention and to avoid going to bed at night. By ignoring his crying behavior, the child's crying at bedtime was gradually eliminated.

As demonstrated by the Williams study, extinction has been effective with very young children. Others have demonstrated the effectiveness of extinction with older preschoolers (three to five years old) (Higgins, Morris, & Johnson, 1989) and with young adults (Barrett, Deitz, Gaydos, & Quinn, 1987).

Extinction will not be effective for behaviors that are intrinsically reinforcing. Examples of behaviors that are intrinsically reinforcing include thumbsucking, daydreaming, and self-stimulatory behaviors. Also, extinction should not be used for physical aggression, even if it is determined that attention is the motivating factor. Physical aggression is a behavior that should never be ignored. Also, some behaviors, such as severe self-injury or behaviors that may cause injury to others, may require a more direct intervention approach than extinction.

Extinction and Consistency

Consistency is the most important factor related to the efficacy of extinction. For extinction to be effective in reducing a target behavior, caregivers must be willing to ignore the behavior each and every time the behavior is observed. Caregivers must alert other caregivers about the extinction program so that all caregivers consistently withhold reinforcement following the target behavior. Accidental reinforcement must be prevented. Caregivers must determine if the child's primary source of reinforcement is from caregivers or peers. If the primary source of reinforcement is from the child's peers, caregivers may not be in a position to control the delivery of reinforcement, and extinction is unlikely to be an effective procedure in reducing the target behavior. For example, if a child exhibits disruptive behavior within an educational setting in order to gain recognition from friends, an extinction program initiated by the teacher without the cooperation of the child's friends is unlikely to be effective.

As with other behavior reduction procedures, extinction should not be used in isolation and must be paired with the reinforcement of appropriate behaviors. By consistently ignoring the inappropriate behavior, the behavior will be extinguished over a period of time. The child will learn that inappropriate behaviors are ignored and only appropriate behaviors are followed by access to the desired attention or reinforcement.

Other Factors Affecting Extinction

Kazdin (1989) cited several factors that may influence a behavior's resistance to extinction:

- The schedule of reinforcement that previously maintained the behavior (continuously reinforced behaviors decrease more rapidly than intermittently reinforced behaviors).
- The amount or strength of reinforcement that previously maintained the behavior; the greater the amount or strength of reinforcement associated with the behavior the more resistance to extinction.
- The length of time the reinforcement was previously associated with the target behavior; the longer the association between the reinforcement and the behavior, the more resistance to extinction.
- The frequency of extinction used in the past to disassociate the reinforcement and the behavior; the greater the number of times, the more rapid the extinction.

Extinction Burst

Extinction is an effective procedure for reducing inappropriate attention-getting behavior in children. However, one aspect of the procedure may make extinction very difficult for some caregivers to use. Often a child has learned that demands will eventually be met if he or she is persistent and engages in the inappropriate behavior until caregivers "give in" or "give up."

What happens when a caregiver decides to ignore behavior that has previously been reinforced? The child is likely to repeat the behavior with greater frequency and intensity in hopes that the caregiver will eventually give in (again). This is called an *extinction burst*. An extinction burst is a temporary increase in the frequency or intensity of a target behavior immediately after the introduction of extinction. For example, when a teacher decides to ignore a student's talking-out behavior, which previously resulted in getting the teacher's attention, the child's behavior may initially increase. By being consistent and reinforcing the child for appropriate methods of getting the teacher's attention (raising hand), the student's talking-out behavior will decrease. Unfortunately, many caregivers do not know about extinction bursts and, at this point, incorrectly judge the extinction program as ineffective. On the contrary, the extinction burst demonstrates that the caregiver has identified at least some of the primary reinforcements maintaining the target behavior, that these reinforcers have been effectively withheld, and that the extinction procedure is having an impact on the child's behavior. With a little persistence and patience on the part of the caregiver, once the extinction burst period is over, the child's behavior will improve. Caregivers must decide *prior* to using extinction if they will be able to ignore the inappropriate behavior through the extinction burst phase. If this is not possible, then another procedure is recommended.

Spontaneous Recovery

Spontaneous recovery refers to the temporary recurrence of a target behavior during extinction even though the behavior has not been reinforced. The frequency or intensity of the behavior is usually not significant during spontaneous recovery. The biggest danger during this time is that the behavior will receive significant caregiver attention or other forms of reinforcement. This, of course, will increase the likelihood of the behavior recurring in the future. However, if caregivers are consistent with the extinction procedure, the behavior is less likely to recur. Figure 8.2 demonstrates an example of both an extinction burst and spontaneous recovery during an extinction program used to reduce the frequency of a child's tattling behavior.

Advantages of Extinction

Extinction has many advantages over other behavior reduction procedures, especially procedures that are considered "intrusive" or "aversive." First, extinction may be effective in reducing inappropriate behavior without the use of any physical or verbal consequences (for example, repeatedly telling the child "No!") that may decrease the child's self-esteem or establish a "battle" between the caregiver and the child. Second, since extinction does not involve the use of any "aversive punishments," negative side-effects from these procedures are avoided. Third, while the effects of extinction may be gradual, the duration of effects is usually long-lasting. Last, reinforcement of appropriate behaviors, while ignoring the inappropriate target behavior, is a critical ele-

Figure 8.2. *Demonstration of extinction burst and spontaneous recovery during extinction program for reduction of tattling behavior.*

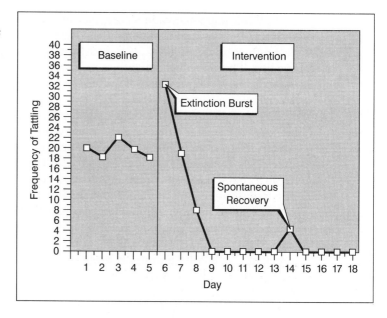

ment of extinction. Next to positive reinforcement, this makes extinction, in our opinion, a procedure of first-choice when caregivers are trying to reduce minor inappropriate behaviors.

Potential Side-Effects and Disadvantages of Extinction

Except for the temporary increase in the target behavior that occurs during the extinction burst, the extinction procedure has only minor potential side-effects. For example, the child may become frustrated when caregivers no longer provide attention that has come to be expected following a target behavior. This may lead to a significant extinction burst and the demonstration of other inappropriate behaviors (e.g., aggression) as well. As long as caregivers are providing reinforcement for other appropriate behaviors and are consistent with the extinction procedure, these side-effects should be only temporary setbacks.

In summary, extinction may be effective when caregivers are able and willing to:

♦ Identify all reinforcers that typically follow the target behavior.
♦ Withhold all reinforcers that typically follow the target behavior.
♦ Be consistent. The target behavior must be ignored each and every time it is exhibited.
♦ Identify and reinforce appropriate behaviors during the extinction program.
♦ Maintain the procedure through the expected extinction burst and spontaneous recovery periods beyond.
♦ Teach and demonstrate to the child that caregiver attention follows appropriate behavior.

Extinction may not be effective or should not be used when:

◆ The reinforcers that typically follow the target behavior cannot be identified.

◆ The withholding of reinforcement following the target behavior is not possible.

◆ Other caregivers who come in contact with the child are not willing or able to follow the extinction procedure.

◆ Peer reinforcement in maintaining the target behavior cannot be controlled.

◆ There is a high probability of accidental reinforcement.

◆ An extinction burst of the behavior cannot be tolerated given the child's behavior or other factors within the environment.

◆ It is inappropriate or dangerous to ignore the target behavior (e.g., aggression, severe self-injury).

Time-out from Positive Reinforcement

Time-out from reinforcement refers to the removal of an individual's access to sources of reinforcement for a specific period of time contingent on inappropriate behavior. Caregivers may deny access to reinforcement in two primary ways—caregivers can remove the child from the reinforcement or remove the reinforcement from the child. Time-out from positive reinforcement has proven effective in reducing many kinds of inappropriate behaviors (Crespi, 1988; Harris, 1985).

Note that if the initial environment or activity is *not* reinforcing to the child, then removing the child's access to that reinforcement would *not* be considered time-out or a behavior reduction procedure. In fact, if a child does not want to be in an environment to begin with, removing the child may actually be reinforcing. As stated by Nelson and Rutherford, "Perhaps the most common problem with all levels of timeout is the lack of a sufficiently reinforcing timein environment" (1983, p. 62). For example, if a student does not like his or her classroom and wants to get out of the classroom, then removing the student from the classroom (e.g., sending the student to a time-out area outside the classroom) contingent on inappropriate behavior may serve as a reinforcer, not a punisher. The use of "time-out" in this case may, in fact, increase the student's inappropriate behavior.

> Time-out may function as a reinforcer for undesired behavior if behaviors that result in timeout allow the student to escape from a minimally reinforcing environment; or the opportunity to engage in highly reinforcing behavior during time-out may be a more powerful contingency than positive reinforcement for appropriate classroom performances. (Nelson & Rutherford, 1983, p. 62)

As with any behavior reduction procedure, the effectiveness of time-out is measured by the reduction of the target behavior for which the time-out serves as a consequence. By monitoring the target behavior, caregivers should be able to determine if the time-out procedure is effective. Unfortunately, many caregivers continue to use time-out with individual children even when the evidence is clear that time-out has not been an effective behavior reduction procedure for those individuals. Because some types of time-out involve the removal of a challenging child from the environment, some caregivers may use time-out as a method of taking a temporary "break" from the child. This, however, is not time-out from positive reinforcement and is unlikely to serve as an effective behavior reduction procedure. In fact, the temporary "break" from the child may be negatively reinforcing for caregivers and, despite a lack of effectiveness, they continue to use the procedure.

One of the primary issues regarding time-out is the length of the time-out period. Two- to eight-minute time-out periods are suggested for young children contingent on inappropriate behavior. Time-out periods should be given in increments of one minute per year of age (e.g., two years = two minutes of time-out) for children 10 years and younger. Longer periods of time are not more effective and may even lead to an increase in inappropriate behavior (Harris, 1985). Caregivers should use an alarm clock, timer, or other method of time keeping to act as a cue to the end of the time-out period and to ensure that the child does not spend more time in time-out than scheduled.

Several types of time-out procedures are available. There are also some terminology issues concerning other procedures incorrectly identified under the heading of "time-out." These will be discussed here.

Exclusion Time-Out

Exclusion time-out refers to the *physical removal* of a child from a reinforcing environment or activity for a specific period of time. In our opinion, exclusion time-out is the only "true" time-out procedure since, by definition, time-out is the removal of the child from reinforcement. Within exclusion time-out, there are three widely accepted subtypes.

Contingent Observation Time-Out   A *contingent observation time-out* is a type of exclusion time-out that involves removing the child from a reinforcing activity (e.g., story time, game) to the "sideline" contingent on the target behavior (Porterfield, Herbert-Jackson, & Risley, 1976). Rather than isolating the child, the child is allowed to remain on the periphery of the group and observe the other children participating in the activity and behaving appropriately (Brantner & Doherty, 1983). After a short period of time, the child is allowed to return to the group. For example, when a hockey player commits a foul, he or she must sit on the sideline for a specific time period. The hockey player may observe other members of the team play, but he or she may not rejoin the activity until the time-out period is over. White and Bailey (1990) used a contingent observation time-out procedure called "sit and watch" to decrease disruptive behaviors with elementary students during physical education classes. Disruptive behavior included noncompliance, aggression, and throwing objects.

Mathews, Friman, Barone, Ross, and Christophersen (1987) used a playpen as a time-out area to reduce successfully unsafe behavior with one-year-old infants. The time-out procedure was used in conjunction with parent training on how to child-proof the home and increase positive parent-child interactions. Use of the playpen as a time-out area allowed the child to observe caregivers and other environmental reinforcers without the ability to interact with these reinforcers for several seconds. This procedure was seen as one step beyond a partially successful procedure described by Powers and Chapieski (1986) in which mothers were taught to just remove their 14-month-old infants from unsafe objects.

Isolation Time-Out   Isolation time-out is a procedure that requires the caregiver to remove the child totally from the reinforcing activity contingent on the target behavior. This procedure is one step beyond contingent observation and the child is *turned away* from the reinforcing activity. An isolation time-out area may be a designated corner or other isolated space in the environment. The children need to know beforehand that they are placed or sent to this area as a result of their inappropriate behavior.

This technique is especially effective in decreasing physically aggressive behavior in young children. When the child exhibits the target behavior (e.g., hitting others), he or she is immediately removed from the activity and placed in the time-out area for a predetermined time period. For young children, caregivers should gently, but firmly, take the child to the predetermined area, briefly tell the child why he or she is being placed in time-out, and how long he or she must remain in time-out (e.g., "You may come out of time-out when the timer goes off"). Older children may simply be instructed "You (target behavior). Go to time-out." Other general guidelines for using isolation time-out include:

♦   The time-out area should be set up so that the caregiver can clearly observe the child but the child cannot observe the activity from which he was just removed. Isolation time-out may include placing the child behind a partition within the environment or other open space next to the environment. School hallways are usually not good time-out areas since the classroom teacher may not be able to monitor the child during the time-out period.

♦   The isolation time-out area may contain a chair for the child to sit on so that expectations for what the child will do while in the time-out area are clear (i.e., sit on the chair).

♦   A timer should be set by the caregiver for the amount of time the child is to spend sitting in the time-out area. Use of a timer clearly delineates to the child how long he or she must stay in time-out and also eliminates the possibility that the caregiver will lose track of how long the child has been in time-out. Again, it is important to note that longer time-out periods do not mean that the child will be less inclined to engage in the inappropriate behavior in the future. Time-out periods that last longer than 10 minutes are unlikely to be any more effective than 2-minute periods. As stated above, one minute of time-out per year of age of the child is a good guideline to follow (Wacker, personal communication, January 9, 1989).

♦   The most important factor regarding the effectiveness of time-out is the reinforcement value of the environment from which the child has been removed. Children should not be allowed to play with toys or interact with others while in the time-out area. Remember, the purpose of time-out is to remove the child from reinforcement.

♦   If the child refuses to remain in the time-out area, the caregiver should return him to the area and tell the child that he may not return to the group until he completes his time in time-out. If this does not work, the child may be given a choice between sitting in the time-out area or being completely removed from the environment. This may be enough of a deterrent that the child will choose to stay in the less restrictive area. Also, other backup consequences may be employed to reinforce appropriate time-out behavior. Keep in mind that the child will want to return to the activity if he or she has learned that reinforcement may be earned through appropriate behavior.

Seclusion Time-Out   Seclusion time-out involves the complete removal of the child to a separate, usually closed, room or cubicle (i.e., time-out room) "outside the individual's normal educational or treatment environment that is devoid of positive reinforcers and in which the individual can be safely placed for a temporary period of time" (Cooper, Heron, & Heward, 1987, p. 445). An example of seclusion time-out is sending a child to her bedroom or to a time-out room within the educational setting. Some may argue that sending a child to the bedroom is not an appropriate time-out room because it is not devoid of positive reinforcers. However, if the child does not want to be in his or her bedroom and would rather be playing with friends, the bedroom may be appropriate. If not, other less reinforcing areas of the house, such as a parent's bedroom, the stairway, or a chair placed in an isolated area of the home may be used. Small areas (e.g., closets) that are too confining and are not well ventilated or lighted are *not* recommended and may be considered abusive. In the classroom environment, where an appropriate time-out room is not available, a special chair or carpet square placed in an isolated area of the classroom may be considered a form of seclusionary time-out.

From our personal observations, the use of seclusion time-out has been and continues to be misused and abused in many educational settings. First, children are being removed from environments or activities they do not find reinforcing. By removing a child from an unpleasant environment contingent on inappropriate behavior, caregivers may be negatively reinforcing inappropriate behavior. Second, children are frequently sent to seclusion time-out for periods of time that are too long and serve only to provide caregivers with a break from the child. Third, in many cases time-out continues to be used despite data indicating its ineffectiveness in reducing specific inappropriate behavior in individual children. Fourth, time-out is frequently used across schools and other educational settings with disregard for individual differences across children and behaviors. A procedure perceived as punishing for one child may be perceived as reinforcing for another and vice versa.

Nonexclusion Time-Out

Nonexclusion time-out is discussed in several texts and articles as a procedure in which the child is *not* removed from the reinforcing environment, but in some way or another, attention and other forms of reinforcement are removed from the child (Alberto & Troutman, 1990; Cooper, Heron, & Heward, 1987; Kazdin, 1989). At first reading, some readers may be confused by the similarity of nonexclusion time-out and extinction. While extinction refers to the withholding of reinforcement previously associated with a target behavior, nonexclusion time-out refers to the temporary removal of *all* reinforcement for a short period of time. For example, as a result of an extinction program, Julia is ignored by her teacher when she speaks in class without first raising her hand. While Julia was previously able to receive her teacher's attention in this manner in the past, her teacher now calls on Julia only when she raises her hand. If the same teacher were using a nonexclusion time-out procedure, the teacher would remove all attention and other reinforcement from Julia for a specific period of time (e.g., two minutes) each time Julia speaks in class without first seeking recognition by raising her hand. With extinction, a specific reinforcement (teacher's attention) previously associated with the target behavior (speaking-out) is withheld. With nonexclusion time-out, all attention and reinforcement is removed for a limited time period contingent on the target behavior.

There are several variations of nonexclusion time-out. The three most common variations are planned ignoring, removal of a specific reinforcer, and the time-out ribbon.

Planned Ignoring   *Planned ignoring* refers to the removal of any social attention for a short period of time contingent on the occurrence of an inappropriate behavior. For example, when working with a child or a group of children, a teacher may look away from the child/children for 30 seconds contingent on inappropriate behavior.

Removal of Specific Reinforcers   *Removal of specific reinforcers* refers to the removal of such reinforcers as food, toys, or materials for a short period of time contingent on the occurrence of an inappropriate behavior. For example, a caregiver may remove a child's food for 60 seconds contingent on inappropriate behavior during mealtime. In a second example, a caregiver may remove a toy from a child for two minutes after the child throws the toy at another child.

The Time-Out Ribbon   The *time-out ribbon* refers to a procedure first used by Foxx and Shapiro (1978) in which all the children in a classroom were given a ribbon to wear. In addition, the children received edibles and praise for appropriate behavior and for wearing their ribbon. When targeted inappropriate behavior occurred, a teacher removed the ribbon and attention from the child for three minutes or until the inappropriate behavior was terminated. Inappropriate behavior decreased from 42% during baseline to 6% during the time-out ribbon program.

Salend and Gordon (1987) used one large ribbon for a whole group of children and demonstrated the effectiveness of an interdependent group-oriented time-out ribbon procedure. While the class had possession of the ribbon (on display in front of the class), a token system was employed whereby the group received one token for every two minutes they refrained from inappropriate verbalization. However, when a group member engaged in inappropriate verbalization the ribbon was removed for a one-minute period. The students could not earn tokens during this one-minute period. Inappropriate verbalizations were significantly reduced.

The time-out ribbon procedure has been effective both with groups and with individuals. For example, McKeegan, Estill, and Campbell (1984) used the time-out ribbon procedure to eliminate stereotypic behavior of a single child. The child learned that, contingent on stereotypic behavior, the ribbon, along with any associated attention or reinforcement, was removed. Caregivers may employ many variations to the time-out ribbon. For example, Fee, Matson, and Manikam (1990) used a wristband covered with smiling-face stickers, instead of a ribbon, with preschool children. The wristband was removed for three consecutive minutes contingent on targeted inappropriate behaviors.

Advantages of Time-Out

Time-out from positive reinforcement has several advantages. The primary advantages of time-out include the following:

- ◆ It is easy to integrate a time-out procedure with a positive reinforcement program to increase appropriate behaviors.
- ◆ Effects from time-out procedures are usually rapid and the duration of effects is usually long-lasting.

◆ The nonexclusion time-out process may be employed without removing the child from the educational environment.

◆ Nonexclusion time-out involves little or no physical contact with the child following inappropriate behavior.

◆ Time-out provides caregivers with an alternative to more intrusive behavior reduction strategies.

Potential Side-Effects and Disadvantages of Time-Out

A primary concern about the use of time-out is the removal of children from the instructional setting, which may affect the child's academic performance. Skiba and Raison examined the relationship between time-out usage with elementary children and academic achievement. They found that "considerably less instructional time was lost to time-out than to other sources of classroom absence, such as suspension or truancy" (1990, p. 36). The amount of time-out usage was stated as "low to moderate for the majority of students" or an average of seven time-out periods (74 minutes) per month per student. When time-out usage is high, caregivers should not only begin to question the impact on educational performance, but the effectiveness of the time-out procedure for the individual students.

In summary, time-out from positive reinforcement may be an effective behavior reduction procedure if the following results:

◆ The use of time-out is paired with a positive reinforcement program for appropriate behaviors.

◆ Caregivers make the child's environment and activities reinforcing so that the child will want to remain in the current environment and activities. That is, the current environment and activities are perceived by the child as more reinforcing than the time-out area.

◆ Caregivers monitor the effectiveness of time-out and discontinue its use when data indicate no effect on behavior.

◆ Caregivers do not abuse time-out as a method of removing a child with challenging behavior.

Potential disadvantages and side-effects of time-out include:

◆ Possible abuse, especially the duration of the time-out period.

◆ Use by some caregivers as a 'break' period.

◆ May be viewed by some children as more reinforcing than the time-in environment.

◆ Frequent time-out usage removes the child from educational settings and may effect academic performance.

◆ The child may exhibit other inappropriate behaviors when caregivers remove positive reinforcement or remove the child from a reinforcing environment.

Response Cost

Response cost is the systematic removal of reinforcers, sometimes in the form of tokens, points, money, or check marks, contingent on inappropriate behavior. Response cost is a behavior reduction procedure often used in conjunction with a token economy program (described in Chapter 5). This intervention requires the systematic removal of tokens as a consequence of inappropriate behavior (Walker, 1983). The number of tokens lost per inappropriate behavior is predetermined and usually depends on the severity of the behavior.

The response cost system should be explained to the child prior to implementation; moreover, it is a wise idea to list and post both the behaviors that will result in a removal of reinforcers and the number of reinforcers that will be lost per inappropriate behavior. A response cost program should always be employed in conjunction with a token economy program. Thus, along with a list of inappropriate behaviors that will lead to the removal of reinforcers, a list of appropriate behaviors that will warrant the earning of additional reinforcers should also be posted. Research has repeatedly indicated that the combination of response cost with other reinforcement programs is more effective than response cost alone (Phillips, Phillips, Fixsen, & Wolf, 1971; Walker, Hops, & Fiegenbaum, 1976; Walker, 1983).

Caregivers should ensure that a child does not have all reinforcers removed or "go in the hole." For example, a child on a response cost program should not owe caregivers 10 tokens at the end of the day. This is ensured by reinforcing appropriate behavior at a higher rate than the removal of tokens for inappropriate behavior. Caregivers should reinforce appropriate behavior four times for every response to inappropriate behavior. In this way, the primary focus of the educational setting will be on reinforcing appropriate behaviors rather than the punishment of inappropriate behaviors.

Walker (1983, p. 52) outlined several guidelines for implementing response cost (RC) programs:

- RC should be implemented immediately after the target behavior occurs.
- RC should be applied consistently.
- The child should not be allowed to accumulate negative points.
- The ratio of points earned to points lost must be controlled.
- The subtraction of reinforcers should not be punitive or personalized.
- The child's appropriate behavior should be praised frequently.

Table 8.1 provides a comparison of response cost with extinction and time-out. While all three involve the removal of reinforcement, response cost removes a specific reinforcement in increments. Also, the amount of the reinforcement removed is directly proportional to the frequency of inappropriate behavior. As explained by Pazulinec, Meyerrose and Sajwaj:

Table 8.1.   *Comparison of extinction, time-out, and response cost procedures.*

Procedure	Definition	Example
Extinction	Removal of attention and other reinforcement previously associated with a target behavior.	Caregiver ignores child during tantrum behavior.
Time-out	Removal of all reinforcement for short, specific time period contingent upon a target behavior.	Caregiver removes child from activity contingent upon hitting others.
Response cost	Removal of predetermined number of reinforcers (tokens, points, check marks) contingent upon a target behavior.	Caregiver removes one token from child contingent upon off-task behavior.

In both extinction and timeout procedures, the reinforcing consequence following a response is withheld. In contrast, response cost involves the removal of a positive stimulus contingent upon the occurrence of an undesirable behavior. . . .in timeout the individual is restricted from receiving reinforcement or from participating in ongoing setting activities, whereas the response cost condition imposes no restrictions. (1983, p. 71)

Pazulinec, Meyerrose, and Sajwaj (1983) outlined several variations to response cost. In the first variation, a child is noncontingently provided with reinforcers at the beginning of a specific period of time (e.g., day, class period). Then, the child must give back reinforcers contingent on the occurrence of specific target behaviors. This variation may also be used with a group of children. For example, a classroom teacher may give the students 10 points and state that if the class still has 5 points by the end of the day the students will receive a special reinforcement. Points would be removed throughout the day contingent on inappropriate target behaviors. This first variation is not recommended for several reasons

◆ By providing the children with reinforcers noncontingently, it does not allow for the teaching of appropriate behaviors through the contingent presentation of reinforcers.

◆ A program that removes tokens without a procedure for children to earn tokens increases the chance that a child will develop a negative balance of tokens. Moreover, after a caregiver has taken away all of a child's tokens, what will he or she do following the next inappropriate behavior?

◆ This variation provides attention only for inappropriate behaviors.

In a second variation of response cost, children earn reinforcers throughout the response cost program. Thus, unlike the first variation, children are not provided with "free" reinforcers, which may be taken away contingent on inappropriate behavior. Rather, reinforcers must be earned contingent on appropriate behavior and, at the same time, reinforcers may be taken away contingent on inappropriate behavior. This second variation may be considered a combination token economy and response cost program, and may also be employed with a group or classroom of children. Walker (1983, p. 48) reported that the two variations of response cost described above were "equally effective" in school settings.

In a third variation, caregivers may divide their children into smaller groups and give each group opportunities to earn reinforcers and, contingent on inappropriate behavior, lose reinforcers. Special reinforcers may be provided to the group of children who ended the day with the most tokens or points. For example, many classroom teachers have activities (e.g., a companion reading program) throughout the day when students are divided into several small groups. These group periods provide teachers with opportunities to use a group token economy and response cost program to manage classroom behavior. Each group could earn or lose tokens contingent on behavior. At the end of the lesson, the group with the most tokens could earn a special reinforcer (e.g., extra time on the computer). An example of a combination token economy and response cost classroom program is provided in Vignette 8.3.

Vignette 8.3.   Example of a Combination Token Economy and Response Cost Classroom Program.

Marie was a first-grade teacher in a classroom of 28 students. As part of her classroom behavior management program, Marie divided her students into groups of four. She varied group membership throughout the school year in an effort to find the best student combination per group. The desks of the four students were placed in a circle. For each group, Marie placed a small glass jar on one of the group member's desks. Contingent on appropriate behavior demonstrated by either an individual member of a group or a whole group, the teacher dropped a token into the jar. Also, when inappropriate behavior was observed, a token was removed from the jar. Because the jars were made of glass, the students could see the tokens accumulate in (or disappear from) their group jars. Marie tried to maintain a higher rate of giving tokens than removing tokens. A special pencil was provided to each member of the group who ended the day with the most tokens. An extra special reinforcer was provided to the group who ended the week with the most tokens.

Advantages of Response Cost

There are many advantages to using response cost programs to modify behavior. However, the advantages listed here assume the use of response cost in conjunction with a positive reinforcement program:

♦ Response cost programs are easily integrated with token economy or other positive reinforcement programs.

♦ Response cost programs are easily implemented in both home and classroom settings.

♦ The effects of response cost programming on target behaviors are usually rapid and long-lasting.

♦ During response cost programs, caregiver attention is directed at specific target behaviors that need modification (Rapport, Murphy, & Bailey, 1982).

♦ During response cost programs there is little delay between inappropriate behavior and caregiver-produced consequences (Rapport, Murphy, & Bailey, 1982).

Potential Side-Effects and Disadvantages of Response Cost

The most significant potential side-effect of response cost is that the procedure may place the focus of caregiver attention on inappropriate behavior. Since the major element of response cost is the removal of reinforcers as a consequence of inappropriate behavior, too much caregiver attention may be directed toward inappropriate behavior rather than appropriate behavior.

A second disadvantage of response cost programs is the potential for some children to lose all reinforcers and then "give up." Both of these disadvantages may be avoided when opportunities to earn positive reinforcers are also available whenever response cost programs are employed.

Restitution, Positive Practice, and Overcorrection

In many behavior management references, restitution and positive practice are considered subtypes or components of overcorrection (Foxx & Azrin, 1972, 1973; Foxx & Bechtel, 1983). Thus, the terms *restitutional overcorrection* and *positive practice overcorrection* are frequently used in the literature to describe procedures designed to decrease inappropriate behavior (Alberto & Troutman, 1990; Cooper, Heron, & Heward, 1987). In this chapter the terms are presented separately in order to clarify their definitions and expand on their practical applications.

Restitution or Simple Correction

Restitution, also known as *simple correction,* refers to a procedure that requires an individual to return the environment to its state prior to a behavior that changed the environment (Azrin & Besalel, 1980). The classic example is asking a child who spills a glass of milk to clean up the spill. Whether the child spilled the milk deliberately or by accident, restitution teaches children to be responsible for their behavior. It is recommended here that restitution not be employed in a punitive manner. Rather, restitution should be carried out in a matter-of-fact manner, especially if the behavior was an accident. Examples of restitution are provided in Table 8.2.

Table 8.2.   *Examples of restitution and restitution overcorrection.*

If the child:	Restitution only—Ask child to:	Restitutional Overcorrection—Ask child to:
Damages family car	Pay for repair.	Pay for new car.
Throws things	Pick up the items thrown and return to appropriate storage place.	Pick up all items in environment and return to appropriate place.
Makes a mess during play or other activities	Clean play area to condition prior to activity.	Clean play area and beyond.
Writes on the wall	Wash the writing from the wall.	Wash the entire wall.
Drops food on the floor during lunch	Sweep up food after lunch.	Sweep entire floor.
Damages school materials	Repair or replace materials.	Repair or replace materials plus repair other damaged materials.
Damages school property	Repair property to condition prior to behavior.	Repair property damaged and perform additional service to school property.
Throws litter on the playground	Pick up the litter thrown on the playground.	Pick up all litter on the playground and around the school.

Very young children may not be able to complete the restitution of the environment independently. However, it is important that caregivers ask the child to help as much as possible, depending on age and ability, while the caregiver repairs the environment. This may be called *assisted restitution*. For example, a caregiver may ask the child to put the wet paper towels in the trash after the spill is wiped up.

Restitutional Overcorrection

Restitutional overcorrection was defined by Foxx and Azrin (1973) as a step beyond simple correction of the environment. Contingent on inappropriate behavior, the child is not only required to perform restitution, but to "restore the situation to a state vastly improved from that which existed before the disruption" (Foxx & Azrin, 1973, p. 2). Restitutional overcorrection should not be used as a consequence of unintentional spills or other accidents. Rather, restitutional overcorrection is intended to serve as a "punishing" consequence for deliberate inappropriate behaviors. Table 8.2 provides examples of restitution overcorrection.

Foxx and Bechtel (1982, p. 231) listed the following conditions for the overcorrection procedure:

♦   The response required of the child should be "directly related" to the child's "misbehavior."

◆ The child should experience "the effort normally required of others to correct the products of his misbehavior."

◆ The overcorrection procedure should be "instituted immediately following the misbehavior."

◆ The child should be required to perform the overcorrection procedure "rapidly so that consequences constitute an inhibitory effort requirement."

◆ The child "is instructed and manually guided through the required acts, with the amount of guidance adjusted on a moment-to-moment basis according to the degree to which he/she is voluntarily performing the act."

Foxx and Bechtel (1983, p. 135) later reduced the procedures of restitution overcorrection to three steps:

◆ Identify the specific and general disturbances created by the misbehavior.

◆ Identify the behaviors needed to vastly improve the consequences of the disturbance.

◆ Require the individual to perform these corrective actions whenever the misbehavior occurs.

The use of restitutional overcorrection has been most frequently cited in the literature as a procedure to decrease inappropriate behaviors with individuals having disabilities (Foxx & Bechtel, 1983). The most frequently cited behaviors targeted with this population were aggression and disruption (Foxx & Azrin, 1972), toileting accidents (Azrin & Foxx, 1971), and self-stimulatory behaviors (Barrett & Shapiro, 1980). With nondisabled populations, restitutional overcorrection is most often cited in the literature as an intervention for toileting accidents and aggression and/or disruption (Foxx & Bechtel, 1983). For example, a child who has a toileting accident may be required to clean the entire room where the accident occurred. In a second example, a child may be required to apologize to all students in a classroom as a consequence for aggression directed at one student.

Restitutional overcorrection has been extensively documented as effective in the elimination of many inappropriate behaviors. Yet, while the use of restitution is recommended, restitutional overcorrection is not recommended as an acceptable behavior reduction procedure for the following reasons:

◆ Overcorrection has questionable educational value beyond the lessons learned during the restitution phase of the child's response (Carey & Bucher, 1986).

◆ Overcorrection places a great deal of attention on the child's inappropriate rather than appropriate behaviors.

◆ It may be difficult or impossible to force a child to perform an overcorrection procedure.

- ◆ Overcorrection may require a caregiver to use physical force if a child refuses to participate or cooperate in the overcorrection procedure. As a result, the child may become aggressive.
- ◆ Forcing a child to perform overcorrection may provide the child with opportunities for inappropriate attention, especially if completed in the presence of peers.
- ◆ Because the overcorrection procedure will probably require considerable caregiver effort, teachers will find the procedure disruptive to their teaching and to the other children within the educational setting.

Positive Practice

Positive practice refers to practicing an appropriate behavior as a consequence for inappropriate behavior. The behavior practiced is the correct, or positive, behavior the child should have exhibited instead of the observed inappropriate behavior. "It means stopping all activities, whenever an error occurs, and then carefully performing the correct behavior several times" (Azrin, Besalel, Hall, & Hall, 1981). For example, when a child throws a piece of paper across the classroom toward a wastepaper basket, the teacher may ask the child to pick up the paper, walk to the wastepaper basket, place the paper into the basket, and return to his or her seat. On the completion of this appropriate behavior, the teacher should reinforce the child ("Thank you") for performing the behavior correctly. This example provides a nonpunitive approach to positive practice. The caregiver corrects the inappropriate behavior, informs the child of an appropriate alternative, allows the child to practice the appropriate behavior, and praises the child for correct performance of the behavior.

Positive practice was not meant to be a positive consequence for inappropriate behavior. Forcing the child to practice the correct response was intended to be a punitive procedure. Also, Foxx and Azrin (1972) and Foxx and Bechtel (1982) stated that the use of reinforcement for correct responses during positive practice may encourage the child to behave inappropriately (in order to have additional opportunities for positive practice and reinforcement). Foxx and Bechtel (1983) recommended that the term "positive practice" be discontinued since the word "positive" gave the wrong impression about the procedure. Lenz, Singh, and Hewett recommended that the term "directed rehearsal" be used "instead of the generic term overcorrection" (1991, p. 71).

Positive Practice Overcorrection

While many texts do not make a distinction between positive practice and positive practice overcorrection, a distinction is made here between the use of positive practice as described above and positive practice overcorrection. While positive practice may be completed with a nonpunitive, educational intent, positive practice overcorrection is clearly intended as a punishing consequence for inappropriate behavior. With overcorrection, the student is required to perform the correct or appropriate behavior repeatedly. The operative word here is "repeatedly." Using our example above, the child may be required to repeat the steps of putting the paper in the wastepaper basket 10 times. The child is not reinforced for correct responses during the positive practice overcorrection procedure.

In a second example, Ollendick, Matson, Esveldt-Dawson, and Shapiro (1980) used positive practice overcorrection to decrease spelling errors. In keeping with the original intent of positive practice, Ollendick et al. did not reinforce students for correct spelling during positive practice. Asking a student to simply repeat the spelling of a word correctly is an example of positive practice. Asking a student to repeat the spelling of a word 100 times (orally or in writing) is an example of positive practice overcorrection.

Carey and Bucher (1986) compared the use of positive practice overcorrection with and without the reinforcement of correct responses during the procedure. They found that reinforcing correct performance during the procedure was effective for increasing appropriate behavior and for reducing inappropriate behavior. Carey and Bucher found that nonreinforced positive practice "showed no advantages over the reinforced variation, and resulted in a greater incidence of undesirable side effects such as aggression and emotionality" (p. 85).

Foxx and Bechtel (1982) voice some concerns about the reinforcement of children for correct responses during positive practice. Their primary concern was that children might choose to behave inappropriately in order to receive reinforcement during the positive practice procedure. However, it is hoped that children will be reinforced for appropriate behavior outside the positive practice procedure and not have to depend on the positive practice procedure for caregiver attention. The use of positive reinforcement during positive practice makes both variations of positive practice less punitive and increases the educational value of the procedures. While not consistent with the initial intent of positive practice, the procedure may be employed in a less punitive manner to teach and reinforce appropriate social skills. These variations are outlined in Figure 8.3.

Medications

The use of medications to control inappropriate behavior has recently received a significant amount of public attention. This attention has focused on the use of methylphenidate (Ritalin) and other stimulants used to control the behavior of children diagnosed as hyperactive or having attention-deficit hyperactive disorder (ADHD). It is clear that the prescription of medications has helped some children, especially children considered hyperactive (Henker, Astor-Dubin, & Varni, 1986; Tannock, Schachar, Carr, Chajczyk, & Logan, 1989). It is also clear that, at times, medications are overprescribed and that many children are taking medication when less intrusive behavior management interventions would prove effective (Hackenberg & Thompson, 1991; Hollander, 1983; Williams, 1988). Many argue that ADHD and hyperactivity are being overdiagnosed and misdiagnosed and "then prescribed medication that cannot help them and could harm them" (Wicks-Nelson & Israel, 1991, p. 203).

Figure 8.3. *Punitiveness of different variations of positive practice with and without the use of positive reinforcement.*

	With Reinforcement	Without Reinforcement
Positive practice	Least punitive	Punitive
Positive practice overcorrection	Punitive	Most punitive

There is considerable evidence that behavior management procedures are more effective for children with attention deficits or hyperactivity than medication (Rapport, Murphy, & Bailey, 1982; Rumain, 1988). Yet, medication remains the primary intervention for the majority of these children (Cullinan, Epstein, & Lloyd, 1983; Friedman & Doyal, 1989; Vyse & Rapport, 1989). It is estimated that 1 to 2% of students take medication for hyperactivity (Epstein & Olinger, 1987). Caregivers frequently look for quick solutions when faced with inappropriate behaviors, and the use of medication appears to offer caregivers quick results. Medicating a child, however, does not change the antecedents and consequences within the child's environment—an environment that may be reinforcing inappropriate behaviors or that seldom teaches and reinforces appropriate behaviors. In this case, the effects of medication may only mask the real problems, which remain unsolved.

Categories of Medications

The medications most frequently used to alter the behavior of children were categorized by Epstein and Olinger (1987) into three types: stimulants, antidepressants, and antipsychotics. Common stimulants include Ritalin, dextroamphetamine (Dexedrine), and pemoline (Cylert). Stimulants are used most frequently to increase attention span and decrease hyperactive, disruptive, and impulsive behavior (Trockman, 1987). Common antidepressants include amitriptyline (Elavil) and imipramine (Tofranil). Antidepressants are frequently used for enuresis, childhood depression, and anxiety (Gadow, 1986). Common antipsychotics include chlorpromazine (Thorazine), haloperidol (Haldol), and thioridazine (Mellaril). Antipsychotics are frequently used to treat severe behavior disorders in children such as psychosis and childhood schizophrenia. Gadow (1986) stated that antipsychotics are also used to treat self-injurious and aggressive behaviors in individuals who have mental and emotional disorders.

Of the three medication categories discussed here, Epstein and Olinger (1987) stated that stimulants were considered the mildest and antipsychotic medications the strongest, with the most side-effects. However, the use of stimulant medication is not recommended for children under the age of three years and is questionable for children between three and five years (Barkley, 1989). Also, while the effectiveness of stimulants as a behavior modifier in children has been clearly demonstrated, their effectiveness in modifying academic performance remains questionable (Barkley, 1989; Gadow, 1986).

Caregivers should be knowledgeable about the potential side-effects associated with any medication prescribed to the children placed in their care. A text by Gadow (1986), titled *Children on Medication: Epilepsy, Emotional Disturbance, and Adolescent Disorders,* provides a more complete understanding of medications used to modify the behavior of children. The following list outlines potential side-effects for all three categories of medications—stimulants, antidepressants, and antipsychotics (Epstein & Olinger, 1987; Gadow, 1986):

Stimulants

  Loss of appetite

  Insomnia

  Growth inhibition

  Nervous tics

  Motor restlessness

Antidepressants

  Loss of appetite

  Insomnia

  Dry mouth

  Nausea

  High blood pressure

  Heart problems

  Poisoning

Antipsychotics

  Increased appetite and weight gain

  Lethargy/apathy

  Dry mouth

  Impaired cognition

  Motor disorders (may be temporary or permanent).

Other precautions include:

- Monitoring and documenting observed side-effects;
- Requesting periodic blood tests to determine if amount of medication is too high or low for child's body weight; and
- Requesting periods of "drug holidays" to reassess child's behavior without the medication and to give the child's body a "rest" from the medication's side-effects.

Throughout this text caregivers have been encouraged to review and evaluate their own behavior and the child's overall environment, and to seek professional advice on modifying these variables before trying to modify the child's behavior. The same approach should be followed before placing a child on medication. Caregivers are advised to question professionals who are quick to prescribe medications before a thorough evaluation of environmental variables and before proven behavior management techniques have been explored. Medications should not serve as the treatment of first-choice for inappropriate behavior. Unfortunately, in many cases, medications have become the "quick-fix" solution for many caregivers who wish to modify the behavior of children.

Physical Restraint

There are two categories of physical restraint. *Manual restraint* involves the use of person-to-person physical contact between a caregiver and the individual being restrained. In this procedure, the child is physically restrained by a caregiver or caregivers. *Mechanical restraint* involves the use of some apparatus used by caregivers to restrain the individual. Straps, belts, and blankets are just a few examples of mechanical restraints.

Schloss and Smith (1987) outlined four primary limitations of manual restraint. First, manual restraint, when used in isolation, does not promote the acquisition of prosocial skills that may be learned through positive strategies such as modeling, direct instruction, and so on. Second, the physical contact and social interaction involved in a manual restraint procedure may serve as reinforcement for inappropriate behavior. Placing an individual in a mechanical restraint may also draw significant attention to the individual. A child who does not have the social skills to gain attention through positive behavior may find the restraint procedure very reinforcing. Third, the restraint procedure is very likely to produce additional inappropriate behaviors, such as aggression, which may be reinforced by caregivers during the restraint procedure. In this case, the child's overall inappropriate behavior may increase. Last, restraint procedures may lead to physical injury to the child and/or caregiver. Schloss and Smith stated that manual restraint may be the most "potentially dangerous behavior management procedure practiced in educational programs" (p. 211).

An additional limitation is the significant physical and emotional trauma caused to children who are restrained. Caregivers who are using physical restraint or considering the use of restraint procedures are encouraged to think about how they would feel if a similar procedure were employed against them.

It is important to understand the difference between using restraints as a temporary, emergency measure and as a planned consequence for inappropriate behavior within a behavior reduction procedure. While there may be situations when restraining a child is necessary in an emergency situation, the use of restraints as a behavior reduction strategy or planned consequence for inappropriate behavior is not recommended. Programming limitations and side-effects overwhelmingly condemn the use of restraints as an acceptable behavior management strategy. Using manual or physical restraints as a planned behavior reduction strategy may also be considered physically and emotionally abusive. In the rare emergency situations when restraints are necessary, only caregivers who have received appropriate training in the proper and safe use of restraints should participate in restraining a child.

Corporal Punishment

Corporal punishment involves hitting an individual with a hand or object (e.g., belt or paddle) with the intent to cause pain or injury. The following is a sample list of some of the professional organizations that have condemned the use of corporal punishment:

- American Association on Mental Retardation
- American Bar Association
- American Educational Association
- American Psychological Association
- American Public Health Association
- Council for Exceptional Children
- National Association of School Psychologists
- National Education Association
- National Parent and Teachers Association
- The Association for Persons With Severe Handicaps

Corporal punishment continues to be a common, although unacceptable, consequence for inappropriate behavior in the United States (Baker, 1987; Rose, 1983; Zirpoli, 1986). Less than half of the 50 states in America prohibit corporal punishment in their public schools (Baker, 1987). In contrast, some countries, such as Norway and Sweden, have national laws against the hitting of children by adults.

While other less aversive procedures have been proven significantly more effective, corporal punishment has very little empirical support regarding its effectiveness as a behavior reduction procedure. Caregivers are urged to resolve against the use of corporal punishment in all settings and support efforts to ban the hitting of children.

While some caregivers may view the short-term punitive effects of corporal punishment as beneficial, the long-term problems and negative side-effects of corporal punishment are numerous. A brief list is presented here:

- As a behavior reduction procedure, corporal punishment does not involve the reinforcement of appropriate behavior and places the focus of caregiver attention on the child's inappropriate behavior.
- Emotional reactions from corporal punishment may interfere with academic learning and appropriate social skill development (Kazdin, 1989).

- ◆ Emotional reactions from corporal punishment may interfere with bonding between caregivers and child (Bayless, 1986).
- ◆ Corporal punishment decreases the self-esteem of the victim (Bayless, 1986).
- ◆ Corporal punishment provides an inappropriate model for behavior and teaches children to solve problems through aggression (Bandura, 1969).
- ◆ The victim of corporal punishment may become aggressive toward the punishing caregiver (Kazdin, 1989).
- ◆ The use of corporal punishment may lead the victim to avoid or escape the punishing environment (Kazdin, 1989).
- ◆ The use of corporal punishment may elicit a fear response in the child when interacting with the punishing caregiver (Newsom, Favell, & Rincover, 1983).

The side-effects of corporal punishment certainly outweigh any short-term benefits. Corporal punishment is not only an ineffective behavior reduction strategy, but given all the other more positive alternatives, corporal punishment is unnecessary.

SUMMARY

The term "behavior reduction strategies" is used in this chapter instead of "punishment" due to the perceived association between punishment and aversive procedures. Punishment is technically any response that reduces the occurrence of preceding behaviors. However, the punishing response does not have to be aversive or even punitive in nature to reduce target behaviors effectively.

The use of positive reinforcement is promoted as the intervention of first-choice for the reduction of inappropriate behaviors. When other behavior reduction strategies are employed, they should always be used in conjunction with a positive reinforcement program. In addition, establishing internal and external committees to safeguard the rights of children is strongly recommended before caregivers attempt to modify or eliminate a child's behavior.

General guidelines for behavior reduction strategies include the fair pair rule, consistency, avoiding too much child-focused attention following inappropriate behavior, providing consequences that are effective, and immediate delivery of consequences. Caregivers are urged to consider environmental modifications before trying to modify the behavior of children within the environment.

A number of behavior reduction strategies are available to caregivers. These include extinction, time-out, response cost, restitution, positive practice, and overcorrection.

Extinction is the withholding of reinforcement from a previously reinforced behavior. Time-out refers to the removal of an individual's access to sources of reinforcement for a specific period of time. Response cost is the systematic removal of reinforcers, such as tokens and points, contingent on inappropriate behavior. Note that all of these interventions should be used in conjunction with positive reinforcement of appropriate behaviors.

Restitution is the act of returning the environment to the condition prior to inappropriate behavior. Restitutional overcorrection refers to a step beyond simple restitution and vastly improving the environment contingent on inappropriate behavior. The nonpunitive use of restitution is supported, while the use of restitutional overcorrection is not.

Positive practice refers to the required practice of appropriate behaviors contingent on inappropriate behavior. Positive practice overcorrection refers to the punitive, repeated practice of appropriate behavior. Although not part of the historic or technical definition of positive practice or overcorrection, reinforcing correct performance of behaviors during and outside of the practice procedures is recommended.

Medications are frequently employed to modify the behavior of children. The most common medications used include stimulants to control aggressive and disruptive behaviors, antidepressants, and antipsychotics to treat children with severe behavior disorders. Caregivers are encouraged to become knowledgeable about the associated side-effects of any medications prescribed to their children. Medications should not serve as a treatment of first-choice or a "quick-fix" solution to behavior challenges that may be remedied by environmental modifications or the employment of basic behavior management strategies.

Manual and mechanical restraints are not recommended, except for rare emergency situations, for the management of inappropriate behaviors. Restraints should never be used as a planned strategy or consequence for inappropriate behavior. Because of the potential physical and emotional trauma restraints may cause to children, the use of restraints as a behavior reduction strategy is considered abusive.

Corporal punishment involves the hitting of children with the intent to cause pain or injury. While many parental and professional organizations have condemned the use of corporal punishment, it continues to be a common consequence for inappropriate behavior. The use of corporal punishment has many negative side-effects, has no educational value, and interferes with learning and social development. Thus, the practice of hitting children in any setting or situation is not an acceptable behavior management strategy.

For Discussion

1. Discuss the difference between programs that focus caregiver attention on reinforcement of appropriate behaviors and programs that focus caregiver attention on inappropriate behaviors.
2. Discuss the importance of establishing internal and external review committees when caregivers attempt to modify or eliminate children's behavior.

3. List and discuss the general guidelines for behavior reduction strategies.
4. Discuss the following behavior reduction strategies and give examples of each: extinction, time-out, response cost, restitution, positive practice, and overcorrection.
5. Discuss the reasons why mechanical restraint and corporal punishment are not recommended strategies for behavior reduction.

REFERENCES

Alberto, P. A., & Troutman, A. C. (1990). *Applied behavior analysis for teachers.* Columbus, OH: Merrill/Macmillan.

Axelrod, S. (1990). Myths that mis(guide) our profession. In A. C. Repp & N. N. Singh (Eds.), *Perspectives on the use of nonaversive and aversive interventions for persons with developmental disabilities* (pp. 59–72). Sycamore, IL: Sycamore Publishing Company.

Azrin, N. H., & Besalel, V. A. (1980). *How to use overcorrection.* Austin, TX: Pro-Ed.

Azrin, N. H., Besalel, V. A., Hall, R. V., & Hall, M. C. (1981). *How to use positive practice.* Austin, TX: Pro-Ed.

Azrin, N. H., & Foxx, R. M. (1971). A rapid method of toilet training the institutionalized retarded. *Journal of Applied Behavior Analysis, 4,* 89–99.

Baker, J. N. (1987, January). Paddling: Still a sore point. *Newsweek.*

Bandura, A. (1969). *Principles of behavior modification.* New York: Holt, Rinehart & Winston.

Barkley, R. A. (1989). Attention deficit-hyperactivity disorder. In E. J. Marsh and R. A. Barkley (Eds.), *Treatment of childhood disorders.* New York: Guilford.

Barrett, D. H., Deitz, S. M., Gaydos, G. R., & Quinn, P. C. (1987). The effects of programmed contingencies and social conditions on response stereotype with human subjects, *Psychological Record, 37,* 489–505.

Bayless, L. (1986). *Discipline: The case against corporal punishment.* King George, VA: American Foster Care Resources.

Berkman, K. A., & Meyer, L. H. (1988). Alternative strategies and multiple outcomes in the remediation of severe self-injury: Going "all out" nonaversively. *Journal of The Association for Persons with Severe Handicaps, 13,* 76–86.

Brantner, J. P., & Doherty, M. A. (1983). A review of time-out: A conceptual and methodological analysis. In S. Axelrod & J. Apsche (Eds.), *The effects of punishment on human behavior* (pp. 87–132). New York: Academic Press.

Carey, R. G., & Bucher, B. D. (1986). Positive practice overcorrection: Effects of reinforcing correct performance. *Behavior Modification, 10,* 73–92.

Cooper, J. O., Heron, T. E., & Heward, W. L. (1987). *Applied behavior analysis.* Columbus, OH: Merrill/Macmillan.

Crespi, T. D. (1988). Effectiveness of time-out: A comparison of psychiatric, correctional, and day treatment programs. *Adolescence, 23,* 805–811.

Cullinan, D., Epstein, M. H., & Lloyd, J. W. (1983). *Behavior disorders of children and adolescents.* Englewood Cliffs, NJ: Prentice-Hall.

DeLuke, S. V., & Knoblock, P. (1987). Teacher behavior as preventive discipline. *Teaching Exceptional Children, 19*(4), 18–24.

Donnellan, A. M., & LaVigna, G. W. (1990). Myths about punishment. In A. C. Repp & N. N. Singh (Eds.), *Perspectives on the use of nonaversive and aversive interventions for persons with developmental disabilities* (pp. 33–57). Sycamore, IL: Sycamore Publishing Company.

Donnellan, A. M., LaVigna, G. W., Negri-Shoultz, N., & Fassbender, L. L. (1988). *Progress without punishment: Effective approaches for learners with behavior problems.* New York: Teachers College Press, Columbia University.

Donnellan, A. M., Mirenda, P. L., Mesaros, R. A., & Fassbender, L. L. (1984). Analyzing the communicative functions of aberrant behavior. *Journal of The Association for Persons with Severe Handicaps, 9,* 201–212.

Doss, L. S., & Reichle, J. (1989). Establishing communicative alternatives to the emission of socially motivated excess behavior: A review. *Journal of The Association for Persons with Severe Handicaps, 14,* 101–112.

Durand, V. M., & Crimmins, D. M. (1988). Identifying the variables maintaining self-injurious behaviors. *Journal of Autism & Developmental Disorders, 18,* 99–117.

Epstein, M. H., & Olinger, E. (1987). Use of medication in school programs for behaviorally disordered pupils. *Behavioral Disorders, 12,* 138–144.

Evans, I. M., & Meyer, L. H. (1985). *An educative approach to behavior problems: A practical decision model for interventions with severely handicapped learners.* Baltimore, MD: Paul H. Brookes.

Evans, I. M., & Meyer, L. H. (1990). Toward a science in support of meaningful outcomes: A response to Horner et al. *The Journal of The Association of Persons With Severe Handicaps, 15,* 133–135.

Fee, V. E., Matson, J. L., & Manikam, R. (1990). A control group outcome study of a nonexclusionary time-out package to improve social skills with preschoolers. *Exceptionality, 1,* 107–121.

Foxx, R. M., & Azrin, N. H. (1972). Restitution: A method of eliminating aggressive-disruptive behaviors of retarded and brain damaged patients. *Behavior Research and Therapy, 10,* 15–27.

Foxx, R. M., & Azrin, N. H. (1973). The elimination of autistic self-stimulatory behavior by overcorrection. *Journal of Applied Behavior Analysis, 6,* 1–14.

Foxx, R. M., & Bechtel, D. R. (1982). Overcorrection. In M. Hersen, R. M. Eisler, & P. M. Miller (Eds.), *Progress in behavior modification* (Vol. 13, pp. 227–288). New York: Academic Press.

Foxx, R. M., & Bechtel, D. R. (1983). Overcorrection: A review and analysis. In S. Axelrod & J. Apsche (Eds.), *The effects of punishment on human behavior* (pp. 133–220). New York: Academic Press.

Foxx, R. M., & Shapiro, S. T. (1978). The time-out ribbon: A nonexclusionary time-out procedure. *Journal of Applied Behavior Analysis, 11,* 125–136.

Friedman, R. J., & Doyal, G. T. (1989). *Attention deficit disorder and hyperactivity.* Danville, IL: Interstate Printers and Publishers.

Friman, P. C. (1990). Nonaversive treatment of high-rate disruption: Child and provider effects. *Exceptional Children, 57,* 64–69.

Gadow, K. D. (1986). *Children on medication: Epilepsy, emotional disturbance, and adolescent disorders.* San Diego, CA: College-Hill Press.

Gaylord-Ross, R. (1980). A decision model for the treatment of aberrant behavior in applied settings. In W. Sailor, B. Wilcox, & L. Brown (Eds.), *Methods of instruction for severely handicapped students* (pp. 135–158). Baltimore, MD: Paul H. Brookes.

Gilliam, J. E. (1989). Positive reinforcement and behavioral deficits of children with autism: C.B. Ferster's thoughts versus current practice. *Focus on Autistic Behavior, 4,* 1–16.

Hackenberg, T. D., & Thompson, T. (1991). Psychotropic drugs and developmental disabilities: From form to function. *Impact, 4,* 12–18.

Harris, K. R. (1985). Definitional, parametric, and procedural considerations in time-out interventions and research. *Exceptional Children, 51,* 279–288.

Henker, B., Astor-Dubin, L., & Varni, J. W. (1986). Psychostimulant medications and perceived intensity in hyperactive children. *Journal of Abnormal Child Psychology, 14,* 105–114.

Higgins, S. T., Morris, E. K., & Johnson, L. M. (1989). Social transmission of superstitious behavior in preschool children. *Psychological Records, 39,* 307–323.

Hollander, S. K. (1983). Patterns of interest in the pharmacological management of hyperactivity. *American Journal of Orthopsychiatry, 53,* 353–356.

Iwata, B. A., Vollmer, T. R., & Zarcone, J. R. (1990). The experimental (functional) analysis of behavior disorders: Methodology, applications, and limitations. In A. C. Repp & N. N. Singh (Eds.), *Perspectives on the use of nonaversive and aversive interventions for persons with developmental disabilities* (pp. 301–330). Sycamore, IL: Sycamore Publishing Company.

Kazdin, A. E. (1989). *Behavior modification in applied settings.* Pacific Grove, CA: Brooks/Cole.

LaVigna, G. W., & Donnellan, A. M. (1986). *Alternatives to punishment.* New York: Irvington Publishers.

LaVigna, G. W., & Willis, T. J. (1991, February). *Nonaversive behavior modification.* Workshop presented by the Institute for Applied Behavior Analysis, Minneapolis, Minnesota.

Lenz, M., Singh, N. N., & Hewett, A. E. (1991). Overcorrection as an academic remediation procedure. *Behavior Modification, 15,* 64–73.

Long, N. J., & Newman, R. G. (1976). Managing surface behavior of children in school. In N. J. Long, W. C. Morse, & R. G. Newman (Eds.), *Conflict in* the classroom: The education of the emotionally disturbed children (3rd ed., pp. 308–317). Belmont, CA: Wadsworth Publishing Company.

Mathews, J. R., Friman, P. C., Barone, V. J., Ross, L. V., & Christophersen, E. R. (1987). Decreasing dangerous infant behaviors through parent instruction. Journal of Applied Behavior Analysis, 20, 165–169.

McKeegan, G., Estill, K., & Campbell, B. (1984). Use of nonseclusionary time-out for the elimination of stereotypic behavior. Journal of Behavior Therapy and Experimental Psychiatry, 15, 261–264.

Meyer, L. H., & Evans, I. M. (1989). Nonaversive intervention for behavior problems: A manual for home and community. Baltimore, MD: Paul H. Brookes.

Morgan, R. L., & Striefel, S. (1988). Restrictiveness of procedures to decrease behavior: Views of school psychologist, administrators, teachers, and specialists. Journal of Special Education, 21, 108–119.

Nelson, C. M., & Rutherford, R. B. (1983). Time-out revisited: Guidelines for its use in special education. Exceptional Education Quarterly, 3, 56–67.

Newsom, C., Favell, J. E., & Rincover, A. (1983). The side effects of punishment. In S. Axelrod & J. Apsche (Eds.), The effects of punishment on human behavior (pp. 285–316). New York: Academic Press.

O'Brien, S., & Repp, A. C. (1990). Reinforcement-based reductive procedures: A review of 20 years of their use with persons with severe or profound retardation. The Association for Persons with Severe Handicaps, 15, 148–159.

Ollendick, T., Matson, J., Esveldt-Dawson, K., & Shapiro, E. (1980). Increasing spelling achievement: An analysis of treatment spelling utilizing an alternative treatment design. Journal of Applied Behavior Analysis, 13, 645–654.

O'Neill, R. E., Horner, R. H., Albin, R. W., Storey, K., & Sprague, J. R. (1990). Functional analysis of problem behavior: A practicial assessment guide. Sycamore, IL: Sycamore Publishing Company.

Pazulinec, R., Meyerrose, M., & Sajwaj, T. (1983). Punishment via response cost. In S. Axelrod & J. Apsche (Eds.), The effects of punishment on human behavior (pp. 71–86). New York: Academic Press.

Pfiffner, L. J., & O'Leary, S. G. (1987). The efficacy of all positive management as a function of the prior use of negative consequences. Journal of Applied Behavior Analysis, 20, 265–271.

Pfiffner, L. J., Rosen, L. A., & O'Leary, S. G. (1985). The efficacy of an all-positive approach to classroom management. Journal of Applied Behavior Analysis, 18, 257–261.

Phillips, E. L., Phillips, E. A., Fixen, D. L., & Wolf, M. (1971). Achievement place: Modification of behaviors of pre-delinquent boys within a token economy. Journal of Applied Behavior Analysis, 4, 45–59.

Porterfield, J. K., Herbert-Jackson, E., & Risley, T. R. (1976). Contingent observation: An effective and acceptable procedure for reducing disruptive behavior of young children in a group setting. Journal of Applied Behavior Analysis, 9, 55–64.

Rapport, M. D., Murphy, A., & Bailey, J. S. (1982). Ritalin vs. response cost in the control of hyperactive children: A within-subject comparison. *Journal of Applied Behavior Analysis, 15,* 205–216.

Rose, T. L. (1983). A survey of corporal punishment of mildly handicapped students. *Exceptional Education Quarterly, 3,* 9–19.

Rosenberg, M. S. (1986). Maximizing the effectiveness of structured classroom management programs: Implementing rule-review procedures with disruptive and distractible students. *Behavioral Disorders, 11,* 239–248.

Rumain, B. (1988). Efficacy of behavior management versus Methylphenidate in a hyperactive child: The role of dynamics. *American Journal of Orthopsychiatry, 58,* 466–469.

Sabatino, D. A. (1987). Preventive discipline as a practice in special education. *Teaching Exceptional Children, 19*(4), 8–11.

Salend, S., & Gordon, B. (1987). A group-oriented time-out ribbon procedure. *Behavioral Disorders, 12,* 131–137.

Sasso, G. M., Melloy, K. J., & Kavale, K. A. (1990). The effects of social skills training through structured learning: Behavioral covariation, generalization, and maintenance. *Behavioral Disorders, 16,* 9–22.

Schloss, P. J., & Smith, M. A. (1987). Guidelines for ethical use of manual restraint in public school settings for behaviorally disordered students. *Behavioral Disorders, 12,* 207–213.

Schuler, A. L. (1980, August). *Communicative intent and aberrant behavior,* Paper presented at the Council for Exceptional Children's Topical Conference on the Seriously Emotionally Disturbed, Minneapolis, Minnesota.

Skiba, R. J., & Deno, S. L. (1991). Terminology and behavior reduction: The case against "punishment." *Exceptional Children, 57,* 298–312.

Skiba, R., & Raison, J. (1990). Relationship between the use of timeout and academic achievement. *Exceptional Children, 57,* 36–46.

Snell, M. E., & Zirpoli, T. J. (1987). Instructional strategies. In M. E. Snell (Ed.). *Systematic instruction of persons with severe handicaps* (pp. 110–149). Columbus, OH: Merrill/Macmillan.

Stainback, W., Stainback, S., & Froyen, L. (1987). Structuring the classroom to prevent disruptive behaviors. *Teaching Exceptional Children, 19,* 12–16.

Tannock, R., Schachar, R. J., Carr, R. P., Chajczyk, D., & Logan, G. D. (1989). Effects of methylphenidate on inhibitory control in hyperactive children. *Journal of Abnormal Child Psychology, 17,* 473–491.

Trockman, R. W. (1987). *The use of stimulant medication for AD-HD children: The educators' responsibilities.* Unpublished manuscript, Minneapolis, Minnesota.

Turnbull, A. P., & Turnbull, H. R. (1990). A tale about lifestyle changes: Comments on "Toward a technology of 'Nonaversive' behavior support." *The Association for Persons with Severe Handicaps, 15,* 142–144.

Underwood, L., & Thyer, B. (1990). Social work practice with the mentally retarded: Reducing self-injurious behaviors using non-aversive methods. *Arete, 15,* 14–23.

Vyse, S. A., & Rapport, M. (1989). The effects of methylphenidate on learning in children with ADHD: The stimulus equivalence paradigm. *Journal of Counseling and Clinical Psychology, 57,* 425–435.

Wacker, D., Berg, W., & Northrup, J. (1991). Breaking the cycle of challenging behaviors: Early treatment key to success. *Impact, 4,* 10–11.

Walker, H. M. (1983, February). Application of response cost in school settings: Outcomes, issues and recommendations. *Exceptional Education Quarterly,* 47–55.

Walker, H. M., Hops, H., & Fiegenbaum, E. (1976). Deviant classroom behavior as a function of combinations of social and token reinforcement and cost contingency. *Behavior Therapy, 7,* 76–88.

White, A. G., & Bailey, J. S. (1990). Reducing disruptive behaviors of elementary physical education students with sit and watch. *Journal of Applied Behavior Analysis, 23,* 353–359.

White, O. R., & Haring, N. G. (1976). *Exceptional teaching.* Columbus, OH: Merrill/Macmillan.

Wicks-Nelson, R., & Israel, A. C. (1991). *Behavior disorders of childhood.* Englewood Cliffs, NJ: Prentice Hall.

Williams, C. D. (1959). The elimination of tantrum behavior by extinction procedures. *Journal of Abnormal and Social Psychology, 59,* 266–272.

Williams, L. (1988, January 15). Parents and doctors fear growing misuse of drug used to treat hyperactive kids. *Wall Street Journal,* 21.

Wolery, M., & Gast, D. (1990). Defining the role of social validity. In A. C. Repp & N. N. Singh (Eds.), *Perspectives on the use of nonaversive and aversive interventions for persons with developmental disabilities* (pp. 129–143). Sycamore, IL: Sycamore Publishing Company.

Zirpoli, T. J. (1986). Child abuse and children with handicaps. *Remedial and Special Education, 7,* 39–48.

CHAPTER 9
Specific Behavior Challenges

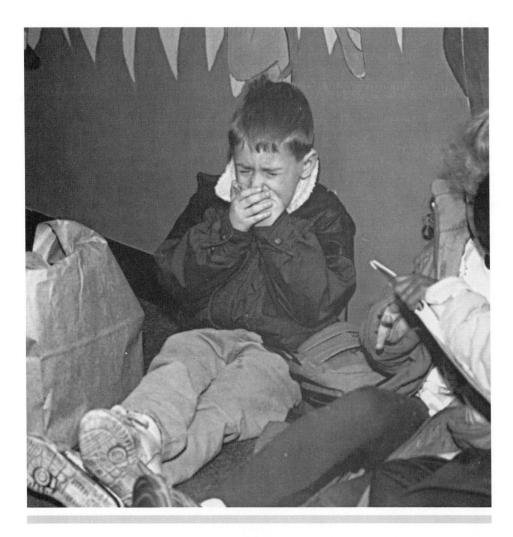

I like to fight. I'm not happy unless I'm fighting something or someone. Sometimes the issue is important, other times I just need the struggle. When I was a kid the fights were usually with other kids and most of the time it was a fist fight. I didn't have the verbal prowess I now possess. I did a lot of fist fighting until I was a sophomore in high school. Then I hurt someone. Not real bad. There'd been plenty of other times when it was worse. But I could see pain and resignation in the guy's eyes and I hit him again. It was the first time I'd ever really thought about what I was doing. That was the beginning of the end for me. Every fight after that I could see that guy's eyes waiting to get blasted again.

—Taylor, 1990, p. 20

This chapter focuses on behaviors that are problematic to children, parents, and teachers. These behaviors are termed "challenging behaviors" because, in general, when a child demonstrates a problem with behavior, adults are required to develop interventions that will both decrease inappropriate behaviors and increase appropriate behavior (see Part Two). Also, when a child engages in behavior that is deemed inappropriate, everyone involved (e.g., the child, adults, peers) is placed in circumstances that are highly stressful and usually unpleasant.

Specific challenging behaviors discussed in this chapter include *aggression, disruptiveness, noncompliance, temper tantrums, impulsivity, inattention, hyperactivity,* and *stereotypic behavior.* A majority of children will demonstrate more than one of these behavior problems at the same time. For example, a child who is considered disruptive in a classroom may also be described as someone who does not follow teacher directions (i.e., noncompliant behavior) and as a child who trips his classmates when they walk by his desk (i.e., aggressive behavior).

Each of the challenging behaviors will be discussed separately in terms of definition, etiology, and interventions. Chapters 5, 6, 7, and 8 of this text provide numerous ideas for increasing appropriate behaviors and decreasing inappropriate behavior based on behavioral and social learning theories.

AGGRESSIVE BEHAVIOR

Definition

Whenever the term "aggressive" is used to describe a child's behavior, images of physical injury to another automatically come to mind. In truth, there is no one globally accepted definition of aggressive behavior (e.g., Bandura, 1973; Kerr & Nelson, 1989; Lancelotta & Vaughn, 1989). Some consensus seems to exist, however, that aggressive behavior is either meant to injure another, gain something for the aggressor, or result in both injury and extraneous gains. Bandura distinguished instrumental and hostile aggression. He described instrumental aggression as those actions "aimed at securing extraneous rewards other than the victim's suffering" (1973, p. 8). Hostile aggression, on the other hand, was described as actions that are "used to produce injurious outcomes rather than to gain status, power, resources, or some other types of results" (Bandura, 1973, p. 8).

In a study conducted by Lancelotta and Vaughn, aggression was divided into five behavior categories. "Provoked physical aggression" was characterized as fighting, but only if attacked first by someone (1989, p. 87). An example of provoked physical aggression is a child who hits another individual when he is hit first. "Outburst aggression" was described as an uncontrolled verbal or physical outburst that had no apparent provocation (p. 87). A child who gets so angry that he or she does not seem to know what is happening provides an example of this category of aggression. "Unprovoked physical aggression" was described as aggressive acts directed at another person with no apparent provocation (p. 87). For example, a child may initiate a fight with another child for no apparent reason. Children who were verbally aggressive toward another person, in order to attack or intimidate, were described as demonstrating "verbal aggression" (p. 87). An example of verbal aggression is a child who says "You are dumb!" to a classmate during a classroom activity. Finally, "indirect aggression" was described as indirectly responding to attack or injury through another person (p. 87). A common example of indirect aggression is tattling on someone to the teacher.

Aggressive behavior was defined by Sasso, Melloy, and Kavale (1990) in a study conducted with children who had behavioral disorders. Physical aggression was described as hitting, kicking, striking another with an object, and striking objects or self behaviors. Verbal aggression was characterized as arguing using a loud and/or nasty tone of voice with a teacher, teacher aide, or peer for more than 30 seconds.

Kerr and Nelson (1989) described behaviors that are generally associated with aggressive behavior. Aggression was characterized by behaviors such as slapping, striking, kicking, and "karate" move behaviors. Property abuse was described by behaviors such as taking something that belonged to someone else. Nonverbal aggression was characterized by behaviors such as destruction of objects and hurtful teasing.

In this chapter, aggressive behaviors refer to those behaviors–verbal, nonverbal, or physical—that injure another indirectly or directly and/or result in extraneous gains for the aggressor. These behaviors are typically described in terms such as those used by Kerr and Nelson (1989), Lancelotta and Vaughn (1989), and Sasso, Melloy, and Kavale (1990). The child's body language for all of these aggressive behaviors is a stance that clearly communicates anger, rage, frustration, humiliation, and/or other feelings that motivate aggressive behavior. For example, the children's faces may become red, they may be crying, their breathing may become faster and harder, their muscles tensed. In instances where verbal aggression is manifested, children will not always demonstrate the body language described (e.g., tattling) but the intent of the behavior is still clearly to hurt another person. It is also important to keep in mind that even playful hits, kicks, punches, and sarcastic statements are forms of aggressive behavior. Parents and educators should encourage children and reinforce them for using alternative behaviors to express affection and liking for others. The following is a list of common physical aggressions and the observable characteristics of the behaviors:

- *Kicking:* A child uses his or her foot/feet to make contact with another's body in a manner that inflicts discomfort, pain, and/or injury.

- *Hitting:* A child uses his or her hand(s) (i.e., open or in a fist) to strike another person's body with the intention of inflicting discomfort, pain, and/or injury.

- *Spitting:* A child projects saliva onto another person, which causes the other person's body parts or clothing to become wet. (Note that sometimes children may pretend to spit on another and even though no saliva is actually projected, the behavior is considered aggressive because it may result in the same effect—degradation and discomfort on the part of the other person.)

- *Biting:* The child's teeth make contact with another's skin and causes discomfort, pain, and/or injury.

- *Grabbing/holding:* A child forcibly takes another person with his or her hand(s) and then inhibits the movement of the other in a manner that results in discomfort, pain, and/or injury.

- *Fighting:* Two or more children are engaged in hitting, kicking, grabbing, and/or holding behavior, which may result in one or more children falling to the ground or being shoved against a structure (e.g., wall, door, ledge, cupboard). This behavior results in discomfort, pain, and/or injury to the aggressor and aggressee. (Note that wrestling behavior in which one or more children are engaged in grabbing and holding each other while they roll on the ground is not considered physical aggression unless the prerequisite body language is present and/or physical injury or pain results.)

- *Throwing:* A child directs materials (e.g., book, pencil, objects, furniture, papers) toward a person by sending the object through the air with a motion of the hand or arm. This is considered aggressive behavior (1) if the prerequisite body language is present and (2) whether or not the object actually strikes the targeted person causing pain or injury—the intention is enough to consider the behavior to be aggressive.

Some examples of verbal aggression and their observable behavior characteristics are as follows:

- *"Bossy" verbal behavior:* The child commands others in a demanding voice tone.

- *Teasing others:* The child makes fun of another person(s) by verbally expressing words that result in emotional discomfort, pain, and/or injury of the other person. The other person demonstrates his or her feelings of hurt by crying, running away, verbal aggression, and/or pretending to ignore the aggressor.
- *Tattling:* The child repeatedly reports on trivial behaviors of others that are not endangering others to an adult who is in authority (e.g., teacher, parent). An example would be a child who reports to the teacher that "Billy is pulling Susan's hair" in an exaggerated tone of voice.
- *Criticizing the work of others:* The child puts down the work of others using condescending terms (e.g., "That's a stupid idea"), which results in the other person expressing hurt feelings or anger.
- *Picking on others:* The child says things to another person that emphasizes a perceived fault of the other (e.g., "Boy, where did you get those UGLY shoes? They aren't even worn on this planet by anyone who's awesome!"), which results in the person feeling humiliation, hurt feelings, and/or anger. Behaviors of the person being picked on that demonstrate these feelings include a dejected look, verbal retorts, and/or anger outbursts.
- *Making sarcastic remarks:* The child uses phrases to comment on another's appearance, performance, etc., that are derogatory in nature and result in emotional discomfort and/or pain in the person to whom the remarks were directed. The remarks are generally made in a "sarcastic tone of voice" (e.g., words exaggerated, nasty tone). An example of a sarcastic remark is "Look at Colleen, don't you just LOVE her pretty, pink dress?"), which is voiced in a nasty tone of voice. Sarcastic remarks can also be made in a pleasant tone of voice but the result is that the other person is hurt or humiliated by the remark (e.g., a teacher remarks, "Wow, isn't it nice that Lori could join us again?" after a child returns from time-out for behaving aggressively). Hurt and humiliation are demonstrated by behaviors such as putting one's head down, getting a red face, or crying.

Etiology

Modeled Aggressive Behavior

On any given day, children are faced with many instances that result in feelings of anger, frustration, and/or humiliation. These feelings often result in children reacting aggressively. The most commonly accepted cause for aggressive behavior is that these behaviors are learned through modeling (e.g., Bandura, 1973; Wicks-Nelson & Israel, 1991; Widom, 1989). For example, children observe aggressive behavior models when caregivers engage in verbally abusive or physical punishment of children. Vignette 9.1 provides a common example in which a child models verbal aggression.

Vignette 9.1.   Example of Child Modeling Verbally Aggressive Behavior.

Mr. Ryan, a teacher, yells at Charlene when she makes an error during reading class. After reading class, Charlene yells at a peer when the peer makes a mistake during a game the two children are playing. To prevent future verbal aggression, Mr. Ryan could model a more acceptable way to solve problems. He could quietly tell the child she made an error and help her find the correct answer. Using this approach, the teacher provides all the children in the class with an alternative behavior model. Also, children should be taught social skills that offer alternatives to verbal aggression. Children may then practice these social skills when they feel frustrated or angry. When these skills are modeled and reinforced by teachers, children are more likely to resolve their own feelings of frustration and anger in an acceptable manner.

Another common example of adult-modeled aggressive behavior is when a child is slapped or spanked as a consequence of hitting another person. When a child is hit in response to his own hitting behavior, the child receives a mixed message that it is acceptable for adults to hit but the child must not hit. Children cannot be expected to expand their repertoire of responses to anger if they only see a limited number of inappropriate responses modeled. Teachers and parents can model appropriate alternatives to aggressive behavior by remaining calm in anger-inducing situations, talking out the problem, or walking away from the problem until they feel calm enough to discuss the situation. This alternative to aggression can be modeled and practiced in a formal social skills training (see Chapter 7) program.

Widom (1989) cautioned that many of the studies that have been conducted to determine if aggressive behavior is modeled were methodologically flawed. However, she suggested that even though most of the studies relied heavily on self-reports for retrospective accounts of such things as family violence, the results indicated that in many cases children who had experienced or been exposed to aggressive acts were at risk for becoming aggressive themselves. According to Widom (1989) children who observed marital aggression were rated higher on measures of behavior problems than children who did not experience this exposure. Children of battered women were also rated higher on these measures and were rated lower on measures of social competence than children who did not witness this type of abuse (Widom, 1989). Finally, children who experienced physical abuse in addition to battering of their mothers and/or extreme marital discord were more likely to report marital aggression as adults (Widom, 1989).

Developmental Perspective on Aggressive Behavior

Other research findings indicated that antisocial behavior, including aggression, "appears to be a developmental trait that begins early in life and often continues into adolescence and adulthood" (Patterson, DeBaryshe, & Ramsey, 1989, p. 329). According to Patterson et al. (1989) and Wahler and Dumas (1986), antisocial behavior develops as a result of the child's behavior and interaction with the social environment. Patterson and colleagues maintained that these behaviors occur in stages and that behaviors of one stage will result in certain predictable reactions from the child's social environment, leading to further actions from the child.

During the first stage of aggressive behavior development, family variables, such as harsh parental discipline and poor adult supervision, result in the child being "trained" to engage in aggressive behavior such as hitting. These behaviors become functional in the sense that the child may be allowed to escape from tasks when he or she acts aggressively. For example, a child may be sent to her room after hitting her brother while they do dishes. Also, aggressive behaviors may be positively reinforced through laughter, attention, and approval, which results in maintenance of the behaviors. Children in these situations do not learn socially skillful responses to others, but they learn aggressive behavior that results in meeting their needs.

Following this stage, children who are aggressive often find themselves rejected by their peer group and experiencing academic failure (Patterson et al., 1989). Having learned aggressive behaviors in early childhood, these children become rejected because they do not demonstrate the social skills that allow them to be socially competent with peers. This idea is in contrast to that of others who believe that children become aggressive after they are rejected by their peers and/or fail academically. Patterson et al. (1989) reported that children who engaged in aggressive behaviors spent less time on academic tasks and had more difficulty with classroom survival skills (e.g., staying in seat, answering questions). These behaviors resulted in a higher incidence of academic failure. Once children have learned aggressive behavior and experienced peer rejection and academic failure, they are at a higher risk for developing delinquent behavior (Lancelotta & Vaughn, 1989; Patterson et al., 1989; Wahler & Dumas, 1986). These children have a tendency to become involved with deviant peer groups who also engage in aggressive behaviors (e.g., fighting, property damage). The members of the groups positively reinforce these actions, thus increasing the probability of their repeated occurrence. Unfortunately, long-term outcomes for children who seemingly follow this developmental sequence of aggressive behavior are not generally desirable.

These findings have important implications for children and their parents and teachers. Reports have found that children who engage in antisocial behavior throughout childhood and adolescence are at an extremely high risk for becoming school dropouts, having difficulty maintaining employment, committing crimes, and having marital difficulties. Figure 9.1 provides a model for the development of aggressive behavior based on the developmental perspective.

Media Influence on Aggressive Behavior

The media also offer plenty of aggressive models for children through TV programs geared to the interest of young persons. Widom (1989) reviewed the literature on the relationship of TV violence to aggressive behavior in children. Her conclusions were that television violence was clearly related to aggressive behavior:

> Exposure to television violence has been found to increase levels of aggression in the viewer, to have long-term effects as well as effects immediately after exposure, and to lead to emotional desensitization, making the viewer less likely to respond both physiologically and behaviorally to aggression in others. (Widom, 1989, p. 23)

Friedrich-Cofer and Huston (1986) reviewed studies that focused on the relationship of viewing TV violence and subsequent manifestation of aggressive behavior in children. Their review included laboratory studies that generally demonstrated a causal link between TV violence and aggressive behavior. These studies have been criticized, however, for a number of factors including experimenters not using real-world television stories as stimuli in their experiments. A review of the literature revealed that laboratory studies do in fact have high internal validity and therefore offer an important contribution to the information on the cause of aggression. Friedrich-Cofer and Huston also reviewed field experiments and found a correlation between children's viewing of TV violence and the demonstration of aggressive behavior. They reported that this was more often the case with children who demonstrated a high rate of aggression before viewing the TV show. In these children, the rate of aggressive behavior increased after viewing the shows. A review of longitudinal stud-

Early Childhood		Middle Childhood	Late Childhood and Early Adolescence	
⇩	⇩	⇩	⇩	⇩
Poor parental discipline and ⇒ monitoring	Child conduct ⇒ problems	Rejection by normal peers ⇒	Commitment to deviant ⇒ peer group	Delinquency
		⇩		
		Academic failure		

Figure 9.1. *A developmental progression for antisocial behavior.*

Source: From Patterson, G. R., DeBaryshe, B. D., & Ramsey, E. (1989). A developmental perspective on antisocial behavior. *American Psychologist, 44*(2), 329–335. Copyright 1989 American Psychological Association. Adapted with permission.

ies revealed that viewing TV violence at one age correlated with aggressive behaviors demonstrated at a later age. "Of a large number of parent, family, and socioeconomic variables measured at age 8, television was the single best predictor of aggression in 18-year-olds" (Friedrich-Cofer & Huston, 1986, p. 367).

Findings also indicated that children who demonstrated a predisposition for aggressive behavior were likely to choose a diet of violent television programs. Friedrich-Cofer and Huston noted that viewing of television violence generalized to serious forms of aggression including "firing a revolver at someone, attacks with a knife, setting fire to a building, hitting someone in the face with a broken bottle, and knocking someone off a bike" (1986, p. 369). These findings present serious implications to our society in the face of more and more violent television being made available to children and adolescents through cable television and videotape rentals. Even the television shows that are available to children on broadcast television are filled with violent acts against persons, property, and animals.

Peer Reinforcement

The literature offered other explanations for the cause of aggressive behavior. Several authors proposed that the likelihood that aggressive behavior will be repeated is strengthened through peer reinforcement of the behavior (Fremont, Tedesco, & Trusty, 1988; Quay, 1986). This is seen in situations where the probability of engaging in aggressive behaviors is increased when children are given attention for their behavior. The example in Vignette 9.2 illustrates the effects of positive reinforcement on aggressive behavior.

Vignette 9.2.   Example of Peer Reinforcement of Aggressive Behavior.

Joe begins a fight with a peer, named Peter, in the school parking lot during the lunch break. Peter was seen talking to Joe's girlfriend during Spanish class earlier that morning. When this was reported to Joe, he became angry and sought Peter out to "take care of that jerk." As Joe and Peter took off for the parking lot, a large gathering of peers assembled to witness the fight. Afterward, Joe relished in the limelight when he clearly was declared the winner by his peers and was encouraged for fighting with Peter. Joe was positively reinforced for his aggressive behavior.

Social Skills Deficits

Others have proposed that children act aggressively because they lack alternative skills that would allow them to choose a socially acceptable behavior to deal with a provocative situation in an assertive rather than aggressive manner (Dubow, Huesmann, & Eron, 1987; Hollinger, 1987; Strain, Guralnick, & Walker, 1986). Dubow, Huesmann, and Eron (1987) reported the need for children to develop social competence before they experience a history of reinforcement for solving problems with aggressive behavior. Strain, Guralnick, and Walker (1986) outlined a number of reasons for aggressive behavior in children that focused on development of social behavior. They maintained that children often have a limited repertoire of social problem-solving behaviors. Often, due to environmental interactions and opportunities for modeling, aggressive behaviors are manifested as the only behavioral choice for situations that require problem-solving for frustration, anger, and humiliation.

Neel, Jenkins, and Meadows (1990) found results that conflicted with those of researchers who reported that aggressive behavior was caused by deficits in social skills. In their study of 19 preschoolers, aged 3-1/2 to 4-1/2, Neel and his colleagues found that children who were aggressive demonstrated similar usage of social skills compared to their nonaggressive peers. Neel, Jenkins, and Meadows concluded that children who were aggressive used a number of social problem-solving strategies just as their nonaggressive counterparts did. The difference was that children who were aggressive used more intrusive types of strategies (e.g., barging into a game) compared to the more socially acceptable strategies used by their nonaggressive peers (e.g., asking for information and questioning before joining the group). A number of authors have suggested this in previous research (e.g., Melloy, 1990; Strain, Guralnick, & Walker, 1986). The findings of Neel, Jenkins, and Meadows suggest that the development of social competence in children who are aggressive should concentrate on strategy content rather than on the number of strategies within the child's repertoire. For example, a child who demonstrates intrusive group joining-in skills will need to learn social skills that are more acceptable. Children who manifest aggressive behaviors with their peers do not always fail in their social goals—the child may be allowed to join the group even if he or she uses intrusive means. However, these children more often earn a reputation that results in deviant peer acceptance.

Melloy (1990) described several types of peer acceptance of children who demonstrated aggressive behavior. Some children who are aggressive are accepted as leaders by their peers because their peers are afraid to reject them. In other words, a child who is aggressive may threaten his peers with taunts such as "If you don't let me play, I'll beat you up." On the other hand, children who are aggressive are often rejected by their peers. A common scene on a playground is for a group of children to terminate their play and move to another area when they see a peer who is aggressive approaching the group.

In the long run, a history of rejection by one's peers can lead to a dependence on less desirable peers and membership in deviant subcultures, which often leads to social maladjustment (Center, 1990; Weinberg & Weinberg, 1990). Children in these subcultures are frequently reinforced for engaging in aggressive behaviors.

Examples of Interventions for Aggression

Social Skills Training

Landy and Peters (1990) outlined a number of interventions that have been effective in treating preschoolers who manifested aggressive behavior. They suggested that, depending on the individual needs of children, these interventions could be applied one-on-one, in group settings, and with a component of parent training. Landy and Peters recommended that children who engage in aggressive play themes be taught, through play therapy and social skills training (e.g., modeling, role playing), how to incorporate nonaggressive themes into their play. They also suggested that some children, who demonstrated extremely aggressive behavior, be assigned a "special person" (1990, p. 34) to provide one-to-one assistance. The special person could teach the child alternative behaviors to aggression and reinforce the child for appropriate behavior.

According to Landy and Peters (1990) physical exercise and movement may provide children with acceptable ways to express frustration and other feelings. Social games and action songs assist children in learning language so that they can verbalize their feelings, thoughts, and anxieties. Also, breaking activities into small units enhances children's learning with lots of opportunities for reinforcement of achievements.

Sasso and his colleagues (1990) demonstrated that social skills training could assist elementary and junior high students in acquiring, maintaining, and generalizing social skills that were alternatives to aggression. The authors reported a study that took place over an entire school year with three children, ages 8, 10, and 13, who were behaviorally disordered. The subjects were part of a larger class of eight students that was housed in a large, midwestern elementary and junior high. The children were all integrated into regular classes for at least one class period per day. Students were taught social skills using the structured learning approach and the curriculum from *Skillstreaming the Elementary School Child* (McGinnis & Goldstein, 1984). Pertinent to the Sasso, Melloy, and Kavale study was the training of social skills, which included accepting consequences, dealing with accusations, negotiating, responding to teasing, asking permission, and staying out of fights. These skills were determined to be alternatives to aggressive behaviors.

Following treatment, all of the children in the study reduced levels of aggressive behavior in comparison to baseline levels. During the maintenance phase of the study, the children maintained treatment levels of appropriate behaviors and generalized these behaviors to their regular classroom settings and other school settings. Use of social skills training along with positive reinforcement for appropriate behaviors are among the current best practices in teaching children alternative behaviors to aggression.

Cognitive Behavior Management

Using this intervention, children are taught to use techniques such as self-talk and self-instruction to deal with stressful situations. Dubow and his colleagues

(1987) conducted a study with 104 boys, ages 8 through 13, who were aggressive. Each of the children was assigned to one of four training groups: (1) cognitive training, (2) social skills training, (3) combined cognitive and social skills training, and (4) attention/play condition.

In the cognitive training condition, children were shown cue cards that detailed problem-solving steps. Included on the cards were procedures for defining the problem, generating possible solutions to the problem, thinking about the alternative solutions, choosing a solution, and reinforcing self for use of an effective solution or correcting a mistake. Following this phase of training, children were given an opportunity to role play problem situations (e.g., you argue with your brother; you lose a game). Children in the social skills training intervention had opportunities to model and role play situations of sharing, helping, and providing positive verbal support. The cognitive and social skills training condition used a combination of the procedures described above. In the attention/play intervention, children received modeling, role playing, coaching, feedback, and discussion about improving game strategies. Children in this group played card and board games together.

The results of this study indicated that aggressive behaviors were reduced and prosocial behaviors increased in the cognitive-social skills training and attention/play conditions. However, after six months, only the children in the attention/play group were observed to maintain improvement. The authors suggested that the reason for the short-lived effect of the cognitive-social skills treatment was the time period in which training took place—only 10 sessions. They suggested that the unexpected carryover effects of the attention/play group was that these children were taught cognitive and social skills strategies in natural conditions and realized natural consequences (i.e., real-life, immediate payoff). This study has important implications for generalization of effects of treatment using social skills training and cognitive behavior management.

Etscheidt (1991) used cognitive behavior management with 30 adolescents, ages 13 to 18, who demonstrated aggressive behavior. The purpose of the study was (1) to determine the effectiveness of cognitive behavior management on the reduction of aggressive behavior and increases in prosocial behavior and (2) to determine if the addition of positive consequences would increase the effectiveness of cognitive training.

One group of students was exposed to cognitive training from the *Anger Control Program Model* (Lochman, Nelson, & Sims, cited in Etscheidt, 1991). The intent of the program was to assist students "in modifying their aggressive behaviors by altering their cognitive processing of events and response alternatives" (Etscheidt, 1991, p. 110). During training, children in Group I participated in 12 lessons with goals of:

- self awareness
- exploration of reactions to peer influences
- identification of problem situations
- generation of alternative solutions to problems
- evaluation of solutions

- ◆ recognition of physiological awareness of anger arousal
- ◆ integration of physiological awareness
- ◆ self-talk and social problem-solving techniques to reduce aggressive behavior

The students were taught to use the following strategy in problem situations:

Step 1.   *Motor Cue/Impulse Delay:* Stop and think before you act, cue yourself.

Step 2.   *Problem Definition:* Say how you feel and exactly what the problem is.

Step 3.   *Generation of Alternatives:* Think of as many solutions as you can.

Step 4.   *Consideration of Consequences:* Think ahead to what might happen next.

Step 5.   *Implementation:* When you have a really good solution, try it! (Etscheidt, 1991, p. 111)

The students in Group II received cognitive training and were positively reinforced for use of the skills taught. A control group received no cognitive training or positive consequences for use of the training strategy. The results of the study indicated a significant decrease in aggressive behavior and a significant increase in self-control behavior in Group I and Group II students compared to the control group. No significant differences between Group I and II were noted. The author attributed this to the fact that, prior to cognitive training, a behavior management program existed in the students' classroom. Adding additional positive consequences may not have been as effective due to this factor.

Use of cognitive behavior management intervention strategies is highly recommended for treatment of aggressive behavior in children. Descriptions of cognitive behavior management curricula that are available for use in school settings are outlined in Chapter 6.

Behavior Reduction Strategies

Frankel and Simmons (1985) reported on a number of behavior modification procedures that have been used to decrease aggressive behavior in young children. They reviewed research articles on aggression that had been published between 1965 and 1985. The interventions reported to be effective in reducing aggressive behavior in children included extinction, time-out, and environmental manipulations. These behavior reduction strategies are discussed in Chapter 8.

Frankel and Simmons reported that extinction (i.e., removal of reinforcement previously associated with the aggressive behavior) had been used in a number of studies designed to evaluate the effectiveness of removing reinforcing events from aggressive responses. Although this intervention was effective in reducing aggressive behavior, the authors suggested that part of this effectiveness could have been attributed to the fact that peers seemed to avoid contact with the child who was aggressive. Since there were no victims at which to direct aggressive behavior, a concomitant reduction in aggressive behavior resulted in the child who was aggressive. Also, this intervention was found to be more effective when the victim was comforted and separated from the child who was aggressive. Frankel and Simmons reported that extinction was effective when appropriate interaction behaviors were positively reinforced and aggressive behavior ignored.

Frankel and Simmons (1985) reported that time-out (removal from a reinforcing environment) was much more effective than extinction in reducing aggressive behavior. They reported that use of contingent observation time-out and isolation time-out periods ranging from 1 to 30 minutes were effective in the reduction of aggression.

Sherburne, Utley, McConnell, and Gannon (1988) conducted a study with 11 preschoolers to determine the effects of two different treatments on aggressive theme play—use of time-out and verbal prompts. The study was prompted by a growing concern among teachers and parents "regarding the effect of aggressive stimuli on young children's lives" (Sherburne et al., 1988, p. 166). These concerns were "based on mounting evidence that rates of verbal and physical aggression by children may be increased by viewing aggressive or violent acts (either live or enacted) or by having access to toys or games that represent violent or aggressive themes" (Sherburne et al., 1988, p. 166). The purpose of Sherburne's and her colleagues' research was to assess the effects of two different treatments—verbal prompts and contingency statements—on the violent and aggressive theme play of young children. Their work was conducted at a daycare center for children. Data were collected daily for 1-1/2 months during two free-play sessions. During the contingency statements treatment phase, children were instructed to play on a specific rug in the play area if they were observed to be engaging in aggressive theme play. (If children were observed to demonstrate physical aggression against a peer, such as hitting and/or biting, they were sent to time-out, which was a chair in the corner of the room.) These statements were made in a pleasant manner and no time limits were put on how long the child could play aggressively on the rug. During the verbal prompts treatment phase, children did not have a rug where aggressive behavior was allowed. When a child or children engaged in aggressive theme play they were redirected through verbal prompts to play something else. Both treatments were effective in decreasing aggressive theme play compared to baseline rates. However, the intervention involving the use of contingency statements (e.g., "If you want to play guns, go play on the rug," p. 169) was more effective in decreasing rates of aggressive theme play than the use of verbal prompts. The authors pointed out that the effects of contingency statements could be enhanced by a teacher's social praise for more acceptable behavior.

Environmental manipulations combined with positive reinforcement for appropriate behavior were effective in reducing aggressive behavior. For example, Frankel and Simmons (1985) reported that increasing space to play and the number of toys to play with was effective in increasing appropriate behavior and decreasing inappropriate behavior in young children. They concluded, however, that the results of the studies they researched were equivocal. Vignettes 9.3 and 9.4 offer examples of behavior reduction strategies for aggression.

Vignette 9.3.   Example of Contingent Observation Time-Out Used as an Intervention to Reduce Aggression.

A two-year-old child manifested aggressive behavior toward her infant sister on the arrival of her aunt for a visit. The child's mother reported that the child had never done this prior to this incident. Within the first two hours of the visit, however, the toddler attempted to act aggressively toward her sister at least five times. Telling her "No, you can't do that to your sister, it will hurt her" was not effective in reducing the aggressive behavior. However, a combination of increased attention for appropriate behavior and time-out for aggressive behavior resulted in the immediate and lasting decrease of aggressive behavior by the toddler. In this example, contingent observation time-out was employed. When the child attempted to hit her sister, she was told to sit in a small chair placed against the wall in the room. Her mother set a kitchen timer for two minutes to signal when the child could leave the time-out chair and return to the family activity.

Time-out can also be used effectively even when the child is out of the classroom or home setting. Teachers and teacher assistants responsible for children on a playground may tell a child that "Because you hit your friend, you need to stand next to the building for ___ minutes." This type of intervention, paired with positive social praise and natural attention for appropriate behavior, has been effective in reducing aggressive behavior in school age children.

Vignette 9.4.   Example of an Environmental Manipulation as an Intervention to Reduce Aggression.

Five children receiving English tutoring met with their teacher in a very small resource room. The teacher reported that it was so cramped in the room, there was hardly room for a table and chairs for each student. Each time she met with more than two or three students at one time, the children became verbally and physically aggressive. The behaviors they exhibited included pushing and shoving, and yelling at each other to "move over." In an attempt to improve the children's behavior, the teacher changed her schedule so that no more than two children came to the room at one time. This was effective in reducing most of the aggressive behaviors. The teacher also requested a larger room for the following school year so that she could meet with larger groups of children.

DISRUPTIVE BEHAVIOR

Definition

Disruptive behavior has been defined as any behavior that "serves to disrupt the ongoing learning process in a classroom" (Kerr & Nelson, 1989). We often think of children manifesting disruptive behaviors in educational settings, but these behaviors can occur in varied settings. A number of authors described disruptive behaviors (e.g., Friman, 1990; Kerr & Nelson, 1989; Sasso, Melloy, & Kavale, 1990; White & Bailey, 1990). Note that some of the behaviors described in the following list are identified by the same behavioral terms used in the lists of physical and verbal aggressions already discussed. In order for this behavior to be defined as disruptive versus aggressive, however, no intent to harm or injure another person is associated with disruptive behavior.

- *Off-task talking:* The child speaks out without permission or interrupts others who are talking.
- *Getting out-of-seat behavior:* The child lifts his buttocks off the chair and walks around the classroom without permission. He or she may stop to chat with peers or may just continue to walk around with no purpose related to an academic task.
- *Making noises:* The child elicits sounds, either verbally or physically, that are clearly not related to the task (e.g., tapping a pencil repeatedly, tipping chair back until it falls over).
- *Playing with objects:* The child engages in play with things such as pens, pencils, or small cars, that may be related or unrelated to the task. To constitute an inappropriate behavior, the play must not be part of the task and clearly not appropriate for the time.
- *Throwing objects:* The child projects things, such as pencils, paper airplanes, or furniture, into the air or across the floor when this behavior is not related to an educational task.
- *Climbing:* The child ascends to the top of furniture or other objects/persons in the room for no reason related to a classroom task.

Etiology

Inconsistent Reinforcement of Disruptive Behavior

Behaviors considered to be disruptive often occur in school settings. The cause of this behavior appears to stem from inconsistent behavior management—most often, positive reinforcement for inappropriate behavior (McMahon & Wells, 1989; White & Bailey, 1990). Children who demonstrate disruptive behaviors (e.g., talking out, being noisy, playing with things) are often reinforced for this behavior by peers (Smith & Fowler, 1984). Often a child will receive attention in the form of laughter from his or her peers or teachers. This serves to reinforce positively the disruptive behavior and increases the possibility that the behavior will be repeated. Unfortunately, children who are described as "class clowns" often say and do funny things, but usually at an inappropriate time. When the child is laughed at, this serves to reinforce the behavior. Rather than develop interventions that squelch the child's sense of humor, it would be better to teach him to manifest his behavior at appropriate times (e.g., when the class is waiting in line to go to the lunchroom), in an appropriate manner (e.g., not meant to hurt others feelings), and in appropriate places (e.g., on the playground). The example in Vignette 9.5 is one that teachers have often witnessed in their classrooms.

Vignette 9.5.   Example of Disruptive Behavior Reinforced by Peers.

Kevin frequently mimics the teacher whenever she turns her back to the students. His peers are entertained and laugh when Kevin puts on his show. The teacher, unaware of what caused her students to respond in this manner, turns to the class and demands to know what is so funny. Of course, no one confesses and the teacher is left to draw her own conclusions, which probably leaves her somewhat frustrated. She notices that this behavior occurs whenever she turns her back to write on the board or to answer the door. Kevin's behavior has been reinforced by his peers. He will probably continue to engage in this behavior until the teacher catches him and intervenes, or until the behavior is no longer reinforced by his peers.

Frequently, teachers and others recognize children only when they exhibit disruptive behavior. Even though the teacher may view a reprimand as a behavior reduction strategy, the child often views this attention as reinforcing. When teachers attend to children's appropriate behavior and ignore disruptive behavior, there is generally an increase in appropriate behavior and a decrease in the disruptive behavior (McMahon & Wells, 1989).

Social Skills Deficits

Children who lack competence in classroom social skills often demonstrate disruptive behavior (McGinnis & Goldstein, 1984). Children who were deficit in skills such as raising their hand, asking permission, and listening to others were noted to engage in frequent disruptive behavior. However, when these children were taught social skills and became competent in them, their disruptive behavior decreased significantly (Melloy, 1990).

Examples of Interventions for Disruptive Behavior

Behavioral Strategies to Increase Nondisruptive Behavior

A number of authors reported on the effectiveness of behavior management techniques in reducing disruptive behavior in children. Friman (1990) described the use of differential reinforcement of incompatible behaviors (DRI) (see Chapter 5) with a four-year-old boy with severe disabilities who was very disruptive in his preschool classroom. Using DRI, the child was able to remain seated for up to 20 minutes compared to baseline rates of less than 1 minute. This allowed him to participate in activities with his peers. Although toy play was not targeted for intervention, the results indicated that the child's appropriate toy play increased when his disruptive behavior decreased.

White and Bailey developed an intervention called "sit and watch" (1990, p. 353) that they used in an elementary physical education class to reduce disruptive behavior. The intervention consisted of removing the child from the activity as a consequence for disruptive behavior. The teacher told the child why he or she was being removed. The child then picked up a timer, walked to an area away from the other students, sat down, and watched the activity. When the sand had flowed through the timer, the child was allowed to rejoin the class. The authors reported that this intervention was effective in reducing disruptive behavior by 95%. Another example of a behavioral intervention designed to reduce disruptive behavior is provided in Vignette 9.6.

Vignette 9.6.   Example of Behavioral Intervention to Reduce Disruptive Behavior.

Zachary is a preschooler who poured paint on a peer during art time. To eliminate further opportunities for Zachary to engage in this behavior, his teacher moved Zachary's easel and materials just out of the area where his peers were painting. This allowed Zachary to be part of the group, but made it more difficult to access the other children in his class—therefore he wouldn't be able to pour paint on them. His teacher then positively reinforced Zachary's appropriate behavior (i.e., painting on the paper rather than his peers) with qualitative social praise ("Zachary, you painted a nice flower on your art paper. Your friends like it when you paint on the paper.") Eventually, his teacher was able to move Zachary's easel closer to the other children, continuing to reinforce him positively for his appropriate behavior, until Zachary was able to work next to his peers during painting activities.

Social Skills Training

Fowler, Dougherty, Kirby, and Kohler (1986) reported that assigning children as peer monitors was effective in reducing the disruptive behavior of three seven-year-old boys. The boys were taught social skills for interacting with their peers and then taught to monitor their peers' behavior. The boys were able to award points to their peers for appropriate behavior. Concomitantly, the boys' disruptive behavior decreased. Two of the boys also increased their rates of positive interactions. Although, initially, this behavior failed to generalize, adjustments to the intervention resulted in generalization of appropriate behavior to other school settings. Social skills training was effective in reducing disruptive behavior in the example provided in Vignette 9.7

Vignette 9.7.   Example of Reduction of Disruptive Behavior Through Social Skills Training.

The children in Mr. O'Neill's class became very disruptive during transitions between class periods (e.g., when they changed from math to reading class). The noise that ensued while children slammed desktops, talked loudly to classmates, and ran up to the teacher for directions became unacceptable. Mr. O'Neill decided to teach his students some social skills for making smooth transitions (e.g., following directions, making conversation in an appropriate voice volume, listening). Following the suggested format for teaching social skills (see Chapter 6), Mr. O'Neill modeled the skills for his class, allowed them to role play these skills, provided feedback for their performance, and assigned homework that allowed children to report on their progress in using their new skills during transition periods. As each skill was learned and practiced, the children became much more competent in making smooth transitions and were amazed at how pleasant the classroom environment became.

Cognitive Behavior Management

Brigham, Hopper, Hill, de Armas, and Newsom (1985) reported on a three-year study that involved 79 adolescents in grades six, seven, and eight. The students were all characterized as disruptive in the classroom setting. Cognitive behavior management strategies were taught in a self-management class to students who received 12 detentions in one quarter. Students who attended this class met after school with the instructor for one-hour classes, three days a week. During the classes, students chose a self-management project aimed at increasing an appropriate behavior or decreasing inappropriate behavior. The projects consisted of behavior analysis of the problem, a written set of intervention procedures, and a behavioral contract between the student and the instructor. Role playing, modeling, study guides, and quizzes were used to teach the students alternative behaviors. If, on completing the unit, they passed a quiz with 80% or better, they went on to the next unit. The results of the study suggested that the self-management training program was effective in reducing the number of detentions earned for disruptive behavior.

NONCOMPLIANCE

Definition

Teachers and parents often report that children will not do what they have been told or asked to do. According to Forehand (1977), children comply with only about 60 to 80% of parental requests and commands. Kuczynski, Kochanska, Radke-Yarrow, and Girnius-Brown reported that "serious noncompliant behavior is the most frequent reason for psychiatric referral of young children" (1987, p. 799).

Compliance is generally defined as obedience to adult directives and prohibitions, cooperation with requests and suggestions, and/or the willingness to accept suggestions in a teaching situation (Rocissano, Slade, & Lynch, 1987). Noncompliance then is comprised of behaviors that are opposite—disobedience to directives, uncooperativeness with requests and suggestions, and unwillingness to accept suggestions. One facet of compliance/noncompliance is the issue of teaching children how to become independent and make appropriate choices regarding their own behavior. These characteristics are admired in our society. Regardless, noncompliant behavior becomes challenging when a child is frequently defiant and this behavior is expressed in an unpleasant, negative manner.

Kuczynski et al. (1987) described four categories of noncompliance in a study with young children and their mothers. A child was described as engaging in *passive noncompliance* when she did not overtly refuse or defy the request, but rather went on about her business as if she had not been addressed. A child who overtly refused requests with angry, defiant, or negative facial, body, and/or verbal expressions was described as behaving with

Teacher praise for on-task student behavior often results in increased on-task behavior.

direct defiance. Children who replied "no" or "I don't want to" with no apparent negative verbal or body language were described as engaging in *simple refusal* behavior. Finally, *negotiation* behavior was defined as attempts by the child to convince the parent to issue a new directive through bargaining. A case example, in which Beth's teacher asks her to put her science project away and get ready for math, shows each of these types of noncompliance.

♦ *Passive noncompliance:* Beth continues working on her science project.

♦ *Direct defiance:* Beth throws her pencil to the floor, yells at her teacher that she isn't finished with her project, and looks away from her teacher.

♦ *Simple refusal:* Beth tells her teacher that she is not going to stop work on her science project. Beth is smiling and doesn't raise her voice.

♦ *Negotiation:* Beth asks her teacher if she can work on her science project for 10 more minutes before doing math. When her teacher says "no," Beth asks for 5 minutes, then 3 minutes, etc.

Etiology

Developmental Perspective

Kuczynski and others (1987) found a link between developmental factors and noncompliance. In a study conducted of 70 mothers and their toddler-aged children, the authors found that passive noncompliance and direct defiance decreased with age. Negotiation, a more sophisticated level of resistance, however, increased as the child got older.

Interactional Patterns

The interactional patterns of adults and children are often associated with the causal factors attributed to noncompliance. Holden and West (1989) observed the interactional styles of mothers and their children and the consequences of those styles within a play setting. The mothers were given directions to be either "directors" or "forbidders" in separate trials in which the mother and child were placed in a setting with toys that were either out of bounds or in bounds. In the proactive trial, mothers were instructed to direct their child's attention to objects, suggest activities, or play games. In the reactive trial, mothers were not allowed to direct their child in play and were instructed to interact with their child only when the child needed to be prohibited from playing with a toy that was out of bounds.

The authors reported that children were more likely to comply with requests and suggestions for play in the proactive trial than in the reactive trial. This research has important implications related to the causes of noncompliance in children. It provides confirmatory data for the idea that attending to the child for appropriate behavior (i.e., compliance) will prevent the need for the child to engage in inappropriate behavior (i.e., noncompliance) in order to get the attention of the adult.

Lay, Waters, and Park (1989) conducted two studies with four-year-olds and their mothers to determine if the mother's mood had an impact on children's compliant behavior. In the first study, 32 mothers and their children were assigned to either a responsive play condition or standard play condition. Mothers in the responsive play condition were trained to respond positively to their child in play and to let their child take the lead in the play situation. Mothers were told to model their child's behavior rather than give commands, instructions, or ask questions. The standard play condition required the mothers to play with their child as they would at home.

Lay and colleagues (1989) reported that children found more pleasure in playing when their mother's engaged in responsive play. The opposite effect was found in situations where a negative mood was induced. The authors reported that neither of these conditions had a significant effect on compliance.

Study 2 was conducted with 24 four-year-olds and their mothers to determine if compliance tasks would be affected by putting a child into a positive or negative mood through verbalizations. In this study (Lay, Waters, and Park, 1989, p. 1408), a "mood inducer" talked with the child about their feelings and thoughts when they heard words such as "happy" (i.e., positive mood) and "upset" (i.e., negative mood). After instructing the child to think about these feelings, the experimenter left the room where the child and mother had been in close proximity. The mother then commanded the child to sort blocks. Results of the study indicated that children who were in a positive mood complied with their mothers' commands more quickly than their peers who were in a negative mood. Children in a positive mood also sorted more blocks (i.e., complied more) than those in a negative mood.

The authors realized that the responsive play situations created in the clinic setting would not be amenable to home play settings since their experimental situation required constant attention on the part of the mother to her child and his or her play behavior. However, the results of the study provided important clues about the effect of mood on a child's compliant behavior.

McMahon and Wells (1989) reported similar causes of noncompliance in classrooms where teachers attended to inappropriate behavior verses appropriate behavior. Children tended to comply more with requests and commands when teachers interacted with them in a proactive manner rather than a reactive manner. Vignette 9.8 provides an example of a teacher giving a student too much attention for noncompliance.

Vignette 9.8.   Example of Inappropriate Attention for Noncompliant Behavior.

Joshua is a 13-year-old junior high student in Mr. Smith's class. Joshua has demonstrated tremendous difficulty in following his teacher's directions. It has been noted that Joshua receives a lot of negative attention from his teacher whenever Joshua fails to follow directions. For example, the teacher tells Joshua that he'll "never amount to anything" unless he learns to follow directions. During these "lectures," Joshua hangs his head and says, "What do you expect, I'm so stupid—how do you think I can remember directions?" The teacher then usually says, "Joshua, you are not stupid and you know it. You just need to concentrate more." Joshua's noncompliant behavior results in a significant amount of teacher attention. Meanwhile, the children who are following the teacher's directions are being ignored. The teacher might observe a greater amount of compliance if attention were directed at Joshua when he followed directions, instead of when he did not follow directions. In addition, a quiet reminder, directed to Joshua with minimum attention, would serve as a more appropriate response to his inappropriate behavior.

Inconsistent Follow-up for Noncompliant Behavior

Wahler and Dumas (1986) reported that noncompliant behavior may be maintained by an adult's indiscriminant attention. They reported that when children cannot predict how an adult will react to their behavior (i.e., the adult sometimes attends, other times ignores), they have no way of knowing what is expected of them. Wicks-Nelson and Israel (1991) also suggested that adults who were not consistent in follow-up on commands/requests realized a higher incidence of noncompliance. The opposite effect was experienced when adults positively reinforced children for compliance. Vignette 9.9 provides an example of the effects of inconsistent follow-up for noncompliant behavior.

Vignette 9.9.   Example of the Effects of Inconsistent Follow-up for Noncompliant Behavior.

Kelli's third-grade teacher tells Kelli that she cannot go to recess until her math project is completed. However, at recess time, Kelli has not completed her math project and she goes to recess anyway. The teacher realizes this, but decides to ignore Kelli's noncompliant behavior. The next day, Kelli tries to attend recess before completing her assignments. But this time, Kelli's teacher makes her stay in the classroom. Kelli responds by yelling and crying. As a result, the teacher allows Kelli to go outside. Finally, on the third day, once again, Kelli is told she cannot join the others for recess unless her math assignment is completed. Once again, Kelli doesn't finish her work. Her teacher responds to Kelli's behavior by sending her to the principal's office. Kelli becomes angry and responds by kicking and screaming on the way to the principal's office. Kelli is confused and believes that if she cries hard enough, her teacher will, once again, change her mind. Because Kelli's teacher was inconsistent in her management of Kelli's behavior, Kelli's noncompliant behavior escalated. In addition, the teacher's inconsistent response to Kelli's noncompliance reinforced Kelli's tantrum behavior, which escalated into aggression. Had Kelli's teacher been consistent from the beginning, Kelli would have known what was expected of her, and the teacher could have avoided much of the negative behavior that ensued.

Examples of Interventions for Noncompliance

Behavioral Strategies to Increase Compliance

Pfiffner and O'Leary (1987) investigated the effects of an all-positive behavior management program on the noncompliant behavior of eight first through third graders. Prior to the study, these children had no experience with negative consequences for their inappropriate behavior, which was operationally defined as off-task and academic inaccuracy. Using an alternating treatments design, the authors applied interventions within four conditions. In the "regular positives alone" (Pfiffner & O'Leary, 1987, p. 266) condition, children earned positive consequences for on-task behavior in the form of social praise, bonus work, and public posting of completed work. The "enhanced positives alone" (p. 266) condition required that the teachers increase the frequency and quality of positive consequences (described previously). In the third condition, "enhanced positives and negatives" (p. 267), the teachers administered positive consequences for appropriate behavior and reprimands for off-task behavior. The results of the study indicated that children in the third condition improved their on-task behavior significantly when they were positively reinforced for appropriate behavior and received negative consequences for inappropriate behavior. The all-positive behavior management conditions were not effective in changing the behavior of these children. The teacher and students described in Vignette 9.10 used positive and negative consequences to increase compliance during classroom transition periods.

Vignette 9.10.   Example of Positive and Negative Consequences and Their Effects on Compliance During Classroom Transition Periods.

Compliant behavior during classroom transitions and the latency between a direction and compliance were improved in an elementary classroom. The children were told that they would have free-time at the end of the day if they followed directions in a timely fashion during transitions between class periods. Whenever the teacher announced a transition, she started a stop watch to keep track of the amount of time spent making the transitions. If the time was under one minute, the children earned one minute of free-time at the end of the day. However, if the time was more than one minute, the children did not earn the free-time at the end of the day. The teacher and students graphed the time earned for all of the transitions throughout the day. The intervention was effective in significantly reducing the time "wasted" during transition time. Later, the teacher was able to use an intermittent schedule of reinforcement for compliant behavior, eventually fading the need for the stop watch. When children were able to make transitions in a timely fashion, without external reinforcers, the class earned an automatic free period (such as 5 minutes) at the end of the day.

S. Vanourney-Peck, personal communication, 1989.

Cognitive Behavior Management

Another intervention that is effective in increasing compliant behavior and reducing noncompliant behavior is cognitive behavior management. For example, Rhode, Morgan, and Young (1983) observed positive behavior changes in six children with behavior disorders who were served in a resource room. Children in this elementary classroom were taught to use self-evaluation to monitor their classroom rule-following behavior. A token reinforcement program was implemented to reinforce children for compliance. The intervention consisted of modeling, role playing, feedback, correction, and clarification of classroom rules. Initially, the teacher awarded points for following rules and the children tallied these points on a point card. Points were traded for secondary reinforcers. In the next phase of the study, the children were asked to evaluate their academic work and behavior by awarding themselves points. The teacher also continued to rate the children. Eventually, the children were taught to evaluate their performance without the teacher matching the ratings. The program was successful in increasing compliant behavior. In addition, the children generalized their compliant behavior and the self-evaluation strategy to regular classroom settings.

TEMPER TANTRUMS

Definition

Temper tantrum behavior was often included in literature regarding the characteristics of aggressive and/or noncompliant behavior (for example, Kerr & Nelson, 1989; Kuczynski et al., 1987; McMahon & Wells, 1989; Sasso, Melloy, & Kavale, 1990). Temper tantrums have been defined as noxious behavior demonstrated by children when their demands are not met or when they are tired (Sasso, Melloy, & Kavale, 1990). Blechman defined temper tantrums as taking place "when a child, who has not been mistreated, is out-of-control for at least 1 minute, screaming, crying, throwing things, or hitting" (1985, p. 89). Although tantruming behavior is exhibited by persons of all ages, we often affiliate this behavior with toddlers and young children. Temper tantrums are characterized by a variety of acting-out behaviors including crying, stamping, throwing self, screaming, kicking, clinging, jumping up and down, shouting, pounding, and other annoying behaviors. Temper tantrums are among the most common challenging behaviors of young children (Blechman, 1985).

Children manifest tantrums most often when their wishes for edibles or privileges are not met. For example, two-year-old Tyler requests to go to the store with his mother. When he is told he cannot go, he throws himself to the ground, screams and cries, demanding in a loud voice that he be allowed to go along. This behavior may be manifested from a few seconds to several hours depending on the child's history of reinforcement for tantrum behavior (D. Wacker, personal communication, 1989).

Etiology

Inconsistent Reinforcement Consequences

The cause of temper tantrums is often attributed to theories of learning. Temper tantrum behavior can often be traced directly to an adult's pattern of giving into the child's wishes as soon as he or she begins to tantrum. In the case of Tyler, his mother did not like the tantrum behavior, so she let Tyler accompany her to the store. Tyler promptly stopped his tantrum, got his coat, and smilingly accompanied his mother. By giving in to Tyler's behavior, his mother reinforced his behavior. In the future, Tyler will be more likely to engage in tantrum behavior when he is told "no" as a result of the positive consequences he experienced for his tantrum behavior.

A more common scenario is the battle that young children and parents engage in at bedtime. Children may manifest tantrum behavior when they are told it is time to go to bed. The tantrum may begin when the parent and child attempt to put on the child's pajamas. The parent may let the child get out of bed (for just a little while longer) when the child engages in tantrum behavior. Unfortunately, this only exacerbates the problem as the child will continue to engage in tantrums whenever the parents try to put the child to bed. Parents who are consistent in their behavior (i.e., not allowing the child to get out of bed once he has gone to bed), will be more successful in helping the child comply with behavioral expectations. Of course, it is helpful if the child is properly prepared for bed (such as brushed teeth, glass of water, snack, bedtime story) using a regular routine. Otherwise the child's protests or expressions of needs may be warranted.

Examples of Interventions for Tantrum Behavior

Consistent Reinforcement and Use of Extinction

Temper tantrums occur most frequently when a child does not get his or her own way or when he or she is very tired. Ironically, both of these factors exist at bedtime—a time when some children manifest tantrum behavior. According to Edwards (1991), one out of four preschoolers exhibits tantrums at bedtime. The problem is that children want to stay up, but they are often too tired to stay up. Occasionally, however, parents will experience problems with their child when the child has had a late nap and is not tired at bedtime. It is extremely important for adults to be consistent when trying to decrease tantrum behavior. When a child is told "no," adults must be prepared to follow through with the command. If the parents do not really mean "no" then they should not say "no."

Tantrum behavior can be significantly decreased through the use of extinction (see Chapter 8). When reinforcement for tantrum behavior is withdrawn, and the child's behavior is ignored, the tantrum behavior will probably be greatly reduced or eliminated. To avoid tantrum behavior at bedtime, a routine for getting to bed should be established and then consistently followed

(Edwards, 1991). Generally, the child is given a warning that bedtime is in ___ minutes. This gives the child a chance to finish what he or she is doing before the bedtime routine begins and to let the child know that a pleasant time with a parent or other adult is soon to take place. Consistent bedtime routines are effective in reducing tantrum and noncompliant behaviors at bedtime, and in making bedtime a pleasant time for children and parents (Edwards, 1991). An example of a bedtime routine for a five-year-old child follows:

1. Tell the child that bedtime is coming about 15 minutes before bedtime.
2. Offer the child a small snack "before you go to bed."
3. Tell the child "It is time to brush your teeth."
4. Help the child put on his or her pajamas.
5. Tell the child to "use the bathroom and wash your hands."
6. Read the child a story from a book the child selects.
7. Offer the child a drink of water.
8. Exchange good night hugs and kisses while tucking the child into the bed.
9. Turn on the night light and turn off the room lights.
10. Leave the room.

If the child gets out of bed following the routine, the parent should gently and quietly lead the child back to bed. It is important that the parent be firm, but gentle, in efforts to assist the child back to bed. Additional interactions with the child, especially reinforcing interactions, should be kept to a minimum.

IMPULSIVITY

Definition

Teachers and parents who refer to a child as being "impulsive" usually conjure up images of children who rarely stop to think before they act, who attempt tasks before they fully understand the directions, who often demonstrate remorse when their actions have led to errors or mishaps, who call out frequently in class (usually with the wrong answer), and who have difficulty organizing their materials. Impulsivity, although difficult to define as a separate construct of behavior (Campbell & Werry, 1986; Olson, Bates, & Bayles, 1990), is often referred to when persons consider the types of behavior that cause problems for adults and children.

Kauffman (1989) pointed out that impulsive behavior is normal in young children, but that as children grow older, they are able to learn alternative responses. Olson and colleagues pointed out that two-year-old children will begin to "inhibit prohibited actions owing to remembered information" (1990, p. 318), but stated that "self-regulation does not develop until the 3rd or 4th year of life" (p. 318). Campbell and Werry defined impulsivity as "erratic and poorly controlled behavior" (1986, p. 120). Kauffman defined impulsivity as behavior demonstrated by children who are "unable to keep from responding quickly and without thinking to academic tasks and to social situations. Typically, these children's impulses are wrong, and they get them into trouble" (1985, pp. 198–199). In other words, children who act impulsively are often observed to fail to inhibit their response to target stimuli.

Shafrir and Pascual-Leone (1990) reported that children who had deficits in postfailure reflective behavior made more errors than children who stopped and reflected on the errors they made in initial efforts to complete academic tasks. Likewise, children who make errors on academic tasks and reflect on them right away will learn from their mistakes, therefore reducing the probability of making further errors on the task (Shafrir & Pascual-Leone, 1990). On the other hand, Shafrir and Pascual-Leone found that children who did not reflect on errors made even more errors on the subsequent tasks.

Children who manifest impulsive behavior often get into trouble in social situations such as games and play activities (Melloy, 1990). Since they demonstrate poor impulse control, these children are apt to take their turn before its

Children who demonstrate behavior problems associated with impulsivity, inattention, and hyperactivity often appear to be unorganized and "lost" compared to their peers.

time, or to respond incorrectly to game stimuli (e.g., questions). Some children who have poor impulse control may respond to teasing, for example, by hitting the person who teases them. They are often sorry for their actions and can discuss what they should have done had they taken time to think about their action.

Children who manifest impulsive behavior are also described as not being able to delay gratification (Shafrir & Pascual-Leone, 1990). The example in Vignette 9.11 demonstrates this characteristic of impulsive behavior.

Vignette 9.11.   Example of Impulsive Behavior.

Jeff has just been given his weekly allowance. He immediately rides his bicycle to the convenience store and spends all his money on candy and baseball cards. Later, he regrets his actions because he doesn't have any money to play video games with his friends. In comparison to Jeff's impulsive behavior, Jeff's brother has saved some of his allowance and is able to play at the video arcade.

Etiology

Multiple Factors

According to a number of authors, no one actually knows what causes impulsivity (Kauffman, 1985, 1989; Campbell & Werry, 1986). Kauffman (1985) suggested that impulsivity is most likely caused by multiple factors, including biological, psychological, environmental, and social learning factors. Assessment of impulsivity is usually achieved through the use of behavioral checklists, behavior ratings, mazes, match-to-sample tasks, and behavioral observations (Campbell & Werry, 1986; Olson, Bates, & Bayles, 1990; Shafrir & Pascual-Leone, 1990; Vitiello, Stoff, Atkins, & Mahoney, 1990).

Attention to Errors

Shafrir and Pascual-Leone (1990) conducted a study with 378 children of 9, 10, 11, and 12 years of age. The purpose of the study was to determine the effect of attention to errors on academic tasks and the relationship to reflective/impulsive behavior. Shafrir and Pascual-Leone administered a number of measures, including mazes and match-to-sample tasks, to determine response behavior, and tests of academic achievement to evaluate arithmetic abilities. The authors reported that children who completed tasks quickly and accurately tended to take time to check their answers. If an error occurred, they took time to correct the error and used the information learned in correction of the error to assist them in completing the rest of the task. This resulted in fewer errors overall and completion of the task in a more timely fashion. They called these children "postfailure reflective" (Shafrir & Pascual-Leone, 1990, p. 385).

In comparison, children who were referred to as "postfailure impulsive" (Shafrir & Pascual-Leone, 1990, p. 385) were found to complete tasks slowly and inaccurately. These children plodded through the task without checking answers for correctness. They simply went on to the next problem with no reference to previously completed tasks. Shafrir and Pascual-Leone concluded that the lack of postfailure reflection by this group lead to more errors because they did not learn from their previous errors. The implications of the results of this study are that children possess some type of "reflection/impulsivity cognitive style" (Shafrir & Pascual-Leone, 1990, p. 386), which was first proposed by Kagan (1966). Also, children who appeared to be taking their time (slow thinkers) in actuality made more errors than the children who completed the tasks quickly (reflective thinkers). Vignette 9.12 provides an example of a child who behaves in an impulsive manner after receiving an assignment from his teacher.

Vignette 9.12.   Example of a Child Who Behaves in an Impulsive Manner.

Kyle begins to work on his paper as soon as it touches his desk. He does not read the directions at the top of the page and he does not wait for the teacher to give directions on how to complete the work. Since Kyle has completed similar worksheets in the past, he responds to the presented stimuli in a similar manner. Unfortunately, today's worksheet requires a different format for responding and, as a result, Kyle made many errors. Had he waited and listened to the teacher's directions, he would have made fewer errors.

Interactional Patterns Associated with Impulsivity

Olson and his colleagues (1990) attempted to identify the antecedents of impulsivity in children. They assessed parent-child interactions through behavioral observation to determine if parental interaction style was a predictor of impulsive behavior. According to Olson, Bates, and Bayles, the purpose of their study was to "identify the relative contributions of different parent-child interaction antecedents to children's later self-regulatory abilities" (1990, p. 320). This longitudinal study involved 79 mother-child dyads. Their findings indicated that "responsive, sensitive, and cognitively enriching mother-child interactions are important precursors of childhood impulse control" (p. 332). Children, especially boys, were more likely to develop impulsivity if their mothers manifested punitive and inconsistent behavior management styles.

Examples of Interventions for Impulsivity

Consistent Reinforcement for Behavior

Impulsivity may be reduced by teaching children appropriate "waiting" behaviors, and by consistently reinforcing children for appropriate responding behavior. For example, after an assignment has been passed out, a teacher may teach a student to place her hands on her desk, establish eye contact with the teacher, and listen for directions. The teacher should praise the student for demonstrating "waiting" behaviors. A child who hurries through an assignment without stopping to read the directions or to check for errors could be given small amounts of a task to accomplish rather than the whole task at once. This would give the child a smaller chunk of the problem to deal with and more opportunities for reinforcement since the child would be more likely to solve the problem correctly. Sometimes, a child can handle solving only one problem at a time. In this case, the child should be allowed to solve the problem and receive feedback immediately. As the child becomes more confident and is able to pace himself or herself more efficiently, the child may be able to handle larger portions of projects and assignments.

Social Skills Training and Relaxation Techniques

Children who manifest impulsive behavior will benefit from training in social skills such as self-control. At the same time, children may be taught relaxation techniques. Reinforcement will increase the possibility that a child will demonstrate behaviors that are alternatives to impulsivity. Targeting behaviors for intervention that are positive and incompatible with the undesirable behavior may also be effective with children who demonstrate impulsive behavior (Schaub, 1990). Vignette 9.13 provides an example of teaching social skills incompatible with impulsive behavior.

Vignette 9.13.   Example of Teaching Social Skills Incompatible with Impulsive Behavior.

Several students in a fourth-grade classroom shouted out answers to questions before the teacher had a chance to ask the entire question. Consequently, the answers were often incorrect. The teacher decided to teach the children behaviors that were incompatible with the students' current behaviors. The target behaviors that she chose to teach were "Waiting until an entire question has been asked" and "Raising hand to answer a question." The teacher and the students discussed the new skills and decided on a plan. The plan stated that the teacher would model the appropriate behavior, the students would role play the skills, the teacher would provide the students with feedback, and the students would record, on a chart on their desks, whenever they used their new skills. As a result of this new program, the students waited for the entire question to be asked and then raised their hands to answer. Consequently, the children answered more questions correctly and the classroom environment was improved.

INATTENTION

Definition

Attention has been defined as the ability to remain oriented to a task or activity for the length of time required to complete the task or activity or for an amount of time that seems socially acceptable (Ruff, Lawson, Parrinello, & Weissberg, 1990; Kounin, 1970). McGee, Williams, and Silva identified behavioral dimensions associated with inattention: "planning, organization, and execution of tasks or activities" (1985, pp. 487–488). Children who manifest inattentive behavior will often have problems that fall along three dimensions: (1) coming to attention, (2) making decisions, and (3) giving sustained attention (Brown, & Wynne, 1984; Hallahan, Kauffman, & Lloyd, 1985). Parents and teachers often describe children that they consider to have problems with attention as having trouble starting and/or finishing things.

Another problem often cited by parents and teachers of children with attention problems is that they are easily distracted. These children may become off task at even the slightest noise (e.g., someone's pencil dropping on the floor) or change in the environment (e.g., someone comes to the door of the classroom to talk to the teacher). Being distracted is not always a problem. These children, however, often have trouble getting back to work once they have been distracted. As a result, they may have difficulty completing academic tasks, possibly resulting in poor academic achievement.

McMahon (1989) observed children on a playground in a study on social skills, and found that one of the children seemed easily distracted. This child rarely initiated play activities with other children. When he did become involved in a game or activity, he switched groups every few minutes. For instance, the child started playing kickball with one group of children, then moved to another group playing on the swings before the kickball game was over.

Children who have attention problems are also described as poor listeners. For example, 10-year-old Matthew rarely uses any body language (e.g., eye contact) to indicate that he is listening to another person. At school, the children have been instructed to look at a person who is talking (e.g., a peer reading in front of the class). During these situations, Matthew is often observed to stare out the window. In Matthew's home, where he is expected to stand in close proximity to the adult speaking but not to make eye contact, Matthew often runs around the room while someone talks to him.

Inattention is a problem that often exists with other behavioral deficits such as impulsivity and hyperactivity. Its existence as an independent construct has been debated (Kauffman, 1985). Regardless of its definition, inattention is a problem that seems to be a common characteristic among children with challenging behaviors.

Etiology

Developmental Perspective on Inattention

Ruff and Lawson (1990) investigated the development of attention in preschoolers. Two studies of attention involved 67 children, ages one through five. The studies were conducted using observations of free-play as the measure of focused attention. They found that as children got older, their attention became more focused when they were presented with a variety of activities that involved complex problem-solving aspects. Effective treatment of children with attention problems usually involves the presentation of novel and interesting tasks at a pace that is geared toward motivating children (Kerr & Nelson, 1989).

Examples of Interventions for Inattention

Cognitive Behavior Management

Self-instructional training with children who demonstrate inattentive behavior has been very effective in reducing this behavior (Davis & Hajicek, 1985; Lloyd, Bateman, Landrum, & Hallahan, 1989). In a study conducted by Davis and Hajicek (1985), they found that seven children who had problems with attending to tasks were able to learn self-instructional verbalizations. This strategy helped the children to significantly improve their attending and accuracy rate on academic tasks. Lloyd and his colleagues (1989) assisted five upper elementary children in changing their attending behavior through self-recording. Using self-recording, the children's arithmetic productivity and attention to task improved significantly.

HYPERACTIVITY

Definition

"Hyperactivity is one of the most common problems of elementary school children" (O'Brien & Obrzut, 1986, p. 281). Controversy has arisen over whether or not hyperactivity exists as an independent behavioral construct, and it is often associated with inattention and impulsivity in children's behavior (e.g., Gaynor, 1990; Kauffman, 1985, 1989; Kohn, 1989). Hyperactivity has been defined as "a class of heterogeneous behavior disorders in which a high level of activity is exhibited at inappropriate times and cannot be inhibited upon command" (Ross & Ross, 1982, p. 14). Johnson (1989) described children who were hyperactive as "having trouble remaining seated, running in the room, fidgeting, manipulating objects, and twisting and wiggling in their seats" (p. 471). Most of these behaviors are expected of very young children in many environmental contexts. These same behaviors, however, prove troublesome for school-age children and adolescents in home, school, and community environments. Kohn (1989) pointed out that symptoms of hyperactivity often seem to disappear when the child is engaged in something he or she likes to do such as watching TV or engaging in free-play. The following list presents a number of behaviors that are often associated with hyperactive behavior in children:

♦ *Problems in school:* The child who is disruptive, aggressive, constantly out-of-seat, and often off-task.
♦ *Restlessness:* The child does not sit still for more than several minutes at one time.
♦ *Childish or immature behavior:* The child may choose to play with younger children.
♦ *Problems keeping friends:* The child does not know how to join a group for play.
♦ *Overasserts self:* The child goes overboard trying to please adults with offers to help.
♦ *Perfectionism:* The child erases answers on a math worksheet so often that holes appear in the paper.

Often parents and teachers label an "active" child hyperactive. For a child to be considered truly hyperactive, we need to consider more than the activity level. A child who exhibits high levels of activity may be very bright, enthusiastic, socially acceptable, and a high achiever (Kauffman, 1989). The difference between an active child and a hyperactive child is the dimension of appropriateness of the activity. Children who are hyperactive often act inappropriately in the context of the situation. An example is provided in Vignette 9.14.

Vignette 9.14.   Example of a Child Who Demonstrates Hyperactive Behavior.

Jackie is 12 years old. She is described by her parents and teachers as always on the go, fidgety, and restless. Jackie often gets into trouble for her behavior as was evidenced at a recent family anniversary party. During the party, Jackie ran around the room, slid down the lobby bannister, and ran into the cake table when she ran across the room to tell her mother something. In school, Jackie does not stay in her seat for longer than two consecutive minutes, has great difficulty paying attention to directions, and is unable to complete a task or project without considerable assistance. Jackie's parents are afraid to take her places, such as shopping or to church, because her behaviors are very disruptive. In comparison, Jackie's 10-year-old sister is also very active. However, she attends to tasks in school, gets good grades, and behaves in an age-appropriate manner during most social situations. For example, although she is fidgety at church, she is not overly disruptive to others.

Etiology

Multiple Factors

No one really knows what causes hyperactivity even though a number of theories have been researched. Brain damage, biological factors, food additives, difficult temperament, and psychoanalytic factors have all been proposed as explanations for hyperactivity (Kauffman, 1989). None of these explanations, however, has been supported by sufficient research data to conclude that any one of them is a cause for hyperactivity. Other explanations for hyperactive behavior revolve around theories of modeling, imitation, and environmental interaction (Campbell & Werry, 1986; David & Wintrob, 1989; Kauffman, 1985, 1989; Kohn, 1989). It has been proposed that the most plausible explanation for hyperactive behavior is that it is caused by a combination of factors.

Environmental Factors Associated with Hyperactivity

Kohn (1989) suggested that hyperactive behavior is caused by environmental factors such as classroom dynamics and/or family dynamics. He stated that children demonstrate hyperactive behavior in classrooms where the work is not stimulating and where the pace of instruction is not conducive to the ability of the child. Kohn also suggested that hyperactive behavior may be the result of academic failure rather than the cause of that failure. Kohn further reported that "warped family patterns often accompany hyperactivity" (1989, p. 94). These patterns were described in terms of difficulty with mental health among family members, a heavy emphasis on punitive and authoritative approaches to management of children's behavior, and experience of marital problems between the child's parents.

Interactional Patterns Associated with Hyperactivity

David and Wintrob (1989) studied the role of mother-child communication patterns in the development of hyperactive/conduct-disturbed behavior. The authors conducted research with 30 boys who had been diagnosed as hyperactive/conduct-disordered and their mothers. Mothers and their sons were given pictures to discuss while their interactions were videotaped. Examples of the exchanges that were taped included an interaction about a picture that could have been described as a type of flying animal. The following interaction was considered to demonstrate a disturbed communication pattern between a mother and her son: "That's a bat" (son); "Don't be stupid! That's not a bat, that's a butterfly" (mother) (David & Wintrob, 1989, p. 386). In comparison, this interaction was considered to be a positive interaction between the mother and her son: "That is a bat" (son); Very good! That's what it looks like" (mother) (David & Wintrob, 1989, p. 386).

The authors found that the communication patterns of sons were disturbed in dyads consisting of mothers and sons with hyperactivity in comparison to the communication patterns of mothers and their sons without hyperactivity. David and Wintrob commented that even though their study was conducted with mothers and sons, there is a possibility that others who communicate with children may influence children's behavior (e.g., fathers, siblings, teachers). They pointed out that "in most instances the primary caretaker will be most influential in this regard" (1989, p. 390).

Examples of Interventions for Hyperactivity

A number of effective strategies are available for decreasing hyperactivity. Few studies are available in current literature that focus solely on hyperactivity. Most of the research focuses on hyperactivity combined with inattention and impulsivity as constructs of attention deficit hyperactive disorder (ADHD). This section will describe the literature that is available on behavioral interventions that were effective in decreasing hyperactive behavior. The most popular of these interventions includes consistent reinforcement consequences, social skills training, and cognitive behavior management.

Consistent Reinforcement Consequences

Children who have hyperactivity will respond best in settings where the rules for behavior have been clearly established. In these settings, rules are consistently enforced and children are reinforced for their use. Children with hyperactivity were most successful in structured classroom settings where the rules were obvious and enforced (Gordon, 1991; Schaub, 1990).

Along with structure, children with hyperactivity respond well in educational programs that include token economies. Children who are positively reinforced for appropriate behavior (e.g., staying in seat, asking permission, following rules) were more likely to engage in behaviors incompatible with hyperactivity (McIntyre, 1989; Melloy, 1990; Schaub, 1990).

Paniagua, Morrison, and Black (1990) reported on the effective use of positive reinforcement to reduce the hyperactive behavior of a seven-year-old boy. They found that offering a toy as positive reinforcement for promising to inhibit behavior and actual inhibition of the behavior was effective in reducing hyperactive behavior.

Social Skills Training

Children who are hyperactive often receive low social status ratings from their peers and deviant scores on teacher ratings of behavior (McConnell & Odom,

1986). These children benefit from training in social skills using a structured learning approach (McGinnis & Goldstein, 1984). Social skills that are incompatible with hyperactive behavior include "staying in seat," "task completion," "joining in a group," and "offering help to others." Modeling, role playing, receiving feedback, and generalization training in these skills can reduce hyperactive behavior in children.

Cognitive Behavior Management

Hinshaw, Henker, and Whalen (1984) reported that cognitive behavior management was effective in decreasing hyperactive behavior in 21 boys, ages 8 through 13 years. All of these boys took Ritalin to reduce hyperactive behavior. The boys were trained in self-instructional and problem-solving strategies during twice a week, two-hour training sessions over a three-week period. During the intervention, the boys were assigned to either Ritalin or placebo conditions for the three weeks. The results of the study suggested that cognitive behavior management strategies were effective in helping children to solve problems. There was no significant advantage for groups who received both cognitive behavior management training and Ritalin.

STEREOTYPIC BEHAVIOR

Definition

Children who demonstrate stereotypic behavior typically engage in repetitious, invariant responses that occur at an excessively high rate and do not appear to have any adaptive function (Baumeister, 1978). Specific responses vary from child to child and include self-injurious behavior and self-stimulatory behavior. The major implication for children is that these behaviors often interfere with the child's level of attention to environmental stimuli. This often limits the effectiveness of educational and other programming efforts. Stereotypic behaviors that interfere with educational goals are most commonly observed in children who are autistic or severely mentally disabled. In fact, we all engage in stereotypic behavior whenever we flip a pencil repeatedly or swing a leg.

Self-injurious behaviors (SIB) inflict harm on the person exhibiting them. Behaviors of this type include "striking oneself, biting or sucking various body parts, pinching, scratching, poking or pulling various body parts, repeatedly vomiting, or vomiting and reingesting food, and consuming nonedible substances" (Kerr & Nelson, 1989, p. 280). These behaviors are often of such high intensity that they inflict permanent tissue damage to the person's body or even death (Berkman & Meyer, 1988; LaVigna & Willis, 1991). Zirpoli and Lloyd (1987) described two types of SIB. They characterized indirect SIB as including "alcohol abuse, drug abuse, repeated vomiting, pica, and self-induced seizures" (1987, p. 46). Zirpoli and Lloyd further characterized direct SIB as "banging, cutting, biting, abrading, severing, inserting, burning, and hitting" (1987, p. 46).

Self-stimulatory behaviors (SSB) are stereotypic behaviors that are repetitive and frequent but do not cause physical injury to the child exhibiting them. These behaviors are often manifested as "screaming, running, hopping, finger wiggling, looking out the corner of the eye, public masturbation, rocking and other repeated movements" (Kerr & Nelson, 1989, p. 282). Lovaas, Newsom, and Hickman reported that SSB "takes the form of prolonged body-rocking, head-nodding, flapping the hands at the wrist, tapping or shaking objects, gazing at lights, and jumping up and down" (1987, p. 45). Self-stimulatory behaviors are not always intrusive behaviors for the person engaging in them or others around them. For this reason, professionals and parents need to consider two rules in order to make decisions about treatment of SSB: (1) If the behavior has developed into SIB, there should be no question of treatment and (2) if SSB is interfering with the child's progress in educational programming, then treatment is warranted.

Etiology

Reinforcement, Sensory Arousal, or Organic Origination

Bellfiore and Dattilio (1990) reviewed the literature on SIB from the past 30 years. They reported that the literature revealed three explanations for the "onset, maintenance, and continuance of self-injury" (1990, p. 29). According to Bellfiore and Dattilio's review, SIB seems to originate from one of the following sources:

◆ SIB is learned behavior that is maintained by operant contingencies of either the "positive reinforcement paradigm" (Bellfiore & Dattilio, 1990, p. 24) or the "negative reinforcement paradigm" (p. 25). In other words, children learn to manifest self-injurious behaviors, which are maintained by positive reinforcement (e.g., attention from others) or negative reinforcement (e.g., withdrawal of parent/teacher abuse) contingent on eliciting SIB.

◆ SIB is elicited as an attempt to increase or decrease sensory arousal. It has been theorized that persons who engage in SIB have a need to provide neurological stimulation and that these behaviors assist in meeting this need. Others suggested that SIB is manifested as an attempt to reduce aversive stimuli. For example, children who suffer from otitis media (i.e., inner ear infection) may resort to head-banging as an attempt to reduce or replace the pain experienced from the ear infection (Demchak & Halle, 1985).

◆ SIB is related to organic origination such as is present in genetic anomalies or biochemical imbalances. SIB has been manifested by some persons who experience genetic flaws that are present in Lesch-Nyhan syndrome or Cornelia de Lang syndrome. Individuals who exhibit Lesch-Nyhan syndrome engage in SIB characterized by "severe repetitive mutilation of fingers, lips, and tongue" (Bellfiore &

Dattilio, 1990, p. 27). Persons experiencing Cornelia de Lang syndrome exhibit irregular patterns of SIB that are characterized as "eye picking, face hitting, and [sic] self-biting" (Bellfiore & Dattilio, 1990, p. 28). It should be noted that these types of syndromes are very rare and effect a very small number of persons who engage in SIB.

Bellfiore and Dattilio (1990) noted that although each of these causative factors all have some empirical backing, none have been identified as the primary etiology for SIB.

Motivating Conditions of Self-Injurious Behavior

Durand and Carr (1985) offered supported evidence that SIB has four motivating conditions. Their theories have received support in the literature (e.g., Favell, McGimsey, & Schell, 1982; Iwata, Dorsey, Slifer, Bauman, & Richman, 1982; Rincover & Devany, 1982; Sasso & Reimers, 1988; Sasso, Reimers, Cooper, Wacker, Berg, Steege, Kelly, & Allaire, in press). According to Durand and Carr (1985), SIB is motivated by:

- ◆ *Social attention:* SIB appears to be shaped and maintained by attention (e.g., from others) as a consequence.
- ◆ *Tangible consequences:* Some children exhibit SIB in order to gain access to tangible rewards such as playing with a desired toy.
- ◆ *Escape from aversive situations:* Children who engage in SIB in order to remove themselves from an unpleasant task (e.g., an academic task) are said to be motivated by escape.
- ◆ *Sensory consequences:* Sensory feedback (e.g., auditory, visual, tactile), which reinforces the child, appears to be another motivating condition that maintains SIB.

A number of authors completed a functional analysis of SIB by exposing children who exhibit SIB to analogue conditions in which each of the motivating conditions is simulated (Iwata et al., 1982; Sasso & Reimers, 1988; Wacker, Steege, Northup, Reimers, Berg, & Sasso, 1990). They reported that interventions based on findings from the functional analysis were effective in reducing SIB in children. These results lend credence to Durand and Carr's theories of motivation for SIB.

Motivating Conditions of Self-Stimulatory Behavior

Lovaas and others (1987) reported that SSB is learned behavior that is maintained by *perceptual reinforcers* or *automatic reinforcers* (Iwata, Vollmer, & Zarcone, 1990). Considerable controversy surrounds the operant learning theory as a cause for SSB. Lewis, Baumeister, and Mailman (1987) argued that Lovaas's and his colleagues' theory of SSB was flawed and failed to take into account biological factors.

Demchak and Halle reported that SSB is maintained by the level of stimulation received by the individual during the behavior. The individual, according to this theory, is unable to receive this stimulation through other, more appropriate methods. They concluded that SIB may be "an extreme type of sensory self-stimulation" (1985, p. 30).

Horner (1980) hypothesized that SSB is exhibited within environments that are not enriched with activities, materials, and manipulatable toys. Horner concluded that, when individuals were exposed to enriched versus austere environments, SSB and SIB decreased in the enriched environment and increased in the austere environment.

Examples of Interventions for SSB and SIB

Durand and Carr (1985) outlined several treatment guidelines that have been used to treat the self-injurious behavior of children. These guidelines include the teaching of appropriate social skills and interactive behaviors depending on the motivating condition that seems to be maintaining the child's SIB. For example, Durand and Carr suggested that if the SIB is maintained by social attention, the teacher should teach the child appropriate attention-seeking behavior. Children have been taught to ask if they are doing good work, and other appropriate phrases, for gaining teacher attention. Children who are nonverbal have been taught to use sign language or to play a taped message that is an alternative to seeking teacher attention.

Before persons responsible for educational programming decide to reduce a child's SSB, it should be determined that this behavior is interfering with the child's educational performance and social interactions with others. Also, a functional analysis of the SSB will likely lead professionals and parents to the conclusion that environmental variables, not the child's behavior, should be the focus of an intervention plan. Teachers are encouraged to first modify the environment before trying to reduce the child's behavior directly. Increasing environmental stimulation by providing a greater array of stimulating activities and materials is likely to prove effective in reducing these behaviors. Also, children who engage in SSB may be redirected to other incompatible behaviors with verbal and physical prompts. These appropriate behaviors should then be reinforced. For a more extensive review of SSB and SIB, and related interventions, readers are referred to Repp and Singh (1990) and Zirpoli and Lloyd (1987).

SUMMARY

Aggressive behavior was divided into five categories by Lancelotta and Vaughn (1989). These five different types of aggression included provoked physical aggression, outburst aggression, unprovoked physical aggression, verbal aggression, and indirect aggression. Examples of physical aggression included kicking, hitting, spitting, and biting. Examples of verbal aggression included bossy behavior, teasing others, tattling, and criticizing the work of others. Aggression is modeled by persons when they are verbally and physically abusive in their interactions with others. Aggression may develop through a child's early experiences, starting with exposure to family aggression and associations with aggressive peers. Children are frequently reinforced by peers for their aggressive behavior. Television shows often teach children to use aggression as a primary problem-solving strategy. In addition, the lack of appropriate social skills is a primary cause of aggression for some children who lack acceptable skills to deal with provocative situations. Intervention strategies for aggressive behaviors include environmental modifications, social skills training, cognitive behavior modification techniques, and direct behavior reduction strategies.

Disruptive behaviors include off-task talking in the classroom, out-of-seat behavior, making noises, and throwing objects. Disruptive behaviors interrupt the classroom learning process. Causes of disruptive behavior include the inconsistent reinforcement of disruptive behaviors by adults and peers, and social skills deficits. Intervention strategies for disruptive behavior include behavioral techniques that teach and reinforce appropriate behavior, social skills training, and cognitive behavior modification.

Noncompliance is defined as disobedience to parent/teacher directives and prohibitions. Kuczynski and others (1987) described four categories of noncompliance: passive noncompliance, direct defiance, simple refusal, and negotiation behavior. The etiology of noncompliance was found to be related to inconsistent interaction patterns between adults and children. Adults who were identified as more responsive to their children had fewer problems with noncompliance. Also, children were more responsive to teachers who interacted with them in a proactive rather than a reactive manner. Intervention strategies to increase compliant behavior include the environmental modifications described above, provision of consistent consequences for noncompliance, and various cognitive modification techniques.

Temper tantrum behavior was defined as noxious behavior demonstrated by children when their demands are not met or when they are tired. Tantrum behavior may include crying, screaming, kicking, and so on. Tantrum behaviors are learned by children as an effective means of manipulating others. Adults who comply with the demands of a child having a tantrum are reinforcing the tantrum behavior. This reinforcement increases the probability that the child will have additional tantrums in similar situations. Interventions for tantrum behavior include extinction and consistent interactions with adults.

Impulsivity is used to define a child who responds to environmental stimuli in a quick manner, without thinking. The response for impulsive behavior is usually incorrect and, thus, these children may perform poorly, academically and socially. Impulsive behaviors are related to multiple factors that include biological, psychological, environmental, and social learning variables. Intervention strategies for impulsivity include teaching "waiting" behaviors, consistent reinforcement of appropriate behavior, social skills training, and relaxation techniques.

Inattention may include problems with coming to attention, making decisions, and giving sustained attention. Inattention often exists with other behavioral deficits such as impulsivity and hyperactivity. As children grow and develop, their attention increases and becomes more focused. Increasing attention skills involves the presentation of novel and interesting tasks at a pace geared toward motivating children. Self-instruction training, and other cognitive behavior modification methods, have also been successfully used to increase attention in children.

Hyperactivity describes a child who seems to be unable to sit or work on a task for even a short period of time. These behaviors may include restlessness, running, fidgeting, and so on. Some secondary problems of children who are hyperactive include academic and social problems. Like impulsivity and attentional problems, no one variable has been found to cause hyperactivity. Rather, a multifactorial etiology and intervention approach must be assumed. The most common intervention strategies for hyperactivity include environmental manipulations, behavioral strategies, social skills training, cognitive behavior modification, and medication.

Stereotypic behaviors include self-injurious behavior and self-stimulatory behavior. Self-injurious behaviors inflict harm on the person exhibiting them. These behaviors may be used to gain attention, gain tangible consequences, escape from aversive situations, and receive sensory feedback. Self-stimulatory behaviors include repetitious responses that do not appear to have a functional purpose. These behaviors may be maintained by self-induced sensory stimulation reinforcement. SSB and SIB have been identified with individuals who have severe disabilities, and individuals living in austere, nonstimulating environments. Intervention strategies include environmental modifications and behavioral reduction strategies.

For Discussion

    1. Discuss the definitions and etiology of aggression, disruptiveness, temper tantrums, noncompliance, impulsivity, inattention, hyperactivity, and stereotypic behaviors.

    2. Describe interventions that are effective in modifying the following challenging behaviors:

       aggressiveness
       disruptiveness
       temper tantrums
       noncompliance
       impulsivity
       inattention

hyperactivity
stereotypy

3. Discuss reasons for assisting children in modifying challenging behaviors.

REFERENCES

Bandura, A. (1973). *Aggression: A social learning analysis,* Englewood Cliffs, NJ: Prentice-Hall.

Baumeister, A. A. (1978). Origins and control of stereotyped movements. In C. E. Meyers (Ed.), *Quality of life in severely and profoundly mentally retarded people* (pp. 353–384). Washington, DC: American Association on Mental Deficiency.

Bellfiore, P. J., & Dattilio, F. M. (1990). The behavior of self-injury: A brief review and analysis. *Behavioral Disorders, 16*(1), 23–31.

Berkman, K. A., & Meyer, L. H. (1988). Alternative strategies and multiple outcomes in the remediation of severe self-injury: Going "all out" non-aversively. *Journal of the Association of Severely Handicapped, 13*(2), 76–86.

Blechman, E. A. (1985). *Solving child behavior problems at home and at school.* Champaign, IL: Research Press.

Brigham, T. A., Hopper, C., Hill, B., de Armas, A., & Newsom, P. (1985). A self-management program for disruptive adolescents in the school: A clinical replication analysis. *Behavior Therapy, 16*, 99–115.

Brown, R. T., & Wynne, M. E. (1984). An analysis of attentional components in hyperactive and normal boys. *Journal of Learning Disabilities, 17*(3), 162–167.

Campbell, S. B., & Werry, J. S. (1986). Attention deficit disorder (hyperactivity). In H. C. Quay & J. S. Werry (Eds.), *Psychopathological disorders of childhood* (3rd ed., pp. 111–155). New York: John Wiley & Sons.

Center, D. B. (1990). Social maladjustment: An interpretation. *Behavioral Disorders, 15*(3), 141–148.

David, O. J., & Wintrob, H. L. (1989). Communication disturbances and hyperactive/conduct-disordered behavior. *Psychiatry, 52*, 379–392.

Davis, R. W., & Hajicek, J. O. (1985). Effects of self-instructional training and strategy training on a mathematics task with severely behaviorally disordered students. *Behavioral Disorders, 10*, 275–282.

Demchak, M. A., & Halle, J. W. (1985). Motivational assessment: A potential means of enhancing treatment success of self-injurious individuals. *Education and Training of the Mentally Retarded, 20*(1), 25–38.

Dubow, E. F., Huesmann, R., & Eron, L. D. (1987). Mitigating aggression and promoting prosocial behavior in aggressive elementary schoolboys. *Behavioral Research Therapy, 25*(6), 527–531.

Durand, V. M., & Carr, E. G. (1985). Self-injurious behavior: Motivating conditions and guidelines for treatment. *School Psychology Review, 14*(2), 171–176.

Edwards, V.N. (1991). Changes in routine can ease bedtime tantrums. *Growing Child Research Review, 9*(1), 5.

Etscheidt, S. (1991). Reducing aggressive behavior and improving self-control: A cognitive-behavioral training program for behaviorally disordered adolescents. *Behavioral Disorders, 16*(2), 107–115.

Favell, J. E., McGimsey, J. F., & Schell, R. M. (1982). Treatment of self-injury by providing alternate sensory activities. *Analysis and Intervention in Developmental Disabilities, 2,* 83–104.

Forehand, R. (1977). Child noncompliance to parental requests: Behavioral analysis and treatment. In M. Hersen, R. M. Eisler, & P. M. Miller (Eds.), *Progress in behavior modification* (Vol. 5, pp. 111–147). New York: Academic Press.

Fowler, S. A., Dougherty, B. S., Kirby, K. C., & Kohler, F. W. (1986). Role reversals: An analysis of therapeutic effects achieved with disruptive boys during their appointments as peer monitors. *Journal of Applied Behavior Analysis, 19,* 437–444.

Frankel, F., & Simmons, J. Q. (1985). Behavioral treatment approaches to pathological unsocialized physical aggression in young children. *Journal of Child Psychiatry, 26*(4), 525–551.

Fremont, T., Tedesco, J. F., & Trusty, N. (1988). Understanding conduct problems. *Behavior in Our Schools, 2*(2), 17–19.

Friedrich-Cofer, L., & Huston, A. C. (1986). Television violence and aggression: The debate continues. *Psychological Bulletin, 100*(3), 364–371.

Friman, P. C. (1990). Nonaversive treatment of high-rate disruption: Child and provider effects. *Exceptional Children, 57*(1), 64–69.

Gaynor, J. (1990). Attention deficit hyperactivity disorder may be etched in sand. *Beyond Behavior, 2*(1), 17–18.

Gordon, M. (1991). *ADHD/Hyperactivity: A consumer's guide for parents and teachers.* DeWitt, NY: GSI Publications.

Hallahan, D. P., Kauffman, J. J., & Lloyd, J. W. (1985). *Introduction to learning disabilities* (2nd ed.). Englewood Cliffs, NJ: Prentice Hall.

Hinshaw, S. P., Henker, B., & Whalen, C. K. (1984). Self-control in hyperactive boys in anger-inducing situations: Effects of cognitive-behavioral training and of methylphenidate. *Journal of Abnormal Child Psychology, 12*(1), 55–77.

Holden, G.W., & West, M.J. (1989). Proximate regulation by mothers: A demonstration of how differing styles affect young children's behavior. *Child Devleopment, 60,* 64–69.

Hollinger, J. D. (1987). Social skills for behaviorally disordered children as preparation for mainstreaming: Theory, practice and new directions. *Remedial and Special Education, 8,* 17–27.

Horner, R. D. (1980). The effects of an environment "enrichment" program on the behavior of institutionalized profoundly retarded children. *Journal of Applied Behavior Analysis, 13,* 473–491.

Iwata, B. A., Dorsey, M. F., Slifer, K. J., Bauman, K. E., & Richman, G. S. (1982). Toward a functional analysis of self-injury. *Analysis and Intervention in Developmental Disabilities, 2,* 3–20.

Iwata, B. A., Vollmer, T. R., & Zarcone, J. H. (1990). The experimental (functional) analysis of behavior disorders: Methodology, applications, and limitations. In A. C. Repp & N. N. Singh (Eds.), *Perspectives on the use of nonaversive and aversive interventions for persons with developmental disabilities* (pp. 301–330). Sycamore, IL: Sycamore Publishing Company.

Johnson, H.C. (1989). The disruptive child: Problems of definition. *Social Casework: The Journal of Contemporary Social Work, 70*(8), 469–478.

Kagan, J. (1966). Reflection-impulsivity: The generality and dynamics of conceptual tempo. *Journal of Abnormal Psychology, 71*, 17–24.

Kauffman, J. M. (1985). *Characteristics of children's behavior disorders* (3rd ed.). Columbus, OH: Merrill/Macmillan.

Kauffman, J. M. (1989). *Characteristics of children's behavior disorders* (4th ed.). Columbus, OH: Merrill/Macmillan.

Kerr, M. M., & Nelson, C. M. (1989). *Strategies for managing behavior problems in the classroom.* Columbus, OH: Merrill/Macmillan.

Kohn, A. (1989, November). Suffer the restless children. *The Atlantic Monthly,* 90–97.

Kounin, J. (1970). *Discipline and group management in classrooms.* New York: Holt, Rinehart, and Winston.

Kuczynski, L., Kochanska, G., Radke-Yarrow, M., & Girnius-Brown, O. (1987). A developmental interpretation of young children's noncompliance. *Developmental Psychology, 23*(6), 779–806.

Lancelotta, G. X., & Vaughn, S. (1989). Relation between types of aggression and sociometric status: Peer and teacher perceptions. *Journal of Educational Psychology, 81*(1), 86–90.

Landy, S., & Peters, R. D. (1990). Identifying and treating aggressive preschoolers. *Infants and Young Children, 3*(2), 24–38.

LaVigna, G.W., & Willis, T.J. (1991, February). *Nonaversive behavior modification.* Workshop presented by the Institute for Applied Behavior Analysis, Minneapolis, Minnesota.

Lay, K. L., Waters, E., & Park, K. A. (1989). Maternal responsiveness and child compliance: The role of mood as mediator. *Child Development, 60,* 1405–1411.

Lewis, M. H., Baumeister, A. A., & Mailman, R. B. (1987). A neurobiological alternative to the perceptual reinforcement hypothesis of stereotyped behavior: A commentary on "self-stimulatory behavior and perceptual reinforcement". *Journal of Applied Behavior Analysis, 20*, 253–258.

Lloyd, J. W., Bateman, D. F., Landrum, T. J., & Hallahan, D. P. (1989). Self-recording of attention versus productivity. *Journal of Applied Behavior Analysis, 22*, 315–323.

Lovaas, I., Newsom, C., & Hickman, C. (1987). Self-stimulatory behavior and perceptual reinforcement. *Journal of Applied Behavior Analysis, 20*, 45–68.

McConnell, S. R., & Odom, S. L. (1986). Sociometrics: Peer-referenced measures and the assessment of social competence. In P. S. Strain, M. J. Guralnick, & H. M. Walker (Eds.), *Children's social behavior:*

Development, assessment, and modification (pp. 215–284). Orlando, FL: Academic Press.

McGee, R., Williams, S., & Silva, P. A. (1985). Factor structure and correlates of ratings of inattention, hyperactivity, and antisocial behavior in a large sample of 9-year-old children for the general population. *Journal of Consulting and Clinical Psychology, 53*(4), 480–490.

McGinnis, E., & Goldstein, A. (1984). *Skillstreaming the elementary school child.* Champaign, IL: Research Press.

McIntyre, T. (1989). *A resource book for remediating common behavior and learning problems.* Boston, MA: Allyn and Bacon.

McMahon, C. (1989). *An evaluation of the multiple effects of a social skills intervention: An interactionist perspective.* Unpublished doctoral dissertation, University of Iowa.

McMahon, R. J., & Wells, K. C. (1989). Conduct disorders. In E. J. Mash & R. A. Barkley (Eds.), *Treatment of childhood disorders* (pp. 73–132). New York: Guilford Press.

Melloy, K. J. (1990). *Attitudes and behavior of non-disabled elementary-aged children toward their peers with disabilities in integrated settings: An examination of the effects of treatment on quality of attitude, social status and critical social skills.* Unpublished doctoral dissertation, University of Iowa.

Neel, R. S., Jenkins, Z. N., & Meadows, N. (1990). Social problem-solving behaviors and aggression in young children: A descriptive observational study. *Behavioral Disorders, 16*(1), 39–51.

O'Brien, M. A., & Obrzut, J. E. (1986). Attention deficit disorder with hyperactivity: A review and implications for the classroom. *The Journal of Special Education, 20*(3), 281–297.

Olson, S. L., Bates, J. E., Bayles, K. (1990). Early antecedents of childhood impulsivity: The role of parent-child interaction, cognitive competence, and temperament. *Journal of Abnormal Child Psychology, 18*(3), 317–334.

Paniagua, F. A., Morrison, P. B., & Black, S. A. (1990). Management of a hyperactive-conduct disordered child through correspondence training: A preliminary study. *Journal of Behavior Therapy and Experimental Psychiatry, 21*(1), 63–68.

Patterson, G. R., DeBaryshe, B. D., & Ramsey, E. (1989). A developmental perspective on antisocial behavior. *American Psychologist, 44,* 329–335.

Pfiffner, L. J., & O'Leary, S. G. (1987). The efficacy of all-positive management as a function of the prior use of negative consequences. *Journal of Applied Behavior Analysis, 20,* 265–271.

Quay, H. C. (1986). Conduct disorders. In H. C. Quay & J. S. Werry (Eds.), *Psychopathological disorders of childhood* (3rd ed., pp. 35–72). New York: John Wiley & Sons.

Repp, A. C., & Singh, N. N. (1990). *Perspectives on the use of nonaversive and aversive interventions for persons with developmental disabilities.* Sycamore, IL: Sycamore Publishing Company.

Rhode, G., Morgan, D. P., & Young, K. R. (1983). Generalization and maintenance of treatment gains of behaviorally handicapped students from
resource rooms to regular classrooms using self-evaluation procedures.
Journal ofApplied Behavior Analysis, 16, 171–188.

Rincover, A., & Devany, J. (1982). The application of sensory extinction
procedures to self-injury. *Analysis and Intervention in Developmental
Disabilities, 2,* 67–81.

Rocissano, L., Slade, A., & Lynch, V. (1987). Dyadic synchrony and toddler
compliance. *Developmental Psychology, 23*(5), 698–704.

Ross, D. M., & Ross, S. A. (1982). *Hyperactivity: Research, theory, action* (2nd
ed.). New York: Wiley.

Ruff, H. A., & Lawson, K. R. (1990). Development of sustained, focused attention in young children during free play. *Developmental Psychology, 26*(1),
85–93.

Ruff, H. A., Lawson, K. R., Parrinello, R., & Weissberg, R. (1990). Long term
stability of individual differences in sustained attention in the early
years. *Child Development, 61,* 60–75.

Sasso, G. M., Melloy, K. J., & Kavale, K. A. (1990). Generalization, maintenance, and behavioral covariation associated with social skills training
through structured learning. *Behavioral Disorders, 16*(1), 9–22.

Sasso, G. M., & Reimers, T. M. (1988). Assessing the functional properties of
behavior: Implications and applications for the classroom. *Focus on
Autistic Behavior, 3,* 1–15.

Schaub, J. M. (1990, March). *ADHD: Practical intervention strategies for the
classroom.* Presentation to the East Metro Special Education
Cooperative, Edina, Minnesota.

Shafrir, U., & Pascual-Leone, J. (1990). Postfailure reflectivity/impulsivity and
spontaneous attention to errors. *Journal of Educational Psychology,
82*(2), 378–387.

Sherburne, S., Utley, B., McConnell, S., & Gannon, J. (1988). Decreasing
violent or aggressive theme play among preschool children with behavior
disorders. *Exceptional Children, 55*(2), 166–172.

Smith, L. K., & Fowler, S. A. (1984). Positive peer pressure: The effects of peer
monitoring on children's disruptive behavior. *Journal of Applied
Behavior Analysis, 17,* 213–227.

Strain, P. S., Guralnick, M. J., & Walker, H. M. (1986). *Children's social
behavior: Development, assessment and modification.* New York:
Academic Press.

Taylor, G. (1990). Candy kisses and jaw breakers. *Beyond Behavior, 2*(1),
20–21.

Vitiello, B., Stoff, D., Atkins, M., & Mahoney, A. (1990). Soft neurological signs
and impulsivity in children. *Developmental and Behavioral Pediatrics,
11*(3), 112–115.

Wacker, D., Steege, M., Northup, J., Reimers, T., Berg, W., & Sasso, G. (1990).
Use of functional analysis and acceptability measures to assess and treat

severe behavior problems: An outpatient clinic model. In A. C. Repp & N. N. Singh (Eds.), *Perspectives on the use of nonaversive and aversive interventions for persons with developmental disabilities* (pp. 349–359). Sycamore, IL: Sycamore Publishing Company.

Wahler, R. G., & Dumas, J. E. (1986). "A chip off the old block": Some interpersonal characteristics of coercive children across generations. In P. S. Strain, M. J. Guralnick, & H. M. Walker (Eds.), *Children's social behavior: Development, assessment, and modification* (pp. 49–91). Orlando, FL: Academic Press.

Weinberg, L. A., & Weinberg, C. (1990). Seriously emotionally disturbed or socially maladjusted? A critique of interpretations. *Behavioral Disorders, 15*(3), 149–158.

White, A. G., & Bailey, J. S. (1990). Reducing disruptive behaviors of elementary physical education students with sit and watch. *Journal of Applied Behavior Analysis, 23,* 353–359.

Wicks-Nelson, R., & Israel, A. C. (1991). *Behavior disorders of childhood* (2nd ed.). Englewood Cliffs, NJ: Prentice Hall.

Widom, C. S. (1989). Does violence beget violence? A critical examination of the literature. *Psychological Bulletin, 106*(1), 3–28.

Zirpoli, T. J., & Lloyd, J. W. (1987). Understanding and managing self-injurious behavior. *Remedial and Special Education, 8*(5), 46–57.

PART FOUR

Special Considerations for Special Populations

CHAPTER 10

Issues in Early Childhood Behavior

Susan B. Zirpoli

Thomas J. Zirpoli, University of St. Thomas

Children require food, shelter, health care, educational opportunities, and
an environment that is free from harm. For a child to successfully learn
and grow—no matter what his or her biological risk status—the child
must have these basic requirements. Thus, every policy affecting children
must be based on this basic bill of rights.

—*Howard, 1990, p. 3*

The importance of understanding and effectively managing the behavior of young children cannot be overemphasized for several reasons. First, many caregivers of young children report that their biggest challenge is behavior management (Hersh & Walker, 1983). Most caregivers, however, have not received even the most basic training in this area. It is interesting how preoccupied we are with birthing classes and other methods of getting parents prepared for the delivery of their children, but how little attention—and even less education and support—society provides to parents during the critical preschool years. Even most professional educators have had little or no behavior management education during their preservice training. Thus, they are unable to provide appropriate guidance to the parents of the children they serve.

Second, appropriate social behaviors are positively correlated with academic performance. Children who stay on task, listen to their teachers, and follow classroom rules are more likely to be liked by both adults and peers (Bugental & Shennum, 1984) and succeed in the classroom (Hersh & Walker, 1983). Indeed, researchers have identified significant relationships between children's individual characteristics and how adults evaluate children's intelligence, personality, and other attributes (Zirpoli & Bell, 1987). These findings are especially significant when one studies the relationship between children's social behaviors and caregiver-child interaction patterns (Zirpoli, Snell, & Loyd, 1987). Children who have learned appropriate social behaviors have significant educational advantages over children who have not learned these basic skills. For example, children who have learned at home how to sit quietly and listen when a story is being read are likely to sit and listen to a story read by caregivers within the educational setting. Skills such as this can be learned at home, within a preschool setting, or both. Regardless of where they learn them, these children will have the social readiness skills that will help make them ready to learn and be successful in school.

Third, caregivers should have a good understanding of children's behavior because of the significant role caregivers play in the development of those behaviors. Young children learn appropriate and inappropriate social skills from many sources (Sasso, Melloy, & Kavale, 1990). The educational setting may provide the only structured setting in which prosocial behaviors are modeled and reinforced. Thus, the caregiver's role in the educational setting may take on additional significance for many children. Also, many early childhood programs are becoming less center-based and more home-based. Caregivers must be able to model and teach effective behavior management skills to the families they visit and serve.

Last, the best time to teach appropriate social behaviors effectively and prevent the development of inappropriate behaviors is when children are young. During these critical years of early development, children establish behavioral patterns while they learn the response value of appropriate and inappropriate behaviors. For example, children who learn at a young age that tantrum behaviors "work" are likely to use tantrum behaviors throughout childhood and into adolescence. Thus, it is important to teach children when they are young which behaviors are considered appropriate and which are not, and that appropriate behaviors are reinforced and inappropriate behaviors are not. We will talk about the efficacy of early intervention later in this chapter.

All children misbehave at times. This, of course, is normal. A caregiver's response to inappropriate behaviors, however, will frequently determine the future course for both the misbehavior and the child. As we mentioned, when a caregiver provides candy to a child following a temper tantrum, the child is likely to exhibit tantrum behavior in the future as a means of getting adult attention and having demands met. In fact, the frequency and intensity of tantrums will increase over time as the child learns how to use tantrum behavior to manipulate adult behavior. On the other hand, when a caregiver refuses to "give in" to a child's demands following a temper tantrum, the child is unlikely to demonstrate tantrum behavior in the future. Thus, the relationship is clear between the rate of children's misbehavior and the response they receive from significant caregivers.

When children misbehave, caregivers frequently focus on assessing and identifying what may be wrong with the *child,* what treatment or intervention might be best for the *child,* and so on. This focus-on-the-child approach fails to recognize the significant role of the child's *environment* and the people in that environment in shaping the child's behavior. In our fast-paced and busy world, caregivers seem to have less time to devote to the needs of their children than in previous times. Frequently, caregivers look for quick and easy answers to questions regarding children's inappropriate behavior. Today we believe that the blame-the-victim syndrome places too great an emphasis on how to "fix" children; instead we need greater emphasis on improving the quality of children's environments.

Much of the information in this text regarding understanding and management of behavior is applicable to children of all ages. Special understandings, however, apply to newborns and infants. Taking care of a newborn, especially for inexperienced caregivers, may be stressful. A basic understanding of infant behavior will help caregivers maintain realistic expectations *and* meet the needs of their children.

THE GROWING POPULATION OF YOUNG CHILDREN AT RISK

Today, more children are considered to be at risk for developing antisocial behaviors than ever before. Although this may seem impossible in view of the significant advances we have made in general health care and education, a growing population of children does not have access to the opportunities these advancements offer. For example, G. Miller (1989) noted a decrease in the number of women receiving prenatal care in America, especially among least-educated women.

In 1974, children replaced the elderly as the poorest subgroup of our nation's population. By 1980, the rate of poverty among preschool children was six times that of the elderly (Schorr & Schorr, 1989). The Center for the Study of Social Policy (1991) reported that more than 12 million children, or 20.1% of all American children, were growing up in poverty. Children raised within impoverished environments are at great risk for academic failure and challenging behavior problems. These children are living and developing in neighborhoods where there are limited positive role models for appropriate social behaviors. Frequently, the only adults they see who are making a "decent" living are making it in illegal activities, such as selling drugs and prostitution. The majority of these children do not have a father living in the home, and, each year, 500,000 children are born to mothers who themselves are children under the age of 18. Most of these mothers will drop out of high school, and the poverty cycle will continue for another generation. Schorr & Schorr (1989) suggested, however, that this cycle of poverty and "rotten outcomes" can be broken; we only need the will and resources to support the social programs that have proven effective both in cost and effect for at-risk children.

Premature/Dysmature Infants

Infants who are born premature (too soon) or dysmature (low birth weight) are likely to be especially challenging (i.e., frequent crying, poor sleeping patterns, difficult to feed). About 2% of all babies born in the United States are born prematurely and about 7% are classified as low birth weight (Batshaw & Perret, 1986). The majority of these births are to women who did not receive adequate nutritional and prenatal care. For example, the prematurity rate for babies born to teenage mothers is 20%. These infants frequently have trouble establishing regular sleeping patterns. They may be especially difficult to feed and, in general, to comfort. Crying behavior may be constant and irritating due to the high-pitched nature of the premature child's cry. It is no wonder that these infants are at risk for maltreatment by caregivers.

Caregivers need to know that these behaviors will decrease as the infant develops beyond the normal ninth month of gestation. Patience, support from others, and a sense of humor will get most caregivers through this difficult time. The behavior of most children born prematurely will be consistent with their peers before their second birthday.

Drugs and Alcohol

About 11% of all births, or approximately 400,000 infants, in the United States each year are affected by alcohol and other drugs (Weston, Ivins, Zuckerman, Jones, & Lopez, 1989). Rosenthal (1990) conservatively estimated the number of children born with fetal alcohol syndrome at 8000 per year, or 2.7 per 1000 live births. In some minority populations, the rate is significantly higher. For example, within the native American Indian population, 25% of all babies are reportedly alcohol-damaged (Rosenthal, 1990).

The long-term detrimental consequences on these children may include permanent neurobehavioral and affective disorders (Adler, 1989) and many other developmental disabilities. According to Howard (1990), approximately one-third of these children are born prematurely. Another one-third have been found to have some level of brain damage, primarily within the frontal lobe, which is the hub of higher cortical functioning. "Behavioral observations of these children indicate problems in the areas of impulsivity, increased activity levels, language dysfunction, social affective dysfunction, and disorganization in play" (Howard, 1990, p. 1). Rosenthal (1990) confirmed that these children tend to be impulsive, distractible, and uninhibited. Vignette 10.1 outlines other behavioral outcomes for children born addicted to cocaine.

Vignette 10.1.   Cocaine in the Womb: Some Behavioral Outcomes.

Cocaine is far more damaging to unborn babies than it is to their mothers. For her there is a brief high and the effects of the drug on her body are over within 48 hours. However, the drug remains in a concentrated form in the fluid surrounding the unborn infant for 4 to 5 days, constantly exposing the baby during critical months of development.

Damage to the baby is most severe during the first 3 months of pregnancy when organs are forming. There is increased likelihood for many things to go wrong. These include a) brain vessels burst causing a prenatal stroke, b) malformed kidneys and limbs, c) damage to the digestive and nervous system, d) deformed heart and lungs, and e) impaired muscle development.

These infants are irritable and jittery. With emotions "right on the edge," they can scream and be inconsolable one moment and fall asleep the next. They are unable to remain in a calm, alert state unless left alone. When a parent tries to talk or play with them, they get upset or fall asleep.

This is not only a profound negative effect on the baby's ability to form relationships, but can discourage the mother from trying to interact with her baby. A normal parent-child attachment lays the groundwork for developing trust and the ability to interact with others. These babies will not develop those basic skills and will be "at risk" in terms of getting along with others.

Drugs can interfere with memory, attention, and perception so these children are often easily distracted and frustrated. Observers see them as hyperactive and having difficulty in organizing information.

Source: Fact Find Sheet # 4. "Children of Cocaine: Facing the Issues," April 1990, by Erna Fishhaut, Center for Early Education and Development, University of Minnesota, Minneapolis, Minnesota. Reprinted by permission.

In addition to drugs and alcohol, other external substances pose a threat to the health and behavior of young children. For example, the National Health/Education Consortium (1991, p. 4) reported that "One American child in six has toxic levels of lead in his or her blood. Each year, 400,000 newborns are delivered with toxic levels of lead" which can be transferred from mother to fetus. Needleman and Gatsonis (1990) found that many children who had elevated lead levels demonstrated disorderly classroom behavior and had more need for special services such as behavioral counseling.

The increase in the number of children exposed to drugs, alcohol, and lead—placing them at risk for developmental and behavioral problems—is not occurring in isolation. Indeed, these are interrelated with more general societal problems. Between 1979 and 1986, the poverty rate for children under the age of five years rose 23%. Today, the poverty rate for children continues to increase to include 20% of all American children (The Center for the Study of Social Policy, 1991). "One in every five children lives in an environment characterized by substandard housing, poor nutrition, high social stress, and inadequate or nonexistent primary/preventive health care" (Baumeister, Kupstas, & Klindworth, 1990, p. 5). The effects on children's social behavior are significant. Again, preschool and other educators face far greater challenges from the children they serve than ever before (Howard, 1990).

Understanding the Maltreatment of Children

Child maltreatment, a generic term, may be used to describe negligence, physical injury, emotional or psychological injury, and sexual molestation by caregivers. Clearly, child maltreatment is the ultimate example of a dysfunctional interaction between caregivers and the children in their care. More than 2.5 million cases of child maltreatment are reported in the United States each year. This figure compares to one million cases reported in 1980 and half a million reported in 1976 (Zirpoli, 1990).

The study of child maltreatment allows researchers to understand the many and interacting variables associated with caregiver-child relationships and interaction patterns. These variables include social and cultural factors, environmental factors, characteristics of the caregiver, and the characteristics of the child or victim.

Social/Cultural Variables

Social and cultural factors have been noted as a significant contributing variable in the maltreatment of children in the United States. Straus, Gelles, and Steinmetz (1980) referred to the culturally sanctioned violence within families where spouse and child maltreatment are learned and are acceptable forms of interaction. Zigler and Hall (1989) and Rose (1983) reviewed the acceptance of physical punishment of children and found that the willingness of caregivers to employ physical punishment is the most significant determinant of child maltreatment in America. Violence seems to be embedded in our society, and this social acceptance of violence is directly related to the high prevalence of child maltreatment in America (Zirpoli, 1986).

Environmental Variables

Environmental conditions are frequently thought of as trigger variables in child maltreatment. That is, maltreatment is likely to occur under certain environmental conditions, which, given an already dysfunctional caregiver-child relationship, trigger inappropriate and abusive caregiver behavior. These conditions may include unemployment, household poverty, frustration, lack of social support, and general lack of family structure (Straus, Gelles, & Steinmetz, 1980).

Environmental conditions are especially problematic when there is little or no support system to help buffer the caregiver against the effects of these conditions. Neighborhood support groups, quality daycare and preschool programs, and other community services may provide assistance to caregivers and reduce environmental burdens to a tolerable level. Garbarino (1982) and Belsky and Vondra (1989) talked about the importance of social support systems for healthy families and noted that, as society has become more mobile, many caregivers find themselves separated from the natural support systems of their extended family and long-term friendships.

Caregiver Variables

Child maltreatment research has historically focused on the characteristics of the abusive caregiver. Current research, however, views the caregiver as a single, although significant, variable within a model of many interacting variables that cannot be separated and understood in isolation from each other (Pianta, Egeland, & Erickson, 1989).

Many abusive caregivers have unrealistic expectations about children and their behavior. This is especially true with new caregivers (e.g., adolescent parents) who have little or no knowledge of child development or of effective parenting. When combined with their own immaturity and the lack of appropriate social support, new caregivers may not be able to cope with the responsibilities of parenthood, and the children in their care may be considered at risk for maltreatment.

Caregivers who abuse their children are often victims of maltreatment themselves (Straus, Gelles, & Steinmetz, 1980). Many caregivers have only their own abusive caregivers from which to model and learn the skills of caring for children and how caregivers and children should interact. For example, Egeland, Jacobvitz, and Papatola (1984) followed 47 women who were physically maltreated as children and found that 70% were maltreating their children at two years of age. As long as other environmental and sociocultural factors continue to exist, the cycle of maltreatment is likely to continue.

Child Variables

Although children who are maltreated should never be blamed for the maltreatment they receive from caregivers, it is helpful to understand the variables that may place some children at greater risk. The idea that children affect caregiver behavior (known as *child effects*) has received considerable attention during the past two decades beginning with Richard Bell's review of the parent-child relationship as a reciprocal relationship (Bell, 1968; Bell & Harper, 1977). As professionals began to realize the significant contribution children make toward caregiver-child interactions, interest in the characteristics of children maltreated by caregivers has increased considerably (Rusch, Hall, & Griffin, 1986; Zirpoli, 1986; Zirpoli, Snell, & Loyd, 1987).

Research has shown that younger children are at greater risk for maltreatment than older children. Premature infants, representing less than 10% of all births, have been reported to represent up to half the cases of child maltreatment (Fontana, 1971). Pianta, Egeland, and Erickson (1989) reported that toddlers are more likely to be maltreated than school-age children.

Premature infants present an excellent example for understanding child effects. These infants are prone to colic, irritability, and restlessness. They have irregular sleeping and eating patterns and may be difficult to feed. Premature infants may have an annoying and irritating cry and usually require additional parental care and attention. Combined with certain caregiver, environmental, and sociocultural factors, one can easily understand how premature infants may be at greater risk for maltreatment by caregivers who are already stressed by other family and environmental challenges.

Some debate exists concerning the extent or degree of child effects on caregiver behavior, specifically concerning the role of child effects in child maltreatment. Some professionals believe that child effects are short term and situational and that child effects do not account for the quality of caregiving over time (Starr, 1982). It is generally agreed, however, that some child characteristics have been associated with maltreatment, but that these characteristics alone are not enough to predict future child maltreatment. The following statement reinforces this point:

> To the extent that the child with extreme individual differences is placed in a family which may not be ready to parent, characteristics of that child may exacerbate an already difficult situation. This child may become the victim of maltreatment, not because of its own behavior, but because the child places added burdens upon an already stressed or incapable family system, resulting in a breakdown in the processes of good parenting. (Pianta, Egeland, & Erickson, 1989, p. 203)

An overview of antecedents and consequences of child maltreatment is provided in Vignette 10.2.

Vignette 10.2.   Antecedents and Consequences of Maltreatment.

Mother-Child Project at the University of Minnesota   The Mother-Child Project is a longitudinal study of high risk children and their families. The parents were at risk for child abuse, neglect and other forms of maltreatment and the children were at risk for poor developmental outcomes. The children currently are 13 and 14 years old. The mothers were at risk due to their low socioeconomic status and all the risk factors associated with poverty. For example, the mean age of mothers at birth of their child was 20.5, range 12 to 37 years; 62 percent were single; only 13 percent of the biological fathers were in the home at 18 months; and 40 percent had not completed high school.

Comprehensive assessments of the family began during the last trimester of pregnancy and have continued at regularly scheduled intervals through the sixth grade. Briefly, some selected findings from our studies of the antecedents and consequences of maltreatment are as follows:

1. The incidence of maltreatment appears to be much greater than the figures commonly reported in the literature.
2. The consequences of maltreatment were severe and none of the children were invulnerable to the negative effects of maltreatment.
3. At each assessment from infancy through the sixth grade there were increasing numbers of children who were having problems.
4. By third grade 60 percent of the children were receiving some form of special education services. Despite receiving services these children continue to fall further behind. The problems they bring to school make it difficult for them to profit from special services regardless of how good the teacher or curriculum. Intervention with these children needs to include more than good educational services. It must include a comprehensive, intensive approach which also involves their families.
5. The effects of neglect and emotionally unresponsive caretaking were as devastating as physical abuse.
6. A major antecedent of maltreatment was the parent's history of having been abused as a child. The factors related to breaking the cycle of abuse have implications for intervention and prevention.
7. The child's environment (e.g., an organized, predictable home environment, secure attachment between mother and infant) was associated with resilience in the early elementary grades.

8. Most parents of the children who are having difficulty in school have no involvement with the school. This needs to be a consideration in educational planning.

9. To some degree an organized classroom where the teacher provides clear expectations for the child seems to serve as a protective factor.

Source: Egeland, B. (1990). Summary of findings from the Mother-Child Project and implications for program and policy (pp. 1–2). In *Crossing the boundaries between health and education.* Washington, DC: The National Health/Education Consortium. Reprinted by permission.

Breaking the Cycle of Child Maltreatment

Given the variables associated with child maltreatment, how can we help in breaking the cycle? Some solutions require significant changes in national priorities and attitudes. Caregivers, however, are in the best position to advocate for these changes.

First, we must put an end to the widespread tolerance of physical punishment of children. As caregivers, we can start in our own homes and educational settings. Second, we must advocate a highest priority status for our nation's children and the issues related to their protection and enrichment (physical, mental, and emotional). This means full funding for Head Start, the Women, Infants and Children (WIC) program, and other effective programs that serve our nation's impoverished children. Third, we must ensure that all caregivers, regardless of background or income, have the appropriate, necessary community support to provide their children with a protecting, healthy, and enriching environment. This means appropriate prenatal care for *all* women, appropriate medical care for *all* children, and quality educational settings for *all* children, regardless of family income or ability to pay. These are sound investments for the future of our nation's children.

THE EFFICACY OF EARLY INTERVENTION

More and more young children are attending some type of preschool setting outside the home. The increase in maternal employment outside the home, single-parent families, and families with two working parents are the primary reasons for the greater demand for early childhood programs. For many children, these programs provide early, quality intervention with many beneficial outcomes, for example, the opportunity to develop appropriate social skills necessary for success in elementary school and beyond. Weikart (1990) said that the demand for greater quality programs is directly related to the growing recognition that good early childhood programs produce positive outcomes for children's development.

Although more children are attending preschool than ever before, the number of children entering kindergarten or first grade without basic readiness skills is also increasing. These readiness skills include basic social behaviors such as listening, compliance, following directions, and staying-in-seat and on-task behaviors. Caregivers, especially educators and pediatricians, report a significant increase in children who are considered "behavior problems," especially children considered hyperactive and aggressive (Newacheck, Budetti, & Halfon, 1986). Also, the number of preschool children labeled with some type of disability, especially a behavioral disability, is increasing at an alarming rate.

At least some of the increase in behavior problems may be attributed to both the growing number of children living in impoverished environments and the numbers of children born addicted to drugs, such as cocaine, or suffering the effects of maternal alcoholism. These children represent a new population of preschoolers and young elementary school children with challenging behaviors and other disabilities not yet totally understood. Although the long-term outcome for these children is unknown, educators must now be prepared to serve this new and challenging population.

Children considered at risk because of prematurity, dysmaturity, alcohol and drug effects, and general poverty are best served early in life. The earlier intervention begins, the better the short- and long-term outcomes for children and their families. Early childhood intervention programs such as Head Start have had and continue to have dramatic effects on the lives of children considered at risk for developmental problems and antisocial behaviors (Gallagher & Ramey, 1990; Smith, 1990). Unfortunately, because of lack of funding, only 20 to 30% of children who qualify for programs such as Head Start are able to receive these services (Smith, 1990).

Long-term studies have found that high-risk children who participated in quality preschool programs had a 40 to 60% reduction in crime, a 50% reduction in teen-age births, a 50% reduction in welfare payments, a 30 to 50% increase in high school graduation and college attendance, and a 50% increase in employment compared to their high-risk peers who did not have the same early intervention opportunities (Hodgkinson, 1989; K. Miller, 1989). Weikart (1990), in a review of eight long-term studies on the effects of quality early childhood programs, also found a reduction in crime, teen pregnancy, and welfare utilization, as well as an increase in high school graduation rates and employment.

In a four-year study of 985 premature babies who weighed five and a half pounds or less at birth, the children and families that received early intervention and services were found at the age of three to have IQ scores that averaged 13 points higher than those children who did not participate in an early intervention program. Babies in the control group were nearly three times more likely to be mentally disabled (Sparling, Lewis, Ramey, Wasik, Bryant, & LaVange, 1991).

Several studies have shown that immediate IQ gains attributed to participation in early childhood intervention programs were followed by a steady decline. Three to four years after the termination of early intervention, IQ scores do not differ between children who participated in early intervention and children who did not (Lazar, Darlington, Murray, Royce, & Sniper, 1982). However, children who had early intervention did perform better on achievement tests, were less likely to need special education services or be retained in a grade, and had more positive attitudes toward achievement and school (Scarr & Weinberg, 1986). The following list provides a summary of numerous research studies relating to the impact of the Head Start program.

- ◆ *Cognitive effects:* Children involved in Head Start make substantial gains in all cognitive components during their Head Start experience. They demonstrate a test score advantage over control groups of children who did not attend Head Start.
- ◆ *Socioemotional effects:* Children involved in Head Start make meaningful gains in self esteem, achievement, motivation and especially in social behaviors during their Head Start experience.
- ◆ *Health effects:* Children involved in Head Start are healthier as a result of their participation in Head Start. They have a level of general pediatric and dental health comparable to more advantaged children. Their nutritional intake is better than children who do not attend. Significant improvements can be seen in the motor coordination and development of all participating children and particularly among children with physical handicaps.
- ◆ *Family effects:* Parents are generally positive about their children's experience and are satisfied with the benefits they receive from Head Start. Parents who actively participate in the program feel better about themselves, improve their economic and social status and have children with high levels of developmental achievement. Head Start programs also link families with a wide range of health and social services. Head Start has also had mixed success in influencing parental child rearing practices in the home.
- ◆ *Community effects:* Head Start has a positive impact on providing increased social and health services for the poor and affecting more responsive educational programs among public school institutions.[1]

Variables Associated With Effective Early Intervention

Quality early childhood programs have several major components. First, in addition to serving children during their early development, effective programs aim to serve children at the prenatal and early infancy periods—and, again, the earlier services are provided, the better the outcome for child and family.

___

[1] *Source:*   Smith, A. N. (1990). Summary impact of Head Start on children, youth, and families (pp. 1–2). Washington, DC: The National Health/Education Consortium. Reprinted by permission.

Research has clearly demonstrated that mothers who receive quality prenatal care have babies who are at lower risk for developmental and behavioral disorders (Bricker, 1982; Ensher & Clark, 1986; Garbarino & Ramey, 1990; Schorr & Schorr, 1989). Second, effective programs have a low caregiver-to-child ratio, with no more than 16 to 20 three- to five-year-olds for every two adults (Weikart, 1990). Third, parental participation is essential to the effective early childhood program. Professional caregivers must work with parents as *partners* in their children's development, and effective programs provide services to the *family* in addition to the children (Egeland, 1990; Lazar, 1981; Weikart, 1990). Last, research has also found that home-based programs are more effective than center-based programs (Smith, 1990).

McDonnell & Hardman (1988) outlined six best practice guidelines for the most effective early childhood services:

◆ Services must be *integrated*. Children with mental and behavioral disabilities should receive supported placement in generic early childhood sites where there is planned and systematic contact with nondisabled peers.

◆ Services, including assessment, planning, programming, and evaluation, must be *comprehensive* and delivered using a transdisciplinary model.

◆ Services must be *normalized* with age appropriate skills and instructional strategies, avoidance of artificial reinforcement and aversive control techniques, and support for the parenting role.

◆ Services must be *adaptable* and *flexible*. Programming must meet individual needs and support different family structures.

◆ Services must be *peer and family referenced*. Curricula must be referenced to the individual child, family, and community. Parents must be full partners with ongoing communication between family and service providers.

◆ Services must be *outcome-based* and evaluated using a variety of outcome measures. Curricula must be functional for current and future needs, and include transitional training.

UNDERSTANDING THE BEHAVIOR OF YOUNG CHILDREN

By the time of birth, an infant's brain, at two-thirds the size of an adult brain, is remarkably complete. Recent research has found that three months before birth, a fetus has already developed 10 billion neurons, nearly the full complement of brain maturity. Neurons are the single nerve cells that serve as the functional unit of the nervous system. They are created at the average rate of 40,000 every minute for the first 180 days after conception. (National Health/Education Consortium, 1991)

Newborns are totally dependent on others. For the most part, their behavior is directly related to their physical condition and environment. Newborns cry when they need to be changed, when they are hungry, or when they are in some sort of discomfort (Pomeranz, 1986). Newborns do not cry in order to manipulate their parents into giving them excessive attention. A newborn's crying is not a learned behavior that will increase if parents or other caregivers respond to the child's needs. In other words, you cannot spoil a newborn. The newborn needs lots of caregiver attention, warmth, and love. He or she will develop a sense of security knowing that there are caregivers willing and able to care for his or her basic needs.

Attachment in infants has been studied extensively by Ainsworth (1979) and Bowlby (1982). Ainsworth (1979) found that mothers of securely attached infants were more responsive to their infants' basic needs, and that the infants were more cooperative and less aggressive in their interaction with their mothers than "anxiously attached" infants.

Between the third and sixth months, infants begin to develop an understanding of the relationship between their behavior and responses from others (Ensher & Clark, 1986). About this time, infants may begin to use a variety of behaviors, including crying, simply to seek the attention of others, especially significant others such as parents. At this time, caregivers may begin to regulate their response to these behaviors so that appropriate behaviors are reinforced and inappropriate behaviors are not.

At around six months of age, children may exhibit several inconvenient or even irritating behaviors that represent a passage through normal cognitive and motor stages of development. For example, the child may enjoy dropping things from the high chair and looking to see where the object goes. With this simple behavior, the child begins to learn about cause and effect and object permanence. Thus, a six-month-old child should not be punished for these "learning" behaviors.

A significant milestone for the seven- to eight-month-old infant is the development of anxiety toward strangers. It is during this time that the infant demonstrates a strong attachment to the primary caregiver, usually the mother. Parents frequently feel the need to apologize for their child's crying and clinging during separation. Caregivers should be assured that the child is developing normally and understand that, especially during this period, the child needs reassurance and comfort (Woolfolk, 1987). By the time the infant approaches 18 months, he or she will be able to cope with separation from the primary caregiver. Attachment to many others is evident in their ease at being with other familiar caregivers.

At 6 to 8 months, children want to crawl around and explore (learn). Caregivers should provide safe places for the child to explore rather than confine the child to a playpen or crib for long periods. At 9 to 12 months, the child will be cruising furniture and, by 12 to 18 months, walking. Again, providing a safe environment allows children to explore and develop new cognitive and motor skills.

Feeding time for infants and young children is likely to be challenging for caregivers. At 6 months of age, the infant may push the spoon away from the feeder to show that he is finished. The 9-month-old is beginning to feed himself crackers and toast. By 15 months, finger feeding is typical. Being able to use a cup without spilling may be seen by 18 months. The point is that learning to eat and drink is part of normal development and that opportunities for self-feeding should be allowed. Young children are not neat eaters, but rather than punishing them for their messes and spills, caregivers should make cleanup easier by pouring only small amounts of liquids into cups, putting drop cloths under high chairs, and using appropriate child-sized utensils. If children start to throw food or drop it on the floor, remove the food for a short time (two to three minutes) and say, "No throwing food on the floor." Children will soon get the message that this is unacceptable behavior.

By the end of the first year, children begin to show interest in other children. They frequently enjoy being around other children and playing beside them. Expecting a one-year-old to play with other children, however, is unrealistic. They delight in exploring other children, which may take the form of hair pulling, poking (particularly around the face), and grabbing toys. Putting objects in their mouth is still a primary means of exploration for the one-year-old—and that may even include biting other children. Although these actions may appear to be aggressive, they are simply the child's way of exploring his environment.

Language development is a critical component of early development. By the end of the first year, the child typically speaks one-word utterances (which consist primarily of nouns) and can name familiar objects such as "bottle," "cup," "milk," "ball," and "mommy." By the second birthday, children are usually capable of speaking two-word utterances such as "mommy go," "kitty run," "bite finger," and "dolly hat." Parents frequently understand the language of their young children even when no one else can. For example, a child who points to the refrigerator and says "milk" is understood by the parent to mean "Mommy, I'm thirsty. Could you please give me a glass of milk." Unfortunately, because of limited language development, a child is often unable to communicate his wants and needs to caregivers. The young child who is tired, unhappy, wet, or in need of a hug may become frustrated and express himself through crying, tantrums, or other means that caregivers judge inappropriate. But they must understand that the child may not possess the words to express himself. Caregivers are usually on the right track to comfort distressed toddlers and try to read the body language which may be saying "I'm tired" or "I'm wet." Providing basic needs such as warmth, food, sleep, and physical contact should be the first intervention when comforting young children.

By the time children reach their second birthday, they should be on the way to developing an awareness of some basic behaviors considered appropriate and inappropriate. Behavior rules may apply to the home, car, preschool, grocery store, and so on. The toddler learns these rules when caregivers verbally repeat the rules and praise compliance. On the other hand, toddlers learn not to follow rules if they do not clearly understand them and when caregivers are inconsistent with enforcement. For example, young children learn that they must always sit in the car seat when traveling by hearing about the importance of the car seat, consistently using the car seat, and never, under any circumstances, traveling in the car without using the car seat (regardless of crying or other tantrum behaviors).

Young children are quick to learn their limits and their ability to amend the limits established by caregivers. It is up to caregivers to set clear limits and be consistent in enforcing of those limits. Children develop an understanding of the word "no" by their first birthday. Caregivers should avoid saying "no" when they don't really mean "no." Children quickly learn that the word "no" may have a different meaning for some caregivers. For example, a child may learn that for some caregivers, "no" means "maybe." Around these caregivers, children are likely to be noncompliant and exhibit other challenging behaviors.

During the first two years of life, children progress rapidly in many areas. By the end of the second year, the child is beginning to develop a sense of self; however, young children continue to need structure in their environments as much as they need room and freedom to explore. Some caregivers believe the two are incompatible; they are not. In fact, young children who feel secure within a structured environment will feel free to explore and take risks within

Children model the behavior of significant others such as parents, siblings, and friends.

the boundaries established by loving care-givers. Table 10.1 provides an overview of some of the important behavioral milestones in young children.

APPROPRIATE CAREGIVING FOR YOUNG CHILDREN

Establishing a Caring and Loving Environment

Children need to know that they are loved and accepted. Even very young children develop an understanding about how caregivers feel about them. They listen to what caregivers say to them and to others about them, and they observe how caregivers behave. Children who feel secure in their environment and in their relationships with caregivers are less likely to misbehave as a way of getting inappropriate attention.

Behavior	Age of Onset Range (months)	Behavior	Age of Onset Range (months)
Responds positively to comfort	0–1	Uses words to make wants known	14–27
Looks at face	0–1	Plays independently for short time	16–20
Vocalizes	0–6	Develops multiple attachments	16–20
Demonstrates social smile	.5–3	Knows when a familiar person is gone	16–22
Can quiet self with sucking	.5–3	Able to put away toys when asked	17–23
Shows distress and excitement	.5–3	Obeys simple commands	18–23
Discriminates mother from others	2–4	Shows that he/she is jealous	18–24
Cries real tears	2–4	Wants to help with simple jobs	18–24
Aware of strange situations	2–6	Enjoys listening to short stories	18–24
Laughs	3–5	Answers questions	18–29
Discriminates strangers	3–8	Refers to self by name	18–30
Vocalizes to self in mirror	5–7	Demonstrates parallel play	18–30
Laughs at games (peek-a-boo)	5–7	Begins to share toys	20–26
Cooperates in games	5–12	Initiates own play activities	24–36
Follows simple directions	6–12	Relates experiences	24–36
Makes facial expressions to others	7–9	Demonstrates parallel play and role play	28–32
Shows separation and stranger anxiety	8–10	Plays cooperatively at K-level	36–48
Tugs at adults to get attention	8–12	Helps at little household tasks	36–48
Understands the word "No"	8–18	"Performs" for others	36–48
Jabbers expressively	9–18	Asks questions rhetorically	30–42
Imitates words	9–18	Demonstrates group play	36–48
Shows affection	10–14	Plays cooperatively with other children	42–54
Shows interest in other children	10–14	Plays competitive exercise games	48–60
Throws toys on the floor	11–15	Calls attention to own performance	48–60
Uses gestures to make wants known	11–19	Shows affection and hostility with peers	46–50
Enjoys showing things to adults	12–16	Has many fantasy fears	46–50
Discriminates edible substances	12–24	Increases in cooperative play	58–62
Shows mood	13–17	Shows many real fears	58–62
Sits at table for short time	14–18	Increases in organized play with rules	68–76

Table 10.1.   *Important behavioral milestones in young children.*
Sources: From Bayley, N. (1969). *Bayley Scales of Infant Development.* New York: The Psychological Corporation; Frankenburg, W., and Dodds, J. (1981). *Denver Developmental Screening Test-Revised.* Denver, CO: Ladoca Publishing Foundation; and Sparrow, S., Balla, D., and Cicchetti, D. (1985). *Vineland Adaptive Behavior Scales.* Circle Pines, NY: American Guidance Service.

When a child misbehaves, caregivers are likely to focus on the child and the child's behavior in an effort to stop the inappropriate behavior and prevent its recurrence. It may be difficult for the caregiver to understand how the environment may be a contributing factor to the misbehavior (Barkley, 1987; LaVigna & Donnellan, 1986). Environmental variables that may contribute to the misbehavior include:

◆ the behavior of the caregiver (e.g., is misbehavior reinforced?);
◆ the behavior of others in the environment (e.g., how do peers respond to the child's behavior?); and
◆ factors relating to the environment in which the child exhibits the behavior (e.g, physical environment, cognitive and social demands).

We will look at three suggestions as to how caregivers can demonstrate to young children that they are loved, liked, and accepted.

Tell Children You Like Them

A caregiver cannot assume that children know someone likes them—you must tell them! Caregivers should get into the daily habit of telling children that they are liked. Some caregivers may have a very difficult time saying "I like you" or expressing positive feelings to the children placed in their care. If expressing feelings in this way becomes part of the daily routine, however, caregivers will find it becomes easier to do so. Children should leave their educational setting saying "My teacher really likes me!"

Families who communicate their feelings about each other when children are young will have an easier time expressing feelings when the children become adolescents. Thus, efforts to communicate affection when children are young provide an investment for future parent-child communication patterns.

Educators can help children establish healthy attitudes about expressing their feelings in the classroom. Talking about feelings and giving children opportunities to talk about how they feel teach children that their feelings are real and part of being a person. It also gives educators a chance to teach children how to identify, be sensitive to, and respect the feelings of others. These lessons will help provide a solid foundation for the development of appropriate social skills.

Set Aside Individual Time

Set aside some special time, if only a few minutes per day, with each child. Use this time to talk and listen to the child and to let that child know how important he or she is. These private conversations also give children a chance to express any feelings, concerns, or reactions to the day's events. Moreover, regardless of how difficult the day has been for both of you, this special time provides an opportunity for at least one positive caregiver-child interaction.

Many children do not have a significant adult in their lives outside the school environment. They may live in a single-parent household with a parent who is busy and preoccupied with trying to support the family. We all know how important it is for children and adolescents to have one special adult to talk to, share their feelings, and provide positive feedback and support. Often that adult is a teacher or counselor from the child's school. Educators need to be aware of these social needs and willing to give some time (even a few minutes each day) to show a student that someone cares.

Give Children Affection

With all the attention to and appropriate concern about the sexual abuse of children, some caregivers are hesitant to touch, hug, or otherwise express affection toward the children in their care. Some schools have even told educators not to touch their students. This is very unfortunate. Children need affection to develop normally and to be emotionally happy and secure. Children in today's society spend more and more time out of their homes and away from loving parents. Thus, the affection of other caregivers becomes even more crucial, especially for infants and young children. Schools are encouraged to develop policies that also outline acceptable touching (e.g., pats on the shoulders, handshakes).

Building Self-Esteem

Children who have healthy self-esteem are usually happy children who feel good about themselves and others. Happy, self-assured children are likely to interact positively with caregivers and other children. In addition to the social and behavioral benefits, healthy self-esteem is positively related to academic achievement.

Demonstrating to children that they are loved, liked, and accepted is the first step to building their self-esteem. We can now look at some specific suggestions for increasing children's self-esteem.

Allow and Enable Children to be Competent

Hendrick said, "the purpose of early education is to foster competence in young children" (1990, p. 4). Competence is the self-assured feeling that one is capable of doing something "all by myself." Teachers and parents alike can help children participate in competence-building activities by allowing them to do things for themselves. Caregivers who provide opportunities for children to wash dishes after snacks or meals at low sinks, or who give preschoolers jobs (e.g., feeding the family dog, being the leader at school) are providing children with opportunities to feel competent.

Tell Children About the Good Things They Do

Too often caregivers focus on children's *inappropriate* behaviors instead of *appropriate* behaviors. When this happens, children are taught to associate caregiver attention with inappropriate behaviors. As a result, inappropriate behaviors increase. Unfortunately, it seems easier to focus on inappropriate behaviors than appropriate behaviors. Caregivers must make every effort to give greater attention to the appropriate things children do. This can be accomplished by telling children "You're such a good worker" or "I like the way you played with John" or "I liked the way you solved that problem with Mary." Make it a point to attend to the good things children are doing. Teach the children that there is an association between caregiver attention and *appropriate* behavior.

Speak to Children Appropriately

Many caregivers do not understand how their own behaviors teach appropriate and inappropriate behaviors to children. Caregivers influence children's learning every time they interact with them. Two things are important to keep in mind when speaking to children. First, *what* you say is important. Sarcastic, negative statements promote feelings of worthlessness. If a child does something inappropriate and you must say something, talk about the *behavior,* not the child. Although their behaviors may sometimes be bad, children are never bad. To maintain a child's dignity and self-worth, describe what the child did that you don't like, but don't criticize the child as a person. Inappropriate statements from a significant caregiver may severely damage a child's self-esteem.

Second, *how* you speak to children is very important. Some caregivers believe that the louder they shout, the more effective they will be in changing children's behaviors. However, talking to children firmly, but calmly, is more effective in both the short and long term. In addition, when caregivers stop shouting, the environment becomes a calmer place for children to learn and develop. Children exhibit less inappropriate behavior within calm, positive environments where they are getting lots of attention for appropriate behaviors (Hetherington & Martin, 1986).

Teach Children that Mistakes Are Normal

Everybody makes mistakes. When children make mistakes, tell them that everyone makes mistakes and that no one is perfect. Caregivers have opportunities to model appropriate ways to deal with mistakes whenever they commit an error, for example, by saying "I was wrong and I am sorry" when a mistake is made. Children who observe this behavior are more likely to say "I was wrong" or "I am sorry" when they make mistakes because they will feel confident that it is all right to make mistakes. Also, children will not be afraid to try new things when they are not worried about successful outcomes (Woolfolk, 1987).

Teaching young children that it is normal to make mistakes and to talk about their mistakes will help them confront and talk about mistakes as adolescents and adults. Being able to say "I was wrong and I am sorry" will serve as a functional behavior throughout the child's life and across all social settings.

Allow Children to Have Choices

Children will learn how to make good choices if they are allowed to practice making choices from an early age. Some choices young children can make include selecting books or stories to read before bedtime, choosing juice to drink during snack time, deciding what clothes to wear, and so on. Giving children choices is an excellent way to reduce power struggles. Caregivers frequently feel that, to be in control of children's behavior, they must resort to giving directives. Sometimes, directives are appropriate; however, young children who are struggling to develop their independence may respond negatively to a lack of choices, leading to a cycle of caregiver versus child battles. Of course, caregivers should limit the range of choices. For example, when we say that children may choose what to drink, the caregiver first limits the choice ("Do you want orange juice or apple juice?"). In this way, mature adults remain in control while providing opportunities for children to make safe choices.

Everyday events provide opportunities to discuss choices. For example, when children fight over a toy, caregivers can use the event to help children think about alternative behaviors and choose appropriate behaviors on their own. Asking questions about their behaviors (such as "Can you think of another way of telling John that you want to play with that toy?") and giving them an opportunity to explore alternatives and consider the consequences of their behaviors ("How do you think John would feel about that?") are other ways to teach children how to make choices about their behaviors.

Hendrick reported that children who are allowed to make choices are more creative. She says that "for an experience to be creative for children, it must be generated from within them, not be an experience 'laid on' from outside" (1990, p. 250). For example, rather than providing children with coloring books during art activities in a classroom, the teacher could provide collage materials for children to create their own original artwork. Sometimes, caregiver-directed activities provide limited opportunities for problem-solving. Indeed, children who are given choices may have an advantage when it comes to solving problems related to their social behavior. For example, the child who divides and shares his blocks with a friend is able to plan a solution to the problem (i.e., both children wanting to play with blocks), rather than acting on the immediate impulse to be possessive.

Let Children Know You Value Their Opinions

When children are reinforced for expressing their own opinions, they learn the value of their personhood, in addition to the value of their feelings, beliefs, and opinions. Children can be encouraged to develop their own feelings and ideas and to express their own opinion when caregivers ask "What do you think?" or

"How do you feel about that?" These kinds of queries let children know that they (and their feelings) are important, too. In addition, this is a great way to teach and practice how to interact and converse appropriately with adults and other children.

Respect Individual Differences

Caregivers must teach that all children are unique, that their own differences should be recognized and appreciated, and that they should recognize and appreciate the differences in others. Lyle (1990) suggested the following activities to encourage children to recognize and appreciate their differences:

◆ Ask the children to talk about things that make their families special.
◆ Have the children develop and share their autobiographies.
◆ Have the children interview each other about their backgrounds, physical differences, and so on.
◆ Encourage children to express their ideas even when they are different from their peers.

VARIABLES ASSOCIATED WITH APPROPRIATE BEHAVIOR IN YOUNG CHILDREN

Several variables are associated with appropriate behavior in young children. The absence of these variables has been found to place children at risk for antisocial behaviors. These variables include the level of adult supervision, consistency of consequences, readiness for academic achievement, and environmental considerations.

Supervision

The strongest predictor of appropriate behavior in children is the quantity and quality of caregiver supervision (Kauffman, 1989; Patterson, 1971, 1982). When caregivers monitor children's behavior—where the children play and who their children play with—they are showing children that they care about their well-being, that there are specific physical and behavioral boundaries, and that there are caregivers who will monitor their safety. Caregivers must strive for a healthy balance between restrictiveness and permissiveness. When caregivers are overly restrictive, children tend to be submissive, dependent, and unable to take risks. When caregivers are overly permissive, children tend to be noncompliant, delinquent, and careless. Lack of caregiver supervision is also related to children's association with property destruction (e.g., breaking toys) (Patterson, 1982). Hetherington and Martin (1986) stated that children will have positive outcomes when parental discipline is firm, consistent, but loving and responsive.

Consistency

Perhaps the most significant variable in managing young children's behavior is consistency. "Consistency helps make an environment predictable" (Bailey & Wolery, 1984, p. 242). Consistency builds understanding and trust between caregivers and children. Children learn what to expect and what is acceptable and unacceptable behavior when caregivers are consistent in what they say and how they respond. Children learn the likely consequences for their behaviors when caregivers consistently follow through.

In the absence of consistency, children are likely to be rebellious when caregivers finally do try to respond to inappropriate behaviors. Research has shown that caregivers who are inconsistent when disciplining children tend to be harsh and hostile in responding to inappropriate behaviors (Doke & Flippo, 1983). This inconsistent and hostile relationship is associated with children's aggressive, noncompliant, and delinquent behavior (Martin, 1975). Zirpoli (1986) found that inconsistent discipline is associated with dysfunctional and abusive caregiver-child interactions.

Readiness Skills

When young children enter school, at either the preschool or elementary level, educators have certain expectations about their skills and behavior. Unfortunately, many young children do not have the skills or behaviors to meet even minimal teacher expectations. The percentage of young children entering educational settings without basic readiness skills is increasing (Hodgkinson, 1989). The potential outcome for these children includes social and academic failure, poor relationships with educators and peers, and the risk of falling further and further behind the norm throughout their school years.

Parents and early childhood caregivers can improve the chances of success for young children entering school by teaching them basic readiness skills and behaviors. These school readiness or academic survival skills include:

- appropriate social interactions with caregivers (listening, compliance, following directions),
- appropriate social interactions with peers (sharing, playing, turn-taking), and
- appropriate environmental behaviors (use of toys and other materials, in-seat behavior, attention to environmental cues).

Caregivers teach these skills through verbal instructions and practice. We have already provided the example about children who have been read to from an early age; they are likely to sit and listen when caregivers read a story within an educational setting. Sitting and listening are not just behaviors; they are skills that children must learn. Children who learn to share and cooperate from an early age are likely to get along with their peers in later years. Children who learn to take care of their toys and not to be destructive are likely to generalize these skills and behaviors to the school environment. These children will be ready to learn and ready to expand their social relationships with new caregivers and peers.

Environmental Considerations

Both teachers and parents alike need to realize the importance of environmental influences on young children's behavior. The purpose of considering these influences is to establish an environment that serves to *prevent* inappropriate behaviors in preschoolers (McEvoy, Fox, & Rosenberg, 1991; Nordquist & Twardosz, 1990). Of course, prevention is the best form of intervention. While structuring the physical environment, one should keep in mind that the preschool child is struggling to become independent, yet still requires the close support and guidance of caregivers.

Although the preschool setting is the most typical educational environment outside the home, the passage of Public Law 99-457 (1989) has promoted the provision of early childhood services within the context of the family. Thus, many early childhood intervention programs are home-based. Consequently, we will discuss environmental considerations for both educational and home settings.

Educational Settings

The preschool classroom should provide opportunities for children to explore the environment independently with challenging yet age-appropriate materials. The classroom should be safe, obviating too many restrictions set by the teacher. Areas should be set up where a child can retreat to or pull himself together when feeling overwhelmed from too much activity or involvement with many others.

In the typical preschool classroom, a great portion of the child's day is spent waiting for an activity to begin, waiting for an activity to end, waiting in line to go to the bathroom, and waiting for others to settle down quietly for group times. These frequent transitions are one of the high-risk periods for behavior problems. Young children have great difficulty sitting quietly and waiting for long durations. Finding ways to reduce transition periods can significantly reduce behavioral problems in the classroom.

Rather than wait, insisting that children be seated quietly before beginning group activities such as story times, teachers should instruct children to join the group for story time and begin reading when most are seated.

The behaviors of young children
are shaped by a variety of internal and environmental influences.

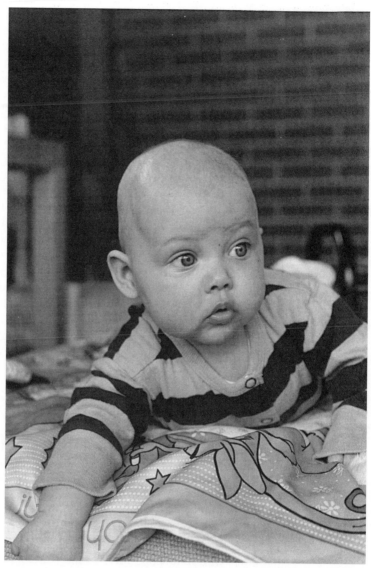

Beginning a group activity with familiar songs or active finger plays will entice
most children. When young children demonstrate lack of interest in an activity, the teacher should be flexible and change the activity. McEvoy and Brady
(1988) recommended that children rotate through activities independently
rather than as a group. McWilliam, Trivette, and Dunst (1985) noted a positive
relationship between the level of a child's engagement with the environment
and the efficacy of early intervention, including appropriate behavior. Small
group, child-directed activities, rather than large group, teacher-directed activ-

ities generally are recommended when trying to reduce the amount of transition time and prevent disruptive behavior during the transition.

Young preschoolers are usually just beginning to share toys at playtime. Teachers who expect children to share toys without guidance have unrealistic expectations. Children in a preschool class typically sit alongside one another but play by themselves. The teacher can facilitate the children's learning to respect others and their playthings. Many schools use small carpet squares or rugs for children to sit on and place their play materials (Bailey & Wolery, 1984). The children are taught that they must wait for materials to be placed back on the shelf or ask permission to play with materials. Children are more likely to ask or allow other children to share playthings on "their" rug if they are not forced to share and if they are given time when they may play with the materials alone. With limited and preferred items, teachers may use timers. Children are usually compliant in turning over playthings to others when their time is up as long as the same rule applies to the other children as well.

Throughout the day, many children feel overwhelmed by high levels of activity, noise, or ongoing contact with other children and caregivers. Providing safe, cozy areas for time alone is encouraged. Bean-bag chairs, rocking chairs, cushioned areas with tape recorders and earphones, book nooks, and lofts can provide a great escape for young children. Sand and water tables are frequently effective for calming an overstimulated child. The soothing, tactile sensation of warm water on the hands is a great stress reducer for many children.

Teachers' expectations for young children are often too high. Teaching readiness skills, such as sitting and listening, are frequently overdone during the traditional "circle time" or group activities. Classrooms should be active places where young minds can explore and young bodies can exercise the need to move. Group times should be fun, but optional. If your activities are inviting and stimulating, young children will readily join in song or story time. In many settings, however, there is considerable variance in children's developmental levels. Hence, not all children will be able to sit or be interested in the same materials. Small groups, whenever possible, are recommended. Reading times should not only be shared during large group times, but should be incorporated throughout the day on a one-to-one basis.

One cannot discuss environmental factors in the classroom without addressing the issue of scheduling. Young children are likely to be more comfortable in the preschool classroom if they know what to expect. By following routines, children learn to expect snacks, free-time, group times, stories, outdoor play, lunch, nap time, and so on. McEvoy, Fox, and Rosenberg recommended that the preschool schedule "be divided into short time segments, depending on the length of the child's attention span and the nature of the activity" (1991, p. 21). Schedules should follow the natural rhythm of the child. Active play and group times should occur when children are well rested and fed. Passive and quiet activities, such as story times, should be utilized when children are tired or as a means of entertaining children during transition times (e.g., waiting for parents to pick up the child from school). Other recommendations for setting up the preschool environment to prevent inappropriate behavior are provided in Vignette 10.3.

Vignette 10.3. Setting Up the Preschool Environment.

By Mary McEvoy

In our classroom we began by focusing primarily on how we could arrange our classroom setting so that it was inviting and supportive. We were also interested in arranging the classroom setting so that it would encourage appropriate behavior.

We started by organizing our space. We put compatible interest centers near each other. For example, we made sure that the block area was not right beside the quiet book/music area. Next, we made sure the areas were well defined. It was important that children knew where the art area began and ended so they would have cues to assist them in remembering to keep the crayons in a certain area. We used small room dividers, carpet squares, or even tape on the floor to designate areas. Finally, we made sure that we could scan the room and see all of the children at all times. This was important as we wanted to be able to intervene immediately in situations where we were needed.

After we had the room organized, we made a schedule of activities. The schedule was important for two reasons. First, it helped us structure the day somewhat for the children. Second, it helped the teachers to know where they should be and when. Free-play activities were scheduled for almost all of the day. In addition, small and large group activities were scheduled. Children were allowed to move through activities individually. For example, during a small group activity such as pasting or coloring, some children would finish before other children, and they were allowed to leave an activity as they finished. They did not have to wait. In addition, children were encouraged during free-play to practice skills that were introduced to them in small or large group settings.

Once we had a schedule, we chose materials to support our activities. We tried to select materials that were social or that required children to play cooperatively. For example, we had children share puzzle pieces or make joint block structures. We made sure that we rotated the toys in our classroom to keep them interesting; we did not put all the toys out on the shelves. We always made sure that the toys worked and were safe. Finally, we placed some very desirable materials on a shelf out of children's reach. The children could see the toys; however, they had to ask us for a toy or find a friend with whom to share a toy. This was a great way to encourage language and social skills.

Last, we assigned staff to certain areas of the classroom rather than assigning children to staff. By using a "zone" coverage strategy, teachers were able to work with an individual child when he or she entered a certain area of the classroom. In this way, all teachers were able to work with all the children. This promoted generalization of skills as well as a sense of community.

Not all of the children's inappropriate behaviors were eliminated when we had a well-organized classroom. However, many problems that were related to disorganization were eliminated. For example, children did not have to wait while teachers gathered materials for an activity or were deciding where to go or what to do. We were ready for the children when an activity began. In addition, while our free-play setting looked like "free choice" to the children, for us it was a great opportunity to help children practice skills. If we did find it necessary to use a specific intervention for inappropriate behavior, we found the interventions to be much more effective when they were implemented within an organized setting. For us, having an organized environment helped us work more effectively with all the children, regardless of their behavioral needs.

Source: Mary McEvoy, Ph.D., is an associate professor of early childhood at the University of Minnesota. St. Paul, Minnesota.

Home Settings

As in the classroom, appropriate measures for setting up the environment in the home can prevent undesirable behaviors. Many of the recommendations for the classroom are also appropriate for the home setting. Other considerations are specifically for families.

Allowing and facilitating competence in the child should also be encouraged within the home. Minor physical modifications to the home can make it possible for the young child to do some things independently. Placing a step-stool at the bathroom sink enables children to wash their hands and brush their teeth independently. Putting small pitchers of juice in the refrigerator enables children to pour their own juice.

Giving children simple, age-appropriate responsibilities is also effective in building confidence and independence. Feeding a pet and putting away toys are appropriate. The environment should be conducive to carrying out chores. For example, expecting a three-year-old to pick up an entire room full of toys without parental guidance and an organized method for maintaining the toys (shelves, toy boxes, and containers for small objects such as blocks) would be an unrealistic expectation.

Daily routines are as important in the home as in the classroom. For example, children are generally more cooperative about going to bed if a daily routine or a special nighttime ritual is included. Children usually enjoy relaxing in a warm bath, rocking in a parent's lap, and having a short story read to them before bedtime. Many parents know that when these rituals are interrupted, children frequently exhibit behavior problems. For example, when a parent insists that a child go to bed without these comforting rituals during out-of-town visits, problems can be expected. Children find a great deal of comfort in these simple routines.

Timing is also important when planning daily activities, such as family outings or a trip to the grocery store. Young children are more likely to be cooperative and enjoy these outings if they are planned for a time when the child is well rested and fed. Taking a child to the grocery store during the normal nap period may be asking for trouble.

Parents who have more than one child can expect a healthy amount of "sibling rivalry." Issues of ownership are frequently at the root of these sibling arguments. For example, parents who insist that their seven-year-old child share toys with a preschooler are likely to observe the older sibling resenting the younger child. Allowing children to have a special space, such as a shelf in their room, where they can maintain personal possessions or nonsharing items will be helpful. Having some special possessions that they do not have to share will help decrease arguments among children. Moreover, teaching children to ask permission to play with toys and respecting "no" for an answer teaches appropriate social skills and respect for the property of others (Williams, 1985).

Transition periods at home can be a source of problem behaviors. A child who is ready and on the way to the playground with his father is likely to become agitated when Dad is interrupted by a phone call. Keeping a special basket filled with playthings by the phone to be used only during phone calls is one method for easing the transition or waiting time. Hurrying children during transition times is also likely to cause some behavior problems. For example, when moving children from one situation (e.g., a play activity) to another (getting ready for lunch), scheduling time for putting toys away and washing hands will save caregivers the need to rush the children. Caregivers must be sensitive to the needs of children who, based on their developmental age, will need varying degrees of time to move from one activity to another. Allowing for some transition time and advance preparation will decrease the challenges.

In summary, environmental modifications suggested for the prevention of inappropriate behaviors include:

- Allow adequate room for children to move within activity areas and from one area to the next. Children should not feel that they have to fight for their physical space.
- Employ rules that will reduce fighting over materials.
- Reduce transition or waiting times for activities—plan for transition.
- Keep children busy—busy children have little time for inappropriate behaviors (Bailey & Wolery, 1984).
- Provide a predictable and consistent environment through effective scheduling (McEvoy, Fox, & Rosenberg, 1991).
- Engage children in interesting activities at their developmental levels (Bailey & Wolery, 1984).
- Employ the Premack principle (see Chapter 5).

- ◆ Reinforce appropriate behaviors (see Chapter 5).
- ◆ Maintain a safe environment for children. This reduces the frequency of having to say "no," "Don't touch that," "Stay away from there," and so on.
- ◆ Allow children to rotate through activities independently, rather than as a group (McEvoy & Brady, 1988).
- ◆ Promote competence, confidence, and independence.
- ◆ Give children simple, age-appropriate responsibilities.
- ◆ Use daily rituals and routines to help make the home setting predictable and comforting.
- ◆ Allow children to have special things they don't have to share. Encourage—do not force—children to share.

PARENT-TEACHER RELATIONSHIPS

Facilitating Relationships: What Teachers Can Do

The role of professional caregivers in facilitating positive and effective parent-child interactions cannot be overstated. When teachers and others make positive comments to parents regarding their children, parents tend to feel good about their child and to interact with him or her more frequently and positively. On the other hand, when teachers make many negative comments to parents about a child, parents tend to feel negatively about their child and interact with them less frequently and positively (Bell & Harper, 1977; Zirpoli & Bell, 1987).

Unfortunately, teachers tend to view parents and parental involvement in mainly negative terms. Instead of viewing parents as partners in the challenge of educating children, teachers tend to perceive parents as an obstacle to their work (Williams & Chavkin, 1985). Teachers must understand, however, that there are significant gains to be had from encouraging parental involvement. In one intercity study, Walberg (1980) found that when parents were encouraged to provide a work space at home for their child, praise their child's school work, and cooperate with the teacher, students achieved twice the grade level gain than those in a control group. Sattes (1985) found that, as parents became more interested and involved in their children's school and achievement, their children's attitudes and achievement also improved.

Parents tend to reduce contact with teachers who always have "bad" news about their child's current performance or behavior. For example, parents may stop attending teacher-parent conferences if they consistently hear only negative news about their child. A good rule of thumb for teachers is to balance negative statements to parents with at least an equal number of positive statements. For example, when talking to a parent about their child's inappropriate behavior, mention situations during which the child's behavior was appropriate. Try to make parents feel good about their children. Be sup-

portive. Parenting is a difficult job even with well-behaved children. Parenting a child who has challenging behaviors may be all that a parent can handle. Adding to the parents' already stressful feelings and anxiety about the child's behavior will not be helpful.

Facilitating Relationships: What Parents Can Do

One of the most important things a parent can do to help their children succeed in school is to maintain regular and positive contacts with the children's teachers. When parents take their young children to daycare or preschool, they should take a moment to greet the teachers and express their interest and concern about their children, the teachers, and the educational setting. Even for older children and adolescents, regular contact with teachers lets the children and teachers know that Mom and Dad care and are supportive.

When parents do not maintain contact with teachers or are not supportive, teachers should take the initiative to contact parents. These initiatives may go unrewarded, and parents may continue to be unresponsive; nonetheless, it is still the teacher's professional responsibility to maintain regular and positive contact with the students' home environments. Although teachers may not realize or perceive any significant outcomes from these efforts, they must understand the potential positive influence these efforts have on parent-child relationships.

SUMMARY

With more and more young children attending some form of daycare service, preschool, or early childhood intervention program, an understanding of some special behavioral considerations for newborns, infants, and young children is necessary. In addition, a new and growing problem with premature infants and infants born addicted to drugs (and related behaviors) is emerging. Research has demonstrated the effectiveness of early intervention in helping children develop academic readiness and appropriate social skills. Effective early intervention programs are integrated, comprehensive, normalized, adaptable, family-referenced, and outcome-based.

For the most part, the behavior of newborns is directly related to their physical situation and environment. Their cry is their primary means of communication to significant others. As infants develop, their understanding of the relationship between their behavior and the behavior of others increases. By their second birthday, young children are developing an awareness of appropriate versus inappropriate behavior. Much of their behavior is shaped by caregivers who establish limits and guidelines.

Premature and dysmature infants may be especially challenging for caregivers. Drugs, alcohol, and lead also place children at risk for developmental and behavioral problems. Poverty is, perhaps, the greatest handicap facing children in the United States. Indeed, 20% of all American children live in poverty.

Child maltreatment, a significant problem in the United States, is influenced by social/cultural, environmental, caregiver, and child variables. Breaking the cycle of child maltreatment involves the termination of widespread acceptance of physical punishment and making the needs of our children a national priority through the provision of early intervention to all at-risk children and families.

Appropriate caregiving for young children includes the establishment of a caring and loving environment for children as they develop. This is accomplished by letting children know they are liked and loved, setting aside individual time, and giving children affection. Self-esteem may be developed in children by allowing and enabling children to be competent, telling children about the good things they do, speaking to children appropriately, teaching children that it is all right to make mistakes, allowing children to make choices, letting children know that their opinions are valued, and teaching children to respect individual differences.

Variables associated with appropriate behavior in young children include the provision of appropriate supervision, establishing a consistent and predictable environment, and teaching readiness skills for academic success. A greater emphasis must be placed on the prevention of inappropriate behaviors through a sensitivity to children's developmental stages, environmental considerations, and special attention to daily routines and children's physical needs.

Teachers are encouraged to facilitate parent-child-teacher relationships by making frequent contacts with parents and having positive comments to share about their children. Negative statements to parents about their children should always be balanced with positive comments to make parents feel good about their children and reinforce parent-teacher contacts.

For Discussion

1. Discuss some of the social problems placing newborns and young children at greater risk than ever before.
2. Discuss the effectiveness of early intervention and the long-term benefits, especially with regard to costs.
3. Discuss the factors related to child maltreatment.
4. List and discuss the elements of effective caregiving for young children.
5. List and discuss some of the variables of classroom environments and associated influences on young children's behavior.
6. How may parents facilitate effective parent-child-teacher relationships?

REFERENCES

Adler, T. (1989, July). Cocaine babies face behavior deficits. *The American Psychological Association Monitor, 20*(7), 14.

Ainsworth, M. D. S. (1979). Attachment as related to mother-infant interaction. In J. S. Rosenblatt, R. A Hinde, C. Beer, & M. C. Busnel (Eds.), *Advances in the study of behavior* (Vol. 9, pp. 1–51). New York: Academic Press.

Bailey, D. B., & Wolery, M. (1984). *Teaching infants and preschoolers with handicaps.* Columbus: Merrill/Macmillan.

Barkley, R. A. (1987). *Defiant children: A clinician's manual for parent training.* New York: Guilford Press.

Batshaw, M. L., & Perret, Y. M. (1981). *Children with handicaps: A medical primer.* Baltimore, MD: Paul H. Brookes.

Baumeister, A. A., Kupstas, F., & Klindworth, L. M. (1990). New morbidity: Implications for prevention of children's disabilities. *Exceptionality, 1,* 1–16.

Bayley, N. (1969). *Bayley Scales of Infant Development.* New York: The Psychological Corporation.

Bell, R. Q. (1968). A reinterpretation of the direction of effects in studies of socialization. *Psychological Review, 75,* 1171–1190.

Bell, R. Q., & Harper, L. V. (1977). *Child effects on adults.* Hillsdale, NJ: Lawrence Erlbaum.

Belsky, J., & Vondra, J. (1989). Lessons from child abuse: The determinants of parenting. In D. Cicchetti & V. Carlson (Eds.), *Child maltreatment: Theory and research on the cause and consequences of child abuse and neglect* (pp. 203–253). New York: Cambridge University Press.

Bowlby, J. (1982). *Attachment.* New York: Basic Books.

Bricker, D. D. (1982). *Intervention with at-risk and handicapped infants: From research to application.* Baltimore, MD: University Park Press.

Bugental, D. B., & Shennum, W. A. (1984). Difficult children as elicitors and targets of adult communication patterns: An attributional-behavioral-transactional analysis. *Monographs of the Society for Research in Child Development, 49*(1, Serial No. 205).

Doke, L. A., & Flippo, J. R. (1983). Aggressive and oppositional behavior. In T. H. Ollendick & M. Hersen (Eds.), *Handbook of child psychopathology.* New York: Plenum Press.

Egeland, B. (1990). Summary of findings from the Mother-Child Project and implications for program and policy. In *Crossing the boundaries between health and education* (pp. 1–2). Washington, DC: The National Health/Education Consortium.

Egeland, B., Jacobvitz, D., & Papatola, K. (1984, May 20–23). *Intergenerational continuity of parental abuse.* Proceedings from the Conference on Biosocial Perspectives on Child Abuse and Neglect, Social Science Research Council, York, ME. May 20–23.

Ensher, G. L., & Clark, D. A. (1986). *Newborns at risk.* Rockville, MD: Aspen.

Fishhaut, E. (1990, April). Children of cocaine: Facing the issues. *Fact Find.* Minneapolis, MN: Center for Early Education and Development, University of Minnesota.

Fontana, V. J. (1971). *The maltreated child.* Springfield, IL: Charles C. Thomas.

Frankenburg, W., & Dodds, J. (1981). *Denver Developmental Screening Test—Revised*. Denver: Ladoca Publishing Foundation.

Gallagher, J. J., & Ramey, C. T. (1990). *The malleability of children*. Baltimore, MD: Paul H. Brookes.

Garbarino, J. (1982). *Children and families in the social environment*. New York: Aldine.

Garbarino, J.J., & Ramey, C.T. (1990). *The malleability of children*. Baltimore, MD: Paul H. Brookes.

Hendrick, J. (1990). *Total learning: Developmental curriculum for the young child*. Columbus: Merrill/Macmillan.

Hersh, R. H., & Walker, H. M. (1983). Great expectations: Making schools effective for all students. *Policy Studies Review, 2,* 147–188.

Hetherington, E. M., & Martin, B. (1986). Family factors and psychopathology in children. In H. C. Quay & J. S. Werry (Eds.), *Psychopathological disorders of childhood*. New York: Wiley.

Hodgkinson, H. L. (1989). *The same client: The demographics of education and service delivery systems*. Washington, DC: Institute for Educational Leadership.

Howard, J. (1990, May 29). Substance abuse. *Crossing the boundaries between health and education*. Washington, DC: The National Health/Education Consortium.

Kauffman, J. M. (1989). *Characteristics of behavior disorders of children and youth* (4th ed.). Columbus, OH: Merrill/Macmillan.

LaVigna, G. W., & Donnellan, A. M. (1986). *Alternatives to punishment: Solving behavior problems with non-aversive strategies*. New York: Irvington Publishers.

Lazar, I. (1981). Early intervention is effective. *Educational Leadership, 38,* 303–305.

Lazar, I., Darlington, R., Murray, H., Royce, J., & Sniper, A. (1982). Lasting effects of early education: A report from the Consortium for Longitudinal Studies. *Monographs of the Society for Research in Child Development, 47*(2–3, Serial No. 195).

Lyle, C. (1990). *The impact of hearing impairment on children's self-concept and strategies for building self-esteem*. Unpublished manuscript. St. Paul, MN: College of St. Thomas.

Martin, B. (1975). Parent-child relations. In F. D. Horowitz (Ed.), *Review of Child Development Research* (Vol. 4). Chicago: University of Chicago Press.

McDonnell, A., & Hardman, M. (1988). A synthesis of "best practice" guidelines for early childhood services. *The Journal for the Division of Early Childhood, 12,* 329–339.

McEvoy, M. A., & Brady, M. P. (1988). Contingent access to play materials as an academic motivator for autistic and behavior disordered children. *Education and Treatment of Children, 11,* 5–18.

McEvoy, M. A., Fox, J. J., & Rosenberg, M. S. (1991). Organizing preschool environments: Suggestions for enhancing the development/learning of preschool children with handicaps. *Topics in Early Childhood Special Education, 11,* 18–28.

McWilliam, R. A., Trivette, C. M., & Dunst, C. J. (1985). Behavior engagement as a measure of the efficacy of early intervention. *Analysis and Intervention in Developmental Disabilities, 5,* 59–71.

Miller, G. (1989). *Giving children a chance: The case for more effective neonatal policies.* Lanham, MD: University Press of America.

Miller, K. (1989, January 15). Are we doing enough? *Sunday Magazine: Star Tribune,* Minneapolis, MN.

National Health/Education Consortium (1991). *Healthy brain development: Precursor to learning.* Washington, DC: National Education/Health Consortium.

Needleman, H., and Gatsonis, C. (1990, February). Low-level lead exposure and the IQ of children. *The Journal of the American Medical Association, 263,* 673–687.

Newacheck, P. W., Budetti, P. P., & Halfon, N. (1986). Trends in activity-limiting chronic conditions among children. *American Journal of Public Health, 76,* 178–184.

Nordquist, V. M., & Twardosz, S. (1990). Preventing behavior problems in early childhood special education classroom through environmental organization. *Education and Treatment of Children. 13,* 274–287.

Patterson, G. R. (1971). *Families.* Champaign, IL: Research Press.

Patterson, G. R. (1982). *Coercive family process.* Eugene, OR: Castalia.

Pianta, R., Egeland, B., & Erickson, M. F. (1989). The antecedents of maltreatment: Results of the mother-child interaction research project. In D. Cicchetti & V. Carlson (Eds.), *Child maltreatment: Theory and research on the cause and consequences of child abuse and neglect* (pp. 203–253). New York: Cambridge University Press.

Pomeranz, V. E. (1986, January). You're going to spoil that child. *Parents,* p. 100.

Rose, T. L. (1983). A survey of corporal punishment of mildly handicapped students. *Exceptional Education Quarterly, 3,* 9–19.

Rosenthal, E. (1990, February). When a pregnant woman drinks. *The New York Times Magazine.*

Rusch, R. G., Hall, J. C., & Griffin, H. C. (1986). Abuse-provoking characteristics of institutionalized mentally retarded individuals. *American Journal of Mental Deficiency, 90,* 618–624.

Sasso, G. M., Melloy, K. J., & Kavale, K. A. (1990). The effects of social skills training through structured learning: Behavioral covariation, generalization, and maintenance. *Behavioral Disorders, 16,* 9–22.

Sattes, B. (1985). *Parent involvement: A review of the literature.* Appalachia Educational Laboratory.

Scarr, S., & Weinberg, R. (1986, November). The early childhood enterprise: Care and education of the young. *American Psychologist, 41,* 140–146.

Schorr, L. B., & Schorr, D. (1989). *Within our reach: Breaking the cycle of disadvantage.* New York: Anchor Books.

Smith, A. N. (1990). Summary impact of Head Start on children, youth, and families. *Crossing the boundaries between health and education.* Washington, DC: The National Health/Education Consortium.

Sparling, J., Lewis, I., Ramey, C. T., Wasik, B. H., Bryant, D. M., & LaVange, L. M. (1991). Partners: A curriculum to help premature, low birthweight infants get off to a good start. *Topics in Early Childhood Special Education, 11,* 36–55.

Sparrow, S., Balla, D., & Cicchetti, D. (1985). *Vineland Adaptive Behavior Scales.* Circle Pines, NY: American Guidance Service.

Starr, R. H., Jr. (1982). A research-based approach to the prediction of child abuse. In R. H. Starr, Jr. (Ed.), *Child abuse prediction: Policy implications* (pp. 105–134). Cambridge, MA: Ballinger.

Straus, M. A., Gelles, R. J., & Steinmetz, S. K. (1980). *Behind closed doors: Violence in the American family.* New York: Anchor Press.

The Center for the Study of Social Policy (1991). *Kids count data book: State profiles of child well-being.* Washington, DC: The Center for the Study of Social Policy.

Walberg, H. J. (1980). School based family socialization and reading achievement in the inner city. *Psychology in the Schools, 17.*

Weikart, D. P. (1990, May 29). Early childhood programs for disadvantaged children. *Crossing the boundaries between health and education.* Washington, DC: The National Health/Education Consortium.

Weston, D. R., Ivins, B., Zuckerman, B., Jones, C., & Lopez, R. (1989, June). Drug-exposed babies: Research and clinical issues. *Zero to Three, 9,* 1–7.

Williams, D., & Chavkin, N. (1985). *Guidelines and strategies to train teachers for parent involvement.* Austin, TX: Southwestern Educational Development Laboratory.

Williams, R. L. (1985). Children's stealing: A review of theft-control procedures for parents and teachers. *Remedial and Special Education, 6,* 17–23.

Woolfolk, A. E. (1987). *Educational psychology.* Englewood Cliffs, NJ: Prentice-Hall.

Zigler, E., & Hall, N. W. (1989). In D. Cicchetti & V. Carlson (Eds.), *Child maltreatment: Theory and research on the cause and consequences of child abuse and neglect* (pp. 203–253). New York: Cambridge University Press.

Zirpoli, T. J. (1986). Child abuse and children with handicaps. *Remedial and Special Education, 7,* 39–48.

Zirpoli, T. J. (1990). Physical abuse: Are children with disabilities at greater risk? *Intervention in School and Clinic, 26,* 6–11.

Zirpoli, T. J., & Bell, R. Q. (1987). Unresponsiveness in children with severe
    disabilities: Potential effects on parent-child interactions. *The
    Exceptional Child, 34,* 31–40.
Zirpoli, T. J., Snell, M. E., & Loyd, B. H. (1987). Characteristics of persons
    with mental retardation who have been abused by caregivers. *The
    Journal of Special Education, 21,* 31–41.

CHAPTER 11
Issues in Adolescent Behavior

In the crossing zone between childhood and adulthood stands adolescence, with its many celebrated troubles. Most of these troubles are, happily, transient. But not all. Adolescents in trouble because they drop out of school, engage in criminal acts, or have children too soon are embarked on a rocky life course. Their troubles are a source of pain for themselves and their families, and often a burden for the rest of us. But much of that private pain and public cost can be prevented. With knowledge now at hand, society could improve the childhood experiences of those at greatest risk, and thereby reduce the incidence of school failure, juvenile crime, and teenage childbearing—and some of their most serious consequences.

—Schorr, 1988, p. 1

As adolescents search for their new identities and adjust to rapid changes in physical, emotional, and social growth, behaviors emerge that often are in conflict with those behaviors desired by persons in their environments. Persons who live and work with adolescents in homes, schools, and communities may often be observed to throw up their hands in futility as their efforts to develop constructive relationships with these youth are thwarted. Although adolescents and their behavior can often be exasperating, they also can foster exhilaration, excitement, enthusiasm, and joy as they embrace life with vigor and resiliency and offer it to all those around them. A positive attitude toward youth is evident in the words of Benson, Williams, and Johnson:

> Many who work with youth think of early adolescence less in terms of agitation and trouble than in terms of excitement and discovery. They see it as that crucial and challenging time when one begins to catch a glimpse of the emerging adult side by side with the child, when leadership begins to make itself visible, when the capacity for abstract thought develops, and when, perhaps for the first time, a parent or a teacher can hold a conversation with the young person that has the tone of adult-to-adult communication. (1987, p. 4)

A number of adolescents, commonly defined as youth who are ages 11 through 19, receive the proper support and experience relationships that are crucial to healthy mental, social, and physical development. However, the increases in adolescent violent crime, teenage parenthood, homelessness, school dropout, adolescent suicide, and alcohol and drug abuse tell us that all is not right with today's teenagers. Factors that have been blamed for these increases include the lack of communication among adolescents and adults, inadequate education, the "generation gap," lack of appropriate role models, and insufficient funding for youth programs that promote positive growth (Benson, Williams, & Johnson, 1987; Brendtro, Brokenleg, & Van Bockern, 1990; Bower, 1991).

Researchers indicated that unless adolescents develop "backbone," problems in behavior and social development emerge (Backbone, 1991). They described backbone as the development of skills that allow an adolescent to stand up for what he or she believes and to resist peer pressure. The essential components of backbone are being committed to doing well in school, possessing positive values, and being socially competent. Figure 11.1 depicts the three categories of backbone and the behaviors associated with each of the components. Unfortunately, a number of adolescents do not possess these necessary academic and social behaviors. This chapter addresses the issues facing adolescents and their families in terms of behaviors that are expected and apparent in youth. This chapter also explores some ideas for effective intervention with adolescents who demonstrate behaviors that are deviant from what is considered appropriate for persons in this age group.

BEHAVIOR OF ADOLESCENTS

Independent Behavior

Many persons who live with and work with adolescents find it difficult to define what is acceptable and unacceptable in terms of expected behavior. Adolescents, in their efforts to express independence, very often exhibit behaviors described as rebellious by the adults in their environment (Brigham, 1989). For example, Tom was a child who loved doing things with his family. Now, as a 14-year-old, he argues with his parents anytime he is expected to do things with his family (e.g., visit relatives, shopping). Tom says that "it is totally uncool to be seen with his parents." What if his friends saw him!

Figure 11.1. Components necessary for development of backbone in adolescents.

Source: From Backbone: Essential for survival on the troubled journey. (1991, April). *Source, a quarterly information resource on issues facing children, adolescents, and families,* pp. 1–3. Search Institute, 122 West Franklin, Suite 525, Minneapolis, MN 55404. 1-800-888-7828. Reprinted with permission.

Educational Commitment	I	School performance
	N	Achievement motivation
	T	Homework
	E	Educational aspiration
	R	
Positive Values	N	Values sexual restraint
	A	Values helping people
	L	Concerned about world hunger
	S	Cares about other people's feelings
	U	
	P	
Social Competence	P	Self esteem
	O	Assertiveness skills
	R	Decision-making skills
	T	Friend-making skills
	S	Planning skills
		Positive view of personal future

Actually, teenagers are expected to spend less and less time with their families and more time with their peers. This independence is a behavior correlated with growing into adulthood (Larson & Richards, 1991). Even though independent behavior is sanctioned among adolescents, adults still consider it necessary to control to a certain extent the activities in which adolescents engage. Enforcing curfews, providing input about the adolescent's peers, keeping track of what the young person is up to—all of these adult behaviors often result in conflict between the adult "in charge" and the adolescent. Often, however, adolescents express their need for someone to discipline them. They feel that it is a sign of love and care when an adult spends the energy necessary to be informed about the adolescents' activities and to help them make decisions about friends and other crucial factors in the young person's life. Some adolescents experience a great deal of support from family, school, and community while others receive significantly less support.

The level of support an adolescent receives is often in direct correlation to the type of behavior demonstrated by the adolescent. According to Benson and colleagues (1987, p. 154), "the single most powerful factor in non-use of alcohol and other drugs among this group [adolescents in high school] was the degree to which the young person believed her or his parents would be upset to discover they had been drinking." Vignette 11.1 provides a comparison between the behavior of two adolescents who receive varying degrees of support and the differences in their behavior.

Vignette 11.1. Comparison of the Behaviors of Two Adolescents.

Kerry and David are two 17-year-old juniors at Central High School. Kerry, an honor student and basketball player, was arrested over the weekend for possession of alcohol by a minor. She was released into the custody of her parents after paying a $100 fine. This was Kerry's first encounter with the law for delinquent activity. As a result of Kerry's arrest, she was suspended from extracurricular activities for the remainder of the semester in compliance with Central's discipline policy and High School Athletic Rules. She also met with the guidance counselor once a week to discuss the potential problems associated with drinking and talked about other things that teenagers can do as alternatives to drinking for entertainment. Kerry was also disciplined at home. To pay her parents back the fine money, Kerry completed extra chores around the house for her parents. Also, Kerry's parents sat down with her and discussed the problems associated with drinking as a minor. Together, Kerry and her parents worked out some ideas for alternative activities for Kerry and her friends to engage in on weekend nights.

Initially, Kerry was angry about the consequences for her behavior and her grades began to slip. With encouragement from her parents and teachers, however, Kerry was able to bring her grades back up and maintain them. Kerry reported that she felt support from both her parents and school personnel. After six months, Kerry reported that she no longer chose drinking as a weekend activity. She and her friends took turns having alcohol-free parties at each others houses as one alternative to drinking parties.

David, a classmate of Kerry's, experienced many run-ins with the law for delinquent behavior. David was bright and noted for his great sense of humor. David's teachers reported that he had the potential for good grades but that he didn't seem to try very hard. As a result, David was on the verge of failing two classes and barely making C's in three others. He went out for football but had to quit to get a job to help support his father and younger siblings. David's mother had died in the previous year from cancer. David's father felt bad that his son had to quit football. It was necessary, however, for David to help supplement his father's income, as David's mother had. David's father explained that he was already working 60 hours a week and couldn't do any more if he was to spend time with his children. David explained that he understood, but felt that if he had adult responsibilities he should be allowed more freedoms including staying out until 3:00 A.M. on weekend nights. Even though his father gave David a curfew of 12:00 midnight on weekend nights, David often broke the curfew and wouldn't come home until 3:00 A.M. or later. Several nights, David stayed overnight with friends without telling his father. David and his friends often drank heavily all weekend and had begun vandalizing property when they were drunk. David had been arrested several times for his behavior.

Each time his father bailed him out of jail by paying his fine and then grounded David from use of the family car for two weeks. One night, David's father told the police to keep David in jail overnight—thinking that would teach him a lesson. When David's father picked David up the next morning, neither of them talked to each other, except to say how betrayed each of them felt by the other. When David got home, he went to his room and didn't emerge until evening to go out with friends. His father looked at him dejectedly as David left the house and didn't even try to enforce the punishment he had given David (i.e., grounding for two months). David was recommended to meet with the school counselor on a weekly basis to talk about his behavior and grades. David showed up for his session once and didn't return. His grades continued on their downward slide and he failed two classes. He maintained his job but was rarely at home. David and his friends continued to vandalize property. David eventually wound up in a correctional facility after he stole a car and took it for a joyride.

Kerry and David could be described as typical teenagers—both preferred the company of their friends, were involved in school activities, and both experimented with alcohol. Kerry, however, received supports from significant adults in her life and was able to get back on track inspite of making some mistakes in her behavior. David, on the other hand, did not have the necessary level of support from family and school personnel. As a result, David made some choices in behavior that led to serious consequences—alienation of his father and spending time in a correctional facility.

Downs and Rose reported direct correlations of commitment to school activities and delinquent behavior. Their research suggested that adolescents who were actively involved in school activities were labeled in positive terms such as "fun" and "academic" (1991, p. 474). In comparison, they found that adolescents who were not involved in school activities were associated with negative behaviors including delinquency and alcohol abuse.

Interpersonal Relationships

Young persons' interpersonal relationships with others have also been cited as a source of harmony or conflict (Cullinan, Epstein, & Kauffman, 1984; Miller, 1991). Often, adolescents are described as having a difficult time getting along with adults and peers. Adolescents who demonstrate disruptive, aggressive, and uncooperative behavior are often described as lacking prosocial behavior. These behaviors take on added significance with adolescents since they are

Adolescents who are supported by significant adults in their lives have a better chance for coping with major changes that occur during the teen years.

confounded by other adolescent factors including physical, cognitive, social, and emotional changes.

Teachers and parents of adolescents are faced with ever-increasing rates of behavior problems ranging from "mild behavioral disruptions to criminal activity" (Blumberg, 1986, p. 67). These behavior problems have resulted in unsatisfactory interpersonal relationships and low self-esteem among adolescents (Hirsch & Rapkin, 1987; Lamke, Lujan, & Showalter, 1988; Wise, Bundy, Bundy, & Wise, 1991). Although similar behaviors are demonstrated by younger children, these problems intensify during adolescence. Adolescents are approaching adulthood and the time when they will leave school and their families—the supportive environments in which satisfactory interpersonal relationships can be guided and shaped.

Even in situations where the adolescent has not received adequate support within these environments, his or her chances for involvement with supporting individuals decreases tremendously when he or she leaves home and school. Once the adolescent leaves even a somewhat supportive environment, many opportunities are lost for teaching adolescents prosocial behaviors that would assist them in the development of satisfactory relationships with others.

Adolescents will often seek out other supportive persons if they don't get support for their behavior in school and at home. Unfortunately, the choices adolescents make in terms of alternatives to home and school sometimes result in increased involvement in alcohol and drug abuse, delinquent acts, teen pregnancy, and gang involvement (Benson, Williams, & Johnson, 1987; Downs & Rose, 1991; Hirsch & Rapkin, 1987; Margalit, Weisel, Heiman, & Shulman, 1988; Snodgrass, 1991). Vignette 11.2 offers an example of an adolescent who demonstrated behaviors typical of someone who has deficits in prosocial behavior.

Vignette 11.2.   Addolescent Behavior Related to Deficits in Prosocial Skills.

Fourteen-year-old Devon experienced considerable teasing by his peers due to the fact that he was about six inches taller than they were and was described as being "fat." Prior to reaching puberty, at which point Devon's body started a tremendous spurt in physical growth, Devon was described as a fairly happy child who had lots of friends and did okay academically. Seemingly overnight, however, he started growing in height and gained a lot of weight. His friends started to tease him incessantly and, although Devon's physical size grew in leaps and bounds, his social-emotional growth lagged behind. Devon did not have the skills for coping with his friends when they teased him. Often he would yell at them or hit them and then run away from them and begin to cry. Devon's feelings were hurt by the taunting remarks of his friends, but he did not have the social skills to reply in an age-appropriate manner (i.e., tell his friends how he felt, walk away without crying).

As a result of Devon's deficits in social skills, his relationships with his friends deteriorated considerably to the point where he would hide during transitions in the hall until everyone had gotten to class. Consequently, Devon was often late to class, which required him to procure a pass from the office—thus making him arrive in class even later. Devon began to do poorly in his course work since he was missing out on so much of the class. Also, Devon would sneak out a back door when school was dismissed to avoid contact with his friends. He would then run home, go to his room, and stay there until called for dinner. Devon became increasingly despondent, not only to his friends and teachers, but to family members.

Delinquent Behavior

The aggressive and disruptive behaviors exhibited by youth who commit delinquent offenses increase during the junior high years (Heward & Orlansky, 1992). According to several authors, the rate and seriousness of crimes committed by children under the age of 18 have increased considerably in the past several years (Heward & Orlansky, 1992; Snarr & Wolford, 1985). Arrests of adolescents for violent crimes (e.g., murder, armed robbery) have also increased. Although children under age 15 have also increased in their rate and seriousness of delinquent behavior, older adolescents still account for the majority of crimes committed by juveniles (Nelson, Rutherford, & Wolford, 1987). Some examples of the most common delinquent behaviors that result in arrests of adolescents are as follows:

> Runaway
> Petty and grand larceny
> Auto theft
> Breaking and entering
> Attempted rape
> Rape
> Stealing
> Shoplifting
> Arson
> Destroying private and public property
> Truancy
> Curfew violation
> Carrying a deadly weapon
> Carrying a concealed deadly weapon

Robbery (armed; unarmed)

Operating motor vehicle without license

Forgery

Habituation to drugs

Public intoxication.

INFLUENCES ON ADOLESCENT BEHAVIOR

Major Life Changes

During puberty, adolescents are faced with major life changes in the context of biological change, social definition, and organizational context (Simmons, Burgeson, Carlton-Ford, & Blyth, 1987). In many adolescents, these changes occur simultaneously, leaving no time to learn to cope with one set of changes before the others occur. Adolescents are often forced to deal with their rapidly changing bodies and the move from elementary school to junior high without a gradual transition. Peterson (1987) reported that students who changed schools within six months of pubertal change reported more depression and anxiety than other students. When other life changes occur as well (e.g., death in the family, divorce) the adolescent noted similar feelings.

Physiological Aspects

Body changes do not occur at the same rate for all adolescents. This in and of itself is disconcerting to adolescents in that their peers are changing, but at different rates. Some adolescents become very frustrated in the fact that they are either changing too fast or not fast enough. Peterson (1987) reported that girls perceived pubertal change as a negative experience, while boys viewed this change as positive. While girls tended to be embarrassed by maturing early, boys tended to be proud of early development.

An adolescent's level of self-esteem and self confidence is often influenced by body image (Benson, Williams, & Johnson, 1987). Adolescents may become more outgoing if they feel that they are keeping in step with what they perceive as "normal" physical development while others lock themselves in their rooms until they look like others in their peer group. Adolescents, especially girls, will often dress alike in efforts to boost confidence in themselves by looking like everyone else rather than standing out in the crowd.

Puberty also seems to have an effect on girls' relationships with their parents. As girls advance in physical development, they talk less to their parents and have less positive feelings about their family (Peterson, 1987).

In Vignette 11.2, Devon became the target for his peers' teasing when he began to look too different. Devon's reactions to his peers' teasing demonstrated lowered self-esteem. On the other hand, his peers' teasing may have been brought on by their own lack of self-esteem—not knowing for sure how their own bodies would look once they entered puberty.

The physiological changes that occur during puberty may cause changes in behavior as the adolescent searches for ways to cope with her or his roller-coaster-type emotions. One minute the adolescent may delight in childlike play and activity, the next he or she may scoff at such "childishness." Parents and teachers often complain about the tremendous mood swings demonstrated by adolescents. Often these mood swings are attributed to increased hormone levels. Although adolescents do experience physiological changes in hormone levels, their behavior cannot be solely attributed to this fact. During this time adolescents experiment with many behaviors to find their new identity (e.g., boys and girls flirting with each other, dressing in the latest fad, becoming boisterous and disruptive). The fact that their emotions and behaviors seem to be influenced by physiological changes is an easy explanation for this phenomenon. However, these changes are very complex and involve a multitude of physical, social, and emotional factors (Blumberg, 1986; Simmons et al., 1987; Smetana, Braeges, & Yau, 1991; Spirito, Hart, Overholser, & Halverson, 1990).

Adolescents often feel pressured by their peers (and society) to have a boyfriend or girlfriend and may feel ostracized if they aren't involved in an intimate relationship. In a study involving 8,165 adolescents, Benson, Williams, and Johnson and others found that many fifth through ninth graders responded positively to a survey question that they were "in love with someone of my age who is of the opposite sex" (1987, p. 54). Figure 11.2 provides the number of adolescents who responded affirmatively to this question. Also, many adolescents are involved in sexual relations at earlier and earlier ages as indicated in Figure 11.3.

Figure 11.2. *Percent of adolescents who responded "yes" to a survey question about being in love.*

Source: From Benson, P., Williams, D., & Johnson, A. (1987). *The quicksilver years, the hopes and fears of early adolescence* (p. 55). San Francisco, CA: Harper & Row, Publishers. Copyright by Search Institute, 122 W. Franklin, Suite 525, Minneapolis, MN 55404. 1-800-888-7828. Reprinted with permission.

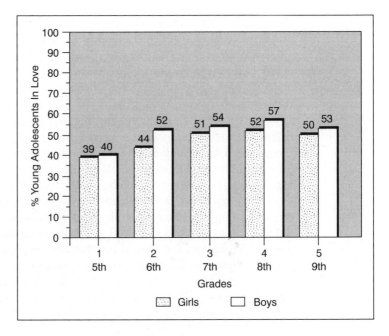

Grade	Percent of sample (N = 8,165) reporting sexual intercourse one or more times	Percent (Girls, N = 4,237; Boys, N = 3,807) reporting sexual intercourse one or more times:	
		Girls	Boys
5th	17%	no information	no information
6th	16%	no information	no information
7th	15%	9%	22%
8th	17%	9%	26%
9th	20%	13%	28%

Figure 11.3.   *Fifth through ninth graders who engaged in sexual intercourse.*

Source: From Benson, P., Williams, D., & Johnson, A. (1987). *The quicksilver years, the hopes and fears of early adolescence* (p. 58). San Francisco, CA: Harper and Row, Publishers. Copyright by Search Institute, 122 W. Franklin, Suite 525, Minneapolis, MN 55404. 1-800-888-7828. Reprinted by permission.

The behaviors exhibited by adolescents when they involve themselves in intimate relations with others are often in direct conflict with adult ideas about these types of relationships—generally parents and teachers do not sanction sexual behavior among adolescents. Although engaging in sexual intercourse is regarded as deviant behavior in unmarried adolescents, in recent years there seems to have been a shift in acceptance of adolescent use of birth control and parenthood. In reality more and more teenagers are becoming parents when they are children themselves. Many of these adolescents are not giving up their children and therefore often receive support from their parents and school personnel (e.g., provision of daycare in high schools; grandparents' assistance in raising their grandchildren). Obviously, the shift in attitude about adolescent parenthood among adolescents, their parents, and other adults correlates with an increase in adolescent sexual behavior.

Organizational Context

Another major life change that effects most adolescents is the switch from elementary school to junior and senior high school. In elementary school, most children are taught in situations where they have only one or two teachers and a stable set of classmates. In junior high school and high school the organization changes to one of increased numbers of classmates and teachers. The adolescent changes classes, classmates, and teachers throughout the day. Adolescents, already faced with having to cope with physiological changes, must also cope with changes in their school structure and social relationships. Whereas in elementary school children are able to form close bonds with their teachers and peers, the likelihood of this happening in later school years is confounded by the very structure and organization of high schools. Simmons and her colleagues (1987) concluded that when adolescents face these multiple changes at the same time, they experience a greater sense of discomfort than if these changes are buffered by adult and peer support and significant levels of comfort in one or more life changes.

Social Definition

We have already discussed the increased level of dating and sexual behavior engaged in by adolescents during puberty. Adolescents not only struggle with the increased pressures of defining their sexual identity but also their relationships with their peers who are going through the same changes. Life would probably be substantially easier if all teenagers went through major life changes at the same pace. However, as in all levels of development and growth, adolescents experience a continuum of what is considered normal physical, social, and emotional development. Friends that the adolescent may have had during one phase of adolescence may change dramatically as a result of "going through adolescence." Vignette 11.3 depicts an example of how friends change among adolescents.

Vignette 11.3.   Social Relationship Change for Lindsey.

Lindsey is a 15-year-old sophomore in high school. She is quite popular and has several close friends, including Tiffany and Jaclyn. Lindsey has been frustrated lately by her friends' behavior. Only a month ago Lindsey, Tiffany, and Jaclyn enjoyed riding their bikes and shopping at the local mall for fun clothes. The three were actually inseparable in all their activities—it seemed the only time they were apart was when they didn't have classes together (actually only two class periods per day) and when they went home to sleep. Now, however, it seems that all Tiffany and Jaclyn want to talk about is clothes and boys. Instead of riding their bikes to get to places, Tiffany and Jaclyn catch a ride with some of their newfound friends who have driver's licenses. More and more they leave Lindsey out of their plans because she has objected to hanging around with older kids, especially boys. Lindsey is torn about her desire to be part of the crowd, but is very unhappy that her close friends no longer include her. Lindsey has tried to become friends with others in her class but feels left out just the same since the girls she really wants to be with don't seem to feel the same about her.

Adolescents' relationships with adults also seem to need redefining during this period in their lives. As they grow closer to adulthood, adolescents are expected to take on more adult-like responsibilities (e.g., caring for younger siblings, getting a part-time job, planning for careers once they graduate from high school). Parents and teachers expect to see these behaviors demonstrated by adolescents, and when the behaviors aren't up to par, the adolescent opens him or herself to criticism. The adolescent can often be heard to express frustration with adults always telling them what to do when they use such phrases as "get off my back."

According to Smetana and her colleagues, conflict within parent/adolescent relationships often occurs because of the difference in how conflict is treated by parents and their children. Parents often treat conflict as "issues of social convention" (Smetana et al., 1991, p. 277). In other words, parents seem to be more concerned that the adolescent's behavior is within generally accepted social norms. In comparison, adolescents often treat conflict "as issues of exercising or maintaining personal jurisdiction" (i.e., able to make their own decisions about what is right for them) (Smetana et al., 1991, p. 277). To illustrate, consider the case of Mrs. Major and her son Jeff. Mrs. Major feels that she should have some say about Jeff's choice of friends. In exercising this responsibility, Mrs. Major tells Jeff that he shouldn't hang around with Mike, a peer who gets into trouble in school (for example, suspended for fighting with peers in the school setting). Jeff argues that Mike is truly a good friend. Further, Jeff tells his mother that Mike doesn't fight with him. So far, Jeff argues, he hasn't been suspended from school for engaging in aggressive behavior like Mike. In other words, Jeff argues that Mike's negative behavior hasn't rubbed off on him.

Adult Influence on Behavior

Parents

Contrary to popular belief, adolescents are strongly influenced by their parents wishes, desires, expectations, and needs for appropriate behavior (Papini, Sebby, & Clark, 1989; Snodgrass, 1991). Researchers indicated that adolescents were influenced by their parents in behaviors including academic behavior, choice of friends, drug and alcohol use, and sexual activity (Benson, Williams, & Johnson, 1987). As previously stated, adolescents tended to engage in more appropriate, acceptable behavior if they perceived their parent(s) as being supportive (e.g., expressing concern about their choices of friends, expecting them to do well in school, placing time parameters on bedtime and curfews). Again, in homes where parental support was low, adolescents tended to engage in more inappropriate behavior, such as disruptiveness in school, delinquent acts, and lower academic achievement (Blumberg, 1986; Snodgrass, 1991).

Teachers

Next to parents, teachers are the adults most likely to influence the behavior of adolescents if the adolescent is still in school. Miller (1991) found that adolescents with behavior disorders demonstrated helpful, cooperative, sharing, comforting, defending, donating, and rescuing prosocial behaviors when they had teachers who engaged in prosocial behaviors. In comparison, fewer prosocial behaviors were demonstrated by a group of students who were not disabled and whose teachers did not report that they engaged in prosocial behaviors.

Teachers have also been influential through their teaching and discussions with adolescents in helping them to change irrational thought patterns that lead to inappropriate behavior (Schmitz & Hipp, 1987). Jones reported that teachers "can have a dramatic and positive impact on students at risk" (1991, p. 17) when they use behavior management strategies to help adolescents acquire appropriate behavior. In a study conducted by Blumberg (1986), teachers used behavior management techniques to assist students in changing from low achieving and disruptive behavior to more acceptable school-related behaviors.

Brendtro and his colleagues reported that "the school is the only institution providing ongoing, long-term relationships with all of our young" (1990, p. 10). Teachers and other adults in the school can play a major role in the lives of young persons.

Teachers and parents can be positive or negative influences for adolescents. Vignette 11.4 is a quotation from 17-year-old Richard's diary—an adolescent who had experienced failure in his home, school, and community. Richard hanged himself shortly after writing this passage.

Vignette 11.4.   Richard.

I had four hours before I would leave my family and friends behind. I went into the bedroom and dug out my old harmonica. I went down to the barn-yard and sat on the fence. I began to play real slow and sad-like for the occasion, but halfway through the song my lower lip began to quiver and I knew I was going to cry. And I was glad so I didn't even try to stop my self. I guess that my foster mother heard me and must have come down to comfort me. When she put her arm around me, I pulled away and ran up the roadway.

I didn't want no one to love anymore. I had been hurt too many times. So I began to learn the art of blocking out all emotions and shut out the rest of the world. The door would open to no one.

I'm skipping the rest of the years because it continues to be the same. I want to say to people involved in my life, don't take this personally. I just can't take it anymore.

Love can be gentle as a lamb or ferocious as a lion. It is something to be welcomed, it is something to be afraid of. It is good and bad, yet people live, fight, die for this. Somehow people can cope with it. I don't know. I think I would not be happy with it, yet I am depressed and sad without it. Love is very strange. (Brendtro, Brokenleg, & Van Bockern, 1990, p. 9)

Peer Influence on Behavior

According to adult perceptions, peers seem to have the greatest influence on adolescent behavior. Although peers do increase their level of influence during adolescence, they actually take a back seat to the level of influence provided by supportive adults in the adolescent's environment (Benson, Williams, & Johnson, 1987; Larson & Richards, 1991). Larson and Richards (1991) reported that even though adolescents spend less and less time with their family, they do not necessarily spend more time with their peers. Adolescents reported that they spent a great deal of time alone. Researchers found that this increase in "alone time" could be considered constructive or a sign of increased alienation from others.

Peers seem to have a greater influence on adolescents who do not have a strong adult support system. Unfortunately, adolescents who turn to peers for the kind of support needed from adults are prone to become involved with "other outcast and unclaimed youth" (Brendtro, Brokenleg, & Van Bockern, 1990, p. 11). A number of authors reported that adolescents who rely on peers for social and emotional support often end up engaging in unacceptable behavior (e.g., substance abuse, delinquent behavior including aggression); see, for example, Botvin & Dusenbury, 1989; Brendtro, Brokenleg, & Van Bockern, 1990; Downs & Rose, 1991; Hirsch & Rapkin, 1987; Stouthamer-Loeber & Loeber, 1989.

On a more positive note, several authors reported that peers could be a positive influence on adolescent's behavior (e.g., Downs & Rose, 1991; Kerr & Nelson, 1987). These influences generally are in the guise of peer modeling of behaviors deemed acceptable by parents, teachers, and youth themselves. High-status peers (that is, peers who are popular) were noted to be most influential on other adolescents' prosocial behavior in school and other settings (Kerr & Nelson, 1987). Downs and Rose reported that peer groups label themselves as positive ("fun" and "academic") or negative ("delinquent") (1991, p. 474).

PREDICTORS OF BEHAVIOR IN ADOLESCENTS

Friendships

Adolescents who have friends are predicted to grow into adulthood as better adjusted and able to demonstrate more acceptable behaviors than adolescents who do not have friends (Benson, Williams, & Johnson, 1987). When supports are in place, such as those described previously in this chapter, adolescents have a good chance of engaging in healthy interpersonal relations with peers. However, as noted previously, adolescents who become friends of peers who engage in unacceptable behaviors may model those same behaviors. It is interesting to note that although adolescents in these groups may continue to demonstrate aggressive and other undesirable behaviors, they seem to develop higher self-esteem since they are able to engage in relationships with persons from their peer group.

Parental Involvement

Adolescents who experience parental involvement in education and social arenas are predicted to engage in acceptable behaviors (Margalit et al., 1988; Snodgrass, 1991). Parents who are supportive of their adolescent will often experience a more rewarding relationship with their child than if they aren't supportive. Conflict is still a part of normal parent-child relationships. Arguments will still take place in situations including use of the family car, curfew, chores and responsibilities, school work, and careers. In supportive relationships, however, it is more likely that these conflicts will be resolved using appropriate problem-solving strategies rather than resorting to loss of self-control in parents and their adolescent.

Teacher Involvement

Teachers have also been cited as influential adults in adolescent behavior. Teachers and others in educational settings were responsible for promoting acceptable behaviors among adolescents through the following (DeLuke & Knoblock, 1987):

- ◆ Modeling of appropriate social behavior,
- ◆ Teaching from a curriculum that promoted acceptable behavior,
- ◆ Using behavior management techniques that focused on increasing positive behaviors,
- ◆ Addressing the individual needs of their students, and
- ◆ Respecting their students.

Later in this chapter, we will discuss curricula and interventions designed to enhance teacher/student relationships.

Mental Health

Predictions have been made that, given appropriate supports, adolescents will maintain good mental health as opposed to development of depression and other emotional disturbances (Weissberg, Caplan, & Sivo, 1989). The supports that we refer to include adult and peer support and supportive environments (i.e., home, school, and community). Weissberg and his colleagues suggested that schools incorporate social competence training into educational programming for all adolescents in order to promote mentally healthy individuals. They back their suggestion with the fact that "7.5 million to 9.5 million youngsters, i.e., 12% to 15% of all individuals under the age of 18, experience emotional or behavioral problems that warrant treatment" (Weissberg, Caplan, & Sivo, 1989, p. 256). This statistic should be a warning to individuals responsible for adolescents' educational programming that there are a significant number of children who would benefit from social skills training offered as part of the school curriculum.

EFFECTIVE BEHAVIORAL INTERVENTIONS FOR ADOLESCENTS

Recently interest in researching and working with adolescents has increased. This interest has been motivated by findings that suggested that adolescence is not a time to give up on trying to change children's behavior. On the contrary, parents, teachers, and others see this time as one last effort to influence adolescents in behaviors that are acceptable in society and promote success in adulthood. The remainder of this chapter will focus on interventions that have been effective in maintaining and modifying the behaviors of adolescents. Many of these interventions have been described in depth in other chapters of this text. The information shared in this chapter focuses on the effective application of these interventions with adolescents.

Behavior Management Interventions

A number of authors reported behavior management interventions that were effective in increasing appropriate behavior among adolescents (e.g., Blumberg, 1986; Carpenter & Sandberg, 1985; Jones, 1991; Welch & Holborn, 1988). Note that much of the available research on effective interventions with adolescents reported combinations of behavior management techniques with social skills training and cognitive behavior management strategies. The examples provided in this section focus on effective use of behavior management.

Daily Progress Report

Blumberg (1986) suggested that the disruptive behavior of adolescents could be modified through use of a "Daily Progress Report" (DPR; p. 67). The DPR was developed to meet the need for monitoring low achievement and disruptive behavior of students in junior high school settings. These students met with the guidance counselor each day in efforts to monitor their behavior and discuss alternative behaviors. The students' teachers marked the DPR with grades that reflected the adolescents' performance in a specific class. Parents were also given the opportunity to sign the DPR and to make remarks with regard to their child's behavior. An example of the DPR is provided in Figure 11.4. Figure 11.5 presents a graph of hypothetical data for a student whose nondisruptive behavior increased as a result of using the DPR for intervention with disruptive classroom behavior. Blumberg reported that initially students were rewarded with material rewards (e.g., pens, pencils, erasers) for each favorable item recorded on the DPR. Reward with material items was phased out as the students' behavior improved. In their place, activities such as being escorted to an administrator to show him or her the positive DPR were used to reward appropriate school behavior. Use of the DPR was effective in improving students' grades, and increasing appropriate school behaviors (e.g., conduct, completion of assignments) and decreasing inappropriate behaviors. Several parents reported improved behavior in the home environment, demonstrating generalization of the effects of the DPR.

Student's name   Grade   Date

To Teacher: Please evaluate this student in the areas stated during your class. Use appropri-
                 ate words such as:

                 Poor   Fair   Good   Excellent

To the Student: This form is to be presented to each teacher at the beginning of the class and
                 picked up at the end of the class. The completed form is to be returned to:

                 (name of counselor/teacher)

                                          Behavioral Criteria:
                                                  a = On time for class
                                                  b = Brought materials to class
                                                  c = Completed homework
                                                  d = Conduct

                                          (Place a "+" in spaces of behaviors
Teacher's signature for each class period: demonstrated in your class)

                                          a   b   c   d   e   Comments

1

2

3

4   Lunch

5

6

7

Parent Signature:_____   Comments:_____

Figure 11.4.   *Daily Progress Report.*

Source: Reprinted from T. L. Blumberg (1986). Transforming low achieving and disruptive adolescents into model students. *The School Counselor, 34,* 67–72. American Association for Counseling and Development, 5999 Stevenson
Avenue, Alexandria, VA 22304. Reprinted with permission.

Contingency Contracting

Contingency contracting (see Chapter 5) is another effective behavior management strategy used to affect adolescent behavior. These interventions were effective in modifying the behavior of adolescents described as juvenile delinquents.

A group of adolescents was rewarded for attending group therapy sessions designed to improve self-control behaviors (Carpenter & Sandberg,

Figure 11.5.   *Graph showing the effectiveness of the DPR in increasing nondisruptive class-room behavior.*

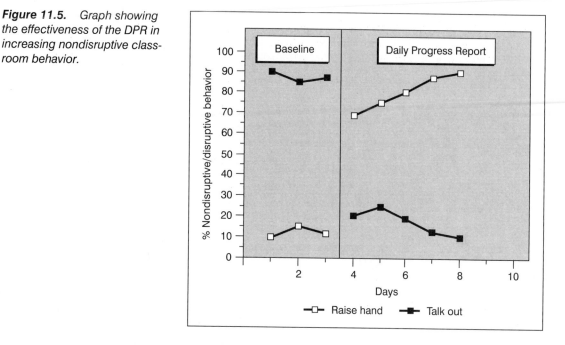

1985). Members of the group signed contracts stating their commitment to attend and participate in group sessions. In addition, the contract stated that each participant would be paid $5.00 for attendance at 9 of the 12 sessions and $0.50 for each additional session. If the adolescent played a role during the session, he or she was paid an additional $0.50. The results of the study indicated that contingency contracting, monetary reinforcement, and behavioral rehearsal increased participation among the group members and increased self-control behaviors.

Welch and Holborn (1988) conducted experiments to demonstrate the effectiveness of a program to train caregivers in the use of contracts with adolescents who demonstrated delinquent behavior (e.g., aggression, truancy). The youth were treated in residential care facilities. The authors were also interested in the ability of the caregivers to apply negotiating and contracting skills with the youth. Their findings indicated that training in these skills did improve the caregivers ability to use contracting with adolescents. Also, use of contracting improved adolescent behavior. Figure 11.6 provides the steps for negotiation with adolescents proposed by Welch and Holborn (1988). Wording of several of the steps has been adapted for use in school settings with youth who demonstrate aggressive, acting-out type behaviors.

Social Skill Interventions

Social skills interventions have been described as effective in modifying the behavior of adolescents. Chapter 7 of this text focused on development of social

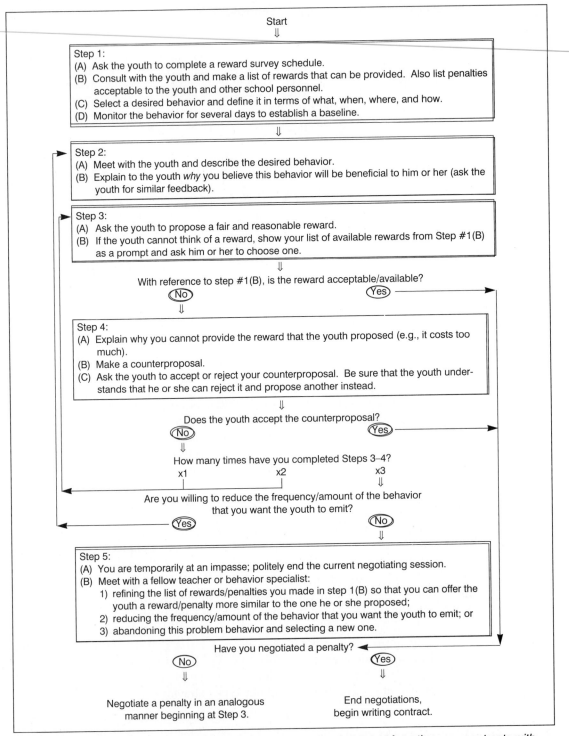

Figure 11.6. *Flowchart for negotiation behaviors used in development of contingency contracts with adolescents.*

Source: Adapted from Welch, S. J., and Holborn, S. W. (1988). Contingency contracting with delinquents: Effects of a brief training manual on staff contract negotiation and writing skills. *Journal of Applied Behavior Analysis, 21,* 357–368. Department of Human Development, University of Kansas, Lawrence, Kansas 66045. Reprinted with permission.

competence in children and youth. In this section, specific applications of these interventions with adolescents will be reviewed.

Skills for Adolescents

Gerler (1986) described a multimodal approach for teaching social skills to adolescents that would assist them in becoming competent in appropriate behaviors including school attendance, classroom behavior, and academic achievement. The author suggested that this approach was effective in reducing inappropriate behaviors (e.g., poor school performance, drug and alcohol abuse) while increasing appropriate behaviors.

The program, entitled *Skills for Adolescents* (Quest International, 1988), includes eight units of instruction designed to prevent alienation behaviors in adolescents in grades 6 through 8. Each unit includes 10 detailed lessons of instruction. Examples of the unit titles include "Entering the Teen Years: The Challenge Ahead," "Friends: Improving Peer Relationships," and "Strengthening Family Relationships" (Gerler, 1986, p. 438). Activities in each unit include readings in a student text, homework assignments, writing assignments, and ideas for a student service project. Through discussion, reading, activities, and projects, adolescents learn to recognize and appreciate their own uniqueness and similarities to others in their environment, thus providing adolescents with skills for dealing with the difficulties they face during the turbulent adolescent years. A number of schools throughout the country have adopted the *Skills for Adolescents* program and reported its effectiveness in helping adolescents in their behavior.

Assertiveness Training

Another social skills training program was designed to teach adolescents assertiveness skills, i.e, expressing one's self in socially acceptable ways (Wise et al., 1991). The authors presented lessons in assertiveness training to sixth graders during six 40-minute lessons during social studies class. Each session was conducted using instructional handouts, lecture, discussion, homework, and activities. Several lessons were presented in a game show format, which seemed to appeal to adolescents in the sixth grade. Other materials and activities including oversized posters, cartoon homework, puppet interviews, self-sticking panels, videotapes, and role plays were implemented to enhance learning of the social skills by the adolescents. Figure 11.7 depicts the lessons, objectives, and activities used to teach assertiveness. The results of the study indicated that the adolescents learned basic understanding of the concept of assertion. In a six-month follow-up, the students demonstrated that they had retained this information and were able to use the skills they had learned.

Houchens Daily Personal Growth Curriculum

The *Houchens Daily Personal Growth* curriculum (Houchens, 1982) is another example of effective social skills training materials for adolescents. This curriculum addresses the affective education needs of high school students who

Lesson	Learning Objective	Activity
1	Recognize definitions and examples of rights	Scripting game
2 and 3	Recognize definitions and examples of assertion, aggression, and nonassertion	Puppet demonstration Videotape presentation
4	Recognize definitions and examples of nonverbal components associated with assertion, aggression and nonassertion	Directed role-plays
5	Recognize feelings associated with assertion, aggression, and nonassertion	Videotape presentation Cartoon worksheet
6	Recognize description and examples of responsible use of assertiveness	Improvised group role-play

Figure 11.7. *Assertiveness training: learning objectives and activities.*

Source: Wise, K. L., Bundy, K. A., Bundy, E. A., & Wise, L. A. (1991). Social skills training for young adolescents. *Adolescence, 26,* 233–241. Libra Publishers, Inc., 3089C Clairemont Dr., Suite 383, San Diego, CA 92117. Reprinted with permission.

demonstrate behavior problems. The areas included in the curriculum are "identity," "interpersonal relationships," and "values." Included in the curriculum are 42 course objectives that relate to the goals for each of the three major areas covered in the curriculum. Each unit has detailed daily lesson plans, which include the following (Houchens, 1984, p. 101):

- ◆ Topic
- ◆ Area of Personal Growth
- ◆ Method of Presentation
- ◆ Goal and Instructional Objective
- ◆ Strategy and Materials
- ◆ Music to be Used with Topic

During the lessons, the teacher and up to 10 students sit in a circle to participate in class activities that address unit topics such as "feelings, thought, behavior," "friendship," "decision-making," and "risk-taking" (Houchens, 1984, p. 101). Houchens described methods of instruction that included brainstorming, discussion, rank ordering, dramatization, open-ended stories, and role playing.

The *Houchens Daily Personal Growth* curriculum has been offered as a course in the East Detroit Schools for a number of years. Students who take the course earn English communication credits, which are applied to graduation requirements. Research on the curriculum showed student gains in positive self-concept and ability in communication skills (Houchens, 1984).

Further research is needed to demonstrate the efficacy of this curriculum with other populations of adolescents.

Fighting Invisible Tigers

Schmitz and Hipp (1987) described their 12-part course in lifeskills development in a curriculum entitled *Fighting Invisible Tigers*. The purpose of the course is to prevent mental and physical illness brought on by stress in the lives of adolescents. Adolescents learn social skills that focus on decreasing stress and increasing use of strategies that foster good mental and physical health. The curriculum includes a teacher's guide and a student text designed to "develop and teach a course on lifeskills development" (Schmitz & Hipp, 1987, p. 1).

Throughout the curriculum, lessons are provided that allow adolescents to become aware of stress in their lives and to learn how to manage stress. One or more 50-minute sessions has been developed to cover each of five lifeskill areas (Schmitz & Hipp, 1987, p. 14):

- Physical activity,
- Relaxation,
- Assertiveness,
- Supportive relationships,
- Life planning.

Twelve teaching units are provided in the curriculum along with learning activities presented through small group exercises and discussion. The format of the learning activities includes role play and direct experience in such things as meditation and aerobic exercise. The goals of the course are to enable students to:

- Differentiate between a state of stress and a state of relaxation.
- Understand the origins and nature of stress.
- Describe their physical and emotional responses to stress.
- Evaluate their current stress levels and their current methods for coping.
- Recognize the difference between positive and negative coping and proactive stress management.
- Identify the benefits of a range of lifeskills: physical activity, relaxation, assertiveness, supportive relationships, and life planning.
- Practice new skills for stress management.[1]

---

[1]   *Source:*   From C. Schmitz and E. Hipp (1987). *A teacher's guide to fighting invisible tigers, a 12-part course in lifeskills development* (p. 14). Free Spirit Publishing Inc., 400 First Avenue North, Suite 616, Minneapolis, MN 55401. Reprinted with permission.

The following provides an example of a reading from the student text that accompanies the unit on building supportive relationships with peers and family members:

Weaving a Safety Net

Many people never change their lives for the better, and it's not because they lack brains or motivation. Instead, they lack support. Pressure from others to "stay the way you are," the force of habit, and those inevitable moments of weak resolve can wear down even the most enthusiastic and determined individual.

Making changes solo is tough going. We need other people. We need them to encourage us, celebrate with us, cry with us, and give us a good swift kick in the pants when it's called for.

Relationships help us to deal with fear, frustrations, stress, isolation, and other blocks to personal growth. Together they form a "safety net" which gives us the freedom to take risks and experiment with new behaviors.

When you're teetering along a tightrope, it's great to know that there's something beneath you to break your fall. Like people who love and accept you for the daredevil you are.[2]

Each student who finishes the course is expected to complete two final projects: a relaxation tape, which is scripted, directed, and recorded by the student, and a personal growth plan.

Refusal Skills Curriculum

Goldstein, Reagles and Amann (1990) developed a social skills curriculum designed to prevent drug use in adolescents. The philosophy of the curriculum is that many adolescents have social skills deficits that hinder their efforts to refuse drug use when pressured by their peers or high-status adults. The curriculum incorporates the teaching of prosocial skills through modeling, role playing, performance feedback, and transfer training. It is based on Goldstein's and others earlier *Skillstreaming* curricula (Goldstein, Sprafkin, Gershaw, & Klein, 1980; McGinnis & Goldstein, 1984). The use of the structured learning approach proposed in these curricula has been effective in teaching prosocial skills to children and adolescents (see Chapter 7).

The teacher's guide includes lessons for each of the 20 core refusal skills that are included in the curriculum. Suggestions for modeling, role play, and transfer of training for each of the skills are also included in the teacher's guide. Teacher and student refusal skill checklists are included in the guide. These checklists can be used for assessment of present levels of performance for the adolescents who are candidates for training in refusal skills. Training suggestions are offered as well as characteristics of trainers. Goldstein and his colleagues (1990, p. 60) offer the following trainer skills that are essential for group training success:

---

[2]   *Source:*   From E. Hipp (1985). *Fighting invisible tigers, a stress management guide for teens* (p. 77). Free Spirit Publishing Inc., 400 First Avenue North, Suite 616, Minneapolis, MN 55401. Reprinted with permission.

◆ Oral communication and teaching ability,

◆ Flexibility and capacity for resourcefulness,

◆ Enthusiasm,

◆ Ability to work under pressure,

◆ Interpersonal sensitivity,

◆ Listening skills, and

◆ Knowledge of the subject (adolescent development, drug use, peer pressure on adolescents, etc.).

The following list provides the reader with a list of the 20 core refusal skills and Figure 11.8 shows an example of a refusal skill lesson:

1. Asking for help.
2. Giving instructions.
3. Convincing others.
4. Knowing your feelings.
5. Expressing your feelings.
6. Dealing with someone else's anger.
7. Dealing with fear.

Steps	Trainer notes
1. Think about how you will feel during the conversation.	You might be tense, anxious, or impatient.
2. Think about how the other person will feel.	He or she may feel anxious, bored, or angry.
3. Think about different ways you could say what you want to say.	
4. Think about what the other person might say back to you.	
5. Think about any things that might happen during the conversation.	Repeat Steps 1 through 5 at least twice, using different approaches to the situation.
6. Choose the best approach you can think of and try it.	

Suggested modeling display
Main actor prepares to tell parent about out-of-control drug habit.

Comments
In preparing for difficult or stressful conversations, it is useful for youngsters to see that the way they approach the situation can influence the final outcome. This skill involves rehearsing a variety of approaches and then reflecting upon which approach is likely to produce the best results. Feedback from group members on the effectiveness of each approach can be particularly useful in this regard.

Figure 11.8. *Refusal skills lesson example: Getting ready for a difficult conversation.*

Source: From *Refusal skills, preventing drug use in adolescents* (p. 50) by A. P. Goldstein, K. W. Reagles, and L. S. Amann, 1990, Champaign, IL: Research Press. Copyright 1990 by the authors. Reprinted by permission.

8. Using self-control.
9. Standing up for your rights.
10. Responding to teasing.
11. Avoiding trouble with others.
12. Keeping out of fights.
13. Dealing with embarrassment.
14. Dealing with being left out.
15. Responding to persuasion.
16. Responding to failure.
17. Dealing with an accusation.
18. Getting ready for a difficult conversation.
19. Dealing with group pressure.
20. Making a decision.[3]

Figure 11.9 presents the homework form used to assist in generalization of the refusal skills learned through social skills training.

Cognitive Behavior Management Interventions

Cognitive behavior modification strategies were thoroughly discussed in Chapter 6. These procedures have been especially effective in modifying the behavior of adolescents as evidenced in classrooms for adolescents and in the

Figure 11.9. *Refusal skills homework sheet.*

Source: From *Refusal skills, preventing drug use in adolescents* (p. 50) by A. P. Goldstein, K. W. Reagles, and L. S. Amann, 1990, Champaign, IL: Research Press. Copyright 1989 by the authors. Reprinted by permission.

Name_____ Date _____
Group Leaders_____
_____

Fill in during this meeting
1. What skill will you use?
2. What are the steps for the skill?
3. Where will you try the skill?
4. With whom will you try the skill?
5. When will you try the skill?

Fill in before the next meeting
6. What happened when you did the homework assignment?
7. Which steps did you actually follow?
8. How good a job did you do in using the skill? (Check one.)

___ Excellent   ___ Good   ___ Fair   ___ Poor

9. What do you feel should be your next homework assignment?

---

3   *Source:*   From *Refusal skills, preventing drug use in adolescents* (p. 32) by A. P. Goldstein, K. W. Reagles, and L. S. Amann, 1990, Champaign, IL: Research Press. Copyright 1990 by the authors. Reprinted by permission.

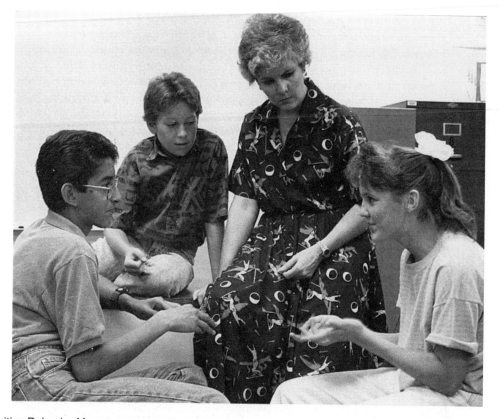

Cognitive Behavior Management curricula provide lessons that motivate student participation in discussions and activities directed on feelings and behavior.

literature (e.g., Brigham, 1989; Etscheidt, 1991). This section will explore several applications of CBM strategies with adolescents.

Thinking, Feeling, Behaving Curriculum

Vernon (1989) presented a curriculum for students in grades 7 through 12 that was designed to promote positive mental health. Lessons in *Thinking, Feeling, Behaving: An Emotional Education Curriculum for Adolescents, Grades 7–12* (Vernon, 1989) are an extension of the first- through sixth-grade program. Based on CBM theory, the curriculum includes 90 lessons, which are divided into topics including the following (Vernon, 1989, p. 1):

- Self-Acceptance
- Feelings
- Beliefs and Behavior
- Problem Solving/Decision Making
- Interpersonal Relationships

Adolescents are encouraged to change their thinking about issues and conflicts they face through simulation games, role playing, stories, written activities, brainstorming, and art activities. Expected outcomes of the training provided in this curriculum include being able to identify irrational beliefs. Through discussion and participation in activities then, adolescents develop the ability to look at the situations they face in a more realistic, rational manner.

The lessons are designed to be presented during classroom or small-group sessions by teachers, counselors, school psychologists, or school social workers. Figure 11.10 provides a sample lesson from Vernon's curriculum.

Self-Management for Adolescents

Brigham (1989) presented a self-management training program for adolescents. In this program, Brigham outlined instructional strategies based on CBM concepts that would train adolescents to become self-managers of their behavior. Brigham (1989) suggested that the curriculum was suited for adolescents in tenth through twelfth grades. The program text offers assessment instruments for use in evaluating youths' current level of performance in their ability to describe and manage their own behavior. The curriculum for teaching self-management included 33 units of instruction on topics including "measurement and definition of behavior," "operant behavior and consequences," "punishment and response cost," and "designing and conducting a self-management project" (Brigham, 1989). The lessons in each unit are designed to teach adolescents the concepts of behavior analysis so that they may apply these concepts to the management of their own daily lives. An instructor's guide outlining each unit and unit activities as well as a student workbook are included in the curriculum. The format for instruction is lecture, discussion, and individual and group projects. Figure 11.11 provides a sample lesson from *Self-Management for Adolescents, A Skills Training Program* (Brigham, 1989).

Thinking, Changing, Rearranging Curriculum

Anderson (1981) offers a curriculum for children and adolescents ages 9 to 17 that is designed to assist students in changing their irrational "junk" thoughts to more rational, helpful thoughts. *Thinking, Changing, Rearranging: Improving Self-Esteem in Young People* (Anderson, 1981) guides teachers and other educational personnel in conducting small group lessons in improving self-esteem in young persons. The teacher's guide outlines nine chapters that include 30 sessions designed to help adolescents change their thinking and behavior in relation to common situations and relationships they face in daily life. The format for each lesson offers an objective, student text reading, and activities for reinforcing the learning for each chapter/unit. Chapters in the student text and teacher guide are entitled as follows:

- ◆ Chapter 1: Self-Esteem
- ◆ Chapter 2: Where Does Hurt Come From?

- Chapter 3: Thoughts, Feelings and Thunderclouds
- Chapter 4: But, What About Vanilla?
- Chapter 5: Junk-Thought: Food for Misery
- Chapter 6: Beliefs That Cause Problems
- Chapter 7: "I Hope Your Mouth Falls Off!"
- Chapter 8: New Language
- Chapter 9: Making Changes

Interpersonal Relationships Activity 4

Resolving relationship issues:

Objective
To identify the techniques to handle interpersonal relationship difficulties.

Materials
Paper and pencil as needed.

Procedure
1. Have students pair up and briefly brainstorm examples of relationship problems they have had with others in the past 3 months. These could include problems with peers, parents, teachers, employers, etc.
2. Invite students to share examples of these difficulties. List them on the chalkboard, categorizing them as follows: peer, parent, stepparent, sibling, employer, teacher/principal, police, etc. (Use additional categories as they become apparent.)
3. Next encourage students to brainstorm methods they have used to resolve these difficulties. List alternatives beside the categories to which they correspond so that, ultimately, you can determine which methods work best with which problems.
4. Once all ideas have been generated, go back and discuss pros and cons of the methods suggested, making sure to help students assess the consequences of the various alternatives.

Discussion

Content questions
1. Which alternatives seem most viable to you?
2. Do certain methods work with one type of problem but not with another? Why do you suppose that is?
3. Do you think there is always a way to resolve differences in relationships?

Personalization questions
1. Which of the suggested alternatives have worked best for you? Which have not worked?
2. Have you learned some new alternatives that you might try in resolving relationship issues? Share.

To the Leader
Understanding that there are alternatives for working out conflicts in relationships will empower students to deal more effectively with issues as they arise.

Figure 11.10.   *Sample lesson from* Thinking, Feeling, Behaving. Interpersonal Relationships, *Activity 4.*

Source: From Thinking, feeling, behaving: An emotional education curriculum for adolescents, grades 7–12 (p. 159) by A. Vernon, 1989, Champaign, IL: Research Press. Copyright 1989 by the author. Reprinted by permission.

Unit 19. Applying Behavior Analysis Skills with Others

Objective: Teach the students the concepts of reciprocity and equity and that how a person acts influences how other people respond to him/her.

Reciprocity and equity
These are key concepts for understanding and improving social interactions. Adolescents generally have a limited perspective on how their behavior affects other people.
Instructional Activities: This is essentially a discussion unit to prepare the students to conduct the behavior modification project in the next unit. Nonetheless, it is very important that the students understand these concepts. In addition to discussing the study guide and reviewing the questions concerning equity and reciprocity, it is important that the questions be stated both from the perspective of the student and from that of other people. The following example questions cover both perspectives: "Suppose you bought a tape recorder from a friend, it didn't work, and he refused to give your money back. How would you feel about this? Would it affect your friendship?" "Suppose you had promised to help a friend on some task, then had a chance to do something really fun and did that instead without telling your friend. How do you think the friend would feel? Would this affect the future of the friendship?" In short, it is hoped that the students will learn how their behavior influences other peoples' future responses.

Figure 11.11. *Sample lesson from self-management curriculum.*

Source: From Brigham, T. A. (1989). *Self-management for adolescents, a skills training program.* New York: Guilford Press. Reprinted with permission.

Figure 11.12 provides a sample lesson from the student text, Chapter 4. The curriculum includes a teacher's guide, student text, posters, reward stickers, and bookmarks.

A number of interventions for adolescent behavior have been reviewed in this chapter. To assist the reader in making decisions about appropriate strategies for the adolescents they work with, these interventions are summarized in Table 11.1.

SUMMARY

Adolescents are both a challenge and a joy to be around and to work with. They face tremendous physical, social, and emotional changes during the adolescent phase of their life. Adults and adolescents are often in conflict due to the nature of behavior demonstrated by youth as they search for new identities and adjust to changes in their lives. With supportive environments, adolescents can look forward to a brighter future in the development of satisfying interpersonal relationships, physical and mental health, and social behavior. It was suggested that development of "backbone" would allow for adolescents to become competent in life's environments.

Adolescents are expected to demonstrate greater levels of independent behavior when they spend less time with their families and become more

---

But, What About Vanilla?

We understand now that our bad feelings aren't caused by what happens, but by what we think about what happens. So, if we want to say good-bye to some of those bad feelings, then the first step is to start paying more attention to what we're thinking. We will look first at our beliefs, then at our language and vocabulary. That's where we'll find clues as to why we feel the way we do.

There is a difference between a *Fact* and *Belief*. A *Fact* is known to be true, can be proven, and is accepted by almost everyone.

Here are some Facts:

1. Ice cream is a food.

2. Bicycles do not create pollution.

3. Math is a subject taught in school.

People would not generally argue with those facts, and it is hard to imagine anyone getting upset over them. Can you imagine someone being angry because grass is green? Of course not.

A *Belief* is an idea felt to be true by some people, but maybe not by others. A belief may be true at one time, but not at another. It is like an opinion. People might not say this part out loud, but a belief usually has "I think..." in front of it. Beliefs are often what people think about facts.

Here are some Beliefs:

1. Chocolate ice cream is great!

2. Bicycles are better for transportation than cars.

3. Long division is a waste of time.

These are beliefs that make sense. They may not be true all the time, or may not be true for everyone; but they can be true for some people some of the time. Because they make sense, we call them *Rational beliefs*. People don't usually get upset over rational beliefs.

Here are some Beliefs that don't make sense:

1. The best ice cream is CHOCOLATE. Everyone must like chocolate! All the other flavors are awful! Anybody who doesn't like Chocolate is stupid!

2. Everybody should ride a bike all the time. People who drive cars are ruining everything! They should be fined.

3. I flunked my math test 'cause my Mom made me runny eggs for breakfast! It made me so upset that I forgot all the long division facts! It's all her fault!

These beliefs don't make sense. They are not true; they are ridiculous. We call them *Irrational beliefs*. People who have irrational beliefs probably get upset a lot, just because of the way things are.

Figure 11.12.   *Sample lesson from the student text* Thinking, Changing, Rearranging.

Source: From Anderson, J. (1981). *Thinking, changing, rearranging, improving self-esteem in young people.* (pp. 15–16). Timberline Press, Box 70187, Eugene, OR 97401. Reprinted with permission.

involved in environments outside their home. Pressure to become more independent added to other changes in the adolescents' lives can inhibit their ability to build good relationships with adults and peers. When support is lacking in home and school, adolescents turn to support groups outside their home and

Table 11.1. *Interventions for adolescent behavior.*

Name of Intervention	Age appropriate for	Grade appropriate for	Intervention type	Source
Daily Progress Report	11–14	Junior High	Behavior management	Blumberg, T. L. (1986). *The School Counselor,* 67–72.
Contingency Contracting	11–18	Junior High and High School	Behavior management	Welch, S. J., & Holborn, S. W. (1988). *JABA,* 21, 357–368.
Skills for Adolescents	11–14	6–8	Social skills	Quest National Center, 537 Jones Road, Granville, OH 43023–0566.
Assertiveness Training	11–12	6	Social skills	Wise, K. L., Bundy, K. A., Bundy, E. A., & Wise, L. A.(1991). *Adolescence,* 26, 233–241.
Houchens Daily Personal Growth Curriculum	14–18	High School	Social skills	Houchens, C. J. (1982). *A secondary curriculum for personal adjustment.* Mafex Publishers, Johnstown, PA.
Fighting Invisible Tigers	11–18	Junior High and High School	Social skills	Free Spirit Publishing, Inc., 400 1st Ave N., Suite 616, Minneapolis, MN 55401.
Refusal Skills, Preventing Drug Use in Adolescents	11–18	Junior High and High School	Social skills	Research Press, 2612 N. Mattis Ave., Champaign, IL 61821.
Thinking, Feeling, Behaving: An Emotional Education Curriculum for Adolescents	12–18	Junior High and High School	Cognitive behavior management	Research Press, 2612 N. Mattis Ave., Champaign, IL 61821.
Self-Management for Adolescents. A Skills Training Program	15–18	10–12	Cognitive behavior management	1989 The Guilford Press, A Division of Guilford Publications, Inc., 72 Spring St., New York, NY 10012.
Thinking, Changing, Rearranging: Self-Esteem Skills for 9–17	9–17	4–12	Cognitive behavior management	Timberline Press, P.O. Box 70071, Eugene, OR 97401.

school. Often these groups engage in delinquent behavior. There has been a significant increase in violent crimes committed among adolescents.

During the adolescent years, young persons experience varying influences on their behavior. Youth are faced with major life changes in the form of biological change, social definition, and organizational context. If too many of these changes occur simultaneously, the adolescent may be overwhelmed. This can result in loss of self-esteem and self-confidence for individuals. Supportive adults and teachers have more influence on adolescent behavior than peers. However, youth often turn to peers for supportive relationships when adults have failed them.

Adolescent behavior can be predicted by several factors. Adolescents who have friends should grow into better adjusted adults. Acceptable behaviors are demonstrated by adolescents who have parents who support them in academic and social arenas. Teachers who model appropriate social behavior and attend to individual needs of their students will experience appropriate adolescent behavior. Mental health will be maintained if adolescents receive proper support in terms of adults, peers, and appropriate educational programming.

A number of curricula and strategies based on behavior management, social skills, and cognitive behavior management were reviewed. These techniques are considered as best practice ideas when working with adolescents in home, school, and community settings.

The behavior management strategies reviewed included positive reinforcement of school-related behavior using a Daily Progress Report and contingency contracting for group attendance.

Social skills curricula reviewed included *Skills for Adolescence* (Quest National Center), assertiveness training (Wise et al., 1991), *Houchens Daily Personal Growth Curriculum* (Houchens, 1982), *Fighting Invisible Tigers* (Schmitz & Hipp, 1989), and *Refusal Skills* (Goldstein et al., 1990). Each of the curricula incorporated modeling, role playing, discussion, homework assignments, and other effective interventions for development of social competence.

Several curricula based on cognitive behavior management strategies were reviewed. These included curricula entitled *Thinking, Feeling, Behaving* (Vernon, 1989), *Self-Management for Adolescents* (Brigham, 1989), and *Thinking, Changing, Rearranging* (Anderson, 1981). Discussion, scripting, and activities were among the suggested interventions for modifying adolescents' thoughts and behaviors.

For Discussion

1. Discuss the major issues that adolescents face as they experience physical, emotional, and social changes.
2. Describe the importance of supportive relationships in the lives of adolescents.
3. Discuss major influences on adolescents' behavior.
4. Discuss effective strategies and curricula that have been used in working with adolescents experiencing behavior problems.

REFERENCES

Anderson, J. (1981). *Thinking, changing, rearranging: Improving self-esteem in young people.* Eugene, OR: Timberline Press.

Backbone: Essential for survival on the troubled journey. (1991, April). *Source, a Quarterly Information Resource on Issues Facing Children, Adolescents, and Families, 7*(1), 1–3.

Benson, P., Williams, D., & Johnson, A. (1987). *The quicksilver years, the hopes and fears of early adolescence.* San Francisco, CA: Harper & Row.

Blumberg, T. L. (1986). Transforming low achieving and disruptive adolescents into model students. *The School Counselor, 34,* 67–72.

Botvin, G. B., & Dusenbury, L. (1989). Substance abuse prevention and the promotion of competence. In L. A. Bond and B. E. Compas (Eds.), *Primary prevention and promotion in the schools* (pp. 146–178). Newbury Park, CA: Sage Publications.

Bower, B. (1991). Teenage turning point. *Science News, 139,* 184–186.

Brendtro, L. K., Brokenleg, M., & Van Bockern, S. (1990). *Reclaiming youth at risk, our hope for the future.* Bloomington, IN: National Education Service.

Brigham, T. A. (1989). *Self-management for adolescents, a skills training program.* New York: Guilford Press.

Carpenter, P., & Sandberg, S. (1985). Further psychodrama with delinquent adolescents. *Adolescence, 20,* 599–604.

Cullinan, D., Epstein, M. H., & Kauffman, J. M. (1984). Teachers' ratings of students' behaviors: What constitutes a behavior disorder in school. *Behavioral Disorders, 10,* 9–19.

DeLuke, S. V., & Knoblock, P. (1987). Teacher behavior as preventive discipline. *Teaching Exceptional Children, 19*(4), 18–24.

Downs, W. R., & Rose, S. R. (1991). The relationship of adolescent peer groups to the incidence of psychosocial problems. *Adolescence, 26,* 473–492.

Etscheidt, S. (1991). Reducing aggressive behavior and improving self-control: A cognitive-behavioral training program for behaviorally disordered adolescents. *Behavioral Disorders, 16,* 107–115.

Gerler, E. R. (1986). Skills for adolescence: A new program for young teenagers. *Phi Delta Kappan, 67,* 436–439.

Goldstein, A. P., Reagles, K. W., & Amann, L. S. (1990). *Refusal skills, preventing drug use in adolescents.* Champaign, IL: Research Press.

Goldstein, A. P., Sprafkin, R. P., Gershaw, N. J., & Klein, P. (1980). *Skillstreaming the adolescent, a structured learning approach to teaching prosocial skills.* Champaign, IL: Research Press.

Heward, W. L., & Orlansky, M. D. (1992). *Exceptional children* (4th ed.). Columbus, OH: Merrill/Macmillan.

Hipp, E. (1985). *Fighting invisible tigers, a stress management guide for teens.* Minneapolis, MN: Free Spirit Publishing.

Hirsch, B. J., & Rapkin, B. D. (1987). The transition to junior high school: A longitudinal study of self-esteem, psychological symptomatology, school life, and social support. *Child Development, 58,* 1235–1243.

Houchens, C. J. (1982). *A secondary curriculum for personal adjustment.* Johnstown, PA: Mafex.

Houchens, C. J. (1984). A personal adjustment curriculum for secondary behaviorally disordered students. In S. Braaten, R. B. Rutherford, & C. A.

Kardash (Eds.), *Programming for adolescents with behavioral disorders* (pp. 97–104). Reston, VA: Council For Exceptional Children.

Jones, V. (1991). Responding to students' behavior problems. *Beyond Behavior, 2*(1), 17–21.

Kerr, M. M., and Nelson, C. M. (1987). *Helping adolescents with learning and behavior problems.* Columbus, OH: Merrill/Macmillan.

Lamke, L. K., Lujan, B. M., & Showalter, J. M. (1988). The case for modifying adolescents' cognitive self-statements. *Adolescence, 23,* 967–974.

Larson, R., & Richards, M. H. (1991). Daily companionship in late childhood and early adolescence: Changing developmental contexts. *Child Development, 62,* 284–300.

Margalit, M., Weisel, A., Heiman, T., & Shulman, S. (1988). Social skills and family climate of behaviorally disordered adolescents. *Behavioral Disorders, 13,* 253–262.

McGinnis, E., & Goldstein, A. P. (1984). *Skillstreaming the elementary school child.* Champaign, IL: Research Press.

Miller, D. (1991). Do adolescents help and share? *Adolescence, 26,* 449–456.

Nelson, C. M., Rutherford, R. B., Jr., & Wolford, B. I. (1987). *Special education in the criminal justice system.* Columbus, OH: Merrill/Macmillan.

Peterson, A. C. (1987). Those gangly years. *Psychology Today,* 28–34.

Quest International (1988). *Skills for adolescence: Middle and Junior High Schools.* Granville, OH: Author.

Schmitz, C., & Hipp, E. (1987). *A teacher's guide to fighting invisible tigers, a 12-part course in lifeskills development.* Minneapolis, MN: Free Spirit Publishing.

Schorr, L.B. (1988). *Within our reach, breaking the cycle of disadvantage.* New York: Anchor Press, Doubleday.

Simmons, R. G., Burgeson, R., Carlton-Ford, S., & Blyth, D. A. (1987). The impact of cumulative change in early adolescence. *Child Development, 58,* 1220–1234.

Smetana, J. G., Braeges, J. L., & Yau, J. (1991). Doing what you say and saying what you do reasoning about adolescent-parent conflict in interviews and interactions. *Journal of Adolescent Research, 6,* 276–295.

Snarr, R., & Wolford, B. I. (1985). *Introduction to corrections.* Dubuque, IA: William C. Brown.

Snodgrass, D. M. (1991). The parent connection. *Adolescence, 26,* 83–87.

Spirito, A., Hart, K., Overholser, J., & Halverson, J. (1990). Social skills and depression in adolescent suicide attempters. *Adolescence, 25,* 543–552.

Stouthamer-Loeber, M., & Loeber, R. (1989). The use of prediction data in understanding delinquency. In L. A. Bond and B. E. Compas (Eds.), *Primary prevention and promotion in the schools* (pp. 179–201). Newbury Park, CA: Sage Publications.

Vernon, A. (1989). *Thinking, feeling, behaving: An emotional education curriculum for adolescents, grades 7–12.* Champaign, IL: Research Press.

Weissberg, R. P., Caplan, M. Z., & Sivo, P. J. (1989). A new conceptual framework for establishing school-based social competence promotion programs. In L. A. Bond and B. E. Compas (Eds.), *Primary prevention and promotion in the schools* (pp. 255–318). Newbury Park, CA: Sage Publications.

Welch, S. J., & Holborn, S. W. (1988). Contingency contracting with delinquents: Effects of a brief training manual on staff contract negotiation and writing skills. *Journal of Applied Behavior Analysis, 21,* 357–368.

Wise, K. L., Bundy, K. A., Bundy, E. A., & Wise, L. A. (1991). Social skills training for young adolescents. *Adolescence, 26,* 233–241.

CHAPTER 12

Cultural Influences on Behavior

**Douglas F. Warring, Sally M. Hunter, Thomas J. Zirpoli,
University of St. Thomas**

You damage a child still more when you destroy his first stone of identity, when you tell him his language is no good, when you tell him that his color is not right or imply it by surrounding him with people of a different color, habits and status. You tell him that what his parents have taught him is no good, that he should not do so and so, or be what is.

—Menninger, 1980

By the year 2000, 30% to 40% of public school students in the United States will be from an ethnic minority family (Hodgkinson, 1990; Ramirez, 1988). In many states students of color will comprise the majority of the student population. For example, Yates (1986) found that half the students in Texas kindergarten programs are Hispanic. Plisko and Stern (1985) found that in many urban schools, 80% of the students were people of color. These demographic changes have brought both unique and diverse needs to America's public schools, along with many opportunities. Are educators prepared for these challenges and opportunities? A significant first step, perhaps, is for educators to learn about their students' cultures and the cultural influences on their behaviors.

DEFINITION OF TERMS

An *ethnic group* is a group that is bound together by common characteristics such as values, political interests, economic interests, language patterns, religious beliefs, and other factors that contribute to a sense of group identification (Banks, 1991). A *cultural group* is defined "as people with common origins, customs, and styles of living" (Randall-David, 1989, p. 1). Behavior is learned within the framework of a particular ethnic group or culture and usually taught within a family structure. "Culture is a broad concept encompassing all of the learned, shared, and transmitted behaviors characteristic of a group of people" (Henderson, 1982, p. 69). According to Banks and Banks, culture is "the ideations, symbols, behaviors, values, and beliefs that are shared by a human group" (1989, p. 327). The Minneapolis Multicultural Task Force (Minneapolis Public Schools, 1989) stated that culture is:

> . . .that complex whole which includes behavior patterns, values, beliefs, symbols, expressions of creativity, institutions and other human-made components of society. There are unique achievements of a human group within this framework that "culturally" distinguish one group from another. Culture is learned. (p. 25)

MYTHS AND STEREOTYPES

Many myths are associated with individual ethnic groups. These myths, along with a lack of appreciation for different cultural norms, contribute to frequent misunderstanding and misinterpretation of children's behaviors. Often a child who has been reared in a strong cultural environment becomes frustrated when teachers and peers consider him or her backward or slow for following the behavioral traditions of his or her culture—the only behavior he or she knows. An examination of individuals within the context of their own cultural background, conducted from a descriptive rather than ethnocentric point of view, is essential for understanding behavior (Hale-Benson, 1987). Randall-David warned:

> There is always the danger of overgeneralizing or stereotyping when cultural information such as this is described. It is vitally important that none of these groups be seen as a monolith, but rather as a collection of individuals who share a common cultural heritage. (1989, p. 35)

Educators also need to examine the effects of racism and stereotyping on children's behaviors. Many children have damaged self-images because their unique, individual cultures are not recognized within their school or community. All children need to be connected to family and cultural values and belief systems. Showing respect for these values and beliefs is a way of showing respect for the individual child, his family, and his culture.

This chapter will briefly examine the demographics, history, and other cultural components affecting the behavior of African-Americans, American Indians or native Americans, Asian-Americans, and Hispanic-Americans. The following list defines other terms used to describe cross-cultural principles of behavior:

◆ *Acculturation:* "The degree to which people from a particular cultural group display behavior which is like the more pervasive American norms of behavior" (Randall-David, 1989, p. 3). "The process of conditioning a child to the patterns or customs of a culture" (Guralnick, 1986, p. 10).

◆ *Assimilation:* "The cultural absorption of a minority group into the main cultural body" (Guralnick, 1986, p. 84).

◆ *Cultural relativity:* "The idea that any behavior must be judged first in relation to the context of the culture in which it occurs" (Randall-David, 1989, p. 2).

◆ *Ethnocentrism:* "The tendency to view one's cultural group as the center of everything, the standard against which all others are judged. It assumes that one's own cultural patterns are the correct and best ways of acting" (Randall-David, 1989, p. 2).

◆ *Enculturation:* "To cause to adapt to the prevailing cultural patterns of one's society" (Guralnick, 1986, p. 461).

AFRICAN-AMERICANS

Demographics

African-Americans, the largest minority group in the United States, comprise 28.9 million people or about 12% of the total population (Hodgkinson, 1990). The African-American population is expected to grow almost twice as fast as the total U.S. population by the year 2000, resulting in a rise from 12.4% of the population to 13.4% between 1988 and 2000 (Hodgkinson, 1990). African-American children represent 16% of all public school students (DBS Corporation, 1987).

The educational status of African-Americans has improved significantly over the past 30 years. In 1960, the average African-American adult had an eighth-grade education. By 1986, the average African-American adult had a high school diploma (Hodgkinson, 1990). Although they represent 12.2% of the total population, only 7.2% of African-Americans held a college degree in 1984, compared to 15.5% of the total population (Hodgkinson, 1990). And the number of African-American high school graduates actually going to college declined in the 1980s. The share of college students who are African-American fell from 9.4% to 8.6% (Hodgkinson, 1990; Wilson & Carter, 1988).

An African-American child is 40% more likely than a European-American child to be behind a grade level in school, and 15% more likely to drop out of school (Hodgkinson, 1990). The gap between test scores of African-Americans and European-Americans, however, is narrowing. In 1975, the average SAT score for African-Americans were 332 (verbal) and 354 (mathematics), compared to 451 (verbal) and 493 (mathematics) for European-Americans. In 1987, African-Americans averaged 353 (verbal) and 384 (mathematics), compared to 447 (verbal) and 490 (mathematics) for European-Americans (Hodgkinson, 1990). While African-Americans make up only 16% of the U.S. student population, they represent 31% of all corporal punishment cases; 25% of all student suspensions; 35% of students categorized as mentally disabled; and just 8% of students in gifted and talented programs (Hodgkinson, 1990).

Nearly one of every two African-American children lives in poverty and almost two-thirds live in homes relying on some form of public assistance (Children's Defense Fund, 1987). Educationally, African-American children are three times as likely as European-Americans to be placed in special education programs and have the highest dropout rate (28%) (Children's Defense Fund, 1987).

Brief Historical Overview

African-Americans are drawn from a diverse range of countries and cultures including Africa, the Caribbean, and Central and South America. For African-

An African-American child learns at an early age that behavioral expectations of the predominantly white school community may vary significantly from that of his or her neighborhood community.

Americans in the United States the reality is that race, as it has been biologi-
cally and socially defined, has been a major determining factor in institutional
arrangements. This is particularly true with respect to what is considered to
be appropriate educational policies, programs, and practices (Anderson, 1988).

Historically, the economic and political needs of the larger society dictat-
ed an educational policy of "compulsory ignorance" for African-Americans
(Bond, 1970). Schooling was forbidden for most people of color under the caste-
like laws that supported the southern agricultural economy. Since most
African-Americans lived in the South and the majority of them were slaves,
this discriminatory educational policy affected most of them.

Education that was permitted occurred in the name of religion and was
designed to "Christianize the heathens." A few African-Americans were infor-
mally educated in the households of European-Americans who ignored or
deliberately violated the laws against educating slaves (Butts, 1989). Although
northern African-Americans were allowed to be educated, schooling for them
was uneven in quality, often separate, and usually unequal (Woodson, 1968).

White industrialists and philanthropists felt that universal schooling for
all children would be complementary to an economy that was changing from

an agricultural to an industrial base. However, their vision of education for African-Americans was one that emphasized vocational training to ensure economic productivity. This was coupled with a plan to socialize them into subordinate societal roles, thereby contributing to social stability. Yankee missionaries, guided by democratic idealism, believed that African-American children had the right to quality education as well as political and civil equality.

In 1896 the *Plessy v. Ferguson* decision constitutionally established the "separate but equal" doctrine that dominated social and educational policy until the passage of *Brown v. Topeka (Brown I)* in 1954. For 58 years constitutional law protected the existence of *de jure* school segregation in the South and *de facto* school segregation in other parts of the country. While the separateness of this concept was enforced, the equality portion was not. The resulting inequalities were maintained through the transition to an industrial economy, through more than half the twentieth century, the Great Depression, and two world wars. These inequalities became entrenched in our society through law, habit, custom, tradition, expediency, and attitude formation. Second-class citizenship for African-Americans was seen as right and good, natural and normal, and supportive of societal stability which included gradual progress for African-Americans (Felice, 1981).

After the *Brown I* and *Brown II* decisions in 1954 and 1955, formal, constitutional, and legal discrimination in educational policy came to an end. However, many southern white policymakers elected not to obey the law. Initially there was massive resistance to desegregating public schools in the South and to making access to education equal. Such concepts as "nullification" and "interposition" were resurrected, and southern governors literally and figuratively stood in schoolhouse doors to bar entry of African-American students at all levels of the educational enterprise.

White flight from desegregating schools often leaves urban schools without sufficient resources to accomplish the tasks of education. Gerrymandering of northern school boundary lines was common as school boards manipulated and regulated school attendance patterns to contain African-Americans within certain districts. The social/educational practice of busing was extended to give African-American students access to schools of higher material quality—better buildings, equipment, libraries, laboratories, and the like. However, as the practice of tracking (sometimes camouflaged under other rubrics) spread and the trend toward the intellectual grouping of students escalated, the policy of busing often resulted in the resegregation of African-American students in the receiving schools based on these students' underachievement and alleged inability to learn academic subjects (Wilson & Carter, 1988).

The African-American family was held to be the prime cause of student underachievement because of alleged deficiencies due to deprivation, difference, and poverty. The old debate about genetically caused African-American mental deficiencies was reopened with the publication of Jensen's (1969) article in the *Harvard Educational Review*.

Federal legislation and executive orders of the 1960s were designed to help African-Americans overcome severe past discrimination. These included the Civil Rights Act of 1964, the Voting Rights Act of 1965, the Elementary and Secondary Education Act of 1965 (amended in 1974), the Higher Education Act of 1965 (amended in 1972), and the affirmative action policies rooted in Executive Order 11246.

Historically, African-Americans have taken advantage of opportunities to become better educated. They migrated from the South to other regions of the country, from rural to urban areas, always seeking better educational opportunities, along with more opportunities for meaningful employment, desirable housing, and improved quality of life (Wilson & Carter, 1988). African-Americans often sent their children to live in the homes of relatives who resided in cities that offered better educational opportunities than the communities in which they lived. They maintained family support systems whereby parents educated their older offspring, who in turn contributed greatly to the education of younger family members. Many older offspring had to forego their own formal educational development to help meet their families' economic needs so that younger offspring could obtain a higher education. This traditional emphasis on the collective family community is very different from the American emphasis on the individual.

Cultural Influences on Behavior

The majority of critiques and discussions of African-Americans have generally portrayed their families as disorganized, matriarchal, and single-family directed. This view has resulted in a deficiency model for studying the culture and behavior of African-Americans. Any explanation of behavior, however, must consider the environmental context and larger social systems. Low social status, less respect, and less power and influence on a societal level have certainly made an impact on the culture of the African-American community.

Community Influences on Behavior

African-American children who grow up in predominantly black communities are raised to believe in the collective view of success that is concerned with the black community as a whole. They, like many other families, want the best that life has to offer in terms of education, finances, spirituality, politics, and social interaction.

African-American children start their educational lives with cognitive, sensory, and motor skills equal to children of other cultures (Jones, 1985). But since an individualistic rather than a collective, cooperative learning environment exists in most schools, these children must first unlearn or modify their own culturally sanctioned interactional and behavioral styles if they wish to be rewarded in the school context and subsequently achieve academic success. This is a very difficult choice for most children, especially adolescents.

A type of kinship exists in African-American culture based on reciprocal social, political, and economic relationships. The term used to convey this kinship is "brotherhood" or "sisterhood." Simply being black, however, does not guarantee good standing in the community. One can be denied membership based on behavior, attitude, and activities if they are perceived to be at variance from group norms or expectations.

Children learn about this kinship from their parents and peers while they are growing up. They acquire a sense of cooperation within the community and work for the good of the group. For many adolescents, the mere act of attending school may place them in competition with the expectations of their community peers. This often results in a conscious or semiconscious rejection of the indigenous African-American culture.

Conflict Between Cultures

At age five or six years, children are learning how to make sense of their world from a culture-specific perspective. At a time when African-American children are learning who they are, where they are, and how they fit into the world, they are introduced to formal schooling, which promotes acculturation. Many of these youngsters quickly become aware of hostility toward their race at an early age. To succeed in school, some students develop a minimal connection to their own culture and assimilate into the school culture. Others, like Bryan in Vignette 12.1, refuse to do so and may be stigmatized by school personnel.

Vignette 12.1.   Conflict in the Classroom: A Student's Perspective.

By Bryan James

I remember when I was in fifth grade. Ms. Jones was my social studies teacher. I was considered the class clown. I would never do my homework or listen in class. I would always talk to others around me and distract them from their work. I thought I was doing pretty well until my grades came. That's when my dad and I had a very serious talk about school. My teachers put me on a program where they signed a daily progress report on my performance in school. I studied hard and my grades slightly improved.

Social studies class was still the hardest for me. I sat in the back row. I would often talk to myself or repeat aloud things I needed to learn. This helped me remember things. One day, however, Ms. Jones gave us an assignment. I started talking to myself, repeating the directions, to help me along. Ms. Jones looked up from her desk and said, "Out!" I looked at her and she said, "You are disturbing the class." "No I wasn't," I said, "I was working." But Ms. Jones said, "You can't work with your mouth open." At that point she sent me to the principal's office. I felt cold and alone, like I was stupid. No one would listen to me or take me seriously. The more I thought about it, the more mad I became. My way of getting back at Ms. Jones was to be disruptive in class. The more I did this, the worse my grades got. But I did not care—I wanted to get back at her for not listening to me.

After a while I slowed down and my anger dried up. I began to realize why my teachers would not listen to me about thinking aloud and repeating things. It was because of all those years of goofing off and not paying attention. I also realized that if you challenge authority you will always lose.

Source: Bryan James is a seventh-grade, African-American student in Maple Grove, Minnesota.

Children who don't develop a strong connection with their school community may find it easier to drop out—intellectually, emotionally, and physically. For many African-Americans, the knowledge learned in school has no direct relationship to their own real world and culture. Frequently, knowledge learned through their cultural environment is not valued by the school. For example, many educators are critical of native dialects and want all students to learn standard English. "Until recently a major function of the public school was the Americanization of immigrants. Rigid adherence to standard English in the classroom was one of the school's defensive responses to its inundation by culturally different immigrant children" (Erickson, 1972, p. 19). In Vignette 12.1, Bryan's use of repeating directions and thinking aloud, an auditory learning strategy frequently used by African-Americans, conflicted with the teacher's expectations of appropriate classroom behavior. These conflicts, communicated through teachers' verbal and nonverbal messages (Graham, 1984), may have a significant impact on a child's socialization and self-esteem. Perhaps his teacher could have asked him why he was repeating her directions, listen to his explanation, and reach an agreement with Bryan that would allow him, when necessary, to *quietly* talk to himself as not to disturb the other students.

Parental Alienation

A high sense of alienation among parents of color and the school (along with other public institutions) is common. This alienation should be examined in light of the school's culture and the parents' perception of that culture. Parents of color often report higher levels of alienation, isolation, and normlessness in their relationship with public schools than white parents (Jones, 1985). For example, parents of color viewed school regulations as arbitrarily determined and applied according to the prevailing white, middle-class culture. Furthermore, they perceived the school's organizational policies and procedures as hostile and identified a lack of "friendliness" and overt attempts by teachers not to relate to them in a positive fashion (Jones, 1985).

Teachers often contact parents only when their children are in trouble. Since the teachers become associated with predominantly negative information about their children, the teacher-parent relationship becomes strained. As a result, parent-teacher interactions may become dominated by confrontation rather than mutual respect.

A consistent pattern of discrimination is also established by administrators who make changes in school assignments, policy, or instructional methods without first consulting people, including people of color, from the larger school community. One way to alleviate some of these concerns is to have an active and effective parent/community involvement advisory board for each school that looks at the whole or general needs of the school rather than isolated parts (Banks & Banks, 1989).

Due to disparities in economic conditions, African-Americans and their children often are treated as clients and not as consumers by school personnel. Educators often attribute poor academic performance of African-Americans to a lack of parental interest. Banks (1991) found that African-American parents may not want to be passive participants, and their children passive recipients, in the education process. As with other parents, however, many African-American parents feel that they lack the personal knowledge or confidence to confront a large, bureaucratic institution, as evidenced by Vignette 12.2.

Vignette 12.2.   Conflict Between Cultures: A Parent's Perspective.

By Kerry Frank

I have two little boys, ages 7 and 9 years. In order for me, anyone actually, to fully understand the complexities involved in their experiences, it is necessary to realize the context within which they must exist on a day to day basis. I would like to reflect on three major points. They are: (1) the context that Black Americans must understand in order to live in America and achieve at certain levels; (2) the point at which my little boys realized how being a Black-American affects them; and (3) what I hope for and would want my children's teachers to realize.

As I see it, Black-Americans constitute a unique minority, not only in the United States, but in the world. This fact has been recognized by a number of researchers and writers. Black-Americans experience a special type of marginality in the United States (Pettigrew, 1988). That is, they are part of the society, but are often treated as though they are not part of the society.

I grew up in the South—a place where discrimination, race, slavery, and segregation are brought to a Black-American's mind on a fairly regular basis. I know that my experiences as I was growing up affects how I feel about race relations and how I communicate this to my children. I do not harbor any animosities toward any given persons. I have never had problems getting along well with members of the dominant culture. That has meant, however, that I have had to either pretend that certain experiences were not painful or acknowledge that living in the United States means having to endure, grow stronger, hurt, and be angry. I did all of the above.

I want my children to be able to do the same. I know that I do not want my children to alienate themselves from their peers. When discussing issues related to slavery, or their African ancestors, or issues related to prejudice and racism, I know that my children are very special, and that their ancestors were special. I know that certain acts were committed by certain people. But I also know that hate is morally wrong and reprehensible regardless of who harbors it.

I believe my little boys realized their uniqueness very early in their development. They were the only Black-American children in their preschool which they started attending at around three years of age. During their upper-Midwest preschool experience they encountered the kinds of reminders I encountered. They did not seem to be affected by their uniqueness. Even now, most of their experiences are with diverse groups and members of the dominant culture. The only time they are able to interact with a predominantly Black audience is when they attend church.

I want my children's teachers to recognize my children's uniqueness as something positive and highly valued. As their father, I have serious doubts about my family ever being assimilated into the U.S. society. I am not a separatist. Having studied this society (as a means of survival), however, I know that certain things, at this point in time, are simply not possible. I want my children's teachers to expect and require of them the same that is expected and required of white, middle-class children. But, I also want my children's teachers to realize that there are many subtleties existing in our society that encourage members of the dominant culture to treat others, especially Blacks, a certain way.

Source: Kerry Frank is an assistant professor at the University of St. Thomas, St. Paul, Minnesota.

Most school administrations fail to recognize that all parents, regardless of color, whether single or married, employed or unemployed, want a good education for their children. African-American parents, however, are more alienated than white parents from the American public school system. Traditionally, American urban public school systems have attempted to meet the needs of African-American students through busing, hiring African-American teachers and administrators, eliminating tracking systems, and initiating programs designed to raise the academic performance and encourage students to remain in school. Jones (1985) found, however, that many African-American parents continue to believe that the school officials covertly maintain discriminatory attitudes that reflect cultural biases against them and their children. Attempts to mask these attitudes have not been successful, and many parents have developed a passive attitude to help their children survive in the public school environment. This passive attitude may be translated as a "negative attitude" by many educators. In that sense, parental attitudes may also be a factor in the high dropout rate among African-American students (Rumberger, 1983). The following list, adapted from Randall-David (1989) and Berry and Asamen (1989), outlines behaviors associated with African-American culture. African-Americans are likely to:

- ◆ Look away while listening.
- ◆ Stand close to others when talking.
- ◆ Be reluctant to talk about family problems and personal relationships.
- ◆ Be concerned with present more than the future goals.
- ◆ Consider family and extended family very important.
- ◆ Be influenced by many adults within the family and extended family.
- ◆ Consider Mother's role as the most significant in the family.
- ◆ Live in a female-headed household.
- ◆ Consider elderly members of the community especially important and respected.
- ◆ Consider religion an important part of life, and consider the church minister to be the most influential member of the community.
- ◆ Embrace cultural norms if they are living in low SES conditions but not if they live in middle or upper-class conditions.
- ◆ Believe that most individuals within the white culture do not understand or want to understand their culture.
- ◆ Find it difficult to operate within predominantly black settings if they grow up in white, middle-class settings.

AMERICAN INDIANS

Demographics

The population of American Indians is small compared to Hispanics or African-Americans, but is growing at unprecedented rates. The U.S. Census Bureau (1991) reported a 60% increase in the American Indian population from 1970 to 1980 and a 38% increase from 1980 to 1990. The current American Indian population stands at approximately 2 million people or 0.8% of the total U.S. population (U.S. Census Bureau, 1991). American Indian children represent approximately 1% of public school students.

Many American Indians have recently moved from rural to urban homes. The urban population of American Indians increased from 0% in 1890 to 49% in 1980 (Thornton, 1987). As of 1990, 62.3% of American Indians were living in urban areas or lands off the reservations (U.S. Census Bureau, 1991). There is a prevalence of young families among the Indian population. For example, Attneave (1982) found that only 10% of American Indians were 55 or over.

Brief Historical Overview

American Indian heritage is rich, beautiful, and overflowing with respect for persons and all creation. It is, however, constantly changing, adapting, and diverse. The indigenous people of the American continent, grouped and designated as American Indians in legal references with the government, have adopted the term Native American. While both these terms are technically incorrect, because they allude to either anyone born on this continent or to inhabitants of India, they are used interchangeably in the literature. Caregivers should learn the preferred language of the students and families with whom they work. Also, when referring to individual groups, both nation and tribe will be used interchangeably in this chapter.

In the varied belief systems and religions of individual American Indian nations, a value that remains constant is the belief that American Indian people were always on the North American continent. This contradicts the commonly held stereotypes and theories which conclude that Indians are descendants of Asians. Indian people reject this conclusion and some leaders suggest this stereotype is an attempt by Eurocentric scientists and the government policymakers to further deny Indian land claims. Continual Indian habitation of North America is now further substantiated by scientific theories such as the continental drift.

Beginning with the emigration of Europeans to America, conflicts occurred between white populations and tribal people. Land ownership has been the main issue of conflict along with other issues stemming from different values and belief systems. The Dawes Act of 1887 divided American Indian land into individual ownership lots rather than tribal land held in common. American Indians were expected to become farmers of their own individual allotment of land. This gave land speculators an opportunity to extort land from individuals rather than tribes. Many unscrupulous schemes were used to gain American Indian land. This "divide and conquer" tactic worked and many Indian resources were lost. Without a land base, American Indians were frequently destined to early deaths and poverty.

The Termination Act of the 1950s was enacted to end the laws guaranteeing special status of American Indian land. Consequently, more land was taken from American Indians. The demoralizing policy of termination was stopped through the work of activists and as a result of President Nixon's proclamation to halt this practice. Today, however, land and resources are continually coveted by the non-Indian populations, businesses, and government.

American Indians gained the right to vote in 1924 after many returned from service with American forces overseas during World War I. More changes occurred when the federal government began to allow self-government through the Wheeler-Howard Act of 1934. This law was the first to provide some semblance of American Indian self-rule. Constitutions were written under governmental tutelage for most Indian nations. However, the majority of positive legislation began in the 1970s. For example:

◆ In 1975 Congress passed the Indian Self-Determination Act, which provides some autonomy and recognizes American Indian's special relationship with the federal government.
◆ In 1978 Congress passed the Indian Freedom of Religion Act making it legal to practice Indian religions and they could be openly celebrated (Banks, 1991, p. 135).

◆ In 1978 Congress passed the Indian Child Welfare Act, which allows American Indians to control adoptions and foster placements of their own children.

The struggle to keep or improve American Indian rights and the land base as it remains today is continuous. Fishing and hunting rights, religious rights, and land and educational issues are still major concerns for which American Indians struggle. These issues are further complicated by the diversity of people, tribes, religions, and diverse adaptations to American culture.

Some American Indian elders and leaders do not see multicultural education as the correct method of education for American Indians in the twenty-first century. Instead, they hope that the non-Indians will eventually leave them alone to run their own affairs and live without interference. As stated by Deloria, the United States and its inhabitants regarded the Indians as "another domestic minority group." American Indians do not see themselves as such. Instead, many "remain fully intent on raising their claims of national independence" (Deloria, 1985, p. 3).

The U.S. government, along with churches and missionaries, used various means to keep American Indian children from learning their culture, its values, and behaviors. Boarding schools, for example, made every effort to negate native American culture and tribal languages and replace them with the culture of the dominant society. Many scholars of earlier times believed American Indians did not have the desirable means to educate and rear their own children. As stated by Johnston:

> The line generally taken by the instructors was that Indian culture was inferior, and Wilson boasted that "not a word of Indian [language] is heard from our boys after six months." This was achieved through strict discipline and rigorous punishment. Punishment was given every night at seven to those who broke any of the rules. (1989, p. 7)

Physical punishment for children was contrary to American Indian philosophy and was considered inappropriate to American Indian parents. However, it was the preferred method for European-Americans and their children during this era. Through these violent methods, it was surmised that the Indian child would be "civilized."

Today, due to a multimedia proliferation of native American stereotypes, many non-Indians continue to hold these perceived negative views of Indians being savage and uncivilized. This is further reinforced through the stereotypes perpetuated in cartoons and old Hollywood movies. As stated by Hirschfelder:

> It also should come as no surprise that Indian children who constantly see their people stereotyped or treated in unfair ways grow into adults who begin to feel and act as if they were not as good as other people. These Native children are hindered in developing healthy self-images and racial identities. (1982, pp. x–xi)

These stereotypes must be corrected and the classroom is a great place to start. Unfortunately, they are usually ignored as demonstrated in Vignette 12.3.

Vignette 12.3.   The Proliferation of Stereotypic Materials.

Joan Phelps, a sixth-grade teacher, required her class to write a history paper and report on a story written about the days of the "Wild West." On the day of their reports, one of Joan's students began to talk about a story she found in the school library. The story was about the many fights European-Americans had with native Americans and the idea of "killing Indians" was significantly glorified.

Although Ms. Phelps had a native American student in her classroom, she did not think about how the story would affect the student. Moreover, Ms. Phelps missed an ideal opportunity to correct several myths and stereotypes about native Americans and their relationships with the early European settlers. An educational opportunity for her students and a chance to promote understanding and appreciation for cultural diversity was lost. In fact, incorrect myths and stereotypes were reinforced.

Cultural Influences on Behavior

Considering all the behaviors of all the Indian people and nations across America would be unmanageable because there are approximately 400 different nations with their own languages, dialects, and customs. American Indians do not share the same culture, they do not all look the same, and they do not have the same behavioral traits. American Indians are conservatives, liberals, urban, rural, traditional, contemporary, and so on; and they raise their children accordingly.

While American Indians have a unique culture, many individuals have not been exposed to their own tribal customs. Much of the subtleties of Indian behavior, however, can be found in the children regardless of their cultural knowledge. These behaviors are learned and nurtured within Indian families and their communities.

Some traditional cultural behaviors of American Indians are described next. Again, not all American Indians will exhibit all these characteristics—it is not the purpose of this chapter to generalize nor stereotype American Indian behavior. However, there are some cultural influences on American Indian behavior of which educators should be aware.

Respectful Behavior

Although similarities are found in the outward submission conveyed to authority, such as church figures, business leaders, and elderly family members, American Indians view "respectful behavior" differently than non–Indian Americans. For American Indians, demonstrating respect of elders, with their more powerful spirits and a wealth of knowledge obtained through longevity, is based on religious and cultural values. Respect is an integral part of the native American culture and transfers into all aspects of life. Respect for others has a significant effect on individual behavior and on social mores within the American Indian culture.

One of the most unique expressions of respect is that of "noninterference." This includes a tolerance for others that allows family and friends to make their own mistakes and live their own lives without interference. Respect has precedence over all aspects of the American Indian child and the family's behavior, underlying the thoughts and actions observed by caregivers. Although each Indian nation has its own customs, this powerful value is the foundation of most American Indian cultures.

Eye Contact

American Indian children may look away from an adult or hold their heads down during initial interactions with adults. Traditional children will not raise their heads to their teachers because the teacher is an adult who should be respected. Also, adults may gaze away from the person with whom they are speaking as a sign of respect and religious custom. Maintaining eye contact for American Indians may be considered an act of disrespect, hostility, or rudeness (LaFromboise, 1982).

Nonaggressive Behavior

Traditionally, and in some homes today, American Indian children learn not to argue with or criticize parents or offer views different from parents' views in their presence. For many children, this respect carries into all adult relationships, especially relationships with figures of authority and elders. Consequently, elderly people, who are not to be challenged in public, are treated with respect regardless of their social status. Displays of disrespect of elders may result in a reduction of credibility throughout the American Indian community.

In this framework of relationships, traditional Indians perform in American society in a nonassertive or passive manner. American Indians may walk away from a potential problem whenever they feel uncomfortable. For example, one may walk away from a situation that has the potential for aggressive behavior. Also, although they may have very strong feelings and emotions about an issue, they may refrain from expressing these feelings in order to keep the human relationships respectful. Opinions and feelings are sometimes better expressed to other perceptive people with the use of body language and other subtle gestures and movements (LaFromboise, 1982, p. 10).

LaFromboise (1982), with the help of many American Indian professionals from across the country, produced a manual called *Assertion Training with American Indians: Cultural/Behavioral Issues for Trainers.* One of the strategies within this manual provides American Indians with skills in assertiveness so that they are better prepared to exercise personal rights without denying the rights of others. LaFromboise stated that:

> Through effective communication, Indians can protect their heritage, reach compromises acceptable to both Indian and non-Indian cultures, and prosper through self-determination. Indian people can still be quiet and self-disciplined, using bravery (assertiveness) when necessary to stand up for the rights of all Indian people. (1982, p. 12)

Sharing Behavior

Traditionally, tribal people worked for the good of the group. Indian tradition teaches that a life well lived should be for the family and others in the clan and tribe—individuals should not stand out from the group. This is a trait or quality not fully understood by many within American society where individuals are encouraged to stand out and be the best.

Sharing is a cultural expectation within American Indian culture because of the traditional sharing of food, ideas, knowledge, material, wealth, and time. Also, others are expected to reciprocate. If this does not happen, one's cultural heritage may be suspect. Indian women may offer nourishment to guests without concern for their modest homes or furnishings. Mothers and grandmothers worry aloud about their ability to provide for guests. Through this behavior, children are taught indirectly particular cultural mores. An example of sharing was experienced by the second author during a professional visit to a home in one of the poorest of neighborhoods in Minneapolis in 1983. The homemaker had only one kitchen chair and one can of juice to share. The visitor was given the chair and the can of juice with sincere expressions of hospitality. The author could not refuse, but could offer to share her portion with the children.

Speaking Behavior

Privately, American Indians laugh, gossip, and verbalize as much as anyone else. But, while family siblings and cousins may converse very freely, respectful behavior is maintained with parents and elders. Other guidelines vary from tribe to tribe. For example, Winnebago people have rules about teasing and other restrictions apply for in-laws and other relatives in the extended family.

Educators may experience children who are very quiet within the school setting. This may be because of the child's unsure assessment of his or her situation. Silence may also be a way of expressing respect for the teacher as an elder and authority figure. For example, one teacher told the story of a 6-year-old girl who moved from an Indian reservation to Minneapolis. She did not talk aloud in the classroom for many months. During the same period of time, however, she was observed talking to her cousins and sisters on the playground. After five months in the school, she began to whisper in her teacher's ear. It was not until the following school year that she was able to participate verbally in classroom discussions. LaFromboise (1982) advised educators to watch for visual clues from American Indian children, along with encouraging them to express their feelings and attitudes.

Disclaimers are frequently used in American Indian conversation—this is an essential method of showing one's humility. Pepper stated that "Many Indian people believe all people are of equal social value, therefore, each person has inherent rights to mutual respect and equal treatment. These values are generally learned in an informal manner and unconsciously applied" (1986, p. 5). American Indians typically disavow, deny, and repudiate any attempts at bragging or placing themselves above anyone else. Disclaimers may also be used when asked to express their opinion. Again, the purpose here is to nullify any attempt to raise one's status above others (LaFromboise, 1982).

American Indians believe that conversation should not be interrupted. For example, in an American Indian home it was observed that the husband would let his dinner get cold when he received a phone call from a salesman. He would not interrupt the sales pitch until it was finished. Then he would politely tell them he was not interested in their product.

When elders or others are speaking, they continually use allegorical phrases, stories, and anecdotes, and may speak for long periods of time. The traditional Indian will talk around the point and expect the listener to locate the meaning (LaFromboise, 1982). Many times, elders will refrain from joining the conversation in a school faculty meeting. Instead, they may expect to be asked their opinion and expect others to wait patiently for their full response.

The use of stories in teaching and everyday conversation is common in American Indian culture. Children develop listening skills at an early age. Children are encouraged to draw their own conclusions and find the hidden meaning in the rhetoric or allegories often found in the traditional stories. Intense listening skills and analytical powers were needed to find the meanings in an ancient culture with an oral rather than written tradition.

Educators are encouraged to allow for longer waiting periods when questioning Indian students. In a study of children living on an Indian reservation, Tharp (1989) found that Navajo teachers allowed a longer waiting period before an answer was expected of Navajo children than Anglo teachers working with the same children. American Indians believe that, when given an opportunity to speak, verbalization should not be hurried.

Observing and Listening Behavior

Observing and listening are essential skills in the American Indian culture. Traditionally, children observed their elders working or attending other "adult" activities and meetings. Parents used cradleboards to wrap children securely so they would be immobile and snug, yet transferrable and safe for travel with their parents as they worked. "Although you in Western society may argue that such a method serves to hinder motor-skill development and abstract reasoning, we believe it forces the child to first develop his intuitive faculties, rational intellect, symbolic thinking and five senses" (Lake, 1990, p. 50). Today, American Indians will frequently bring children along rather than leaving children to the care of relatives or enlisting the services of a babysitter. Community events are usually planned with the whole family in mind (Light & Martin, 1985).

Traditionally, Indian children were taught to value stillness and quiet in preparation for learning. Family elders had a certain "look" for children that reminded them their behavior at that moment was not appropriate and they must remain still and quiet, observing and listening. Although some of this has changed, listening still is an important characteristic of Indian people. For example, when involved in a conversation, an American Indian may sit with his eyes closed and simply listen and think about what others have to say. This should not be considered a sign of rudeness or inattention.

Initiation and Participation Behavior

Typically, American Indians must feel they can succeed at a task before they will initiate a task. This is different from the European-American try-and-try-again-until-you-succeed virtue. For example, before participating in a new game, American Indian children may spend a significant amount of time just watching and learning how to play. They may not participate in the activity unless they believe they can succeed.

Traditionally, Indian mothers and grandmothers demonstrated skills repeatedly before children were given opportunities to perform the task. When elders were assured the child was ready, then they would provide the opportunity to proceed. Needless to say, children were carefully prepared for a successful experience.

Timing Behavior

Indian culture teaches an acute sense of timing. Before speaking or taking action, American Indians are taught to assess the situation. Non-Indians are able to be curt and abrasive with constant interruptions, quick questions, and short answers. This behavior is not congruent with Indian culture. While it is not uncommon for non-Indian people to be abrupt or straightforward in the business world or in a professional setting, this style is offensive to Indians because it contrasts with their traditional means of communication and interactions with others (LaFromboise, 1982).

American Indians are sometimes perceived as having a very relaxed perspective of time. Actually, for Indian people, time has a people-centered focus. They feel that, first and foremost, priority should be given to people and their needs rather than the clock. Indian traditionalists carefully consider the present time and do not worry about the distant future. For example, it would be inappropriate to interrupt an elder's storytelling in order to be on time for a meeting. To the American Indians, the present is considerably more important than the future. This way of living contrasts with the fast-paced, dominant society.

Physical Appearance and Behaviors

Hair length was important to the Ojibwe Indians. Furthermore, this outward appearance had spiritual meaning. Even today, some tribes believe that hair length is a symbol of one's lifeline while others consider hair length a sign of health, knowledge, and adherence to traditions. Unfortunately, government boarding schools and public schools often did not allow Indian children to wear their hair long. This is another example of how many children of Indian cultures were forced to follow the expectations of the dominant, white society.

Indians are very respectful of body space. They believe that people need only to be within listening distance and communications do not have to be face-to-face. For example, conversations may be more comfortable when held while members are working side-by-side, not staring into each other's face. Two or three feet is a respectful distance during communications. To be closer may be considered rude. Even the modern adoption of the handshake is done with a very gentle clasping of the hands and one small up and down movement. This gesture may also include a tiny up and down movement of the head. The gentleness of the handshake is a demonstration of respect. A firm and dynamic handshake may be perceived as an expression of aggression (LaFromboise, 1982).

From an Indian's perspective, body position and movements can reveal a person's feelings and attitudes. Likewise, the fewer movements and expressions on the face, the more successful one is in keeping emotions hidden. This is perceived by American Indians as a respectful way of presenting oneself.

Public displays of affection are a rarity for traditional Indians. In school, however, a gentle touch or a pat of encouragement on the student's shoulder is very acceptable. Hugging is also acceptable for young children.

Social Behaviors

Socializing occurs in all community gatherings. Many people incorporate socializing at work. Work can be the place for humor and friendship because Indians are functioning as "whole" persons at all times and do not separate their business or religious lives from the rest of their personhood. To be strictly business-like, or to keep religion separate from education, is incongruent to many Indian cultures.

Today, many myths are still associated with native Americans. Some of these myths versus the facts are outlined as follows:

Myth	Fact
American Indians are shy.	They are taught to be respectful.
American Indians are stoic.	They are taught to keep emotions and feelings to themselves or to share only with family members.
American Indians are dependent on the government.	The government has never finished paying for Indian land.
American Indians are wild and aggressive.	They are generally nonaggressive.

American Indians are dirty.

They bathed daily while the Pilgrims did not.

American Indians are lazy.

Their land base and natural resources have been diminished. As a result, unemployment is high among the American Indian population.

ASIAN-AMERICANS

Demographics

The Asian-American population was the fastest growing ethnic group between 1970 and 1980 and continued to be one of the fastest growing groups between 1980 and 1990 (Banks, 1991). During this period, the number of Asian-Americans grew from 3.8 million to an estimated 6.9 million. Since 1980, Asian-Americans have grown from 1.7% to 2.8% of the U.S. population (Hodgkinson, 1990). Three percent of all public school students are Asian-Americans (DBS Corporation, 1987). Chinese Americans comprised the largest group of Asian-Americans (21%) followed by Filipino (21%); Japanese (19.2%); Asian Indians (10.4%); and Samoan, Guamanian, and others (6.8%) (Hodgkinson, 1990).

While 60% of Asian-Americans are foreign born, the average Japanese American speaks English as his or her native language, while almost no Indochinese do (Hodgkinson, 1990). Because of the increasing Indochinese immigration, language problems among Asian-American youth are expected to increase (Nicassio, 1985). The average age of Asian-Americans is just 30 years, compared with 36 for European-Americans (Hodgkinson, 1990).

Twelve states (California, Hawaii, New York, Illinois, New Jersey, Texas, Massachusetts, Pennsylvania, Virginia, Florida, Michigan, and Washington) have more than 100,000 Asian-Americans. The largest Asian-American population centers include Honolulu (60.7% of total population), San Francisco–Oakland (10.3%), and Salinas-Seaside Monterey, California (7.0%) (Hodgkinson, 1990).

Almost 30% of Asian-Americans arrive in the United States with four years of college education completed. Thirty-nine percent of all Asian-American adults are college graduates (Hodgkinson, 1990). Asian-American youth are heavily enrolled in public schools and a high percentage graduate and attend college (Hodgkinson, 1990). While Asian-American SAT verbal scores are below white averages, their math SAT scores are higher (Hodgkinson, 1990). Because of their competence in math and the physical sciences, Asian-Americans represent a disproportionate share of minority students at many colleges and universities (Tollefson, 1986).

Asian-Americans are frequently perceived by others, especially the American media, as the "model minority" in terms of educational achievement (Banks, 1991). This, however, is not the case for many Asians. While it is true that 21% of Asian-Americans have completed four years of college, compared to 13% of all Americans (Hodgkinson, 1990), these data obscure the immense diversity within Asian communities and ignore many existing problems. For example, in Philadelphia, 40% to 50% of Asian-American students drop out of high school. And while Vietnamese students in Orange County, California, are disproportionately overrepresented as high school valedictorians, this same group also has the highest rate of truancy and suspensions of any ethnic group (Rumbaut & Kenji, 1988).

Brief Historical Overview

Asian-Americans are one of the most diverse and interesting ethnic groups in America today. Asian-Americans include the Chinese, Japanese, Indochinese, Koreans, Asian Indians and Pakistanis, and Filipinos (Banks, 1991).

Chinese

The Chinese first arrived in the United States in great numbers between 1849 and 1870. Some came from the Toishan district in Guandong, but most came from the provincial area of Kwangtung on the south China coast. This was a commercial port city that routinely gathered news from around the world. When word came about the gold rush in California, many citizens decided to seek new opportunities in America.

Emigration often involved many hardships since both America and China had strict laws against it. Additionally, Confucian doctrine, which was an integral part of Chinese life during that time, taught that a young man should value his family above all else and should not leave. Political unrest, famine, excessive taxes, and a depressed economy, however, motivated many Chinese to leave. Many of these hardships continued after their arrival in America. Many of the new arrivals moved inland to find jobs in the mines as laborers and cooks and in laundry services (Banks, 1991).

After the mining industry slowed, many Chinese found jobs working on the railroad. The owners were so impressed by their efficiency that other Chinese were recruited. When the major railroad construction projects were completed, many Chinese turned to other enterprises in agriculture and fishing. A large number settled in urban areas—the most notable of which was San Francisco where Chinatown became a social, political, and cultural center for the Chinese. It provided the Chinese immigrants with a community of shared language and tradition.

Exclusionary laws that were discriminatory against the Chinese were passed in the late 1800s on local, state, and federal levels. As a result, segregated schools and detainment facilities for new arrivals became the norm. It was not until after World War II that these laws were changed.

Many Chinese Americans who are descendants of earlier immigrants have experienced upward mobility. The Chinese community has faced an influx of new immigrants in the last 25 years. This makes them one of the largest Asian groups in the United States (Haines, 1985).

Japanese

In the late 1800s Japan faced overpopulation, political turmoil, and depressed agricultural conditions. Its citizens began immigrating to Hawaii and the U.S. mainland in search of better opportunities. The largest number of Japanese immigrants arrived in the United States between 1891 and 1924.

After the anti–Chinese exclusionary act stopped Chinese immigration, the continued need for seasonal farm laborers existed. The Japanese immigrants filled this need. One of the differences from the Chinese community was the especially strong families established through traditional arranged marriages. The marriages worked well in bonding families and developing strong family ties in the United States.

After arrival in the United States, the Japanese worked in a variety of fields including agriculture, railroads, gardening, small business, and as domestics. Because of job discrimination they worked in self-employment types of occupations. They were initially praised for their industry but were later seen as a threat and much anti–Japanese feeling surfaced (Haines, 1985).

In the early 1900s a number of legislative acts were passed that were discriminatory against the Japanese. The most devastating of these was the Executive Order 9066 signed by President Roosevelt in 1942, which resulted in the internment of Japanese Americans.

Compared to other Asian groups, few Japanese have emigrated to the United States in the last 25 years. This is because of the highly developed economy in Japan and its ability to provide necessary employment. As a result of these factors, the Japanese in the United States are one of the smallest Asian groups (Kan & Liu, 1986).

The success of the Japanese in American society is widely recognized but its future is uncertain. Their success has probably resulted from traditionally held Japanese values, attitudes, and beliefs. With a relatively low rate of immigration, structural assimilation into the American mainstream is quite likely.

Indochinese

Each nation in Indochina has its own unique sociocultural traditions and political structures. All the nations have been strongly influenced by both Chinese and Indian cultures. So while there are many differences, there are also many similarities. These influences and similarities can be seen in art, music, food, government, literature, and religion (Chuong, 1988).

The first refugees from Indochina fled to the United States in 1975. Their journey was directly related to the Vietnam War. Nearly one-half million immigrants from Vietnam, Laos, and Kampuchea (Cambodia), including many Hmong, settled in the United States in the 1980s (Cambodian Women's Project, 1984).

The Vietnamese are one of the fastest growing Asian groups in the United States. Indochinese refugees have been coming from the camps and resettlement efforts have been quite successful. The Indochinese resettled for many different reasons such as political, economic, and personal concerns.

Many of them were personally touched by the Vietnam War and its aftermath. The U.S. government had originally planned only to admit those Vietnamese who worked for the United States in Vietnam or were dependents of U.S. citizens. The criteria were expanded for other groups such as the Hmong because lives were in danger. When the Communists took over, they targeted the Hmong for annihilation because the Hmong fought with the United States against the Communists (Bilatout, Downing, Lewis, & Yang, 1988). Most of these refugees came to the United States as family groups, and a wide range of socioeconomic and educational levels were represented. Refugee camps were established to process the refugees and to provide for a transition period (Brick, 1984).

One of the major goals of the refugee camps was to provide a rapid assimilation of the refugees into American society. English as a second language programs were used and many of the resettlement sponsors were employers (Nguyen, 1984). These camps had been closed by 1975 and immigration after that point occurred through dispersal of refugees throughout the United States rather than concentrations in any single area.

Compared to the refugees arriving before 1975, those coming after 1975 received less government support. The adjustments have been great in psychological, social, and economic areas (Beare, 1984). As with other minority groups, conflicts emerged between the values children learned at school and those taught at home. In traditional Indochinese homes, the children are taught to respect older people and to be quiet, polite, modest, and humble. The conflicting behavioral expectations of the home and school sometimes confuse the children and put them in a position of forced choice. This often results in conflict at home and in the school (Caplan, Whitmore, Bui, & Trautman, 1985).

Koreans

The number of Koreans in the United States has increased in the past 25 years. The first Koreans came to the United States in 1881 and, later, many more came as students. A significant number of Koreans were also recruited to work in the sugar plantations of Hawaii in the early 1900s. Few Koreans, however, immigrated to the United States until 1965.

Asian Indians and Pakistanis

Only a small number of immigrants from India and Pakistan had settled in the United States prior to 1965. Since that time mostly highly educated, English-speaking Asian Indians have settled in the United States (Banks, 1991).

Filipinos

After the United States acquired the Philippines from the Spanish in 1898, farmers in Hawaii and mainland U.S. began to lure Filipinos away from their island homes to work as cheap laborers. Because of the chronic unemployment and widespread poverty in the Philippines, many willingly immigrated (Yu, Doi, & Chang, 1986).

Like other Asians, the Filipinos came to do work that was labor intensive. They also were involved in domestic jobs that were menial and low paying. They were however, unable to develop tight-knit communities like those the Japanese and Chinese created. This was a result of the high rate of mobility caused by seasonal jobs and because few female Filipinos were present. They faced many of the hardships and problems encountered by their other Asian counterparts (Nicassio, 1985).

Today, most Filipinos live in urban areas of California and Hawaii. More recently, Filipino immigrations have included professionals and led to a significantly higher level of socioeconomic status.

Cultural Influences on Behavior

As we have just demonstrated, Asian-Americans are a very diverse group. One way to begin to understand Asian-Americans, however, is to examine their social structure (Kan & Liu, 1986). In China, Japan, and Korea, Confucianism has served for centuries as the essential basis for its ethical, social, cultural and political life. This structure provides a framework for understanding motivation and behavior, which is essential for communication in education.

The foundation of Confucianism is the dictum of the so-called "five cardinal relationships" between father and son, wife and husband, elder and younger brother, friend and friend, ruler and subject. The dictum decrees that these relationships, except that between friends, are inherently unequal. The husband is superior to his wife by virtue of sex, the father is superior to his son and the elder to the younger brother by virtue of age, and ruler is superior to subjects by virtue of status. In this framework of relationships, where there are only superiors and inferiors, a superior holds absolute authority over an inferior. At least in theory, if not always in practice, an inferior is expected to obey the superior. It is from this absolute premise that Confucian society is organized. This is why the concept of equality before God or supreme law or the value of human rights (or individual rights) has never evolved in the tradition of Confucianism.

In this system, the worth of a person is primarily determined by sex, age, or social status, not by the intrinsic value of life or the individual self. A strong emphasis on the hierarchy of a relationship, as well as on the family group rather than the individual, is built into many aspects of Confucian culture. For example, in Korea as in Japan and China, one's family name precedes one's personal name.

Perhaps the most important example of the effects of Confucian culture is language. In Korean and Japanese, it is not essential for a sentence to indicate singular personal pronouns, particularly that of first person. Thus, these elements are often omitted in daily conversation. The function of a Korean verb is also drastically different from that of an English verb. A Korean verb comes at the end of a sentence and changes forms according to the status of the speaker in relation to the listener. Since language binds cultures to belief systems, this has a significant impact on the entire system.

Standards for social behavior between the sexes are probably most contrasting in Confucian and American cultures. In Confucian tradition boys and girls are brought up in strict separation from an early age. This custom is deeply rooted in the Confucian teachings, starting with the Confucian dictum of the five cardinal relationships mentioned above. This is further reinforced by the Confucian precept that boys and girls must not sit together after the age of seven.

Although today there are some signs that this custom is changing in some urban segments of the country, the Confucian teaching on the male-female relationships still has a formidable hold on the mind and manner of Asian people and virtually dominates the social fabric of their lives. Traditionally and at the present time, the separation between boys and girls in Asian countries is strictly enforced in elementary school. In the lower grades boys and girls may share the same classroom, but the boys are seated on one side of the classroom and girls on the other. Some teachers may even try to make a boy sit with a girl as punishment. One 16-year-old girl who came to the United States at age 11 reported that her former teachers would say "You guys keep quiet or I'll mix you boys and girls and make you sit by each other." She stated that the students were terrified by this.

In the upper classes, boys and girls are grouped separately in different classrooms. In school or out, boys and girls do not play with one another. One American mother who adopted two sisters at ages 8 and 10 reported that the girls were very uncomfortable in the presence of boys, they did not know how to play with boys, and found it difficult to cope with their teasing.

Needless to say, the enforcement of strict division between the sexes influences interactions and relationships. For example, when an Asian child sees another child of the opposite sex in school or in the street, one neither greets nor talks to the other, even though they know each other (Spero, 1985). Of course, this behavior exhibited in the United States might be misinterpreted as inappropriate. Some children of mixed parentage, or children who have lived outside the mainstream of Asian culture, may not follow traditional behavior (Overbeck, 1984).

Traditionally, and still today in most cases, Asian teenagers receive little or no sex education at home or in school, other than the instruction girls receive from their mothers about menstruation. Biological changes in adolescent years, as well as the emotional experiences of young people, are paid little attention and largely ignored. Girls rarely discuss matters of sex with others, although some girls may read about sex or talk sex with their close girlfriends. Discussing sex-related matters is often considered in bad taste. Platonic relationships are much admired and romanticized in Korea and in Japan, where open sexual expressions are generally looked on with contempt. This often carries over into social interactions by Asian-Americans in the United States. Unless others bring up this subject, married women do not openly talk about their pregnancies or send birth announcements. Pregnancy is accepted as the natural course of marriage, just as growing old is the course of life.

How do the youth channel their youthful energies? Most of their energies are expended in study and, to a limited extent, in sports and in developing relationships with peers of their own sex. This may account for the apparent work/study ethic held by many Asian-Americans. Girls are more free in expressing affection for each other, such as holding hands while walking, but almost never hug or kiss one another.

Dating between the sexes is generally permitted after graduation from high school. At this time girls are permitted to use makeup and face cream or powder, but in a modest manner. They may change their hair style from pigtails to permanent waves, and wear clothes of their choice instead of school uniforms. However, girls are careful not to expose their bodies.

Methods of discipline in the Asian-American culture are primarily determined by their social structure. Since the types of social structure differ between Confucian and American cultures, the methods of discipline used in each culture are correspondingly different. In the United States, where the individual is the most basic social unit, individual rights and responsibilities are emphasized. Accordingly, American parents train their child to stand up for their own rights and the rights of others, to be autonomous, and to become independent of them. In contrast, in Korea and other east Asian countries where the family is the basic social unit, the individual is primarily part of the family. Accordingly, Asian parents teach their children not to think for themselves but to think of themselves as part of the group. They put greater emphasis on teaching their children to be loyal to their group—whether family or nation—than on individual rights or responsibilities. As a result, they tend to become easily aroused when they feel their group or nation is criticized, but not when the human rights of their fellow citizens are violated. The concept of "our" rather than "my" is emphasized. For example, Asian children say "our mother" or "our family," instead of "my mother" or "my family." In school and at home the child is exhorted to obey authority and to conform to group norms and be like everyone else (Quan, 1986). The value of uniformity and conformity is strongly instilled in children from an early age.

Asian parents often use commanding, exhortation, fear-inspiring tactics, or, as the last resort, physical punishment. During the preschool years, Asian mothers tend to be excessively indulgent and often do not discipline their children. They may believe that the child is too young to know better and that discipline is more appropriate for older children. Instead, mothers may try to pacify their children with candy or toys or fear-inspiring tactics as a primary method of behavioral control (Prendergast, 1985; Walker, 1987). As a result, some of these young children may have some problems adapting to the strict guidelines employed in some educational programs.

Despite the many differences Asians and Americans have in their cultural values and behavior, they share the importance of education. In Asia, traditionally and today, the attainment of a good education is a common dream. It is regarded as the ultimate key to success and social status (Gallagher, 1986). For example, one might hear an Asian mother tell her children to "study hard" or "obey your teacher" when the children go to school. When the children return from school the mother may ask "Did you study hard?" Relatives and peers may greet children by asking "Are you studying hard?" The child lives in a social milieu highly charged with innate respect for learning and the drive toward achievement in education. The importance of education has been handed down largely by the legacy of Confucianism. In traditional Asia, education was synonymous with a mastery of the Confucian classics, which defined the hierarchy of relationships, familial duties, and rules for propriety of conduct.

In the legacy of Confucianism, the worth of the individual is primarily determined by sex, age, or social status. Since sex and age are fixed by birth, if a person wants to attain superiority above and beyond, he or she has to attain social status. In traditional times, the highest social status was attained by becoming a Confucian scholar. Only wealthy landlords could afford to educate their sons on Confucian ethics because such an education required funds. At the end of his study, the student took a series of civil service examinations that tested his ability to repeat the text of the Confucian classics and exegesis in the most literal sense. If he passed the examinations, he was able to obtain a position in the bureaucracy. The rationale behind this system was that those who mastered Confucian ethics automatically became moral persons who had the ability to rule the people. Through his bureaucratic position, the scholar-bureaucrat exerted his political and economic power (Phillips, 1987). Although today's education in Asia is not based on mastery of Confucian classics, much of its character, approaches, and effects are inherited from the past. An example of how this attention to social status and respect for elders may influence a child's classroom behavior is provided in Vignette 12.4.

Vignette 12.4.   Asking Questions in the Classroom: A Sign of Disrespect?

Ha, an 8-year-old child in third grade, was described by her teacher, Ann, as respectful, obedient, and motivated to learn. Although she was fairly proficient in the English language, English was not Ha's primary language. In the beginning of the school year, however, Ann reported that Ha was having problems completing classroom and homework assignments. Ann noticed that although Ha consistently made significant efforts to complete the assignments, mistakes in how or when the assignments were completed made Ann believe that Ha was not following directions.

In an effort to solve this problem, Ann began to ask Ha if she understood her directions whenever she gave the class an assignment. Ha would always say "yes." But the problem continued. Why, Ann thought, would Ha say she understood her directions when she clearly did not.

Ann then decided to have a conference meeting with Ha and her parents to discuss possible solutions to Ha's "problem." During the meeting, Ann noticed that Ha was very respectful to her parents and agreed with everything Ann and her parents said during the meeting. Ann was sure, however, that Ha did not understand many of the issues they discussed. Ann also noticed that Ha did not ask any questions and, in thinking about Ha's classroom behavior, remembered that Ha seldom asked questions in the classroom. At that time Ann asked Ha why she did not ask questions in the classroom when she did not understand assignments or when other directions were given. Ha's response surprised Ann. "I think you are a great teacher," said Ha. Ann got the message. She now understood that Ha believed that saying she did not understand Ann's directions or asking questions about Ann's directions was, in Ha's mind, not polite and, perhaps, a sign of disrespect.

Ann discussed with Ha and Ha's parents the importance of asking questions in school. In the classroom, Ann's questions to Ha were more direct. For example, instead of asking Ha if she understood the assignment, she would ask Ha to repeat the directions or certain parts of the directions. In this way, Ann could determine whether or not Ha understood her directions. In addition, Ann specially requested that Ha ask at least one question per day during class. Ann verbally reinforced Ha for these questions and made Ha understand that, as a teacher, she was very happy to hear Ha's questions.

Not surprisingly, teachers frequently described the behavior of Asian children, like the behavior of Ha in Vignette 12.4, as respectful and obedient, as well as highly motivated to learn. The results of one parent and teacher survey found that more than 64% of Asian children was rated high to above average in motivation, while 23% were rated average and 13% low (Tollefson, 1986).

Teachers should take extra precautions with their language when communicating with Asian parents about their children. The choice of words and the order of discussion is important. Yao (1988) has suggested that strengths be discussed first and then problems or weaknesses, explaining the remediation plan and enlisting the support of the parents. Indeed, this is good advice for all teacher/parent interactions. Also, note that because of the high regard most Asian parents have for educators, the choice of words is crucial. Nonverbal communication such as posture, gestures, time and space, and facial expressions may convey specific meaning to the parents (Yao, 1988). The following list, adapted from Randall-David (1989, pp. 40–47) outlines other behaviors associated with Asian-Americans. Asian-Americans are likely to:

- Not shake hands with each other.
- Consider the touching of strangers as inappropriate.
- Consider eye-to-eye contact between strangers shameful.
- Smile or laugh to mask other emotions or avoid conflict.
- Consider emotional restraint, formality, and politeness as essential for appropriate social behavior.

◆ Show deference to others and try to be nonconfrontational.
◆ Hide emotional expressions and personal feelings because these are seen as a sign of immaturity.
◆ Consider time as flexible and not hurry or consider it important to be punctual except in very important cases.
◆ Consider family and extended family as very important.
◆ Consider the behavior of an individual member of a family as a reflection on the entire family.
◆ Respect learning and have high educational standards.
◆ Be very modest.

HISPANIC

Demographics

The term "Hispanic" refers to a population that embodies Dominicans, Cubans, Puerto Ricans, Central and South Americans, and Mexican Americans. The population originates from Central and South America, Mexico, and the islands of the Caribbean.

> Hispanics came from all different racial groups. They were of European, African, Asiatic and native American extraction. Thus the Hispanics do not constitute one race but rather a mix of races. Within the various countries and in different areas of each country, the degree and variety of racial mixes changes according to the historical realities of the locality. (National Catholic Educational Association, 1987, p. 17)

The Hispanic population grew faster than any other racial or ethnic group in the United States between the 1980 and 1990 census (U.S. Census Bureau, 1991). During this time, the Hispanic population increased at five times the rate of the non–Hispanic populations and did so all throughout the 1980s. The Census Bureau (1991) reported that Hispanics have approximately doubled their population in the decade between 1980 and 1990. Their total population increased from 14.6 million to an estimated 22.4 million during this time period and now comprises 9.8% of the U.S. population in 1990 compared to 6.4% in 1980. Hispanic children represent 10% of all public school students (DBS Corporation, 1987). The large population increase may be attributed to immigration and a high birth rate among Hispanic families.

The largest group within the Hispanic population consists of Mexican Americans who account for 62.6% of Hispanics (Vobejda, 1991). Other groups that make up the Hispanic people in America and their current population are (De La Rosa & Maw, 1990, p. 5):

Hispanic Subgroup	Percent of Hispanics in United States
Mexican	62.6
Central/South American	12.7
Puerto Rican	11.6
Cuban	05.3
Other	07.8

According to De La Rosa and Maw (1990) the Hispanic population is now the youngest major ethnic group in the United States. While Americans have a median age of 31.9 years, Hispanics have a median age of 25.1. Traditionally, Hispanic families are large and children are valued as an important part of the extended family system.

Brief Historical Overview

Each culture has a cultural domain from which it draws knowledge. The dimensions of this body of knowledge are shared and it is from this concept that the perspective of the ethnic people is derived (Banks & Banks, 1989). An influential force in the Hispanic communities is the Roman Catholic church. It is the national religion of the people of Latin America. Since the conquest of the new world began, the Spanish transported Roman Catholicism to the indigenous people of the continent. Consequently, most countries of both Central and South America have Roman Catholic majorities. Although some encroachments are being made from other Christian groups, the Catholic church has been the prominent religion for centuries.

In the early sixteenth century, before the Pilgrims arrived, Spanish-speaking settlers had colonized in the southwestern United States. The prominence of the Spaniards and their culture conveyed a new philosophy to the western hemisphere. This type of thinking gave rise to a pride and honor based on conquest and glory through adventure. It was not a culture that valued manual labor and, from this basic belief, the class system was institutionalized. "The Indians and the vast number of people who performed manual labor formed the disenfranchised masses with no political or economic rights" (National Catholic Educational Association, 1987, p. 130). Some of these strong class distinctions continued even after each nation obtained its independence (National Catholic Educational Association, 1987, p. 12).

Religious participation and education for the young did not happen for the masses of people in the Spanish territories. Due to the small numbers of trained religious personnel, the huge population experienced long periods without priests and clergy to train the children and celebrate the religious services. As the land barons gained more control of the wealth and land, the vast majority of people suffered.

Because there are many Spanish-speaking nations in the western hemisphere, there are large numbers of Hispanic immigrants in the United States. However, many Mexican Americans were born in the United States before the southwestern section of the country was annexed and as a result have been citizens since this initiative was enacted. Immigrating Hispanics joined with generations of Hispanics who had been living mostly in the western and southern states of Texas, California, and Florida. Many Americans inappropriately lump native-born generations of Mexican Americans, who have lived on American soil for hundreds of years, with those who are new immigrants. Along with new immigrants, native-born Mexican Americans have experienced racism and discrimination in housing, education and other areas of society in America.

While some Mexican Americans have resided for generations in the southwestern states of Texas, New Mexico, Arizona, and California, their culture has been modified as a result of exposure to American culture. Many older generations of Hispanic-Americans are on a different socioeconomic level than recent immigrants. For example, Cuban families that have been in Florida for generations are part of the upper classes. After the Cuban revolution, when many of the educated social classes were ostracized, many well-educated citizens of Cuba found refuge in the United States. They have continued to prosper at various educational and economical levels. For many other Hispanics, however, the attainment of educational and economical success has been more difficult. Historically, the intermixing and close proximity of Indians and Spaniards in Mexico produced interconnections that are now an integral part of the culture. After the Mexican-American War in 1848, the United States annexed Mexican land inhabited by Mestizos, Spaniards, and Indians. These people were made U.S. citizens. "Thus, by virtue of the Treaty of Guadalupe Hidalgo in 1848, Mexican Americans residing in the Southwest became American citizens and were guaranteed equal protection and treatment under the American Constitution" (Ramirez and Castaneda, 1974, p. 2).

While Mexican Americans are primarily related to American Indians and are considered Mestizos (indicating an American Indian and Spanish heritage), some Hispanics have more European ancestry (people from the southern tip of South America). Yet others, from the Caribbean, for example, could have African-American ancestry. In addition, many combinations make race an undefinable ingredient for many Hispanic people.

As conditions for the lower socioeconomic classes continued to deteriorate in Mexico, immigrants from the poverty areas of Mexico poured across the border into the United States. Geographic proximity and daily migration allowed the firm attachments between families separated by the Mexican border to continue. Conversely, Central and South American immigrants had a different geographical experience as a result of the great distances separating them from their homelands.

Many Mexican American children from recently immigrated families are born into economically deprived homes. Many Mexican Americans toil in the vegetable and fruit farms of America for minimal wages. As these families move from one agricultural region to another, they are likely to join an Hispanic community already established.

Another example of Hispanic citizenship is that represented by Puerto Ricans who are found primarily in large population centers such as New York.

"Since 1917, Puerto Ricans have been U.S. citizens. In the period between the two world wars, they started migrating to the mainland in large numbers, mainly to New York City. In 1988, about 42% of all Puerto Ricans lived in the U.S. mainland" (Banks, 1991, p. 348).

Hispanic workers and their families have moved throughout the United States. As far north as Minnesota, migrant farm workers have been brought into Midwest farming and factory communities and have stayed to become permanent residents. In addition, new immigrants continued to cross the borders. The most recent immigrants have been the Haitians. Most Hispanics come looking for a livelihood denied them in their native land due to the poor economic conditions.

Cultural Influences on Behavior

Because of the immense diversity of the Hispanic population, and because Mexican Americans comprise the majority of Hispanics, this section focuses on the Mexican American people. Commonality across Hispanics, however, is found in the Spanish background, language, geographic ancestry, and religion or faith. Although some similarities are found in the behaviors of children from various Hispanic cultures, teachers are cautioned to recognize the individuality of all their students.

The Importance of the Family

For Mexican Americans the family represents their highest priority and strongest allegiance. Whenever a child needs to make a choice between school or family, the family holds the strongest position and will likely take precedence over school obligations. When there is a family celebration, special function, or circumstance requiring participation, the family members must be in attendance. According to Mexican American traditions, family loyalty comes before adherence to any schooling or job obligation.

Bonding and loyalty tie the family together. "Being children of the same Father, familiarly called 'Papa Dios' or 'Papacito Dios,' every other person is seen within the context of God's family as brother and sister" (National Catholic Educational Association, 1987, p. 31). The Hispanic extended family consists of parents, siblings, grandparents, aunts, uncles, cousins, and in-laws. Especially high regard is awarded grandparents and other elderly adults. Furthermore, family life stresses dependence on one another and sharing the joys and sorrows among family members. Blood relatives and godparents are joined to the family through such events as baptism and confirmation (see Vignette 12.5). Godparents are considered to be members of the family and they participate in all family events as if they were blood relatives:

> Though variations exist in family patterns, the Hispanic family is characterized by authority on the part of the father, loyalty and compassion on the part of the mother, obedience and submission on the part of the children. The individual gains identity and self-esteem in relation to the family group. The collective inter-

est of the family takes precedence over the individual's goals. Caring, sharing, obedience, respect, loyalty, responsibility, and interdependence are stressed (National Catholic Education Association, 1987, p. 15)

Vignette 12.5.   Interactions with the School Community: A Hispanic Parent's Perspective.

By Ramona A. de Rosales

What I tell you may not be the same thing that other Hispanic parents tell you. The Hispanic population is very diverse. Much of this depends on a parent's educational level. Some of our Hispanic parents accept everything the teachers say at face value. They may not know what to ask or how to ask.

My advice to teachers is to get to know the parents of their Hispanic children. Make them feel welcome in the school and in the classroom. This is very important to them because this is how guests are treated when they visit a Hispanic household. Sit and talk with them.

I think that many teachers do not expect Hispanic children to ask questions and challenge them. When they do, the teachers may become defensive. In our culture we teach our children to respect authority. But I think it is important to teach children the difference between disrespectful behavior and appropriate questioning or challenging behavior. I don't want my children to be aggressive, but I want them to be assertive. I think that teachers have a problem with this kind of behavior.

Hispanic people are much more interdependent in nature than other people. In our family we encourage interdependence. In school, they encourage independence. For example, sometimes my children want more help from the teacher than the teacher expects them to need. The teacher may think that the children are being babies. This is an example of how my children's behavior, behavior that is based upon Hispanic values, has been misinterpreted by teachers.

In our culture we teach our children to worry about others and take care of others. Within the school this behavior may get them into trouble. I have also heard this from other Hispanic parents that sometimes our children try to reach out and help other children with their school work when they were told to work independently. Then we are told that our children do not stay on task. What is more important is that our children think of others and help others. This is how we bring up our children. This is another behavior that is misunderstood.

Hispanic people are very warm and social and we have a desire to relate to others. Teachers must understand that the children want to socialize. This is important to them. Although they need to work on their academic tasks, this could be integrated into the presentation of the academic tasks. I think this is a strength, a gift, that our children have. The teachers should use this to their advantage. Working in groups, for example, instead of working independently all of the time.

As a parent, I want to stress to teachers that the school environment must welcome Hispanic parents. This means being sensitive to parents who have poor English language skills. For example, find someone to translate notes you send to parents. The approach is so important. You have to have good people skills when working with Hispanic parents. Also, be sensitive to the amount of negative information you communicate to parents about their children. Show respect for the child and the parent. Otherwise, the parents will stop coming to your school. This has happened already with our first-generation parents—their experiences with schools have been so negative that many have given up on the schools. We must reach out to them and try to regain their trust. You don't have to be an expert on Hispanic culture. You just need to be a sensitive person.

_____

Source: Ramona A. de Rosales is director of the Hispanic Pre-College Project, University of St. Thomas, St. Paul, Minnesota.

Festivals and Celebrations

Church festivals and important family events become major celebrations for Hispanics and their communities. The family celebrations are of both life and death. For example, celebrations of life are those of baptism, marriages, or when a young girl comes of age in a *Quinceanera* celebration. The festival sometimes occurs early in the young girl's life. Following this celebration and a traditional church ceremony, young women are ready to be courted and married. In some regions of the United States, families have incurred great debt in their dedication to provide a major gala occasion for their daughters. Similarly, men are introduced to society at age 18 when they are supposedly ready to support and care for a wife and family. These ceremonies and celebrations may be held within the home, church, or other community setting.

Personal Dignity

Personal dignity, pride, and self-worth and self-esteem are important to Hispanic people. Children are taught to show respect for others, especially to older family members and other adults in authority roles. Elders frequently remain in the family home, not nursing homes. Elders are valued for their wisdom and for imparting the Hispanic culture and language to the children. The home is considered a richer environment if it contains grandparents.

The Sense of Space

When Hispanics are engaged in conversation, they normally stand close together. As a result there may be some contact such as a gentle touching or hugging. The Hispanic is approximately eight inches closer than the European-American in face to face conversation. "'Abrazos' (hugs), touch, body distance are reflective of the desire to communicate with the other in a familiar way" (National Catholic Education Association, 1987, p. 32).

Conversation

For Hispanic people, much adherence is given to speaking Spanish. When one is accustomed to holding conversations in his or her native language, the communication will be much more animated. Mexican Americans are very visual and prefer to use more of the senses while communicating. This visual skill continues to enrich the use of the senses. The people tend to be practical and want a meaningful interpretation to their work and conversation. A sensual conversational style is intimate and carries more emotion so that conversation is lively when spoken within the native language and familiar vocabulary. Speaking Spanish is also an expression of pride in one's culture and self. In Spanish or in English, conversations may be animated when expressing emotional events or feelings in a situation where there is trust.

Open participation is the rule for joining a group discussion. One doesn't need to wait patiently for a timely pause in order to join the conversation. Interruptions in Hispanic culture are not considered rude. These conversational expectations are direct opposites to mainstream politeness, along with Asian and American Indian correct modes of behaviors. For Hispanics, these cultural expectations are meant to bring people together and engage them to participate in conversations and interactions with one another.

Relationships with Others

Family relationships and duties have an all-encompassing importance. The status of the older sibling, for example, depends on her or his ability to care for the smaller children. Likewise, the well being of the younger sibling depends on the help and assistance given by the older siblings.

Mexican American students and family members are accustomed to sharing and helping one another. Rosales (personal communication, June 6, 1991), the director of an Hispanic elementary program, reported that her students were frequently busy helping each other instead of listening to the teacher. Mexican American children would probably be comfortable in a cooperative and dependent environment (i.e., cooperative learning, sharing tasks, peer teaching). "Many traditional Mexican American children tend to perform poorly in situations that demand individual competition" (Ramirez and Castaneda, 1974, p. 114).

Hispanic people consider personalized and humanized knowledge more appealing than abstract knowledge (Banks & Banks, 1989). When a child is completing a task, the teacher may want to first demonstrate the whole picture. Once the purpose and the relevance are known, the teacher may divide the tasks into specifics.

Many Hispanic-American children prefer working more in cooperative groups than on independent assignments.

Authoritative Behavior Styles

In Hispanic culture, a strong authority system has always existed. The order of allegiance is to God, king or president, and Catholic authority (e.g., priest or bishop). For the traditional Hispanic family, the father is the head of the household. While this patriarchal style appears to relegate the mother to a lesser position, this is not the case. The mother is the main source of love and nurturing and she yields loyalty to the father. In addition, Hispanic mothers have significant control of family events and activities. Today, many Mexican American families have mothers as the head of the household.

Recommendations to teachers and other professionals for success when working with the Hispanic would include establishing personal rapport, working in groups, and having group discussions. Once trust has been established, then tasks could be divided into smaller units. At first, the student must understand the group goal, then can be asked to perform something individually. It is important to define the totality and ensure that each task is well defined and understood before proceeding with smaller units in the lesson.

To be the most effective, the teacher and professional must make personal, caring efforts to attend to the cooperative nature of the Hispanic. One must know the loyalties and structure of the family along with the ideas and beliefs that are most important to each family. Once again, the traditional values and belief systems must be familiar so that teachers may affect the behaviors of the children. How much each individual adheres to these values and behaviors will be the mystery discovered in the classroom. For many, "generalizations have instilled in the minds of most educators a picture of a typical Mexican American and a stereotype of a homogeneous folk culture" (Carter, 1970, p. 46). It is a popular myth that caregivers must eradicate for themselves and others:

> Although membership in a gender, racial, ethnic, social class, or religious group can provide us with important clues about individual's behavior, it cannot enable us to predict behavior. Knowing one's group affiliation can enable us to state that a certain type of behavior is probable. Membership in a particular group does not determine behavior but make certain types of behavior more probable. (Banks & Banks, 1989 p. 13)

Behaviors associated with the Hispanic culture are presented in the following list, adapted from Randall-David (1989, pp. 55–59). Hispanic-Americans are likely to:

- Touch people with whom they are speaking. May engage in introductory embrace, kissing on the cheek, or back slapping.
- Stand close to people with whom they are speaking.
- Interpret prolonged eye contact as disrespectful.
- Keep family or personal information from strangers.
- Have a high regard for family and extended family.
- Treat the elderly with respect.
- Help other family members and friends with child care.
- Be nonconfrontational.
- Be emotionally expressive (especially Hispanic females).
- Have traditionally prescribed sex roles for males and females.
- Consider children a family priority.
- Expect their children to consult parent's advice on important issues.
- Be more concerned with present than future time.
- Be very modest.

SUMMARY

Within the next 10 years, 30% to 40% of the students attending public schools in the United States will be non–European-Americans. They will be students from various ethnic and cultural backgrounds including African-Americans,

American-Indians, Asian-Americans, Hispanic-Americans, and many others. Before we can begin to understanding a child's behavior we must first have at least a basic understanding of the child's ethnicity and culture. Otherwise, our behavioral expectations will be invalid and we will be guilty of ethnocentrism and enculturation. We believe, however, that, in addition to the challenges, educators should consider the many educational opportunities of working with an increasingly diverse population of students. The first step, however, is for educators to learn about their students' cultures and the cultural influences on their behavior.

African-Americans are the largest minority group in the United States. They represent about 12% of the current U.S. population and, by the year 2000, will represent 13.4% of the population. African-American children represent about 16% of all public school students.

Although their educational status has improved significantly, African-Americans are still disproportionately represented in programs for students with special academic and behavioral needs. They are still more likely than white children to be behind a grade level in school and drop out of school. Nearly one of every two African-American children lives in poverty and they are less likely than white children to have the benefits of a college education.

The African-American culture has many influences on the behavior of African-American children. These behaviors have their foundation in the black family and community. Unfortunately, African-American parental attitudes and student behaviors are influenced by years of alienation. African-American children frequently find themselves trying to juggle the relationship between the European-American culture found within the school and their own culture taught within the black community. African-Americans are often treated as clients, not consumers, by school personnel. As with other parents, many African-American parents feel that they lack the knowledge or confidence to confront school personnel regarding their needs. While many have developed a passive attitude, translated as a negative attitude by white school personnel, educators must recognize that all parents, regardless of color, want a good education for their children.

The native American or American-Indian population is a small, but growing, population. They make up 0.8% of the total U.S. population and about 1% of the public school population. The American-Indian population consists of approximately 400 different nations, languages, dialects, and customs. Many American-Indians do not share the same culture and certainly not the same behavioral traits. There are, however, some cultural influences on American-Indians of which educators should be aware.

American-Indians view respectful behavior, especially as demonstrated to their elders, as one of the most important social mores of Indian culture. Other behaviors frequently associated with American-Indians include the lack of eye contact when talking to others, and nonaggressive, sharing, observing, and listening behaviors. Many inaccurate myths continue to persist about American-Indians. These myths are frequently reinforced by the media, especially the visual media.

The Asian-American population is one of the fastest growing ethnic groups in the United States. Asian-Americans make up 2.8% of the U.S. population and 3% of all public school students. Asian-Americans include the Chinese-Americans, Filipino-Americans, Japanese-Americans, Korean-Americans, and many other ethnic groups. While it is true that many Asian-Americans are model students and almost 30% of these students arrive in the United States with four years of college education, these facts often obscure the immense diversity within Asian-American communities and ignore many existing challenges for Asian-American students.

Asian-Americans are also a very diverse group. For the Chinese, Japanese, and Koreans, however, Confucianism serves as the foundation for most social and cultural issues. According to Confucian society, the worth of a person is primarily determined by sex, age, and social status, not by the intrinsic value of life or self.

In many Asian cultures, boys and girls are grouped separately within educational settings. The lack of sexual segregation within the European-American culture directly contradicts social mores of many Asian-Americans. Other differences with regard to U.S. customs include the amount of sex education, dating behaviors, and methods of discipline.

The Hispanic-American population grew faster than any other racial or ethnic group during the last 10 years and now comprises almost 10% of the U.S. population and 10% of all public school students. Hispanic-Americans include Dominicans, Cubans, Puerto Ricans, Central and South Americans, and Mexican Americans. Mexican Americans account for the largest percent of Hispanic-Americans.

The primary influences on Hispanic behaviors include the Hispanic family, the Spanish language, and the Roman Catholic church. Family relationships and duties have an all-encompassing importance. Hispanics are noted for their festivals and celebrations, usually centered around family, church, or community.

Personal dignity and pride are important elements of the Hispanic character. Touching and hugging are common during interactions, as is sharing and helping others within the community. Thus, Hispanic children are usually comfortable within cooperative learning environments and may perform poorly in situations demanding individual competition.

The Hispanic culture has a strong authority system. The order of allegiance is God, king or president, priest or bishop, and the father of the household. Establishing personal rapports with Hispanic students and their families is essential to effective teacher-student and teacher-parent relationships.

For Discussion

1. Discuss the history and treatment of African-Americans since their introduction into America. How has this history influenced African-Americans today and, perhaps, the behavior of some African-American students?

2. Frequently, the social skills learned by children within the home environment conflict with behavioral expectations within the school environment. Discuss some examples of these conflicts and how they may be resolved in a way that is sensitive to cultural differences.

3. Discuss the influence of traditional "cowboys and Indians" movies on the perceptions and behaviors of children toward native Americans. How may these stereotypes affect the self-esteem and behavior of native American students?

4. What are some family influences for Asian-American students that may have a positive effect on their academic performance?

5. Discuss the most significant influences on Hispanic students' behavior (e.g., family, church). How may these influences be incorporated into the school environment to facilitate more effective interactions between the home and school?

REFERENCES

Anderson, J. D. (1988). *The education of Blacks in the South, 1860–1935.* Chapel Hill, NC: University of North Carolina Press.

Attneave, C. (1982). American Indians and Alaska native families: Emigrants in their own homeland. In M. McGoldrick, J. K. Pearce, & J. Giordano, (Eds.), *Ethnicity and family therapy.* New York: Guilford Press.

Banks, J. (1991). *Teaching strategies for ethnic studies.* Boston, MA: Allyn & Bacon.

Banks, J., & Banks, C. M. (1989). *Multicultural education: Issues and perspectives.* Boston, MA: Allyn & Bacon.

Beare, S. (1984). ESL instruction for refugee employment. *TESL Talk, 15*(3), 12–16.

Berry, G. L., & Asamen, J. K. (1989). *Black students: Psychosocial issues and academic achievement.* New York: Sage Publications.

Bilatout, B. T., Downing, B. T., Lewis, J., & Yang, D. (1988). *Handbook for teaching Hmong.* California State Department of Education.

Bond, H. M. (1970). *The education of the Negro in the American social order.* New York: Octagon Books.

Brick, J. (1984). *Language and culture: Laos.* Sydney, Austrailia: Adult Migrant Education Service.

Butts, R. F. (1989). *The civic mission in educational reform: Perspectives for the public and profession.* Stanford, CA: Hoover Institution Press.

Cambodian Women's Project. (1984). *Bibliography of materials relating to Cambodia and the Cambodian people.* New York: Cambodian Women's Project, The American Friends Service Committee.

Caplan, N., Whitmore, J., Bui, Q., & Trautman, M. (1985). Study shows boat refugees' children achieve academic success. *Refugee Reports, 6,* 1–6.

Carter, R. (1970). *Mexican Americans in school: A history of educational neglect.* New York: College Entrance Examination Board.

Children's Defense Fund. (1987). *A children's defense budget: An analysis of the FY' 87 federal budget and children.* Washington, DC: Children's Defense Fund.

Chuong, C. H. (1988). *Working with Vietnamese high school students.* Clio Project, Graduate School of Education, University of California, Berkeley.

DBS Corporation (1987, December). *1986 Elementary and Secondary School Civil Rights Survey National Summaries* (Contract Number 300-86-0062). Washington, DC: Office of Civil Rights, U.S. Department of Education.

De La Rosa, D., & Maw, C. E. (1990) *Hispanic education: A statistical portrait.* Washington, DC: National Council of La Raza.

Deloria, Jr., V. (1985). *Behind the trail of broken treaties: An Indian declaration of independence.* Austin, TX: University of Texas Press.

Erickson, F. D. (1972). "F'get you Honky!": A new look at Black dialect and the school. In A. L. Smith (Ed.), *Language, communication, and rhetoric in Black America* (pp. 18–27). New York: Harper & Row.

Felice, L. (1981). Black student dropout behavior: Disengagement from school rejection and racial discrimination. *The Journal of Negro Education, 50,* 415–424.

Gallagher, D. (1986). Refugees: Issues and directions. *International Migration Review, 20*(2), 141–147.

Graham, M. (1984). *Educational teleconferencing in Canada.* (Paper #14). Toronto, Canada: TV Ontario.

Guralnick, D. B. (1986). *Webster's new world dictionary of the American language.* New York: Simon & Schuster.

Haines, D. (1985). *Refugees in the United States: A reference handbook.* Westport, CT: Greenwood Press.

Hale-Benson, J. (1987). Self-esteem of Black middle-class women who choose to work inside or outside the home. *Journal of Multicultural Counseling and Development, 15,* 71–80.

Henderson, R. (1982). *Teacher relations with minority students and their families.* Washington, DC: Office of Special Education and Rehabilitative Services, U.S. Department of Education, Washington, DC.

Hirschfelder, A. (1982). *American Indian stereotypes in the world of children: A reader and bibliography.* Metuchen, NJ: The Scarecrow Press.

Hodgkinson, H. L. (1990). *All in one system: Demographics of education—kindergarten through graduate school.* Washington, DC: Institute for Educational Leadership.

Jensen, A. R. (1969). How much can we boost IQ and scholastic achievement? *Harvard Educational Review, 39,* 1–123.

Johnston, B. H. (1989). *Indian school days.* Norman, OK: University of Oklahoma Press.

Jones, S. (1985). *Parent partnerships and children at risk.* Topeka, KS: Education Service Division, Department of Education, University of Kansas.

Kan, S. H., & Liu, W. T. (1986). Issues in Asian and Pacific American Education. In N. Tsuchida (Ed.), *The educational status of Asian-Americans: An update from the 1980 census* (pp. 153–164). Minneapolis, MN: Asian and Pacific Learning Resource Center.

LaFromboise, T. (1982). *Assertion training with American Indians: Cultural/behavioral issues for trainers.* ERIC Clearinghouse on Rural Education and Small Schools.

Lake, R. (1990, September). An Indian Father's Plea. *Teacher Magazine, 2,* 48–53.

Light, H., & Martin, R. (1985). Guidance of American-Indian baseline essays: Their heritage and some contemporary views. *Journal of American Indian Education, 25,* 42–46.

Menninger, K. (1980). Testimony before the Senate Subcommittee on Indian Education. *Report to The Legislature.* St. Paul, MN: Minnesota Department of Education.

Minneapolis Public Schools. (1989). *Multicultural and gender-fair education plan.* Minneapolis, MN: Minneapolis Public Schools.

National Catholic Educational Association. (1987). *Integral education: A response to the Hispanic presence.* Washington, DC: National Catholic Educational Association.

Nguyen, T. (1984). Positive self-concept in the Vietnamese bilingual child. *Bilingual Journal, 8*(3), 16–17, 36.

Nicassio, P. M. (1985). Psychosocial adjustment of the southeast Asian refugee: An overview of empirical findings and theoretical models. *Journal of Cross-Cultural Psychology, 16*(2), 153–173.

Overbeck, C. (1984). A survival kit for teaching English to refugees. *Lifelong Learning, 8*(2), 29–30.

Pepper, F. (1986). *Cognitive, Social and Cultural Effects on Indian Learning Style: Classroom Implications.* Paper presented at the Mokakit Conference, Indian Education Research Association, Winnipeg, Manitoba, Canada.

Pettigrew, T. F. (1988). Integration and pluralism. In P. A. Katz & D. A. Taylor (Eds.), *Eliminating racism* (pp. 19–29). New York: Plenum Press.

Phillips, J. (1987). From learning to read to reading to learn: The native language literacy program. *Passage, 3*(3), 61–65.

Plisko, V. W., & Stern, J. D. (1985). *The condition of education: A statistical report.* Washington, DC: U.S. Government Printing Office.

Prendergast, N. (1985). *A Vietnamese refugee family in the United States from 1975–1985: A case study of education and culture.* Ph.D. dissertation, Loyola University, Chicago, IL. University Microfilms International, Ann Arbor, MI.

Quan, C. A. (1986). *Crisis intervention for the ESL teacher: Whose problem is it?* Alexandria, VA: ERIC Reproduction.

Ramirez, B. A. (1988). Culturally and linguistically diverse children, *Teaching Exceptional Children, 20,* 45.

Ramirez III, R., & Castaneda, A. (1974) *Cultural democracy, bicognitive development, and education.* New York: Academic Press.

Randall-David, E. (1989). *Strategies for working with culturally diverse communities and clients.* Rockville, MD: The Association for the Care of Children's Health.

Rumbaut, R. G., & Kenji, I. (1988). *Adaptation of southeast Asian refugee youth: A comparative study. Final Report to the Office of Refugee Resettlement.* San Diego, CA: San Diego State.

Rumberger, R. (1983). Dropping out of high school: The influence of race, sex, and family background. *American Educational Research Journal, 20,* 199–200.

Spero, A. (1985). *In America and in need: Immigrant, refugee, and entrant women.* Washington, DC: American Association of Community and Junior Colleges.

Tharp, R. G. (1989). Psychocultural variables and constants: Effects on teaching and learning in schools. *American Psychologist, 44,* 349–351.

Thornton, R. (1987). *American Indian holocaust and survival: A population history since 1942.* Norman, OK: University of Oklahoma Press.

Tollefson, J. W. (1986). Functional competencies in the US refugee program: Theoretical and practical problems. *TESOL Quarterly, 20*(4), 649–664.

United States Census Bureau. (1991) *Resident population distribution for the U.S. by race and Hispanic origin.* Washington, DC: Cendata Data Base.

Vobejda, B. (1991, March 11). *Ethnic/Multicultural Diversity is Growing.* (Vol. 1 pp. A & 4A). St. Paul, Minnesota: St. Paul Pioneer Press.

Walker, W. D. (1987). *The other side of the Asian academic success myth: The Hmong story.* Qualifying paper. Harvard Graduate School of Education, Boston.

Wilson, R., and Carter, D. (1988). *Minorities in higher education* (Seventh Annual Status Report). Washington, DC: American Council on Education.

Woodson, C. G. (1968). *The education of the Negro prior to 1861.* New York: Arno Press and *The New York Times.*

Yao, E. L. (1988, November). Working effectively with Asian immigrant parents. *Phi Delta Kappan,* 223–225.

Yates, J. R. (1986). Current and emerging forces impacting special education. In H. J. Prehm (Ed.), *The future of special education* (pp. 13–74). Reston, VA: The Council for Exceptional Children.

Yu, E.S.H., Doi, M., & Chang, C. (1986). *Asian-American education in Illinois: A review of the data.* Chicago, IL: Pacific/Asian-American Mental Health Research Center.

Subject Index

Author Index